❧ COAT OF MANY CULTURES

COAT OF MANY CULTURES

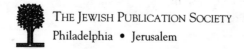 The Story of Joseph
in Spanish Literature
1200–1492

Selected, Translated, and Introduced by
MICHAEL McGAHA

THE JEWISH PUBLICATION SOCIETY
Philadelphia • Jerusalem

Manufactured in the United States of America

Library if Congress Cataloging-in-Publication Data

Coat of many cultures : the Joseph story in Spanish literature,
     1200-1492 / selected, translated, and introduced by Michael McGaha.
          p. cm.
     Translated from Spanish, Arabic, Hebrew and Ladino.
     ISBN 0-8276-0570-6
     1. Joseph (Son of Jacob) - Literary collections.   2. Spanish
literature - To 1500 - Translations into English.   3. Spanish
literature - Translations into English.   4. Spain - Literatures -
Translations into English.   5. Mozarabic literature - Translations into
English.   6. Spain - Literatures - History and criticism.
I. McGaha, Michael D., 1941 -
     PQ6174.9.J6C3   1996
     808.8'0351 - dc20

Typeset by Circle Graphics, Inc.
Printed by Text Press

TO MY FIRSTBORN SON
JOSEPH PATRICK MCGAHA

יְשִׂמְךָ אֱלֹהִים כְּאֶפְרַיִם וְכִמְנַשֶּׁה:

➤ Contents

⇒ Acknowledgements

I was inspired to undertake the research that led to the writing of this book by reading Muslim versions of the story of Joseph in a brilliant seminar on Sufism taught by Professor Carl Ernst at Pomona College in the spring of 1992. I shall always be grateful to Carl Ernst for introducing me to some of the most beautiful and inspiring literary works I have ever read. A grant from the Pew Charitable Trust, administered by Pomona College's Curriculum Committee, provided important assistance in obtaining the costly materials needed to begin the research. I would certainly never have written this book without the encouragement of my dear friend Dr. Élie Chemtob. Dr. Chemtob generously shared his vast knowledge of Arabic and Hebrew literature and closely collaborated with me on the translation of the *Sefer ha Yashar*, heroically continuing that work even during his final illness. I miss Élie more than I can say, and I deeply regret that he did not live to see the book completed. Professor Sylvian Castel de Oro has taught me most of what I know of Arabic and has cheerfully helped me track down much important information about the Muslim texts included in this book. Jennifer Goldstein, one of the most talented and memorable students I have taught during the past twenty five years, kindly obtained copies of materials I needed from Harvard's Widener Library. Professor Albert Sicroff very generously loaned me his copy of the *Biblia de Alba*—the priceless copy personally dedicated to Américo Castro by the Duke of Alba. My colleague and friend María Donapetry has often assisted me in translating very difficult passages from the Spanish. Professor David M. Gitlitz read the entire manuscript with great care and gave me several excellent suggestions for its improvement. Professor Helena Percas de Ponseti gave me some helpful comments on the text by Roiç de Corella. My beloved rabbis, Dr. Hershel Brooks and Sholom Harlig, have patiently answered many questions about the Jewish texts in this volume. Finally, the students who have participated in three seminars on the subject of this book that I have taught at Pomona College have given me many new and valuable insights into these texts. Some of them are acknowledged by name in the following pages.

⟫ Introduction

The story of Joseph in Genesis 37–50 forms an important part of the epic origin myth of the Jewish people and sets the stage for the most formative event in Jewish history: the exodus from Egypt. It is also one of the oldest and most beloved folktales in all of world literature. As the great French orientalist Ernest Renan observed, it is not only the oldest of novels, but the only one that never grows old.[1] The great themes it embodies—sibling rivalry resulting in betrayal, revenge, and ultimate reconciliation; the triumph of honor and chastity over sexual temptation; the Cinderella-like rise of a member of a despised minority to a position of almost unimaginable power and influence in one of the mightiest empires the world has ever known—have never ceased to inspire the imagination of later writers, ranging from Philo in first-century Alexandria to Thomas Mann in twentieth-century Germany. Nowhere, however, has the story of Joseph been more extensively studied, rewritten, and debated than in the Spain of the Middle Ages and Renaissance, when Jews, Christians, and Muslims all claimed Joseph as their own and produced astonishing new interpretations of his saga in romance, poetry, and drama.

Research carried out during the past fifty years has demonstrated beyond the shadow of a doubt that what is most distinctive about Hispanic civilization is its essentially hybrid nature. The culture we now know as "Spanish" is the product of over half a millennium of religious and ethnic pluralism, during which Christians, Jews, and Muslims lived side by side in relationships ranging from grudging tolerance to genuine mutual respect and admiration. In spite of sometimes fierce opposition from religious leaders of all three faiths, Christians, Jews, and Muslims read each other's books, ate and drank together, did business, employed each other, formed military alliances, had illicit sex, intermarried, feuded, proselytized, and converted from one religion to another. When Spain's national hero, Rodrigo Díaz de Vivar, significantly known as El Cid (from the Arabic *sayyidi*, "my lord"), was exiled by King Alfonso VI of Castile, he spent five years as a mercenary soldier in the service of the Muslim king of Saragossa, and no one at the time saw anything unusual about this. As T. A. Perry has noted, "Coexistence was not modeled on the melting-pot

---

[1]Cited in Jean Spiro, *L'histoire de Joseph selon la tradition musulmane* (Lausanne: Th. Sack, 1906), p. 6.

ix

theory, but rather on the interchange of different points of view, on a dialogue that could range from commonly shared tenets of moral philosophy to religious confrontation and polemic. This attempt at cultural *convivencia* has not only historical interest, but also ongoing importance for modern pluralistic culture in search of models of coexistence."[2]

For the first four centuries following the Muslim invasion of the Iberian peninsula in 711 C.E., religious tolerance was the general rule in both Muslim and Christian territories. Muslim rulers extended protection to their Jewish and Christian subjects as "peoples of the Book," provided only that those religious minorities acknowledge the superiority of Islam by paying a special tax and practicing their creeds relatively inconspicuously. Many Christians and Jews rose to high offices in Muslim Spain. As the Christians of the north began to win back some of the territories wrested from them by the Muslim invaders, they followed suit, allowing subject minorities freedom of religion in return for tribute. The Jews of Christian Spain were protected by the kings and were even viewed as their personal property. Bilingualism and even trilingualism were relatively common.

In Muslim Spain, known as al-Andalus, the language of culture was Arabic, while Spanish (or *mozárabe*, as the dialect spoken in al-Andalus was known) was largely restricted to domestic use. The earliest lyric poetry in any modern European language, the so-called *kharjas*, consisted of bilingual poems, the main part in Arabic or Hebrew, with a refrain (*muwashshaha*) in *mozárabe*. These refrains are the earliest literary texts we possess in the Spanish language, and, significantly, they were written in Arabic or Hebrew characters. The Catholic Church, of course, continued to use Latin for all official purposes, though knowledge of that language became increasingly restricted to the clergy. Culturally, the Christians of al-Andalus were almost indistinguishable from their Muslim and Jewish neighbors. The prestige of Muslim culture eventually led a majority of Christians and Jews in al-Andalus to convert to Islam. In ninth-century Córdoba a fanatical group of Christians led by a certain Eulogius and his companion, a Jewish convert to Christianity named Alvaro, viewing this tolerance and cultural assimilation as a greater threat to their faith than persecution, deliberately provoked the Muslim authorities to martyr them. Most of their fellow Christians were horrified by such outrageous behavior, and a church council forbade Christians to seek martyrdom. In an attempt to rival Arabic literature, Jewish authors wrote

[2]*The Moral Proverbs of Santob de Carrión: Jewish Wisdom in Christian Spain* (Princeton: Princeton Univ. Press, 1987), p. 4.

the first secular poetry in Hebrew as well as the first scientific studies of Hebrew grammar. The great Jewish philosophers and theologians of medieval Spain, such as Maimonides (1135–1204), wrote most of their works in Arabic; only later were they translated into Hebrew. Al-Andalus became the most civilized region in Europe and great advances were made in all branches of learning, as well as literature and architecture. In the twelfth century the rationalism of the Cordoban Aristotelian philosopher Averroes (Ibn Rushd) was so influential that it was viewed as a threat to the orthodox beliefs of all three faiths.

The first serious menace to this fruitful period of tolerance and coexistence came in the late eleventh and early twelfth centuries, when, in response to the Christian conquest of the ancient capital of Toledo in 1085, fanatical Muslim groups from North Africa invaded al-Andalus, wiping out both Christian and Jewish communities in their wake. An indirect result of this conflict was that the Christian kingdoms now reaped many of the benefits of Andalusian civilization. Many of the educated Jews who then fled to the Christian kingdoms knew Arabic, Hebrew, and Spanish, but few knew Latin. Likewise, many educated Christians knew Latin and Arabic, but few knew Hebrew. King Alfonso VII of Castile-León (1126–58) and Raimundo, second archbishop of Toledo, took advantage of this influx of learned refugees to create a School of Translators. Jewish scholars translated the masterpieces of Arabic, Hebrew, and Greek thought into Spanish, and these Spanish drafts were then rendered into Latin by Christian monks. A century later, Alfonso VII's great-grandson Alfonso X (1252–1284) would take the bold step of eliminating the Latin versions, thus producing the first scholarly writings in a modern European language and making those works accessible to all of his literate subjects. The brilliant court of Toledo replaced Córdoba as the intellectual capital of Spain and soon attracted scholars from all over Europe, paving the way for the Renaissance.

Collaboration among Jews, Muslims, and Christians thus produced a new, hybrid form of civilization that encouraged the highest achievements of all three cultures. That cooperative spirit, made possible by a tolerance for difference and an openness to new ideas and artistic forms, enabled Spain to enter the world stage with a burst of creative energy that has never since been equaled. What transformed Spain from a great, pluralistic center of intellectual and religious freedom to one of the most backward, repressive, monolithic societies the world has ever known?

It is very difficult to pinpoint exactly when and how this terrible reversal occurred. Somehow, over a relatively short period of time, Christian Spaniards ceased to view their Jewish and Muslim compatriots as fellow human beings, sharing common feelings, needs, and aspirations, and instead came to demonize them as enemy aliens. The evidence suggests that as long as the Muslim kingdoms of the south were viewed as a serious threat, and as long as Christian rulers found their Muslim and Jewish subjects useful (sometimes even indispensable), those rulers somehow managed to keep the aggressiveness of the Catholic clergy in check. As the balance of power shifted to the north, the reconquest—which formerly had been mostly a political and economic power struggle—became marked by a new spirit of crusader zealousness. The introduction of the French monks of Cluny into the kingdom of Navarre under Sancho the Great (970–1035) planted the seeds of this transformation. As William Atkinson has noted, "Cluny's reports to Rome on the progress of the Christian cause in Spain led the Pope in 1063 to commend the reconquest throughout western Europe as a holy crusade, and in the following year contingents from France and Italy, forerunners of the many which would share in later campaigns, entered Spain a generation before the first crusade to the Holy Land."[3] Surely one important factor in Christian Spain's ultimate rejection of its Jewish and Muslim minorities was an inferiority complex vis-à-vis the other nations of western Europe and an ardent desire to be fully integrated into western Christendom. Alfonso X squandered much of his fortune and energy in a futile attempt to be elected Holy Roman Emperor. Christian Spaniards were mortified by the widespread view that "Africa begins at the Pyrenees."[4] The first crusade (1096) had been accompanied by massacres of the Jews in the Rhineland. Edward I expelled the Jews from England in 1290; only a few years later, in 1306, the much larger and more prominent Jewish population was expelled from France. Though there was no general expulsion from Germany, numerous communities there were massacred, especially after they were blamed for the Black Death in the fourteenth century. In view of these events, one might well ask not why Spain turned against its Jews (and its Muslims), but rather, what took it so long.

Nevertheless, the fact remains that the Jews had not made such important contributions to the developing cultures of England, France, or Germany, nor had they ever enjoyed such prosperity and prominence in those lands as in Spain. Significantly, England, the last European country to which Jews had emigrated, was also the first to expel them. By contrast, Jews had lived in the Iberian peninsula in significant numbers since Roman times. The Marxist historian Ellis Rivkin has explained Spain's rejection of its Jews as resulting from the social unrest brought on by the decline of feudalism. Jews became the

---

[3]*A History of Spain and Portugal* (Harmondsworth: Penguin Books, 1970), p. 69.

[4]Though it gives succinct expression to an age-old idea, the saying is attributed to Alexandre Dumas.

scapegoats for the chaos and suffering that in fact were brought on by the cat-
astrophic power struggle between the nobility and the crown. "Since the Jews
were especially singled out to bear the responsibility for the major stresses and
strains of a disintegrating society," Rivkin writes, "they were accused of whatever the various groups in society needed to accuse them. The accusations were
created to meet the need; their truth or falsity was of absolutely no conse-
quence."[5] In a similar vein, the Portuguese historian António José Saraiva has
argued that the expulsion of the Jews and the later persecution of Jewish converts to Christianity were really just an attempt by the church and the feudal
aristocracy to defend their entrenched power against the threat of an emerging urban bourgeoisie, which consisted mostly of Jews, and, later, Jewish converts to Christianity, known as "New Christians."[6]

Still another factor that must be taken into account is the intense efforts
made in the twelfth century by the recently founded mendicant orders (especially the Franciscans and Dominicans) to convert the Jews of Christian Spain.
Many of the zealous new converts to Catholicism used their knowledge of Hebrew and Judaism against their former coreligionists and stirred up anti-Jewish
fervor among the masses. Finally, we cannot discount the bitterness aroused by
envy of Jewish wealth and intellectual attainments.

Hatred of the Jews seems to have had little real basis in religious differences,
although it initially took the form of demands that they convert to Catholicism. Even after large numbers of Jews—perhaps 200,000—converted to
Catholicism in 1492 as a condition of remaining in the country, the hatred
continued unabated and indeed may even have intensified. The promulgation
of laws of blood purity (*limpieza de sangre*) now extended the limitations and
exclusions formerly applied to Jews to the New Christian converts. Only those
who could prove that all four of their grandparents were born Christian could
qualify to hold public offices, join religious orders, and enjoy the privileges of
noble rank.[7]

These laws effectively prevented converted Jews from assimilating into the
mainstream population. At the same time, the Inquisition's zealous efforts to
stamp out all sorts of nonconformity—intellectual, religious, and even sexual—led to a state of national paranoia, since people were encouraged to de-
nounce their neighbors—and even their closest relatives—anonymously, and

---

[5]"The Utilization of Non-Jewish Sources for the Reconstruction of Jewish History,"
Jewish Quarterly Review 48 (1957–58): 188–89; see also Rivkin's *The Shaping of Jewish
History: A Radical New Interpretation* (New York: Charles Scribner's Sons, 1971).

[6]See his *História da Cultura em Portugal* (Lisbon: Jornal do Fôro, 1962).

[7]For details see Albert A. Sicroff's important book *Les controverses des statuts de
"pureté de sang" en Espagne du XVᵉ au XVIIᵉ siècle* (Paris: Didier, 1960).

hardly anyone could be absolutely certain that her or his closet did not contain a skeleton or two.

The experience of Spain's Muslims would closely parallel that of the Jews, with a bit of a time lag. Although guaranteed freedom of religion and all rights of citizenship by the treaty of surrender of Granada in 1491, by 1526 they too had been forced to convert to Catholicism. In the years thereafter, increasingly draconian measures were adopted to wipe out all vestiges of Muslim culture. On the one hand they were driven to absolute assimilation; on the other they were segregated from the Christian population and discriminated against in myriad ways, making assimilation impossible. Ultimately their fate was even worse than that of the Jews. Between 1609 and 1614, all identifiable descendants of Muslims—perhaps 300,000 people—were expelled from Spain.

By expelling the Jews and Muslims and relentlessly persecuting even their descendants, Spain effectively eliminated its intellectual, professional, and commercial élite and its most industrious agricultural workers. Concomitant with the rejection of Jews and Moors was the rejection of the spirit of free inquiry, capitalist entrepreneurialism, and the work ethic. The emerging Spanish nation was thereby doomed from the start to a very bleak future, one from which it is only now emerging.

Yet Spain remained haunted by its Semitic past. In 1517, a quarter century after the expulsion of the Jews, the humanist Erasmus of Rotterdam declined an invitation from Cardinal Jiménez de Cisneros to visit Spain, alleging that the country was so tainted by Jews that "there are hardly any Christians there."[8] A century later the government of King Philip IV's favorite, the Count-Duke of Olivares, was scornfully branded the *sinagoga* because of the notorious Jewish ancestry of some of its members.[9] From the sixteenth century on, many powerful Spaniards were deeply embarrassed by their nation's profound indebtedness to Muslim and Jewish thinkers, writers, and artists and did their utmost to obliterate or at least minimize all traces of it. This book is an attempt to recover a few precious remnants of Spain's former pluralism, to give ear anew to voices long silenced by prejudice and censorship.

The legend of Joseph offers us a unique opportunity to examine the interactions of Jews, Muslims, and Christians in medieval and renaissance Spain. It is a story that all three traditions cherished. Each of these ethnic and religious groups developed new interpretations of the story dictated by the historical cir-

[8]Marcel Bataillon, *Erasmo y España*, trans. Antonio Alatorre (Mexico City: Fondo de Cultura Económica, 1966), p. 78.

[9]J. H. Elliott, *The Count-Duke of Olivares: The Statesman in an Age of Decline* (New Haven: Yale Univ. Press, 1986), p. 556.

cumstances of a particular time and place, yet each was influenced by the versions created by the others. In the thirteenth century knowledge of all three "holy tongues"—Hebrew, Arabic, and Latin—declined drastically among the masses, and writers from all three traditions began to create religious texts in the vernacular. This enabled them to hear and read each other's texts in a way that had rarely been possible before. Each group sought to rival and improve upon versions created by the others; ultimately this grudging collaboration produced a uniquely "multicultural" version of the story.

The story of Joseph lent itself particularly well to such elaboration, for from its first recorded appearance in the Book of Genesis it was a "cross-cultural" story describing a fruitful and problematic encounter between the Jews and the Egyptians. Some parts of the story are remarkably similar to the Egyptian folktale of "Anpu and Bata" (also known as "The Two Brothers"), which, interestingly, is believed to date from approximately the time of the historical Joseph's sojourn in Egypt (c. 1500 B.C.E.), but it is unlikely that it will ever be possible to prove that one story decisively influenced or inspired the other.[10]

The legend of Joseph is the longest, most complex, and probably most interesting single story in the Pentateuch from a purely esthetic viewpoint. Isaac Bashevis Singer has observed that "the masters of the short story, Chekhov, Maupassant, as well as the sublime scribe of the Joseph story in the Book of Genesis, knew exactly where they were going. One can read them over and over again and never get bored."[11] The author(s) of the account in Genesis seem to have viewed it primarily as the wonderful story of a heroic ancestor who embodied the virtues most highly esteemed by the Jews. For later generations of Diaspora Jews the story would take on even greater importance, since it described how a Jew triumphed over adversity and became spectacularly successful in a non-Jewish society, yet always retained his loyalty to his people and used his position of power to help them. Although the story has didactic overtones and is presented as "providential" in a very general way, its tone is emphatically personal and secular. Later rabbinical literature sought to make up for these "deficiencies," examining in microscopic detail every imaginable moral and ethical issue raised by the story, and thereby robbing it of much of its subtlety and ambiguity.

In first-century Alexandria the story was accessible to Hellenistic Egyptians in the Septuagint translation, and they seized upon it for purposes of anti-

---

[10]See Susan Tower Hillis, *The Ancient Egyptian "Tale of the Two Brothers": The Oldest Fairy Tale in the World* (Norman: Univ. of Oklahoma Press, 1990).

[11]"Author's Note," *The Collected Stories of Isaac Bashevis Singer* (New York: Farrar, Straus, Giroux, 1982), p. vii.

Semitic propaganda, arguing that the foreign Jew Joseph had abused his power to exploit the native Egyptians and subject them to the utter tyranny of Pharaoh. Philo of Alexandria sought to answer those charges in his biography of Joseph as the ideal statesman. An anonymous Alexandrian contemporary of Philo penned the romance *Joseph and Asenath* as an argument against assimilation and intermarriage. That romance, which places great emphasis on Joseph's superhuman beauty and stoical self-control (both virtues highly prized by Hellenistic culture), presents the legend primarily as a love story containing a philosophical and mystical allegory. It is believed to have been an important source of inspiration for Muslim versions of the story. The historian Josephus Flavius (c. 38–c.100 C.E.) strongly identified with his biblical namesake and in his version of the story, in the *Antiquities of the Jews*, implicitly defended himself against charges that he had betrayed his Jewish people by siding with the Romans in the Emperor Vespasian's war against the Jews.

Islam regarded Joseph as one of the twenty six prophets who preceded Muhammad. As the only character in the Hebrew Bible to whom the Qur'an devotes an entire chapter (*surah*), Joseph came to figure much more prominently in Muslim literature and folklore than in Jewish writings; indeed much of the later Jewish interest in the story—especially in Spain—must be seen as a reaction to the Muslim use of it. According to Muslim tradition, a Jewish antagonist of Muhammad, hoping to embarrass him, argued that if he were truly a prophet he should be able to recount the story of Joseph. Muhammad was completely ignorant of the story, but the angel Gabriel revealed it to him. Muhammad then asked the Jew: "If I tell you this, will you become a Muslim?" The Jew replied that he would, and the surah "Yusuf" is Muhammad's reply. It therefore has an obvious element of rivalry with the Jewish versions of the story.

"Yusuf" draws on both Genesis and later Jewish folktales. For Muhammad the legend of Joseph was important mainly as a superb illustration of divine providence and retribution. The Qur'anic version of the story is much more concise than that in the Bible (partly because it assumes that the reader is already familiar with the story), but it introduces a few new episodes, the most famous of which is the story of the banquet offered by Potiphar's wife to the court ladies of Egypt. A good indication of the importance the Surah Yusuf acquired among Muslims is 'Abd Allah ibn 'Umar al-Baydawi's (d. 1286 or later) comment: "There is a tradition of the Prophet, 'Teach your slaves the Surah of Joseph, for if any Muslim studies it and teaches it to his household and to those whom he owns, God will lighten for him the pains of death and give him the power not to envy any [other] Muslim.'"[12]

---

[12]*Baidawi's Commentary on Surah 12 of the Qur'an*, trans. A. F. L. Beeston (Oxford: Clarendon Press, 1963), p. 55.

The Muslim popular imagination developed many later elaborations on the legend of Joseph, some of them influenced by rabbinical literature. The first great Muslim literary version of the story is the Persian poet Abu-l-Qasim Mansur Firdawsi's (940–1020) *Yusuf and Zulaikha*, which inspired no fewer than sixteen Persian romances, at least one Judeo-Persian version, and others in Turkish and Hindustani. For Firdawsi and his many imitators, *Yusuf and Zulaikha* became the supreme allegory for the love between God and the human soul. It therefore came to occupy in Muslim tradition approximately the same place that the Song of Songs has held for Jewish and Christian mystics.

Early Christian writers interpreted the story of Joseph principally as foreshadowing the life of Christ:

> Like Jesus, Joseph was hated and cast out by his brethren, and yet wrought out their salvation through the sufferings they had brought upon him. Like Jesus, Joseph obtained his exaltation only after passing through the deepest and most undeserved humiliations; and, in the kingdom over which he ruled, he invited his brethren to join those whom heretofore they had looked upon as strangers, in order that they also might enjoy the blessings which he had stored up for them. Like the Saviour of the world, Joseph had but words of forgiveness and blessing for all who, recognizing their misery, had recourse to his supreme power. It was to Joseph of old, as to Jesus, that all had to appeal for relief, offer homages of the deepest respect, and yield ready obedience in all things. Finally, to the Patriarch Joseph, as to Jesus, it was given to inaugurate a new order of things for the greater power and glory of the monarch to whom he owed his exaltation.[13]

Spanish writers would emphasize parallels between Joseph's salvation of the people through storing up wheat and Jesus's institution of the Eucharist (foreshadowed in Pharaoh's cupbearer's and baker's dreams concerning wine and bread and in the banquet Joseph offered his brothers).

These three great traditions coincided in Spain during the formative period of Spanish literature. In the seven texts contained in this volume, one can observe the growth and development of that literature over a period of three centuries. The earliest text I have included is a twelfth-century Hebrew epic written by a Jew who had sought refuge in Christian Spain from persecution by Muslim fundamentalists in the south. It contains many veiled allusions to contemporary events. The last text in this volume is a Valencian version in

[13]Francis E. Gigot, "Joseph," *The Catholic Encyclopedia* (New York: Universal Knowledge Foundation, 1910), VIII, 508.

poetic prose which, though written on the eve of the conquest of Granada and the expulsion of the Jews, nevertheless boldly incorporates Jewish and Muslim material. In between are a Muslim romance rivaling Christian Spain's romances of chivalry; Alfonso X's history of Joseph, which seeks to harmonize all three traditions; two charming narrative poems offering Muslim and Jewish alternatives to the poems on the lives of the saints penned by thirteenth-century Castilian monks; and a translation and commentary on the biblical text written by a Castilian rabbi (in collaboration with a Franciscan monk) for a Christian nobleman.

All these works are unmistakably Spanish, though many of them are also undeniably Jewish or Muslim. They are not just antiquarian curiosities but truly admirable literary texts. Sadly, I would venture to guess that few Spanish professors, even those specializing in literature of the Middle Ages and Renaissance, are aware of their existence. Only two of these texts have ever previously been translated into English. Most of them are rare and difficult to obtain even in the original languages. I have provided a brief historical-critical introduction to each text and have added footnotes to clarify some of the more obscure allusions. I hope that publication of these texts will help Christian, Jewish, and Muslim readers acquire a new awareness of their common heritage and will contribute to the process of healing the wounds inflicted by too many centuries of misunderstanding and strife.

M. M.
Claremont, California, 1995

❧ COAT OF MANY CULTURES

The Alba Bible. Don Luis de Guzmàn, who commissioned the Bible, sits enthroned in the center, and below is shown receiving the manuscript from Rabbi Moses Arragel of Guadalajara. Photo by Juan Jiménez Salmerón. Courtesy of Fundación Alba, Madrid.

➤ Translation and Commentary, Genesis 37–50 (1422–33)

Rabbi Moses Arragel of Guadalajara

In spite of its late date, Rabbi Moses Arragel's translation of Genesis 37–50 and his commentary on the text is an excellent place for us to begin our survey of the story of Joseph in Hispanic literature. In the first place, it gives us an opportunity to review the biblical text, which is the direct or indirect basis of all subsequent versions of the story. At the same time, Arragel's commentary succinctly summarizes many of the most important insights obtained through close scrutiny of the text by rabbinic exegetes during the previous millennium.

Arragel's commentary, carried out in close collaboration with the Franciscan friar Arias de Enzina, can be considered one of the the the last precarious links in a seven-hundred-year-old chain of fruitful intellectual exchange among the Jews, Muslims, and Christians of Spain. That earlier collaboration had borne rich fruits in the contributions to poetry, philosophy, and science by such writers as Solomon Ibn Gabirol (c. 1021–c. 1070), Judah Halevi (1075–c. 1140), and Moses Maimonides (1135–1204), to mention only three of the most illustrious writers of the so-called Golden Age of the Jews in Spain, universally recognized as the most creative epoch in Jewish history since biblical times.

The thirteenth century had marked a turning point in the history of Spain's previously large and prosperous Jewish community. Two new religious orders—the Friars Minor, or Franciscans, founded by Francis of Assisi in 1210, and the Dominican Order of Preaching Friars, founded by the Spaniard Domingo de Guzmán in 1215—made ardent efforts to convert the Jews of Spain, often learning Hebrew and mastering Jewish texts in order to conduct their missionary campaigns more effectively. These monks obtained royal permission to preach to captive audiences of Jews in their synagogues. Some of their converts were even more fervent in proselytizing their former coreligionists and in stirring up anti-Jewish prejudice among the population as a whole. Matters took a grave turn for the worse after Jews were blamed for spreading the bubonic plague, or Black Death, which decimated the country in 1348. In 1378 the archdeacon of Ecija, Ferrant Martínez, launched a rabble-rousing anti-Jewish campaign that would culminate in the outbreak of a pogrom against the Jews of Seville in 1391. For years the kings of Castile and the local ecclesiastical authorities managed to restrain Martínez, but the deaths of both King Juan I and the archbishop of Seville in 1390 created a power vacuum that Martínez was quick to exploit. Anti-Jewish riots broke out in Seville on June 6, 1391, and quickly spread throughout the country and even to the Balearic Islands. Everywhere, Jews were given the choice of conversion to Christianity or death. The historian Jane S. Gerber has recently noted that "when order was finally restored after about a year of riot, perhaps 100,000 Jews converted, another 100,000 had been murdered, and yet another 100,000 somehow survived by going into hiding or fleeing to Muslim lands."[1]

During the years 1411–1416 the Valencian Dominican friar Vicente Ferrer (1357–1419) terrorized the Jewish population of Spain by leading mobs of fanatical flagellants into the Jewish quarters of various cities of the peninsula and demanding that the Jews convert. Perhaps even more ominous for the future of Judaism in Spain was the famous "Disputation of Tortosa," a show trial held in 1413–1414, at which some of the most prominent rabbis in the land were required to defend their faith against the charges brought by Christian opponents. The disputation was conducted in the presence of Pope Benedict XIII and an intimidating audience sometimes numbering as many as two thousand people, including cardinals, archbishops, and noblemen. Predictably, it ended in a resounding victory for the Christian side and the conversion of fourteen of the rabbis.

Problems resulting from the existence of a large and poorly assimilated *converso* population, some of whom—later to be branded derisively as *Marranos* or "swine"—secretly maintained their adherence to Judaism, alongside the still unconverted Jewish community would ultimately lead to the expulsion of 1492. Mass conversions and large-scale emigration of Spanish Jews to North Africa and the eastern Mediterranean continued throughout the fifteenth century. Jewish writers interpreted the tragic events of 1391 and the following period as God's punishment for the religious laxity of the Spanish Jews, particularly for their materialism, rationalism, and admiration for Greek and Muslim philosophy, and advocated a return to rigid orthodoxy as the only remedy for their ills. It was in this gloomy atmosphere that Rabbi Arragel penned his translation.

The monastic society of knights known as the Order of Calatrava was founded around 1160 by Raimundo Sierra, abbot of the Cistercian monastery of Fitero, with the primary purpose of defending the castle and town of Calatrava from attack by Almohad ("Unitarian") invaders from Morocco. Modeled on the Knights Templars, who had been organized in 1119 to defend territories in the Holy Land wrested from Muslim control during the first crusade, the Order of Calatrava was the first such military order founded in Spain. After

---

[1] *The Jews of Spain: A History of the Sephardic Experience* (New York: Free Press, 1992), p. 113.

Sierra's death, leadership of the order was transferred from the abbot to a Grand Master elected by the knights themselves, although the order remained under the jurisdiction of the Cistercians. The order played an important role in the Christian Reconquest of Muslim Spain and by the fifteenth century had become one of the country's wealthiest landowners and a very powerful political force.

Luis de Guzmán was elected twenty-fifth Grand Master of Calatrava in 1404, but his election was contested and was not confirmed by the General Chapter of the Cistercian Order until 1414. In the spring of 1422, while taking some much-needed rest and recreation in Toledo after his campaigns against the Moors, Guzmán was moved by a desire to become personally acquainted with the Bible. Since he was unable to read the Latin Vulgate comfortably, and furthermore felt the need of a commentary that would explain the more obscure passages, he cast about for a qualified person to prepare a Spanish Bible and commentary for his personal use. One of his associates informed him that a vassal of his, a learned rabbi named Moses Arragel of Guadalajara, who was then serving in the town of Maqueda, within the jurisdiction of the Order of Calatrava, was ideally qualified for the task. Accordingly, Guzmán wrote Arragel on April 5, 1422, offering him generous remuneration if he would kindly undertake this, admittedly massive, job. Nine days later, Rabbi Arragel replied to Guzmán's letter, thanking him profusely for his generous and flattering offer but asking to be excused from the task. He explained that there are irreconcilable differences between the Vulgate—the version of the Bible officially adopted by the Catholic Church—and the Hebrew version. As a good Jew, he could not alter the meaning of the Hebrew, but, since an accurate Spanish translation of the Hebrew text would differ from the Vulgate, the Church would surely find it unacceptable. He therefore argued that Guzmán would be better advised to seek a learned Christian theologian to carry out the translation. He also pointed out that, in spite of their glorious past, the Jews of Castile were now reduced to the most wretched conditions and that nothing remained of their former learning but the merest "remnant of a remnant." Guzmán, however, refused to take no for an answer. Four days later he wrote Arragel that he had discussed his letter with his secretary and close relative Fray Arias de Enzina, Guardian of the Franciscan monastery of St. Francis in Toledo, and that Arias was convinced that the difficulties Arragel had pointed out were not insuperable. Guzmán therefore ordered the rabbi to report to Fray Arias in Toledo at the earliest possible date, reiterating his promise to pay the rabbi well for his services. The letter ended with a not-so-veiled threat: "Even if you didn't live in our lands, it would be to your advantage to please us and not anger us."

Guzmán's letter was accompanied by a letter from Fray Arias himself. Arias offered to provide Arragel "sane and noble advice," explaining whatever needed to be said concerning the Catholic interpretation of scripture to him in cases where it differed from the Jewish one. He promised Arragel that he would be given complete liberty to expound the Jewish viewpoint alongside the Christian one in his commentaries, and indeed acknowledged that interpretations differed even among Christians. Perhaps the most noteworthy observation in Arias's letter is that Guzmán had no lack of learned Christian advisors but was particularly interested in "knowing, and seeing, and becoming informed about the biblical commentaries of your modern doctors, which Nicholas of Lyra neither obtained nor saw." Albert Sicroff has noted that "evidently, Guzmán was not at all inhibited by the fact that only eight years earlier [i.e., at the Disputation of Tortosa] rabbinical interpretations of the Hebrew text of the Old Testament had been thoroughly discredited in Christian Spain."[2] Arias also offered personally to take charge of commissioning illustrations for the Bible from painters in Toledo. Three days later Rabbi Arragel went to Toledo, where he spent two weeks receiving detailed instructions from Fray Arias, who also gave him Latin commentaries on the book of Genesis.

After the translation and commentary had been completed and approved by the Dominican Fray Juan de Zamora of the University of Salamanca, Rabbi Arragel formally presented it to the Order of Calatrava in a ceremony held in the monastery of St. Francis in Toledo on November 5, 1433.[3] Fray Arias graciously thanked Arragel for his endeavors, praising his translation as "beyond any price" and "the best and most famous work that can exist in many kingdoms," and observing that "even if the translation of the Hebrew deviates from St. Jerome's version, that can be accepted as long as it does not prejudice our Roman faith."

Arragel's translation is written in a graceful, clear, literary Castilian notably free of archaisms and obscure vocabulary. While he shows a scholar's concern for the exact meaning of specific words in the Hebrew text, he does not hesitate to paraphrase in order to make his translation more accessible to lay readers. Thus, for example, although the literal meaning of the opening of Gene-

---

[2] "The Arragel Bible: A Fifteenth Century Rabbi Translates and Glosses the Bible for His Christian Master," in Ronald E. Surtz, Jaime Ferrán, and Daniel P. Testa, eds., *Américo Castro: The Impact of His Thought: Essays to Mark the Centenary of His Birth* (Madison, Wis.: Hispanic Seminary of Medieval Studies, 1988), p. 175.

[3] Although the last number of this date is missing from the manuscript, it is assumed to be 1433, because Arragel states that it took him eleven years to complete the translation.

sis 37:2 is "These are the generations of Jacob . . . ," Arragel recognized that this statement would be confusing to readers, since in fact it is not followed by a genealogy but by the words: "Joseph was seventeen years old. . . ." He therefore paraphrases: "This is what happened to Jacob. . . ." Always conscious of his Christian audience, he uses the word *roquete* ("surplice") to translate the Hebrew *ketonet* (Joseph's famous "coat of many colors"). The exact nature of the garment designated by the Hebrew word is in any case unclear, as Arragel points out in his commentary.

Arragel's commentary is derived principally from the many midrashim to the text and the best medieval rabbinical commentaries. The earliest manifestations of the literary genre known as midrash, consisting of a line-by-line interpretation of the biblical text, date from the first century C.E. and may have been inspired by the commentaries of Greek grammarians on the works of Homer and those of Roman rhetoricians on legal texts. The comments contained in the midrashim are of the most varied sort, including explanations of obscure words or grammatical constructions; attempts to resolve apparent contradictions in the text; explanations of the text's legal implications; moral observations; and inferences about material that was thought to be implied, though not stated, in the text. As James Kugel has observed,

> ancient exegetes tended to view the Bible as fundamentally elliptical: it said much in a few words and often omitted essentials, leaving the full meaning to be figured out by readers alert to the tiniest irregularities in the text. The process of fully understanding a biblical text thus consisted of bringing out all possible nuances implied in the precise wording of each and every sentence. With regard to biblical narrative, this often meant "deducing" background details, conversations, or even whole incidents that were not openly stated in a narrative text, but only suggested by an unusual word, an apparently unnecessary repetition, an unusual grammatical form, and so forth.[4]

As time went on, exegetes gave increasingly free rein to their imagination and developed rather elaborate stories very loosely based on some element in the biblical narrative. More seriously, these "narrative expansions," to use the term coined by Kugel, often contradict the obvious meaning of the biblical text, usually in an attempt to gloss over some of the less edifying material recounted in

---

[4] *In Potiphar's House: The Interpretive Life of Biblical Texts* (San Francisco: Harper, 1990), pp. 3–4.

the Bible. The rabbis considered it their duty, as Milton so aptly phrased it, to "assert eternal Providence, and justify the ways of God to men." Like the Duchess in *Alice in Wonderland,* they were convinced that "everything's got a moral if only you can find it." Thus many of the midrashim to the story of Joseph try to clarify what Joseph had done to deserve to be sold into slavery or what Jacob had done to deserve the loss of his beloved son, and at the same time to mitigate the culpability of Joseph's brothers, who, after all, were the ancestors of the Jewish people. Rabbi Arragel rejects the more fanciful of these interpolations, while including those which he found plausible.

He shows a profound reverence for the literal meaning of the text, eschewing interpretations that seem to him to twist or obscure that meaning. Nevertheless, he is far from what would nowadays be called a literalist or fundamentalist in his interpretation of the Bible. Following in the tradition of Maimonides, he considered many of the stories in the Bible—such as Eve's temptation by the serpent—as fables or parables, which, while not literally true, embody spiritual truths in a form that was comprehensible to the ignorant. As Maimonides wrote, "[God] described those profound truths, which His Divine Wisdom found it necessary to communicate to us, in allegorical, figurative, and metaphorical language. . . . It has been treated in metaphors in order that the uneducated may comprehend it according to the measure of their faculties and the feebleness of their apprehension, while educated persons may take it in a different sense."[5]

In spite of the apocalyptic circumstances in which he lived, Arragel remained a committed rationalist, convinced that the truths of philosophy and science were consistent with the truth of revelation. The unusual tolerance and curiosity demonstrated by Luis de Guzmán and Arias de Enzina in sponsoring and encouraging Arragel's work, and Arragel's own courageous pursuit of truth, are heartening glimmers of light in what was otherwise a very dark time. As the historian Américo Castro wrote in a review of the edition of Arragel's translation published by the Duke of Alba in 1920–1922, if such tolerance had prevailed in Spain, "we would have entered the modern era with a great spirit, incompatible with that tribal mentality which ended up turning Spain, culturally, into a vast village, even before the end of the seventeenth century."[6]

I have based my English version of Arragel's translation and commentary on the *Biblia (Antiguo Testamento) traducida del hebreo al castellano por Rabí Mose Arragel de Guadalfajara (1422–1433) y publicada por el Duque de Alba y Berwick* (Madrid: Imprenta Artística, 1920–22), 2 vols.

---

[5] *The Guide for the Perplexed,* trans. M. Friedländer (New York: Dover, 1956), p. 4.
[6] *El sol,* January 23, 1923; I quote from the article by Albert Sicroff cited above.

I. Of How Joseph Had Dreams, and How He Was Sold to the Egyptians

37 **While Jacob was sojourning in the land where his father sojourned, . . .**

Rabbi Solomon[7] says that, while the Law had recounted the generations of Esau briefly,[8] it then goes on to recount the generations and deeds of Jacob at length—at greater length than those of Esau—because God loved Jacob more than Esau. Likewise, you will find that in the ten generations that the Law recounted from Noah to Abraham, it abbreviated its account of all ten; but when it got to Abraham, it recounted his deeds at length, as you have heard. This can be compared to a pearl that fell in the sand, and they can't find it; they take all that sand and sift it until they find the pearl, and they pour out the sand. The midrash gives another example touching on this: it says it is like grain that is already threshed, but to obtain the wheat, they have to flog it, and the wheat goes to one side, and the wind carries off the chaff, and [the wheat] is left clean. Rabbi Abraham[9] wrote that, since the Law had already related how Esau settled in Mount Seir, it now relates how Jacob settled in the blessed Land of Promise. Rabbi Jacob, [author of] the *Turim*,[10] says that because, as has already been stated, Esau's settlement had been recounted, now it mentions how Jacob was a wanderer in a strange land, because he was already beginning to suffer God's sentence of four hundred years of exile.[11] Rabbi Joseph Kimḥi[12] wrote

---

[7] Rabbi Solomon ben Isaac (1040–1105), commonly known by the acronym Rashi. Born in Troyes, France, Rashi was one of the most important commentators on the Bible and Talmud. Rashi's extremely influential commentary on the Pentateuch is the first Hebrew work known to have been printed (1475), and since then most editions of the Hebrew Bible published for Jewish use have included his commentary. He is the source most frequently cited by Arragel in his commentary.

[8] In Gen. 36:40–43

[9] Abraham Ibn Ezra (1089–1164) was born in Tudela, Spain. His long commentary on the Pentateuch, *Sefer ha-Shem*, was first printed in Naples in 1488. Ibn Ezra's commentaries have enjoyed a popularity second only to those of Rashi.

[10] Jacob Ben Asher (1270?–1340) was born in Germany but spent the major part of his career in Toledo, Spain. He is best known as the author of the *Arba'ah Turim (Four Rows)*, an encyclopedic compendium of Jewish laws and customs; but the reference here is to his comprehensive commentary on the Pentateuch.

[11] Cf. Gen. 15:13: "And He said to Abram, 'Know well that your offspring shall be strangers in a land not theirs, and they shall be enslaved and oppressed four hundred years.'"

[12] Joseph Kimḥi (c. 1105–c.1170) was born in Spain but spent most of his adult life in Narbonne, France. His commentary on the Pentateuch, *Sefer ha-Torah*, stresses the literal meaning as opposed to the homiletic school of exegesis prevalent in the Provence of his day.

that the son is obliged by law to dwell where his father dwelled, and the Law told how Jacob kept this commandment. He adds that a man is obliged by law to do fifteen things for his father, as follows. We find two commandments in the Law: first, that they should honor their father;[13] and second, that they should fear him.[14] For a man to honor his father includes five things: to give him food, drink, and clothing; and to help him go in and out—these are five. The five included in the fear of one's father are: the son should not sit in his father's place; he should not speak in his father's presence; he should not contradict what his father says; he should not demand proof to verify what he says; he should always stand in his presence. With the previous five, these make ten. The other five apply after the father's death: if anyone honors the son, he should say that he owes that honor to his father; he should not change the names his father gave things; and he should dwell in the place where his father dwelled, just as Jacob dwelled where his father dwelled. These five make fifteen.[15]

2. this is what happened to Jacob. Joseph, being seventeen years old, was a shepherd with his brothers in the flock.

There is a note in *Midrash Genesis Rabbah*[16] on this passage stating that everything that happened to Jacob, happened to Joseph, that is: Jacob was born circumcised, likewise Joseph; Jacob's mother was wily, Joseph's mother was wily; Jacob's mother had a hard childbirth, Joseph's mother had a hard childbirth; the mother of the first bore two sons, the mother of the second bore two sons; one was hated by his brother, the other by his brothers; one was a shepherd, the other was a shepherd; one was threatened, the other was threatened; one left his land, and so did the other; one was robbed,[17] the other was robbed;[18] one married outside his land, so did the other; one had children outside his land, so did the other; one had dealings with kings, so did the other; one was powerful on account of his dream, so was the other; the house of one man's father-in-law was blessed on account of him, and the same thing happened to

---

[13] Ex. 20:12.

[14] Lev. 19:3.

[15] Arragel seems not to have noticed that the duties applying after the father's death are really only *three*, not five.

[16] A midrashic collection on the book of Genesis compiled at the end of the fourth or early fifth century C.E. Since there are midrashim called "Rabbah" (i.e., "Great") on all five books of the Pentateuch (though they were compiled at different times, *Genesis Rabbah* being the oldest), Arragel refers to them collectively as "Rabot." The present reference is to *Genesis Rabbah*, chapter 84, paragraph 6.

[17] Gen. 31:39.

[18] Gen. 40:15.

the other one;[19] one went down to Egypt, so did the other; one put an end to famine, so did the other; one died in Egypt, so did the other; one was embalmed; so was the other; they brought one's bones out of Egypt, and the same thing happened to the other. This was a great miracle, for these similarities reveal that the ascendants of father and son were in accord in the signs of the twelve houses [of the zodiac].

> **Joseph was brought up with the sons of Bilhah, and with the sons of Zilpah, his father's wives. And Joseph brought bad reports about his brothers to the attention of his father.**

Since Joseph was a lad, the sons of the concubines[20] made him serve them, and this was the bad report he brought his father about them; for if he had served his brothers, the sons of the ladies,[21] there would have been nothing wrong with that. Rabbi Solomon says that what he said about them was any fault he found in them, such as that they dismembered living cattle and ate them, and that they called their brothers sons of slaves, and that they were fornicators. Joseph was punished for all three statements: when they cut the throat of the kid to bedaub his tunic with blood, the Law testifies that they didn't eat it alive; because he accused them of calling their brothers sons of slaves, he was sold as a slave; because he suspected them of fornication, he was suspected of fornication.

> **3.   And Israel loved Joseph more than all his brothers, because he had had him when he was already an old man;**

The Targum Onkelos[22] states that his father loved him because he was wiser than his other sons. The Hebrew says only that he was the son of his old age, and the Master[23] says that that is the same as to say that he served him in his old age.

> **and he made him a tunic of silk embroidered with checks (*tunicam polymitam*).[24]**

---

[19] This is based on the identification of Potiphar (Gen. 39:5) with Joseph's father-in-law Poti-phera.

[20] The sons of Rachel's maid Bilhah were Dan and Naphtali; those of Leah's maid Zilpah were Gad and Asher.

[21] That is, Leah and Rachel.

[22] Rabbi Arragel uses the Christian term "Chaldean Gloss" for the Aramaic translation of the Bible known to Jews as the Targum Onkelos (first–second century C.E.).

[23] The Franciscan monk Fray Arias de Enzina of Toledo, whom Arragel often consulted about the Christian interpretation of Scripture.

[24] Citation from the Vulgate. The Latin *polymitam* means "wrought with many threads." The precise meaning of the Hebrew *ketonet passim* is unclear.

The Hebrew says only "tunic of pieces," and Ibn Ezra says "of silk." The rabbis deduce from this that no one should favor one of his children over the others, for one can easily see what Joseph's brothers did to him out of envy of this tunic, notwithstanding the fact that all of this had to happen, according to the sentence pronounced concerning the captivity in Egypt.

> **4. When his brothers saw that their father loved him more than all his brothers, they hated him and could not speak to him in peace.**

Even though they hated him, the Law testifies to their nobility, for they didn't have one thing in their hearts, and show him something else with their mouths.

> **5. And Joseph had a dream, and they began to hate him even more. 6. He said to them: "Hear me now this dream which I have dreamed, 7. which is that we were making sheaves in the field, and my sheaf stood up and was erect, and your sheaves surrounded it and bowed down to my sheaf." 8. His brothers said to him: "Are you going to reign over us, or will you have power over us?"**

Will we appoint you our king, or will you seize power over us by force?

> **And their hatred of him increased because of his dreams and his words. 9. And he had another dream and told it to his brothers. He said: "I have had yet another dream: that the sun and moon and eleven stars bowed down to me."**

You can easily see that his own father interpreted this dream [as meaning that] he and his mother would obey him; but since Bilhah, Rachel's handmaid, had taken her place in the house of Jacob and Rachel after Rachel died, [Joseph] considered her his mother. *Genesis Rabbah* argues that Joshua benefited greatly from the power of this prophecy when he told the sun to stand still at Gibeon.[25] You should know that Joshua was of the tribe of Joseph, and this is what he told the sun at Gibeon: "Friend, you should know that what Joseph saw about the sun and moon bowing down to him was said in reference to this time; for you know very well that it was never fulfilled." Then the sun and moon stood still, as the story recounts.

---

[25] Cf. Josh. 10:12: "Sun, stand thou still upon Gibeon; And thou, Moon, in the valley of Aijalon."

10.   And he told it to his father and his brothers, and his father be-
rated him and said to him: "What is this dream you have
dreamed? Are we to come, I and your mother and your brothers,
and bow low to you to the ground?"

Jacob said this for two reasons: to get it out of his brothers' minds—and hence
he said: "Sons, pay no attention to the words of this man, for the sun and the
moon were I and his mother Rachel. Since his mother is dead, this prophecy
cannot be fulfilled with regard to her; and hence, the rest of it is equally impossible. For you should know, my sons, that dreams are often absurd." Second,
so that Joseph would not consider himself superior to his brothers, for as the
Master adds, the moon commonly signified only Jacob's wives, and the eleven
stars, his eleven brothers.

11.   And his brothers envied him for that reason, but his father kept
the matter in mind. 12. And one day his brothers went to pasture
their father's flock at Shechem. 13. Israel said to Joseph: "It is
certain that your brothers are pasturing at Shechem. Go, for I
want to send you to them." He said: "I am ready." 14. He said to
him: "Go now and see how your brothers are and how the flocks
are faring, and bring me back word." And he sent him from the
valley of Hebron, and he came to Shechem. 15. A man found
him, for Joseph was wandering lost in the field, and that man
asked him: "What are you looking for?"

Rabbi Solomon states that it was the angel Gabriel. And don't be perplexed by
the word "man," for Daniel said: "the man Gabriel."[26] In this regard Master
Alfon[27] observed that the Jews apply the word "man" to an angel, calling him
Gabriel; but it is important to understand the etymology of "Gabriel." And it
is true that Gabriel consists of two words, namely *gabri*,[28] which in Hebrew
means "man," and *El*, which means "God." Hence we can deduce that this one
was God and man, and therefore we can argue that he had a revelation that
the angel of God appears to man.

16.   He said: "I am looking for my brothers. Tell me where they are
pasturing." 17. That man said: "They have gone from here, and I

---

[26] Dan. 9:21: "yea, while I was speaking in prayer, the man Gabriel whom I had seen
in the vision at the beginning, being caused to fly swiftly, approached close to me about
the time of the evening offering."

[27] Another Franciscan friar consulted by Arragel.

[28] That is, *gever*.

heard them say: Let us go to Dothan." Joseph went after his brothers and found them at Dothan.

This was as much as to say that he should be careful, for they had left off being his brothers.[29]

18. **And they saw him from afar, and before he came close to them, they conspired to kill him. 19. They said to one another: "Here comes that dreamer! 20. Now let's kill him and throw him in one of these pits; and we will say that a savage beast devoured him, and we'll see what comes of his dreams!"**

It's easy to see that if they had killed him, his dreams would have come to nothing. Hence this saying is superfluous, unless one attributes it to Gabriel: "You say: 'Let's kill him,' but I say: 'I want to see what comes of his dreams.' Which will be fulfilled—my plan or yours?" But Rabbi Abraham says that this man of whom we have spoken was merely a passerby.

21. **When Reuben heard it, he pulled him out of their hands and said: "Oh, for the love of God, let us not wound him mortally!" 22. Reuben told them: "Friends, shed no blood! Cast him into this pit that is in this wilderness, and do not lay a hand on him." And he said this in order to get him out of their hands, so that he could restore him to his father. 23. As soon as Joseph reached his brothers, they stripped him of the checkered tunic he was wearing, 24. and took him, and cast him into a pit, which had no water in it and was empty.**

You can see, friend, that if it states that this pit was empty, there was no need to go on and say that there was no water in it; but that was to indicate that it was full of snakes and lizards and reptiles.

25. **And they sat down to eat.**

Nine of the brothers, for Joseph was already in the pit, and Reuben wasn't there, and Benjamin was still with his father. The Master says that if Joseph's brothers had known about the snakes that were in the sides of the pit where they cast Joseph, they wouldn't have thrown him there to die, for they all agreed not to wound him mortally.

---

[29] This interpretation is based on the ambiguity of the Hebrew text, which merely says: "Nas'u mi-zeh" (They left from this).

> **They looked up and saw a caravan of Moors coming from Gilead,**
> **with their camels loaded with wax and theriaca[30] and acorns (aro-**
> ***mata et resinam et stacten*)[31] which they were taking to Egypt.**

Rabbi Abraham says that this theriaca was made and composed of seventy
seven ingredients. Others say that it is a balsamic oil. Others say it is a resin.
Rabbi Solomon says: here we can see the great mercy that God willed to do
Joseph, for these Arabs were always accustomed to transport castoreum and
myrrh, which smell bad, but because our Lord God knew that these men were
to take Joseph captive, He arranged for them to buy sweet-smelling merchandise, so that the bad odor would not kill him, for he was a delicate man.

> **26. Judah said to his brothers: "What do we gain by killing our**
> **brother and covering up his blood? 27. Let us sell him to these**
> **Moors, and not lay our own hands on him, for he is our flesh."**
> **And his brothers agreed to that. 28. And some other men of Mid-**
> **ian, merchants, passed by, and they took their hooks[32] and pulled**
> **Joseph out of the pit, and they sold him to the Moors for twenty**
> **pieces of silver, and they brought Joseph to Egypt.**

Those of Midian and the Moors are all [the same] Moors, but the Law says they
were from Midian. Rabbi Solomon doesn't agree, arguing that the Midianites
bought him from the Moors, and that Joseph was sold many times from one to
another.

> **29. And Reuben returned to the pit, and when he didn't find Joseph**
> **in the pit, he rent his clothes.**

Reuben had left, because that day it was his turn to serve his father, for his sons
took turns serving him one day each.

> **30. And he returned to his brothers and said: "Since this lad is not**
> **here, where shall I go, or what will become of me?" 31. And they**
> **took Joseph's tunic, and cut the throat of a kid, and smeared [the**
> **tunic] with its blood. 32. And they sent the checkered tunic that**
> **they had taken from him to his father, [ordering that] they tell**

---

[30] An antidote to poison, compounded of many drugs and honey.

[31] Knowing that the meaning of the three Hebrew words is uncertain, Arragel cautiously cites the Vulgate as an alternative to his version. The Latin *stacte* means "myrrh
oil."

[32] Or poles (Sp. "garauatos").

him that they had found it, and they told him: "Examine whether this is your son's tunic or not." 33. And he recognized it, and said: "This is my son's tunic! Some evil animal has devoured him, or Joseph has been captured by robbers."[33]

This prophesied that Joseph would be persecuted by the evil animal, his master's wife, as you will hear further on. Many raise the question that, since Jacob was a prophet, it was to be expected that God would reveal all these things to him. Rabbi Solomon says that all the brothers excommunicated anyone who should reveal the secret, and they said: "This includes even God," and God willed to respect the excommunication. This is a figurative way of saying that men should be obedient, and should refrain from trespassing or violating excommunications, not that God was forced to do so. His brothers didn't remember that Isaac was alive, and [he too was] a prophet and knew about the matter of this sale; but he chose not to reveal it, because he saw that if God wanted to reveal it to Jacob, He could do so, but Isaac decided that "since God chose not to reveal it, I won't reveal it."

34. Jacob rent his clothes, put sackcloth on his loins, and observed mourning for his son many days.

The Law doesn't say how many, but the sages say that it was twenty two years, the same number of years that Jacob was in the house of Laban, and didn't honor his father and his mother.

35. And all his sons and daughters went to comfort him;

Some affirm that with each of Jacob's sons a [twin] daughter was born, and that the brothers married their sisters; and hence it said: "his sons and his daughters." Others say that it is customary for fathers-in-law to call their daughters-in-law "daughters."

> but he refused to be comforted, and he said: "Because he went down into the grave (hell), likewise I will go down with mourning over my son."

I based this translation on the gloss of Ibn Ezra and on the sense of the Hebrew text; but St. Jerome argues that the text means: "I will go down with my son to hell," and they have deduced from this that all the holy fathers up to the com-

---

[33] Alternately, "has been the prey of an animal" (Sp. "es tomado en alguna rapiña").

ing of Jesus Christ went to hell, and that he took them out of there and put them in paradise. St. Jerome interpreted the Hebrew *Sheol* as meaning "hell."

His refusal to be comforted was natural, not voluntary. For if a man is in fact dead, even if he lives a thousand leagues away so that there is no way his father could know it, it is as if the heart could guess, and because he sees that such a misfortune is irremediable, he takes comfort. But if a man is alive or in captivity without ever being heard from, men cannot be comforted.

And his grandfather wept for him.

This refers to Isaac, and there is no doubt that Isaac did not die until Joseph was twenty nine years old. Others say that [the spirit of] prophecy had abandoned both of them—I mean both Jacob and Isaac—on account of the terrible shock they suffered because of Joseph, for there is no doubt that unhappiness deprives prophets of [the power of] prophecy.

36. And the Moors sold him in Egypt to Potiphar, Pharaoh's servant,[34] master of his police and executioners.

[Chapter 38 is a digression having to do with Judah's marriage, the birth and death of his sons Er and Onan, and how his daughter-in-law Tamar deceived him into having intercourse with her, and as a result of this, gave birth to the twins Perez and Zerah. I have translated a few verses from the chapter, because Arragel's commentary relates them to the story of Joseph.]

1. While matters were in this state, Judah left his brothers . . .

They say that his brothers expelled him, seeing how greatly their father suffered on Joseph's account, and said to him: "Oh, traitor! Why did you order us to sell him instead of killing him? If you had ordered us to bring him to his father, we would have brought him; hence you do not deserve to be with us."

7. Er, Judah's firstborn, was wicked before God . . .

Er and Onan, Judah's sons, are the names he gave them, which mean "solitude" and "weeping," and they say that he gave them these names out of pity for Jacob's grief over Joseph.

23. Judah said: "Let her take it, so that we won't be dishonored, for I sent this kid, but you didn't find it."

---

[34] Or eunuch (Sp. "çiclauo").

Rabbi Solomon says that, just as he deceived his father with the blood of the kid that he put on Joseph's tunic, he too was deceived with a kid.

II. Of How Joseph's Mistress Fell in Love with Him, and How He Was Imprisoned Because of That

39. **When Joseph was taken down to Egypt, Potiphar, Pharaoh's servant, the chief of his police and executioners, bought him. And he was an Egyptian man, and he bought him from the Moors who had taken him down there. 2. And the grace of God was with Joseph, for he was a man who succeeded in everything he undertook, and he was there in the house of his master, the Egyptian. 3. His master saw that the grace of God was with him in everything he did; God made him prosper by His hand.**

Rabbi Solomon said that the name of God was constantly in his mouth, for on every occasion he said: "with God's help," "if God please," "God willing," and because of all this, it was only to be expected that he would obtain the grace of God. Others say that his master saw that the grace of God was with him because, whenever he served wine or meat, if the meat was in the pot, and his master said: "Give me some of that very hot food," even if it was cold, it would be hot when he gave it to him. And if he requested cold or lukewarm food, it turned that way. And the same thing happened when he mixed the wine with water. If he didn't have water, he gave it to his master, and it became just the way his master wanted it. Everyone who saw this said that he did it by witchcraft, until one day his master actually saw a sort of cloud that spoke and a great brightness that hovered over Joseph; and this explains how his master saw that the grace of God was with Joseph.

4. **And Joseph found favor in his master's eyes and served him, and he made him majordomo of his house, and put him in charge of everything he owned. 5. And from the time that he put him in charge of his house and of everything he owned, the Lord blessed the Egyptian's house on account of Joseph, and the Lord's blessing was upon everything he owned, in the house and in the field. 6. And he left everything he owned in Joseph's power, and he didn't deny nor forbid him anything except the bread that he ate.**

Rabbi Solomon says that since the Law sometimes applies the word "bread" to woman, it means that he didn't withhold anything from him except his wife.

Others say that the majordomo is not in charge of baking bread in his master's house, but only serving bread; but he doesn't count it out or decide how much food should be served each day. Ibn Ezra says that the Egyptians avoided eating bread that a Jew had touched, and it was for that reason that he withheld and forbade the bread he ate to Joseph.

Nevertheless, I translated this verse: "he didn't deny nor forbid him anything except the bread that he ate," literally. The Hebrew says only: "He knew nothing else with him but the bread that he ate." The Master paraphrased this as follows: "Although Joseph was in charge of the whole house, no other authority or delight reminded[35] his master of Joseph [so much as] that bread that he ate."

And Joseph was beautiful in body and beautiful to look upon.

Rabbi Solomon says that when Joseph saw himself in power he combed his hair and shaved.[36] God said: "Be still, Joseph. Your father is in mourning for you, and I will take you to a place where you won't be so arrogant." Then his master's wife looked Joseph over and told him to sleep with her, and he would be imprisoned because of this.

> 7. **After this, his master's wife looked him over. She told him: "Lie with me." 8. But he refused, and he told his master's wife: "Truly, with me here, my master doesn't know what he has in his house, and I am in charge of everything he owns. 9. No one is greater in this house than I, and he has withheld or forbidden me nothing except you, because you are his wife. How then could I do something so wicked, and sin before God?"**

He gave two excuses: one concerning men and the other regarding God. The one concerning men was that, since his master had entrusted his house to him, he would give a poor account of himself. As regards God, he told her: "Friend, know that, even if I escaped human justice and its shame I would sin before God." If anyone should ask why he didn't come forward first with the excuse concerning God, you should know that in defending their civil suits, men usually present the less compelling argument first, and then say: "If I am not ab-

---

[35] Literally "tasted of Joseph." The Spanish verb *saber* means both "to know" and "to taste."

[36] Or "put on makeup." The Sp. *afeitarse* is ambiguous. *Midrash Genesis Rabbah* 87:3 states: "He was like a man sitting in the marketplace bedaubing his eyes and smoothing back his hair and lifting his heel; he says, 'I am quite the man!' Said [God] to him: 'If you are quite the man, behold, there is a bear prancing before you!'"

solved for this reason, surely I will be for this second one." How then could one do less in a suit affecting the soul?

> 10.   **Although she kept on day after day, he would not be persuaded to lie with her, or near her, or to be with her.**

Notice that he said three things: to lie with her, or near her, or to be with her. She demanded that he lie with her; he said no. Then she said: "You wear your clothes and I'll wear mine, but let's go to bed together." He told her no. Then she said: "Let's just chat for a while." He told her no.

> 11.   **And one day, when he was going in the house to attend to his affairs, and none of the household was in the house, 12. she caught hold of him by his garment, saying: "Lie with me!" But he left his garment in her hand, and fled, and went out to the street.**

Some say that his affairs were his accounts. Others say that this refers to sleeping with her, but that his father Jacob appeared to him and prevented him from doing so.

> 13.   **And then, when she saw that he had left her his garment and gone out to the street, 14. she called the men of her house and told them: "Have you ever seen such a thing? He brought us a Jewish man to mock us. He came to lie with me, but I cried out. 15. And as soon as he heard me crying out for help, he left his garment by me and fled and went out to the street." 16. And she kept Joseph's garment by her until his master came home. 17. And when he came, she told him thus: "That Jewish slave that you brought us to mock me attacked me. 18. But when I cried out for help, he left me his garment and fled to the street." 19. And when his master heard his wife's words, saying: "Thus and so your slave did to me," he was aggrieved.**

Doing and saying are two different things; hence, all she had to say was: "your slave said thus and so to me;" but instead she said "did," whence Rabbi Solomon states that her husband was with her doing you-know-what, so it was the same as to say that he had gone to bed with her.

> 20.   **Joseph's master took him and put him in the jail where he kept the king's prisoners, and Joseph remained in that jail. 21. But God was with Joseph, and showed him mercy, and gave him favor in the eyes of the jailer. 22. And the jailer put Joseph in charge of all the prisoners who were in the jail, and he did everything**

that was done there. 23. And the jailer found no fault with him, because God was with him, and he was successful in all his work.

III. Of the Dream Pharaoh's Cupbearer and Baker Had, and How Joseph Interpreted It

40. **After that, the king of Egypt's cupbearer and baker fell out of favor with the king because of a certain matter.**

It doesn't say what they did wrong. Rabbi Solomon says that the baker's failure was letting a piece of dirt get into the king's bread, and the cupbearer failed to detect a fly in the cup in the king's hand, and this was the matter.

2. **And Pharaoh was angry with his two officials, his chief cupbearer and his chief baker, 3. and he ordered them imprisoned in the house of that chief of police where Joseph was imprisoned. 4. That chief of police entrusted these men to Joseph, and he attended them, and they were in prison like that for some days.**

It doesn't say how many, but by reckoning, one finds that it was a year.

5. **And it happened that both of them had a dream on the same night, and each one dreamed what was interpreted for him later— for this cupbearer and baker of the king of Egypt who were imprisoned in the jail.**

That is, each one dreamed approximately what was to happen, and Joseph interpreted it as follows. The cupbearer saw grapes in his dream, and he was making them into wine, and wine is joy, so the interpretation was joyful. The baker saw something unpleasant and annoying—that birds were eating the bread he had to take before the king—so Joseph rightly interpreted that something unpleasant was going to happen to him: that he would be hanged. Concerning how and why dreams occur, and which men have the gift of understanding them, please God, I shall write in the book of Job.

6. **And when Joseph came in to see them in the morning, he found them sad and trembling. 7. And he asked those two officials who were imprisoned in his master's house: "Why are you in a bad mood and sad today?" 8. They told him: "Friend, we had a dream, and we can find no one to interpret it." Joseph told them: "Although the Lord God is the true interpreter, I beg you to tell it to me."**

Here the Law shows us Joseph's capability and his self-confidence in revealing his knowledge to such great men as these. Joseph could see very well that if he misinterpreted their dreams he would be condemned to death, especially in the case of the baker, if he escaped; but it seems that he trusted in his knowledge and was not afraid to interpret their dreams, albeit he protested that he left the matter to God's better judgment.

> 9. **And the chief cupbearer began telling Joseph. He told him: "I saw in my dream that I had a vine in front of me. 10. On that vine were three branches. It seemed to me that the vine was blooming and budding, and that it had clusters of ripe grapes.**

Understand well what I'm saying: he didn't say that he saw something like a vine, but that he saw a real vine. However, he said: "it seemed to me that it was blooming, and budding, and producing grapes, and that in an instant this vine changed from one state to another, and still a third, that is, the ripening." Thus Joseph understood that God would not delay this matter for long. Because there were three branches and three states, [he knew] it would only be three days, and he didn't interpret them as three months or three years. Rabbi Abraham says that Joseph knew that Pharaoh's birthday was in three days and that the prisoners had an audience then, and that's why he said three days. And the *Midrash Genesis Rabbah* says: "See how great are the miracles of God, who causes a master to become angry with his servants in order to pay honor to a just man! Likewise, he makes the lord's servants become angry so that a just man may be honored. The case of the lord of vassals who became angry for the honor of a just man was that of Pharaoh. The anger of the lord's vassals refers to the cupbearers of Ahasuerus for the sake of Mordecai's honor."[37] The *Midrash Genesis Rabbah* says that this vine and branches stand for the people of Israel and their adventures. The vine means Israel, as the Psalmist said: "You brought a vine from Egypt,"[38] and doubtless he said it with Israel in mind. And the three branches were Moses, Miriam, and Aaron. And in the Talmudic tractate *Ḥullin* it is said that the vine signifies this earthly world; the three branches, Abraham, Isaac, and Jacob; the flowers, Jacob's wives; and the ripe grapes, the twelve tribes.

---

[37] Reference to the book of Esther. When Esther gave a "banquet of wine" to implore King Ahasuerus to spare the Jews who had been condemned by Haman, Haman threw himself on Esther's couch to implore mercy. Ahasuerus believed that Haman was attempting to rape Esther, and Harbonah, "one of the eunuchs" (interpreted here as a cupbearer at the banquet) told him: 'Behold also, the gallows fifty cubits high, which Haman hath made for the king, standeth in the house of Haman.' And the king said: 'Hang him thereon.' " (Esther 7:9).

[38] Ps. 80:8.

Rabbi Joshua[39] said: "when a man tells of things that are past, this is not termed revelation or interpretation; this term is used to refer to things to come." Hence, he still interprets the vine as Israel; the three branches as Moses, Aaron, and Miriam; the flowers, the seventy elders[40]; the ripe grapes, the just who live in all times.

Rabbi Eleazar[41] says: "the vine is not Israel but Jerusalem; the three branches are the temple, the king, and the high priest; the flowers are the children of the priests, i.e., the innocent children. The ripe grapes are the wine with which the sacrifices were mixed." Others say: the vine is the Law; the three branches, a well of water that traveled with Israel and the clouds of glory and fire that traveled with Israel; flower and bud, the first fruits; ripe grapes, the mixtures of the sacrifices. And a cup is mentioned three times here: the first is the one Pharaoh and Egypt drank in the time of Moses;[42] Egypt drank another in the time of king . . . ;[43] she and her provinces will have to drink yet another when the Antichrist comes." Rashba[44] says that since a people cannot succeed, nor endure, nor even truly be called a people unless there are numbered among them those who defend, those who pray, and those who work, the shoots are the defenders, the branches are those who pray, and the leaves are the workers.

Master Alfon applies all of this interpretation to the church and its priests and benefices.

11. **And I had Pharaoh's cup in my hand, and I took the grapes and pressed them into the cup—I mean Pharaoh's cup—and placed the cup in Pharaoh's hand." 12. Joseph said to him: "What it means is this: The three branches mean three days. 13. Before three days it will happen that the king will take account of you along with some other noblemen and restore you to your post and status; and you will place Pharaoh's cup in his hand as was your custom formerly, when you were his cupbearer. 14. When you regain your status, please remember me when all is well with you**

---

[39] The name of at least four different rabbis cited in the Mishnah. I don't know to which one this statement is attributed.

[40] Cf. Ex. 24:1.

[41] At least thirteen different rabbis by this name are cited in the Talmud. I am not sure to which one the present text is attributed.

[42] In the sense of "a cup of bitterness" (i.e., the plagues). Cf. Ps. 11:6: "Upon the wicked He will cause to rain coals; Fire and brimstone and burning wind shall be the portion of their cup."

[43] There is a blank space in the manuscript here.

[44] Acronym for Rabbi Solomon ben Abraham Adret (c. 1235–1310) of Barcelona, the foremost Spanish rabbi of his time. The text has "Rashbag," but I assume this is a mistake for "Rashba."

again, and do me the kindness of mentioning me to Pharaoh, for you will be able to take me out of this prison. 15. For I was kidnapped from the land of the Hebrews, and I was sold here; nor have I done anything here that they should have put me in jail." 16. And the chief baker saw that Joseph had interpreted the dream well.

Rabbi Solomon says that each of these men dreamed what was going to happen to the other; that is, the baker dreamed what was going to happen to the cupbearer, and when he heard Joseph's words he remembered that that was just the way he had dreamed it, and he saw that he had interpreted it well, and considered him wise, and decided it would be a good idea to tell him his dream too.

He said to Joseph: "In my dream, similarly, I saw that I had three white (*farinae*)[45] openwork wicker baskets around my head;

Others translate "of white bread," and hence Master Alfon rectifies that these officials signified the sacrifice of bread and wine,[46] since one saw bread and the other saw the vine from which wine comes.

17. and in the upper basket were all the things that Pharaoh usually eats, I mean, as regards baked goods. And the birds came and were eating out of the basket above my head." 18. Joseph answered: "What it means is this: these three baskets are three days. 19. Before three days, Pharaoh will lift your head, and will hang you on the gallows, and the birds will come, and the birds will pick off your flesh." 20. And three days after that was the feast of Pharaoh's birthday, and he received all his noblemen, and on the list [of them] he saw the chief cupbearer and the chief baker along with the other noblemen. 21. And he restored the cup to the cupbearer, and he placed the cup in Pharaoh's hand; 22. but the chief baker he hanged—just as Joseph had interpreted to them. 23. Yet the chief cupbearer did not mention Joseph; he forgot him.

"Forgot" means that he forgot him in his heart; "mention" refers to the speech of his mouth. Hence it appears that both in his heart and in his mouth he forgot him.

---

[45] The Vulgate translation ("of white bread") of the Hebrew word *ḥori*, of uncertain meaning.
[46] That is, the Catholic Mass.

IV. Of King Pharaoh's Two Dreams, of the Seven Cows and the Seven Ears of Grain, and the Interpretation of Them, and How Because of That He Released Joseph from Jail[47]

41.   After two years, Pharaoh dreamed that he was by the river,

The Law doesn't say from what point the two years up to his dream were counted, just as at the beginning of the prophecy of Ezekiel, it says: "it was in the thirtieth year," and we don't know exactly how that reckoning was made. It may mean two years after Joseph was imprisoned, or two years after the cupbearer was released.

> **2.   and out of the river there came up seven cows, very beautiful and fat, and they grazed in the meadow.**

Since the Egyptians depended on the River Nile, and from it came plenty or famine, he was shown them coming up out of the river. The cows represent farming the soil, and the ears of grain signify the harvest. If he hadn't been shown the other cows, by themselves they might have indicated that he was to be conquered by other peoples; and if he hadn't been shown the other ears of grain, Joseph wouldn't have been sure of the meaning of the dream. The Master wrote that the only place where there was plenty was in the land of Egypt along the shores of the river, and that the produce of that area was insufficient to provide food for the other provinces outside of Egypt proper. This can be seen in Pharaoh's dream, for he saw the goodly cows grazing in the meadow alongside the Nile, and the other bad ones ate up the seven goodly ones. It doesn't say, nor is it known, how far they spread out in the land.

> **3.   And seven other cows came up from the river, ugly and gaunt of flesh, and stood near the other cows on the banks of the river;**

This means that between the years of great plenty and those of famine there would not be an interval of any years.

> **4.   and the cows that were ugly and gaunt of flesh ate up the seven fat, beautiful cows. And then Pharaoh awoke.**

---

[47] The chapter division here corresponds to the break between the first ("Va-Yeshev") and second ("Mikkets") portions of the story of Joseph as read in the synagogue liturgy. Logically, there should have been another chapter division immediately after Joseph's release from jail, but Arragel seems to have become distracted and continued the story uninterruptedly down to the end of the weekly Torah portion.

This was a sign that the years of famine would exhaust all the good and plenty of the seven good years; hence Joseph ordered that they store up the bread of the good years.

5.   **He went back to sleep, and dreamed a second time: Seven ears of grain were sprouting on a single stalk, and they were thick and good.**

Of the seven bad ears of grain, it doesn't say that they were on a single stalk. The reason is that the seven years of plenty were equal in goodness, and hence it said that they were on a single stalk; but each of the seven bad years was worse than the year before, so they were not on a single stalk, because they were not equal.

6.   **And he saw seven other thin ears growing up close behind the first ones, and the east wind scorched them. 7. And the seven thin ears swallowed up the other seven thick, full ears, and Pharaoh awoke, and saw that it was all a dream. 8. In the morning his spirit was broken (*pavore perterritus*),[48] and he sent for all the astrologers of Egypt, and all his wise men; and Pharaoh told them his dream, but they could not interpret it for Pharaoh.**

This means: in a way that he found satisfactory. They offered him the following interpretation of that dream: Sire, you will beget and have seven daughters, and you will bury seven daughters. My lord Master,[49] it is worthwhile for you to understand the difference between this dream of Pharaoh's and King Nabuchodonosor's[50] dream,[51] which is as follows: Nabuchodonosor forgot both the dream and its interpretation, for he was also told the meaning of his dream; and in this case, Pharaoh was told the dream and its interpretation, but he forgot only the interpretation. The issue raised here is: things that are more distant in time require more witnesses and greater certainty, whereas something that is easily proven speaks for itself. In the case of Pharaoh's dream the seven years of plenty began right away, so that whether Joseph spoke truth or falsehood was immediately evident, so it was reasonable to believe Joseph without requiring further signs. However, in King Nabuchodonosor's dream, which sig-

---

[48] The Vulgate version of the Hebrew *tipa'em ruḥo*. The recent Jewish Publication Society translation reads: "his spirit was agitated." In the *JPS Torah Commentary* Nahum Sarna annotates: "Implying that, following his dreams, Pharaoh spent a sleepless night, anxiously awaiting the dawn."

[49] Here Arragel addresses Don Luis de Guzmán, Master of Calatrava, who commissioned the work.

[50] Or Nebuchadnezzar. Arragel uses the form employed in the Vulgate.

[51] Dan. 4.

nified great events that would occur over a long period of time, if Daniel hadn't given him some signs, it would have made no sense to believe him. This is like the old saying: "from great distances, great lies." So, since King Nabuchodonosor's dream signified things that would occur much later, such as the empire of Alexander, and how the world would be divided among four kings after him, and likewise, the great destruction of the people of Israel and the coming of Jesus Christ, and Muhammad's sect, and the Antichrist—as I hope to explain at length, with God's help, in the book of Daniel—therefore, sir, if Nabuchodonosor had forgotten only the interpretation of his dream, and it had been left for Daniel to judge, since he saw nothing at that time, Daniel would not have been believed. But, in order that he might be believed, God made [Nabuchodonosor] forget both the dream and its interpretation; and in order for him to believe the interpretation, he had to be told the dream itself; so this is the difference between these two dreams.

9. **The chief cupbearer said to Pharaoh: "Today I will speak of my faults. 10. Pharaoh was angry with two of his servants, and he put me in prison in the house of the chief of police, me and the chief baker. 11. And he and I had a dream on the same night, each one with its own interpretation.**

He confessed two faults: first, the main reason why he was imprisoned; second, that Joseph had relied on him, but he had done little for him, which is a fault in great men, especially in one who had found a jewel of such price, one that he should have coveted for the king. Hence, I say that there are three faults: the offense against the king for which he was imprisoned; second, not bringing the king's attention to someone as good as Joseph; third, lack of concern for someone who relied on him.

12. **And with us there was a Jewish youth, a slave of the chief of police, and each of us told him our dream, and he interpreted it exactly; 13. for, just as he had interpreted it, so it came to pass: you ordered me to return to my post, and you hanged him."**

A person who is reluctant to speak well of someone always finds a way to say what's really on his mind. This cupbearer called attention to three defects in Joseph: youth, Jew, slave. By saying "slave," he indicated that he did not belong to an honorable estate. [By saying "youth," he deprecated Joseph's knowledge, for] as Aristotle observes in his *Ethics*, "There is no good and perfect knowledge in young men." By saying "Jew," he pointed out that he didn't know the Egyptian language, as if to say that one shouldn't trust someone who speaks a foreign tongue. By saying "slave," he indicated that he lacked the qualifications to be a king, so that the king might recall that the law of Egypt states that a Jew may not be king nor wear honorable or princely robes, because he was a slave in Egypt.

14. And Pharaoh sent for Joseph, and he was rushed out of jail, and they shaved him and gave him other clothing, and he appeared before Pharaoh. 15. Pharaoh said to Joseph: "I had a dream, and I can't find anyone to interpret it for me, but I have heard it said of you that you understand something about dreams and how to interpret them." 16. Joseph answered Pharaoh, saying: "Whatever my interpretation may be, may God preserve Pharaoh's health!" 17. Pharaoh spoke to Joseph, saying: "My dream is that I was on the bank of the river, 18. and seven cows, fat of flesh and beautiful of body, came up out of the river and were grazing in the meadow; 19. and another seven cows came up right behind them, scrawny and very ill-formed, and gaunt in flesh—never had I seen their likes for ugliness in all the land of Egypt! 20. And those scrawny, ugly cows ate up the first seven cows that were fat, and had them in their bellies; 21. but one could not tell that they had eaten them and had them in their bellies, for they looked just as bad as before. And I awoke. 22. And I saw in my [other] dream that seven ears of grain were growing on a single stalk, full and good; 23. and another seven tiny, thin ears, scorched by the east wind, sprouted after them. 24. And the little ears ate the other, good ears. And I told it to my astrologers (*conjectoribus*)[52] but they can't tell me anything about it." 25. Joseph said to Pharaoh: "Pharaoh's dream is one: God is showing Pharaoh what He intends to do. 26. The seven good cows are seven years, and the seven good ears mean seven years; it is all one dream. 27. And the seven empty, ugly cows that followed are seven years. And the seven thin ears, scorched by the east wind, will be seven years of famine. 28. It is just as I have told Pharaoh: God has revealed to Pharaoh what He intends to do. 29. Immediately ahead are seven years of great abundance in all the land of Egypt. 30. After them will come seven years of famine, and the abundance will be forgotten in the land of Egypt, and famine will waste and kill those of the land, 31. and the abundance will not be known in the land because of the famine that will follow it, which will be very severe. 32. As for Pharaoh

---

[52] The Vulgate translation. *Conjector* means "soothsayer" or "interpreter of dreams."

dreaming twice, it means that the matter is certainly from God,
and that He intends to do it very quickly."

One doesn't see that Pharaoh had this dream more than once that night, so
why does it say he dreamed twice? Some say that the word "twice" indicates
that the cows were one revelation, and the ears were another revelation, so it
makes sense to say "twice." Others say that, since cows are one thing, and ears
are something else, one can very well use the word "twice." Furthermore, it has
been deduced from this that when one has a dream two or more times, it is true
and will happen very soon.

33. From this moment let Pharaoh start looking for a man of wisdom
     and understanding, and set him over the land of Egypt. 34. Let
     Pharaoh take this advice and appoint overseers over the land, and
     have them take the fifth part of all the bread during these seven
     years of plenty. 35. Let them gather all the food of these good
     years that are coming; let those overseers gather all the food
     under Pharaoh's authority, and let the food be carefully stored in
     each place on his account.

Farmers say that food cannot be well preserved except in its own soil, and it appears that with each shipment of food they brought soil from its place of origin.

Rabbi Solomon, because of the ambiguity of the Hebrew word *ve-yitzberu*,
paraphrases: "all my people." "That all my people be sustained and supported."

36. Let that food be kept under supervision in the region for the
     seven years of famine, so that the land may not perish in the
     famine." 37. This plan pleased Pharaoh and his servants. 38.
     Pharaoh said to his servants: "Could one find in the world an-
     other like him, a man who has the spirit of God?" 39. Pharaoh
     said to Joseph: "Since God made you know all of this, we believe
     there is none so discerning and wise as you. 40. You will be one
     of the grandees of my house, and your mouth will say when arms
     must be taken up (*imperium cunctus populus obediet*)[53] in all my
     people; I wish to have no other advantage over you but the
     throne of the kingdom." 41. Pharaoh said to Joseph: "See, I put
     you in charge of all the land of Egypt." 42. Pharaoh took off his
     ring from his hand and put it on Joseph's hand; and he dressed
     him in robes of silk (*stola byssina*),[54] and put a gold chain about

[53] The Vulgate version: "all the people will obey the order from your mouth."
[54] The Vulgate version: "a royal robe of fine linen."

his neck. 43. And he had him carried in Pharaoh's second [best] litter, and everyone went before him bowing down and proclaiming that Pharaoh had put him in charge of all the land of Egypt. 44. Pharaoh said to Joseph: "Although I am the king, yet without you no one may put out his hand or foot in all the land of Egypt." 45. And Pharaoh gave Joseph the name of Zaphenath-paneah, which is the same as to say: he who reveals secrets (*Salvatorem mundi*).[55]

It is the custom of kings to give their favorites a new name. Nabuchodonosor did the same thing with Daniel.

And he married him to Asenath, daughter of Poti-phera, who was minister in On (*sacerdotis [H]eliopoleos*)[56] which is Alexandria. And Joseph's fame went out throughout the land of Egypt.

This man was the same chief of police you've already heard about, and he was given this title here for greater honor. The king married Joseph to his daughter, because he didn't tell him that he had been his slave, and his father-in-law was too ashamed to say so. The Master says that this chief of police was a eunuch, and after they castrated him, he was ashamed, and became a monk in one of the temples, and was a minister and priest there.

46. **And Joseph was thirty years old when he was before Pharaoh, king of Egypt. And Joseph left the king's palace and traveled throughout the land of Egypt.**

It means his fame, or else that he went out to take possession of the land entrusted to him and to do as Pharaoh had told him.

47. **And the land prospered in the seven years of plenty throughout the farm lands. 48. And he gathered all the food that was in the land of Egypt, and he put the bread that was in the villages in the city.**

Rabbi Abraham says that he didn't gather all of it, for if he had gathered all of it, they would have died of hunger. The Master states that he did gather it all and brought it under the control of Pharaoh's overseers, and from that they gave them enough so that they wouldn't suffer, and the rest was stored up for the time of famine. He even says that during the seven years of plenty, Joseph bought up

---

[55] The Vulgate version: "Savior of the world."
[56] The Vulgate version: "priest of Heliopolis."

vegetables and fruits, which are another kind of food, cheaply for the king, and then sold them back to them for a high price during the years of famine.

> 49. And Joseph gathered as much food as the sand of the sea, in great quantities, so much that his accountants couldn't count it. 50. Before the year of famine came, two sons were born to Joseph, whom he had by Asenath, daughter of Poti-phera, priest and minister of Alexandria.

There was no reason for the Law to tell us that they were born before the year of famine, except by this saying to teach us that it is sinful for a man to have intercourse with a woman in time of famine, and that Joseph's sons were born in a good year. My student, you will object: If that is so, we find that Levi, Joseph's brother, impregnated his wife with a daughter in a year of famine; and when our father Jacob went to Egypt, two years of famine had already gone by, and this daughter of Levi was born between the wall and the barbican of Egypt. This is proof positive that she was engendered in a year of famine. I reply: Levi was not hungry in his father's house. Furthermore, Levi had no way of knowing how long the famine would last, for he saw only that two years of famine had already gone by. Joseph, however, was well aware of how long the famine would last, because he enjoyed almost the status of a prophet. Joseph was therefore right to exert more self-control than others in this matter, in order to teach men that in times of persecution, they should abstain from carnal vices and turn to God.

> 51. And Joseph called the name of his firstborn Manasseh, which means "forgetfulness," "because the Lord made me forget all my distress, and all the house of my father." 52. And he called the name of the second Ephraim, which means "multiplication," "because God multiplied me in the land where I suffered great distress." 53–55. And when the years of plenty were fulfilled and the seven years of famine began to come, as Joseph had said, the people cried out to the king for bread. Pharaoh said to the Egyptians: "Go to Joseph, and do whatever he tells you."[57] 56. And the famine spread throughout the land, and Joseph opened all the granaries that contained food, and sold it to the Egyptians. And the famine was very severe in the land of Egypt. 57. And all the

---

[57] Arragel compresses vv. 53–55, omitting the second part of 54 ("there was famine in all lands, but throughout the land of Egypt there was bread") and the first part of 55 ("And when the land of Egypt felt the hunger").

> region came to Egypt to buy from Joseph, for the famine was
> throughout the earth.

This means the area surrounding Egypt, for if it had been the whole world, all
would have died but Egypt, because of the remedy you've heard about.

42. And Jacob saw that there was food in Egypt, and Jacob said to
his sons: "Why do you give the impression that you are rich?"
(*negligitis*)[58]

Jacob was not in Egypt to see that there was food there, so the Law should have
said: "Jacob heard," not "saw." To satisfy this objection, Ibn Ezra wrote that the
Law said "saw" meaning "heard." In this case seeing is the same as hearing,
since doubtless the five senses come together in a single place, and one takes
the place of another. When we see honey, we judge it sweet, and when we see
gall, we judge it bitter, even if we don't taste them. When we hear Peter or
John sing, we recognize them, even though we may not see them at that time,
through the use of the sixth sense, which is called "common sense." This explains why it says that Jacob "saw that there was food in Egypt," rather than
"heard tell." Others say that he knew it through revelation; but this is impossible, because Jacob received no revelation from the time of Joseph's departure
until he saw him. Others say that there was a river that went from Egypt to
Canaan, and Joseph, sensing that his brothers and father were looking for
bread, sent straw with ears of grain, and they reached Canaan. When Jacob saw
them, he said: "By this I see that there is food in Egypt," and that is why the
text said: "Jacob saw that there was food in Egypt."

> 2. And he said: "Since I've heard that there was food in Egypt, go
> down there and buy food for us there, and we will live and not
> die." 3. And Joseph's ten brothers went down to buy food from
> Egypt. 4. But Jacob didn't send Benjamin, Joseph's brother, with
> his brothers, for he said: "I would not want some disaster to be-
> fall him." 5. And Israel's sons came together with the others who
> came, because there was famine in the land of Canaan.

Some say that they didn't enter together, because that was what their father
had ordered them, to defend them against the evil eye, and each one entered

---

[58] The Vulgate version ("Why are you negligent?"). Sarna observes in the *JPS Torah
Commentary*: "Since the Hitpael conjugation frequently expresses affectation, the
phrase may be rendered 'Why do you make an outward show' of being well supplied?"

the city through a different gate.[59] Concerning the abuses of believing in the evil eye and similar abominable superstitions, the Church of God rejects all of this. If indeed they entered through different gates, it must have been for another reason, such as so they might not be refused bread if it were known that they were all of a single household, in which case they might not have sold them as much bread.

> 6. And since Joseph was the vizier of the land, and he was the one who sold food to all those of the land, Joseph's brothers came and bowed down to him to the ground. 7. When Joseph saw his brothers, he recognized them, but he pretended not to recognize them, and said harsh things to them. He asked them: "Where do you come from?" They said: "From the land of Canaan, to buy food." 8. Thus it happened that Joseph recognized his brothers, but they did not recognize him.

It's easy to recognize a man with a beard, but when Joseph left them he didn't have a beard. He had grown it in Egypt, and hence they didn't recognize him; and for the same reason, he was able to recognize them.

> 9. And Joseph remembered the dreams he had dreamed. He said to them: "You are spies, and you have come to see the ugliness of the land in order to spread the word about it; or else to learn its secrets." 10. They said to him: "It is not so, my lord, for your servants came to buy food. 11. We are all of us sons of the same man, and we are behaving honestly, and we are not spies." 12. He said to them: "No, you came to see the secrets of the land!" 13. And they said: "We are twelve brothers, sons of a man who is in the land of Canaan; and the youngest of us is today with our father, and the other one died, and we know nothing of him."

Joseph had no reason to accuse the other merchants of being spies, but he had a reason to accuse his brothers—because they had come in through ten different gates. If they were all members of the same group, it made no sense for them to spread out like that. Joseph's purpose in putting them through these tests was to find out whether the dreams he had told them would come true. Oth-

---

[59] This is a Muslim interpretation, based on Qur'an 12:67: "And he said: O my sons! Go not in by one gate; go in by different gates. I can naught avail you as against Allah. Lo! the decision rests with Allah only. In Him do I put my trust, and in Him let all the trusting put their trust."

ers say that when he saw his brothers dressed in purple he asked: "Why would men who can [afford to] dress like this come to buy food? One must presume that you are spies, and have come to spy out the poverty of the land. For the others who come to buy food come wearing inexpensive clothing, but you have come disguised as merchants."

> 14. He said to them: "That just proves what I told you, that you are spies. 15. But, by Pharaoh's life, I mean to put you to a test: you will not leave here until that youngest brother of yours comes here.

He suspected that his brothers had killed his brother Benjamin, and that's why he ordered them to bring him there.

> 16. Send one of you to bring your brother, while the rest of you are confined, and by this I will know whether you are truthful or not; otherwise, by Pharaoh's life, you are spies!" 17. And he put them in jail for three days.

He didn't detain them longer, because he knew by revelation that the Messiah would be resurrected on the third day.

> 18. On the third day Joseph said to them: "Proceed in this fashion if you wish to live, for you should know that I fear God. 19. If you are honest men, one of your brothers will remain imprisoned in the jail where you were, and you go, and take whatever you need for the sustenance of your households. 20. And bring me that youngest brother of yours, and your words will be believed, and you will not die." And they did accordingly. 21. They said to one another: "Surely we are guilty on account of our brother, for we saw the anguish of his soul begging us for pity, yet we paid him no heed, and that is why this distress has come upon us." 22. Reuben said to them: "I told you over and over: 'Don't sin toward this child,' but you paid no heed, and it seems that God has remembered his blood."

They didn't kill him, but because of the great cruelty they had shown him they felt that it was the same as if they had killed him. Doubtless they thought he was dead, for they said: "He was a delicate child, and he surely must have died from so much suffering," and hence they said: "God remembered his blood."

> 23. And they did not know that Joseph understood what they were saying, for they spoke with him through an interpreter. 24. And

> he turned away from them and wept. And he came back to them
> and conversed with them; and he chose Simeon from among
> them, and had him jailed before their eyes.

When errors are committed, the most important of the wrongdoers is doubtless to blame. It was Reuben, who was the eldest, who deserved the blame and
punishment. But since Reuben saved him from death he passed over Reuben
and took Simeon, who was the next oldest after Reuben, and could have
stopped the sale, especially with Reuben on his side, and the brothers would
have submitted to him. He didn't do so, however; and therefore he received all
the blame, as the older brother, which should have gone to the eldest, because
the eldest can always resist wrongdoing and punish it, which Reuben didn't do
in this case.

> 25. And Joseph gave orders, and they filled their bags with food and
>   returned their money, putting it in their bags, and he ordered that
>   they be given food for the journey. 26. And they loaded their
>   food on their asses and departed from there. 27. And one of them
>   opened his bag, for he wanted to give feed to his ass at the inn,
>   and he saw his money at the mouth of his bag. 28. He said to his
>   brothers: "They returned my money, and it's here in my bag!"
>   And they were disturbed, and they all trembled, saying to one an-
>   other: "What can this be that God has done to us?" 29. And they
>   came to Jacob, their father, in the land of Canaan, and they told
>   him all that had befallen them, 30. saying how the lord of the
>   land "spoke harsh words to us and accused us of being spies. 31.
>   And we told him that we were honest men, and not spies, 32. and
>   that we were twelve brothers, sons of one father, and that one [of
>   us] was no [longer] in the world, and how the youngest was with
>   our father in the land of Canaan. 33. But that man who was lord
>   of the land said to us: 'By one thing I shall know that you are
>   honest men: leave one of your brothers with me, and take suste-
>   nance for your households, and go in peace. 34. And bring me
>   your youngest brother, and I will know that you are not spies and
>   that you are honest men, and therefore I will give you your
>   brother, and you will do your business in the land.' "

Joseph didn't tell them to do their business in the land, but they told their father this so that he would be more willing to give them Benjamin.

> 35. While they were emptying their sacks, each one saw his money-
>   bag in his sack, and when they saw their money, they and their

father were frightened. 36. Their father Jacob said to them: "You have left me without sons. I know nothing about Joseph, even less about Simeon, and if you take Benjamin now, all these evils will have befallen me!" 37. Reuben said to his father: "Kill my two sons if I do not bring him back to you. Hand him over to me, for I will return him to you!"

Although Reuben had four sons, he said: "Very well! Kill two of my sons for one of yours!" Reuben said this because he had not participated in the sale of Joseph; but his father didn't want to entrust his son to him, because Reuben had betrayed him on another occasion when he slept with his father's concubine.[60] He preferred to give him to Judah, who was the bravest of them all.

And Judah's advice was good when he said: "Let the bread run out, and the old man will listen to reason," and thus it happened.

38. **He said: "My son will not go with you, for his brother died, and he alone was left; and a disaster might befall him on this journey you will take, for which reason I would die of grief, and my white head would go down with a bad end to hell."**

Here the Latins differ from the Jews, for they say that Jacob seemed to fear that not even circumcision sufficed to obtain pardon for Adam's sin. For, though circumcision restored the lineage of mankind [to some extent], it still did not do so as perfectly as when Jesus suffered death to save mankind. Hence, it seems that the holy fathers before Jesus went to hell—that is, limbo—and Jesus broke [the gates of] hell and took them out of there. The Jewish translation does not confound this opinion. Wherever St. Jerome translated "hell," the Jews translated "grave" or "pit," and even though they translate "grave," it can mean "hell" in the following way. We accept that the Lord raises the soul of the just man to heaven, but the body goes into the grave. In the present instance, when [Jacob] said he would go down to the grave, Jewish opinion interprets this as a reference only to his body, which [nevertheless] suggests that that souls are as if lost and cannot enter heaven until the coming of the Messiah. However, my lord, Jews have opposed all of this, and wherever St. Jerome translated "hell," they translate "grave" or "pit."

43. **And the famine was still severe in that land. 2. And when they had eaten up the food they had brought from Egypt, their father repeated to them: "Go again and buy some food for us." 3. Judah said to him: "That man, lord of the land, swore to us, saying: 'Do**

---

[60] That is, Bilhah. Cf. Gen. 35:22.

not let me see your face, nor appear before me, unless your brother comes with you.' 4. If you will send our brother with us, we will go and buy food, 5. but if you won't send him, we will not go, for that man said to us: 'Do not appear before me unless your brother comes with you.' " 6. Israel said: "Why did you do me so wrong as to tell that man that you had another brother?" 7. They told him: "He asked us in detail about us and our generations, asking us: 'Is your father alive? Have you another brother?' and we had to answer everything in detail. How were we to know that he would say: 'Bring your brother'?" 8. Judah said to his father Israel: "Send this lad with me, and let us go, and that will allow us to live and not die, we and you and our families. 9. I will be responsible for him. Hold me accountable if I don't bring him back and set him before you. I will consider myself a sinner before you forever. 10. For if we hadn't dawdled, we could have been there and back twice." 11. Their father Israel said to them: "Friends, since that's how it is, do this: take the best [things] that are in the land (*de optimis terrae fructibus*)[61] in your baggage, and take this man as a gift some wax (*resinae*)[62] and some honey and theriaca (*storacis*)[63] and acorns and pine-nuts and almonds. 12. And take double the money in your hands, including the money that was put in the mouths of your bags; for perhaps this was a mistake. 13. And take your brother and go to that man. 14. And I ask that abundant (*omnipotens*)[64] God to give you favor before that man, and that he may send and release your other brother and Benjamin, for since I was left without my son Joseph, I imagine I'll be left without the others." 15. These men took the aforementioned present and carried twice the money in their hands, and went to Egypt, and appeared before Joseph. 16. As soon as Joseph saw Benjamin with them, he told his majordomo: "Take these men with you to my house, and slaughter some animals and dress them, for these

---

[61] The Vulgate version: "of the best fruits of the land."

[62] Thus the Vulgate.

[63] The Vulgate version: "styrax," a genus of shrubs and trees, some of them—such as benzoin—yielding resins.

[64] Thus the Vulgate. The Hebrew has *El Shaddai*. In the *JPS Torah Commentary*, Sarna annotates: "The modern conjecture that has gained widest currency connects shaddai with Akkadian *šadu*, 'a mountain,' often used as a divine (and royal) epithet. The name would originally have meant, 'The One of the Mountain,' probably referring to a cosmic mount or corresponding to the divine epithet 'The Rock.' "

men will dine with me at lunch time." 17. And that majordomo
did as Joseph commanded him, and the majordomo took those
men to the house. 18. And once those men had been put inside
Joseph's house, they were very much afraid, and they said: "No
doubt we have been brought here on account of that money that
they put in our sacks before, in order to upset us, and accuse us,
and enslave us, and steal our animals." 19. And they went to that
majordomo of Joseph's and spoke to him at the doorway of the
house. 20. They told him: "Sir, you know very well that we
came before to buy food, 21. and it happened that at the first inn,
we went to open our bags, and each one's money was in the
mouth of his bag—I mean the money we had weighed out—
which we have brought with us. 22. And we are even bringing
double the money to buy food; we do not know who put our
money in our bags." 23. He said to them: "Peace be with you!
Do not be afraid, for your God, who is the God of your
father. . . . I suppose you must have [unwittingly] carried off
some money that was hidden among the food that you were taking, for there is no doubt that I took your money and silver."
And he brought out Simeon to them. 24. And as soon as they entered Joseph's house, they gave them water to wash their feet,
and they gave them feed for their asses.

This was a sign of baptism, by which they would be washed of their sins; and
it said "to wash their feet" for two reasons: one, because the feet are the cause
of all bodily movements, since they are the bases of the columns of the house;
the other, because "feet" may just be a general term rather than referring specifically to feet, and hence the text merely makes mention of what he gave them,
unless the water was specifically for this purpose.

25. And they got the present ready for Joseph's arrival to eat lunch,
for they had heard that they were to eat there. 26. And as soon
as Joseph came home, they gave him the present they had
brought, and they bowed down to the ground. 27. And he asked
them if they were well, and he said: "Is your aged father of whom
you spoke well? Is he still alive?" 28. They said: "Your servant is
well; our father is still alive," and they knelt and bowed down.

Some comment here that Joseph was inquiring about the health of both his father and his grandfather Isaac. When he asked: "Is your father well?" he meant
Jacob; and when he said "aged," he meant his grandfather. They replied that
their father was well, but concerning their grandfather they made no reply, for
he was dead. Hence the Talmudists deduce that one should never answer such

questions with bad news, but should remain silent, for if the listener is intelligent, seeing that they don't answer his question, he will understand by himself.

29. **And he raised his eyes and saw Benjamin, his brother, son of his mother, and he said: "Is this perhaps your youngest brother that you told me about?" And he said: "God give you His grace, my son." 30. And Joseph hurried out, because he was seized by the ardor of mercy toward his brother (*quia commota fuerant viscera ejus super fratre suo*),**[65] **and he sought a place to weep, and went into his bedroom and wept there. 31. And he washed his face, and came out, and took control of himself, and ordered the table set. 32. And they set a table for him on his side, and for them on their side, and separately for the Egyptians who ate with him, for the Egyptians were not accustomed to eat bread with the Jews, for it was abhorrent to them. 33. And they sat down before him, the eldest as eldest and the youngest as youngest,**[66] **and the men looked at each other in astonishment.**

Some are of the opinion that they didn't sit down on their own, but Joseph tapped with a rod on his cup, and said: "It tells me that So-and-so is the eldest, so let him sit in the highest place, and So-and-so, who is younger, should sit below him"; and thus he went on with all of them, and this is what astonished them; for otherwise, there was no reason to be astonished.

34. **And he gave them presents, and Benjamin's present was five times greater than the present of any of the others. And they drank, and got drunk from the refreshments.**

Rabbi Solomon notes that from the day Joseph's brothers had sold him they had never drunk wine until that day out of mourning for him, and therefore they got drunk, because they weren't used to it.

44. **And he ordered his majordomo, saying: "Have these men's bags filled with as much food as they can carry, and put each one's money in the mouth of his bag.**

He ordered him to do this in the presence of each one of them, and the reason was that if he hadn't done it in their presence, they would have been right to say, when they found the goblet, that they didn't know who put it there. But

---

[65] Thus the Vulgate: "for he was inwardly moved over his brother."
[66] That is, in order of seniority.

he wanted them to think that he [realized he] had wronged them by putting them to so many tests, and that now he wanted to make it up to them.

> 2. And you will put that silver (*singular*)[67] goblet of mine in the mouth of the bag of the youngest one, and also the money his food is worth." And he did as Joseph told him. 3. With the first light of morning, they were dispatched and sent off, they and their asses. 4. When they left the city—they hadn't gone far—Joseph told his majordomo: "Go follow those men, and as soon as you catch up with them, ask them: 'Why did you return evil for good?

He didn't wait to give this command until they had traveled far, because if they had been far away, since they were all brave men, no one would have been able to catch them, whereas since they were near the city, they would be frightened.

> 5. You stole that goblet from which my master drank, and which he used to determine whether those who came to his house were thieves, as if he were unconcerned about it; and almost as if by divining, it tells him which ones are thieves. No doubt you have done a wicked thing!' " 6. And as soon as he caught up with them, he told them those very words. 7. They said to him: "Sir, why are you saying things like this, which are better left unsaid? God forbid that we should do such a thing! 8. For we brought you back from the land of Canaan the money we found in the mouth of our bags. How then could we have stolen silver or gold from your master's house? 9. If it be found with any of your servants, let him die! Moreover, may the rest of us be my lord's slaves." 10. He said to them: "What you say is right: let the man who took it be my slave, and you will go free."

Rabbi Solomon says: "What you say is exactly right, for all who are aware of a theft and cover it up must suffer; but I choose to behave more magnanimously. Whoever has the cup will be my slave, and the rest of you can go in peace." But the Master is not satisfied with this commentary, and Master Leon says as follows: "What you say is right, for my master and I suspect you, and therefore, let him who has the cup be my slave, and the rest of you, go in peace."

> 11. And they made haste, and each one put his bag on the ground, and each one opened the mouth of his bag. 12. And he began

---

[67] This word seems to have appeared in the Vulgate text Arragel consulted; standard editions of the Vulgate, however, have "argenteum" ("silver").

looking and searching, starting with the eldest and ending with the youngest; and the goblet was found in Benjamin's bag. 13. And they rent their clothes and loaded their packs back on their asses and returned to the city.

This trial came upon them because they had made Jacob rend his clothes on account of not knowing [what had become] of Joseph.

14. And Judah and his brothers entered Joseph's house, and Joseph was still there, and they threw themselves on the ground before him. 15. Joseph said to them: "What is this that you have done? Do you not know that a man like me tests men? (*quod non sit similis mei in augurandi scientia?*)"[68] 16. Judah said: "What can we say, or how can we justify ourselves? God has passed judgment and remembered the sins of your servants. Here we are, slaves of my lord, both we and the one in whose possession the goblet was found." 17. He said: "Far be it from me to do that; but he in whose possession the goblet was found, let him be my slave, and the rest of you, go to your father in peace."

Judah thought that Joseph intended to sentence Benjamin to death, and he was upset; but when he heard him say that he meant to take him as his slave he said: "I want to be [your] slave in place of him, and let the lad go with his brothers."

V. Of How Judah Spoke to Joseph Until He Made Himself Known to Them, and How They Brought Jacob in Wagons[69]

18. Judah went up to him and said: "Please, my lord, may I have a short audience with my lord, and do not be angry with your servant, for you are as great as King Pharaoh.

He meant: "If I get angry, I will kill both you and him."

19. My lord, you asked your servants, saying: 'Do you have a father or brother?' 20. And we told my lord that we had an old father,

---

[68] The Vulgate version: "that a man like me knows how to divine?"

[69] The chapter division here corresponds to the break between the second ("Mikkets") and third ("Va-Yiggash") portions of the story of Joseph as read in the synagogue liturgy.

> and a son he had in his old age, and how his other brother had
> died, so that he alone was left of his mother, and that his father
> had grown very fond of him for that reason. 21. And you said to
> your servants: 'Bring him here to me, for I want to see him and
> take an interest in him.'

It is the same as to say: "My lord, one can presume that ever since the beginning, you have spoken deceptively with us, for these questions would have
been proper if we had been negotiating to marry our son or daughter to you.
Nevertheless, we never refused to tell you the truth, and we told you that we
had a father and brothers. It is therefore especially incumbent upon you, since
your status is as great as that of the king, to keep your promise that you would
take an interest in the lad."

> 22. We told you, my lord, that this boy could not leave his father, for
> there was no doubt that if he left his father he would die. 23. But
> you said to your servants: 'If your youngest brother doesn't come
> with you, do not appear before me again.' 24. Thus, when we
> went to your servant, our father, we told him what you had said.
> 25. Our father once again told us that we should return to buy
> him some food. 26. And we told him that we couldn't go unless
> he gave us our youngest brother to come with us, saying: 'Friend,
> we cannot appear before that man if our youngest brother doesn't
> go with us.' 27. Your servant, my father, answered us and said:
> 'You know very well that my wife bore me two sons, 28. but one
> of them is gone from me, and I suppose that some animal or
> snake carried him off, for up to now I have never seen him since.
> 29. And if you take this other one from my face, and some disas-
> ter befalls him, you will make me die with a bad end.'

St. Jerome translated: "You will make my white head go down to hell." Hence
they comment that the patriarchs went to hell until Jesus Christ broke [the
gates of] hell and took them out of there, as I have already told you. For "grave"
and "hell" almost seem to be the same thing, since the soul is not mentioned.

> 30. Now, if I go to my father and don't take the boy with me—since
> his soul is bound up with this boy's soul—31. when he sees that
> the boy is not coming, he will die because of that, and your ser-
> vants will send the white head of our father down to the grave
> (*ad inferos*)[70] with grief and sorrow. 32. For, my lord, I took this

---

[70] The Vulgate version.

**boy from my father on my responsibility, saying: 'If I don't bring
him back to you, I will be a sinner before my father forever.'**

Some translate: "I would be excommunicated."

33. **Now, my lord, please let me take the place of this boy as my
    lord's slave, and let the boy go with his brothers;**

He told him: "My lord, if you're looking for a slave, you'd be much better off
to have me than him; for I can do a lot more than he—whether it be manual
labor, fighting, or knowing how to serve in a palace.

34. **for how could I could I go to my father if the boy were not with
    me, or how could I bear to witness the woe that would come and
    overtake my father because of that?"**

45. **And Joseph could not bear what he was hearing, on account of
    those who were present, and he commanded: "Have everyone
    here go outside!" So no one was there with him when Joseph
    made himself known to his brothers.**

Joseph did this so as not to shame his brothers in public. Others say that he
wanted to show them that he was circumcised, so that there could be no doubt
that he was their brother. At that time circumcision was not practiced in
Egypt, as it is now, ever since that confounder of the laws Muhammad; and
even now the Moorish circumcision is not the same as that of the Jew. And
this is how they recognized him.

2. **And he raised his voice in weeping, and the Egyptians heard it; it
   was so loud that it was even heard in Pharaoh's house.**

Because he knew about the cruel death that Christ would suffer; for it is obvious that there was no reason for him to weep on his own account, because at
present both he and his father had great consolation.

3. **Joseph said to his brothers: "I am Joseph. Is my father still
   alive?" But his brothers could not answer him, so dumbfounded
   were they on account of him. 4. Joseph said to his brothers:
   "Come close to me," and they came forward.**

This was because he wanted to show them that he was circumcised, as they
were, so that they could see that he wasn't deceiving them.

**Joseph said: "I am the one whom you sold into Egypt. 5. Now, do
not be sad or reproach yourselves because you sold me hither; it**

was so that you might have life that God sent me ahead of you; 6.
for, although the famine began in the world two years ago, there
are still five years in which there shall be no plowing, or sowing,
or reaping. 7. And God sent me ahead of you that you might remain in the world, and so that you could come and have a great
deliverance. 8. Now you should know that it was not you who
sent me here, but God; and He has brought me to a status where
I am Pharaoh's father and lord over all his house, and ruler in all
the land of Egypt. 9. Make haste, and go to my father, and tell
him these words. Your son Joseph sends you the following message: 'Know that the Lord has made me lord over all the Egyptians. Come to me; do not delay. 10. And you will be in the land
of Goshen, and you will be near me—you and your sons and your
grandchildren and all that you have. 11. And I will provide for
you there—for there are yet five years of famine—for otherwise,
you and your household and all that you have would perish.' 12.
And your eyes and those of my brother Benjamin see that I am
telling you this with my own mouth, without an interpreter.

This means that, though up to now he had spoken with them through a Hebrew interpreter, now Joseph spoke to them in Hebrew himself. Besides the
sign of circumcision that he had already shown them, this was a second sign to
show them that he was Joseph, their brother.

13.   And you will tell my father about all the honor I have acquired in
      Egypt, and all that you have seen; and go quickly and bring me
      my father here." 14. And he fell upon the neck of Benjamin, his
      brother, and wept; and Benjamin wept likewise on Joseph's neck.

Because he saw through the Holy Spirit that the Holy House[71] that would be
located in Benjamin's territory would be destroyed. And Benjamin wept on
Joseph's neck because he saw that the tabernacle of Shiloh, which would be
built in Joseph's territory, would also perish.[72] Others say that both brothers
wept because the Messiah would be crucified in Jerusalem, which was in Benjamin's territory, and their weeping expressed humanity's sorrow over his
death. Yet they also wept for joy because of the great good that his death and
resurrection would accomplish: salvation from the consequences of Adam's sin
and deliverance from hell. There is nothing new about the notion that men

---

[71] That is, the Temple.
[72] Cf. 1 Sam. 4.

would weep for joy, because of the hasty movements of the animal passions, as naturalists have explained very well.

15. **And he kissed all his brothers and wept with them. Then his brothers began to speak at length with him. 16. And the cry and the news rang out in Pharaoh's house, saying: "Joseph's brothers have come," which pleased Pharaoh and his noblemen.**

It pleased them to know that he had honorable brothers, and that they didn't have a slave as governor over them.

17. **Pharaoh said to Joseph: "Tell your brothers: 'Load up your beasts and take them to the land of Canaan,**

Some translate: "Goad your beasts," and they explain that it would have made no sense here to say "load your beasts," for everything was to be transported in wagons, which had already been given them on Pharaoh's command. Others see no problem in this, because they say that even when there are wagons the beasts carry the cargo.

18. **and take your father and your households and come to me, and I will give you the best of the land of Egypt and you will eat the best things of the land'; 19. and I advise you to tell them this on your own: 'Friends, take wagons from the land of Egypt for your families and your wives, and take your father and come. 20. And don't be concerned about your household goods, for the best of all the land of Egypt is yours.' " 21. And the sons of Israel did so, and Joseph gave them wagons by Pharaoh's command, and he gave them food and money for the journey. 22. To each of them he distributed two suits of clothing, and he gave Benjamin three hundred pieces of silver and five suits of clothing.**

He had to give them these because their clothes were torn; they had gotten torn when Benjamin was arrested on account of the goblet. He gave Benjamin three hundred pieces of silver, because the law provides that anyone who sells a slave into a foreign land is fined ten times the value of the slave. The value of a slave is thirty coins, and ten times thirty is three hundred, all of which he gave Benjamin; but he didn't give the others any money. He also gave him five suits of clothing—two suits as in the case of the other brothers; but [Joseph's] wife and his two sons each gave him an additional suit, much finer than those of the others, so this adds up to five suits of clothing.

23. And likewise to his father he sent ten he-asses laden with the best things of Egypt, and ten she-asses laden with food and cooked bread and other provisions for his father for the journey.

Some say that this was a sign of the holy sacrifice of the Temple.

24. And he sent his brothers off, and they left there, and he said to them: "Don't quarrel with each other on the way, saying: 'You sold him,' 'No, you were the one who sold him.' " 25. And they left Egypt and went to the land of Canaan, to their father Jacob. 26. And they told him what had happened, telling him how Joseph was still alive and that he ruled over the land of Egypt. And the movement of his heart and his inner warmth stopped; and he was as if dead, for he refused to believe it. 27. And they told him all that Joseph had said to them, and he saw the wagons that Joseph sent to transport him, and the spirit of Jacob their father revived.

Jacob had two striking indications that Joseph was alive: first, the wagons and the great present of the best jewels of Egypt; and he said to himself that if it were not true, it would be impossible for them to have brought such a great present by any other means. Second, the fact that Joseph was alive was proven because the shock of losing Joseph had made the Holy Spirit depart from him. It is a well-known fact that the Holy Spirit dwells in a man only when he is joyful, not when he is mourning; and that's why the Holy Spirit had abandoned Jacob. Now, when he saw his sons and the wagons, prophecy was restored to him, and that's why the text says: "the spirit of Jacob their father revived."

28. Israel said: "Enough! I have heard great joy and consolation in that my son Joseph is still alive! I want to go and see him before I die."

46. And Israel set out with all that was his, and he came to Beersheba, and there he made sacrifices to the God of his father Isaac. 2. The Lord said to Jacob, who is Israel, in the revelation of the night: "Jacob! Jacob!" He said: "Here I am."

Although the Lord God had told Jacob that he should no longer be called Jacob, here He again called him Jacob. This change of Jacob's name was not the same as the change He made from Abram to Abraham; we can see that He never called him Abram again, but rather Abraham. The reason is that Abraham was called Abram before he knew God, and Abram was his original name, so it would have been wrong to go on calling him by this name of [pagan] agnosticism, instead of the name he received when he knew God: Abraham. Jacob, however, had this name as a believer. Hence, although his name was changed to Israel, Jacob was not a pagan name, for they had given it to him at birth.

> 3. **And He said: "I am the God of your father. Fear not to go to Egypt, for I will make you a great generation there. 4. I will go down with you to Egypt, and I will lift you and raise you up from there,**

Here He repeated Himself, saying: "I will lift you and raise you up." This means that he would raise his soul to heaven, and that He would have his body and his bones brought up from Egypt.

> **and Joseph will put his hand on your eyes."**

It means that he would participate in his burial.

> 5. **And Jacob set out from Beer-sheba, and the sons of Israel took their father Jacob and their families and their wives in the wagons that Pharaoh had sent to transport them. 6. And they took their livestock and the wealth that they had amassed in the land of Canaan, and Jacob and all his offspring came to Egypt: 7. his sons, and his sons' sons, his daughters and his sons' daughters, and all his offspring came with him to Egypt.**

Jacob had only one daughter, but the text said "daughters," in the plural. You should know that the text often does this, that is, gives a plural with a singular meaning, as when it said: "The sons of Pallu: Eliab,"[73] "The sons of Dan: Hushim,"[74] but in each case there was only one son. Others say that it refers to daughters-in-law, because fathers-in-law are accustomed to call them "daughters."

VI. Of the Names of the Children of Israel Who Came to Egypt, and of Their Number

> 8. **These are the names of the children of Israel who came to Egypt, which are as follows: Jacob and his sons. Jacob's firstborn is Reuben. 9. And Reuben's sons were: Enoch and Pallu and**

---

[73] Num. 26:8.
[74] Gen. 46:23.

Hezron and Carmi. 10. And Simeon's sons: Jemuel and Jamin and Ohad and Jachin and Zohar, and Saul the son of a Canaanite.

Rabbi Abraham says that, according to the Law, none of the [founders of the] tribes married a Canaanite. However, Rabbi Solomon says that this Saul was the son of Dinah, who was raped by a Canaanite. Some say that with each of the sons, a daughter was born; but the Law gives no indication of this. Some even say that they married their sisters.

11. And Levi's sons: Gershon and Kohath and Merari. 12. And Judah's sons were: Er and Onan and Shelah and Perez and Zerah—but Er and Onan died in the land of Canaan; and Perez's sons were: Hezron and Hamul. 13. And Issachar's sons: Tola and Puvah and Iob and Shimron. 14. Zebulun's sons: Sered and Elon and Jahleel. 15. These are the sons that Leah bore Jacob in the countryside of Aram, besides his daughter Dinah; so that all the souls of her sons and daughters are thirty three. 16. And the sons of Gad: Ziphion and Haggi, Shuni and Ezbon, Eri and Arodi and Areli. 17. And Asher's sons: Imnah and Ishvah and Ishvi and Beriah and Heber and Malchiel.[75] 18. These are the sons of Zilpah, whom Laban gave to his daughter Leah, and she bore these children to Jacob: sixteen souls. 19. The sons of Jacob's wife Rachel: Joseph and Benjamin. 20. And to Joseph in Egypt were born these sons, whom Asenath, daughter of Poti-phera minister of Alexandria, bore to him: Manasseh and Ephraim. 21. And Benjamin's sons: Bela and Becher and Ashbel, Gera and Naaman, Ehi and Rosh, Muppim and Huppim and Ard. 22. These are the descendants of Rachel who were born to Jacob: fourteen in all. 23. And Dan's sons: Hushim. 24. And Naphtali's sons: Jahzeel and Guni and Jezer and Shillem. 25. These were the sons of Bilhah, whom Laban gave to his daughter Rachel, and she bore these to Jacob: they were seven souls. 26. Thus all the souls that came with Jacob to Egypt, those who came out of his loins, aside from the wives of Jacob's sons, numbered sixty six souls altogether, 27. plus Joseph's two sons who were born to him in Egypt. Thus the number of all the souls that came with Jacob to Egypt is seventy.

By adding them up, one finds that there were really only sixty nine. Some complete the number of seventy with Jacob himself, and others complete it with

---

[75] The biblical text states that Heber and Malchiel were Beriah's sons.

Jochebed, who was born between the wall and the barbican, as they were entering Egypt. This Jochebed was Levi's daughter.

VII. Of How Joseph Saw His Father Jacob, and of How Jacob's Brothers Saw Pharaoh, and of How Jacob Came to Pharaoh

28. Jacob sent Judah ahead of him to show him the land of Goshen,
so that they could go to the land of Goshen. 29. And Joseph ordered his horse saddled, and went out to meet his father Israel, to
Goshen, and he stood before him and threw himself on his neck
and wept while he was like that on his neck. 30. Israel said to
Joseph: "Now I can die, for I have seen your face, and that you
are still alive." 31. Joseph told his father and those of his household and his brothers: "I want to go to give an account to
Pharaoh and tell him that my brothers and my father's household, who were in the land of Canaan, have come to me. 32. And
I will tell him: 'These men are shepherds of sheep, besides having
much livestock; and they have brought with them their sheep and
their cattle and all that is theirs.' 33. I want you to agree that
when Pharaoh summons you and asks you what is your business,
34. you should tell him thus: 'My lord, your servants have been
cattlemen from our youth up to now,' so that you may be and
dwell in the land of Goshen, for you should know that the Egyptians abhor all who are shepherds of sheep."

Here the commentary says that the Egyptians at that time didn't eat meat, nor
did they allow in their midst a man who slaughtered sheep, as is the custom in
India today. And they abhor shepherds because they drink the milk of sheep,
for they don't eat or drink anything that comes from a living thing.

47. And Joseph went and said to Pharaoh: "My father and my brothers, who were in the land of Canaan, have come to me; they are
in the land of Goshen." 2. And he took some of his brothers—
five of them in all—and brought them before Pharaoh. 3.
Pharaoh said to his brothers: "What is your business?" And they
told him: "My lord, we are shepherds of sheep, both we and our
father. 4. And, my lord, we came to dwell in this land because we
couldn't find pasture for our cattle on account of the great famine
that is in the land of Canaan. Please let us stay in the land of
Goshen."

It is surprising that they said they couldn't find pasture, and that is why they came to Egypt, because in Egypt as well, with the famine, they would have found no pasture; so this reason they offered—that they came because they didn't have pasture—was not legitimate. However, the Master concludes that in the land of Canaan, because of the famine, men ate the grass and exhausted it. But since in Egypt they had access to bread, they didn't eat the grasses, and there was pasture—all the more so because it was irrigated land.

> 5. Pharaoh said to Joseph: "Since your father and your brothers have come, 6. you are in possession of the land of Egypt: settle them in the best of the land; let them be in the land of Goshen. And if you know of any reliable men (*viros industrios*)[76] among them, put them in charge of my cattle." 7. Jacob also brought his father and stood him before Pharaoh, and Jacob greeted and blessed Pharaoh.

The Scripture doesn't literally say "greeted," but only "he blessed him." Since, however, the contents of this blessing are not recorded, Rabbi Solomon said that he didn't really bless him, but only greeted him. And the Master says that it is not customary to greet the king, for men who are equals greet each other, but not the king. Therefore he affirms that, even though Scripture doesn't record the blessing, it means that he blessed him nonetheless; for it is customary for old men, when they go before kings, to bless them and ask God to exalt their estates. Some say that the blessing Jacob gave him was that whenever he went to the Nile, it would rise to meet him. Others say that he put an end to the famine.

> 8. Pharaoh asked Jacob to tell him how old he was. 9. Jacob replied to Pharaoh: "The years I have lived are one hundred and thirty years; few and evil have been the years of my life, and they have not come up to the life spans of my ancestors in the way they lived."

There are two strange things about this passage: (1) Why did Pharaoh ask Jacob his age? (2) Why did Jacob complain and say that his days were few and evil—130 years! But the reason is this: Jacob's white hair and old age had come upon him because of the pain and grief he had suffered, not on account of his age. He told Pharaoh that he came to dwell for a while in that land, implying that he still thought he would return to his own land. Pharaoh was amazed at how old Jacob was, and he said that he had never seen such an old man in

---

[76] Thus the Vulgate.

Egypt: "How then can you expect to live long enough to still have hope of returning to your land?" And this is why he asked him how old he was; and
hence, Jacob explained that his white hair and aged appearance were not the
result of his age in years, but of grief and sorrow.

10. **And Jacob blessed Pharaoh and went out from before Pharaoh.
11. And Joseph settled his father and his brothers and gave them
properties in the land of Egypt, in the best of the land, which is
the land of Rameses, as Pharaoh had commanded him.**

He did this at Pharaoh's command, so that the people would not consider them
slaves.

12. **And Joseph sustained his father and his brothers and all his father's household with bread, as much as the family could eat.**

VIII. Of How Joseph Took All the Money in the Land of Egypt, and How He Set Aside a Fifth for the King

13. **Since there was no bread in all that land—for the famine was severe in the land of Canaan, exceedingly so—and those of the land
of Egypt and the land of Canaan were delirious with hunger, 14.
Joseph collected to himself all the money that could be had in the
land of Egypt and in the land of Canaan in exchange for the food
they bought from him, and Joseph took all the money to
Pharaoh's house.**

The Law makes this comment to emphasize Joseph's great goodness and loyalty, that he gave the king all that he collected and kept nothing for himself,
thereby teaching us that a man should give a good account of what is entrusted
to him.

15. **And when the money gave out in the land of Egypt and the land
of Canaan, all the Egyptians returned to Joseph, telling him:
"Why do you want us to die here before your eyes, since there is
no more money?"**

This is what the Egyptians said to Joseph: "My lord, since the money in the
land of Canaan has given out, you have no more hope that they will come from
there to buy bread. What good will it do you if we die and you still have bread
in your barns?" The money ran out at the same time among both the rich and

the poor. The *Midrash Genesis Rabbah* says that Joseph learned from the Holy Spirit how much to charge the rich and how much to charge the poor, so that both ran out of money at the same time.

> **16.** **Joseph told them: "Give me your cattle, for I will give you bread for your cattle, since you say the money has given out." 17. And they brought Joseph their cattle, and Joseph gave them bread in exchange for their horses and sheep and cows and asses; and he sustained them with bread that year in exchange for their livestock. 18. And when that year was over, they returned to him the following year (*anno secundo*)[77] and told him: "My lord, it is public knowledge that the money gave out, and you have the cattle and beasts. My lord, we have nothing left but our bodies and our lands. 19. Why do you want us to die, when you can help both us and our lands? Buy us and our lands in exchange for bread, and we and our lands will be Pharaoh's slaves, and the land will not become a waste."**

According to Rabbi Solomon, this was the second year of the famine. For, although Joseph had told his father that there were five years of famine remaining, when Jacob came to Egypt, the good years came with him. Joseph in his wisdom would have been aware of this, since everyone knew that God performed a miracle for Jacob, in that when he went to the Nile, it rose and came out to meet him. Therefore, plenty came to Egypt because of Jacob, and no one would suspect that this was a failure on Joseph's part. And in the *Tosefta Sotah*,[78] which is a book of the Talmud, they say that as soon as Jacob died, the famine returned to the land. Also in Sifrei[79] we read that the blessing Jacob gave Pharaoh was that there would no longer be a famine in Egypt; but the years of famine were fulfilled when Jacob died. Rabbi Simeon said that it was blasphemy against the honor of God to say that His miracles would endure during the life of the just, but would be annulled when they died. Another rabbi replied, saying: "I disagree. God's honor is better served by His blessing the world during the lifetime of the just, and withdrawing that blessing when the just are missing from the world. Thereby the world is made aware that God brings good things on account of the good." Hence, it is his opinion that the

---

[77] Thus the Vulgate.

[78] Sotah ("Errant Wife") is the sixth—or in some manuscripts the fifth—tractate in the order "Nashim" ("Women") of the Mishnah. The *Tosefta* ("Addition") is a lengthy collection of glosses on the Mishnah that was not edited in its present form before the fourth century C.E.

[79] ("Books"), a midrash to the books of Numbers and Deuteronomy thought to have been compiled around 200 C.E. or shortly thereafter.

five years of famine were fulfilled after Jacob died—particularly since the text doesn't mention more years of famine. Others, however, say that Jacob's coming to Egypt didn't end the famine at all, and they have other arguments to support their view.

> 20. And Joseph bought all of the lands of the Egyptians for Pharaoh, for on account of their great hunger, each one sold his fields, so that the land became Pharaoh's. 21. And he made the people move from one town to another, from the beginning of the kingdom to the end of it. 22. But he did not buy the land of the priests and ministers, because they had an allotment from the king, and they ate from the allotment that Pharaoh gave them, so they did not have to sell their lands.

Although we have translated this as "priests and ministers," we don't really know exactly what their function and duties were; however, it has been argued that they received an allotment from Pharaoh as lawyers and judges who ruled on lawsuits. And it has even been said that this allotment was granted them by Pharaoh after they decided the case of the tear in Joseph's garment, which his mistress tore; and that was as follows. She said that Joseph raped her. Joseph denied this and said she was lying. The torn garment was found to be in her possession. They didn't know which of them to believe; but these sages sentenced that if the tear in Joseph's garment was in the back, it was a sign that she had torn it off him, and he was guiltless; and if the tear was in the front, that Joseph did it himself to run away from her, and she was telling the truth. And they found that the tear was in the back, and therefore Joseph escaped and did not die. And this decision pleased Pharaoh, and hence he gave them that allotment.[80]

> 23. Joseph told the people: "As of today, I have bought you and your lands for Pharaoh. Here is seed; sow the land. 24. And it shall be that when the fruits come, you will give one-fifth to Pharaoh, and four-fifths will be yours to sow the lands, and for you and those of your household and your families to eat."

(1) To sow; (2) to eat; (3) for those whom you have in your house, such as manservants and maidservants; (4) for your families to eat.

---

[80] This is a Muslim interpretation based on Qur'an 12:26–27: "And a witness of her own folk testified: If his shirt is torn from front, then she speaketh truth and he is of the liars. And if his shirt is torn from behind, then she hath lied and he is of the faithful."

25. They said to him: "You have given us life, so we are grateful to you, my lord, and we will be Pharaoh's slaves." 26. And Joseph established this law in the land of Egypt, that they should give Pharaoh one-fifth; but he did not buy the land of the priests. That land alone did not become Pharaoh's. 27. And Israel settled in the land of Egypt, in the land of Goshen, and they put down roots there, and increased and multiplied in it.

IX. Of How Jacob Fell Ill, and of the Years That He Lived in the Land of Egypt, and of How He Made Joseph Swear to Bury Him in the Land of Canaan[81]

28. Jacob lived in the land of Egypt seventeen years, and all of Jacob's life was one hundred and forty seven years.

Jacob's descent into Egypt was a sign to the people of Israel of their third captivity, when they were under the Roman yoke. For there is no doubt that Jacob's sons caused their being in captivity by selling Joseph, and Jacob had to go to Egypt on account of the famine, and he thought he would escape and get out of there once the famine was over, but he didn't leave there. Instead, their captivity was prolonged, and he had to die there, and they had to take his bones from Egypt. The same thing happened to Israel, for they themselves practically caused this captivity by the death of Christ. Likewise, they made a pact and truce with the Romans, for the last king Israel had in the Second Temple was King Agrippa. He surrendered to the Romans and sought asylum with them, and Jerusalem was gripped by famine, and the captivity endures to this day, and no one knows when it will end.

29. And the days were drawing near for Israel to die, and he summoned his son Joseph and said to him: "If I have found grace in your eyes, I beg you to put your hand under my thigh,

The Law does not say that he put it there, in the same way that Eliezer, Abraham's servant, did,[82] so some argue that he didn't mean for him to swear an oath. But the Law explicitly says that he told him: "Swear to me," and that he swore. However, what he was asking him there was to maintain Jacob's house-

---

[81] This chapter division corresponds to the break between the third ("Va-Yiggash") and fourth ("Va-Yeḥi") portions of the story of Joseph as read in the synagogue liturgy.
[82] Cf. Gen. 24:9.

hold and his brothers as well as himself, as long as he lived. Others say that here he was indicating to his son the coming of the true Messiah, who would be a descendant of Jacob, and that he said "thigh" as a euphemism.[83]

> **that you may do me so much good and mercy and truth, that you bury me not in Egypt.**

The good that the living do to other living persons is self-interested, but a good deed done to the dead is truly good, since one can expect no reward from the dead.

30.   **Arrange for me to lie with my ancestors, and take me from Egypt and bury me where they are buried." And he told him: "I will do what you command me."**

It is the same as to say that he assured him that he would do as he commanded him. Others say that he meant: I will do you as you command me, and I will command my sons not to bury me in Egypt, so that they may not make us into gods. And Jacob required this oath of Joseph so that Pharaoh might see it and not prevent him from doing as he wished.

31.   **He said: "Swear it to me," and he swore it to him. And Israel bowed down at the head of the bed, giving thanks to God.**

Hence they say that God's glory is always everywhere, and that he was showing reverence to the Lord God. Rabbi Solomon says that God's glory is always over the head of the sick man, and when Jacob saw it, he bowed down. Others say that he bowed down out of gratitude to Joseph for the assurance he had given him; and here Joseph's dream came true: that "the sun and moon bowed down to me." Jacob was the sun, and up to now only the eleven stars, which were his brothers, had bowed down to him; but now his father bowed down.

48.   **After this, they told Joseph: "Know that your father is ill," and he took his two sons, Manasseh and Ephraim, with him. 2. Likewise they told Jacob: "Your son Joseph is coming to see you." And Israel summoned his strength and sat up in the bed. 3. Jacob said to Joseph: "Almighty God appeared to me at Luz in the land of Canaan and blessed me. 4. And He told me thus: 'I will multiply you and make you increase and will give you as**

---

[83] For penis. It was customary to require a person taking an oath to put his hand on the penis of the man to whom he was swearing, so as to swear by the "sign of the covenant" (i.e., circumcision).

> your estate that communities of peoples will come out of you,
> and I will give this land to your offspring after you as a right of
> perpetual property (*in possessionem sempiternam*).'[84]

He said that he was conferring that same blessing on Joseph, and that it was
necessary to do so for the following reason: Rachel died immediately after God
gave him this blessing, and he never had any more sons. Hence it follows that
the blessing was fulfilled in Joseph.

> 5. And you should know that these two sons, who were born to you
>   in the land of Egypt before I came to you from the land of
>   Canaan, are mine; and let Ephraim and Manasseh be mine as re-
>   gards the inheritance, just like Reuben and Simeon, who are my
>   eldest sons. 6. And let the other sons who were born to you, or
>   will be born to you, after these, be yours; I mean, let them in-
>   herit along with their brothers, who are Ephraim and Manasseh.[85]
>   7. And you should know very well that you should not resent my
>   burying your mother Rachel; for as I was coming from Paddan-
>   aram (*Mesopotamia*),[86] Rachel died suddenly, so I wasn't able to
>   take her to be buried where I buried Leah, for she died in the
>   land of Canaan, one plot of ground away from the entrance to
>   Ephrath; and I buried here there on the road to Ephrath, which
>   Ephrath is Bethlehem.

He wanted to inform him that, although he didn't bury her in the cave, as
Jacob's mother had been buried with his father, he did this so that Rachel
would pray to God [for Israel], since she was buried on the road, when Israel
passed by there on their way into captivity. [There was] all the less reason [to
resent her burial there], for after all, he did bury her in the Land of Promise,
and there is no doubt that anyone who is buried there obtains much greater
spiritual glory, as, God willing, I intend to explain at greater length later. Others say that since he had taken Rachel when he was already married to Leah,
he didn't want to bury her in the cave, because he understood that it was a sin
to marry two sisters.[87]

> 8. And Israel looked over Joseph's sons and said: "Who are these?"

---

[84] Thus the Vulgate.

[85] Sarna explains in the *JPS Torah Commentary*: "They shall not constitute separate
tribal entities but shall partake of the inheritance of either Manasseh or Ephraim."

[86] Thus the Vulgate.

[87] According to the Holiness Code, Lev. 18:18: "Do not marry a woman as a rival to
her sister and uncover her nakedness in the other's lifetime."

He wanted to bless them, but the Holy Spirit left him, and he was unable to bless them, and hence he asked: "Who are these, who are unworthy to receive my blessing?" Joseph answered that he had begotten them by his wife, to whom he was legally married with a contract and dowry, and that there was no impediment in them. And Joseph prayed that the Holy Spirit return to him, and God heard his prayer and sent Jacob the Holy Spirit, and he blessed them.

9. Joseph said to his father: "They are my sons, whom the Lord God gave me here." And he said: "Bring them here, and I will bless them." 10. And Israel's eyes were weary with old age—he could not see—and he drew them to him and kissed them and embraced them. 11. Israel said to Joseph: "I never thought I would see you, and the Lord has shown me both you and your offspring." 12. Joseph took them out from between his legs, and he bowed low to the ground. 13. Joseph took the two of them, Ephraim with his right hand, which was on Israel's left, and Manasseh with his left hand, which was on Israel's right, and brought them close to him. 14. But Israel extended his right hand and put it on the head of Ephraim, who was the younger, and he put his left hand on the head of Manasseh; and he paid attention to what he was doing (*commutans manus*),[88] though Manasseh was the older of the two. 15. And he blessed Joseph, and he said to him: "May that God in whose service my fathers Abraham and Isaac walked, that God who has sustained me since I came into the world— 16. that Angel who redeemed me from all harm, who took Israel out of Egypt before [the appointed] time—bless these lads. And may they take my name and title—that is, Ephraim is titled Israel—and may they be called likewise by the name of my fathers Abraham and Isaac; and may they multiply like the fish in the sea." 17. When Joseph saw that his father put his right hand on the head of Ephraim, it grieved him; and he took hold of his father's hand to remove it from Ephraim's head and put it on Manasseh's head. 18. Joseph said to his father: "My lord, it is not as you think, for this other one is the elder; put your right hand on his head." 19. But his father refused and said: "Son, I know very well, very well indeed, that he too will be multiplied in peoples and will increase greatly; but his younger brother will increase more and will be greater, so that his offspring will be more plentiful and more populous."

---

[88] The Vulgate version: "crossing his hands."

This meant that from him would come Gideon, by whose hand our Lord God would work a miracle.

> 20.   **And he blessed them that day and said: "By you shall Israel bless, and when they are to give a blessing, let them say: 'May God make you like Ephraim and like Manasseh.' " And he put Ephraim before Manasseh in this blessing. 21. Israel said to Joseph: "I am dead, but God will be with you and will return you to the land of your ancestors. 22. And I will give you one portion more than your brothers in the land that will be won (*quam tulli*)[89] from the Amorites with swords and with bows."**

And he mentioned the Amorite here, because it was the strongest of the seven nations whom they were to constrain and conquer. Literally the Law says only: "which I took from the Amorites with my sword and with my bow." Rabbi Solomon says that when Simeon and Levi killed the sons of Shechem, Jacob also took up arms against them, and thus Shechem was won. This Shechem[90] was given to Joseph, and he was buried there. Others say that this sword and bow were the prayers and petitions that Jacob made to God, and that the "portion" means that Joseph's sons, Ephraim and Manasseh, would be counted as two tribes, and would receive the inheritance of two tribes in the Land of Promise; and that his words "which I took from the hand of the Amorite," meant that Israel's first conquest in the Land of Promise would be from the hands of the Amorite, that is, the two kings Sihon[91] and Og.[92] The first battle Joshua won was with the Amorite, and he won it fair and square; and Jacob began this battle; for in this regard, the prophet Elisha, when a king of Israel was going into battle with the king of Aram, made the king take a bow and arrows, and the prophet put his hand on it and said: "Shoot the arrows," and he shot them, and he said: "Thus you will utterly destroy the king of Aram (*Syria*)"[93] and this is the meaning of "with my sword and with my bow."[94]

---

[89] The Vulgate's version: "that I took."

[90] The word *shechem* means "portion" in Hebrew.

[91] Cf. Deut. 1:4.

[92] Cf. Deut. 1:4; Num. 21:33.

[93] The Vulgate translation. The identity of the Arameans with the Syrians is clear in the Bible; however, the Hebrew text always uses "Aram" rather than the Greek "Syria," which was introduced by the Septuagint.

[94] The reference here is to 2 Kings 13:14–18: "Now Elisha was fallen sick of his sickness whereof he was to die; and Joash the king of Israel came down unto him, and wept over him, and said: 'My father, my father, the chariots of Israel and the horsemen thereof!' And Elisha said unto him: 'Take bow and arrows'; and he took unto him bow and arrows. And he said to the king of Israel: 'Put thy hand upon the bow'; and he put his hand upon it. And Elisha laid his hands upon the king's hands. And he said: 'Open the window eastward'; and he opened it. Then Elisha said: 'Shoot'; and he shot. And

X. Of Jacob's Predictions to His Sons Concerning What Would Happen to Them at the End of Days

49. **Jacob called his sons and said: "Come near me, and I will tell you what is to befall you in the last days. 2. And draw near and prepare yourselves, O sons of Israel, and hearken to Israel your father.**

Rabbi Solomon says that he wanted to tell them by way of prophecy about the coming of the Messiah, but the Holy Spirit left him, and he began telling them other things, although he did speak somewhat of that. Some are of the opinion that these words that Jacob said to his sons are a blessing rather than a prophecy, and they support their argument by the fact that in conclusion it said: "This is how their father blessed them," etc. If this be so, show me the blessing he gave Reuben and Simeon; for instead of blessing them, he censured them! Nevertheless, he must have blessed them too, but the Law doesn't state the blessings; so I think it is a prophecy.

3. **Reuben, you are my firstborn, and my might and the beginning of my strength (*doloris mei*);[95] you deserved to be exalted**

Rabbi Solomon says that until he begat Reuben, his father Jacob never experienced pollution in dreams;[96] and that is why he called him "the beginning of my strength." "You deserved to be exalted" means that he deserved the priesthood.

and strengthened in power. 4. But because you were as swift as water, you will not have this advantage, because you went up to your father's bed;

This means that kings, who are called "power," should have come from him. "But on account of your discourtesy, that will not happen, because you were as swift as water being poured out, which stops for nothing. You didn't even refrain from doing that with Bilhah"—for it was already mentioned that he slept with her—and you've already heard what the commentary said about that.

since you did me that discourtesy, my place of honor was usurped!

---

he said: 'The Lord's arrow of victory, even the arrow of victory against Aram; for thou shalt smite the Arameans in Aphek, till thou have consumed them.' "

[95] The Vulgate version: "of my sorrow."

[96] That is, nocturnal emission.

There are two commentaries on this: either it means that Jacob never slept with Bilhah again after that; or, according to others, that the Holy Spirit no longer came to him as usual, and the Holy Spirit was lifted from him.

5. Simeon and Levi are brothers; theirs are weapons of offense against those who submitted to them.

This refers to the fact that Simeon and Levi, after those who lived in the city of Shechem had been circumcised and submitted and made a treaty with the sons of Jacob, went to destroy the city. And this was manifestly an offense; and the Targum agrees with this interpretation. However, Rabbi Solomon says that this offense refers to the sale of Joseph and the fact that only Simeon and Levi fully agreed to it. He explains as follows: "If you say that Reuben and Judah went along with it, the Law testifies the contrary, for it says that they disagreed and preferred to cast him into a well, so that they could draw him out later. And if you say that it was the sons of the handmaids, they didn't dislike him that much, for the Law says that he was brought up with them. And if you say it was Issachar and Zebulun, they would not have dared oppose their older brothers. Hence, a thorough investigation reveals that only Simeon and Levi were guilty of the attempted murder of Joseph."

6. Let not my soul enter into their secret,

This refers to the homicide they perpetrated in Shechem; for if God had not miraculously put fear into the hearts of the people of the region, they would all have come against him to kill him.[97] Some say that Jacob's prayer that his soul not enter into their secret referred to what happened with Zimri, which you will hear later, which was that the tribe of Simeon gathered together and brought an Egyptian woman before Moses, saying: "This Egyptian woman, can we lie with her without sin or not, since she is not an Israelite?" Moses replied that it was a sin, and when they heard him say that, they told him: "O Moses! Then who gave you permission to take the daughter of Jethro as your wife?"[98] Jacob, seeing this great disgrace through the Holy Spirit, prayed God that when the Law recounted this man's name in the time of Phineas, he should not be called "son of Jacob," and hence the Law refers to the man who did this as "Zimri, son of Salu, captain of the house of Simeon," not "son of Jacob," so that his father Jacob would not be disgraced by having a bad son.

---

[97] As Jacob himself pointed out: "You have brought trouble on me, making me odious among the inhabitants of the land, the Canaanites and Perizzites; my men are few in number, so that if they unite against me and attack me, I and my house will be destroyed" (Gen. 34:30).

[98] Num. 25:6–8; 14–15.

Let my honor not join them in their gatherings.

Here "honor" means "soul," for doubtless a clean soul is true honor. Jacob was praying here that his name not be mentioned with reference to the assembly of Korah and the other two hundred and fifty men who joined him. Hence, when the Law relates this, it says: "Korah son of Izhar, son of Kohath, son of Levi . . . challenged [him],"[99] but it doesn't say there that Levi was the son of Jacob, as the Law is accustomed to say when referring to worthy descendants: "So-and-so, son of So-and-so, son of Jacob." This is found in the book called Paralipomenon,[100] when it mentions the choir sharing the priestly benefice as "sons of Korah, son of Izhar, son of Kohath, son of Levi, son of Israel."

for with their anger they killed a man,

This refers to the same men of the city of Shechem that they killed.

and when calm, they ripped out and broke the wall.

This likewise refers to the wall of Shechem. The Hebrew says: "they broke *shor*," and *shor* is ambiguous, sometimes meaning "a wall" and other times "a bull," and the Law called Joseph "bull," and his ensign features a bull, for which reason some translate: "They carried off the bull," saying that this refers to the sale of Joseph.

7.   **Cursed be their anger so fierce, and their wrath so harsh!**

Pay close attention to what I am writing: a curse and a blessing are opposites; and just as a blessing desires an increase in strength, a curse seeks a lessening. Hence Rabbi Abraham says—and the Master agrees with him—that what Jacob meant was: "Cursed be their anger," meaning for God to lessen that anger, so that no harm might come to them from it. Rabbi Solomon says: "If you want to know how patient our father Jacob was, you can see this in the fact that, when he reviewed the evil his sons had done, he didn't say: 'May they be cursed!' but God put it in his mouth to say: 'Cursed be their anger!' And this is as Balaam said to Balak: 'How can I curse someone whom God has not cursed?' "[101]

I will divide them in Jacob and scatter them in Israel.

Literally, it means that they would not have their inheritance in the Land of Promise one next to the other, for it is not right for two bad people to be next

---

[99] Num. 16:1.
[100] The two apocryphal books of Chronicles included in the Vulgate.
[101] Num. 23:8.

to each other, or to be bad neighbors; and hence, when they divided the land, they did not receive adjoining portions.

There is no doubt that when two people agree for good or for evil, they can accomplish a great deal. That's why the patriarch Jacob said: "Since these two brothers agree on wickedness, they should be separated from each other, because if they are together they will destroy the world." And this saying was fulfilled in their separation from each other, for when Joshua divided the land among Israel, Simeon's share of towns fell within Judah's portion, so that Simeon was practically stripped of power; and even those towns that fully corresponded to him were scattered and not together, but, as I say, scattered among the towns of Judah, so that they could not join together to do evil. For the worst deeds done in Israel came from the tribe of Simeon. Likewise the tribe of Levi was given the forty eight consecrated cities, where murderers were given refuge, to dwell in; but, as in the case of Simeon, they were given to them scattered apart. And it is said that these two tribes had another separation, since the tribe of Levi did not go out to battle, but stayed behind to exercise the priesthood and sing in the choir. Others say that they were separated in still another way. For the poor can support little pride, and hence it is found among the Jews that most teachers of children and scribes of books, which are tedious and poorly paid occupations, are of the tribe of Simeon. As for Levi, there is no doubt that he was given a life of poverty, traveling from field to field to collect the first fruits and the tithes, so they had to live frugally and without pride. Just as wealth brings much wickedness with it, poverty brings much goodness, as I could very well testify: O Law of God, all who chose to devote themselves to you were repaid with poverty! Jacob asked only for bread and raiment.[102]

8. You, O Judah, your brothers shall praise;

When Judah heard his father reprimanding Simeon and Levi, he pulled back to leave. When Jacob saw that, he said: "Judah, you are not like them."

your hand shall be on the nape of your foes;

This was fulfilled in the time of King David, for they laid on their hands in the battles and decapitated their foes at sword point.

your father's sons will bow down to you.

---

[102] "Jacob then made a vow, saying: 'If God remains with me, if He protects me on this journey that I am making, and gives me bread to eat and clothing to wear, and if I return safe to my father's house—the Lord shall be my God' " (Gen. 28:20–21).

Since the brothers were the sons of four different mothers, but only one father, he said "sons of your father," so as to include all of them in this subservience.

9.   A little lion, and Judah is that lion;

This could simply refer to Judah's great might. However, since it begins "a little lion, and Judah is that lion," it means more than that. For just as the cub is a little lion, so would Judah be at first; for when Saul was king of Israel, David, who was of Judah's lineage, was a sort of commander-in-chief or general, but in the end he became king, a strong lion.

you usurped my son's prey; he will kneel and will lie like a lion or a lioness:

This can be paraphrased: "You were content to take the prey and the booty." Rabbi Solomon says that this refers to the fact that Judah did not agree to kill his daughter-in-law Tamar; nor did he agree to kill Joseph. Others say that from the moment when David began to kill the bear and the lion,[103] he was already considered king, and hence it said: "you were content to take the prey and the booty." It simply means: he was considered king because he had the strength to be one, for he fought against the Philistine, and conquered him, and came out very well.

who will raise him up?

When the lion is upon its prey, it is at its greatest strength, and there is no one in the world of whom it is afraid. This happened in the time of King Solomon; there was no king who did not pay him tribute, and all Israel enjoyed peace beyond description, without the slightest fear.

10.   The scepter will not be taken from Judah nor the leadership from his haunch (*Hebrew: Shiloh*) until he who is to be sent, comes; and the peoples will draw near to him. 11. He will tether his colt to the vine, and the son of his she-ass to the vine-shoot; he will wash his clothing with wine, and his covering with the blood of grapes. 12. His eyes are redder than wine, and his teeth are whiter than milk.

---

[103] "And David said unto Saul: 'Thy servant kept his father's sheep; and when there came a lion, or a bear, and took a lamb out of the flock, I went out after him, and smote him, and delivered it out of his mouth; and when he arose against me, I caught him by his beard, and smote him, and slew him' " (1 Sam. 17:34–36).

There is a great division between Christians and Jews concerning the meaning of this saying, and it would take a long time and much writing to decide between them. Since, however, the very high lord Don Luis de Guzmán, Master of the Order of Knights of Calatrava, has commanded me here to write the opinions of both Jews and Christians concerning the Law; and since the famous Nicholas of Lyra[104] has already done this very well, I shall follow in his footsteps, as I have done hitherto; and thus I will be able to expound both the Christian and the Jewish opinion. It is up to the theologians, defenders of the law, to decide who is right.

The Christians say that here it is proven that the Messiah, who was Jesus Christ, has come, and this is more or less the proof. The Law said: "The scepter will not be taken from Judah nor the scribe from between his feet until the Messiah comes." They observe that as soon as the Messiah came, the Jews would be deprived of their kings and leaders; and that is what happened, for as soon as Jesus came, there were no more princes or dukes or rulers of any sort in Israel. And he was the true Messiah, but they didn't recognize him as such. This is even more obvious, because it goes on to say: "and the peoples will draw near to him," meaning Jesus Christ, because people from many different parts converted to him, and many different tribes drew near to him, for he preached the word of God to them. Further evidence is provided in the words: "He will tether his she-ass to the vine, the son of his she-ass to the sapling (vine-shoot; Latin, vitem)." This is a sign of St. Mary's coming with her son, as is told in his story and is well known. Additionally, it continues: "They will wash their garments with wine, and their coverings with the blood of grapes." Take here as a premise that the reference is to wine, and keep this saying in mind. Then it goes on: "And they will have their teeth whiter than milk." You must know that the bread of the holy mass is whiter than milk; and hence, we have a basis for wine, and something white, and the Messiah; and that this thing will be changed into the Messiah's very essence. And it said here: "They will wash their coverings with wine." You must know that the covering stops and prevents the eyesight from seeing the substance of the person. It says all of this to indicate that it is important in this sacrifice to wipe clean the covering of the eyes of the heart and leave it cleaner than white teeth so that it can see the meaning of this holy sacrifice. "He will wash his garment with wine" means that the mass is celebrated with wine, and changes it into the substance of the Messiah's blood, for his clothing and garment was washed with blood during his passion. Thus "covering" and "garment" is taken to mean either the holy sacrifice, which is hidden (or "covered") from many who have not enjoyed or

___

[104] (c. 1270–1349), important French Franciscan Bible commentator and theologian, author of De Messia . . . ad Judaei argumenta.

learned the faith of God and the true Messiah; or else it refers to his clothing, which was washed in blood during his passion. Hence this saying signifies the coming of the Messiah and the holy mass. And here concludes the Christian interpretation of these verses. The Jews, however, have a different view, and they say as follows.

"The scepter will not be taken from Judah, nor the scribe from between his feet." Rabbi Abraham Ibn Ezra says that here Jacob assured Judah the preeminence and principality until King David came. Even though they didn't have kings, Judah would have this preeminence. Hence, when they were wandering in the desert, Judah's ensign and standard always went first, and in the battles Judah was the first to fight. But the Master of Gerona[105] disagreed with this interpretation of Rabbi Abraham's and said as follows: "The scepter refers only to the rod that kings and princes hold when they rule, as the psalmist David said: 'your royal scepter is a scepter of equity.' "[106] We do not find that Judah had a ruler's scepter before David, and hence the aforementioned Master interpreted as follows: "the scepter will not be taken from Judah": he wasn't assuring him here that his kingdom and power would never be taken from him, for we find that God told Israel: if you do not obey these words, "May the Lord give you up, you and the king whom you have appointed, to a nation which neither you nor your fathers have known,"[107] etc. It follows that they and their king would go into captivity, and they would be left without a king and without princes, for which reason the aforementioned Master says that he knows that the words "the scepter will not be taken from Judah," etc., mean: "the scepter will not be taken from Judah to be passed on to any of his brothers." Just as David was the first king, the kings of Israel would always be from David's offspring, and not from any other tribe.

"Until the Messiah comes." The Hebrew says: "Until *Shiloh* comes." Some say that *Shiloh* means "his son," who is the king Messiah. Rabbi Abraham says: "Don't think that he would lose the scepter and kingdom when Shiloh came. For it is the same as when they say to someone: So-and-so will not lack for food until he acquires possessions and country houses; or indeed as God told Jacob: 'I will not leave you until I fulfill all that I promised you.' This certainly doesn't mean that He was going to leave him after that. Here Jacob bestowed the kingdom and rulership on Judah more than all the others." And you should know that when Saul reigned before Judah, this was because of [God's] love [for Judah]. For when Israel demanded a king in the time of Samuel, God found it

---

[105] Rabbi Moses Ben Naḥman (1194–1270) of Gerona, Catalonia, known as Naḥmanides, one of the leading Spanish rabbis of the Middle Ages and author of an extensive commentary on the Torah.

[106] Ps. 45:6.

[107] Deut. 28:36.

abominable, and it aggrieved Him, since Samuel was His ruler and fought their battles for them at God's command. And therefore He decided to give the kingdom to a tribe that could give it up without great damage. And what the text says concerning Saul—"If you had [kept the commandment laid on you by the Lord God], He would have established your dynasty over Israel for all time"[108]—means that if he hadn't sinned, the kingship would have endured in his tribe, which is Israel; and he didn't say "over all Israel." And when Israel chose a king from a tribe other than Judah and made Jeroboam king over them,[109] they trespassed their father Jacob's commandment; and God punished them for that. But no kings were ever anointed except those who came from the direct line of David. Others comment: "until Shiloh comes" means that it will not be taken to be Judah's scepter until Shiloh is ruined and done away with. This means: until there is no tabernacle in Shiloh, which was a town in Israel. Thus, my lord, you have heard the opinion of the Latins very fully, as well as the Hebrew opinions on this passage, and I already said in the prologue that everyone should hold firm to the fundamentals and articles of his own faith.

13. Zebulun shall dwell in seaports; and he shall always be in the port where the ships dock, and the end of his port will reach Sidon.

All the tribes were listed and mentioned here in the order of their birth, except for Zebulun, which was listed before Issachar, because his part or allotment in the Land of Promise was between the portions of Zebulun and Dan, and hence it said: "he shall dwell in seaports." This proves that these sayings are prophecies and not blessings, as some hold. Here it informs us that Zebulun would always be in the ports to collect the merchandise with which it helped to support the tribe of Issachar, who were students and scholars. And Jacob revealed here that the sea coast that would be given as a portion to Zebulun would have many ports.

14. Issachar is an ass with good bones, who can lie down with the cargo (accubans inter terminos)[110] and get back up with it.

It compared him to a good, hardworking ass; and thus they exerted themselves to know the secrets of the law and the sciences, and hence it says: "he put his shoulder to the law's task."

---

[108] 1 Sam. 13:13.
[109] 1 Kings 12:20.
[110] The Vulgate translation: "lying down between the borders."

15. **And when he saw how good it was to be idle, and that the land was luxuriant, he remembered to put his shoulder to the task and pay tribute.**

That is: to pay tribute to the other tribes so that they would fight in place of him.

16. **Dan will judge his people, as one of those who are tribes of Israel.**

Some say that this means: Dan will take revenge for the people of Israel, as one of the tribes of Israel. And this was said on account of Samson, who would avenge Israel from the power of the Philistines, as is recounted in the books of Kings and Judges.

17. **Dan will be just like a serpent on the road, like one that bites on the road, that bites the horse's heels so that his rider is thrown backward.**

With the kicks the horsemen give.

18. **I wait for your salvation, Lord!**

There are many commentaries about this. Rabbi Solomon says that Samson would say this when the Philistines gouged out his eyes. And we find that he said when he pulled down the house on the Philistines: "Remember me, Lord God, remember me: for this one occasion, God, give me strength. . . ."[111] Rabbi Abraham says that just as when a man hears something bad, he says "but deliver us from evil," so Jacob, when he understood through prophecy that this Samson was to suffer so much evil, said: "I wait for your salvation, Lord!" Others say that when Jacob saw Dan—the whole tribe just like serpents—he was frightened, and therefore he said: "I wait for your salvation, Lord!" The Targum Onkelos says that although Jacob saw many good things in Israel's future, he was not satisfied with anything but the salvation of the Messiah, son of David. And there is still a division among Latins and Hebrews over whether he has come or not. The Jews say he hasn't come, and they are still waiting for him, but the Christians say he has already come.

19. **Gad: combat pay (an army) will come upon him, but he will defeat it in the end.**

Others translate: "Gad as a general will command us, and he will command at the end."

---

[111] Judges 16:28.

Rabbi Abraham says that this signifies that the tribe of Gad would be pursued, and he says that because the books of battles that have come down to us are incomplete, we don't know what befell Israel in those battles. Most of the histories and books of battles were lost during the Babylonian captivity. Rabbi Solomon says that, although the tribes of Reuben and Gad asked Moses for territory on the hither side of the Jordan,[112] they still had to cross the Jordan to help Israel win the land. This explains this saying, because, although their part of the inheritance was on the hither side of the Jordan, Moses and Israel insisted that they help them win the land, but they were always in the rear guard, and returned to their lands by the same way, and fought a considerable number of battles at the end.

20. Asher: his land will be of abundant, rich bread; and in his land will be the luxuries of a king.

Such as fowl and game and oil. Some say that this corresponds to Gad's battles—that if they couldn't farm, they would receive their sustenance from Asher.

21. Naphtali will be like a running deer let loose, and will speak with elegant rhetoric.

This refers to the canticle[113] that Barak and Deborah composed when they vanquished Sisera together with the ten thousand men they took from the tribes of Naphtali and Zebulun, for there is no doubt that that canticle is well written. Others say that in the land of the East kings order deer hunted and send them as gifts; and when they want to send each other letters, they tie the letters to the deer's necks, and they return to their caves, and they have someone there to go after them and hunt them down, and take the letters from them, and thus they receive news from those kings to whom they are well disposed. And this is what Naphtali's land was like, for when it produced good bread and fruit, since the harvest came early there, they knew that [it would be a good year for] all the land, and they brought the news as swiftly as a deer.

22. Joseph is a growing son, a son that outreaches the eye. He makes the daughters increase on top of the castle (murum).[114]

---

[112] That is, outside Israel proper.
[113] Judges 5, considered the choicest masterpiece of Hebrew poetry.
[114] Thus the Vulgate: "wall."

Because of the great risk and violence [he underwent], Jacob likened Joseph to the branch or tree that is planted by a stream, and its branches rise up over the wall; and this meant that two tribes would come from Joseph's sons. Rabbi Solomon says that when Jacob encountered his brother Esau, when he sent him the present as he was coming from the house of Laban,[115] as you already heard, Esau tried hard to see Rachel, because, since she was beautiful, he wanted to rape her. Although Joseph was only a child, he realized this and stood in front of her. It seems that God performed a miracle for him, making him grow so large that Esau couldn't see his mother Rachel, and that's why it said that Joseph was like a branch that grows exceedingly.

23. **They used him as a target, their target, and the bowmen shot there.**

This refers to the wrong Joseph suffered when his brothers sold him, and to what happened to him when his master's wife accused him and they arrested him.

24. **Yet with all this his bow remained strong, and he had firm hands (*et dissoluta sunt vincula brachiorum et manuum illius*)[116] and arms from the mercy (*manus*)[117] of that mighty God of Jacob, and thence was sustained the Rock of Israel.**

This is a figurative way of saying that God delivered him, and they weren't able to kill him because of the mercy of that mighty God of Jacob; and thereby all the house of Israel was sustained.

The Jews hold that this Rock means "house," and the text meant that Joseph had supported and sustained the House of Israel. And, my lord, here it is worthwhile to recall what we said at the beginning of this prophecy, that Jacob told his children: "Come near me, and I will tell you what is to befall you in the last days." And since this prophecy has a lot to do with the coming of the Messiah, why didn't he tell them and reveal to them the evils of the captivities that Israel was to undergo?

---

[115] Gen. 33.

[116] Thus the Vulgate: "The bands of his hands and arms were loosed by the hand of the Mighty One of Jacob."

[117] Thus the Vulgate: "hand."

Some have tried to explain this by saying that Jacob chose not to tell them about the captivities so that Israel would not fall into despair and abandon the Law and mix with the other nations. Some, however, rejected this solution, on the following grounds: Moses was not restrained by this fear of despair, but very amply told them about all the evils and captivities that Israel was to suffer. However, my lord, this is not a sufficient reason to reject that argument, because Moses could reveal the captivities without fear of despair for two reasons: (1) Moses explained that all the captivities he mentioned were conditional—if they failed to devote themselves to God—and would not necessarily come to pass; (2) Jacob, however, as a prophet would have to say that they would necessarily occur. Besides, Moses had done much good for Israel, and a man is more willing to accept something bad from someone who has already given him something good. In Jacob's time Israel had not yet multiplied nor had they received any good from him, and hence he didn't dare reveal the captivities to them.

25. **May He Who is the God of your father help you, and He Who is a God of abundance bless you with blessings of the heavens above, blessings of the abyss that is below, blessings of the breasts and of the womb.**

This means: let no evil befall his children, either while they are in the womb or when they are nursing at the breast. He said this because those are usually the most dangerous times for infants, when they are in the womb or at the breast.

26. **May the blessings of your father be multiplied above the blessings of my ancestors, and may they be raised as high as the ancient (aeternorum)[118] hills, and may these blessings be and come upon Joseph's head, and the head of him who is the crown (Nazaraei)[119] of his brothers.**

He was asking that God be pleased to fulfill the blessings with which God blessed him even beyond those He gave his ancestors, so that Joseph might be entirely successful. You should know that the Lord told our father Abraham: "All the land you see I shall give to you,"[120] and He showed him only the Land of Promise. To our father Isaac He said: "To you and your descendants I shall give all these lands";[121] but to Jacob He said: "You will spread far and wide, to

---

[118] Thus the Vulgate: "eternal" or "everlasting."
[119] Thus the Vulgate: "Nazirite."
[120] Gen. 13:15.
[121] Gen. 26:3.

west and east, to north and south,"[122] which are the four parts of the world. Hence it follows that the greatest blessing was Jacob's, and he was the one who was to multiply most; and hence he said that his blessing would reach as far as the ancient hills, that is, throughout the world.

27. Benjamin will prey like a wolf;

Here he compared the kingdom of Saul, who was of the tribe of Benjamin, to the wolf that is not secure with the prey it has seized, whereas of David he said the contrary, comparing him to the lion, which fears nothing. And the tribe of Benjamin were generally brave men, for we find that all Israel allied against them, and they defeated Israel three times.[123]

> **in the morning he will eat the prey, and at night he will divide the spoil."**

You should be aware that prophets couch their sayings in figurative language, and the sayings of the prophets often refer to morning and night. Sometimes morning means good and pleasure, and night, woes and pestilence; since the morning is light, and the night, darkness, the Law uses one thing for the other. And since morning is taken to mean the beginning of the day, and night is taken to mean its end, he said here that when Benjamin had begun to reign over Israel, this tribe of Benjamin would win a battle and eat the prey. This was King Saul, who was the first king and was of the tribe of Benjamin, who vanquished the Amalekites,[124] and that was the morning of good. "At night he divided the spoil." Just as night is darkness, captivity is great darkness, and when Israel was captive in the power of King Ahasuerus, Haman quarreled with Mordecai, and God gave Mordecai victory over his enemies and over Haman. This Mordecai was of the tribe of Benjamin, and he obtained great spoils from those people, I mean, his contraries, and this explains "morning" and "night." Others, particularly the Targum Onkelos, say that because the house of the Temple was built in the land of Benjamin, and the priests distributed the rations of the sacrifices every morning and night, that is what this saying meant.

28. All these are the tribes of Israel, which are twelve, and this is what their father said to them, and he gave each one of them his blessing. He blessed them as was appropriate to them.

---

[122] Gen. 28:14.
[123] Cf. Judges 20–21.
[124] 1 Sam. 15.

And these blessings are not found in writing, and we have already pointed out that what he said before was a prophecy, not a blessing; there was no blessing at all in what he said here to the tribes.

29. And he instructed them, and this is what he told them: "I am being gathered to my people. Bury me with my ancestors in the cave of the field of Ephron the Hittite, 30. the double cave which is alongside Mamre, in the land of Canaan, the field that Abraham bought from Ephron the Hittite for burials. 31. There they buried Abraham and Sarah his wife; there they buried Isaac and Rebekah his wife; and there I buried Leah. 32. The purchase of that field included the cave which he bought from the sons of Heth." 33. And when Jacob had finished giving this order to his sons, he drew his feet into the bed and died suddenly, without pain or suffering, and was gathered to his people.

50. Joseph flung himself upon his father's face, and wept over him and kissed him. 2. And Joseph ordered his servants the physicians to embalm his father, and the physicians embalmed Israel. 3. And they showed him honor for forty days, for it was their custom to do so to all those who were embalmed; and the Egyptians wept over him seventy days.

It was their custom to show honor to honorable men for thirty days, and an additional forty days in the case of those who were embalmed.

4. And when the days of weeping were over, Joseph spoke to those of Pharaoh's house, telling them: "If I have found grace in your eyes, I beg you to say this to Pharaoh: 5. 'Since my father made me swear, telling me: "In my grave that I dug for myself in the land of Canaan, bury me there";

Although he didn't actually dig it or even buy it, a man can give whatever name he pleases to what he inherits.

therefore, if it pleases him, I want to go bury my father, and I shall return." 6. Pharaoh said: "Go and bury your father and keep your oath." 7. And Joseph went to bury his father, and all Pharaoh's noblemen and the elders of his house and the elders of the land of Egypt went with him, 8. and all Joseph's house, and his brothers, and his father's household; but they left their families and their sheep and their cattle in the land of Goshen. 9. And with them went cavalcades of great knights, and the host was very great. 10. And they came to a place they call "the threshing-floor of hawthorn," which is beyond the Jordan, and there they made exceedingly great lamentations, and observed a mourning period of seven days, and he wept for him and was tearful for seven days.

This was a threshing-floor that was surrounded by hawthorns. Others say that all the kings of Canaan and all the princes of the Moors had joined together to go and destroy Egypt, but when they saw Joseph's crown on Jacob's bier, they all stopped and put their own crowns on the bier, so that the bier was surrounded by crowns as threshing-floors are surrounded by thornbushes.

11. And when the Canaanites who dwelled in the land of Canaan saw this weeping at that threshing-floor of hawthorn, they said: "This is a great mourning on the part of the Egyptians"; hence this place received the name Abel Mitsrayim, which is the same as to say "mourning of the Egyptians" down to the present day, which town is beyond the Jordan. 12. And his sons did to Jacob as he had commanded them. 13. And his sons carried him to the land of Canaan and buried him in the double cave that Abraham bought, the field of Ephron the Hittite, which is near Mamre.

His sons, and not his grandsons; for he ordered three of his sons to hold each of the four sides of the bier, in the same order that they set out and their standards went forward in the desert. He did not order Levi to carry the bier, for he was to carry the ark of the Law, much less Joseph, for he considered him a king, and Ephraim and Manasseh took the place of those two.

14. Joseph returned to Egypt—he and his brothers and all who went with him to bury his father—after they had buried him. 15. And when Joseph's brothers saw that their father was dead, they said: "Perhaps Joseph will bear a grudge and will pay us back for all the wrong we did to him!" 16. And they commended themselves to Joseph, saying: "Before he died, your father ordered us to tell you on his behalf: 17. 'I beg you to forgive your brothers' error and sin, even though they treated you very badly; yet I beg you to forgive the error of those servants of the God of your father.' " And Joseph wept again while they were telling him this. 18. And then likewise his brothers went to him and flung themselves down before him and told him: "See! We are your slaves." 19. Joseph said to them: "Have no fear, for I fear God, and I live in fear of Him. 20. And even though you meant to do me wrong, God meant it for good, so that so many people might be alive as

of today. 21. Therefore, have no fear; I will sustain you, you and your families." And he consoled them and spoke kindly to them.

Saying: "Friends, by coming here you did me a great service, for if it were not for you, I would have been considered a slave—especially since, as you know well, my father never knew of my being sold.

22. And Joseph dwelled in Egypt, he and his father's household. And Joseph lived one hundred and ten years. 23. And Joseph saw children of the third generation of Ephraim; and furthermore, the sons of Machir, Manasseh's son, were born in Joseph's arms. 24. Joseph told his brothers: "I shall die, and doubtless God will remember you and revive you and take you from this land to the land He swore unto Abraham and Isaac and Jacob." 25. And Joseph made the children of Israel swear, saying: "Since God will remember you and revive you, take my bones up from here."

That when God should revive them, they should take his bones. And he didn't say they should take them as soon as he died, either because they would not be able to arrange that, or because Pharaoh would never agree for them to take him out of Egypt.

26. And Joseph died at the age of one hundred and ten years; and he was embalmed and placed in a coffin in Egypt.

HERE ENDS THE FIRST BOOK OF
THE FIVE BOOKS OF THE LAW OF MOSES,
WHICH HAS THE NAME GENESIS; AND THE
NUMBER OF VERSES IN THIS BOOK
IS ONE THOUSAND, FIVE HUNDRED
AND THIRTY FOUR.

DEO GRATIAS.

Joseph's dreams, from a fourteenth-century Spanish Haggadah. Above, Joseph dreams that his brothers' sheaves bow down to his; below, Joseph's brothers mock him as he tells his father Jacob his dream about the sun, moon, and stars. Sarajevo National Museum, Sarajevo Haggadah, fol. 11v.

➤ The Book of Heroes (c. 1150–1200)

Anonymous

The *Sefer ha-Yashar* is a Hebrew compilation of midrashim and medieval legends believed to have been composed in Spain not earlier than the eleventh and not later than the thirteenth century. It differs from traditional midrashim in that it consists entirely of "narrative expansion" of the biblical text, to use James Kugel's term. It takes the form of a chronicle or history covering the period from the creation of the world to the events immediately following the death of Joshua, and in this sense it is comparable to Alfonso X's *General estoria*. Since, however, it is written in Hebrew rather than Spanish—and therefore addressed to a learned rather than a popular audience—it might perhaps better be compared to a work such as the anonymous Latin biography of the Cid known as the *Historia Roderici*.[1] Richard Fletcher has commented on the unadorned style of the *Historia Roderici* that "in the entire work the only figure of speech is a single simile, used twice: 'Rodrigo remained as still as a stone.' "[2] Interestingly, *Yashar* uses the very same simile to describe Jacob's reaction when he was informed of Joseph's death: "he fell on his face to the ground and was as still as a stone," where it is also repeated; and also to describe Joseph's behavior when he encountered his mother's grave while on his way to Egypt as a slave: "[he wept] until at last he fell silent as a stone on his mother's grave from the bitterness in his heart." *Yashar* may also have been influenced by medieval Latin lives of the saints and royal biographies. It is sometimes termed a pseudepigraphic work (from the Greek *pseudepigraphos*, "falsely inscribed"), because it pretends to be the lost biblical book referred to in Joshua 10:13, 2 Samuel 1:18, and the Septuagint version of 1 Kings 8:53b. This false attribution of course was intended to confer greater authority and prestige on the book.

Although most of the stories *Yashar* contains can be traced to earlier Jewish[3] and Muslim sources, its author has skillfully woven them together to form a

---

[1] Written, according to Ramón Menéndez Pidal, before 1110. See Richard Fletcher, *The Quest for El Cid* (New York: Alfred A. Knopf, 1990), p. 97.

[2] Ibid., p. 94.

[3] According to Moshe David Herr, these include "*Genesis Rabbah*, the Babylonian Talmud, *Pirkei de-R. Eliezer*, *Midrash va-Yissa'u*, Josippon, *Midrash Avkir* (no. 15) as well as ancient sources from the literature of the Second Temple period." See his article "Midrashim, Smaller" in vol. 16 (*Supplementary Entries*) of the *Encyclopaedia Judaica* (Jerusalem: Keter Publishing House, c. 1972).

coherent narrative. Nowhere is this more the case than in the portion dedicated to the story of Joseph, which occupies fully a quarter of the entire book.

The etymology of the Hebrew word *yashar* (which is now interpreted as meaning "upright" or "righteous") is uncertain, and it may be derived from a word meaning "victorious." In titling my translation *The Book of Heroes*, I have followed the lead of Eliezer Goldschmidt, who subtitled his Hebrew edition *Das Heldenbuch*. *Yashar* is above all a celebration of the heroic deeds and military prowess of the early Israelites, very much in the spirit of the French and Spanish epic poems with which it is contemporary. Technically, the fact that it is written in prose disqualifies it from being termed an "epic," but it is in fact closer to the epic in style and content than to any other literary genre of the period.

The anthropologist Timothy Mitchell has written that

> In an ideal world, each human community would be secure in its cultural identity, willing to content itself with a discrete body of lore and customs, predisposed to display a broadminded tolerance for the idiosyncrasies of other communities. In practice, very few peoples arrive at such a healthy relativism. Societies are typically absolutist. People employ their expressive culture, sacred and secular, to glorify themselves and to denigrate others and their sacred or secular expressive culture. . . . All over the world, myths and other forms of folklore do the bidding of their ethnocentric possessors.[4]

No literary genre is more ethnocentric than the epic, which recounts the deeds of a hero who is portrayed as embodying the virtues and values of a particular clan or folk, what the German Romantics termed the *Volksgeist* (spirit of a people, or national character). In his influential book *The Narreme in the Medieval Romance Epic*, Eugene Dorfman demonstrated that the major French (*Gormont et Isembart, Pèlerinage de Charlemagne, Chanson de Guillaume, Couronnement de Louis,* and *Chanson de Roland*) and Spanish epics (*Poema de Fernán González, Gesta de los Infantes de Lara, Gesta de Sancho II de Castilla, Condesa traidora,* and *Poema de mío Cid*) derived from a basic pattern of four "narremes"[5]—the family quarrel, the motive (insults, thefts, murders, inheritance struggles), the act of treachery, and the punishment.[6] Interestingly, these four narremes also provide the underlying structure of the story of Joseph.

---

[4] *Violence and Piety in Spanish Folklore* (Philadelphia: Univ. of Pennsylvania Press, 1988), p. 12.

[5] Defined as "functionally central incidents, linked to each other in an organic relationship." *The Narreme in the Medieval Romance Epic* (Toronto: Univ. of Toronto Press, 1969), p. 5.

[6] Ibid., p. 223.

With regard to the Castilian epic, Angel del Río has observed that "the epic poems are the reflection of a vital and lived situation, of a historical and human tension in which the Castilian affirms himself, whether in contrast to the Arabs, with whom he fights and coexists, or to Leonese conservatism, or in his own person in contrast to others—often the nobility and even the king. Hence, the Castilian bases his values on deeds and on the making of oneself, rather than on any hierarchical authority."[7] These comments are especially applicable to the *Poem of the Cid*, the greatest of the Castilian epics and the only one which has come down to us virtually intact. The similarities between the *Poem of the Cid* and the story of Joseph in *Yashar* are so great that one can only conclude that the anonymous author of *Yashar* set out to portray his Joseph as a Jewish national hero who could rival Castile's Rodrigo Díaz de Vivar, known as El Cid. The portrayal of Joseph as epic hero may also have been partially inspired by the illustrious career of Samuel Ibn Nagrella (993–1055), who rose to the highest position of state in eleventh-century Granada and won great distinction as a general of Muslim armies.

It is noteworthy that in *Yashar* Joseph and his brothers are portrayed from the beginning as mighty warriors. On the very first page of the story we read that "the sons of Jacob settled with their father in the valley of Hebron, and all the inhabitants of the land heard of their strength, and their fame spread throughout the land. Jacob's son Joseph and his brother Benjamin, the sons of Jacob's wife Rachel, were still very young in those days, and hence did not accompany their brothers in their wars against all the cities of the Amorites. Joseph saw the strength and greatness of his brothers, and he praised and honored them." Like many other epic heroes, Joseph undergoes a profound transformation in the course of the story. His external triumphs are paralleled by the more important victory over self. The experience of hardship changes him from a vain, spoiled child to a mature man.

At the beginning of the *Cid*, the hero, Rodrigo, has been betrayed by enemies at court who accused him of pocketing tribute money that was rightly the king's, and the king sentences him to exile from Castile. He is thus initially presented as "a penniless exile, forced to leave home and family behind, the future dark before him."[8] After *Yashar*'s brief initial explanation of Joseph's brothers' hatred for him, we see him betrayed, sold into slavery, and taken to exile in Egypt, where his future looks bleak. The pathetic scene in which the Cid bids farewell to his beloved wife and daughters is paralleled in *Yashar* by Jacob's protracted lament over the loss of his beloved son. Like Joseph, the Cid

---

[7] *Historia de la literatura española* (New York: Holt, Rinehart and Winston, 1963), I, 48; my translation.
[8] Dorfman, *The Narreme*, p. 129.

has a prophetic dream on the eve of his departure from Castile in which the angel Gabriel reassures him with a promise of future prosperity. The Cid begins to recover his honor by conquering enemies and loyally sending a fifth part of the booty back to the king. Joseph begins to prosper in Egypt through his intelligent and loyal service to his master Potiphar.

Both the *Poem of the Cid* and the story of Joseph are complicated by a second affront to the hero's honor, which occurs after a period of success and prosperity. Or, looked at another way, each story involves both a family quarrel and a conflict with higher authority. After resisting Zalikha's temptation, Joseph is falsely accused of attempted rape and imprisoned. The Cid's sons-in-law, the Infantes de Carrión, rape and abandon his daughters. Both Joseph and Rodrigo react to these affronts with *mesura* (dignity, restraint), and both are ultimately vindicated. Rather than taking blood vengeance, Rodrigo summons his sons-in-law to a trial and judicial combat before the king in Toledo. Del Río notes that this scene is "perhaps the most solemn in the poem. The Cid's dignity and courage . . . contrast with the cowardly bluster of his enemies, the Infantes de Carrión."[9] While Joseph is cleared of the charge of attempted rape through divine intervention, he must still confront his original adversaries—his own brothers—and settle the score with them. His dignified behavior toward his arrogant brothers resembles the Cid's attitude toward his sons-in-law. At last the Cid fully recovers his honor, his daughters are remarried to the kings of Navarre and Aragon, and the poet tells us that "Now the Kings of Spain are his kinsmen, / and all advance in honor through My Cid the Campeador. . . ."[10] The story of Joseph likewise states that his two sons "were brought up close to the king's own sons" and ends by recounting the rise to royal status of this hero of humble origins: although "there were some who didn't like him and said: 'No foreigner will rule over us,' . . . Joseph ruled over Egypt, for he could do as he pleased throughout Egypt, and all of Egypt was under his hand and his will."

Both stories fall naturally into three parts (beginning, middle, and end):

Joseph	Cid
1. Early life and sale into slavery; initial success in Egypt.	1. Exile and gradual recovery of honor and status.
2. Temptation, imprisonment, and vindication.	2. Reconciliation with king. Marriage of daughters. Affront committed by sons-in-law.
3. Testing of his brothers and final reconciliation with them.	3. Trial of sons-in-law and final vindication.

---

[9] *Historia*, I, 53.
[10] *Poem of the Cid*, trans. W. S. Merwin (New York: New American Library, 1962), p. 301.

Both of these epic heroes are elevated to mythic stature through the constant, ritualistic repetition of epithets—in the case of the Cid, "el que en buen ora çinxo espada" ("he who in good hour girded on sword"), and in that of Joseph, the biblical words "well built and handsome" (Gen. 39:6). In spite of all these striking similarities, there is an important difference between the *Poem of the Cid* and *Yashar*. The poet of the *Cid* sees the events he narrates as foreshadowing and setting the stage for the eventual emergence of his people as a great power, and the tone of the poem is confidently optimistic. By contrast, *Yashar* is the fantasy of a poet who seeks consolation in his people's—partly imaginary—past glory in a time of defeat and powerlessness.

Both epics define their heroes principally by contrast with the same antagonist—the Muslims, who in *Yashar* are identified with the "sons of Esau," with whom Joseph and his brothers carry on a long serious of fictitious wars after the death of Jacob. After suffering many ignominious defeats, "the sons of Esau never again went to war against the sons of Jacob from that day on, for the sons of Esau knew the strength of the sons of Jacob and were very much afraid of them. Nevertheless, from that day on, the sons of Esau hated the sons of Jacob, and that hatred and deep resentment between them has endured down to the present day." The Egyptians in *Yashar* represent the Castilian Christians, who for the moment seemed to hold out the best hope for the survival of Judaism in Spain; yet the author's attitude toward his Christian protectors is, like that of the author of Genesis toward the Egyptians, ambivalent. Though Genesis tells a story of harmonious coexistence, it ends with the promise of redemption from exile, and the author of *Yashar* perhaps took a rather dim view of the long-term prospects of peace and prosperity for the Jews under Christian rule.

Though the author of *Yashar* sides with the Castilian Christians in their struggle against the Muslims, it is clear that he had been educated in Muslim Spain and was fluent in Arabic. The Hebrew text is strongly influenced by Arabic, and the author draws heavily on Muslim versions of the story of Joseph. Some examples are the story of the wolf whom Jacob falsely accused of devouring Joseph and who miraculously received the gift of speech to defend his innocence; and the greatly elaborated version of the story of Joseph and Potiphar's wife Zalikha,[11] containing two famous anecdotes from Surah XII of the Qur'an. The first recounts how Joseph's innocence of the charge of attempted rape was proven by the fact that his shirt was torn from behind, thus indicating that he had attempted to flee from Zalikha; the second how Zalikha, enraged by the fact that the court ladies of Egypt were gossiping about her attempts to seduce Joseph, gave a banquet at which they were so dazzled by

---

[11] This name comes from the Muslim tradition, and is thought to be of Persian origin.

Joseph's beauty that they cut their own hands with their knives. It is perhaps noteworthy that the story of the tear in Joseph's shirt is told differently in *Yashar*: "Then the priests said to Potiphar: 'Go and bring us Joseph's garment that was torn so that we can examine it and see where it was torn. If it was torn in front, then he must have been facing her, and she grabbed him to pull him to her, and your wife treacherously did all the things she has said.'" This may be a deliberate attempt to make the Qur'an look foolish by turning its own story against itself, in the very same way that the Qur'an had attempted to challenge and improve upon the version of the story in Genesis.

The Jews of Muslim Spain had long taken pride in the tradition that their ancestors had provided important assistance to the eighth-century Muslim invaders, whom they viewed as liberators from their anti-Semitic Visigothic rulers, in conquering the peninsula. The author of *Yashar* goes even further. According to him, when the sons of Tarshish (traditionally identified with Tartessos, near Gibraltar) went to war with the Ishmaelites (Arabs), Joseph went to the aid of the Ishmaelites, defeated the Tarshishites, and conquered their land, "and some of the Ishmaelites have lived there ever since." This story seems to attribute the original presence of Arabs in Spain to Jewish military assistance. Another story in *Yashar* clearly reflects the military situation in early twelfth-century Spain. The story tells how the sons of Esau sought the aid of Angias, king of Dinhabah (identified in the text as "Africa"), and one of Angias's nobles later became king over the sons of Esau. Similarly, the Moroccan fundamentalist Almoravid Yusuf Ibn Tashufin (d. 1106–1107) went to the aid of the Muslim kings against Alfonso VI (the same king who exiled the Cid) in 1086 and returned to Spain four years later to annex the Muslim states. In 1102 Yusuf's general Mazdali would reclaim Valencia, conquered by the Cid in 1094, for Islam. *Yashar*'s portrayal of the "sons of Esau" as treacherous, greedy, and distrustful toward each other would then be a pejorative reflection on the kings of Spain's Muslim city states, or *taifas*, whose internecine quarrels were blamed by Jews for bringing to an abrupt end a long period of tolerance and prosperity. As David Wasserstein has observed, "The Almoravids were very different from the civilized and highly cultured Andalusian Muslims. Barely out of the desert, they were largely illiterate; fired by religion, like many supporters of revivalist religious movements in that area before and since, they were far less tolerant of non-Muslims, which there meant mainly Jews, than other rulers; and they were far more devoted to the ideals of *jihad*, holy war for Islam."[12] The Almoravid invasion sounded the death knell for the Jewish communities of

---

[12] *The Rise and Fall of the Party-Kings: Politics and Society in Islamic Spain 1002–1086* (Princeton: Princeton Univ. Press, 1985), p. 285.

southern Spain, which had long been renowned for their brilliant contributions to philosophy, poetry, science, medicine, and statesmanship. Forty years later their fate was sealed when an even more fanatical group, known as the Almohads, crossed the Straits of Gibraltar and overran Andalusia in 1147, massacring one Jewish community after another and forcing thousands of Jews to accept Islam. It was probably then that the author of *Yashar* fled to the Christian north, perhaps to Toledo, where he wrote the *Sefer ha-Yashar*, a book remarkably similar to the contemporary Abraham Ibn Daud's *Sefer ha-Kabbalah* in its elegiac evocation of the glorious Jewish past and its bitter disillusionment over Muslim Spain's rejection and persecution of the Jews.

The *Sefer ha-Yashar* was first printed in Naples in 1522 and has often been reprinted thereafter. An anonymous British translation was published by M. M. Noah and A. S. Gould in New York in 1840 and is available in a 1972 reprint by Hermon Press, New York. Moshe Lazar has recently published a seventeenth-century Ladino translation in *Joseph and His Brothers: Three Ladino Versions* (Culver City, Calif.: Labyrinthos, 1990). Dr. Élie Chemtob collaborated with me on the present translation, which is based on Eliezer Goldschmidt's edition of the Hebrew text (Berlin: Benjamin Harz, 1923). We have followed that edition's division of the narrative according to the portions designated for weekly reading in the synagogue. For the quotations from the Bible embedded in the text, we have used the new translation published by the Jewish Publication Society (Philadelphia, 1985).

I. Va-Yeshev[13]

At the turn of the year the sons of Jacob left Shechem and went back to Hebron to their father Isaac, and they stayed there. However, whereas they had pastured their sheep and cattle and all their animals in the fields in Shechem, now they had to feed them every day; for there was good and abundant pasture in Shechem in those days. And Jacob and his sons and all his household set-

---

[13] *The Book of Heroes* divides the story of Joseph into four chapters, corresponding to the portions of the book of Genesis assigned for weekly reading in the synagogue service. The title of each reading is taken from a word or phrase occurring near its beginning; thus "Va-Yeshev" means "And he settled." The Jewish calendar is so arranged that the second portion of the story of Joseph (Mikkets, "At the end of") always falls on the intermediate sabbath of Hanukkah. This led the popular imagination to establish connections between the story of Joseph and that holiday's celebration of freedom from Hellenistic oppression. Because Hanukkah is also a winter solstice holiday, Joseph was sometimes portrayed as a conquering "sun hero" (in the first-century Greek romance *Joseph and Aseneth*, for example).

tled in the valley of Hebron. That year Jacob was 106 years old, and it was the tenth year since he had come from Paddan-aram. Jacob's wife Leah died that year at the age of 51 in Hebron. And Jacob and her sons buried her in the cave in the field of Machpelah at Hebron that Abraham had bought from the Hittites to use as a burial place.

And the sons of Jacob settled with their father in the valley of Hebron, and all the inhabitants of the land heard of their strength, and their fame spread throughout the land. Jacob's son Joseph and his brother Benjamin, the sons of Jacob's wife Rachel, were still very young in those days, and hence did not accompany their brothers in their wars against all the cities of the Amorites. Joseph saw the strength and greatness of his brothers, and he praised and honored them. Privately, however, he felt superior to them, and he lorded it over them in his own mind. And Jacob his father **loved him best of all his sons, for he was the child of his old age, and he made him an ornamented tunic**[14] because of his great love for him. And Joseph saw that his father loved him more than his brothers, and his feelings of superiority increased, and he brought bad reports of them to his father. And the sons of Jacob saw what their brother Joseph was doing to them, and that their father loved him best, and **they hated him so that they could not speak a friendly word to him.**[15]

When he reached the age of seventeen, Joseph still felt superior to his brothers and spoke of lording it over them. At this time he had a dream, and he came to his brothers and told them his dream. He said to them: "I had a dream. There we all were binding sheaves in the field, when suddenly my sheaf stood up and remained upright on the ground; **then your sheaves gathered around and bowed low to it.**"[16] And his brothers replied: "What is this dream you have had? Is it your heart's desire to rule over us?" Then he told his father Jacob the same thing, and Jacob kissed Joseph when he heard those words, and Jacob blessed Joseph. When Jacob's sons saw how their father blessed Joseph, and kissed him, and loved him very much, they became jealous of him and hated him even more than before.

After that Joseph had another dream, and he recounted the dream to his father in the presence of his brothers. Joseph said to his father and his brothers: **"Look, I have had another dream, and this time the sun, the moon, and eleven stars were bowing down to me."**[17] And his father heard what Joseph

---

[14] Gen. 37:3.
[15] Gen. 37:4.
[16] Gen. 37:7.
[17] Gen. 37:9.

said about his dream and saw that his brothers hated him because of that. Then Jacob scolded Joseph before his brothers for what he had said, and asked him: **"What is this dream you have dreamed?"**[18] Do you imagine that you will rule over your brothers, who are such great men? Do you think in your heart that I and your mother and your eleven brothers shall come and bow down to you just because you have said something like this?" And his brothers were jealous of him for all his talk and his dreams and hated him, but Jacob kept those dreams in his heart.

One day Jacob's sons **went to pasture their father's flock at Shechem**[19]— for they still pastured them in the fields of Shechem in those days—and that day they tarried too long, and the time to round up the cattle for the night was past, but they didn't come home. And Jacob realized that his sons had been detained at Shechem, and he worried that maybe the men of Shechem had risen and made war against them, and this was the reason for their tardiness. So Jacob summoned his son Joseph and told him: **"Your brothers are pasturing at Shechem**[20] today, and they still haven't come home. Go and see where they are, and bring me back word of how your brothers and the flocks are faring." And Jacob sent his son Joseph out from the valley of Hebron. Joseph went to Shechem seeking his brothers, but he didn't find them. Then Joseph went out into the fields outside Shechem to see if he could find his brothers, but he lost his way in that wilderness and didn't know where he was going. As he was lost in that field, an angel of God stood before him in the way and said: "Joseph, Joseph, where are you going, and **what are you looking for?"**[21] And Joseph said to the angel of God: **"I am looking for my brothers.**[22] Have you heard where they are pasturing?" And the angel of God said to Joseph: "I saw your brothers. They were pasturing here, and I heard them say that they were going to pasture at Dothan." And Joseph heeded the voice of the angel of God, and he went to Dothan, where he found his brothers pasturing the flocks.

As Joseph approached his brothers, they saw him from afar and conspired against him to kill him. And Simeon said to his brothers: "Look, that dreamer is coming to us today. **Come now, let us kill him and throw him into one of the pits**[23] that are in this wilderness, and when our father asks us where he is,

---

[18] Gen. 37:10.
[19] Gen. 37:12.
[20] Gen. 37:13.
[21] Gen. 37:15.
[22] Gen. 37:16.
[23] Gen. 37:20.

we will say that **a wild beast ate him."**[24] Reuben heard what his brothers said about Joseph, and he said to them: "Don't do this thing, for how could we show our faces to our father Jacob afterwards? **Just throw him into this pit**[25] so he'll die there, but don't lay hands on him yourselves to shed his blood!" And Reuben said this **intending to save him from them and restore him to his father.**[26]

When Joseph came up to his brothers[27] and sat down before them, they jumped up and grabbed him and beat him to the ground, and they stripped him of the ornamented tunic he was wearing, **and they took him and cast him into the pit. The pit was empty; there was no water in it,**[28] but there were snakes and scorpions. And Joseph was afraid of the snakes and scorpions that were in the pit, and Joseph cried out in a loud voice, and God made the snakes and scorpions go back into their holes in the pit so that they would not harm Joseph. And Joseph cried out to his brothers from the pit, saying: "What did I do to you? How have I sinned against you?[29] Why do you not fear God on my account? Am I not your own flesh and bone? Is not your father Jacob also my father? Why are you doing this to me today? How do you think you'll be able to face our father Jacob?" And he shouted and cried out to his brothers from the pit, saying: "Judah, Reuben, Simeon, and Levi, my brothers, lift me out of this dark place where you have put me, and look today upon the face of God and the face of my father Jacob! If indeed I have sinned against you, are you not the sons of Abraham, Isaac, and Jacob? Whenever they saw an orphan, they pitied him. If he was hungry, they fed him; and if he was thirsty, they gave him water; and if he was naked, they clothed him. How can you not pity your brother, since I am your own bone and flesh? Even if I did sin against you, you should not do this for the sake of my father." Joseph spoke all these words from the pit, but his brothers paid no attention nor did they lend their ears to any of Joseph's words. And he went on crying and weeping in the pit, and Joseph said: "Who will tell my father today what my brothers have done to me and the things they have said to me today?" Then all his brothers heard his cries and his weeping from the pit, and they went some distance away from the pit so as not to hear Joseph's cries and weeping. They went about a bow shot's distance away, and there they sat down to eat.

---

[24] Gen. 37:20.
[25] Gen. 37:22.
[26] Gen. 37:22.
[27] Gen. 37:23.
[28] Gen. 37:24.
[29] Micah 6:3.

As they ate, they conspired together about whether they should kill him or take him back to his father. **As they discussed this, they looked up and saw a caravan of Ishmaelites coming**[30] from afar, on the road from Gilead on their way to Egypt. Then Judah said to them: **"What do we gain by killing our brother?"**[31] Surely God will take revenge on us. Here is what we can do to him. Do you see this caravan of Ishmaelites coming toward us on their way to Egypt? Let's go now and sell him to them, and our hands will be guiltless, and they will go their way, and he will be lost among all the multitudes in that land; but we won't have to kill him with our own hands." And the brothers accepted these words and did as Judah advised.

While they were discussing this as the caravan of Ishmaelites approached, seven Midianite men also came there, and they were thirsty. Looking up, they saw the pit Joseph was in, and above it were all sorts of birds. Those Midianite men ran to the pit to drink water, for they thought there was water in it.[32] They came up to the pit, and they heard the voice of Joseph, who was crying and weeping in the pit. They looked into the pit and saw a lad who was indeed **well built and handsome.**[33] They cried out to him, asking: "Who are you? Who brought you here? Who put you in this pit in the wilderness?" Then they all joined hands and pulled Joseph out of the pit. Taking him with them, they went on their way.

They passed by his brothers, and the brothers saw that he was in the hands of the Midianites. And they said unto them: "Why are you stealing our slave? We put that lad in the pit because he was rebellious, and you came and drew him out and are taking him away with you. Give us back our slave right now!" The Midianites replied to Jacob's sons: "Is he your slave? Maybe instead all of you are his slaves, for he is a very handsome and very good looking and very beautiful lad—much better looking than all of you! Why do you tell such lies? We have no intention of listening to you. We found the lad in the well in the wilderness, and we are going to take him and go."

Then all the sons of Jacob came up to them and stood before them and said: "Give us our slave or you will all die by the sword!" The Midianites shouted back at them and took hold of their swords and were about to attack the sons of Jacob. But Simeon arose from where he was sitting and went over to them and jumped on the ground and drew his sword. Going up to the Midianites, he

---

[30] Gen. 37:25.

[31] Gen. 37:26.

[32] Cf. Qur'an 12:19: "And there came a caravan, and they sent their water-drawer. He let down his pail (into the pit). He said: Good luck! Here is a youth. And they hid him as a treasure, and Allah was Aware of what they did."

[33] Gen. 39:6.

shouted in a loud voice,[34] and his cry was heard far away, and all the earth shook from Simeon's cry. The Midianites were frightened by Simeon's loud voice, and they fell on their faces before him in sheer terror. Simeon said to them: "I am Simeon, son of Jacob the Hebrew. Singlehandedly I have warred against all the cities of Shechem, and with my brother I have warred against the cities of the Amorites. God will deal with me like this, and will magnify me, so that even if all the men of Midian, your brothers, were to come with you, and all the·kings of Canaan, you would not be able to make war against me. Now give us the lad that you took, or I will feed your flesh to the birds of the air and the beasts of the earth."

Then the Midianites were even more frightened of Simeon, and they approached the sons of Jacob in fear and trembling. Speaking very softly, they asked: "Didn't you say that lad was your slave and that you had found him rebellious and therefore had thrown him in that pit? What can you do with a slave who disobeys his masters? Now why not sell him to us? We will pay you whatever you wish." God willed that this should happen so that at least he would not be killed by his brothers, the sons of Jacob. And the Midianites saw that Joseph was **well built and handsome**, and they lusted after him in their hearts, and they wanted to buy him from his brothers. And the sons of Jacob hearkened to the Midianites, and they sold him their brother Joseph for twenty pieces of silver; but their brother Reuben was not with them.

And the Midianites took Joseph and went on their way, which was toward Gilead. As they were traveling along, the Midianites regretted having bought the lad. One of them said to another: "Why have we done this? Why have we taken this **well built and handsome** lad from the Hebrews? He may have been stolen from the land of the Hebrews, so why have we done this? If they come looking for him and find him in our hands, we may all die! You've seen how strong and hard those men we dealt with today were, and surely you noticed the strength of the one who sold the lad to us. Don't you think that with such strength they might have stolen him from his land, and that is why they sold him to us so cheaply?"

As they were having this conversation, they looked up and saw the same caravan of Ishmaelites coming that the sons of Jacob had seen before, and the caravan was coming in their direction. The Midianites said to each other: "Let's sell the lad to that caravan of Ishmaelites that's coming toward us for the same low price we paid for him, and thus we shall be free of sin," and they did so.

---

[34] The folklore regarding Simeon's powerful voice is probably based on the Bible's association of his name with the stem *sh-m-'*, "to hear." Cf. Gen. 29:33: "[Leah] conceived again and bore a son, and declared, 'This is because the Lord heard that I was unloved and has given me this one also'; so she named him Simeon."

They went up to those Ishmaelites, and the Midianites sold Joseph to the Ishmaelites for the twenty pieces of silver they had paid his brothers for him; and the Midianites went on toward Gilead.

The Ishmaelites took Joseph and set him on one of the camels and were taking him to Egypt. When Joseph heard that they were going to Egypt, he wept and cried on that account, because he was going to be very far from the land of Canaan and from his father. And Joseph shed many tears on the camel he was riding. Seeing how sad he was, one of the Ishmaelites took him down from the camel and set him on his feet, but Joseph kept on weeping and lamenting and crying out: "My father, my father!" Another of the Ishmaelites stood before Joseph and slapped him in the face, but he still kept on weeping. Joseph was exhausted on the road and couldn't go on because of the bitterness in his soul. Then all the Ishmaelites came and beat him and made him suffer on the road in order to frighten him and make him stop weeping. And God saw Joseph's suffering and what was happening to him, and cast a great darkness and astonishment upon those people, and suddenly every hand that had been beating him was paralyzed. And they said to each other: "What is this that God has done to us on this road?" And they didn't realize that it was on account of Joseph that this had happened to them. They continued on their way until they came to Ephrath, were Rachel was buried.

Joseph reached his mother's grave, and Joseph hastened to run to his mother's grave, and he fell upon her grave and wept. And on his mother's grave Joseph cried out: "Mother! Mother! You gave birth to me. Now awake, and get up, and look upon your son, and see how he has been sold as a slave, and there is no one to pity him. Get up and look upon your son, and see the tears running down his face! Mother, mother, awake and rise, and look upon your son, and look upon the cruel heart of my brothers! Awake, mother, awake, and prepare your weapons against my brothers, for they have stripped me of my tunic! Twice they have sold me into bondage, and they have separated me from my father and have had no pity on me! Awake, and prepare your indictment of them before God, and see whom God will find innocent in His judgment, and whom He will find guilty. Arise, mother, arise, awake from your sleep, and see how my father's heart and soul pine for me today, and comfort him, and ease his heart." And Joseph went on in this vein, crying and shedding copious tears on his mother's grave until at last he fell silent as a stone on his mother's grave from the bitterness in his heart.

Then Joseph heard a voice speaking to him from under the ground and answering him with a bitter heart, a voice broken with weeping, and this is what it said: "My son, my son Joseph! I have heard your weeping and lamenting, and I have seen your tears. I was aware of your suffering, my son, and I have been suffering for you, and this has been even more painful than what I suffered before. Now, my son Joseph, my son, hope in God, and wait for Him, and fear not, for God is with you, and He will save you from all misfortune. Arise, my son, and go to Egypt with your masters, and fear not, for God is with you, my son." When she had spoken these words to Joseph, she fell silent. And Joseph listened attentively to his mother's words and was greatly astonished and could not stop weeping.

Then one of the Ishmaelites saw him weeping and lamenting on his mother's grave, and he was very annoyed; and he chased him away from there, and he beat him and cursed him. But Joseph said to the other men: "Please, if I find grace in your eyes, take me back to my father's house, and he will make you very rich." They replied: "You are a slave! Where is your father? If you had such a father, surely you couldn't have been sold into slavery—not once but twice— for such a small sum of money." They were vexed with him again, and they kept on beating him and scolding him, and Joseph wept greatly. And God saw Joseph's suffering, and He again afflicted those men and chastised them. And God caused a very strong wind to blow on them, and all the earth grew dark, and there was thunder and lightning, and the earth trembled from the noise and the wind, and those men were stunned and didn't know where to go. The beasts and camels also stood still. The men pushed and pulled them, but they refused to move. Then they beat the animals, and the animals sat down on the ground. Then they all said to each other: "What is this that God is doing to us? How have we sinned, or what have we done to deserve what is happening now?" One of them answered: "Maybe it is on account of afflicting that poor slave that all of this has happened to us today. Now beg his forgiveness, and we will find out why this evil has befallen us. Perhaps God will take pity on us, and then we will know that it was because of this slave that we have had all this trouble." They took his advice and begged Joseph's forgiveness, saying: "We have sinned against God and against you. Now please pray to your God that He spare our lives, for we have sinned against Him." Joseph did as they asked, and God heeded him and removed the plague He had brought upon them on ac- count of Joseph. All the animals got up from the ground and began to walk, and the terrible wind ceased its violence, and the earth stopped shaking.

The men then continued their journey toward Egypt; and they were then aware that all that misery had befallen them on account of Joseph. They all said to each other: "Now we know that it was because of that slave that we had that misfortune. Why bring such mortal danger upon ourselves? We need to think about what we should do with that slave." One of them replied: "Don't you re- call that he asked us to take him back to his father? Let's follow his instructions and go wherever he tells us. At his home we will be reimbursed for the money we spent to buy him, and then we will go on our way." One of them, however, objected: "That's an excellent idea, but we can't do it now, for it's very far away, and it's in the opposite direction." Another one said: "Here is what we must do. There is no other way out of this dilemma. We shall reach Egypt today, and as soon as we get there, we'll sell him for a high price, and perhaps we shall be free of the evil he has brought upon us." Everyone liked this idea, so they decided to do as he said, and they continued toward Egypt with Joseph.

After selling Joseph to the Midianites, the sons of Jacob were very depressed and regretted what they had done. They decided to go back and get him, but they couldn't find him. Reuben returned to the pit where Joseph had been to draw him out and take him to his father. When he reached the top of the pit, Reuben couldn't hear anything. Then he cried: "Joseph! Joseph!" but there was no answer, only total silence. Reuben said to himself: "Maybe Joseph died of fright, or perhaps a snake bit him." Reuben then went down into the pit himself to search for Joseph. Not finding him there, he came back out. Reuben **rent his clothes and said: "The boy is gone!**[35] How can I go back to my father if he is dead?" He went back to his brothers and found them very nervous on account of Joseph, and they were hesitating about what they should do when they went back to their father. Reuben said to his brothers: "I went to the pit, and Joseph wasn't there. What shall we say to our father, for my father will hold me alone responsible for him?" The brothers replied: "We did thus and so, and we were depressed about what we had done, and after that we sat down to discuss what we could say to our father Jacob." And Reuben said to them: "How could you do such a thing—to drag your father's old age with grief down to *She'ol*! What you have done is not good!" Then Reuben huddled with them for a while, and at last they all stood and swore to each other to tell Jacob as we will explain later—"and if anyone tells this to our father or his household, or makes it known to any inhabitant of the land, we will all rise against him together and put him to death with the sword!" And each one of them was afraid of his brothers—the older as well as the younger ones—but they discussed the matter no further. Nevertheless, it was always in their minds.

As they were on their way back to their father's land, they kept searching for an explanation they could offer their father Jacob. Issachar said to them: "I have a solution if you agree. Take that tunic that was Joseph's and tear it, then slaughter a kid and dip the tunic in its blood. Send it to our father. When he sees it, he will say: '**A savage beast devoured him,**[36] and this is why his tunic is torn—and here is his blood on his tunic!' If you do as I say, we will be saved from our father's curses." They all agreed to accept Issachar's suggestion, and they heeded him and did as he advised. Quickly they took Joseph's tunic and tore it, and slaughtered a kid, and dipped the tunic in its blood and soiled it.

---

[35] Gen. 37:29–30.
[36] Gen. 37:33.

And they sent the tunic to their father Jacob by Naphtali,[37] having instructed him to say: "We had rounded up the animals and we were on the road to Shechem when we found this blood-soaked, dirty tunic in the wilderness by the roadside. **Now please examine it; is it your son's tunic or not?**"[38]

Naphtali went to his father and gave him the tunic and told him everything that his brothers had instructed him to say. When Jacob saw Joseph's tunic, he recognized it, and he fell on his face to the ground and was as still as a stone. After a while he got up and cried out in a loud voice racked by his sobs: "It is my son Joseph's tunic!" Jacob immediately sent one of his slaves to his sons, and he found them on the road with their flocks. That evening the sons of Jacob came to their father. They had rent their garments and put dirt on their heads, and they found their father weeping and lamenting in a loud voice. Jacob said to his sons: "Won't you tell me how this curse and misfortune has befallen me so suddenly?" They answered their father Jacob saying: "We had rounded up the flocks and were on our way to the city of Shechem on the road in the wilderness when we found this blood-soaked tunic on the ground, and we thought it looked familiar, and we sent it on to you to see if you could recognize it." When Jacob heard his sons' words, he cried out in a loud voice: "**My son's tunic! A savage beast devoured him! Joseph was torn by a beast!**[39] For I sent him to you today to see how you and the flocks were faring and bring me back word. He went there, just as I had told him to do, and this happened to him while I thought he was with you." Jacob's sons answered him saying: "He did not come to us. We haven't seen him since we left here."

When Jacob heard these words, he gave a great cry, and stood up and rent his garments and girded his loins with sackcloth and wept greatly. And he mourned and wept in a loud voice saying: "Joseph, my son! My son Joseph! Just today I sent you to see if your brothers were all right, and you were torn apart! My son, I made this happen to you! I grieve for you, my son Joseph, I grieve for you! How sweet you were to me in life, and now how bitter your death is to me! If only I could have died in your place today, my son Joseph, for I am deeply grieved for you! My son, my son Joseph, where are you, and where has your soul wandered? Get up, get up from your place, and come and see how I grieve for you, my son Joseph! Please come and count the tears flowing from my eyes down my cheeks, and and take them before God, so that He may turn His anger away from me. How is it, Joseph my son, that you fell into a hand that no one has fallen into from the day the world was created until now? An enemy blow

[37] The midrash interprets Jacob's poetic statement "Naphtali is a hind let loose" (Gen. 49:21) as a reference to swiftness, and hence he is portrayed as the brothers' messenger.
[38] Gen. 37:32.
[39] Gen. 37:33.

has cruelly struck you down, but now I realize that it was on account of my many sins that this has befallen you, my son! Please awaken and see how bitter to me is your misfortune, my son! I was not able to see you grow to manhood, nor did I fashion you; indeed it was not I who breathed life into you. God created you and formed your bones and added flesh upon them. It was He who breathed the breath of life in your nostrils and gave you to me. It was God who gave you to me, and now God has taken you from me. I can only say that everything God does is well done."[40]

And Jacob went on talking about Joseph, and he wept greatly, and fell to the ground and fainted. All the sons of Jacob saw their father's suffering and were sorry for what they had done, and they too wept greatly. Judah got up and lifted his father's head from the ground and put it in his lap, and he dried the tears from his father's cheeks. Judah also wept bitterly with his father's head in his lap motionless as a rock. And the sons of Jacob saw their father's suffering, and they went on weeping, but Jacob remained on the ground as motionless as a rock. And all his sons, and all his slaves, and all the daughters of his slaves gathered round Jacob to comfort him, but he would not be comforted.

And all the house of Jacob arose and prepared a great mourning on account of Joseph and his father's grief. And word of this reached Isaac, son of Abraham and father of Jacob, and he too wept greatly for Joseph, both he and all his household. Then Isaac and the people of his household left the place where they had been and went to Hebron to comfort his son Jacob, but he refused to be comforted. Jacob managed to get up from the ground, although tears continued to stream down his face, and he said to his sons: "Get up, and take your swords and your bows and arrows, and go out and search the fields. Maybe you can find what remains of my son's body, and bring it to me so that I can bury it. Also hunt down any wild animals that are there, and catch them, and bring them here. Perhaps God, seeing how I have suffered today, will give you the one that ate my son, and you will bring it here, and I can take revenge for my son." The sons did as their father commanded. They got up early the next morning, and each one of them took his sword and his bow and arrows and went out to the field to hunt the animals. Meanwhile, Jacob was still weeping and lamenting and pacing around his house, and striking the fist of one hand in the palm of the other, and saying: "Joseph, my son, Joseph, my son!"

As the sons of Jacob were hunting the beasts in the wilderness, they came upon a wolf, and they caught him, and took him to their father. They told him: "This is the first thing we've caught, and we brought him to you as you commanded; but we didn't find any remains of your son." Jacob took the animal

---

[40] Cf. Job 1:21: "The Lord gave, and the Lord hath taken away; Blessed be the name of the Lord."

from his sons' hands, and he cried out and wept loudly while holding it in his hands. And in bitterness of heart and soul, he said to the beast: "Why did you eat my son Joseph? Why did you not fear the God of all the earth, or at least my sorrow for Joseph my son? You had no reason to eat my son! He never did anything violent. You have rendered me guilty on his account, and God will hold me responsible for what has happened to him." And God opened the wolf's mouth so that it might comfort Jacob with its words. And this is what the wolf said to Jacob: "By the living God, Who created me on the earth, and as your soul lives, my lord, I have not seen your son, nor have I torn him apart. I also have come from a very distant land to look for my son. I've had the very same experience that you've had with my son. I came here ten days ago to look for my son who left me twelve days ago, and I don't know whether he is dead or alive. Today I went out to the field to look for my son, and your sons found me and piled new sufferings on the ones I already had by bringing me to you. I'm telling you everything I know. Now, oh son of man, I am in your hands; do with me as you wish today. But I swear to you by the living God who created me on the earth that I have not seen your son, nor have I torn him apart; and human flesh has never entered my mouth all the days of my life." When Jacob heard the animal's words, he was very much amazed, and he released the animal, and it went on its way. And Jacob continued to weep and to wail every day over Joseph, and Jacob mourned for Joseph many days.

The sons of Ishmael who bought Joseph from the Midianites (who had bought him from his brothers) went on traveling with Joseph until they came to the Egyptian border. As they were about to enter Egypt, they came upon four men who were sons of Medan, son of Abraham,[41] who were leaving Egypt on the same road. The Ishmaelites asked them: "Would you like to buy this slave from us?" and they answered: "All right. Give him to us." They gave Joseph to them, and they saw that he was a very handsome lad, and they bought him for five shekels. The Ishmaelites went on to Egypt, and the Medanites arrived there the same day. The Medanites said that they had heard that Potiphar, **a courtier of Pharaoh and his chief steward,**[42] was looking for a good slave to stand before him and serve him and watch over his household and all his property. "Well," said the Medanites, "let's go and sell him, and perhaps we can sell him to him for whatever price we ask." The Medanites went on to Potiphar's house, and they said to him: "We have heard that you are looking for a good slave to serve you. We have with us a slave who is exactly what you want. We'll sell him to you if you'll give us the price we're asking." Potiphar replied: "Well, bring him here so that I can see him. If he pleases me, I will give you what

[41] By Keturah; cf. Gen. 25:2.
[42] Gen. 37:36.

you're asking for him." Then the Medanites went and brought Joseph, and made him stand before Potiphar, and he saw him, and he was well pleased with him. Potiphar said: "Tell me how much you want for this lad." They replied: "We want four hundred pieces of silver for him." Potiphar said: "I will pay you that price if you will bring me the bill of sale and tell me all about him. Perhaps he was stolen, for this lad is no slave, nor is he the son of a slave; for I can see that he comes from a good bloodline and is very handsome." So the Medanites went and brought him the Ishmaelites who had sold Joseph to them, and they told him that he was a slave. "We sold him to the Medanites," they said. Potiphar heeded the words of the Ishmaelites, and he weighed out to the Medanites the four hundred pieces of silver they had asked for, and he put it into the hands of the Ishmaelites to give to the Medanites. And the Medanites took the silver from the hands of the Ishmaelites and went on their way, and the Ishmaelites also went home. And Potiphar took Joseph into his house, and Joseph served him. And Potiphar **took a liking to Joseph,**[43] and Potiphar had full confidence in him, **and put him in charge of his household, placing in his hands all that he owned.**[44] And God was with Joseph, and he was fortunate, and **God blessed [Potiphar's] house for Joseph's sake,**[45] **And Potiphar left all that he had in Joseph's hands,**[46] and Joseph was in charge of taking things out and bringing things into the house, and his words were law in Potiphar's house.

At that time Joseph was eighteen years old, and he had beautiful eyes and was good looking, and his like was not to be found in all the land of Egypt. While Joseph was coming and going in his master's house and serving his master, Zalikha, his master's wife, **cast her eyes upon Joseph,**[47] and she saw that he was a **well built and handsome**[48] lad, and she coveted his beauty in her heart. And her soul cleaved unto Joseph, and every day she tempted him to be with her, and every day she gave him new garments. Zalikha spoke to him every day, but Joseph never raised his eyes to gaze upon his master's wife. And Zalikha said to him: "How good looking you are! I've seen many slaves, but I've never seen another as good looking as you!" Joseph replied: "My Creator formed me in my mother's belly just like all other men." She asked him: "How is it that you have such lovely eyes that they have dazzled everyone in Egypt, both men and women?" He replied: "Yes, they may be pretty as long as I'm alive, but if you could see how they'll look when I'm in my grave, you'd sing a different tune."

---

[43] Gen. 39:4.
[44] Gen. 39:4.
[45] Gen. 39:5.
[46] Gen. 39:6
[47] Gen. 39:7.
[48] Gen. 39:6.

She said to him: "How lovely and pleasant are all your words! Take the harp that's in the house, and play it with your hands, and we'll see if you can sing too!" He replied: "My words are lovely and pleasant when they sing the praise of God and His glory." She said: "How beautiful is the hair on your head! Here in the house is a golden comb. Please take it, and curl your hair with it." He replied: "How long will you continue to speak to me this way? Spare me your words, and get up and do your housework." She answered: "My housework is unimportant. The only thing I care about is your words and desires."

During all this time Joseph never so much as looked at her nor even raised his eyes to her, for he kept his eyes always on the ground. But inwardly Zalikha longed for Joseph to sleep with her. One day he was in the house **doing his work,**[49] and Zalikha came and sat down in front of him. Every day she kept trying to persuade him to sleep with her—or at least to look at her!—but Joseph would not listen. She told him: "If you don't do as I ask, I will have you sentenced to death, and I will put an iron yoke upon you." Joseph answered: "God, Who created man, sets prisoners free,[50] and He will save me from you, and all your prisons and all your sentences."

When she realized that she could not persuade him to sleep with her, although her soul cleaved to him, Zalikha fell gravely ill out of longing for him. All the ladies of Egypt came to visit her, and they asked her: "What has made you so ill? There is nothing that you lack. Is it possible that the wife of a highly honored courtier whom the king greatly esteems could lack anything her soul desires?" Zalikha replied: "Today I will tell you all about what has happened to me, and you will see the cause of my suffering." Then she ordered her maidens to serve all the ladies food. They did so, serving a sumptuous lunch, and all the ladies were eating in Zalikha's house. Then they served citrons, and gave the ladies knives to use for peeling them so that they could eat them. Zalikha ordered Joseph dressed in priceless robes and brought out before the ladies. Joseph came out, and all the ladies stared at him and couldn't take their eyes off him. They all cut their hands with the knives that were in their hands, and all the citrons were covered with their blood. They didn't even notice this, however, for they were completely captivated by Joseph's beauty and couldn't take their eyes off him. But Zalikha saw what was happening, and she asked them: "What have you done? I gave you those citrons to eat, and you have all cut your hands!" Then the ladies looked at their hands and saw that they were all bloody, and there was also blood on their gowns. They told her: "We were utterly captivated by that slave you have in your house, and we couldn't take

---

[49] Gen. 39:11.
[50] Ps. 146:7: "The Lord . . . sets the prisoner free."

our eyes off him because of his beauty." She replied: "Just seeing him for a moment has affected you this way, and you couldn't even take your eyes off him! So what am I supposed to do? I am always here at home, and I see him walking around the house every day. How then can I keep from falling ill and even dying?" They replied: "What you say is true, for who could endure gazing upon this man's beauty while in the very same house with him? However, he is your slave and serves in your house. Why don't you just tell him what's in your heart instead of agonizing like that?" She answered: "Every day I try to persuade him, but he won't do as I wish, and I've promised him all sorts of good things, but he doesn't respond, and that's why I've fallen ill, as you've seen."

Zalikha fell gravely ill out of longing for Joseph, and her illness grew worse as her love increased. Neither the men of Zalikha's household nor her husband knew any of this, nor were they aware that she had fallen ill out of love for Joseph. All the men of her household asked her: "What has made you so sick? Surely there is nothing that you lack." She replied: "It came upon me gradually, and I didn't realize what was happening." All her women friends came to see her and talk to her every day. She told them: "This is all because of my love for Joseph." They said: "Tempt him, and take hold of him in secret. Perhaps he will listen to you and cure all your fatal symptoms." Zalikha's condition kept worsening out of love for Joseph. Restlessly she paced around the house until she was too weak to stand. One day Joseph was in the house doing his master's work, and Zalikha came to him in secret and fell upon him all at once; but he managed to get out from under her and left her lying on the floor. Zalikha wept and told him the feelings she cherished in her heart for him. She stood before him in anguish as the tears streamed down her cheeks. In a pleading voice and in bitterness of soul, she said: "Have you ever seen, or heard of, or known of a woman more beautiful than I? I have spoken to you every day, and have fallen ill out of love for you. I have shown you every imaginable honor, but you wouldn't even listen to my voice. If you are afraid your master might imprison you, I swear to you by the king's life that he will do you no harm. Now please listen to me carefully, and reward me for all the honor I have shown you, and cure my fatal illness. Why should I die for you?" When she had done speaking, Joseph replied: "Get away from me, and stop trying to make me do this every night. I cannot do this to my master. **Look, with me here, my master gives no thought to anything in this house, and all that he owns he has placed in my hands.**[51] How could I do such things in my master's house? He too has shown me great honor in his house, and has made me steward over his house and has exalted me, so that there is no one with more authority than I in this house,

---

[51] Gen. 39:8.

and he has withheld nothing from me except yourself, since you are his wife.[52] How dare you go on talking to me like that? **How could I do this most wicked thing, and sin against God**[53] and your husband? Now please leave me alone, and don't ever bring this matter up again, for I shall pay no attention to what you have to say." Zalikha, however, refused to heed Joseph's words, and every day she went on trying to make him listen to her.

Shortly afterwards the river of Egypt overflowed its banks, and all the Egyptians went out to see the river with all sorts of musical instruments, as was their custom. Also the king and the courtiers went out with drumming and dancing, for it was a great celebration for the Egyptians and a holiday when the river Shihor[54] overflowed its banks; and they all went out to the river banks to celebrate all day long. And when the Egyptians went down to the river to celebrate, as was their custom, all the men of Potiphar's household went too. Zalikha, however, didn't go, for she said she was ill. She stayed at home by herself in the hope of ensnaring Joseph that day.

When everyone left, Zalikha stayed behind, and there was no one in the house but her. Then she got up and went to her boudoir and dressed up like a queen. On her head she put a tiara of onyx stones set in gold and silver. She painted her face and body using all the best cosmetics known to women. And she perfumed her apartments and the rest of the house with precious incense, and also scented her chamber with myrrh and other fine perfumes. Then she sat down in the doorway of her chamber facing the corridor through which Joseph was sure to pass on his way to do his work. Before she knew it, Joseph returned from the fields and **came into the house to do his** master's **work.**[55] He came to the place where she was waiting for him, and when he saw what Zalikha had done, he turned around to go back the way he had come. When Zalikha saw him going away, she shouted after him: "What's the matter with you, Joseph? Come and do your work. I'll get out of your way so you can go where you wish." Joseph turned around and went back into the house, and went to his room, and sat down to do his master's work as usual. But Zalikha came and stood before him wearing that regal gown, and one could smell her perfume from a great distance away. Quickly she caught hold of him by his garment and told him: "By the king's life, if you won't do as I wish today, you will

[52] Gen. 39:9.
[53] Gen. 39:9.
[54] Originally the name of a lake in the eastern Delta near the Pelusiac branch of the Nile, which formed the westernmost border of Palestine in the south in the time of David (1 Chron. 13:5); the term was later used to designate the Nile (Is. 23:3).
[55] Gen. 39:11.

die!" With her other hand she quickly drew a dagger from beneath her robe and pointed it at Joseph's chest, and said: "Get up and do as I say, or else you will surely die today!" Joseph was afraid she would do just as she said, and he got up and tried to run away from her, but she was still holding on to the front of his garment. As he ran away, the garment tore, but he left it in Zalikha's hand and ran on outside, because he was afraid.

When Zalikha realized that Joseph's garment had torn, and he had left it in her hand and run away, she was afraid for her life in case anyone had heard what had happened. Sneakily, she then got up and took off those fine clothes she was wearing and put on her everyday clothing. Then she took Joseph's garment and put it beside her, and she went and lay down in the place where she had been accustomed to lie while she was ill, and where the men had seen her lying when they went down from the house to the river. She summoned a small boy who was in the house and ordered him to call the men of the household. They came to her, and when she saw them, she shouted in a loud voice and moaning: "**Look**, your master brought **a Hebrew** to the house, and he **came** today **to lie with me!**[56] While you were out, he came to the house and saw that there was no one at home, and he came to me and took hold of me to lie with me. I grabbed hold of his clothes and tore them, and screamed in a loud voice. When he heard me screaming, he feared for his life, and he left his garment in my hand and ran outside."

The men of the household didn't even stay to reply, but, enraged against Joseph, they went straight to their master and told him what his wife had said. Potiphar then went home full of anguish and rage, and his wife shouted at him: "Why did you bring that Hebrew slave to my house? **He came to me today to dally with me!**[57] And he did thus and so to me today." Potiphar heeded what his wife said, and he ordered Joseph whipped, and it was done. While they were whipping him, Joseph cried out in a loud voice, and lifted his eyes to heaven and said: "Oh Lord God, You know that I am innocent of all these things. Why must I die today on account of the lies of these uncircumcised, wicked men whom I don't even know?" As Potiphar's men went on whipping him, Joseph kept on crying and weeping.

At that place there was an eleven-month-old infant with one of Potiphar's slaves. God opened that infant's mouth, and he addressed Potiphar's men who were whipping Joseph, and said to them: "What do you have against this man? And why are you doing him so much harm? For my mother was lying when she

---

[56] Gen. 39:14.
[57] Gen. 39:17.

said: 'he did thus and so to me today.' " That infant went on to tell them the whole truth, recounting everything Zalikha had been saying to Joseph day by day. All the men heeded the infant's words, and were very amazed by them. Then it ceased speaking and went to sleep. Potiphar was deeply troubled by his son's words, and he ordered his men to stop whipping Joseph, and they did so. And Potiphar took Joseph and said he would bring him to trial before the priests who were the king's judges[58] so that they might judge him in this matter.

Potiphar and Joseph went before the priests who were the king's judges, and Potiphar said: "Decide now what sentence should be decreed against this slave, for he did thus and so." The priests asked Joseph: "Why did you do this to your master?" Joseph replied: "I did not do thus and so; what really happened was this . . . ." Then Potiphar said to Joseph: "I put everything I own in your hands, and I kept nothing from you except my wife, so how could you do such a wicked thing to me?" Joseph answered: "No, my master! As God lives, and upon your soul, your wife was not telling the truth when she said that I did thus and so, and this is what really happened today. . . . I have been in your house for exactly a year. Have you ever seen me do anything wrong or anything that might make you demand my life?" Then the priests said to Potiphar: "Go and bring us Joseph's garment that was torn so that we can examine it and see where it was torn. If it was torn in front, then he must have been facing her, and she grabbed him to pull him to her, and your wife treacherously did all the things she has said." Then Joseph's garment was brought before those priest-judges, and they saw that it was torn in front, and then those priest-judges understood that it was she who forced him. Then they said: "There can be no death sentence pronounced against this slave, because he has done nothing. We do, however, sentence him to prison because of the public disgrace your wife has suffered on his account." And Potiphar heeded all those words, **and he had Joseph put in prison, where the king's prisoners were confined.**[59]

And Joseph spent twelve years in prison. During all that time, his master's wife never gave up hope that she might yet persuade him to listen to her. When he had been in prison for three months, she went to see him every day and kept trying to get him to listen to her. Zalikha asked him: "How long do you intend to stay in prison? Just listen to me, please, and I will get you out of here." Joseph replied: "I'd rather stay here in prison than listen to you and sin against my God." She told him: "If you don't do what I say, I'll put out your eyes, and I'll put shackles on your legs, and I will turn you over to strangers." He answered:

---

[58] Cf. Arragel's commentary on Gen. 47:20.
[59] Gen. 39:20.

"Behold, the God of all the earth can save me from anything you would do to me, for He gives sight to the blind, and frees the prisoners,[60] and watches over the strangers who are in a land they do not know." Since Zalikha couldn't get Joseph to listen to her, she finally stopped visiting him, but Joseph remained in prison. Meanwhile Jacob, Joseph's father, and all his brothers who were in the land of Canaan were still weeping and mourning for Joseph in those days, for Jacob refused to be comforted for his son Joseph. And Jacob wept and cried and mourned for Joseph all those days.

At that time, in the same year when Joseph went to Egypt after his brothers had sold him, Reuben, son of Jacob, went to Timnah and married Elyoram, daughter of Evi the Canaanite, and he had intercourse with her, and Reuben's wife Elyoram bore him four sons: Hanoch, and Pallu, and Hezron, and Carmi. And Simeon his brother married his sister Dinah, and she bore him Jemuel, and Jamin, and Ohad, and Jachin, and Zohar—five sons. After that, Simeon had intercourse with Bonah the Canaanite; this was the same Bonah that Simeon had brought with him as a captive from the city of Shechem. Bonah was Dinah's servant. He had intercourse with her, and she bore him Shaul. **About that time Judah** went to Adullam, **and camped near a certain Adullamite whose name was Hirah. There Judah saw the daughter of a certain Canaanite whose name was** Alit, daughter of **Shua, and he married her and cohabitated with her.**[61] And Alit bore Judah Er, and Onan, and Shelah—three sons. Levi and Issachar went to the eastern lands, and there they married the daughters of Jobab, son of Joktan, son of Eber. Jobab, son of Joktan, had two daughters; the elder was named Adinah and the younger was named Aridah. Levi married Adinah and Issachar married Aridah; and they took them to their father's house in the land of Canaan. And Adinah bore Levi Gershon, Kohath, and Merari—three sons. And Aridah bore Issachar Tola, and Phuvah, and Iob, and Shimron—four sons. And Dan went to the land of Moab and married Afilelet, daughter of Hamudan the Moabite, and he brought her to the land of Canaan. But Afilelet was barren for a long time and bore no children. Then God remembered Afilelet, wife of Dan, and she became pregnant, and she bore a son named Hushim. Gad and Naphtali went to Haran, and there they married the daughters of Amoram, son of Oz, son of Nahor. These are the names of the daughters of Amoram: the name of the elder was Merimat, and the name of the younger was Ozit. And Naphtali married Merimat, and Dan married

[60] Ps. 146:7–8: "The Lord . . . sets the prisoner free. The Lord restores sight to the blind."
[61] Gen. 38:1-2.

Ozit, and they brought them to their father's house in the land of Canaan. And Merimat bore Naphtali Jahzeel, and Guni, and Jezer, and Shillem—four sons. And Ozit bore Gad Ziphion and Haggi, Shuni and Ezbon, Eri and Arodi, and Areli—seven sons. And Asher went and married Adon, daughter of Afilel, son of Hadad, son of Ishmael, and brought her to the land of Canaan. But Asher's wife Adon died childless in those days. After Adon's death, Asher crossed the river and married Hadurah, daughter of Abimael, son of Eber, son of Shem. And the young woman was lovely to look at and clever, and she had previously been married to Malchiel, son of Eilam, son of Shem. And Hadurah bore a daughter to Malchiel, and they called her Serah. Then Malchiel died, and Hadurah returned to her father's house. After Asher's first wife died, he went and married Hadurah and brought her to the land of Canaan, and he brought her daughter Serah with her. She was then only three years old, and she grew up in Jacob's house. She was a pretty little girl, and she followed in the holy paths of the sons of Jacob, omitting nothing, and God gave her wisdom and intelligence. Hadurah, Asher's wife, became pregnant, and she bore him Jimnah, and Ishuah, and Isui, and Beriah—four sons. And Zebulun went to Midian, and married Merushah, daughter of Moled, son of Abida, son of Midian, and he brought her to the land of Canaan. And Merushah bore Zebulun Sered, and Elon, and Jahleel—three sons. And Jacob sent to Aram, son of Zova, son of Terah, and took Mehalia, daughter of Aram, as a wife for his son Benjamin, and she came to Jacob's house in the land of Canaan. Benjamin was only ten years old when he married Mehalia, daughter of Aram. Mehalia became pregnant and bore Benjamin Belah, and Becher, and Ashbel, Gera, and Naaman— five sons. After that Benjamin went and married Aribat, daughter of Zimran, son of Abraham, in addition to his other wife; and he was then eighteen years old. And Aribat bore Benjamin Ehi, and Rosh, Muppim, and Huppim, and Ard—five sons.[62]

It was around this time that Judah went to the house of Shem and took Tamar, daughter of Eilam, son of Shem, as a wife for his firstborn son Er. And Er had intercourse with his wife Tamar, and she behaved toward him as a wife. But when he had intercourse with her, he ejaculated his semen on the ground, and this was displeasing to God, and God killed him. After the death of Judah's firstborn son Er, Judah told Onan: **"Join with your brother's wife and do your duty by her as a brother-in-law, and provide offspring for your brother."**[63] And Onan took Tamar as his wife and had intercourse with her. However,

---

[62] The names of Jacob's grandchildren are to be found in Gen. 46:9-24.
[63] Gen. 38:8.

Onan did the same thing his brother had done, and God was extremely displeased with him, and killed him too. When Onan died, Judah told Tamar: **"Stay in your father's house until my son Shelah grows up."**[64] But Judah didn't want to marry Tamar to Shelah, for he said: **"He too might die like his brothers."**[65] But Tamar arose, and went, and stayed in her father's house, and she was in her father's house for a long time. And at the turning of the year **Judah's wife** Alit **died, and Judah completed the mourning**[66] for his wife. After Alit's death, **Judah went with his friend Hirah to Timnah for the sheep-shearing.**[67] And Tamar heard that Judah was going up to Timnah for the sheep-shearing; and by this time Shelah was grown, but Judah had not come for her. Tamar arose, and **took off her widow's garb, and covered her face with a veil, and went and sat down at the entrance to Enaim, which is on the road to Timnah.**[68] And Judah passed by, and he saw her, and took her, and had intercourse with her, and she became pregnant by him. **When the time came for her to give birth, there were twins in her womb!**[69] And they named the first one Perez, and the second one Zerah.

In those days Joseph, son of Jacob, was still a prisoner in the prison in the land of Egypt. At that time Pharaoh's courtiers stood before him. One of them was his chief cupbearer, and the other was the king of Egypt's chief baker. The chief cupbearer took wine and served it to Pharaoh to drink, and the chief baker served Pharaoh bread to eat. And the king drank the wine and ate the bread, both he and all his servants and his courtiers who were accustomed to eat at the king's table. While they ate and drank, the chief cupbearer and the chief baker were sitting with them. Pharaoh's courtiers found many flies in the wine that the chief cupbearer served, and they found nitrous stones in the bread that the chief baker served. Pharaoh saw what his servants had done and ordered them put in prison, and so it was done.

In the tenth year of Joseph's imprisonment the chief cupbearer and the chief baker joined him there. **The chief steward assigned Joseph to attend them,**[70] and they were in prison for a whole year. At the end of the year, they both had dreams **on the same night**[71] in the prison where they were confined. When

---

[64] Gen. 38:11.
[65] Gen. 38:11.
[66] Gen. 38:12.
[67] Gen. 38:13.
[68] Gen. 38:14.
[69] Gen. 38:27.
[70] Gen. 40:4.
[71] Gen. 40:5.

Joseph came to serve them and look after them in the morning, he saw that both their faces were very distraught and gloomy. Joseph asked them: "Why are your faces so distraught and gloomy today?" **And they said to him: "We had dreams, and there is no one to interpret them."**[72] Joseph said to them: "Tell me your dreams, and God will answer so that you will have peace of mind." **The chief cupbearer told Joseph his dream. He said to him: "In my dream, I looked and saw a big vine in front of me. On that vine I saw three branches.**[73] All at once **it budded, and out came its blossoms, and its clusters ripened into grapes.**[74] **I took the grapes, pressed them into Pharaoh's cup, and placed the cup in Pharaoh's hand,**[75] and he drank." Joseph told him: "The three branches that were on the vine are three days. In three days the king will pardon you, and liberate you, and **restore you to your post,**[76] and you will serve the king wine, as was formerly your custom. However, if I have pleased you, be so kind as to mention me to the king, **so as to free me from this place.**[77] **For in truth I was kidnapped from the land of**[78] Canaan and sold as a slave in this place, and everything they told concerning my master's wife was nothing but lies, and they put me in this prison for nothing." The chief cupbearer answered Joseph: "If the king restores me to my former post as you have interpreted, I will do whatever you wish and get you out of this prison." When the chief baker saw that Joseph had interpreted the chief cupbearer's dream favorably, he came to Joseph and told him his dream too. He said: "In my dream, I looked and **there were three openwork baskets on my head.**[79] I noticed that **in the uppermost basket were all kinds of food for Pharaoh that a baker prepares,**[80] but **the birds were eating it over my head."**[81] Joseph told him: **"The three baskets that you saw are three days. In three days Pharaoh will lift off your head and impale you upon a pole; and the birds will pick off your flesh,**[82] as you saw in your dream."

In those days—indeed on that very day—the queen bore a son to the king of Egypt. And it was said: "Pharaoh's first son is born!" And all of Egypt, and

[72] Gen. 40:8.
[73] Gen. 40:9.
[74] Gen. 40:10.
[75] Gen. 40:11.
[76] Gen. 40:13.
[77] Gen. 40:14.
[78] Gen. 40:15.
[79] Gen. 40:16.
[80] Gen. 40:17.
[81] Gen. 40:17.
[82] Gen. 40:18–19.

all of Pharaoh's courtiers and servants rejoiced greatly. **On the third day** after he was born, **Pharaoh made a banquet for all his courtiers**[83] and servants in the land of Zoan and the land of Egypt. All the Egyptians and all the servants of Pharaoh came to eat and drink with the king to celebrate the birth of his son, and to rejoice at the king's celebration. And all the king's courtiers and servants rejoiced greatly at that time during all the eight days of the celebration. They rejoiced with all sorts of musical instruments and danced to the sound of drums in the king's house for eight days.

But the cupbearer whose dream Joseph had interpreted forgot Joseph and did not remind the king of him as he had promised. God brought that about to teach Joseph that he should not trust in a man. Joseph remained in prison for two more years, and at that time he had been in prison for twelve years altogether.

Isaac, son of Abraham, was still living in the land of Canaan in those days. He was very old, 180 years old! His son Esau, Jacob's brother, was in the land of Edom, and he and his sons owned land there among the sons of Seir. Esau heard that his father was near death, and he and his sons and all his household came to the land of Canaan to his father Isaac. And Jacob and his sons left the place where they were living in Hebron, and all went to the tent of his father Isaac, and they found Esau and his sons in the tent. Jacob and his sons sat down before Isaac, and Jacob was still in mourning for his son Joseph. Isaac told Jacob: "Bring me your sons so that I may bless them." And Jacob brought his eleven children before his father Isaac. Isaac laid his hands on each of Jacob's sons, and he embraced them, and he kissed them one by one. And that day Isaac blessed them saying: "May the Lord God of your fathers bless you and multiply your descendants like the stars of the sky." Isaac also blessed the sons of Esau saying: "May God make you the terror and dread of all who see you and all your enemies." Then Isaac called Jacob and his sons, and they all sat down before Isaac. Isaac told Jacob: "The Lord God of all the earth spoke to me saying: 'I will give this land to your descendants as an inheritance if your sons will keep my commandments and my ways, and I will carry out for them the covenant I made with your father Abraham.' And now, my son, teach your sons and your sons' sons to fear God and to walk in the good path so that the Lord God will be pleased with them, for if you faithfully follow God's ways and keep His commandments, He will observe the covenant He made with Abraham, and will be gracious unto you and to your descendants forever."

---

[83] Gen. 40:20.

When Isaac had finished speaking to Jacob and his sons, **he breathed his last, and died, and was gathered unto his people.**[84] Jacob and Esau fell upon the face of their father Isaac and wept. Isaac was 180 years old when he died in the land of Canaan in Hebron. His sons carried him to the cave of Machpelah that Abraham had bought from the Hittites to use as a burial place. All the kings of the land of Canaan went with Jacob and Esau to bury Isaac, and all the kings of Canaan showed Isaac great honor when he died. And the sons of Jacob and the sons of Esau walked barefoot and lamented until they reached Kiriath-arba. Jacob and Esau buried their father Isaac in the cave of Machpelah that is at Kiriath-arba in Hebron; they buried him with the great honor normally shown to kings. Jacob and his sons, and Esau and his sons, mourned for him, and all the kings of Canaan mourned grievously, and they buried him and mourned him for many days.

When he died, Isaac left all his flocks and all his possessions to his sons. Esau told Jacob: "Let us divide all that our father has left us into two parts, and I will choose my part." Jacob said: "Yes, that's what we'll do." Jacob took everything that Isaac had left them, all the animals and other belongings in the land of Canaan, and divided it into two parts before Esau and his sons. He told Esau: "Of all that is before you, choose which half you wish to claim." But then Jacob said to Esau: "Please listen to what I have to say. The Lord God of the heavens and the earth spoke to our fathers Abraham and Isaac, saying: 'I will give this land to your descendants as an inheritance forever.' Before you is everything our father left to us, and all the land. Choose which part you desire. If you want all the land for your sons, take it and I will keep the other belongings. If, however, you prefer our father's wealth, take the belongings, and I will take the land for my sons as an inheritance forever."

Ishmael's son Nebaioth was then in the land with his sons, and Esau went and asked his advice, saying: "Jacob said thus and so to me. Tell me what you recommend, and I will do as you say." Nebaioth replied: "What is this that Jacob said to you? All the sons of Canaan are living securely in their lands, but Jacob said he and his descendants will inherit it forever. Go and take all your father's wealth and leave your brother Jacob in the land he spoke of." Then Esau got up and went back to Jacob and did everything that Nebaioth son of Ishmael had advised him to do. Esau took all the wealth that Isaac had left— the people, and the animals, and the herds, and everything that was of value— leaving his brother Jacob nothing. Jacob took all the land of Canaan from the riverbed of Egypt to the river Euphrates as an eternal possession for his sons and all later generations. And Jacob took from his brother Esau the cave of

---

[84] Gen. 35:27.

Machpelah that was in Hebron, which Abraham had bought from Ephron to use as a burial place for himself and his descendants forever. And Jacob wrote all of that down in the contract he made with Esau, and he sealed it in the presence of reliable witnesses. These are the words that Jacob wrote in the contract: "The land of Canaan, and all the cities of the Hittites, and the Hivites, and the Jebusites, and the Amorites, and the Perizzites, all the seven nations from the river of Egypt to the river Euphrates, and the city in Hebron called Kiriath-arba and the cave that is in it—all of this Jacob has bought from his brother Esau for money as an inheritance for him and his sons and for all later generations forever." And Jacob took that deed of sale with its seal, and all the laws pertaining thereto, and put them in a clay urn where they would remain for many days, and he gave them to his sons. Then Esau took his father's legacy from the hands of his brother Jacob. He took all the possessions—slaves, cattle, camels, donkeys, oxen, sheep, silver, gold, precious stones, and bdellium— all the wealth that had belonged to Isaac, son of Abraham. There was nothing that Esau did not take of the property Isaac left when he died. Esau took all these riches and went to the land of Seir the Horite. He and his sons went to their places so as not to be with Jacob and his sons. And Esau owned land among the sons of Seir, and Esau never returned to the land of Canaan from that day on. Therefore all the land of Canaan belonged only to Israel as an inheritance forever, and Esau and his sons inherited Mount Seir.

II. Mikkets

In those days, after the death of Isaac, God brought a great famine upon all the earth. At that time Pharaoh, king of Egypt, was sitting on his throne in the land of Egypt. And Pharaoh lay in his bed and had dreams. In his dream Pharaoh saw himself **standing by the** edge of **the river** of Egypt, **when out of the Nile there came up seven cows, handsome and sturdy.**[85] After them came seven cows, **ugly and gaunt,**[86] **and the ugly gaunt cows ate up the handsome sturdy cows,**[87] but they still looked just as bad as before they had eaten. Then Pharaoh awoke and went back to sleep, and **dreamed a second time. Seven ears of corn grew on a single stalk,** full of grain **and healthy.**[88] And after them **sprouted**

---

[85] Gen. 41:2.
[86] Gen. 41:3.
[87] Gen. 41:4.
[88] Gen. 41:5.

seven ears, thin and scorched by the east wind, and the thin ears swallowed up the seven solid and full ears.[89] Then Pharaoh awoke from his dream.

Next morning, the king remembered his dreams, and **his spirit was** very **agitated** on account of his dreams, and **he sent for all the magicians of Egypt and its wise men,**[90] and they came and stood before the king. The king told them: "I have had some dreams, but there is no one who can interpret them." They replied to the king: "Tell your servants those dreams, and we shall listen to them." The king told them his dreams, and they answered with one voice: "Long live the king! This is the explanation of your dreams: the seven handsome cows that you saw represent seven daughters that will be born to you in the days to come. The seven ugly cows that came out afterwards and swallowed the first ones mean that all seven of your daughters will die during the king's lifetime. What you saw in your second dream—the seven ears of corn that were full and solid on a single stalk—means that you will build seven cities throughout the land of Egypt in the days to come. What you saw concerning the seven thin and scorched ears that swallowed the solid ones means that your eyes will see all those cities that you have built destroyed during the king's lifetime." But as they spoke these words, the king did not heed them nor take them to heart, for the king knew in his wisdom that their explanation of his dreams was incorrect. When they had done speaking, the king said to them: "What is this that you have said? All the words that have proceeded from your mouths are lies and are false. Now give me the true interpretation of my dreams lest you die."

After that the king commanded that more wise men be summoned, and they came and stood before the king. The king told them his dreams, but they all gave the same interpretation as the previous ones. Then the king became angry and flew into a rage because of that. The king told them: "Everything you are saying is lies; all your words are false!" Then the king ordered a proclamation to be made throughout the land of Egypt, as follows: "If there be any wise man who knows and understands how to interpret dreams, he is ordered to report to the king today on pain of death. He who can give the correct interpretation of the king's dreams will be rewarded with anything he requests of the king."

All the wise men of Egypt reported to the king, together with all the magicians and all the sorcerers that were in Egypt and Goshen and Raamses and Tahpanhas and Zoan and all the borders of Egypt. They all stood before the king, and all the king's courtiers and noblemen and officials gathered there from all the cities in Egypt, and they all sat down before the king. The king recounted his dreams in the presence of the wise men and all the court, and all

[89] Gen. 41:6-7.
[90] Gen. 41:8.

those who were sitting before the king were astonished at the sight. All the wise men that were before the king split into many different factions according to their interpretations of the dreams. Some of them gave the king this interpretation: "The seven handsome cows are seven of the king's descendants who will rule over Egypt. The seven ugly cows are seven princes who will rebel against them in the days to come and destroy them. The seven goodly ears of corn are seven great Egyptian princes who will fall into the hands of seven less powerful enemy princes in the king's wars." Others gave the king the following interpretation: "The seven handsome cows are seven very strong cities in Egypt. The seven ugly cows are the seven nations of the land of Canaan that will come upon the seven cities of Egypt in the days to come and destroy them. The seven solid and thin ears of corn that you saw in your second dream mean that your descendants will retain the rulership of the kingdom of Egypt as at the beginning. The inhabitants of the cities of Egypt will again fight the seven strong cities of Canaan that are stronger than they are, and will destroy them, and the government of Egypt will return to your descendants." Still others gave the king the following explanation of his dreams: "The seven handsome cows represent seven queens whom you will marry in days to come. The seven ugly cows mean that all those queens will die during the king's lifetime. The seven goodly and thin ears of corn that you saw in your second dream are fourteen children who will rise up and make war against each other in the latter days, and the weak ones will conquer the strong." Yet another interpretation was as follows: "The seven handsome cows are seven sons who will be born to you, but seven sons of your courtiers will slay them in the days to come. The seven goodly ears of corn that you saw in your second dream are seven courtiers who will make war against the other seven courtiers who were less mighty, and will destroy them in the days to come, taking revenge for the death of your sons, and the kingship will return to your descendants."

The king listened to all the words of the wise men of Egypt and all their interpretations of his dreams, but none of them satisfied the king, for the king understood in his wisdom that all their speeches were mistaken. Thus God confounded the words of all the wise men of Egypt in order to liberate Joseph from prison and make him great in Egypt. The king saw that none of those wise men and magicians gave him the correct interpretation, and he became angry, and his wrath was enkindled, and his anger burned within him. The king ordered all the wise men and all the magicians led away, and they all left his presence in shame and disgrace. And the king ordered that a proclamation be made throughout Egypt that all the wise men and all the magicians in Egypt be killed so that not one of them should remain. Then the king's courtiers all arose and drew their swords and began slaying all the magicians of Egypt and the wise men.

After that the king's chief cupbearer Mirod came and bowed before the king and sat down before him. The chief cupbearer told the king: "Long live the king, and may his kingdom increase in the land! Oh king, you became angry with your servant about two years ago, and you put me in prison, and I was there for a while with the chief baker. With us in the dungeon was a Hebrew slave who belonged to the chief steward. His name was Joseph. His master had condemned him and put him in prison, and he served us there. While we were in prison, **we had dreams the same night,** the chief baker **and I; each of us a dream with a meaning of its own.**[91] In the morning we went and told that slave, and he interpreted our dreams for us, each one individually, and told us exactly what they meant. **And as he interpreted for us, so it came to pass,**[92] and nothing he said was mistaken. My lord king, don't kill the Egyptian men for nothing. That slave is still imprisoned in the prison of the chief steward, his master. If it please the king, summon and bring that man, and he will give you the correct interpretation of the dream you had." The king heeded the words of the chief cupbearer, and he gave orders that they stop killing the wise men of Egypt. And the king ordered his servants to bring Joseph before him, saying: "Go to him, and don't frighten him, for if he is afraid he won't be able to give me the correct interpretation."

The king's servants went to Joseph and quickly took him out of prison. **He had his hair cut and changed his clothes,**[93] and they brought him before the king. The king was sitting on his royal throne wearing his royal robe with a golden ephod around his waist. The gold on it sparkled, and the carbuncle and the ruby and the emerald, as well as the other precious stones that the king was wearing on his head, sparkled dazzlingly, and Joseph was in great awe of the king. The throne on which the king sat was covered with gold and silver and inlaid with onyx stones, and seventy steps led up to it. And it was the custom throughout the land of Egypt that whenever anyone came to seek an audience with the king, if he was a nobleman who was in good standing with the king, he was allowed to approach the throne as high as the thirty-first step, and the king would come down to the thirty-sixth step to speak with him. Commoners, however, were allowed to go up only as high as the third step, and the king would go down four steps to speak with them. There was one exception to this rule, however. Anyone who knew how to speak all the seventy languages could go up all seventy steps and discuss his request right in front of the king. Each

---

[91] Gen. 41:11.
[92] Gen. 41:13.
[93] Gen. 41:14.

one could go up the number of steps corresponding to the number of languages he knew, and they all knew where to stop. Egyptian law in those days decreed that no one could govern them unless he spoke seventy languages. When Joseph came before the king, he bowed low to the ground and went up only three steps and stopped at the third step. The king went down to him and stopped on the fourth step to speak with Joseph.

The king said to Joseph: **"I have had a dream, but no one can interpret it**[94] correctly. Today I summoned all the magicians of Egypt and all the wise men, and I told them my dreams, but none of them could give me the correct interpretation. Later today, I heard about you—that you are a wise man for whom **to hear** any **dream is to tell its** exact **meaning."**[95] **Joseph answered Pharaoh, saying:**[96] "Let Pharaoh tell me the dreams he has had, but it is up to God to give the interpretation." Pharaoh then told Joseph about his dreams—the one about the cows and the one about the ears of corn. When the king had finished speaking, the spirit of God descended upon Joseph at that very moment in the presence of the king, and Joseph understood everything that was to happen to the king from that day on. Joseph understood exactly what the king's dream meant, and he explained it to the king. Joseph found favor in the king's eyes, and the king inclined his ears and his heart to all that Joseph said.

Joseph said to Pharaoh: "Pharaoh must needs understand that his two dreams are really one and the same, for the God of heaven has shown Pharaoh in his dream what He intends to do throughout the land. This is the correct interpretation of your dream: **the seven healthy cows** and ears of corn **are seven years**, and the seven ugly cows and ears of corn **are likewise seven years.**[97] See, it is all one and the same dream! **Immediately ahead are seven years of great abundance in all the land.**[98] After that **will come seven years of famine** and very great hunger, and the seven good years will be forgotten, and famine will ravage all the inhabitants of the land. The king's dream is therefore one and the same. **As for** the king **having the same dream twice, it means that** the message is absolutely correct, **and God will soon carry it out.**[99] Now, therefore, I beg you to consider this and to protect yourself and the inhabitants of the land from the famine. Search throughout your kingdom for a

---

[94] Gen. 41:15.
[95] Gen. 41:15.
[96] Gen. 41:16.
[97] Gen. 41:27.
[98] Gen. 41:29.
[99] Gen. 41:32.

man of discernment and great **wisdom,**[100] who knows all about how to govern, and appoint him to travel throughout the land of Egypt. That man whom you place over Egypt will appoint officers under his authority, and they will collect all the food of the good years to come, and they will store the grain and put it in granaries. They will keep that food for the seven years of famine so that you and all your people and all the land will not perish from the famine. You should also order all the inhabitants of the land to gather the produce of their fields and all kinds of food during the seven good years and put it into storehouses, and they will find it there during the seven years of famine, and thus they will be able to survive. This is the correct interpretation of your dream, and this is the advice you must follow in order to save your life and the lives of your servants." The king replied to Joseph: "But who can say or who knows whether your words are true?" Joseph told the king: "This is a sign that all my words are true and what I have said is for your good: today your wife will sit upon the birthstool and bear a son unto you in whom you will rejoice. When the child comes forth from his mother's womb, your firstborn son, who was born two years ago, will die, but you will find comfort in the son who will be born today."

When Joseph had finishing saying all those things to the king, he bowed to the king and went out. After Joseph left, the signs he had declared to the king took place that very day. The queen bore a son that day, and the king was told about his son and was very happy. When the messenger left the king's presence, the king's servants found that the king's firstborn son had fallen to the ground and died. A great cry of shock and horror rang out through the king's house, and the king heard it and asked: "What is this noise and commotion that I hear in the house?" They told the king that his firstborn son had died, and then he realized that everything Joseph had told him was true. And he was comforted for the death of his son by the child that was born that day, just as Joseph had told him.

After these things occurred, the king sent for all his courtiers and servants and retainers, and they all assembled before the king. The king told them: "You have seen and heard how all the words of that Hebrew man and all the signs he declared have occurred, and not a single detail was omitted. Now I am convinced that his interpretation of my dreams was correct, and that the things he told us are indeed going to happen. Now please pay attention, and I will tell you what you must do in order to save the land from the famine. Go and see if you can find a man who has wisdom and knowledge in his heart, and I will entrust the land to him. For you have heard the advice of that Hebrew man about how we can save the land from the famine. I am convinced that the land can

[100] Gen. 41:33.

only be saved from the famine through the advice of that Hebrew man who counseled me." They all answered the king in unison: "The advice that Hebrew man gave you about this was good. Now, our lord king, all your land is in your hands; do whatever seems best to you. Let the king choose whomever he wishes, and understands in his wisdom to be wise enough to govern the land under the king's authority." The king told all his courtiers: "I have spoken. God caused that Hebrew man to know all the things he told us. There is no one else as truthful and wise as he in all the land. If you agree, I will entrust the land to him, for he will save the land in all his wisdom." All the courtiers replied to the king: "Is it not written in the laws of Egypt that no one may rule or be the king's viceroy in Egypt unless he knows all the languages of mankind? But, my lord king, this Hebrew man speaks only the Hebrew language. How then can he rule over us if he doesn't even know our language? Send for him, and examine him when he arrives, and act accordingly." The king replied: "This will be done tomorrow, and what you have said is good." Then all the courtiers left the king's presence that day.

That same night God sent one of the angels who serve before Him, and he went to the land of Egypt unto Joseph. The angel came to Joseph, and Joseph was sleeping soundly that night in the house of his master, in the dungeon, for his master had returned him to the dungeon on account of his wife. The angel shook him and woke him up. Joseph got up and stood on his feet and saw that the angel of God was standing beside him. The angel of God spoke to Joseph and taught him all the languages of mankind that same night, and he called his name Jehoseph.[101] Then the angel of God left him, and Joseph went back and slept in his bed, and Joseph was very astonished by what he had seen.

In the morning the king sent for his courtiers and his servants, and they all came and sat down before the king. The king ordered them to bring Joseph, and the king's servants went and brought Joseph before Pharaoh. On the king's command Joseph ascended the steps of the throne, and Joseph spoke to the king in all the languages. Joseph went on talking to the king until he reached the seventieth step, where he stopped before the king. The king rejoiced greatly over Joseph, and all the king's courtiers joined him in his rejoicing, for they had heard everything Joseph had said. Then it pleased the king and the courtiers to appoint Joseph viceroy over all the land of Egypt. The king told Joseph: "You advised me to search throughout the land of Egypt for a man who is wise so that in his wisdom he might save the land from the famine. **Since God has made all this known to you,** and all the words you spoke, **there is**

---

[101] Similarly, Moses changed Hoshea's name to Joshua (Yehoshua); Num. 13:16.

none so discerning and wise as you[102] in all the land. Henceforth your name shall no longer be called Joseph, but Zaphenath-paneah will be your name. You will be my viceroy, and every word that comes forth from your mouth will be as if I myself had spoken it, and at your word my people shall go out and come in. Furthermore, under your authority my servants and courtiers will receive the salaries you give them month by month, and all the men of the land will bow down to you; **only with respect to my throne shall I be superior to you.**"[103] **And removing his signet ring from his hand,** the king **put it on Joseph's hand, and** the king **had** Joseph **dressed in** a royal robe, and he put a golden crown on his head and a gold chain about his neck.[104]

The king ordered his servants to put Joseph in the king's second-best chariot, the one that rode next to the king's own chariot. He had him mount one of the king's big, strong horses and ride through the streets of all the land of Egypt. The king ordered his musicians to accompany Joseph with tambourines and harps and all sorts of musical instruments, and a thousand drummers and a thousand dancers and a thousand lyre-players followed him. Five thousand men carrying swords glittering in their hands joined the parade and made merry before Joseph. Twenty thousand of the grandees of the kingdom clad in leather garments studded with gold marched on Joseph's right hand, and another twenty thousand on his left. All the ladies and the maidens went up on the roofs playing and rejoicing over Joseph, and they admired Joseph's physique and how handsome he was. All the king's men preceded and followed him, perfuming the whole route with frankincense and cinnamon and all sorts of pleasant fragrances, and spreading myrrh and aloes before Joseph all along the route. And twenty men proclaimed in a loud voice before him throughout the land: "This is the man whom the king has chosen to be his viceroy![105] He will have power over all government policies. Anyone who disobeys him, or fails to bow to the ground before him, will quickly be put to death as a traitor to the king and his viceroy." After hearing this proclamation, all the Egyptians bowed down to the ground before Joseph and said: "Long live the king, and long live his viceroy!" All the inhabitants of Egypt bowed down when he passed by, and the criers repeated the proclamation, and the people bowed down and rejoiced before Joseph with dancing to the sound of the drum and the lyre. Sitting on

---

[102] Gen. 41:40.
[103] Gen. 41:40.
[104] Gen. 41:42.
[105] Cf. Esther 6:7–9: "And Haman said unto the king: 'For the man whom the king delighteth to honor, let royal apparel be brought which the king useth to wear, and the horse that the king rideth upon, and on whose head a crown royal is set; . . . and proclaim before him: Thus shall it be done to the man whom the king delighteth to honor.'"

his horse, Joseph lifted his eyes to heaven and cried out: "He raises the poor man from the dust, and lifts the needy from his dunghill![106] Oh Lord of hosts, happy is the man who trusts in You!"[107] Joseph traversed all the land of Egypt with Pharaoh's servants and all his court, and they showed him all the land of Egypt and all the king's treasures. Then Joseph went back and appeared before Pharaoh that day. The king gave Joseph estates in the land of Egypt, estates with fields and vineyards. Additionally, the king gave Joseph three thousand talents of silver and a thousand talents of gold and onyx stones and bdellium, and many other gifts. ·

The next day the king ordered all the Egyptians to bring Joseph gifts and presents, warning that anyone who disobeyed the king's order would be put to death. They erected a big platform on a city street and decorated it with hangings, and everyone brought something to that platform to give Joseph. All the Egyptians piled things on that platform—gold jewelry, ornaments, coins, earrings, and all kinds of vessels made of gold and silver and onyx stones and bdellium. Everyone brought whatever he could give to that platform. Joseph accepted all those things and put them in his treasury. And all the king's courtiers and officials honored Joseph and also gave him many gifts, for they saw that the king had chosen Joseph for his viceroy.

Then the king sent for Potiphar, son of Ahiram, priest of On, and he took Asenath, his youngest daughter, and gave her to Joseph as his wife. The maiden was very pretty, and was a virgin whom no man had known, and Joseph accepted her as his wife. The king **said to Joseph: "I am Pharaoh; yet without you no one shall lift up hand or foot** to go out or come in to my people **in all the land of Egypt."**[108] Joseph was thirty years old when he entered the service of Pharaoh. He left** the king's **presence,**[109] and he became the king's viceroy in Egypt.

The king gave Joseph a hundred slaves to serve him in his house, and Joseph himself bought many other slaves, and they were in his house. Then Joseph built himself a very big house, like the houses of kings, and it was just across the courtyard from the royal palace. In his house Joseph built a spacious reception room. It was lovely to look at, and a pleasant place to live. It took Joseph three years to finish building his house. Joseph also had a beautiful throne made for himself. It was made of much gold and silver and inlaid with onyx stones and bdellium. He also had made on it a map of all the land of Egypt, and a map of the river Nile, showing how it irrigates all the land of

---

[106] Ps. 113:7.
[107] Prov. 16:20: "And whoso trusteth in the Lord, happy is he."
[108] Gen. 41:44.
[109] Gen. 41:46.

Egypt. Joseph spent all his time at home, sitting on the throne he had had made, and God added wisdom to the wisdom Joseph already had. All the inhabitants of Egypt and Pharaoh's servants and his court loved Joseph very much. It was God who made all of this happen to Joseph. God was with Joseph, and his power grew ever greater, and his fame spread throughout the land. Joseph had a private army to use in warfare, numbering 40,600 men, and they fought with all their might to defend the king and Joseph against their enemies. When you add to these forces the king's courtiers and slaves and the other inhabitants of Egypt, they were beyond number! Joseph armed his warriors with shields and spears and helmets and armor and stones to throw.

At that time the sons of Tarshish went to war against all the Ishmaelites, and the sons of Tarshish conquered the Ishmaelites and subjected them for a long time. In those days the Ishmaelites were few in number and were no match for the sons of Tarshish, which made them very unhappy. All the elders of Ishmael sent a letter to the king of Egypt saying: "Please send your slaves and your courtiers and your army to help us make war against the sons of Tarshish, for they have been subjecting us for a long time." Pharaoh sent Joseph and his mighty warriors and his private army, as well as the palace guard. They went to the land of Havilah[110] to help the Ishmaelites make war against the sons of Tarshish. The Ishmaelites fought the sons of Tarshish, and Joseph defeated the Tarshishites and conquered all their land, and some of the Ishmaelites have lived there ever since. After the destruction of the land of Tarshish, all the Tarshishites fled and went to the borders of their brethren, the sons of Greece. But Joseph and his mighty warriors and his private army returned to Egypt without a single casualty.

This happened at the turning of the year, during the second year that Joseph had governed Egypt. God sent great plenty throughout the land for seven years, just as Joseph had said. For God blessed all the fruits of the land in those days for seven years, and they ate and were very satisfied. At that time Joseph had stewards under him, and they took all the food of the good years and set it aside year by year, and stored it up in the granaries that Joseph had built. Whenever they gathered the food, Joseph ordered them to bring the grain in sheaves together with some of the dirt from its own field so that it might not spoil. Joseph continued in this manner year after year. **So Joseph collected produce in very large quantities, like the sands of the sea, until he ceased to measure it, for it could not be measured.**[111] The inhabitants of Egypt also gathered great quantities of all kinds of food on their own during the seven good years, but

---

[110] A vaguely defined region traditionally considered to have lain between Ophir and Hazermaveth, north of Sheba, in Arabia.
[111] Gen. 41:49.

they were not as careful as Joseph in their manner of doing so. All the food that Joseph and all the Egyptians stored up during the seven years of plenty was to compensate for the lack of produce during the seven years of famine, so that the land might survive. All the inhabitants of Egypt individually set aside their own reserves and stored up wheat to nourish them during the famine. Joseph placed all the food he had gathered in all the cities of Egypt, and he sealed all the granaries and appointed guards to watch over them.

Asenath, daughter of Potiphar and Joseph's wife, bore him two sons, Manasseh and Ephraim. Joseph was thirty four years old when they were born. The lads grew up, and they walked in his way and followed his ethics, and never deviated from the way their father had taught them either to the right or the left. God was with the lads, and they grew up and became very intelligent and mastered all branches of scholarship and at the same time acquired practical experience in government. All the king's courtiers and the grandees who lived in Egypt praised those lads, and they were brought up close to the king's own sons.

The seven years of abundance that the whole **land of Egypt enjoyed came to an end,**[112] and after that **the seven years of famine set in, just as Joseph had foretold. There was famine in all**[113] the land, and all the Egyptians saw that the famine was going to spread throughout Egypt. The Egyptians opened all the granaries of wheat that they had, for the famine was already very serious; but they found that all the food they had stored up themselves, without taking the precautions Joseph had taken, was infested with insects and was not fit to eat. The famine raged throughout the land, and all the inhabitants of Egypt complained to Pharaoh that the famine weighed heavily upon them. They told Pharaoh: "Give your servants food! Why should we die of hunger before your eyes, both we and our children?" Pharaoh replied: "Why are you crying to me? Didn't Joseph tell you to store up wheat during all those seven years of plenty for the years of famine? Why didn't you do as he said?" The Egyptians answered the king: "By your life, my lord, your servants did everything that Joseph told us to do. Your servants also gathered up all the food from our fields during the years of plenty and stored it up in granaries where it has remained until now. When the famine began to ravage your servants, we opened the granaries and all our food was spoiled and full of insects and not fit to eat."

When the king heard what had befallen the inhabitants of Egypt, he was very fearful of the famine, and very shocked. The king answered the Egyptians: "Now that all this has happened to you, **go to Joseph; whatever he tells you, you shall do;**[114] and don't dare argue with what he says." Then all the Egyptians went to

[112] Gen. 41:53.
[113] Gen. 41:54.
[114] Gen. 41:55.

Joseph and told him: "Give us food! Why should we die in front of you? For we gathered the produce during the seven years of plenty, as you have seen, and we put it in granaries, and this is what has happened to us." When Joseph heard all the words of the Egyptians and what had befallen them, **Joseph laid open all** the granaries of food that he had, **and rationed out grain to the Egyptians.**[115] The famine spread over the face of all the earth, and there was famine in all lands, but in the land of Egypt there was food to distribute. All the inhabitants of Egypt came to Joseph to procure rations, for the famine was severe, and all their stores of food were spoiled. And Joseph fed all Egypt day by day.

The inhabitants of the land of Canaan, and the Philistines, and those who dwelled on the other side of the Jordan, and the sons of the east, and all the cities of the land, both near and far, heard that there were rations in Egypt. So they all **came to Egypt to procure rations** of wheat, **for the famine had become severe**[116] to them. And Joseph opened the stores of food, and he appointed stewards over them to dispense rations to the people who came every day. Joseph knew that his brothers too would come to Egypt to buy food, **for the famine had become severe throughout the world.**[117] Joseph had his men and his slaves issue the following proclamation throughout Egypt: "By the authority of the king and his viceroy and his grandees, anyone who wants to buy wheat in Egypt must not send his servants to Egypt, but only his sons. Also any Egyptian or Canaanite who comes from any land to buy wheat in Egypt and then goes and sells it elsewhere will be put to death, for everyone may buy only for his own household. Furthermore, anyone who comes with two or three pack animals will also be put to death, for each man may bring only one beast."

Joseph stationed guards at the gates of the city, and he instructed them as follows: "When anyone comes to buy food, don't sell it to him unless he writes down his name, and his father's name, and his grandfather's name. Every evening you will send me the list of names you have written down that day, so that I may know their names." Likewise, Joseph appointed inspectors throughout the land of Egypt and ordered them to do the same thing. Joseph established those decrees and regulations so that he might know when his brothers came to Egypt to buy food. Every day Joseph's servants proclaimed those decrees and regulations that Joseph had commanded throughout Egypt. All the inhabitants of the east and the west and the whole world heard all those decrees and regulations that Joseph had established in Egypt. All the inhabitants of the four corners of the earth came to buy rations in Egypt day by day, and then they returned home. All the guards did as Joseph had commanded; they

---

[115] Gen. 41:56.
[116] Gen. 41:57.
[117] Gen. 41:57.

wrote down the names of all who came to Egypt to buy food, as well as their fathers' names, and the lists were delivered to Joseph every evening.

After that, Jacob heard that food was available in Egypt, and he instructed his sons to go to Egypt to buy food, for the famine had grown severe among them too. Jacob summoned his sons and said: **"Now I hear that there are rations to be had in Egypt,**[118] and the whole world is going there to buy. Why do you consider yourselves better off than the rest of the world? Go down to Egypt too, and buy us food there along with the others, so **that we may live and not die."**[119] The sons of Jacob heeded their father's words, and they arose to go down to Egypt to buy food among the others who went there. Jacob ordered his sons: "When you get to the city, don't enter through a single gate in front of the inhabitants of the land." The sons of Jacob set out and went to Egypt, and the sons of Jacob did just as their father had instructed them to do. But Jacob did not send Benjamin, for he said that some accident might befall him on the road, as had happened to his brother, so only ten of Jacob's sons went. While the ten sons of Jacob were on the road, they felt sorry for everything they had done to Joseph. They said to one another: "We know that our brother went down to Egypt. Now let us look for him wherever we go. If we find him, let us buy him back from his master. If they refuse to sell him, we will take him by force or else die trying." The sons of Jacob all agreed to this, and took courage to liberate Joseph from his masters, and the sons of Jacob went on to Egypt.

When they approached the city, they separated from each other, and entered there through ten different gates. The scribes wrote down their names that day, and that evening they were delivered to Joseph. When Joseph read the names recorded by the city inspectors, he found that his brothers had entered the city through ten different gates. Then Joseph ordered the following proclamation to be read throughout the land of Egypt: "To the guards of the gates: Close all the gates where rations are sold, leaving open only a single gate through which people may enter to buy rations." Joseph's officers followed his orders, closing all the gates but one. Joseph gave the list of his brothers' names to the guard who was assigned to the gate that was left open, and he told him: "Ask the name of everyone who comes to buy rations, and if you find any of the men whose names appear on this list, seize them and send them to me." And thus it was done. The sons of Jacob spread out through the city to look for Joseph before attempting to buy food. Some of them went to the brothels by the city walls, and they searched for Joseph there for three days. They thought that Joseph might be in one of those brothels, since he was **well built and handsome.** The sons of Jacob searched along the walls for three days, but they didn't find him.

---

[118] Gen. 42:2.
[119] Gen. 42:2.

The man who was on guard at the open gate kept looking for the names that Joseph had given him, but he didn't find them. He sent a message to Joseph, saying: "For the past three days those men whose names you gave me haven't come." Joseph dispatched slaves to look for those men throughout Egypt and to bring them before Joseph. Joseph's slaves went out to look for them throughout Egypt, but they didn't find them. They went to Goshen but failed to find them there, nor did they find them in the city of Raamses. They returned to Joseph and told him: "We have searched throughout the land as far as the city of Raamses, but we haven't found them." Joseph assembled sixteen other slaves to search for his brothers, and they spread out through the four corners of the city. Four of the slaves went to a house of prostitution, and there they found the ten men searching for their brother. The four slaves took them and brought them before Joseph, and Jacob's sons came to Joseph's house, and **they bowed low to him, with their faces to the ground.**[120]

Joseph was sitting on the throne in his palace dressed in robes of fine purple linen and wearing a big golden diadem on his head, and all the grandees were sitting around him. Jacob's sons were dazzled by the sight of Joseph's handsomeness and the beauty of his face, and once again **they bowed low to him, with their faces to the ground. When Joseph saw his brothers, he recognized them,**[121] but they did not recognize him, for Joseph appeared so majestic to them that they couldn't recognize him. Joseph asked them: **"Where are you from?"** They all replied: "Your servants have come **from the land of Canaan, to procure food,**[122] for the famine is severe throughout the land. For your servants heard that there was food in Egypt and have come with the others to buy rations that we might live." Joseph replied: "If you came to buy food, as you said, why did you enter the city through ten different gates? Is it not rather that you have come to spy out **the land in its nakedness?"**[123] They all replied together: **"No, my lord!"**[124] We are strangers; your servants are not spies. For we came here **to procure food.**[125] All your servants are brothers, sons of one man in the land of Canaan. Our father ordered us not to enter the city through a single gate in front of the inhabitants of the land when we came here." But Joseph answered them: "It is as I said before. You have come to spy out the land in its nakedness. That's why you all entered the city through ten different gates—to spy out the nakedness of the land! Is it not true that everyone who

[120] Gen. 42:6.
[121] Gen. 42:7.
[122] Gen. 42:7.
[123] Gen. 42:9.
[124] Gen. 42:10.
[125] Gen. 42:10.

comes to buy food goes straight home? You, on the other hand, have already been here three days. What were you doing for three days in the brothels? Isn't this the behavior of spies?" They told Joseph: "Far be it from my lord to say such things! For we were **twelve brothers, sons of** Jacob our father, **in the land of Canaan,**[126] and he is the son of Isaac, son of Abraham the Hebrew. And behold, **the youngest is now with our father** in the land of Canaan, **and one is no more,**[127] for he was lost to us. And we said: 'Perhaps we shall find him in this land, and we will search throughout Egypt,' and thus we came to the houses of prostitution, searching for him there." Joseph answered them: "Had you indeed searched for him throughout the land, so that there was no place left in Egypt to look for him? If in fact he was in Egypt, what business would your brother have in houses of prostitution? Didn't you claim to be descendants of Isaac, son of Abraham? What business have the sons of Jacob in houses of prostitution?" They replied: "We had heard that the Ishmaelites who took him from us had sold him in Egypt. Your servant our brother is very **well built and handsome,** and that is why we supposed that he might be in a house of prostitution, and why we went there to ransom him." Joseph again replied: "Are these not all lies and deceptions that you have fabricated among yourselves? You are sons of Abraham? **By Pharaoh, you are nothing but spies,**[128] and your only reason for going to the houses of prostitution was that no one would know you there." They again replied: "No, my lord! We your servants all went there together to search for our brother and ransom him, as we have told your lordship." Joseph answered: "What if you had found him, and his master had demanded an excessive price for him? Would you have paid it?" They answered: "Yes, we would." Joseph said to them: "Suppose his master were unwilling to sell him, no matter what the price? What would you do then?" They replied: "If he would not surrender him to us, we would kill him, and take our brother, and go." Joseph told them: "**It is just as I have told you. You are spies!**[129] You came here to kill one of the inhabitants of the land. We have heard how two of your brothers killed all the inhabitants of Shechem in the land of Canaan on account of your sister. Now you have come to Egypt to do the same thing on account of your brother. But this is how I shall know whether you are honest men: if you send one of your brothers to get your youngest brother from your father, and present him to me. If you do this, I will know that you are honest men." Then Joseph summoned seventy of his strong men and told them: "Take

[126] Gen. 42:13.
[127] Gen. 42:13.
[128] Gen. 42:16.
[129] Gen. 42:14.

these men and put them in the guardhouse." The strong men took those ten men, and seized them, and put them in the guardhouse, and they remained in **the guardhouse for three days.**[130] **On the third day Joseph** brought them out of the guardhouse, and **said to them: Do this** if you are honest men, **and you shall live.**[131] **Let one of your brothers be held in your place of detention, while the rest of you go and take rations to your households**[132] in the land of Canaan. Then you will take your youngest brother and bring him to me. Thus I shall know whether you are honest men: if you do this thing."

Joseph then left them, and went into his chamber and wept profusely out of pity for his brothers. Then he washed his face and returned to them, **and he took Simeon from among them,**[133] and ordered that he be bound. But Simeon refused to be treated like that, for he was a very strong man, and Joseph was unable to have him tied up. Joseph sent for his strong men, and seventy brave men came, holding their naked swords in their hands; and all the sons of Jacob were terrified. Joseph told his strong men: "Seize that man, and hold him in prison until his brothers return." Joseph's strong men hastened to take hold of Simeon and bind him over to prison. Simeon then howled with a very loud and bitter cry, and it was heard from a great distance. All Joseph's strong men were frightened by that cry, and they fell on their faces, and were terrified and ran away. All the men who were with Joseph fled too, for they feared for their lives; only Joseph and his son Manasseh stayed there. Joseph's son Manasseh saw Simeon's strength, and he flew into a rage. Manasseh, son of Joseph, went up to Simeon and hit him hard on the neck with his fist, and Simeon cowered. Then Manasseh seized Simeon and tied him up and drove him to the prison; and all the sons of Jacob were astonished by the lad's deed. Simeon told his brothers: "Don't say that I took such a beating from an Egyptian, for only some-one from my father's house could have done that."

Then Joseph gave orders, and summoned the man in charge of the stores **to fill their bags with grain,** as much as they could carry, **and return each man's money to his sack, and give them provisions for the journey; and this was done for them.**[134] Joseph ordered them: "Do not go back on your word and fail to bring me your brother, as I have told you. If you bring me your brother, I shall know that you are honest men, and you will have the freedom of the land. I will restore your brother to you, and you will return in peace to your fa-ther." They replied: "As our master has commanded us, so shall we do"; and

---

[130] Gen. 42:17.
[131] Gen. 42:18.
[132] Gen. 42:19.
[133] Gen. 42:24
[134] Gen. 42:25.

they bowed low to him, with their faces to the ground. Each of them then loaded his rations on his donkey, and they left to go to the land of Canaan, to their father. They arrived at an inn, and as Levi **was opening his sack to give feed to his donkey, he saw that all his money** had been returned to his purse and was **right there at the mouth of his bag.**[135] The man was very frightened, **and he said to his brothers, "My money has been returned! It is here in my bag!"**[136] The men were very frightened, and they said: **"What is this that God has done to us?"**[137] They went on: "Where is the loving-kindness that God showed to our fathers Abraham, Isaac, and Jacob? For today God has handed us over to the king of Egypt that he might persecute us." Judah asked them: "Are we not guilty and sinners in the sight of our Lord God for having sold our brother, our own flesh? Why then do you ask where is the loving-kindness that God showed our fathers?" Then Reuben told them: **"Did I not tell you, 'Do no wrong to the boy'? But you paid** me **no heed.**[138] Now you are being called to account for his blood. How then can you ask: 'Where is the loving-kindness that God showed our fathers?' when you have sinned against Him." They slept in that place, and they got up early in the morning and loaded their provisions on their animals, and drove them, and returned to the land of Canaan, to their father's house. Jacob and his household went out to welcome his sons, and they saw that their brother Simeon was not with them. Jacob asked his sons: "Where is your brother Simeon? I don't see him with you." His sons then told him everything that had happened to them in Egypt.

They went to their houses, and each one opened his sack and they saw that **there, in each one's sack, was his moneybag,**[139] and they were very dismayed on account of that, both they and their father. Jacob told them: "What is this that you have done to me? I sent you your brother Joseph to see how you were faring, and you told me that a wild beast had devoured him. Simeon went with you to procure food, and now you tell me that the king of Egypt has put him into prison. Now you speak of taking Benjamin to kill him too, **and you will send my white head down to Sheol in grief**[140] for Benjamin and his brother Joseph. Now **my son must not go down with you, for his brother is dead and he alone is left,** lest **he meet with disaster on the journey you are taking,**[141] as happened to his brothers." **Then Reuben said to his father: "You may kill**

---

[135] Gen. 42:27.
[136] Gen. 42:28.
[137] Gen. 42:28.
[138] Gen. 42:22.
[139] Gen. 42:35.
[140] Gen. 42:38.
[141] Gen. 42:38.

my two sons[142] if I don't bring your son back and restore him to you." Jacob told his sons: "Stay here, and do not go back down to Egypt, for my son will not go down with you to Egypt and will not die like his brother." Judah told them: "Be quiet until the food we have brought is finished, and then we shall see. He himself will tell us: 'Go on down there with your brother,' for he and his own household will be hungry."

But the famine was severe in all the land,[143] in those days, and all the people of the land were journeying back and forth to Egypt to buy provisions, for the famine was very damaging to them. But the sons of Jacob remained in the land of Canaan for many days—indeed two months—until they had eaten up their rations. **And when they had eaten up the rations,**[144] everyone in the house of Jacob was very hungry. The children of Jacob's sons gathered together and went to Jacob and stood around him, and they told him: "Give us bread! Why should we all die of hunger on account of you?" Jacob listened to the words of his grandchildren, and he wept profusely, and he felt sorry for them. Then Jacob summoned his sons, and they all came and sat down before him. Jacob asked them: "Haven't you seen how your children have cried 'Give us bread' to me today, but there is none? Now **go again and procure some food for us.**"[145] Judah answered his father: "**If you will let our brother go with us, we will go down and procure food for you, but if you will not let him go, we will not go down,** for the king of Egypt swore to us: 'You shall not see my face **unless your brother is with you.'**[146] The king of Egypt is very mighty and powerful, and if we go to him without our brother, we shall all die. Don't you know, or haven't you heard, that that king is mighty and very wise, and there is no other like him in all the earth? Look, we have seen all the kings of the earth, but we have never seen another like the king of Egypt. Is it not true that no one is as great as Abimelech, king of the Philistines, among all the kings on earth? Yet the king of Egypt is greater and more powerful than he, so much so that Abimelech is not even equal to one of his princes. Father, you have not seen his palace and his throne and all the servants who wait upon him. You have not seen that king seated on his throne in all his beauty and majesty, clad in royal garments and wearing a big golden crown on his head. You have not seen the honor and glory that God has bestowed upon him; for there is none like unto him in all the earth. Father, you have not seen the wisdom and intelligence and knowledge that God implanted in his heart. If only you could have heard the sweetness of

---

[142] Gen. 42:37.
[143] Gen. 43:1.
[144] Gen. 43:2.
[145] Gen. 43:2.
[146] Gen. 43:4–5.

his voice when he spoke to us! We don't know, father, who taught him our names and told him about everything that has happened to us. He even asked about you, saying: 'Is your father still alive and well?' You haven't seen how all the royal decrees of Egypt issued from his mouth, so that no one even consulted his master Pharaoh. You have not beheld his great stature, nor seen how he dominates all the land of Egypt. As we were leaving him, we threatened to do to Egypt everything we had done to the cities of the Amorites, and we were furious about his words, for he spoke to us as if we were spies. Yet when we appear before him again, we will be so overwhelmed by his majesty that none of us will be able to utter a word, much less a speech. Now, our father, please **send the boy** with us, and we will go down and buy you food, **that we may live and not die**[147] of hunger." Jacob said: **"Why did you serve me so ill as to tell** the king **that you had another brother?"**[148] Why did you do this to me?" Then Judah said to his father Jacob: "Hand the boy over to me, and we will arise and go down to Egypt and buy food rations and come back. If we return and the boy is not with us, **I shall stand guilty before you forever.**[149] You have seen all the little children weeping before you from hunger, and there was nothing you could do. Now we beg you to take pity on them, and send our brother with us, and we shall go. Do you doubt God's loving-kindness toward our fathers and you? If not, how can you say that the king of Egypt would take your son? By the living God, I shall not leave him until I come back and return him to you! But please pray to our Lord God for us that He give us grace and loving-kindness before the king of Egypt and his men. **For we could have been there and back** with your son **twice if we had not dawdled."**[150] Then Jacob told his sons: "By the living God, I trust that He will save you and give you grace in the eyes of the king of Egypt and all his men. Now arise and go to the man, and take him in your hands a gift of what is found in this land, and present it to him. **And may El Shaddai dispose the man to mercy toward you, that he may release to you**[151] Benjamin and Simeon, your brothers."

Then all the men arose and took Benjamin, their brother, and a large gift of the choice products of the land of Canaan, **and they took with them double the money.**[152] Jacob earnestly commended Benjamin to his sons, ordering them: "Watch over him on the road you are traveling, and don't let him get separated from you on the road or in Egypt." Jacob then stood up, and spread his palms and

---

[147] Gen. 43:8.
[148] Gen. 43:6.
[149] Gen. 43:9.
[150] Gen. 43:10.
[151] Gen. 43:14.
[152] Gen. 43:15.

prayed to God on behalf of his sons, saying: "Oh Lord our God, God of the heavens and the earth, remember the covenant You made with Abraham our father and Isaac, my father, and show loving-kindness to my sons, and do not hand them over to the king of Egypt. Please do this, my God, on account of Your mercy, and redeem all my sons, and save them from the hands of the Egyptians, and release their two brothers to them." And all the wives of Jacob's sons and all their children raised their eyes to heaven and wept to God and cried to Him to deliver their fathers from the hand of the king of Egypt.

And Jacob wrote the following letter to the king of Egypt, and gave it to Judah and to his sons to give to the king of Egypt: "From your servant Jacob, son of Isaac, son of Abraham the Hebrew, Prince of God, to the powerful and wise king Zaphenath-paneah, king of Egypt. Greetings! Be it known unto our master the king of Egypt that we are suffering gravely from famine in the land of Canaan; and I am sending my sons to buy food from you so that we may live. For I am surrounded by my seventy family members, and I am very old, and my eyes have grown dim, for my eyelids are heavy with age and from weeping constantly for my son Joseph, whom I lost. I commanded my sons not to enter the gates together when they came to Egypt before the inhabitants of the land. And I commanded them to travel through Egypt searching for my son Joseph in the hope that they might find him there, and they did so. And you treated them as if they were spying out the land. Have we not heard of you that you are very wise and truthful? Can you not tell from their faces that they are not spies? We have also heard how you interpreted Pharaoh's dream and informed him about the famine that was coming, and how everything you told him turned out to be correct. How, then, can you not discern in your wisdom whether my sons be spies or not? Now, my lord king, I am sending you my son Benjamin, as you told my sons. I beg you to look kindly upon him until he comes back to me in peace with his brothers. Don't you know, or haven't you heard, what God did to Pharaoh when he took my mother Sarah,[153] and what He did to Abimelech, king of the Philistines, on her behalf?[154] And what about what our father Abraham did to the nine kings of Elam, when he killed them all, in spite of the fact that only a few men were with him? And what about what my two sons Simeon and Levi did to the eight cities of the Amorites which they destroyed on account of their sister Dinah? Benjamin has consoled them for the loss of his brother Joseph. How terribly then will they punish anyone who dares lift a hand against him! Oh king of Egypt, don't you know that

[153] See Gen. 12:11–19.
[154] See Gen. 20:1–8.

the power of our God is with us, and that He always hears our prayers, and that He will never forsake us? By the living God, when my sons told me about what you had done, I did not call upon God to take revenge; otherwise you would have died along with all your men before my son Benjamin appeared before you. I said to myself that my son Simeon is in your house, and perhaps you have dealt kindly with him, and therefore I did not do unto you as I have threatened. Now my son Benjamin is coming to you with my sons. Take good care of him, and keep an eye on him, so that our God will likewise take good care of you and all your kingdom. Now I have told you everything that is in my heart. My sons are coming to you with their brother. Watch over them throughout the face of the earth, and send them back to me with their brothers in peace." Jacob gave that letter to his sons, handing it over to Judah to give to the king of Egypt.

And the sons of Jacob arose and took Benjamin and all the gifts, and they left and went to Egypt, **where they presented themselves to Joseph. When Joseph saw Benjamin** his brother **with them,**[155] he greeted them, and those men came into Joseph's house. Joseph commanded his house steward to cook good food for them to eat, and so it was done. When it was noon, Joseph summoned the men to come before him with Benjamin. **They went up to Joseph's house steward,**[156] and told him about the money that had been returned to their bags. **He replied: "All is well with you; do not be afraid." And he brought out** their brother **Simeon to them.**[157] Simeon told his brothers: "[The lord of Egypt] has treated me very well, and has not imprisoned me, as you have seen with your own eyes. For as soon as you left the city, he set me free and lodged me comfortably in his own home." Judah then took Benjamin, and they presented themselves to Joseph, bowing low before him with their hands on the ground. The men gave Joseph the gifts they had brought him, and they [all] sat down before him. Joseph asked them: "How are you? And how are your children? **How is your aged father?**"[158] They replied: "All are well."

Then Judah took the letter Jacob had sent and gave it to Joseph. Joseph read the letter, and he recognized his father's handwriting, and he **was on the verge of tears**—for he could not control himself—and he went **into his room and wept**[159] in a loud voice; and then he returned. **Looking about, he saw his brother Benjamin, and asked: "Is this your brother of whom you spoke to**

---

[155] Gen. 43:15–16.
[156] Gen. 43:19.
[157] Gen. 43:23.
[158] Gen. 43:27.
[159] Gen. 43:30.

me?"[160] Benjamin approached Joseph, and Joseph put his hand on his head and said to him: **"May God be gracious to you!"**[161] When Joseph saw his brother, his mother's son, he was again **on the verge of tears; he went into a room and wept there.**[162] **Then he washed his face, reappeared, and—now in control of himself—gave the order, "Serve the meal!"**[163]

In Joseph's hand was a goblet from which he drank. It was of silver inlaid with stones of onyx and very fine bdellium. Joseph struck the goblet while his brothers were watching, just as they were sitting down to eat with him. Joseph told the men: "I have learned from this goblet that Reuben is the eldest, followed by Simeon, Levi, Judah, Issachar, and Zebulun, all sons of the same mother. Sit down to eat in the order in which you were born." And he also seated the others in the order of their birth. Then he told them: "I know that this youngest brother of yours has no [full] brother, and, like him, I too have no brother. Let him then sit down to eat with me." Benjamin got up before Joseph and joined him on the throne, and the men saw what Joseph had done, and were amazed by it. And the men ate and drank with Joseph at that time, and he gave them gifts at that time. But Joseph did even more, giving Benjamin still another gift; and Manasseh and Ephraim saw what their father had done, and they too gave him their gifts, and Asenath also gave him a gift; hence Benjamin received five gifts.

Joseph ordered wine for them to drink, but they did not want to drink it. They said: "Since the day our brother Joseph was lost, we swore not to drink wine nor eat good food." But Joseph entreated them and showed them great kindness, and they drank with him, and even got drunk that day. After that, Joseph turned to his brother Benjamin to speak to him, and Benjamin was still sitting on the throne beside Joseph. Joseph asked him: "Do you have any children?" Benjamin replied: "Your servant has ten sons, and these are their names: Bela, Becher, Ashbel, Gera, Naaman, Ehi, Rosh, Muppim, Huppim, and Ard." He mentioned all their names to his brother Joseph, who had not seen them. Joseph commanded them to bring him his map of the stars by which he could foretell the future. Then Joseph told Benjamin: "I have heard that the Hebrews know all the science of the heavens. Can you tell me about that?" Benjamin replied: "Your servant knows all the science that his father has taught him." Joseph then told Benjamin: "Look into this cup very well, and see if it shows where in Egypt your brother Joseph is, for you told me that he went down to

[160] Gen. 43:29.
[161] Gen. 43:29.
[162] Gen. 43:30.
[163] Gen. 43:31.

Egypt." Benjamin took the cup and the chart of the stars in the heavens, and considered and looked in it to determine where his brother was. Benjamin divided the land of Egypt into four parts, and he found that his brother Joseph was sitting beside him on the throne, and he was greatly astonished. And Joseph saw that Benjamin was greatly astonished, and he asked Benjamin: "What did you see; and why are you astonished?" Benjamin replied: "In this I see that my brother Joseph is sitting beside me here on this throne." Then Joseph told him: "I am Joseph, your brother; but don't tell your other brothers.[164] I am going to send you away with them, and you will go, and I will have you brought back with them to the city, and I will take you from them. And if they are ready to give up their lives, and they fight for you, then I will know that they are sorry for what they did to me, and I will reveal myself to them. But if they abandon you and let me take you like this, I will bring you back to me, and I will send them away, and they will go, and I won't reveal myself to them."

At that time Joseph ordered his officer to fill their vessels with food, and to put each one's money in his bag, and to put his goblet in Benjamin's bag, and to give them food for the journey, and thus it was done to them. The next day the men woke up in the morning and loaded their provisions on their donkeys and set out with Benjamin and traveled toward the land of Canaan with their brother Simeon. **They had just left** Egypt, **and had not gone far, when Joseph** commanded **his steward,** saying: **"Up, go after the men**[165] before they get out of Egypt, and say to them: 'Why have you stolen my master's goblet?' " And Joseph's steward got up and followed them and caught up with them and told them what Joseph had said. When they heard that, they became very angry and said: "Anyone with whom your master's goblet is found shall die; **the rest of us, moreover, shall become slaves."**[166] And they hastened to unload their bags from their donkeys, and they searched them; **and the goblet turned up in Benjamin's bag.**[167] Then they all rent their garments and headed back toward the city, and they beat Benjamin while they were on the road and kept on hitting him until they entered the city and stood before Joseph. Judah was very angry and said: "By the living God, this man has only brought me back to destroy Egypt today!"

And the men went into Joseph's house and found Joseph sitting on his throne, and all his mighty men were standing around him, on his right and on

---

[164] Likewise in the Qur'an (12:69) Joseph reveals himself to Benjamin at this point in the story so that he will not be alarmed when he is accused of stealing Joseph's goblet.

[165] Gen. 44:4.

[166] Gen. 44:9.

[167] Gen. 44:12.

his left. **Joseph said to them: "What is this deed that you have done?**[168] For you have taken my silver goblet and gone off with it. But I knew by divination where your brothers were in all the land and where they had taken my silver goblet." **Judah replied: "What can we say to my lord? How can we plead, how can we prove our innocence? God has uncovered the crime of your servants**[169] today, and this is why He has done this to us today." Joseph stood up and seized Benjamin, and took him from his brothers by force, and went inside his house and closed the door in their faces. And Joseph ordered his house steward to tell them: "Thus says the king: "Go in peace to your father. I have taken the man in whose hand my goblet was found." When Judah saw what Joseph had done to them,

III. Va-Yiggash

he went up to him[170] and broke down that door and appeared before Joseph with his brothers. Judah told Joseph: "Be not angry, my lord, and please let your servant speak to you." Joseph answered him: "Speak." Then Judah spoke before Joseph while his brothers were standing there. Judah said to Joseph: "Don't you remember when we first came before your lordship to buy rations, and you thought we had come to spy out the land, and you wanted us to bring our brother Benjamin to you? You have been against us up to this very day. May the king now hearken to my words and please release our brother that he may go with us to his father. Otherwise you will lose your life and the lives of all the inhabitants of Egypt today. Don't you know what my two brothers Simeon and Levi did to the city of Shechem and to the seven cities of the Amorites on account of our sister Dinah, and what they will yet do on account of Benjamin their brother? And I, who in my might am stronger and greater than both of them today, will attack you if you don't agree to release our brother. Haven't you heard what our God, Who chose us, did to Pharaoh on account of our mother Sarah, whom he took from our father? How he struck him and his household with great plagues that are still being talked about all over Egypt, being discussed by every man and his neighbor down to this day? Our God will do the same thing to you on account of Benjamin, whom you have taken from his father today, and the evil things you are planning to do to us in your land today. Our God will remember His covenant with our father Abraham and will bring evil upon you because you have made the soul of our father suffer today.

---

[168] Gen. 44:15.
[169] Gen. 44:16.
[170] Gen. 44:18.

Now please hearken to the words I shall say to you today, and release our brother and let him go to him; otherwise, you and your land will die by the sword, because all of you together will be unable to overpower me."

Joseph answered Judah, saying: "Why have you filled your mouth with all those words, and why are you boasting about your strength? As Pharaoh lives, I shall command all my mighty men to make war against you. Will you not suffer a great defeat, you and these brothers of yours?" Judah then told Joseph: "Is it not rather you and your men who should fear the living God? For if I draw my sword, I shall not return it to its scabbard until this very day I have slain all of Egypt, beginning with you and ending with your master Pharaoh." Joseph replied: "Do you think you're the only one who is strong? I too am strong, indeed mightier than you! If you draw your sword, I will plunge it into your neck, and into the necks of all these brothers of yours." Judah then told him: "Don't you realize that if I open my mouth against you today, I will swallow you, and you will be destroyed and driven from the land, and today you will lose your kingdom?" Joseph replied: "If you dare open your mouth, I have the power to shut it with a big stone so that you won't even be able to pronounce a single word. Just see how many stones we have before us! Don't you think I can take one of them and shut your mouth with it, and break your jaws?" Judah replied: "As God is our witness, we have never wanted to make war against you until now. Just give us our brother, and we will leave you alone." Joseph answered: "As Pharaoh lives, even if all the kings of Canaan came together with you, you could not take him from me. Now go your way to your father, and your brother will stay here as a slave, because he has stolen from the king's house." Judah then said: "What gives you the right to speak in the king's name? Can't a king take from his house throughout the land silver and gold in great quantities either as a gift or as booty? You are referring to your goblet that you put in our brother's bag, but now you say that he stole it from you. It is inconceivable that our brother Benjamin, or any descendant of the house of Abraham, would do such a thing as stealing from you or any of your companions, whether that person be a king, a prince, or even a commoner. Now stop saying such things, for all the land will hear and will gossip about how the king of Egypt fought with some men over a small amount of silver, and accused them, and took their brother as a slave." Joseph answered: "Take this goblet and go away, and leave your brother as a slave, for slavery is the penalty for theft." Judah replied: "Aren't you ashamed to ask us to leave our brother behind and take your goblet? Even if you gave us a thousand goblets, we would not leave our brother for such a paltry price, but rather would die on his account!" Joseph countered: "Since you left your [other] brother and sold him for twenty pieces of silver, why won't you do likewise with this one?" Judah said: "As God is our witness, we have never sought to make war against you. Give us our brother, and we will leave you without further conflict." Joseph answered: "If you brought together all the kings on earth, they would not be able to take your brother from me." Judah asked: "What shall we say to our father when he sees that our brother has not come back with us? He will be grief-stricken." Joseph replied: "This is what you shall tell your father: 'the rope went after the bucket.' "[171] Judah then asked: "Are you not a king? Why then do you speak such words, which would condemn any king like you for wrongfully passing judgment?" Joseph answered: "No judgment could be so wrongful as the one you pronounced concerning your brother Joseph; for you all sold your brother to the Midianites for twenty pieces of silver, and you concealed that from your father, telling him that a wild beast had eaten him: **'Joseph was torn by a beast!'** "[172] Judah said: "The fire of Shechem is burning in my heart. Now I will destroy you and all your land by fire!" Joseph asked: "Didn't the fire of your daughter-in-law Tamar with which she killed your sons put out the fire of Shechem?" Judah replied: "By the living God, if I should pluck but a single hair from my skin, all of Egypt would be filled with blood!" Joseph said: "You seem to be in the habit of doing that, for you did the same thing to your brother when you sold him, dipping his tunic in blood and bringing it to your father so you could say: **'A savage beast devoured him!**[173] Here is his blood on his tunic!' " When Judah heard that, he was enraged and burning with anger. In front of him in that place was a big stone weighing four hundred shekels. Judah was so furious that he took that stone in his hand and threw it up in the air and caught it with his left hand. After that he took it and put it beneath his legs and sat down on it in his rage, and the stone was pulverized by his might. Joseph saw what Judah had done and was very frightened, but he instructed his son Manasseh to do the same thing Judah had done with another stone. Then Judah told his brothers: "Let no one say that this man is an Egyptian. Only someone from the family of our father could do such a thing as this." Joseph said: "It is not only to you that strength has been given. We are strong men too, so why do all you boast like that?" Judah answered Joseph: "Release our brother to us, and don't destroy your land today." Joseph answered them: "Go and tell your father: **'A savage beast devoured him,'** just as you told him in the case of [your brother] Joseph." Judah turned to his brother Naphtali and told him: "Hurry out and count all the districts of Egypt, and then report back to me." Simeon told him: "Don't be intimidated by what he says. Now I shall go to the mountain, and I

---

[171] A proverbial expression. When a bucket falls into a well, dragging the rope after it, the loss is irretrievable. Joseph (like the bucket) was cast into a well, and was lost to his father. Benjamin (like the rope) went in pursuit of Joseph, and now he too is lost.
[172] Gen. 37:33.
[173] Gen. 37:33.

shall take one huge stone from the mountain, and I shall smash all Egypt with it, and all who dwell therein shall die!"

Joseph was listening to all those words that his brothers spoke before him, but they didn't know Joseph understood them, because they thought he couldn't speak Hebrew. Because of what his brothers said, Joseph was very much afraid that they might destroy Egypt, and he instructed his son Manasseh as follows: "Please go quickly and summon all the inhabitants of Egypt and all my mighty men, and bring them to me, on horseback or on foot with all their weapons." And Manasseh went and did so. Meanwhile, Naphtali went off as Judah had instructed him, for Naphtali was as lightfooted as a deer and could trip fleetingly over the stalks of plants without even bending them. He went and counted all the districts of Egypt, and he found twelve of them, and then he hurried back to tell Judah. Judah told his brothers: "Put on your swords quickly, and we shall go to [the city of] Egypt and kill everyone there, leaving not one of them alive." Judah said: "I in my strength will wipe out three districts singlehandedly, and each of you will wipe out one."

While Judah was saying this, all the inhabitants of Egypt and all the mighty men came together against them with all their armor and many weapons and with loud cries. Their number was five hundred cavalrymen and ten thousand infantrymen and four hundred mighty men who could make war without swords or armor but only with the strength of their hands. Those mighty men came with a loud noise and with shouts, and they surrounded the sons of Jacob, who were terrified, and the earth shook on account of their cries. When the sons of Jacob saw those huge armies, they feared greatly for their lives. Joseph did this to make them afraid so that he might be free of them. Judah saw how frightened his brothers were, and he asked them: "Why are you afraid when the grace of our God is with us?" Judah saw all the Egyptians surround them at Joseph's command to slay them; but Joseph ordered them: "Don't touch any of them!" Then Judah quickly drew his sword, and howled loudly and bitterly, and struck the earth with his sword, and kept howling even more at all the men. While this was going on, all those mighty men and the others who were surrounding the brothers were seized with terror of Judah and his brothers. And they all scattered out of fear at the sound of that shout, and they fell on top of each other, and many of them died from the fall. They all ran away from Judah and his brothers out of Joseph's sight. As they fled, Judah and his brothers pursued them right up to Pharaoh's house, and killed all of them. Then Judah returned to Joseph, and he let out a loud cry and a very bitter shout. That cry was heard from a great distance, and all the inhabitants of Succoth heard it, and all Egypt shook from the sound of that cry. Furthermore, all the walls of [the city of] Egypt and the land of Goshen tumbled down from that trembling of the earth, and even Pharaoh fell from his throne on his face to the ground. And all the women of Egypt and Goshen who were pregnant aborted their fetuses from their wombs when they heard the sound of that trembling, for it was terrifying.

Pharaoh sent out messengers asking: "What is this that has happened in the land of Egypt today?" and they came back and reported everything that had happened from beginning to end. Pharaoh was amazed and speechless with fear when he heard all that. He sent a message to Joseph asking him: "Have you brought me these Hebrews to destroy all of Egypt? What do you care about that thieving slave? Why not just let him go with his brothers so that we will not perish on account of their mischief—we, and you, and all Egypt? If you don't want to do this, then divest yourself of everything I have bestowed on you and go with them to their land if you like them so much. This very day they will destroy all my land, and kill all the men, and all the women will abort their fetuses on account of their shouting. Just look at what they've accomplished merely with their shouting and their words! Without even making war with the sword, they've destroyed most of the land. Now you must choose which you prefer: shall it be me or the Hebrews? Egypt or the Hebrews?"

They went and told Joseph everything Pharaoh said, and Joseph was very much afraid on account of Pharaoh's words. Judah and his brothers were still standing before Joseph with anger and fury and rage, and they roared at Joseph like the roaring of the waves of the sea. Joseph was very frightened both of his brothers and of Pharaoh, and he decided to reveal himself to his brothers so that all Egypt would not be destroyed. Joseph gave instructions to his son Manasseh, and Manasseh went up to Judah and put his hand on his shoulder, and Judah's anger was pacified. Judah then told his brothers: "Let no one say that this is the doing of an Egyptian boy, for this could only be the act of someone of my father's house."

Joseph saw that Judah's anger was pacified, and he went over to speak to Judah in a soft voice. Joseph told Judah: "Everything you have said was true, and you have demonstrated your might today, and may your God, Who delights in you, do you even more good. But won't you please explain why you, of all your brothers, made war against me for the sake of the lad, when none of them had spoken a word to me on his behalf." Judah answered Joseph: "You must know that I pledged myself for the boy to my father, saying that **if I do not bring him back to** him, **I shall stand guilty before** him **forever.**[174] This is why I alone among my brothers approached you today, for I saw that you were unwilling to give him up and release him. Now if I have found grace in your eyes, release him and let him go with our brothers, and I will stay here in place of him and serve you in every way you wish, for I will go anywhere you send

---

[174] Gen. 44:32.

me to serve you with my great strength. Just send me to a harsh king who has rebelled against you, and you will hear what I have done to his land. Whether he be accompanied by cavalrymen or infantry or very strong men, I will kill them all and bring you the head of their king. Don't you know, or haven't you heard, that our father Abraham with his servant Eliezer, just the two of them, killed all the kings of Elam with their armies in a single night, leaving not one of them alive? From that day to the present, we have been given our father's strength as an inheritance for us and our descendants forever." Joseph answered him: "You have spoken the truth, and there is no lie in your mouth, for it has also been told us that the Hebrews have great strength, and that their God takes great delight in them, and no one can stand before them. However, I will release your brother to you on this condition: that you bring me his brother, the son of his mother, who you have said went down to Egypt. When you bring me your brother, I will take him as my servant, for none of you pledged your-self to your father for him. When he comes to me, I will release to you the brother for whom you pledged yourself."

Judah was furious with Joseph on account of these words, and his eyes filled with blood from his rage, and he told his brothers: "What is this? Is he trying to destroy both himself and all Egypt in a single day?" Simeon replied to Joseph: "Didn't we tell you when we first came here that we didn't know where he went, or whether he's dead or alive? Why then is my lord saying things like this to us?" Joseph looked at Judah's face, and he knew that he was getting angrier because Joseph had told him: "Bring your other brother in exchange for this one." Joseph said to his brothers: "Didn't you tell me that your brother died and perished? What if I called him today and he came before you? Would you give him to me in place of his brother?" Then Joseph started speaking and crying out: "Joseph! Joseph! Come before me today, and see your brothers, and stand before them!"

As Joseph was saying these things in front of them, they kept looking each one in different directions, and wondering where their brother Joseph would come from. Joseph saw what they were doing and told them: "Why are you looking around like that? **I am your brother Joseph, he whom you sold into Egypt. Now, do not be distressed or reproach yourselves because you sold me hither; it was to save life** from starvation **that God sent me ahead of you.**"[175] His brothers were terrified when they heard Joseph's words, and Judah was particularly terrified. When Benjamin heard Joseph's words, he was in an inner room, and he ran to his brother Joseph, and embraced him, and fell upon his neck, and they wept. When Joseph's brothers saw Benjamin fall on their

[175] Gen. 45:4–5.

brother and weep with him, they too fell upon Joseph, and embraced him, and wept loudly with Joseph.

The news reached Pharaoh's palace that **Joseph's brothers had come. Pharaoh was** very **pleased,**[176] for he had been afraid that they might destroy Egypt. Pharaoh sent his servants to congratulate Joseph on the arrival of his brothers. And all the knights and grandees in Egypt went to join in Joseph's celebration, and all Egypt rejoiced greatly over Joseph's brothers. Pharaoh sent his servants to Joseph with the following message: "Tell your brothers to bring all their belongings and come to me, and I will settle them in the best part of the land of Egypt," and so it was done.

Joseph ordered his house steward to bring his brothers gifts, and yet more gifts, and garments. He brought them many garments, royal robes, and many gifts, and Joseph distributed them to all his brothers. Joseph gave each of his brothers a change of clothing, like royal apparel, and a hundred pieces of silver each. But to his brother Benjamin he gave five changes of clothing, of cloth of gold, and **three hundred pieces of silver.**[177] Joseph instructed them all to put on those robes, and he brought them before Pharaoh. Pharaoh saw all Joseph's brothers, that they were all brave men and well built, and he was very happy. After that they left Pharaoh to go to the land of Canaan to their father, and their brother Benjamin went with them. Joseph got up and gave them eleven of Pharaoh's chariots. Joseph also gave them his own chariot—the one he had ridden on the day he was made vizier of Egypt—to bring his father to Egypt in it. Joseph sent to each of his brothers' children garments according to their number, and a hundred pieces of silver for each of them. He also sent his brothers' wives gowns according to their number, from the gowns of the king's wives, and he sent them perfume and cosmetics. He gave each of his brothers ten men to accompany them to the land of Canaan, to help and serve them, and to make the necessary preparations for their return to Egypt. And Joseph sent by way of his brother Benjamin ten robes for his ten sons—one portion above that which he sent for the children of Jacob's other sons—and he sent each of them fifty pieces of silver and ten of Pharaoh's chariots. **And to his father he sent ten he-asses laden with the best things of Egypt, and ten she-asses laden with grain, bread, and provisions for his father on the journey.**[178] To his sister Dinah he sent gowns of gold and silver, and perfume, and myrrh, and aloes, and a great quantity of ladies' cosmetics. He also sent similar gifts to Benjamin's wives from Pharaoh's wives. He also gave all his brothers and their wives all kinds of precious stones—onyx, and bdellium, and emeralds, and

[176] Gen. 45:16.
[177] Gen. 45:22.
[178] Gen. 45:23.

topaz, and other items from among the treasures of the grandees of Egypt. There was nothing of beauty that Joseph failed to send his father's house!

And he bade his brothers farewell, and they set out, and he sent his brother Benjamin with them to go to the land of Canaan. Joseph went out with them to accompany them on the road as far as the Egyptian border, and he instructed them to bring his father and his household to Egypt. **He told them: "Do not be quarrelsome on the way,**[179] for God has done all this to preserve many people from hunger, for **there are still five years**[180] of famine in the land." Joseph advised them: "When you get to the land of Canaan, don't spring all this news on my father suddenly, but proceed cautiously and with discretion." When Joseph had finished advising them, he turned around and went back to Egypt, and the sons of Jacob went to the land of Canaan with gladness and joy, to their father Jacob.

When they reached the border of the land, they asked each other: "How shall we tell our father about all this? For if we spring all this news on him suddenly, he will be so dumbfounded that he won't be able to comprehend what we are saying." As they were approaching their homes, they came upon Serah, the daughter of Asher, who was coming out to welcome them. The girl was extremely pretty and intelligent, and she knew how to sing to the accompaniment of the harp. They called her, and she came to them and kissed them, and they took her and gave her a harp, saying: "Please go to our father, and sit down before him, and play the harp while reciting some words we will tell you." They instructed her to go to their house, and she took the harp [and she ran ahead of them] and went and sat down facing Jacob. She took the harp and played it, while singing in a lovely voice: "Joseph, the beloved of God, is governor over all Egypt, and he is not dead." She continued to play and sing in this vein, and Jacob listened attentively to her words, and they pleased him. Jacob listened to her song twice and three times over, and her beautiful song brought joy to Jacob's heart, and the spirit of God came upon him, and he realized that everything she said was true. Jacob blessed Serah for her words, telling her: "My daughter, death will never claim you until the end of time, for you have brought my spirit back to life. But please repeat what you were saying, for all your words have brought me great joy." She continued to sing in the same way, and Jacob listened to her and rejoiced, and was very happy, and the spirit of God was upon him.

As he was talking to her, his sons came to him with the horses and the chariots and the royal robes, and the slaves ran before them. Jacob stood up to greet them, and he saw his sons dressed in royal robes, and he saw all the good things

---

[179] Gen. 45:24.
[180] Gen. 45:6.

that Joseph had sent them. They asked him: "Are you aware that our brother Joseph is alive, and is ruler over all the land of Egypt, and that he is the one who told us everything we are telling you?" Jacob listened to everything his sons said, and his heart was pounding on account of those words, for he didn't really trust them until he saw everything Joseph had given them and sent him, and all the signs that Joseph had told them. They opened [their bags] before him, and he saw everything Joseph had given to each one of them, as well as what Joseph had sent him, and Jacob realized that what they were saying was true, and he was very happy on account of his son. Jacob said: **"Enough! My son Joseph is still alive! I must go and see him before I die."**[181] His sons told him everything that had happened to them. Jacob said: "I will go down to Egypt to see my son and his children." Jacob got up and put on the robes that Joseph had sent him, and put the turban Joseph had sent him on his head—after he had washed and shaved his hair. All the men of the house of Jacob and their wives put on the clothes that Joseph had sent them, and they were very happy that Joseph was still alive and that he was the governor of Egypt. All the inhabitants of Canaan heard the news, and they came and warmly congratulated Jacob that Joseph was still alive, and Jacob gave them a great feast for three days, and all the kings of Canaan and all the grandees of the land ate and drank and celebrated in Jacob's house.

After that, Jacob said: "I will go to see my son in Egypt, and then I will return to the land of Canaan of which God spoke to Abraham, for I must never abandon the land of my birth." But then God told him: "Arise, and go down to Egypt with all your household and dwell there. **Fear not to go down to Egypt, for I will make you there into a great nation.**"[182] Jacob said in his heart: "I will go and see whether my son still has the fear of God in his heart among all the inhabitants of Egypt." But God told Jacob: "Don't worry about Joseph, for he has clung tenaciously to his commitment to serve Me and to please you." Jacob was very, very happy [to hear this] about his son.

Then Jacob commanded his sons and his household to go to Egypt, as God had told him. Jacob and his sons and all his household got up and left the land of Canaan by way of Beer-sheba, with gladness and a happy heart, and went to the land of Egypt. As they approached the Egyptian border, Jacob sent Judah ahead to Joseph to find out where they were to live in Egypt. Judah did as his father told him, and made haste, and ran, and went to Joseph; and he assigned them a place in the land of Goshen for Jacob and all his household; and Judah then went back to his father on the road.

---

[181] Gen. 45:28.
[182] Gen. 46:3.

Joseph sent for his chariot, and summoned all his mighty men and his slaves and all the princes of Egypt to go out to welcome his father Jacob. And Joseph proclaimed throughout Egypt that anyone who didn't go out to welcome Jacob would be put to death. The next day Joseph went out with all Egypt, with a mighty and numerous throng dressed in linen robes and purple, and gold and silver armor, bearing weapons of war. They all went out to welcome Jacob with all kinds of musical instruments and drums and timbrels, and myrrh and aloes spread along the highway, and they all went out in their ranks, and the earth trembled from the sound. All the Egyptian women went up to the rooftops of Egypt and climbed up on the walls to welcome Jacob, and they played the drums and danced. Joseph and all the people that were with him went out to welcome Jacob, and on Joseph's head was Pharaoh's royal crown, which Pharaoh had sent him to wear when he went to welcome his father. When Joseph was about fifty cubits away from his father, he got down from his chariot and went to welcome his father on foot. When all the princes of Egypt and the grandees saw Joseph go to his father on foot, they also got down and walked to welcome Jacob. When Jacob and his sons drew near Joseph's camp, and he saw that multitude coming out to welcome him with Joseph, Jacob was astonished and very happy. Jacob asked Judah: "Who is that handsome man whom I see in the Egyptian camp wearing royal robes? He is wearing a bright red robe and has a royal crown on his head, and he has gotten down out of his chariot and is coming to welcome us." Judah answered his father: "He is your son, Joseph the king," and Jacob was very happy to see the honor bestowed on his son.

When Joseph drew nearer to his father, he bowed to his father, and all the men of his camp bowed down to the ground with him before Jacob. Then Jacob ran quickly to his son Joseph, **and embraced him around the neck**[183] and kissed him, and wept with him. Joseph also embraced his father and kissed him and wept, and all the Egyptians wept with them. Then Jacob told Joseph: "Behold, **now I can die, having seen for myself that you are still alive**[184] and honored." All the sons of Jacob, and their wives and children and slaves and all of Jacob's household wept greatly with Joseph, and kissed him and embraced him, and wept exceedingly with him. Then Joseph and the Egyptian multitude went back to their place, and Jacob and his sons and all his household went to [the capital of] Egypt with Joseph, and Joseph assigned them the best part of Egypt in the land of Goshen.

Joseph told his father and his brothers: "I will go and tell Pharaoh that my father and my father's household have come to me with all their belongings,

---

[183] Gen. 46:29.
[184] Gen. 46:30.

and now they are in the land of Goshen." Joseph did so, and he took his brothers Reuben and Issachar and Zebulun and Benjamin, and presented them to Pharaoh. Joseph told Pharaoh: "My brothers and my father's household and **all that is theirs,** including **their flocks and their herds, have come** to me **from the land of Canaan**[185] **to sojourn in** Egypt, **the famine being very severe**[186] to them." Pharaoh told Joseph: "**Settle your father and your brothers in the best part of the land,**[187] and don't deprive them of any good thing, and they shall eat of the fat of the land." Joseph replied: "I have placed them in the land of Goshen, for they are shepherds. Therefore, settle them in Goshen, where they can watch over their sheep out of sight of the Egyptians." Pharaoh told Joseph: "Do to your brothers exactly as they have said." And the sons of Jacob bowed down to Pharaoh, and bade him farewell, and left. Then Joseph presented his father to Pharaoh, and Jacob came and bowed down to Pharaoh, and he blessed Pharaoh and left. Then Jacob and all his sons and all his household dwelled in the land of Goshen.

In the second year [of the famine], Jacob was 130 years old. And Joseph supported his father and his brothers and all their household with bread for their little ones, so that during all the days of the famine, they lacked for nothing. Joseph gave them the best things the land of Egypt had to offer, and the sons of Jacob ate the tastiest food in the land of Egypt during all Joseph's days, and Joseph also gave all his father's household garments and clothing every year. And the sons of Jacob settled in Egypt to stay during all the days of their brother Joseph. Jacob always ate with Joseph. Jacob and his household were never absent from Joseph's table except when the sons of Jacob ate in their own homes.

All the Egyptians ate bread from Joseph's house during all the days of the famine, for he had bought all the Egyptians' property on account of the famine. Joseph had bought Egypt and its land and its fields for Pharaoh with bread. Joseph provided all of Egypt with bread during the days of the famine. **Joseph gathered in all the silver**[188] and gold that came to him from what he sold, and he found that he had a great deal of gold and silver. This was in addition to the onyx stones and bdellium and costly garments that came to Joseph from all over the land, along with money beyond counting. And Joseph took of all the silver and gold that came into his hands, about seventy two talents of gold and silver, and also a large amount of the onyx and bdellium. Joseph buried all this in four different places. He buried one part in the desert near the Red Sea and another part near the river Euphrates; and he buried the third and fourth parts

---

[185] Gen. 47:1.
[186] Gen. 47:4.
[187] Gen. 47:6.
[188] Gen. 47:14.

in the wilderness near the desert of the Persians and the Medes. Joseph took some of the remaining gold and silver and gave it to all his brothers and all his father's household and to all the women of his father's household, and then he took what was left—about twenty talents of gold and silver—to Pharaoh's palace. Joseph gave that remaining gold and silver to Pharaoh, and Pharaoh put it in his treasury. The days of famine were drawing to an end throughout Egypt, and after that they planted, and they had food as before year after year, and nothing was lacking. Joseph settled permanently in Egypt, and all the land was under his supervision, and his father and all his brothers dwelled in the land of Goshen and settled there. Jacob grew very old, and Joseph's two sons, Ephraim and Manasseh, spent all their time in Jacob's house with Jacob's other grandchildren, their brothers, learning the ways of God and His laws. Jacob and his sons dwelled in the land of Egypt, in the land of Goshen, and they settled down there, and they increased and multiplied exceedingly.

IV. Va-yeḥi

Jacob lived seventeen years in the land of Egypt, so that the span of Jacob's life came to one hundred and forty seven years.[189] Then Jacob felt that the time was coming for him to die, and he sent and summoned his son Joseph from [the capital of] Egypt, and Joseph came to his father. Jacob told Joseph and his sons: "**I am about to die; but** the God of your fathers **will be with you and bring you back to the land**[190] that God promised to give to you and your sons after you. Now when I die, bury me in the cave of Machpelah in Hebron in the land of Canaan with my fathers." Jacob made his sons swear to bury him in Machpelah in Hebron, and all his sons swore to do so. He commanded them: "Worship the Lord your God, for He will save you from all misfortunes as He saved your fathers." Jacob said: "Send for all your sons, and all your grandchildren," and they all came and sat down before him. Jacob blessed them, saying: "May God, the God of your fathers, increase you a thousandfold, and bless you, and give you the blessing of Abraham your father." Then all Jacob's grandchildren left him on the day that he blessed them.

The next day Jacob summoned his sons again, and they all came to him and sat down before him. And Jacob blessed his sons on that day before he died, each one with a particular blessing. Behold, this is written in the book of God's Torah to Israel. Jacob told Judah: "I know, my son, that you are the greatest of your brothers, and you will reign over them, and your sons will reign over their

---

[189] Gen. 47:28.
[190] Gen. 48:21.

sons forever. However, teach your sons to use the bow and arrow and all the weapons of war, so that as kings, they will lead their brothers in warfare against all their enemies." And Jacob commanded his sons again that day: "Today I am to be gathered to my people. Take me up from Egypt and bury me in the cave of Machpelah, as I ordered you. However, be sure not to have any of your children take me, but take me yourselves. This is what you must do for me when you carry my body to take it to the land of Canaan to bury me. Judah, Issachar, and Zebulun will carry my bier on the east side. Reuben, Simeon, and Gad will be on the south side. Ephraim, Manasseh, and Benjamin will be on the west side. Dan, Asher, and Naphtali will be on the north side. Don't let Levi carry me, because he and his sons will carry the ark of God's covenant with Israel in the camp. Neither let my son Joseph carry me, for he is like a king in honor, and his sons Ephraim and Manasseh will take his place. This is what you must do for me when you carry me; don't leave out a single thing that I have commanded you! If you do these things for me, God will do good to you and your sons forever. My sons, let each of you honor his brother and his neighbor, and order your children, and your children's children after them, to serve the Lord God of your fathers all their days, so that your days may be long upon the earth, yours and your sons' and your sons' sons, as long as you do good and behave uprightly in the eyes of the Lord God and walk in all His ways. And you, Joseph my son, please forgive your brothers' wrongdoing, and all the sins and evil things they did to you, because God has turned them into good for you and your children. My son, do not abandon your brothers to the inhabitants of Egypt, and do not shame them, for I have entrusted them to the hand of God, and your hand, to protect them all their days from the Egyptians." The sons of Jacob answered their father: "All that you have commanded us, we will do; and may God be with us." Jacob told his sons: "Indeed God will be with you as long as you keep all His ways, not deviating from all His ways either to the right or to the left, and doing what is good and upright in His eyes. For I know that many misfortunes and evils will befall you in the times to come in this land, as well as your sons and your grandchildren; but serve God, and He will save you from all misfortune. You must follow God, and serve Him, and teach your children and your grandchildren after them to know God. God will raise up for you and your children a savior from among your descendants, and God will deliver you by his hand from all misfortune, and will take you out of Egypt and return you to the land of your fathers to inherit it forever."

When Jacob finished his instructions to his sons, he drew his feet into the bed and, breathing his last, he was gathered to his people.[191] **Joseph flung himself upon his father,** and he cried out, **and wept over him and kissed**

---

[191] Gen. 49:33.

him,[192] and he cried out in a bitter voice: "My father, my father!" Then his sons' wives and all his household came and fell upon Jacob, and wept over him, and cried out in a very loud voice over Jacob. Then all Jacob's sons got up and rent their garments, and girded their loins with sackcloth, and they fell on their faces and threw dust into the sky over their heads. Word of this reached Asenath, Joseph's wife, and she got up and put on sackcloth and came with all the women of Egypt to mourn, and they all wept over Jacob. Also all the men of Egypt who had known Jacob came that day, as soon as they heard what had happened, and all Egypt wept over Jacob for many days. Also men came from the land of Canaan to Egypt when they heard of Jacob's death, **and they bewailed him** in Egypt **seventy days.**[193] **Then Joseph ordered the physicians in his service to embalm his father,**[194] with myrrh and frankincense and all kinds of perfumes, and the physicians embalmed Jacob as Joseph had instructed them. All Egypt and its elders and all the inhabitants of the land of Goshen wept and mourned for Jacob, and his sons and all the children of his household mourned and grieved for their father Jacob during all those days.

After that, **when the wailing period was over**[195] at the end of seventy days, Joseph told Pharaoh: "I will go and bury my father in the land of Canaan, as **he made me swear; then I shall return."**[196] Pharaoh sent Joseph the following message: **"Go up and bury your father,** as he told you and **made you promise on oath."**[197] Joseph and all his brothers set out for the land of Canaan to bury their father Jacob, as he had commanded them. Pharaoh ordered a proclamation made throughout Egypt, saying: "Anyone who fails to go with Joseph and his brothers to the land of Canaan to bury Jacob shall be put to death." All Egypt hearkened to Pharaoh's proclamation, and they all went to accompany Joseph—all Pharaoh's servants, and the elders of his household, and all the elders of the land of Egypt. Pharaoh's princes and noblemen and Joseph's servants went to bury Jacob in the land of Canaan.

Jacob's sons lifted the bier on which he was sleeping, doing everything for him exactly as he had commanded. The bier was of pure gold studded with stones of onyx and bdellium, and it was tightly sealed. The covering of the bier was made of woven work of gold joined together with threads, and on it were hooks of onyx stones and bdellium. Joseph put a big golden crown on the head of [his father] Jacob, and put a golden scepter in his hand, and they surrounded the bier, as was the custom of kings during their lifetime. All the armies of

---

[192] Gen. 50:1.
[193] Gen. 50:3.
[194] Gen. 50:2.
[195] Gen. 50:3.
[196] Gen. 50:5.
[197] Gen. 50:6.

Egypt went before him in this order: first the mighty men of Pharaoh and the mighty men of Joseph, followed by most of the inhabitants of Egypt. All of them had their swords girded on their loins and were dressed in armor and carried their weapons with them. All those who were weeping and mourning went at a distance in front of the bier, weeping and lamenting as they went along, and the rest of the people followed the bier. Joseph and his household walked together near the bier, barefoot and weeping, and the rest of Joseph's servants and his mighty men surrounded him girded with their weapons. Fifty of Jacob's servants preceded the bier, sprinkling myrrh and aloes and all kinds of perfume all along the road. All the sons of Jacob who were carrying the bier walked on that perfume. Jacob's servants preceded them, sprinkling perfume on the road. Joseph went with a heavy camp, and they followed the same procedures every day until they reached the land of Canaan. **When they came to Goren ha-Atad, which is beyond the Jordan, they held a very great and solemn lamentation**[198] in that place. All the kings of Canaan heard about that, and each one went out from his own place—thirty one kings of Canaan—and they all went with their men to mourn [and weep] over Jacob. All those kings saw Joseph's crown on Jacob's bier, and they too took their crowns and put them on the bier all around the first one. And all those kings made a very great and solemn lamentation over Jacob in that place with the sons of Jacob and the Egyptians, for all the kings of Canaan knew the strength of Jacob and his sons.

The news reached Esau that Jacob had died in Egypt, and his sons and all the Egyptians had come to the land of Canaan to bury him. [When Esau heard this,] he was living in Mount Seir, and he and his sons [and his grandsons] and all his men and all his household came with a great multitude to mourn and to weep over Jacob. When Esau came to mourn his brother Jacob, all the Egyptians and all the Canaanites made another great lamentation with Esau for Jacob in that place. Joseph and his brothers carried their father Jacob from that place and went to Hebron to bury Jacob in the cave with his fathers [and they came to Kiriath-arba to the cave.]

When they got there, Esau and his sons and their men prevented Joseph from entering the cave, saying: "Do not bury Jacob in it, for it belongs to us and our father." When Joseph and his brothers heard what the sons of Esau said, they became very angry. Joseph went up to Esau and said: "What is the meaning of this? Didn't my father Jacob buy this from you for a high price after the death of Isaac, exactly twenty five years ago today? Furthermore, he bought all the land of Canaan from you and your sons and your descendants after you. Jacob bought it for his sons and their descendants after them as an inheritance forever, so why are you saying these things today?" Esau answered Joseph: "What

[198] Gen. 50:10.

you are saying is all lies and falsehoods, for I did not sell any of my share in all this land [as you claim], nor did my brother Jacob buy any of my property in this land." Esau said those things to deceive Joseph with his words, for Esau knew that Joseph had not been present in those days when Esau sold all his property in the land of Canaan to Jacob. Joseph then told Esau: "Didn't my father record these transactions [with you] in a bill of sale before witnesses? We had it with us in Egypt." Esau replied: "Go and bring the bill of sale, and whatever I find it in, I will do." Joseph called [his brother] Naphtali and told him: "Hurry, and please run without delay to Egypt and bring back all the documents and the seals and the manifestos. Also bring all the original documents containing all the words concerning the birthright. Bring them to us here, and thereby we will know the truth about everything Esau and his sons have said today."

Naphtali did as Joseph said and hastened to run to Egypt. Naphtali was more fleetfooted than the deer in the wilderness and could run over the stems of plants without breaking them. When Esau saw that Naphtali had gone to bring the documents, he reinforced the guards at the entrance of the cave, and he and his sons and his men prepared to make war against Joseph and his brothers. All the sons of Jacob and the Egyptians fought with Esau and his men, and the sons of Jacob defeated Esau and his men, killing forty of Esau's men. At that time Hushim, son of Jacob's son Dan, was with Jacob's sons, but he was about a hundred cubits away from the battlefield, for he was with Jacob's grandchildren guarding Jacob's bier. Hushim was deaf, but he could still understand when people shouted. He asked: "Why aren't you burying this dead man? And what is this loud shouting about?" [They answered] and told him how Esau and his sons had prevented them from burying Jacob in the cave. When he understood what Esau and his sons had done, [he became very angry, and he quickly took his sword] and ran to Esau in the midst of the fighting, and struck Esau [with the sword], and cut off his head, and it flew a long way off, and Esau fell among the men who were fighting. When Hushim did this, the sons of Jacob prevailed against the sons of Esau. The sons of Jacob then buried their father Jacob by force in the cave, while the sons of Esau looked on. Jacob was buried in Hebron, in the cave of Machpelah **which Abraham had bought** from the Hittites **for a burial site,**[199] and he was buried in very costly garments. No king has been treated with such honor as Joseph showed his father [upon his death, for he gave him a very honorable burial, like the burial of kings]. Joseph and his brothers mourned for Jacob seven days.

After that the sons of Esau made war against the sons of Jacob, and the sons of Esau fought the sons of Jacob in Hebron, while Esau lay dead and unburied. It was a great battle between the two sides, but the sons of Esau finally retreated

---

[199] Gen. 50:13.

from the sons of Jacob. The sons of Jacob killed eighty of Esau's men, but not one of the men of the sons of Jacob died. Joseph prevailed against all the men of Esau's sons, and he took prisoner Zepho, son of Eliphaz, son of Esau, and fifty of his men. He put them all in iron chains and turned them over to his servants to take to Egypt. When the sons of Jacob took Zepho and his men prisoners, all the men of Esau's household were very much afraid that they too might be captured. They ran away with Eliphaz, son of Esau, and his men, and they took Esau's corpse, and made their way to Mount Seir. When they got to Mount Seir, they buried Esau there, but they hadn't brought his head with them, for it was buried on the battlefield in Hebron. When the sons of Esau fled [from the sons of Jacob], the sons of Jacob pursued them as far as the border of Seir, but they didn't kill any of them, for they were carrying the corpse of Esau, and they fled with it.

The sons of Jacob left them and went back to the place where they had left their brothers in Hebron, and they remained there that day and the next day to rest from the battle. On the third day all the sons of Seir the Horite gathered, and they summoned all the sons of Kedem,[200] a multitude as numerous as the sands of the sea, and they set out for Egypt to make war against Joseph and his brothers in order to liberate their brothers. Joseph and all the sons of Jacob heard that the sons of Esau had formed an alliance with the sons of Kedem and were coming to make war against them in order to liberate their brothers. They went out to meet Joseph and his brothers and the mighty men of Egypt and to make war against them in the land of Raamses. Joseph and his brothers won a very decisive victory over [the sons of Esau and] the sons of Seir and the sons of Kedem. They killed 600,000 of their men, slaying all the mighty men of the sons of Seir the Horite, so that only very few of them were spared. They also killed a great many of the sons of Kedem and the sons of Esau, and all of them, including Eliphaz, son of Esau, and the sons of Kedem fled from Joseph and his brothers. Joseph and his brothers pursued them as far as Succoth, and killed thirty more of them in Succoth, and the rest fled, each to his own city. Joseph and his brothers and the mighty men of Egypt went home with rejoicing and happy hearts, because they had defeated all their enemies. Zepho, son of Eliphaz, and his men remained in Egypt as slaves of Jacob's sons, and they were even worse off than before.

When the sons of Esau and the sons of Seir returned to their land, the sons of Seir saw that they had all fallen into the hands of the sons of Jacob and the Egyptians as a result of that war which the sons of Esau had started. Then the sons of Seir told the sons of Esau: "You have seen, and you are aware, that it is your fault that we suffered this battle, and no strong man nor anyone trained in

---

[200] Or "children of the east."

warfare has survived. Now get out of our land, and go away from us to the land of Canaan, the land where your fathers dwelled. Why should your children inherit what rightfully belongs to our children in the days to come?" But the sons of Esau refused to do as the sons of Seir said, and the sons of Seir conspired to make war against them. The sons of Esau secretly sent a message to Angias, king of Africa—which is also known as Dinhabah—saying: "Send us some of your men to join us in making war on the sons of Seir the Horite, for they have decided to fight against us to drive us out of the land." And Angias, king of Dinhabah, did so, for Angias was very fond of the sons of Esau in those days. Angias sent the sons of Esau five hundred strong infantrymen and eight hundred cavalrymen. The sons of Seir sent a message to the sons of Kedem and Midian, saying: "You have seen what the sons of Esau have done to us, and how because of them we were almost all destroyed in their war against the sons of Jacob. Now come to us, and help us, and we shall fight them together and drive them out of the land. Thus we will avenge the deaths of your brothers and our brothers who perished on account of their war against the sons of Jacob, their brothers." All the sons of Kedem answered the request of the sons of Seir, sending them about eight hundred men armed with swords. Then the sons of Esau fought the sons of Seir in the wilderness of Paran, and the sons of Seir defeated the sons of Esau. The sons of Seir killed in that war from among the sons of Esau about two hundred of the men sent by Angias, king of Dinhabah, that day.

The next day the sons of Esau gathered together again to fight a second battle against the sons of Seir. Once again that second battle went very badly for the sons of Esau, and they were greatly distressed on account of the sons of Seir. Then the sons of Esau realized that the sons of Seir were mightier than they, and some of the sons of Esau betrayed their own tribesmen and helped the sons of Seir against them. In that second battle fifty nine men of the sons of Esau fell, from among the men sent by Angias, king of Dinhabah. On the third day, the sons of Esau found out that some of their own brothers had turned against them and fought against them in that second battle, and they were very upset about that. They asked: "What shall we do to our brothers who turned against us and helped our enemies, the sons of Seir?" The sons of Esau got together and sent the following message to Angias, king of Dinhabah: "Send us more men, and we will join them in fighting the sons of Seir, for there are twice as many of them as us." Angias then sent the sons of Esau more reinforcements—about six hundred strong, brave men—and they went and helped the sons of Esau.

Ten days later, the sons of Esau gathered together and went out to fight the sons of Seir in the wilderness of Paran. This time the battle went against the sons of Seir, for now they were outnumbered by the sons of Esau. The sons of Seir fled from the sons of Esau, and the sons of Esau killed about two thousand of them. All the mighty men of the sons of Seir perished in that battle. Not a man of them survived, but only their small children who had stayed behind in their cities. All Midian and the sons of Kedem fled from the fighting and abandoned the sons of Seir and ran away because of the fierceness of that battle. The sons of Esau pursued the sons of Kedem until they reached their land, and the sons of Esau killed about two hundred and fifty of them on the way. Only about thirty of the men of the sons of Esau fell in that battle, but it seemed terrible to them because it was on account of their own brothers who had turned against them and helped the sons of Seir the Horite. The sons of Esau heard more about the wickedness their brothers had done, and once again they were greatly saddened by that.

After the battle the sons of Esau went home to their places in Seir. Then the sons of Esau killed all the survivors of the sons of Seir in the land, even their women and children, and spared not a living soul. However, there were among them fifty small boys and girls, and the sons of Esau didn't kill them, but took the boys as slaves and the girls as wives. The sons of Esau stayed in the land of Seir, in place of the sons of Seir, and they inherited their land and became the owners of it. The sons of Esau confiscated all the property of the sons of Seir in the land. The sons of Esau confiscated their flocks and their herds and their belongings, and all that the sons of Seir possessed, and the sons of Esau have lived in Seir, in place of the sons of Seir, right down to the present day. The sons of Esau divided the land into five parts for the five sons of Esau and their families.

At that time the sons of Esau wanted to crown one of them king of the land they had seized. However, they told each other: "Let's not do that, for a king would reign over us in our own land, and keep us under his yoke, and make us fight his wars against his enemies," so they acted accordingly. All the sons of Esau swore as follows: that none of their brothers should ever rule over them, but only a stranger who was not one of their brothers. This was because each of the sons of Esau held a grudge against their own sons and brothers and companions and neighbors on account of the wicked deed their brothers had done them in the war against the sons of Seir. That is why the sons of Esau have sworn from that day to the present time that none of their brothers would ever rule over them, but only a stranger.

There was a man from the people of Angias, king of Dinhabah, named Bela, son of Beor. He was strong and very brave and handsome and good-looking and very knowledgeable in all the sciences and had good judgment, and there was none like him among the men of Angias. All the sons of Esau took him, and anointed him, and crowned him to reign over them, crying: "Long live the king! Long live the king!" They spread out a cloth, and each one gave him earrings of of gold and silver. Some gave him rings, others gave him bracelets, still others gave him necklaces, and they made him very rich in silver and gold and onyx and bdellium. They made him a royal throne, and put a royal crown on his head, and they built him a palace, and he lived there, and he was king over the sons of Esau. Then the men of Angias took their payment for the war from the sons of Esau and returned to their lord in Dinhabah. Bela reigned over the sons of Esau for thirty years, and the sons of Esau occupied the land that had belonged to the sons of Seir, and they have retained their hold on it up to the present day.

In the thirty-second year after Israel went down to Egypt, Joseph was seventy-one years old. That year Pharaoh, king of Egypt, died, and his son Migron ruled in his place. Before he died, Pharaoh instructed Joseph to be like a father to his son Migron, and he ordered Migron to submit to Joseph's guidance. All Egypt accepted Pharaoh's decree that Joseph should be over them, for all the Egyptians loved Joseph just as before. However, Migron, Pharaoh's son, sat on his father's throne, and succeeded his father as king in those days. Migron was forty-one years old when he became king, and he ruled over Egypt for forty years. All the Egyptians called him "Pharaoh," as they had called his father, for it was the Egyptian custom to give this title to all the kings who ruled over them. When this Pharaoh succeeded his father, he entrusted the laws of the land and all matters of government to Joseph, as his father had instructed him. Hence Joseph ruled over Egypt, for he could do as he pleased throughout Egypt, and all of Egypt was under his hand and his will. For all the Egyptians loved Joseph very much after the death of Pharaoh, and they loved having him as their ruler. Nevertheless, there were some who didn't like him and said: "No foreigner will rule over us!" In spite of this, Joseph was in charge of all the government of Egypt in those days after the death of Pharaoh. He was in complete control and could do as he liked throughout the land, and no one could say anything about it. All Egypt was under Joseph's hand, and he made war against all the enemies around him and forced them to submit to him. Joseph also conquered all the land of the Philistines up to the border of Canaan, and they were all under his control, and they paid taxes to him every year. Pharaoh, king of Egypt, sat on the throne as his father's successor, but he was under Joseph's control and guidance, just as he had been under the control of his father. There was no governor in the land of Egypt who was not under Joseph's control. At that time Joseph reigned over all the land from Egypt to the great river Euphrates. Joseph was successful in all his ways, and the Lord his God was with him. And God increased Joseph's wisdom and honor and respect and love in the hearts of the Egyptians and throughout the land, and Joseph ruled over all the land for forty years. All the land of the Philistines, and Canaan, and Zidon, and the other side of the Jordan brought Joseph gifts all his days, and they paid taxes to him every year, as was customary. Joseph made war against all the enemies around him, and conquered them, and all the land was under Joseph's control. And Joseph sat on his throne [in Egypt] continually. All his brothers, the sons of Jacob, stayed permanently in the land of Goshen throughout Joseph's life. They increased and multiplied greatly in the land, and they served God all their days, as their father Jacob had commanded them.

Many days and years had gone by since the sons of Esau had settled down in their land for good with their king Bela, and the sons of Esau had increased and multiplied in the land. They decided to go and make war against the sons of Jacob and all Egypt and to liberate Zepho, son of their brother Eliphaz, and his men, for they were still in Egypt in those days as Joseph's slaves. The sons of Esau sent ambassadors to all the sons of Kedem to make peace with them, so that all the sons of Kedem would come to them to go to Egypt with the sons of Esau to make war. Some of the men of Angias, king of Dinhabah, also joined them, and they also summoned the sons of Ishmael. All those people gathered together and came to Seir to help the sons of Esau in their war. Their camp was enormous, they were as numerous as the sands of the sea—about 800,000 men, between infantry and cavalry. All these armies went down to Egypt to make war against the sons of Jacob, and they camped at Raamses. Joseph and his brothers went out to meet them with all the mighty men of Egypt—about six hundred men—and they fought them in the land of Raamses.

The sons of Jacob fought against the sons of Esau again at that time, in the fiftieth year since the sons of Jacob had gone down to Egypt, which was the thirtieth year that Bela had reigned over the sons of Esau in Seir. God caused Joseph and his brothers to prevail over all the mighty men of Esau and the sons of Kedem, and Joseph crushed the men of the sons of Esau and the sons of Kedem. Many of the men of Esau and the sons of Kedem fell before the sons of Jacob—about 200,000 men—and also Bela, son of Beor, their king, perished in the battle. When the sons of Esau found out that their king had fallen [and died] in battle, they no longer had the strength to go on fighting. But Joseph and his brothers and all Egypt continued to strike out against the men of the house of Esau, and all the men of Esau were terrified of the sons of Jacob and fled before them. Joseph and his brothers and all the Egyptians pursued them about one day's journey and again killed about three hundred of their men, striking them down on the road, and then they turned away from them. Joseph and all his brothers returned to Egypt without losing a single man with the exception of twelve Egyptians. When Joseph returned to Egypt, he ordered Zepho and his men more heavily bound than before, imprisoning them in iron chains and increasing their suffering.

All the men of the sons of Esau and the sons of Kedem returned to their cities in shame, for all the mighty men who were with them had fallen in battle. Since their king had died in that war, the sons of Esau quickly selected a man from among the sons of Kedem named Jobab, son of Zerach, from the land of Batzrah, and crowned him king over them as successor to King Bela. Jobab sat on Bela's throne after him to reign as king, and Jobab reigned in Edom over all the sons of Esau for ten years. The sons of Esau never again went to war against the sons of Jacob from that day on, for the sons of Esau knew the strength of the sons of Jacob [and were very much afraid of them. Nevertheless, from that day on, the sons of Esau hated the sons of Jacob], and that hatred and deep resentment between them has endured down to the present day. Ten years later, Jobab, son of Zerach, king of Edom, died. Then the sons of Esau selected a man whose name was Chusham from the land of Teman and crowned him their king as successor to Jobab. Chusham reigned over the sons of Esau in Edom for twenty years. Joseph, king of Egypt, and his brothers, and all the children of Israel dwelled securely in the land of Egypt in those days, and during all the days of Joseph and his brothers, no problems or misfortune beset them. There were no more wars in the land of Egypt at that time, in the days of Joseph and his brothers.

V. Shemot[201]

These are the names of the sons of Israel who dwelled in Egypt. All the sons of Jacob **came to Egypt with Jacob, each coming with his household:**[202] the children of Leah were Reuben, Simeon, Levi, Judah, Issachar, and Zebulun, and their sister Dinah. The sons of Rachel were Joseph and Benjamin. The sons of Zilpah, Leah's handmaid, were Gad and Asher. The sons of Bilhah, Rachel's handmaid, were Dan and Naphtali.

These are the children that were born to them in the land of Canaan before they went to Egypt with their father Jacob: **Reuben's sons: Enoch, Pallu, Hezron and Carmi. Simeon's sons: Jemuel, Jamin, Ohad, Jachin, Zohar, and Saul the son of a Canaanite woman. Levi's sons: Gershon, Kohath, and Merari,** and their sister Jochebed, who was born to them while they were on their way to Egypt. **Judah's sons: Er, Onan, Shelah, Perez, and Zerah**—but **Er and Onan had died in the land of Canaan; and Perez's sons were Hezron and Hamul. Issachar's sons: Tola, Puvah, Iob, and Shimron. Zebulun's sons: Sered, Elon, and Jahleel.**[203] **Dan's son: Hushim. Naphtali's sons: Jahzeel, Guni, Jezer, and Shillem.**[204] **Gad's sons: Ziphion, Haggi, Shuni, Ezbon, Eri, Arodi, and Areli. Asher's sons: Imnah, Ishvah, Ishvi, and**

Beriah, and their sister Serah. Beriah's sons: Heber and Malchiel.[205] Benjamin's sons: Bela, Becher, Ashbel, Gera, Naaman, Ehi, Rosh, Muppim, Huppim, and Ard.[206] Joseph's sons, who were born to him in Egypt: Manasseh and Ephraim. All the souls that came forth from the loins of Jacob were seventy souls. These were the ones that accompanied their father Jacob to Egypt, to dwell there.

Joseph and all his brothers settled down securely in Egypt, and they ate the good things of the land of Egypt during all the days of Joseph's life. Joseph was in the land of Egypt for ninety three years, and Joseph reigned over all Egypt for eighty years. When Joseph sensed that he was near death, he sent and summoned his brothers and all his father's household, and they came to him together and sat down before him. Joseph told his brothers and all his father's household: "Behold, **I am about to die. God will surely take notice of you and bring you up from this land to the land which He promised on oath to**[207] give to your fathers. When God takes notice of you to take you up [from here] to the land of your fathers, **you shall carry up my bones from here**[208] with you." **Joseph made the sons of Israel** and their descendants after them **swear, saying: "When God has taken notice of you, [you shall carry up my bones from here** with you.]" Then Joseph died that year, which was the seventy-first year since Israel had gone down to Egypt. Joseph was **one hundred and ten years old**[209] when he died in the land of Egypt. All his brothers and all his servants got up and embalmed Joseph, as was customary, and his brothers and all Egypt wept over him for seventy days. They put Joseph in a coffin that was full of spices and all kinds of perfume, and they buried him beside the river Shihor. His sons and all his servants and all his father's household mourned for him for seven days. After Joseph's death, all the Egyptians began to rule over the children of Israel in those days. Pharaoh, king of Egypt, who had succeeded his father, took all the laws of Egypt and conducted the government of Egypt according to his will, and he reigned securely over his people.

[205] Gen. 46:16–17.
[206] Gen. 46:21.
[207] Gen. 50:24.
[208] Gen. 50:25.
[209] Gen. 50:26.

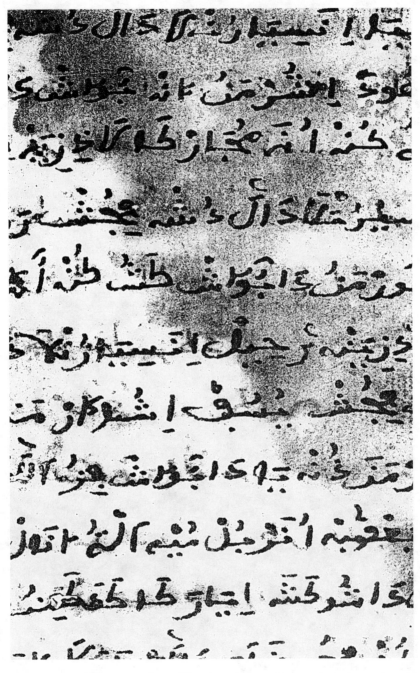

The first page of the manuscript of The Story of Yusuf, Son of Ya'qub. Courtesy of
Biblioteca Nacional, Madrid.

⟫ The Story of Yusuf, Son of Ya'qub (c. 1450–1550)

Anonymous

In the year 711 C.E. an army of Moroccan Berbers, themselves recent converts to Islam, crossed the Straits of Gibraltar and invaded the Iberian peninsula, defeating and killing the Visigothic king Roderic and seizing the capital city of Toledo. Musa, the Arab governor of the Maghreb, then personally crossed over to Spain with a much larger army and completed the conquest of most of the Iberian peninsula by 715. Thus began the Islamic presence in Spain, which would endure for over seven hundred years and irrevocably change the course of Spanish history. Under the terms of the Pact of 'Umar,[1] Christians and Jews—the "People of the Book"—were accorded a somewhat inferior legal status and were required to pay a special tax, but they were allowed to practice their religion without interference. Nevertheless, as time went on, most converted to Islam. It is estimated that by the year 1000 about 75 percent of the population of the Iberian peninsula was Muslim.[2]

At first, Muslim Spain, known as al-Andalus, was subject to the caliphate of Damascus, but after the overthrow of the Umayyad dynasty by the Abbasids, a surviving prince of the Ummayad family named Abd-al-Rahman made his way to Spain, staged a military coup, and established an independent caliphate in Cordova in 756. During the next two hundred and fifty years the caliphate of Cordova would become the most civilized and technologically advanced state in western Europe, and the city of Cordova itself would reach a population perhaps as high as 300,000, making it "far bigger than Paris, which at that time was easily the largest city in Latin Europe."[3]

During the first forty years of the eleventh century, the caliphate broke up into a number of small rival city-states known as *taifa* (Arabic, "party") kingdoms, the most important being Seville, Granada, Badajoz, Toledo, Valencia, and Saragossa. Even as Muslim power began to decline and was increasingly threatened by the Christian kingdoms of the north, the eleventh century saw

---

[1] Compact adopted by 'Umar ibn 'Abd al-Khattab (634–644 C.E.), the second caliph or successor to Muhammad.

[2] See Richard Fletcher, *The Quest for El Cid* (New York: Alfred A. Knopf, 1990), p. 16.

[3] Robert Hillenbrand, " 'The Ornament of the World': Medieval Córdoba as a Cultural Centre," in Salma Khadra Jayyusi, ed., *The Legacy of Muslim Spain* (Leiden: E. J. Brill, 1994), I, 119.

an unprecedented flowering of scholarship, art, architecture, and literature—especially poetry—in the *taifa* kingdoms. At the same time that Muslim Spain was being weakened by division into many small kingdoms, the kingdoms of Christian Spain were becoming more united. Ferdinand I (1035–1065), first king of Castile, subjugated the kingdoms of León and Galicia, thus assuring the future predominance of Castile. Ferdinand's brother Ramiro I (1035–1063), king of Aragon, annexed much of the former kingdom of Navarre.

Unable to defend themselves against Castile, the *taifa* kingdoms of Zaragoza, Toledo, Badajoz, and Seville bought a precarious peace by paying Ferdinand tribute. Unsatisfied with such half-measures, Ferdinand's son Alfonso VI of León (and I of Castile) (1072–1109) conquered the old Visigothic capital of Toledo in 1085, thereafter styling himself "king of the two religions." This event can be said to have turned the tide of the Reconquest, and from then on the days of Muslim domination of Spain were numbered. The *taifa* kings made the grave mistake of seeking help from the fundamentalist Almoravids of Morocco (see introduction to *The Book of Heroes*). Disgusted by the *taifa* kings' willingness to submit to Christian extortion and by their laxity in the practice of Islam, the Almoravids soon dethroned them and managed to reconquer Zaragoza and Valencia and to achieve a short-lived reunification of al-Andalus. By the 1140s Muslim Spain was once again split apart into *taifa* kingdoms. Alfonso VII (1126–1157) of Castile-León conquered Cordova in 1144 and went on to sack Granada and Seville. These traumatic events prompted yet another invasion of Moroccan fundamentalists, that of the Almohads, who temporarily held back the Christian tide and succeeded in reversing most of Alfonso VII's conquests. However, Alfonso VIII's (1158–1214) defeat of the Almohads at the battle of Las Navas de Tolosa in 1212 sounded the death knell for Muslim Spain. As William C. Atkinson has noted,

> the encounter belongs to the category of decisive battles. Al-Andalus never recovered from the blow: to the renewal of its internal discords there would be no further effective answer from Africa. The Christians, picking their objectives at leisure, annexed them thereafter one by one. Between 1229 and 1284 Badajoz fell to León, Cordoba, Murcia, and Seville to Castile, and Valencia to Aragon. . . . Had Castile gone on to reconquer Granada, the reconquest could have been counted at an end, as it was now for Aragon and, within another few years, for Portugal."[4]

As the great historian Henry Charles Lea pointed out almost a century ago, "it has been the fashion to regard the war of the Reconquest, through which Spain

[4] *A History of Spain and Portugal* (Harmondsworth, Middlesex: Penguin Books, 1960), pp. 78-79.

was gradually won back from the Moslems, as a war of religion. . . . In fact, however, the medieval history of Spain shows that in the long struggle there was little antagonism either of race or religion."[5] The Muslim population of the newly conquered territories—known as Mudejars—though forced to pay tribute to their conquerors, were permitted to maintain their language and culture and to practice their religion undisturbed. Even if the Christians had wanted to impose their religion, it would have been virtually impossible because the Muslims in the conquered territories vastly outnumbered their Christian masters, especially in the kingdom of Aragon. Christian noblemen valued their Muslim subjects for their skill and industriousness in agriculture and for their fine craftsmanship. The Catholic Church, however, refused to condone this tolerance and, from the thirteenth century on, exerted increasing pressure on secular authorities to adopt discriminatory measures against Spanish Muslims and segregate them from the Christian populace. For a long time the Muslims escaped persecution because the wrath of the Church was mostly directed against the Jews, whom they considered more dangerous. However, the expulsion of the Jews in 1492 and the conquest of Granada, the last remaining Muslim outpost in Spain, in the same year sealed the doom of the Mudejars.

This fact was not immediately evident because the terms negotiated by Ferdinand and Isabel for the surrender of Granada in the treaty of November 25, 1491, could hardly have been more generous. Indeed, it would be difficult to find a more liberal statute of freedom of religion anywhere in today's world. The treaty granted the conquered Muslims full and equal rights of Spanish citizenship and expressly prohibited all forms of discrimination against them. As soon as the Christians felt secure in their rule over Granada, however, it quickly became clear that the treaty was not worth the paper it was written on.

The historians Antonio Domínguez Ortiz and Bernard Vincent have singled out three decisive events in the subsequent history of the Spanish Muslims: "1500–1502, conversion of the Castilian Mudejars; 1568–70, uprising of the Moriscos[6] of Granada; and 1609–1614, general expulsion."[7] Sporadic attempts to force the Muslims of the former kingdom of Granada to accept Christianity began almost immediately and were met by armed rebellions in many different villages. These rebellions were quickly subdued and the defeated Muslims were forced to convert en masse. These circumstances offered a pretext for a decree of February 12, 1502, requiring all Muslims residing in the kingdom of Castile

---

[5] *The Moriscos of Spain: Their Conversion and Expulsion* (New York: Haskell House Publishers, 1968 [first published 1901]), p. 1.

[6] "Morisco" was originally a pejorative term—"little Moors, or Moor boys"—applied to Muslims who accepted Christianity.

[7] *Historia de los moriscos: Vida y tragedia de una minoría* (Madrid: Alianza Editorial, 1989), p. 17.

to accept Christianity or leave the country. From then on the Mudejars were transformed into Moriscos. Muslim books were burned and ritual slaughter of animals was banned, but the Moriscos were allowed to retain their distinctive style of dress and their bath houses. These measures did not result in the desired assimilation of the Moriscos, so in 1526 a new series of draconian injunctions sought to eliminate all vestiges of a separate culture among the Moriscos. They forbade the use of the Arabic language, the practice of circumcision, and the wearing of distinctively "Moorish" clothing or jewelry, and established a tribunal of the Inquisition in Granada to enforce these statutes. In 1525 the Mudejars of the kingdom of Aragon were likewise ordered to convert and were given a grace period of ten years during which they could continue to use the Arabic language, wear their traditional clothing, and maintain separate cemeteries. By the end of 1526, no Muslims officially remained in Spain. Missionary campaigns were carried out throughout the peninsula to try to achieve a sincere conversion and assimilation of the Moriscos, but these efforts were often subverted by the continued hostility of the "Old Christian" masses, who treated the Moriscos with contempt and refused to accept them as fellow Christians.

After about 1550 the increasing threat posed by the Ottoman empire made many Spaniards view the Moriscos as enemy aliens. Many Moriscos indeed hoped that the Turks would deliver them from their Catholic oppressors. A provincial synod held in Granada in 1565 adopted further drastic measures, prohibiting all Moorish customs, providing for regular inspection of Morisco homes, and requiring that the sons of prominent Morisco families be sent to live in Old Castile, at their parents' expense, to acquire a Christian lifestyle. In 1566 all Arabic books were banned.

These increasingly oppressive measures led in late 1568 to a rebellion among the Moriscos in the Alpujarras mountain range, the remote and sparsely inhabited southern face of the Sierra Nevada. Most of the Moriscos of rural Granada soon joined the rebellion, and during the course of the next two years, using techniques of guerrilla warfare, they spread terror throughout the kingdom of Granada. Heavy losses were sustained on both sides. King Philip II took extraordinary measures to quash the rebellion—even naming his own half-brother, Don Juan of Austria, commander of the government troops—out of fear that the Moriscos in the rest of the country might join in, or that the Moroccans, Algerians, and/or Turks might use the rebellion as a pretext for a full-scale war against Spain. Between 1570 and 1574 all the remaining Moriscos of Granada—some 80,000 people—were deported to Castile, eastern Andalusia, and Estremadura. It is estimated that between 20 and 30 percent of those deported died on the way.[8] By the spring of 1571, the rebellion had been defini-tively put down by the assassination of its leader, Aben Abu, but much of Granada was left in ruins.

After 1570 most of the Morisco population was concentrated in the king-dom of Aragon. The rebellion of 1568–1570 had so traumatized the Christian population that further attempts to assimilate the Moriscos were all but aban-doned. Henceforward the Christian strategy was to disperse, segregate, and dis-arm these "enemy aliens" and to keep them under strict surveillance. With in-creasing frequency even more drastic measures—such as separating all children of Moriscos from their parents, sentencing all Morisco men from the ages of eighteen to forty to serve as galley slaves, or castrating Moriscos—were con-sidered. Gradually, a consensus began to form that the only final solution to the "Morisco problem" was to expel all of them from Spain. This measure was at last adopted by King Philip III, and between 1609 and 1614 approximately 300,000 Moriscos were forced to leave their homeland.

The text I have called *The Story of Yusuf, Son of Ya'qub* has come down to us in a single manuscript, codex number 5292 in the Biblioteca Nacional, Madrid. According to Ursula Klenk, it is evident that the text was originally written in the Aragonese dialect, although the language of the surviving ver-sion has been strongly Castilianized. She argues that the phonetics of the text clearly date it, in its present form, to the sixteenth century.[9] The text is badly flawed, containing garbled passages and obvious omissions. The episode when Yusuf meets an Arab who takes news of him to his father is told twice, first shortly after the king's purchase of Yusuf and again during his imprisonment, suggesting that the text we possess is a composite of at least two earlier textual traditions. The original may therefore antedate the surviving manuscript by as much as a century. By the mid-thirteenth century most of the Mudejars of Castile and Aragon were Romance speakers[10] and had forgotten most of their Arabic, although those of Aragon maintained contact with the community of Valencia, where knowledge of Arabic endured much longer.

The *Story of Yusuf* is one of the most important examples of the type of lit-erature known in Spanish as *aljamiado* (from the Arabic *al-'ajamiyya*, foreign, barbarous [language]), that is, Spanish texts written in Arabic or Hebrew char-acters. In fact the earliest surviving literary texts in Spanish—the poems called *kharjas*, the oldest of which date from the tenth or eleventh century—are of

---

[8] *Historia de los moriscos*, p. 52.

[9] *La Leyenda de Yusuf: Ein Aljamiadotext* (Tübingen: Max Niemeyer Verlag, 1972), p. ix.

[10] See L. P. Harvey, *Islamic Spain, 1250–1500* (Chicago: Univ. of Chicago Press, 1990), p. 15.

this type. Long after literate Moriscos had lost almost all knowledge of the Arabic language, they clung to the use of the Arabic alphabet as a means of retaining their distinctive cultural identity. The *Story of Yusuf* is also bilingual. Approximately 125 Arabic words or phrases, aside from proper names, occur in the text, and some of them are repeated constantly. The vast majority of the Arabic vocabulary items in the text are ritual formulas (peace be upon him, be He exalted, etc.) or represent the specialized religious vocabulary of Islam (blessing, Paradise, prophecy, etc.). There is also, however, a whole constellation of words referring to luxury items (brocade, silk, ambergris, ruby, etc.). Arabic verb stems are regularly conjugated as if they were Spanish (e.g., *asajdó*, "he prostrated himself").

Not long after the death of Muhammad in 632 C.E., legends began to circulate among Muslims concerning the twenty six prophets before Muhammad who are mentioned by name in the Qur'an. Some of the Muslims sought further information about the Hebrew prophets from Jewish converts to Islam, such as Ka'b al-Aḥbar (d. c. 652), a learned Jewish convert from the Yemen, and hence many of these early legends derive from midrashim. Ka'b[11] himself is a figure wrapped in legend. Though very little accurate information exists about his life, he "is considered to have possessed a profound knowledge of the Bible and southern Arabian tradition, as well as a personal wisdom attested by the numerous statements attributed to him without argument because he inspired so much confidence."[12] Ka'b is constantly cited as *the* authority for most of the legends recounted in the *Story of Yusuf*. Because these legends of the prophets circulated orally among both Jews and Muslims long before they were written down (at least in texts that have survived), in many cases it is impossible to determine whether particular legends are of Jewish or Muslim origin.

A whole class of storytellers or street-preachers, known as *quṣṣas* (Arabic, "narrators") soon developed in the Muslim world. It was not until the tenth century, however, that this literary genre, known as *Qiṣas al-anbiya'* (*Tales of the Prophets*) found its way into learned literature. As W. M. Thackston, Jr., has noted, "the oldest extant work of this type is the *Tarikh al-rusul wa'l-muluk* (*Chronicle of Apostles and Kings*) of Muhammad ibn Jarir al-Tabari (839–923) and is a running chronology of all the ancient nations, with their political and prophetic history given in straight chronological order along with variant ac-

---

[11] His name may originally have been Akiba, and *al-aḥbar* appears to be an Arabic version of the Hebrew title *ḥaber*, a scholarly rank immediately below that of rabbi among the Jews of Babylonia.

[12] M. Schmitz, "Ka'b al-Aḥbar," *The Encyclopaedia of Islam* (Leiden: E. J. Brill, 1978), IV, 316-17.

counts."[13] There is an excellent recent translation of the section of al-Tabari's
Chronicle dealing with the prophets.[14] It contains many of the same stories that
occur in the *Story of Yusuf*, but they are loosely strung together as a series of
separate anecdotes or *hadith* (Arabic, "traditions") rather than a continuous
narrative. The stories are much more succinctly told than in the *Story of Yusuf*,
lacking much of the detail and psychological insight that makes the latter work
so admirable, and in each case al-Tabari introduces the story by citing the
whole *isnad*, the "chain of transmission" that guarantees a story's authenticity,
by tracing it back to the time of Muhammad and his earliest companions. This,
and the fact that al-Tabari often cites different versions of the same story and
attempts to determine which is the more reliable, make his version much more
dry and scholarly than the *Story of Yusuf*.

The first Muslim work entirely devoted to the legends of the prophets was
Abu Ishaq Ahmad ibn Muhammad al-Tha'labi's (d. 1036) *'Arais al-majalis:
Qisas al-anbiya' (Brides of the Sessions: Tales of the Prophets)*. Al-Tha'labi's
work is closer to the *Story of Yusuf* in that it includes much more detail. However, "although thorough, [it] is a choppy scholastic compilation that neither
was designed for nor lends itself to smooth, enjoyable reading or listening.
One assumes that it was used as a sort of reference manual for preachers."[15]
The Arabic account that is closest to the *Story of Yusuf* is al-Kisa'i's *Qisas al-
anbiya'*, thought to have been written not long before 1200. Like the *Story of
Yusuf*, al-Kisa'i's text consists entirely of a narrative expansion of the story as
told in the Qur'an and cites few authorities other than Ka'b al-Ahbar and another legendary early commentator on the Qur'an, 'Abdullah ibn 'Abbas
(d. 687). In his edition of al-Kisa'i, Thackston observes that "if not the
scholar that was Tha'labi, Kisa'i was certainly a master storyteller, and his
sense of the dramatic value in ending a narrative section at precisely the right
moment to heighten an important point in the mind of the listener is exhib-
ited throughout."[16] Our *Story of Yusuf* probably originated as a translation or
paraphrase of al-Kisa'i's popular work, which it parallels very closely. Since
manuscripts of al-Kisa'i vary considerably in content and length and the
edition used by Thackston for his English translation is not the most
complete, it is impossible to determine how much original material, or
material taken from other sources, was added by the Spanish editor/translator
or later copyists of the manuscript.

---

[13] *The Tales of the Prophets of al-Kisa'i* (Boston: Twayne Publishers, 1978), p. xvi.
[14] *The History of al-Tabari: Prophets and Patriarchs*, trans. William M. Brinner
(Albany: State Univ. of New York Press, 1987).
[15] Thackston, *Tales of the Prophets*, p. xvi.
[16] Ibid., p. xx.

As a narrative expansion of the sacred text, the *Story of Yusuf* is similar in form to the *Sefer ha-Yashar*. Its tone, however, could hardly be more different. By comparison with the unbridled fantasy of *Yusuf*, *Yashar* seems like a model of austere realism. Like the books of chivalry that captured the Spanish popular imagination at the beginning of the sixteenth century and soon became the rage throughout western Europe, *Yusuf* belongs to the genre known as romance. As Northrop Frye has observed, "the romance is the nearest of all literary forms to the wish-fulfilment dream."[17] Frye goes on to point out that "the perennially childlike quality of romance is marked by its extraordinarily persistent nostalgia, its search for some kind of imaginative golden age in time or space." It is easy to see why the Moriscos of fifteenth- or sixteenth-century Spain would have looked back nostalgically to an earlier, happier age and would have found comfort in the escapist fantasy embodied in the *Story of Yusuf*. The story offered them hope and comfort in a very dark time, for its underlying message is the same as the one enunciated near the end of the Surah Yusuf in the Qur'an: "When the apostles despaired and thought they were made false promises, Our help arrived, and We delivered whom We pleased; but never will Our punishment be averted from the sinners."[18] Frye has noted that romance typically has three main stages: "the stage of the perilous journey and the preliminary minor adventures; the crucial struggle, usually some kind of battle in which either the hero or his foe, or both, must die; and the exaltation of the hero. We may call these stages respectively, using Greek terms, the *agon* or conflict, the *pathos* or death struggle, and the *anagnorisis* or discovery, the recognition of the hero."[19] Both the *agon* and the *pathos* stages in *Yusuf* are doubled, since his antagonists are both his brothers and the temptress Zalikha. Both his sale into slavery and exile and his temptation and imprisonment can by considered symbolic death experiences; Yusuf's father in fact mourns him as dead for years. The climactic *pathos* stage, however, occurs in the life-threatening scene in which he must oppose his brothers' menace with superhuman wisdom and might. The *anagnorisis* stage is of course Yusuf's reunion with his father. A similar threefold structure can be found in the life of Zalikha as recounted in *Yusuf*. In *Yusuf* Zalikha becomes much more than just a character foil for the virtuous Yusuf; her own spiritual odyssey is one of the story's major themes.

Frye explains that

> the central form of quest-romance is the dragon-killing theme exemplified in the stories of St. George and Perseus. . . . A land ruled

[17] *Anatomy of Criticism* (Princeton: Princeton Univ. Press, 1973), p. 186.
[18] 12:110. Trans. Ahmed Ali (Princeton: Princeton Univ. Press, 1988), pp. 209-10.
[19] *Anatomy of Criticism*, p. 187.

by a helpless old king is laid waste by a sea-monster, to whom one young person after another is offered to be devoured, until the lot falls on the king's daughter: at that point the hero arrives, kills the dragon, marries the daughter, and succeeds to the kingdom. . . . The ritual analogies of the myth suggest that the monster *is* the sterility of the land itself, and that the sterility of the land is present in the age and impotence of the king.[20]

Here too the similarities to *Yusuf* are clear. The Messiah figure Yusuf, representing a new people—in this case the Muslims[21]—delivers the ancient kingdom of Egypt from famine. In *Yusuf* he marries the king's widow, once she has been purged of idolatry, and brings renewed fertility to the land, symbolized by the twelve children she bears him.

Francisco Guillén Robles has written of the Morisco legends that

one observes in them a strange mixture of beauties and defects, in spite of which the overall effect is pleasing, as in the case of the Morisco rugs that are still being woven in Rabat, of bizarre designs and color combinations. One observes in them an odd amalgam of simplicity and cleverness, of naïveté and slyness, of melancholy and passion, of materialism and idealism, of originality and imitation— all of which is a delight to the mind. What prevails in them above all is excessive credulity—the marvelous carried to outrageous extremes, the supernatural dominating everything, the *Deus ex machina* perennially at work.[22]

This is certainly an accurate description of the *Story of Yusuf*, yet it would be a mistake to overemphasize the uniqueness of Morisco literature. In fact the same qualities outlined by Guillén Robles are equally characteristic of the romances of chivalry, which were the preferred reading of the Christian Spanish public of the period. As in the case of *Yusuf*, the allure of those romances derives principally from a formula skillfully alternating violence and sensuality in a potentially endless series of adventures. Chandler and Schwartz have noted that some have explained the unprecedented popularity of the romances of chivalry as "due to an escapist urge in the Spanish people, and others [have ar-

---

[20] *Anatomy of Criticism*, p. 189.

[21] The reader may find it odd that the Jew Yusuf is portrayed in the story as a Muslim. However, according to Muslim belief, Islam did not begin with the coming of the prophet Muhammad. Rather, Muslims—the prophets and those who heeded their admonitions and submitted to Allah—have existed since the first age of the world.

[22] *Leyendas de José, hijo de Jacob, y de Alejandro Magno* (Saragossa: Imprenta del Hospicio Provincial, 1888), p. xiii.

gued] that it was due to the nation's insatiable thirst for adventure." They go on to observe that "the chivalric novels are filled with absurdities, recitals of magic, enchantments, the hero's inevitable victory, and improbable incidents which have little appeal to our sophisticated age. Yet at the same time, not all in them was bad, for they taught modesty, bravery, sacrifice, constancy in love, protection of the weak, and fair play at a time when these chivalric ideals were threatened with extinction through the rise of the middle class and the disappearance of the knight on horseback in warfare."[23] Therefore perhaps the best way to understand the *Story of Yusuf* is to view it as a Morisco romance of chivalry in which that originally Christian literary genre is adapted to embody the ideals of Islam. If the Joseph of *Yashar* is the Jewish Cid, Yusuf is the Morisco Amadís.

My translation is based on Ursula Klenk's transcription and edition of the manuscript. I have also consulted Francisco Guillén Robles's edition in modernized Spanish. I have divided the text into chapters in order to make it more manageable. For the passages from the Qur'an embedded in the text, I have used Muhammad Marmaduke Pickthall's translation, *The Meaning of the Glorious Qur'an* (New York: Muslim World League, 1977), emending it when necessary to fit the Spanish text's interpretation.

(The first page of the manuscript is missing)

I. Yusuf's Birth

. . . of his people whose name was Rakhiya, and of her were born unto him two sons, Yahuda and his brother. After her he married a woman named Saduqa, and of her were born unto him two sons, Raubil and his brother. Then he married a woman they called Rahil, and of her were born unto him two sons, Yusuf and his brother Yamin, and their sister Dunya.

II. The Tree and the Rods

After that Allah caused a very tall tree to sprout for Ya'qub in the garden of his house. And it came to pass that every time a son was born unto him, Allah, *be He exalted*,[24] brought forth a rod on that tree. And as the boy grew into a young man, the rod grew; and when he came of age, Ya'qub cut off the

---

[23] Richard E. Chandler and Kessel Schwartz, *A New History of Spanish Literature* (Baton Rouge: Louisiana State Univ. Press, 1961), pp. 166-67.

[24] Words printed in italics are in Arabic in the original text.

rod and gave it to him. And twelve male children were born unto him, and Allah, *glorified and exalted be He*, brought forth from that tree eleven rods, and there was a rod for every one of the sons. And when Yusuf, *peace be upon him*, was born, the earth shone with his comeliness and beauty and the vale of Kin'an was bright, and the rivers lit up, and the trees turned greener with the brightness of Yusuf, *peace be upon him*, and all the beasts rejoiced because of his arrival and his brightness, and the *angels* in their ranks rejoiced and spread their wings, and the mountains shone brightly at the birth of Yusuf, *peace be upon him*.

And Ka'b al-Aḥbar said: and the boy grew and his brightness increased until his brothers and his father and mother could not look upon him on account of the strength of the rays of his brightness and of his comeliness. And those who passed by would say: "Oh, what an advantage Allah, *be He exalted*, gave this youth over his brothers in comeliness and beauty!"

When Yusuf was grown, he said unto his father: "*Oh prophet of Allah*, there is not one of my brothers that doesn't have a rod. Pray then to Allah that He may favor me with a rod from a tree of *Paradise*, that with it I be praised above my brothers." Ka'b said: and Ya'qub lifted up his hands to *heaven* and prayed with secret prayers, and said: "Lord, I beg You, *oh* Lord, that You give Yusuf a rod that he be praised with it above his brothers." Ka'b said: Ya'qub had not finished praying when Jibril, *peace be upon him*, descended with a rod from *Paradise* of green emerald and said: "*Peace be* upon you, *oh* Ya'qub. Allah, noble is His praise, sends you *greetings* and says for you to give this rod to your son Yusuf." And Ya'qub took the rod and said: "*Oh Yusuf*, take this rod and be praised with it above your brothers when they praise themselves above you." He [Ka'b] said: and Yusuf took it and went out with his brothers and accompanied them to keep watch over the cattle. And at that time they loved him with a strong love.

III. Yusuf's Dreams

Ka'b said: One day Yusuf sat down with his brothers and with the rod in his hand. And drowsiness overcame him, and he fell asleep. And he saw in his sleep a dream, and he awoke frightened and terrified. And he [Ka'b] said: and his brothers hugged him to their breasts and kissed him between his eyes and said unto him: "*Oh* beloved, what has happened to you, and what is it that has frightened you?" He said unto them: "*Oh* my brothers, I have seen in my sleep what the sleeper saw in his sleep. I have seen this my rod taken from my hand. Then it was favored, and it sprouted, and it got big, and its branches grew, and it brought forth fruit of all the fruits that Allah, *be He exalted*, cre-

ated. And it was as if Ya'qub and Musa and 'Isa[25] and Muhammad, *Allah's peace be upon them,* and all the *prophets* ate of its fruit, and as if all the rods of my brothers were taken and planted around mine, and they did not sprout nor did they put forth roots, and as if a wind blew from *the sea* and uprooted them from their roots."

Ka'b al-Aḥbar said: The moment when Yusuf's brothers heard that, they said: "Oh son of Rakhila, now you have seen wonders, and we doubt not that you will surpass us, for you are our lord, and we your slaves." And after that they envied him and hated him. And they made known unto Ya'qub his saying and his dream. And Ya'qub never again considered him safe with them after he dreamed that Yusuf was on top of a mountain, and it was as if ten wolves were going toward him, wanting to kill him. The earth broke asunder, and Yusuf went into it and did not come back out until three days had passed. When Ya'qub saw that, he wept, wept mightily out of pity for him. And he made Yusuf sleep at his side.

After Yusuf saw that dream that Allah mentioned in His honored Qur'an, **Yusuf said to his father: "I have seen eleven stars and the sun and the moon all *bowing down* to me."**[26] When Yusuf saw this dream of his, he awoke from his sleep frightened and terrified. And Yusuf was sleeping at his father's side, and his father hugged him to his breast and kissed him between his eyes and said to him: "Oh beloved of Allah, what is it that you have seen in your sleep?" He said: "Oh father, I have seen a dream that has frightened me." He said: "Oh son, may what you have seen be for good." He said: "I saw the gates of heaven open, and a great brightness shone from them, so that the moon shone with that brightness and the stars twinkled, and the mountains were lit up, and the seas flowed and their waves increased and the fish *praised [Allah].*[27] And I was wearing my *cape* and I took the keys of the earth in my hands. And as I was doing this, I saw eleven stars and the sun and the moon, I saw them *bowing down* to me, and their brightness was shining. And the morning star, and al-Mizan, and al-Zahara, and al-Mushtar, and al-Asunbul, and A'utharid, and al-Farqadan, and al-Mayzan, and al-Marih,[28] and the sun and the moon, I saw them *bowing down* to me." He said: When Ya'qub heard his dream, he interpreted it himself and said: "This son of mine is destined for greatness." After that he said just as Allah, *be He exalted,* said in His honored Qur'an: **"Oh son!**

---

[25] Musa=Moses; 'Isa=Jesus.

[26] The passage in bold type is a translation of Qur'an 12:4.

[27] After this phrase in her critical edition, Ursula Klenk transcribes: "kon las espesiyas de sus algos," commenting in a footnote that the last word could also be read "alagos," and that in either case the meaning is not clear. Guillén Robles simply omits the whole phrase.

[28] Names of stars.

Tell not your dream to your brothers, for they will plot against you. For Satan is a declared enemy of man."[29]

IV. Yusuf's Brothers Plot to Kill Him

Ka'b al-Aḥbar said: and Ya'qub's wife heard what Yusuf said to his father. And he said to her: "Conceal, *oh wife*, what he has said. See that you don't let my sons know." She said: "It pleases me, *oh Ya'qub, prophet of Allah*." He said: When Yusuf's brothers came from their cattle, she informed them about Yusuf's dream. She said unto them: "*Oh sons of Ya'qub*, I'll not interpret this dream, but I will say unto you: what can the sun mean but myself, and the moon your father, and the stars you?" When they heard that, their hair stood straight up, and their veins swelled, and they felt rage and a great hatred for Yusuf. They said: "*Oh Yusuf, son of Rahil*, we doubt not that you will lord it over us and say: 'I am your lord, and you are my servants, and I am the greatest among you.' " He [Ka'b] said: and they spoke of slaying him, as Allah said in His honored Qur'an: **"Kill Yusuf or cast him to some (other) land, and your father's face will look favorably upon you, and you will be his people."**[30]

Yahuda, who was the eldest of them in days, said: "Slay not Yusuf. Throw him inside the cistern that a passing caravan may find him if you do it." Raubil said unto them: "Our father will not entrust Yusuf to us, but let us go and play before Yusuf, and when he sees our games, he will long to play with us." And they came to Yusuf, and they found him *praising* Allah, *be He exalted*, and sanctifying Him. And they pretended to play before him, and they laughed with one another. When they had played, Yusuf came to them and said: "*Oh my brothers*, do you play like that in the sheep-folds and pastures?" They said unto him: "Yes, and if you, Yusuf, come unto us while we are playing, you will long to play with us." He said: "*Oh brothers*, when it is morning, *Allah willing*, I will go with you." And he said unto them: "*Oh my brothers*, let us go unto our father Ya'qub and ask him, peradventure he will send me with you." And they came unto their father Ya'qub, and they all stood in *a row* before him and all *greeted* him. And Ya'qub said unto them: "*Oh sons*, and what is your business, and what is your request? They said unto him just as Allah, *be He exalted*, says that they said: " '**Oh father, send Yusuf with us, and we will be his teachers. Send him with us tomorrow, and he will tend the cattle with us and play with us. And we will be his guardians.' He said: 'It saddens me that you should go away with him. And I am afraid that the**

[29] Qur'an 12:5.
[30] Qur'an 12:9.

wolf will eat him, while you are heedless of him.' They said: 'And how will the wolf eat him when we are so strong a band? If so, we should already have perished.' "[31]

He [Ka'b] said: when they heard his words, they said unto him: "*Oh our father, Yusuf is like one of us, and he has the advantage over us because of your great love for him and because he is so small.*" He [Ka'b] said: then he pressed Yusuf to his breast and kissed him between the eyes, and said: "*Oh son, commend yourself to Allah.*" Then he withdrew from them and watched them until they were out of sight.

As soon as Ya'qub was out of sight, they ran ahead of Yusuf until they tired him out. And Yusuf trailed behind them, now falling, now getting back up. Then Shama'un took his vessels of water, and he emptied them all out onto the sand, and Yusuf realized that he was lost. Then they took counsel among themselves about what they would do. When Yusuf saw them take counsel, he wept and realized that he was going to die. Then he said: "*Oh brothers, how quickly you have forgotten that oath my father Ya'qub required of you, when he admonished you concerning me and said: 'If Yusuf be hungry, give him to eat; if he be thirsty, give him to drink; if he be tired, give him rest.' Oh my brothers, I am tired, give me rest, and sit with me till I be rested. Oh brothers, I am hungry, give me to eat. Oh my brothers, I am thirsty, give me to drink.*" They said unto him: "*Oh son of Rahil, you of the lying dreams, we have brought you here to kill you and to sever your head from your body.*" He said unto them: "*Oh brothers, do not do such a thing. Fear Allah, be He exalted, and have pity on the grey head of your father Ya'qub. Oh my brothers, why do you slay me?*" They said unto him: "Because of your lying dreams." Yusuf said unto them: "*By the authority of the grey head of Ibrahim, our grandfather, I have not lied in what I have said.*" But they accepted not his saying, and he complained unto them of hunger and of thirst. And they took the bread Yusuf had given them and gave it to their dogs and said: "*We fast to thank Allah, be He exalted, for having given us dominion over you, oh lying son of Rahil.*" When Yusuf was very thirsty, he said unto them: "*Oh my brothers, give me a drink of water to drink before you kill me, lest I die thirsty.*" They said unto him: "We have no water."

And they turned aside to consider with what sort of death they would kill him. And as they did so, behold, a bird flew by, saying: "*Oh sons of Ya'qub, how quickly have you forgotten your oath and your promise. Are you not ashamed before Allah, glorified and exalted be He?*" But they heeded not its words, which only increased their rage and enmity. Ka'b al-Aḥbar said: then they went with him to a mountain of the mountains of Kin'an, and they said: "Let us kill Yusuf

---

[31] Qur'an 12:11–14.

on this mountain." And the mountain cried unto them: "*Oh sons of Ya'qub, I conjure you by Allah the Great, and by the authority of your grandfather Ibrahim, the friend of Allah, that you slay not Yusuf upon me, for it would be the same as slaying a prophet,* for Allah, *be He exalted,* would hold you responsible." He [Ka'b] said: "And they listened not to his words." Behold, a brown beast said unto them: "*Oh sons of Ya'qub, by Allah, if you slay Yusuf, even we beasts will be enraged with you.*" And they heeded not his saying.

Ka'b said: then they came to their sheep-folds, and they tied Yusuf's hands behind him, and they struck him in the face, and he conjured them by Allah, *glorified and exalted be He,* and said unto them: "*Oh my brothers, take me back to old Ya'qub, and I swear by the authority of my grandfather Ibrahim, the friend [of Allah], that I will not let Ya'qub know any of the things you have done unto me.*" They said unto him: "*Are you still dreaming your lying dreams?*" Yusuf said: "*Oh my brothers, take me back to old Ya'qub, and I will be your servant, and I will pray for you after every prescribed prayer as long as I live. Oh my brothers, do not kill me, for I am frightened of you. If you kill me, may I stand tomorrow before Allah, be He exalted,* and say unto Him: '*Oh Lord, avenge me upon them, for they killed me.*' *Therefore, fear Allah, oh my brothers, and slay me not. Oh sons of Ya'qub, be mindful of the place of the pure and the chosen, Ibrahim and Isma'il and Ishaq and Ya'qub, those who were sent and shed no blood. Let not my blood make you infidels, for it will be held up as an example to those who went before you, and the nations that will come after you. Oh my brothers, slay me not, for if you kill me, you will be bandits. Take pity upon me because of the shortness of my days. Slay me not, fear Allah, and take me back to old Ya'qub.*"

V. Yahuda Intervenes

And they heeded not his words. Ka'b al-Ahbar said that at that moment Shama'un lifted up his hand and struck him in the face and said: "*What are we waiting for?*" He [Ka'b] said: and they set upon him and stoned him with stones. And he began to conjure them by Allah, *be He exalted,* but it availed him nothing. Then Yahuda, the eldest among them, attacked him. And he said: "*Oh my brother Yahuda, are you not the eldest of my brothers? And are you not the son of my maternal aunt, the closest of them to me? Oh my brother Yahuda, when they kill me, you will be the one accused and held responsible on the Day of Judgment.*" Ka'b al-Ahbar said: Yahuda took pity upon him and said unto them: "*By the authority of the grey head of Ibrahim, if you kill him, I will kill many men of you, and I will be your enemy so long as I shall live, and I will tell Ya'qub what you have done to Yusuf. Fear Allah, and slay him not, for if you* kill him, you will bear the shame until the Day of Judgment, and before those of the *nations* that come after you, and they will say that the *prophets* of the *Children of Israel*, the sons of Ya'qub, killed their brother. If there be any doubt in your mind, just hurt him to the point that he will never again lie about his dream, and return him to old Ya'qub."

VI. Yusuf in the Cistern

When they saw that Yahuda had grown angry with them, they were frightened and afraid of him. They surrounded him and said unto him: "Oh Yahuda, advise us with your advice, for you are the eldest of us all." He said unto them: "*Oh* my brothers, if you do as I say, it will be better for you than killing your brother, for you would be killing a soul upon which Allah, *be He exalted*, already *took pity*." They said unto him: "What, then, shall we do?" Yahuda said: "Throw him into the cistern so that a caravan may find him, and I give you my oath to Allah that I will not let your father Ya'qub know what you have done unto Yusuf." They said unto him: "*Oh* Yahuda, give us the lad." He said: "I will not give him to you until you are all of one mind about this." And they all agreed to throw him into the cistern, and they took him and stripped him naked as when his mother bore him. And Yusuf reached for the grass of the earth to cover his shame with it or with his hand until they tied his hands behind his back with ropes. And they tied a rope around his neck so that he feared he was going to die. Then they lowered him into the cistern.

And the cistern was at a crossroads, and it was solitary, very dark, and its water was salty and murky; and it was the cistern dug by Sam, son of Nuh,[32] *peace be upon him*. And it was called the Cistern of Sadness. And they lowered him into the cistern, and he held tightly onto one after another of them, and said unto them: "Do not do this, *oh* my brothers. Do not leave me here! Kill me, for death is better than leaving me in this cistern." But they listened not unto his words, and they lowered him, and as he was suspended, before he reached the water, they let go of the rope, hoping that he would fall upon a boulder in the cistern and die, and they would be rid of him. He [Ka'b] said: Allah, *be He exalted*, brought a white boulder, made soft for him, to the face of the water, and ordered it to rise up under Yusuf's feet. And the boulder rose up till it reached Yusuf's feet. Then, with the permission of Allah, *be He exalted*, he returned with it to its place.

---

[32] That is, Shem, son of Noah.

Then his brothers came unto him and stoned him with stones, and Yahuda defended him and said unto them: "*Oh* brothers, where is that oath and promise you gave me and offered me, that you would not slay him?" They said unto him: "Then let us speak with him." He said unto them: "Speak to him, and stone him not." They said: "It pleases us." And Shama'un looked down into the well and said to him: "*Oh* Yusuf, praise be to Allah, who has permitted us to have mastery over your wicked dreams. *Oh* Yusuf, this is the reward of liars." Yusuf said from the bottom of the cistern: "As for what you have said regarding the praise due to Allah, *oh* Shama'un, you speak truth, for one must thank Allah in all circumstances. I thank Allah and multiply my thanks and praise to Him, and I beg Him for patience, for Allah, *be He exalted,* has promised the patient a very great reward and much good. Allah, *be He exalted,* said in His honored Qur'an: '**Verily the patient will be paid their wages without stint.**' "[33]

Then Shama'un stepped aside, and Raubil came and said unto him: "Oh Yusuf, thus is affronted the man who lies before Allah, *be He exalted,* and your infamy, *oh* Yusuf, is very great." Yusuf said unto him: "Allah, *blessed and exalted be He,* when He loves His servant, hastens to send him a *misfortune* and gives him patience to endure it and gives him good fortune. And, by Allah, I have never lied about my dream." Then Raubil stepped aside, and his brother Lawiya came and said: "*Oh* Yusuf, you loved to have the advantage and sway over us, and you claimed to have seen eleven stars and the sun and the moon *bowing down* to you. What, then, did you desire, *oh* Yusuf, but to claim what the haughty and those *Pharaohs* who went before claimed? And you have not the slightest basis for such pride." Yusuf said unto him: "I swear by Allah that if you were merciful, you would have taken pity on me. Nonetheless, I am content with His will and His portion, and I will suffer His command on account of what He has promised the patient."

Then Lawiya stood aside, and Yahuda came and looked down upon Yusuf, and his tears fell abundantly into the cistern upon Yusuf. And he knew that Yahuda wept for him, and he cried out unto him, and said to him: "Oh brother, be not sad nor frightened, for I am afraid that *misfortune* will befall you later with hunger and strong fear. *Oh* my brother, *oh* Yahuda, make not known unto old Ya'qub what my brothers have done to me, for I will pray to Allah concerning them, and they will be lost. *Oh* brother, *oh* Yahuda, I beseech you by Allah that whenever you see an emaciated wretch, you remember me and weep for me. *Oh* brother Yahuda, whenever you see brothers joined together, remember me and weep for me. *Oh* brother, *oh* Yahuda, whenever you hear someone beg for help and be refused help, remember me and weep for me. *Oh*

---

[33] Qur'an 39:10.

brother Yahuda, whenever you see someone beg for food and be denied food, remember me and weep for me. *Oh* brother, *oh* Yahuda, whenever you see a thirsty man beg for drink and be refused it, remember me and weep for me. *Oh* brother Yahuda, if you should pass the grave of my mother Rahil, *greet* her for me. *Oh* brother, *oh* Yahuda, give my *greetings* to my father, old Ya'qub, and my brother, Yamin, and kiss him between his eyes, and tell him how he is bereft and alone. *Oh* brother Yahuda, give my sister Dunya my *greetings*. *Oh* brother Yahuda, I fear that death will track me down in this cistern and I will have no *shroud* to die in. I will die alone, wretched. As for my father Ya'qub, after me he will suffer a long sadness."

He [Ka'b] said: And Yahuda wept then until he feared that he would fall into the cistern. And when his brothers heard what Yusuf said, they came to him and said unto him: "Oh Yahuda, arise from the top of the cistern and leave this lad, for he is but a little child, and when no one speaks to him, he will be quiet and rest." And they wanted to stone him with stones. Yahuda said unto them: "Where is that oath you swore unto me?" Then they went away and left him in the cistern alone, with no one to console him but Allah, *glorified and exalted be He.*

VII. The Brothers Return to Ya'qub

Then they went and took one of the cattle and beheaded it and wiped Yusuf's shirt with the blood, and they roasted its flesh and ate it. Then they went unto Ya'qub, and he was sitting at the crossroads awaiting the coming of Yusuf. When they saw their father and drew near unto him, they all cried out together as if it were the cry of a single man, and Ya'qub heard their cries and the raising of their voices, and there were six *miles* between them and Ya'qub. And Ya'qub knew that a *misfortune* had befallen them, and he grew sad with a mighty sadness. And his sons[34] reached him, and they had torn their cloaks, and they wounded each other on their breasts, and they said, as Allah, *glorified and exalted be He,* says in His honored Qur'an that the sons of Ya'qub said: **"Oh our father, we went before and left Yusuf by our cattle, and the wolf devoured him; and you believe not our sayings even when we speak the truth."**[35] And Ka'b al-Aḥbar said: and at that moment Ya'qub cried out a very shrill cry, and fell in a swoon to the ground. And he remained in a swoon for

---

[34] The manuscript has "ermanos," clearly a mistake for "hijos."
[35] Qur'an 12:17.

three hours without waking up; and they thought he had departed this world for the other one.

After Ya'qub awoke from his swoon, he wept, wept very shrilly and loudly. And Ya'qub said in his weeping: "My beloved Yusuf, may Allah, *be He exalted*, take not my hope from you. My beloved Yusuf, your dreams were true." And he began to turn Yusuf's shirt over and over, and said: "My beloved Yusuf, your dreams were true, and you were snatched out of my hands. *Oh*, my beloved Yusuf, I took comfort in you for all my *troubles*, but guarding you has profited me not." Ka'b al-Ahbar said: then they gave him the shirt, and he began to smell its smell, and he bellowed as a cow lows over its calf.

Then Ya'qub left them and ran away to the mountain of Kin'an and cried out in his loudest voice: "*Oh* beasts and birds and animals, Ya'qub has lost his son Yusuf! Now pleasure and joy are *forbidden* to me until I find out what has become of my beloved Yusuf." Ka'b al-Ahbar said: That day no bird nor beast that heard him failed to join him in weeping over Yusuf. Then Ya'qub returned and went to his house and took the shirt and said: "*Glory be to Allah, the Excellent*, this wolf was gentle to my beloved Yusuf, for he didn't tear his clothing at all." Then he said unto his sons: "If you speak the truth, catch me the wolf that ate my son Yusuf."

He said—he [Ka'b] said: and they went to hunt the wolf and caught him, and he was a miserable wolf, and they came with him to Ya'qub and threw him down before him. Behold, the wolf turned and complained and wept with the rope tied around its neck, and said unto Ya'qub: "Let me go my way, for I am wrongly accused." And Ya'qub said unto him: "Say you, *oh* wolf, whether you ate my beloved Yusuf. [If so,] you have given me a heritage of long sadness." He [Ka'b] said: and the wolf spoke by the power of Allah, *glorified and exalted be He*, and the first thing he said was: "*There is no god but Allah.* How longsuffering is Allah to the man who disobeys Him! *Oh* Ya'qub, by the honor of my Lord and His nobility, I never ate your son, and I am falsely accused and defamed without reason and miserable among the towns of Misra.[36] And by your authority, *oh prophet* of Allah, I have never before come to a town where the *prophets* lie about *creatures* while swearing by the Lord." When Ya'qub heard that, he released him, and he ran away.

And Ya'qub went, and came weeping to his sons, and said unto them as Allah, *glorified and exalted be He*, says in His honored Qur'an that he said: **"Nay, but your minds have beguiled you into something. (My course is) comely patience. And Allah it is Whose help is to be sought in that (predica-**

---

[36] That is, Egypt.

ment) which you describe."[37] Then he turned away weeping and said: "Oh, how bad for me! What mountain have they taken you into, or in what cavern have they put you? My beloved Yusuf, if you are alive, I commend you to Allah, *be He exalted*; if you are dead, I call upon Allah, *be He exalted*, to reduce the weight [of my sins thereby] on the Day of Judgment."

VIII. Allah's Promise to Yusuf in the Cistern

He said: when the night grew dark upon Yusuf in the cistern, he wept, he wept mightily until the *angels* in heaven wept for his weeping, and they said: "Oh our Lord and our Master, the weeping is the weeping of a lad, [but] the prayer is the prayer of a *prophet*." Then Allah, *be He exalted*, sent a *revelation* to Jibril, *peace be upon him*, saying: "My servant, oh Jibril, [give] my servant Yusuf patience and comfort in the solitude of the cistern." He [Ka'b] said: and Jibril, *peace be upon him*, descended and said unto him: "Oh Yusuf, Allah, *be He exalted*, sends you *greetings* and says unto you not to weep nor be aggrieved, for by My Honor and My Nobility I will take you out of the cistern and I will favor you above the sons of Ya'qub, and I will give you dominion over the lands of Misra, and I will humble its king for you, and he will turn his kingdoms over to you." Then he showed him prayers so that with them he might pray and beseech his Lord Allah, *blessed and exalted be He*, and said unto him: "Oh Yusuf, say!" he said, and he said: "What shall I say?" He said: "say: *Oh Maker of all things made, Repairer of all things broken, oh Answerer of all prayers, oh Great above all the great, oh Who has no partner in His Kingship nor viceroy, oh Creator of the sun and the shining moon, oh Provider of sustenance to small creatures, oh Helper of everything broken, oh Guardian of every court, oh Consoler of all the lonely, oh Companion of all the wretched, oh Conqueror of all the conquered, oh Near One, Far One, oh Living One, Eternal, there is no Lord but You!* I beg You to remedy what has happened to me, and to give me success and a good outcome, and that You imprint Your love in my heart till I love none other than You. *Oh Merciful and Compassionate One, there is no power and strength but in Allah, the High, the Great.*"

Ka'b said: when Yusuf prayed to his Lord with this prayer, the cistern grew larger and its water became sweet and turned for him as clear as the moon on the night when it is full, and the cistern became for him like a meadow of the meadows of *Paradise*. And Jibril came unto him with provisions and he ate, and

---

[37] Qur'an 12:18.

[Jibril] dressed him with the shirt of Ibrahim, *peace be upon him*, the one he wore the day he was thrown into the fire, and the fire passed over him, and the fire was for him cold and safe. And Allah, *be He exalted*, sent Yusuf seventy *angels* to console him in the cistern. And Yahuda consoled him and dressed him, keeping it secret from his brothers, and spoke unto him, and he took comfort from him. And Yusuf remained in the cistern three days.

IX. The Brothers Sell Yusuf to a Merchant

Ka'b said: while Yusuf was sitting in the well, a caravan from Misra stopped, and they camped near the well. And the lord of the caravan was Malik Ibnu Dugzi Alhuza'imu. And he saw that the bottom of the well was shining, for it shone brightly, and he looked at the brightness that came from the well, and he noticed the birds and beasts and animals around the well, and they said: "Oh Yusuf, would that the cistern had never been dug, that it might serve as a prison for you." When Malik noticed that, he said unto his servants: "Take the bucket and go you to this well, for I see that its water has turned sweet and has turned very good." And they went and hung down the bucket. When it reached Yusuf, he grabbed hold of it, and the servant lad tugged on the rope, but he couldn't pull it up. And the lad looked down into the well and saw Yusuf sitting in the bucket as if he were the moon on the night when it is full. And he was frightened of him and said unto him: "Who are you, *oh* you who are coming up? Are you a person or are you a *genie?*" He said: "I am indeed a person, as I will show you with my story." When the lad heard that from Yusuf, he cried: "Oh men of the caravan, come help me draw out this youth." And the people heard his cries and came to the well and gazed upon the youth, and saw his comeliness and beauty, and drew on the rope and pulled him out, and they all shouted when they pulled him out.

And Ya'qub's sons heard their shouts from the mountain and came down to them and said unto them: "What have you to say for yourselves?" They said: "We have found this youth in this cistern." "Oh company, this youth is a slave of ours who ran away from us three days ago, and we have searched for him and have not found him, and there is no doubt but that when he ran away, he threw himself into the well. Return him then unto us." He [Ka'b] said: when the merchant heard their saying, he said unto them: "By Allah, *be He exalted*, I swear that this youth is not these people's slave; I think not but that he is the son of kings." And Shama'un turned to Yusuf and spoke unto him in Hebrew and said unto him: "If you do not declare that you are our slave, we will kill you." Yusuf said: "Oh company of merchants, these are my masters, and I am their slave." Then the merchant said: "Oh sons of Ya'qub, for what price will you give him to me?" They said: "Take him for whatever you wish to give, for he has [bad] qualities." The merchant said: "And what are those qualities he has?" They said: "He is a thief and a liar." The merchants said: "We will take him in spite of those qualities. What is his price to be? For we will sell him in our land, and he will remain with us but a few days." The sons of Ya'qub said: "Give us whatever you wish for him." Ka'b al-Aḥbar said: the merchant put his hand in his sleeve and brought out for them twenty *dirhams*, which counted according to their weight were worth seventeen *dirhams*. And that is as Allah, *glorified and exalted be He*, said: **"And they sold him for a low price, a number of *dirhams*; and they attached no value to him."**[38] Ka'b said: it has come down to us that our *prophet* Muhammad, *may Allah grant him peace and save him*, said: "How cheaply was *the prophet* of Allah Yusuf sold, when they sold him for this price!"

He [Ka'b] said: when they took the *dirhams*, they divided them among themselves while Yusuf watched them. And each one of them took two *dirhams*, for its weight was one *dirham* and two grains. When Yahuda put out his hand to take his share, Yusuf said unto him: "I charge you by Allah the Great, *oh* brother, *oh* Yahuda, that you take nothing of my price, for I fear that Allah will hold you accountable for me on the Day of Judgment." And Yahuda refrained from taking it and took none of it. The merchant said unto them: "*Oh* sons of Ya'qub, write me a letter of sale promising me and giving me your word that you will never, never go back on the sale." Shama'un then said: "Bring me ink and paper." And he wrote, as he sat on the edge of the well: "*In the name of Allah, the Merciful, the Compassionate.* This is what the sons of Ya'qub, Allah's *Israelite*, son of Isḥaq, son of Ibrahim, friend of Allah, sell: They sell a slave of theirs to Malik Ibnu Dugzi Alhuza'imu, lord of the caravan of Misra, for twenty *dirhams*, by count not by weight. They have already given him over into his custody and have received his price, and hence they cannot go back on the sale for a small price. And they have divided his price among themselves."

Then they took the letter and closed it and sealed it with Ya'qub's seal. Then they gave it to the merchant. Ka'b said: the letter never ceased to be in Yusuf's possession until his brothers were reunited with him in Misra, Yusuf then being king, as the story tells further on. And it was Malik who trusted not to give the letter to anyone save Yusuf, and gave it to him, and Yusuf kept it until he brought it out to his brothers in Misra.

He [Ka'b] said: when the merchant wanted to move on, Yusuf's brothers said unto him: "*Oh* merchant, we have warned you of his faults." He said unto them: "He has faults?" They said: "Yes, we warned you that we were giving you a runaway slave and a thief and a liar. Be careful with him, then, and keep him hand-

---

[38] Qur'an 12:20.

cuffed and in chains, for we have warned you." Then they left him. And when Yusuf saw them, he gave up all hope in his brothers, when he saw that they were passing him by, and he cried out to them, and they answered him not. And Yusuf wept, wept mightily. Malik said unto him: "Oh young man, what is the matter?" Yusuf said: "Grief has overtaken me. What do you want of me?" He said: "Come close to me, and sit down before me." And Yusuf drew near the merchant and sat down before him. And he brought him a woolen tunic, and he put it on, and it scratched the flesh of his back. And then he brought handcuffs and handcuffed him.

When he was ready to go, Yusuf said: "Oh merchant, give me license to go and bid my family and my brothers farewell and wish *peace* upon them, and exhort them concerning a little brother I have—we have the same father and mother—called Yamin, and a sister called Dunya." The merchant said: "Go and give them your *greetings*." And Yusuf went before them—and he had irons on his legs—hoping they would pity him when they saw him in chains, and he cried out unto them. When he cried unto them, they fled and drew away from him. When he saw that they were not stopping, he shouted to them, and hastened after them, hoping to catch up with them, and he fell upon his face and lacerated his eyebrows and his face, and blood flowed from him, and he cried out: "Oh my brothers, stop a little for me till I bid you farewell and take some provision from you, at least a word that may be some comfort to me while I live." Yahuda, who pitied him, said unto them: "Oh sons of Ya'qub, I conjure you by Allah the Great, the Noble, that you wait a little for your brother Yusuf, till he wish *peace* upon you." And they stopped. And he reached them, and he stood before each one of them, and he kissed their heads and their hands and their feet, and he said: "Oh my brothers, may Allah have mercy upon you, though you have not had mercy on me. I love you. May Allah not persecute you, though you have persecuted me; may Allah not torment you, though you have tormented me. I beg Allah's pardon for you, for me and for you, *and peace be upon you*. And give my *greetings* to my brother Yamin and my sister Dunya." Then the merchant came and took him and put him upon his *she-camel* and set out for Misra.

X. Yusuf's Lament at His Mother's Grave

And their path led them by the grave of his mother Rahil. When he drew near his mother's grave, he could not resist throwing himself off his *she-camel*, and, sometimes crawling on his knees and other times walking upright, he came to his mother's grave. And he began to lament on the grave of his mother Rahil, saying: "Oh mother, *oh* Rahil, untie the knot of your *shroud* and raise your head from the grave. Oh my mother, *oh* Rahil, if you could see how short a time I have lived and what has befallen me since I lost you, you would weep over me and take pity on me. *Oh my mother, oh Rahil,* if you could see me—for there is no one on the face of the earth more humiliated than I—you would weep over me and take pity on me. *Oh my mother, oh Rahil,* if you could see your son Yusuf, and how they have separated him from his father Ya'qub, you would weep over me and take pity on me. *Oh my mother, oh Rahil,* if you could see how they stripped my shirt from off my back and left me naked, how they threw me in the cistern and threw stones at me and took no pity on me! *Oh my mother, oh Rahil,* they struck me on the cheeks of my face! *Oh my mother, oh Rahil,* if you could have seen me! They left me alone, wretched, and did not see Allah, *be He exalted,* in me. *Oh my mother, oh Rahil,* if you knew what has been done to your son Yusuf, who has been sold as a slave after being *a free man,* handcuffed and chained without having sinned! *Oh my mother, oh Rahil,* if you could see how I am being led as slaves are led or as captives from town to town! *Oh my mother, oh Rahil,* they sold me and handcuffed me with irons, and dressed me in rough clothing till the flesh of my back was scratched!" Ka'b said: and Yusuf heard a cry that said: "Suffer, for your suffering is from Allah, *be He exalted.*"

XI. Allah Protects Yusuf with a Storm

Then the merchant looked for him and found him not. And he cried unto his company in the caravan and said: "And where is the *Hebrew* lad? Has he already returned to his people?" Then the people began to look for him. While they were thus occupied, a man of those of the caravan saw him and came to him and said unto him: "Oh lad, your masters told us when they sold you that you were a thief and a runaway, and we didn't believe them until we saw it in you." He said: "By Allah, I have not run away. However, I have passed by the grave of my mother, and I could not resist throwing myself on it." He [Ka'b] said: he hearkened not unto him nor did he understand his saying, and he raised his hand and struck him upon his cheek, and Yusuf fell upon him in a swoon. Then he raised his head and fell *prostrate* and said in his *prostration:* "Oh my Lord, take pity on the smallness of my *state* and the slightness of my strength. Take pity on my loneliness and the abasement of my condition. *Oh my Lord,* grant my petition. *Oh my Lord,* You see what a loss I have suffered, You are the most Merciful of the merciful. *Oh my Lord,* if my sins have brought me to this state, I approach You with my honored fathers Ibrahim and Ishaq and Ya'qub, to whom You have shown grace above all *creatures.*"

Ka'b said: and Allah, *be He exalted,* took pity on his exile and loneliness. And Allah, *blessed and exalted be He,* sent upon that caravan a black, dark cloud and strong and fierce wind and many powerful thunderbolts. And the *angels* were in them, and the earth shook with them. And a great and powerful darkness passed over them so that they could in no way assist each other. And both the people and the beasts stopped. And in the cloud was a very great serpent and it had a very rough voice, like the voice of a lion. When the company saw that, they were shaken. And the merchants said: "Oh people: whoever among you has sinned, repent unto Allah, *be He exalted*, before we are all lost." The merchant who had struck him said: "I am the one who struck this *Hebrew* boy in the face." They said: "How could you have done that? By Allah, did you desire only our perdition? Now repent unto Allah, *be He exalted*, and go to the lad, that he may either forgive you or take *revenge* upon you."

He said. He [Ka'b] said: then the merchant came to Yusuf and kissed his head and his hands and said unto him: "I am the one who did this injustice unto you. Spare me and forgive me." When Yusuf heard his saying, he said unto him: "Woe unto you, *oh* merchant, for I am of a House which one should not treat this way. Nonetheless, I spare you; may Allah, *be He exalted*, spare you." Then Yusuf raised his head toward *heaven* and said: "Lord, persecute not this company for what they have done unto me." And then the storm and the *misfortune* left them. And they looked one unto another, and they traveled with him.

When they saw his *excellence*, and the honor in which his Lord held him, they released him from his bonds, and persevered in serving him and honoring him in everything. And the other merchants sold their shares in Yusuf, and Malik Ibnu Dugzi Alhuza'imu bought him for the price of a thousand doubloons and four hundred *dirhams*. He said: "Oh company, know that I have heard the *angels greeting* him morning and evening, and I have seen a white cloud above his head that gave him shade and traveled with him, and the cloud stopped whenever Yusuf stopped, and I have therefore neither lifted camp nor pitched my tents without acknowledging Yusuf's *blessedness*. And when Yusuf's weeping grew stronger, I said to myself: there is no doubt that this lad is destined for greatness."

XII. Arrival in Misra

He [Ka'b] said: when the merchant reached Misra, they camped at one of its rivers which they call Alkhalij. And the merchant called Yusuf and said unto him: "Oh Yusuf, this is Misra, for we have already entered it. Therefore, arise and take off that woolen tunic and bathe in this river till your body be cleansed of all filth, and all the weariness and travail of the journey be taken from you." He [Ka'b] said: and Yusuf took off his clothes and bathed in that river. And the fish began to kiss him on his back and played before him and rejoiced with him.

When he finished bathing, the earth shone with his beauty and comeliness, and the gates of *heaven* were opened, and the *angels* of *mercy* descended upon him, and his face was filled with brightness, and his face was then like the moon on the night when it is full. And the enlightener Jibril, *peace be upon him*, descended upon him and congratulated him and gave him patience and dressed him in Ibrahim's shirt. And the merchant was amazed by what had happened, and was bewildered by Yusuf's beauty and comeliness, and he rejoiced with a very great joy.

Ka'b al-Aḥbar said: and the merchant put him on a red camel and took him to Misra, the worst of all of Allah's cities, and the least prosperous, and he entered Misra on the day of *'Ashura'*.[39] And it happened that the trees had withered, and the rivers had dried up, and prices in the markets had risen. When Yusuf entered it, Allah, *be He exalted*, delighted to show the inhabitants of Misra Yusuf's honor and the favor in which he was held by Allah, *be He exalted*. And Allah, *be He exalted*, lit up the cities with his brightness, and made the rivers run, and made their kings just, and the cities abounded in his brightness. And He made the rivers run, and their waters abounded, and their cities were well provisioned, and their markets grew cheap, and their trees turned green again. And their *blessings* increased. He said. He [Ka'b] said: and the people were amazed by all that, and they said: "Do you not see that the cities are shining brightly and overflowing with goods upon the entrance of this lad and this merchant (i.e., Malik Ibnu Dugzi Alhuza'imu)?"

He [Ka'b] said: and the people banded together to go to Malik and to see what merchandise he brought. And they went to him, and they found him sitting on the porch of his house on a golden chair with a crown studded with pearls and *rubies* on his head. And they jointly *greeted* him, and he returned their *greetings*. And he spread out for them *silk* and *brocade* and prepared for them tables of reddish gold and put on them cups of many kinds of white *seed pearls* and he gave them the best meat to eat and gave them a cold beverage to drink, and said unto them: "Oh men of Misra, if you be in need of anything, I will remedy your need." They said unto him: "Yes. And know, *oh* merchant, that you came to our town in a time of great scarcity and great *misfortune*, and it was the worst of Allah's cities, and the least prosperous, and the one with the most expensive markets. As of today, however, it is the best of all of Allah's cities, the cheapest, the most prosperous and the brightest. We would love for you to tell us what is this merchandise that you bring with you from the lands of al-Sham."[40] He [Ka'b] said: and Malik lowered his head toward the ground for a moment. Then he raised his head and said: "This abundance

[39] Tenth day of the month of Muharram, a beneficent holy day possibly derived from the Jewish Day of Atonement.
[40] = Syria.

and *blessedness* that you see is due to the blessing of this lad whom I bought in the towns of al-Sham in the mountains of al-Ardun in the valley of Kin'an from the sons of Ya'qub." They said: "*Oh* merchant, let us see this boy that we may look upon his beauty and comeliness, and if you want to sell him, we will buy him from you along with the copious goods and great profit [he has brought us]. And if you won't sell him, [at least] let us see him." Malik said unto them: "*Oh* men of Misra, as for what you say about selling him, there is no doubt that I shall sell him, *Allah willing*." They said unto him: "Then point out to us on what day we shall buy him." He said unto them: "On *Friday* morning, *Allah willing*."

XIII. Malik Sells Yusuf to the King

The land of Misra is very flat; there are no hills or mounds in it nor anything elevated. The merchant chose a very flat place, and in it he laid out an area with a yardstick and ruler, and he erected on it marble pillars, and he hung on it *hangings* of *brocade*, and on top of the turrets he put balls of gold and silver. And he set upon the *pavilion* a chair of enameled gold and upon it cups of gold and golden swords with rods of green emerald, on each of the corners of the throne a pillar of reddish gold, and on each pillar a peacock of yellow gold, with their wings spread out over the pillars, and on the throne cushions of *brocade* filled with musk and *ambergris* for Yusuf, *peace be upon him*, to sit upon. Ka'b al-Aḥbar said: but Malik did that in order to derive the utmost benefit from his merchandising of Yusuf, and to put him in a high place and enhance his value so that the great and small and all the people should come to see him.

He [Ka'b] said: and the men of Misra wrote to the cities and towns and villages that they should come on the appointed *Friday* to see Yusuf, *peace be upon him*. And the people came from land and sea to see his beauty and comeliness. And when Allah caused that *Friday* to dawn, there was not a single village or city that didn't show up in that place which was made for Yusuf, *peace be upon him*. There was neither *free man* nor slave, neither man nor woman in Misra and its region who didn't show up in that place to look upon the beauty of Yusuf, *peace be upon him*, and his comeliness. And even the recluses came out of their hiding places.

And word of that reached King al-'Aziz and his wife Zalikha. And she asked permission of King al-'Aziz to go, and he gave her permission. And Zalikha adorned herself together with her handmaidens. And she went out, and the king went out with all his host, and the men and women stood [as they passed], and so it was in every village, and Zalikha ordered them to open their doors

and raise their curtains. And the cry went out among the people: there will be
no confiscation [of our property] today, for the king's wife is going out, and the
king likewise, with their adornments and their entourage to see Yusuf, *peace be
upon him*. And the king sent word to Malik Ibnu Dugzi Alhuza'ima to bring the
lad out, for he wanted to see him.

He [Ka'b] said: and Malik turned to Yusuf and *caressed* his head and kissed
him between the eyes and said: "My beloved Yusuf, know that the people
have assembled, wanting to see you. Be careful, then, what you say to the people, for I have bought you with my money from the sons of Ya'qub and
brought you from the towns of al-Sham." He said: "Yes, you speak truth, *oh
merchant*. Do what you like with me, for nothing happens that was not written in the *book* of Allah, *be He exalted*, before I was *created*." He [Ka'b] said:
and the merchant wondered at his teachings and his words. He said unto him:
"Fear not nor be sad, for I will yet adorn you and honor you, and I will bring
you to the highest honor." After that he made him sit down before him, and
he dressed him in very rich clothing, the best that could be. Ka'b al-Aḥbar
said: and he dressed him in a shirt of very thin linen, and in green camlet
breeches, and a yellow brocade burnoose, and a necklace with two gold
chains, and in the middle of each chain a white pearl that made his face shine
like the moon on the fourteenth night of the month. And he put ten rings on
his fingers with their red *rubies*. And at that time men dressed just like
women. He put on him bracelets such as kings wear, and he put on him a
headdress of gold garnished with *seed pearls*, and he gave him a scepter like
the scepters of kings, and had a horse saddled for him with a golden saddle
and with silver stirrups and bridle. And the merchant came to his companions, the seventy men, and they led him by his stirrups until he began to ride.
And when he was seated on his horse, he raised his head toward heaven, and
smiling with joy, said: "Allah, *be He exalted*, and his messenger speak truth."
They said unto him: "And what is that, *oh* Yusuf? And has a messenger come
unto you?" He said: "Yes." And it was said unto him: "And when was that?"
He said: "When the sons of Ya'qub threw me into the cistern. Ya'qub my father let me know all of this, for I saw a dream which I told my father, and he
informed me of all the misfortunes I have undergone, and of all the honor I
shall yet obtain. And when my brothers heard that of me, they were envious
of me, and took me away from my father and tried to kill me. Afterwards they
threw me in the cistern and stripped the shirt off my back. And there the messenger of my Lord, Jibril, *peace be upon him*, came to me and said unto me:
'Your Lord says to be patient, for He will take you out of the cistern and will
favor you above the sons of Ya'qub and will give you dominion over all the
land of Misra, and the people of Misra will be beneath your stirrups.'" When
they heard his saying, they marveled at it. And the merchant said: "*Oh* joy of
my eyes, know that when the people hear your words, they will refrain from

buying you." Yusuf said: "Do what you like, *oh* merchant, but that is my Lord's saying concerning me."

Kaʻb al-Aḥbar said: then Malik Ibnu Dugzi gave orders for the doors to be opened, and the doors of the palace were opened. He said: "*Oh* men of Misra, this is Yusuf who is coming out to you and looking out at you." He [Kaʻb] said: and the people stretched their necks and stood on tiptoe and strained their eyes until Yusuf came out above them, with seventy servants on his right hand and likewise on his left hand. And the merchant took his bridle, and the king's doorman pushed the people back from the road. When the people saw him, they were dazzled, and they could not resist making obeisance to him, and they said: "We have not seen another such lad." Afterwards the merchant came to the *pavilion* and took Yusuf down from his horse and set him upon his throne. Then the merchant took him inside the *pavilion*. And the people came from every place, and the merchant raised the *curtains* of the *pavilion*, and the people's faces shone with Yusuf's brightness and the power of his radiance, and the peacocks spread their wings over him.

And the merchant raised Yusuf's right arm, and a crier cried out: "*Oh* men of Misra, whoever wants to buy this lad, let him speak!" And the people were confused and said: "And who will be able to afford this boy and the raiment he is wearing?" And there came a *maiden* called Annaziga, daughter of Talut Ibn Qaysi, daughter of 'Ad, daughter of Shadad the Greater, and said: "*Oh* Malik, I'll buy this boy from you for ten times his weight in gold and silver." Malik said: "I shall not sell him until I inform King al-'Aziz." And he said unto him: "*Oh* king, buy this boy, peradventure he will be a son unto you." And the king came to the merchant and said: "*Oh* Malik, I will buy this boy from you for one hundred times his weight in gold." Malik said: "I will sell him to you for this price." He [Kaʻb] said: and the merchant had the scale brought, and he said to Yusuf: "Would you like to know your weight, *oh* joy of my eyes?" Yusuf said: "Do what you wish." And he set him in the scale, and he found that he weighed four hundredweights.[41] And Yusuf was fourteen years old, but his weight was that of his *prophethood*. And the king bought him for a hundred times his weight in gold and silver with brocade and silk and pearls and musk and *ambergris*, and the merchant thought it but little on account of the beauty and comeliness he saw in him.

And there was a crown of reddish gold studded with pearls and *rubies* and *seed pearls* on the king's head, and he took it off and put it on Yusuf's head, and its brightness gleamed. When the merchant saw the richness and beauty of the crown, he said: "*Oh* king, I would rather have your crown than the hundred times his weight that you have weighed out." The king said: "Let the crown be

---

[41] That is, 400 pounds.

permitted unto you." And the merchant stretched out his hand to take the crown from Yusuf's head, and his hand withered, and he could not move it, and he was troubled by that, and he said: "Oh Yusuf, my hand has withered. Pray then to Allah, *be He exalted*, that He release my hand and return it to me as it was before." And Yusuf prayed to Allah, and Allah restored him to his original condition. And the people were bewildered by that and said: "Oh, how blessed is this lad! There is no doubt that he is destined for greatness." And this bewildered the king.

He [Ka'b] said: and the king ordered a steed saddled for him with a golden saddle garnished with pearls and *seed pearls* and a bridle of white silver, and the banners waved around him and the ensigns above his head, and the knights and the hosts surrounded Yusuf until he arrived where Zalikha the queen was waiting. And the king said unto her as Allah, *glorified and exalted be He*, recounts in His honored Qur'an: **"Honor, oh Zalikha, his estate. Perchance he may prove useful to us or we may adopt him as a son."**[42] He [Ka'b] said: and the daughters of kings who were with Zalikha came and said unto the king "May Allah, *be He exalted*, give you lasting joy and fulfill your pleasure, for you are already fortunate in this lad."

Ka'b al-Aḥbar said: Yusuf went out riding in the morning and the evening every day until there was no one left in the king's kingdom who had not seen him except for seven daughters of kings, of the kings of Misra; those had not seen Yusuf, *peace be upon him*, those whom Allah, *be He exalted*, mentioned in His honored *book*. And it says that: **"Women in the city said. . . ."**[43] And those were these daughters of kings who had not seen Yusuf nor his beauty nor comeliness. And they reproached Queen Zalikha for having tried to seduce Yusuf, as the story says, when we get to that part, *Allah willing, be He exalted*. Ka'b said: when the king brought Yusuf to his palace, he honored him with very great honors and did him many good turns, and his honor was great before him for a time of five years.

XIV. Yusuf and the Arab

And one day Yusuf wanted to set out on the road to al-Sham, in case perchance he might hear some news of his father. And he asked permission from the king, and the king gave it to him. And the king said unto him: "Oh son, do what you like." And he had a horse saddled for Yusuf, and Yusuf rode out, and the king beside him at the head of his slaves and his people. And they set

---

[42] Qur'an 12:21.
[43] Qur'an 12:30.

out on the road to al-Sham, and they camped at a crossroads in the road. And while Yusuf was sitting there, an *Arab* passed by on his *she-camel*. And when the *she-camel* saw Yusuf's radiance and the great beauty and comeliness Allah, *be He exalted*, had given him, she came up to him and did obeisance before him, and began to rub and lick his feet, and bellowed loudly and pointed to Yusuf. When the king saw that, he said unto Yusuf: "What is the reason that this *she-camel* does that before you?" He said unto him: "*Oh* king, there is no doubt but that she saw me one day sitting before my father Ya'qub." Then the *Arab* said: "This is a great thing." And he whipped his *she-camel* with his rod that he had in his hand to make her get up, and she refused. And the *Arab* marveled at that and turned to Yusuf, *peace be upon him*, and said unto him: "Who are you, *oh* lad, you for whose cause my *she-camel* bows down before you?" And Yusuf wept, and the *Arab* said: "Oh, wonder above all wonders! You weep in the midst of so much honor and favor, crowned with a crown of honor? And there is no doubt but that you are the son of a king." The king said: "Indeed he is not my son, but he is my head slave, and I have adorned him and dressed him in this clothing." When the *Arab* heard that, he said unto Yusuf: "One such as you is a slave? Tell me: where are you from, or from whence have you been brought?" Yusuf said: "From lands of al-Sham of the mountains of al-Ardun and the valley of Kin'an." He said: "And of whom are you of the valley of Kin'an, for I know its peoples?" He said unto him: "*Oh Arab*, do you know in the valley of Kin'an a big tree which I will describe to you?" The *Arab* said: "Describe it to me that I may hear your saying." He said unto him: "And do you know in the vale of Kin'an a tree whose root is firmly planted in *heaven* that shines, and the heavens are open to it, and the earth shining, and the sun looks down upon it, and its rivers are sweet, and the water flows to its leaves and branches, and the *angels* water it; which tree has twelve branches, eleven of them closed and one open?" He said: "Do you know this tree, *oh Arab*? And do you know its branch?" He [Ka'b] said: and the *Arab* wept very mightily. He said: "*Oh* lad, you have done a good job of describing that tree to me, and according to your description of that tree, it must be Ya'qub, *peace be upon him*. As for what you say about the branches, they are the sons of Ya'qub. As for the open branch, it must be Yusuf, *peace be upon him*, the one who was eaten by the wolf." Yusuf said: "Know that I am Yusuf, son of Ya'qub, *peace be upon him*." As soon as the *Arab* heard his saying, he threw himself upon Yusuf's head, and kissed him, and said: "Allah preserve me from drowning out your voice. Oh Yusuf, and how did you become a head slave?" Yusuf said: "A great story has happened to me, and it would take a long time to recount it. But, *oh Arab*, do you know the place where my father Ya'qub is?" He said: "Yes, *oh* beloved of Allah, I left him on a mountain, and his person is now bent over with sadness and weeping over you. And he has built himself three houses: the first one he calls the House of Sadness; the second, the House of Weeping; the third, the House of Loneliness."

He said: when Yusuf heard that, he wept until he fainted. When he revived from his faint, he said unto him: "*Oh Arab,* please take a message from me to my old father Ya'qub." He said unto him: "My beloved Yusuf, what do you want me to tell him when I find him?" He said: "*Oh* my brother, *oh Arab,* when you go, *Allah willing,* and you reach the vale of Kin'an, don't go where Ya'qub is until nightfall, at that hour when the gates of *heaven* open and the *angels* come down with *mercy* and honor. And when you reach him, wish him *peace* and tell him: 'Oh Ya'qub, I have seen a lad in the lands of Misra, and of all people he is the one who weeps most mightily for you, and the one who most longs to see you.' And if he should ask you how I am, describe my condition and tell him: 'your son Yusuf says to you: if your back has become bent and your sight has grown dim with weeping, then know that the green birthmark, the one that was on his cheek, has worn away from so much weeping and sadness over you, *oh prophet* of Allah.' " The *Arab* said unto him: "It pleases me, *oh Yusuf.*" And he left. And Yusuf said unto him: "*Oh* brother, *oh Arab,* deliver my message that I have entrusted to you!"

Ka'b al-Aḥbar said: and the *Arab* rode away on his *she-camel* and said: "*Oh* my *she-camel,* ride on, ride on, and sleep not until Yusuf's message reaches his father Ya'qub, the *prophet* of Allah!" And the *Arab* rode on, and he didn't pass anything that did not speak to him, nor beast nor bird that did not cry out unto him. And the *Arab* reached Misra, and when he finished his affairs and had done his dealings, he returned to the vale of Kin'an to the place where Ya'qub's tent was, and he stopped before the door of the tent, and it was toward sunset, and he cried out in a loud voice and said: "*Peace be upon you, oh* men of Ya'qub!" And he said: "I have seen a lad in Misra who looks more like you than anyone, and he sends you *greetings.*"

Ka'b al-Aḥbar said: and Dunya heard his voice and went out to the door of the tent; and she had lost her coloring, and her body had grown thin, and she had lost her eyesight from weeping. And she was Yusuf's sister by father and mother. When the *Arab* saw her in that state, he wept for her weeping and for what he saw of her sadness. And he said unto her: "*Oh maiden,* are you perchance Yusuf's sister?" She said: "Yes. And have you perchance seen him?" He said unto her: "I have seen a lad, and I bring you a message from him and a *request.*" She said: "From whom, *oh Arab?*" He said: "From your brother Yusuf." When she heard that, she fainted away crying: "Oh my master and joy of my eyes! I ask you by Allah the Great, *oh Arab:* have you seen him?" He said: "Yes, I have seen him." She said unto him: "And where have you seen him, *oh Arab?*" He said: "I have seen him in Misra, for he has been sold as a slave, and he has become a head slave. And he sends you many *greetings.* And King al-'Aziz has already bought him." The *maiden* said: "*Oh Arab*, may Allah, *be He exalted*, reward you on my behalf with good. I know not how to repay you for this, except that I shall pray to Allah that he give you an easy death." He said unto her: "*Oh* servant of Allah, and how is the *prophet* of Allah, Ya'qub?" She said: "*Oh* brother, *oh Arab*, the *prophet* of Allah, Ya'qub, has sworn by himself never again to go under a roof since he was separated from his beloved Yusuf." He said unto her: "And where is he, that I may take him the message from his beloved Yusuf?" She said: "Do you see that green *pavilion* that is on top of this mountain?" He said: "Yes." The *maiden* said: "Ya'qub is living in it. His body is ruined, and his color is gone, and his back is bent, and he has lost his eyesight from the strength of his sadness over Yusuf. Go therefore to him, and you will see that he is like a dead man and is nothing but a living corpse."

Ka'b al-Aḥbar said: and the *Arab* went along until he reached the tent. And he looked at Ya'qub, who was stretched out face down, *prostrate*, weeping, and the birds and beasts wept on account of his weeping. And he said: "Every exile, however long he may be away from home, as long as he be alive, there is no doubt that he will return home; for the exile in a land where he has no relatives, eventually remembers his absence from home." Then he said: "Oh, how terrible; oh, exile; oh, what a *misfortune*; oh, how bitter it is; and oh, what grief; and oh, how strong it is!"

He [Ka'b] said: and the *Arab* cried out: "*Peace be upon you, oh Ya'qub, and Allah's mercy and His blessing!*" And he didn't lift up his head to him. And he cried out a second time: "*Peace be upon you, oh prophet of Allah!*" And he didn't raise his head to him. And he cried out a third time and said: "*Peace be upon you, oh sad one!*" And he raised his head to him and said: "You speak truth. By Allah, I am the sad one." Then he returned his *greeting* and said unto him: "Are you in need of something?" He said unto him: "*Oh prophet* of Allah, I have a message." And Ya'qub wept a great weeping. Then he said: "*Oh Arab*, and how can there be a message for me? Are you joking with me?" He said: "No, by Allah, nor by the authority of Ibrahim's grey hair, I am not joking with you; I have indeed seen Yusuf." He [Ka'b] said: and Ya'qub lost control and fell upon him in a faint and bellowed as the bull bellows. And when he recovered from his fainting spell, he said: "*Oh Arab*, you have seen my beloved Yusuf?" He said: "Yes, *oh prophet* of Allah, I have seen him." He said: "And where have you seen him?" He said: "In the land of Misra, and he sends you *greetings*." Ya'qub said: "Come close to me." And he drew near unto him, and he hugged him to his bosom and kissed him between his eyes and said: "These are the eyes that have seen my beloved Yusuf." Then he said: "I ask you in the name of Allah, *oh Arab*, did he touch your hand with his hand?" He said: "Yes, *oh prophet of Allah*, I took him by the hand with this hand of mine." And Ya'qub took the *Arab's* hand and held it to his face and smelled it. Then he said: "You speak truth, *oh Arab*, for his smell is on your hand. But describe unto me his figure as if I were gazing upon him." He said: "It pleases me, *oh prophet of Allah*. In Misra I have seen a lad of beauteous face, with very beautiful eyes, a long, slender nose, very beautiful teeth, beardless, with a broad forehead, [his complexion is a perfect blend of] white and red, his throat is like a chiseled pearl, his arms are very muscular but slender as palm trees, the palms of his hands are elongated, his face is round like the roundness of your face, *oh prophet of Allah*. His arms and legs shine brightly, and it is as if grains of *seed pearls* dripped from the tips of his hair, and as if his face were the moon, and as if his legs were canes of white silver. And he says unto you that that birthmark that was on his cheek has been worn away from the abundance of his weeping over you, *oh prophet of Allah*."

He said: then Ya'qub wept a very great weeping and said unto him: "Oh brother, *oh Arab*, may Allah reward you on my behalf, for you have completed your description, and I am indebted to you and would like to repay you. See then if there is anything you need of your Lord." The *Arab* said unto him: "And how desirous I am of that, *oh prophet* of Allah, for I am one of the honored men of my tribe, one of the esteemed, and I am very rich and well provided with *sustenance*, and I have twelve wives, but I have not received the *blessing* of a single son. Pray then to Allah, *be He exalted*, that He give me the *blessing* of good sons." Ka'b said: and Ya'qub lifted up his hands toward the *heavens* and prayed with secret prayers and *rubbed* the *Arab's* back with his hand. The *Arab* said: "Oh prophet of Allah, I have a second need." He said: "And what is it?" He said: "Pray to Allah, *be He exalted*, that He give me a palace in *Paradise* between your palace and the palace of your father Ibrahim, the friend of Allah." And Ya'qub prayed to Allah about that and said: "Lord, give him as *a blessing* a palace in *Paradise*." The *Arab* said: "I have yet a third need." He said: "What is it?" "This *she-camel* of mine, since she is the one that caused me to meet your son Yusuf, peradventure you could also say a prayer for her." And Ya'qub prayed to his Lord and laid his hand upon her and said to her: "On your way, now; peradventure you will be one of Yusuf's *she-camels* in *Paradise*."

Then the *Arab* rode away from Ya'qub on his *she-camel*. And from that day on, the *she-camel* never passed another beast without lording it over them on account of Ya'qub's prayer. He [Ka'b] said: and the *Arab* came to his house and copulated with all twelve of his wives in one night. When nine months had passed, each one of them gave birth to two sons—twenty-four male children—on account of Ya'qub's prayer. And we have heard, *but Allah knows [if it is true],* that the *Arab* lived to ride with a thousand [of his descendants] on horseback: all his sons, and his sons' sons, down to seven generations of great grandsons.

XV. Zalikha Falls in Love with Yusuf

Ka'b said: when King al-'Aziz returned to his palace with Yusuf, the king said to Zalikha, the queen: "**Honor his estate. Perchance he may prove useful to us, or we may adopt him as a son,**[44] that he may be king after me." And the fact is that King al-'Aziz was an impotent man who did not approach women, and for that reason he adopted Yusuf as his son. *He said:* then the king left [the room] where Zalikha was, and Zalikha summoned Yusuf and made him sit down in front of her and took off all the clothes that he was wearing. And she dressed him in a shirt of very fine linen and breeches of green camlet, and she put golden rings and golden bracelets and bracelets of silver on him. And she girdled him with a belt studded with *seed pearls* and *rubies*. And she set the king's table for him, and she gave him to drink from the king's vessels, and she crowned him with the king's crown, and she put chains [around his neck], the king's chains. And she said unto him: "Oh Yusuf: did you not hear the king when he said unto me: 'honor his estate'? By the king's authority, then, I shall yet honor you with the king's own honor and with an even greater honor than the king has sub-jects, and I shall even serve you with my own hands!" Ka'b said: then Yusuf wept, wept very mightily. Then he said unto her: "Oh Zalikha, do not love me with a love that will bring me bad fortune." She said: "Why so?" Yusuf said: "Be-cause my father loved me, and my brothers sold me, and I am afraid that you will love me with a love that will be my downfall." She said: "Oh Yusuf, it was not for the kind of service you are performing that I bought you with my money." "Then order me to serve you in a task wherein my body may work and my person may sweat, but while doing it, I may think upon my Lord, for I love that better than this business of honor." Zalikha said: "Oh Yusuf, when kings love a servant, they honor him and they don't use him for manual labor. And I, *oh* Yusuf, am delighted with your service." Yusuf said: "Oh Zalikha, that may be, but I prefer labor and hard work." Zalikha said: "Well, then, I have a garden that contains flowing rivers and fruit trees with different kinds of fruit. Abide there, and pick the fruit with your hands."

Ka'b said: and Zalikha had a garden which the first men had planted. In it were all fruits and myrtles and rosebushes and jasmines and all the different kinds of flowers and good odors and fruit that are upon the face of the earth. And between the *rows* of the trees was a river, and on the banks of the river were all the good odors, and in the garden were all the birds that Allah, *be He*

---

[44] The rather awkward repetition of Qur'an 12:21 here suggests that the long digres-sion about Yusuf's encounter with the Arab and the latter's visit to Ya'qub were later accretions to the original story. James Kugel has termed this device—repetition of an earlier sentence in order to return the narrative to where it was before an interruption—*narrative resumption*.

exalted, created. And in the midst of the garden were two big fountains, one fountain full of honey and the other fountain full of milk. By each fountain was a cushioned platform, and surrounding it all was a wall. And when Zalikha decided to send Yusuf to the garden, she summoned a hundred virgin servants and adorned them with the best of adornments, and bejeweled them with different kinds of jewels, and dressed them in precious clothing, and had them perfumed with different kinds of perfume. And she ordered them to go with Yusuf and to sport with him. Then she said unto them: "As soon as Yusuf starts to stare at you, you must let me know." When the maidens went with him to the garden, they flattered him and gave him gifts and tried to sport with him. And he refused to laugh with them, and said unto them: "*Oh* company of *maidens:* Allah, *be He exalted, created* both me and you from the dirt, and to dirt we must return. Therefore, fear Allah the Great." And when Yusuf *praised* Allah, *glorified and exalted be He,* in the whole garden there were no birds nor beasts nor trees that did not *praise* with him, and when he performed his *prescribed prayers,* the *maidens* performed *prayer* with him and *bowed down* in unison with his *bows.* And Zalikha sent him golden vessels and silken tablecloths. And when Zalikha desired to see Yusuf, they opened the doors of the platforms so that she could go to him, and they hung up the *hangings* and she rode with her servants until she caught sight of Yusuf. And when she saw him, she rejoiced with a very great joy.

XVI. She Attempts to Seduce Him

Ka'b said: the king had five retreats: one retreat of gold, another of silver, another of white marble, another of ivory and ebony, and another of [black?] marble. And these five retreats were dwellings which were called the "Solitary Dwellings," for when the king wanted to be alone, he shut himself up in them all alone. As for the golden dwelling, its lower and upper parts and its doors and walls were all of gold. In it was a golden throne, studded with pearls and *rubies.* Likewise the silver dwelling: above and below, it was of silver, and its doors and walls and everything in it were silver, garnished with white *seed pearls.* And so it was with all the other dwellings. And *silk* and *brocade* were spread about them. And over their doorways were *hangings* of *brocade* adorned with heavy gold, and they were hung over all the doorways, and in each of the rooms were five lamps of *seed pearls,* their chains being of reddish gold.

And [Zalikha] had two maidservants stand at each door. And she had placed in each of the five retreats a portrait of herself and a portrait of Yusuf. Then she sent for Yusuf. When he had come, she made him sit down in front of her, and she said: "*Oh* Yusuf, I have summoned you today to honor you with the greatest honor. These are the estates and solitary rooms where the king goes to be alone. By the authority of the king, I shall yet exalt you in esteem." Then she took Yusuf by the hand and led him into the golden retreat and made him sit upon the chair of gold and *seed pearls*, and bejeweled him and perfumed him and put a crown upon him and put bracelets on him. And, filled with lust, she kept staring provocatively at Yusuf. And Yusuf lowered his head and said: "Oh Zalikha, fear Allah, for it is not *permitted* for you to be alone with me in the king's house." And she begged him for his body, and he refused.

And she made him enter the silver dwelling, and made him sit upon the throne, and said unto him: "Oh Yusuf, the king bought you to be obedient unto me." Yusuf said: "Oh Zalikha, but the king doesn't know what you want from me. Fear Allah, *be He exalted*, and take me away from this house." She said: "There is no chance of that, *oh Yusuf*." Yusuf said: "*Glory be to Allah, the Great, the Wise!* If Allah, *be He exalted*, so willed, I would ruin you, for you are leading me into something *forbidden*. Fear Allah, oh Zalikha, and take me away from this house, for I am afraid of sinking in the sea of those who go astray."

Ka'b al-Aḥbar said: she did not cease to lead him from retreat to retreat, saying unto him: "Oh Yusuf, do as I command, and do not disobey me, for I must discipline you. Therefore fill my need and take pity on my weeping, for you, *oh Yusuf*, are today in the rooms of honor, in the Solitary Dwellings. Why don't you come close to me? Why won't you satisfy my desire?" He [Ka'b] said: then Yusuf lowered his head and said: "Defend yourself with Allah, *be He exalted*, from those who disobey Him, for that is your duty. I conjure you by Allah, oh Zalikha, to take me away from this house, for shame has already abandoned you, and I fear that if [word of] this reaches the king, he will punish you with the punishment of sinners. And if you want this desire to leave you, then take me away from this dwelling, for when you no longer see me, this desire you have for me will leave you." She said: "Oh Yusuf, come and pleasure me, for you know that when the servant fails to please his master, he punishes him with the strongest torture." Yusuf said: "He whom Allah protects is protected, but he whose heart neglects to think on Him is lost."

Then he lowered his gaze to the floor, and the floor of that retreat was white marble, and he saw Zalikha's beauty and loveliness in the marble, as if it were a mirror. Then he looked up at the walls of the room, and she raised her head, and he saw her in the walls, and he saw her everywhere he turned. And he couldn't help weeping, *may Allah grant him peace and save him*, and he cried out: "Oh my Lord, help me, for I am terribly lost! Oh Lord, protect me with Your great protection and let me never be shaken, for it is to the wretched that You love to give good fortune!" Zalikha said: "Oh Yusuf, raise your head, and open your eyes, and look at me." He said: "Oh Zalikha, leave me alone. Don't draw me into something *forbidden*, for I am afraid that this house which the king meant to be a house of happiness and rejoicing will turn out instead to be a place of the fire of *hell*. Oh Zalikha, I am afraid of the king who has honored my estate." Then she said: "*Oh* Yusuf, if you are afraid of the king who has honored your estate, then give him a drink to drink so that he will die of it."[45] Yusuf said: "*Oh* Zalikha, do you want to kill the king for my sake? *Allah forbid!*" Then Yusuf noticed a part of the room, and he saw *a curtain* hanging there, and he said: "*Oh* Zalikha, what is behind that *curtain?*" She said: "*Oh* Yusuf, it is an idol that I put there so that it would help me win you over." *He said:* and Yusuf wept and said: "*Oh* Zalikha, I blush for Him who *created* me and made my body good and comely, for I had nothing to do with it. And He sees me wherever I be, even underneath the covers or shut up in a house, if I disobey Him. And He knows what is in my imagination, and knows my secrets." She said: "*Oh* Yusuf, will your Lord punish you if you disobey Him?" He said: "Yes, for He has promised fire for the disobedient. Therefore fear Allah, *oh* Zalikha, and revere Him, for He is very noble and great." She said: "*Oh* Yusuf, I have gold and silver and different kinds of *seed pearls* and musk and camphor and *ambergris* and *brocade* and *silk* and harnessed horses and cattle which I will give as *charity.*" He said: "*Oh* Zalikha, my Lord does not accept *charity* except from the good."

Ka'b al-Aḥbar said: and Zalikha greatly lusted after him, and demanded his body, and said unto him: "*Oh* Yusuf, how beautiful is your face!" He said: "*Oh* Zalikha, my Lord formed it in the womb." She said unto him: "And how lovely is your hair!" Yusuf said: "It will be the first thing to fall from my body in the grave." Zalikha said: "How good you smell!" Yusuf said: "*Oh* Zalikha, if you were to look in on me in the grave after three days, you would flee from me, vomiting." She said: "How beautiful are your eyes!" Yusuf said: "They will be the first things to run down my cheeks." Zalikha said: "And how sweet are your words!" Yusuf said: "Fear Allah, and remember death." She said: "*Oh* Yusuf, my tongue thirsts for you! Get up, *oh* Yusuf, for the fire is blazing in my heart. Get up then, so you can quench it. *Oh* Yusuf, lift up your head and look at me." He said: "I am afraid I will be blind in the other world." She said: "*Oh* Yusuf, just look at how lovely and beautiful I am." And Zalikha was white and very beautiful, with her eyes *darkened with kohl,* and she had eighty [. . . .][46] And she had adorned herself that day with very rich adornments. When she finally despaired of him, she said: "If this is not to be, then at least play with me."

---

[45] Some of the arguments Zalikha employs in her attempts to seduce Yusuf closely parallel those attributed to her in the second-century B.C.E. Greek *Testaments of the Twelve Patriarchs*. There too she threatens to murder her husband by giving him a drug, offers to convert to Judaism if Joseph will have intercourse with her (similar to Zalikha's offer to give charity), and finally threatens to commit suicide. See *The Old Testament Pseudepigrapha*, ed. James H. Charlesworth (Garden City, N.Y.: Doubleday, 1983), I, 819–28.

[46] The following word is "feletas," but neither Guillén Robles nor Klenk was able to ascertain its meaning.

It is said—but Allah *knows*—that Yusuf reached under his skirt and tied the ties of his breeches, and made sure they were securely tied, and he tied seven knots: the first knot in the name of Ibrahim, and the second knot in the name of Isma'il, and the third knot in the name of Ya'qub. . . .[47] and the fifth knot in the name of Musa, and the sixth knot in the name of 'Isa, and the seventh knot in the name of Muhammad, *may Allah grant them all peace and save them.* Then Yusuf began to weep again, and he bowed down to Allah, *be He exalted,* saying: "*Oh my Lord, oh Lord:* preserve me and let me not be shaken, nor place *demons* in my path, for You are All-Powerful." Then he said: "*Oh Zalikha, fear Allah* and save yourself with Him, for I fear that if I fell to the ground, I would be *erased* from the Book of the Good and sealed in the Book of Sinners. And I am also afraid to see written on the gates of *Paradise: 'Do not enter.'* " Zalikha said: "*Oh Yusuf,* I have given you the king's own bed to lie in, I have seated you on the king's throne, and I have adorned you with the king's ornaments. If you don't do what I ask, I will stab my body with this dagger until I die. And when I am dead, the king will slay you after me." Yusuf said: "*Oh Zalikha, Satan* is the declared enemy of man. Therefore, fear Allah, and don't make me one of the lost." And he began to console her and to urge patience on her so that she should not slay herself with the knife.

Ibn al-'Abbas,[48] *may Allah be pleased with him,* said: "Declared is the saying of Allah, *glorified and exalted be He,* that stated: **"She verily desired him, and he would have desired her if it had not been that he saw the declaration of his Lord."**[49] The declaration refers to the fact that when Yusuf decided to untie the knot in his breeches, the knot cried out: "*Oh Yusuf,* remember in whose name you tied me." And when he started to untie the second knot, the palm of a hand appeared unto him saying: "Approach not *adultery,* for it is ugliness and an evil path." And as he untied the third knot, a[nother] palm appeared unto him, and written on it was: "To the woman who commits *adultery* and to the man who commits *adultery,* give each one of them a hundred lashes." When he untied the fourth knot, [still another] palm appeared unto him, and written on it was: "He who commits adultery, let him marry only an adulteress or an infidel." When he untied the fifth knot, it cried out to him: "*Oh Yusuf,* you are falling into error, and you will be *erased* from the Book of the *Prophets!*"

Ka'b al-Ahbar said: and the *angels* in *heaven* cried out, imploring Allah, *be He exalted,* and Allah sent word to them: "I foresee that he will be preserved, and I will make no separation between him and his grandfathers and his fa-

---

[47] The author forgot to mention the fourth knot.
[48] 'Abdullah Ibn al-'Abbas (d. 687), known as the "father of Koranic exegesis," is credited with the first philologically oriented commentary on the Qur'an.
[49] Qu'ran 12:24.

thers, Ibrahim and Isma'il and Isḥaq." The *angels* said: "Oh Lord, let him see that declaration that You showed unto the chosen and the pure and the obedient." And then Allah, *be He exalted*, sent for Jibril, *peace be upon him*, and said: "Go down, *oh* Jibril, to My servant Yusuf, and show him the declaration so that he may be saved from the *misfortune* of perdition."

He [Ka'b] said: while Yusuf was in this state, with his head lowered, not knowing what to do, he turned and saw Jibril, *peace be upon him*, who had appeared unto him in the form of his father Ya'qub. And he put his hand on his thumb and said unto him: "Oh Yusuf, since you have chosen to fall into error, your name is wiped out from the Book of the Good and of *Prophecy*." And Yusuf could not bear it any longer. And he had already untied five knots, and there were two knots remaining. And he ran for the door of the retreat. And Zalikha had locked it with very strong locks. And Allah, *be He exalted*, gave Yusuf strength, and he broke down the door and ran away. And she hastened to run after him and caught him by the shirt and tore it down the back.

XVII. Zalikha Falsely Accuses Yusuf

And they encountered their lord the king as they went out the door. And the king encountered Yusuf as he came out the door, and he saw that he was red,[50] and his shirt was torn, and he was fleeing. When the king saw that, he said unto him: "*Oh* lad, what has happened to you?" Yusuf said: "*Oh* king, I have seen a harsh and ugly side of your wife." And Yusuf was embarrassed, and he was very honorable, *may Allah grant him peace and save him*. The king said unto him: "Come back, don't worry." And he took him by the hand and led him back into the house. When Zalikha saw the king coming, and Yusuf with him, she said: "*Oh* king, what recompense shall be made unto him who turns against his master?" And she threw herself upon the king, kissing his feet and kissing him between the eyes, and saying, as Allah, *be He exalted*, recounts when He says: **"What recompense shall be made unto him who seeks to do wickedness with your wife, save that he be imprisoned or fiercely tortured?"**[51] The king said: "And who sought to do wickedness with you?" She said: "This lad tried to seduce me." And the king turned to Yusuf and said unto him: "*Oh* lad, is this how you reward me for having bought you with my money and placed you in an honorable estate? You try to seduce Zalikha, your mistress?"

Yusuf said: "*Oh* king, it was she who tried to seduce me." The king said: "How is that?" He said: "She brought me to this house and lured me to her

---

[50] Literally, "his color was changed" (permutado su color).
[51] Qur'an 12:25.

body, but I resisted. And she is the one who tried to rape me." Ka'b said: Zalikha kept on kissing the king's feet and hands, and she said unto him: "By your authority, *oh* king, he is the one who tried to seduce me." When she swore, the king believed her, and he turned to Yusuf and said unto him: "I shall torture you with the strongest torture in punishment for what you have done."

Then he sent for his torturer. When he came, he said: "Take this lad and torture him fiercely." And he took Yusuf by the hand and said: "You have done very badly for yourself in trying to seduce your mistress." And Yusuf wept mightily. Then Yusuf said: "Let me at least make two *cycles* of *prayer* and beseech my Lord, for He is near and answers prayer." The torturer said unto him: "Do as you like." And Yusuf raised his hands to *heaven* and said: "Oh my Lord, help me, most Pious of the pious, by the authority of the grey hair of Ibrahim and Ishaq and Ya'qub, for you are All Powerful." Ka'b said: and the *angels* in *heaven* wept out of pity for Yusuf.

XVIII. An Infant Testifies for Yusuf

He said: Zalikha had a sister who had given birth to a child seven days before and it was in the crib in Zalikha's quarters. And Allah, *be He exalted*, sent word to Jibril, *peace be upon him*: "Go down, *oh* Jibril, to this child and order it to speak, for it will testify truthfully for Yusuf." *He said:* and Jibril went down to the child and said: "*Oh* child, your Lord says for you to testify for Yusuf with the truth, for this case will be judged by your account." He [Ka'b] said: and the baby stood up on its feet and began to walk, until it stood before the king and said: "*Oh* king, why have you ordered this lad Yusuf to be tortured?" The king said: "Because he tried to seduce your mistress." The child said: "*Oh* king, it is not just for you to believe and give credit to Zalikha, and disbelieve and not give credit to Yusuf, for peradventure he speaks the truth, and Zalikha speaks not the truth." The king said: "Tell me then how I will know which of them speaks the truth." The child said: "Observe, *oh* king, whether Yusuf's shirt is torn in the front; [if so,] she speaks the truth, and he is a liar. And if his shirt is torn from behind, then she lies, and he is truthful." When he saw his shirt torn from behind, he said that that was [an example] of the wiles of women, for their wiles are great. He said unto Yusuf: "Stay away from her." "And beg pardon, *oh* Zalikha, for you are among the wayward." Then the king swore not to speak to her for forty days in punishment of what she had done.

Then the king left his palace and busied himself with the business of his kingdom, and he took Yusuf from where he was and took him with him. And Zalikha stayed behind and could not see Yusuf. And she was dying of desire for him. And she closed the doors of the chambers of honor with the great sadness

she felt and because of her love for Yusuf. And she ceased not to weep with desire for Yusuf. And her maidens and servants said unto her: "*Oh* madam, what
has happened to you that you weep so much?" Zalikha said: "I used to see Yusuf
every day, and now I don't see him; a barrier has been placed between me and
him." They said unto her: "*Oh* madam, we will arrange for him to come where
you can see him." And they went to Yusuf and said unto him: "*Oh* Yusuf, you
have made your mistress fall ill and grow disconsolate, and her body has grown
thin. Therefore, do what she commands you." He said: "Haven't you seen what
Allah, *be He exalted*, has demonstrated, the miracles He has performed? Fear
Allah, *be He exalted*, and let Zalikha turn to Allah, *glorified and exalted be He*."

XIX. Women Gossip About Zalikha

He said: Zalikha was unable to cover up her love, and it became public knowledge in the city. And it is as Allah, *glorified and exalted be He*, said in His honored Qur'an where it says as follows: **"And the women in the city said: The
ruler's wife is asking of her slave-boy an ill deed. Indeed he has smitten her
to the heart with love. We behold her in plain aberration."**[52] Ka'b said: and
there were in the city nine tribes[53] of daughters of kings, and they had never
seen Yusuf. And these women gossiped a lot about Queen Zalikha and talked
about her. And word of this reached Zalikha, and she sent for them and prepared a cushioned couch for each one, and placed Yusuf behind a screen.
When they entered the room where Zalikha was, she made each one sit down
in her chair, and for each one she had set out a knife and a grapefruit. Then
she had the screen where Yusuf was removed, and she said to Yusuf, as Allah,
glorified and exalted be He, recounts in His honored Qur'an that Zalikha said to
Yusuf: **"Come out unto them,"**[54] and he came out. When they saw him, they
magnified him greatly, and they cut their hands and said: "This is not a person
but an honored *angel*." The compiler [of this story] said: and they fell into a
faint when they saw him. And when they awoke, they began to cut their grapefruit, and they stained their hands but did not notice it, so greatly were they
upset from seeing Yusuf's comeliness and his beauty. Then they said unto
Zalikha: "*Oh* Zalikha, we have not seen the likes of this lad among the peoples.
How blessed is his *Creator*!" Zalikha said unto them, as Allah, *be He exalted*,
recounts: **"This is he on whose account ye gossiped about me. I tried to seduce him, but he has preserved himself and refused. But if he does not do**

---

[52] Qur'an 12:30.
[53] This in the manuscript. But it is clear that there were really only nine *women*.
[54] Qur'an 12:31.

as I command, he will yet be imprisoned, and verily shall be of those brought low."[55] The compiler said: when Yusuf heard her saying, he said as Allah recounts in His Qur'an that Yusuf said: **"Oh my Lord! Prison is dearer to me than that unto which they urge me, and if You fend not off their wiles from me, I shall incline unto them and become of the foolish."**[56] He [Ka'b] said: and the *angels* in *heaven* wept out of pity for Yusuf.

XX. Yusuf Goes to Prison

When he prayed for prison, Jibril, *peace be upon him*, came down and said unto him: "Oh Yusuf, the Most High Sovereign sends you *greetings* and says that since prison is dearer to you, because you prayed to be preserved, the Lord of Honor says to you: by My Honor and My Nobility, I shall yet test you with prison, as you have chosen it for yourself. Therefore, prepare yourself for it." And it is as Allah, *glorified and exalted be He*, says: **"So his Lord heard his prayer and fended off the wiles of women from him. Lo! He is Hearer, Knower."**[57]

The compiler said: Zalikha asked license from the king and said unto him: "Oh king, the whole city has heard about the case of this lad. Give me, therefore, license to imprison him until people stop talking and lose interest in this matter." And the king gave her license to imprison him. And the king had three jails: a Jail of Torture, and a Jail of Pardon, and a Jail of Death. As for the Jail of Torture, it was dug under the ground, and in it there were many snakes and *scorpions* and it was very dark and deep; one could not tell night from day in it. And the Jail of Death was dug forty cubits into the ground. And when the king was angry with anyone in his kingdom and wanted to kill him, he sent him to that jail and had him thrown into it, and he was dead by the time he hit the floor. As for the Jail of Pardon, it was next to the king's house. In it he imprisoned those involved in civil cases.

When Zalikha wanted to imprison Yusuf, she sent for the jailer of the Jail of Pardon and said unto him: "Prepare for Yusuf in the jail a very strait and narrow place, for I want to imprison him in it." He *said:* and the jailer prepared a very strait place, with only room enough for a single man to sit down. And she sent for Yusuf and made him sit down in front of her and said unto him: "Oh Yusuf, by the authority of the king's honor, I shall yet hand you over to the torturers to torture you, just as you have tortured me, and I shall take you out of

---

[55] Qur'an 12:32.
[56] Qur'an 12:33.
[57] Qur'an 12:34.

the House of Honor to the House of the Wicked." Then she had him stripped of his clothing and the jewels he was wearing, and ordered him to put on a woolen tunic, and handcuffed him with very heavy iron handcuffs. Then she sent for her maidens and said unto them: "Go and place yourselves where Yusuf is to be led to jail, and when he passes by, cry out: 'This is the reward of him who disobeys his mistress!'"

When they came to the jail with him, he lowered his head and wept, wept very mightily. And [Ka'b] said that he was put in jail, and he said: "*In the name of Allah, there is no strength nor power but in Allah, the High, the Great.*" Then he sat down and wept, and the men in jail wept with him and marveled at his comeliness and beauty. And Jibril, *peace be upon him*, came down and said unto him: "*Oh Yusuf*, He Who is High, the Sovereign, sends you *greetings* and asks why you are weeping." Yusuf said: "My beloved Jibril, I am weeping because I don't see a clean place where I can make my *prescribed prayers.*" Jibril, *peace be upon him*, said: "*Oh Yusuf*, your Lord says you can perform *prayer* wherever you like, for Allah, *be He exalted*, has made the earth a mosque, and it is clean for you." And Yusuf made *prayer* wherever he chose in the jail, and every *Friday* he came and made *prayer* facing the doorway of the jail.

One day when Yusuf was facing the door of the jail, an *Arab* passed by on his *she-camel.* And he was saying: "I praise my Lord, and He is the praised Doer of whatever He wills. All good is from Him, and He is the Beginner and the Returner." *He said:* and Yusuf heard him from within the jail and wept, wept very mightily, and cried out unto him, and said: "*Oh Arab*, I beseech Allah on your behalf: *Allah have mercy on you.*" And he repeated his prayer. And Yusuf said unto him: "Where are you from, *oh Arab?*" He said unto him: "From the towns of al-Sham, from the vale of Kin'an." When Yusuf heard that, he fainted away. Then he awoke and said unto him: "*Oh Arab*, do you know in the vale of Kin'an an old man who is called Ya'qub?" He said: "Yes, I know him, for he is a very great old man who is called Ya'qub." He [Ka'b] said: and the *Arab* wept, wept very mightily, and said: "The old man Ya'qub has lost his eyesight out of sadness over his son Yusuf." Yusuf said: "By Allah, I am Yusuf, son of Ya'qub, son of Ishaq, son of Ibrahim, friend of the Merciful. If Allah, *be He exalted*, preserve you, and you reach the vale of Kin'an, go to Ya'qub and give him my *greetings* and tell him: '*Oh prophet* of Allah, I have seen a young lad imprisoned in the jail of Misra, handcuffed with irons, and he sends you *greetings*, and tells you: *oh father, I have followed after you in the state of the unfortunate.*'"

And Ya'qub had made himself a tent at the crossroads of the road, and no one passed by the road without his asking whence he came. And when this *Arab* passed by Ya'qub's tent, he cried out unto him: "*Oh Arab*, speak to me!" And the *Arab* walked over until he was standing before him, and said unto him: "*Peace be upon you, oh prophet of Allah!*" He answered: "*And peace be upon you, oh Arab!* Where are you coming from?" He said: "I am coming from the lands of Misra, and I have seen in the jail of Misra a young lad, beardless, of beauteous face, grown tall, with a face that is white and round as the circle of the moon on the night when it is full. Radiance shines from his face like rays of the sun. When he speaks, his tongue shows knowledge. His neck is like a white pearl, and when he speaks, his words are like pearls that come out of his mouth. If only you could see him, *oh prophet of Allah*, in the jail of Misra handcuffed and imprisoned, whence he sends you his *greetings!*" He [Ka'b] said: and Ya'qub fell upon him in a faint, weeping. And he came to with prayer on his lips, saying: "My beloved Yusuf! Lord, watch over him in his solitude, for You are All Powerful." Ka'b said: as for Yusuf, he kept weeping in jail until his body was disfigured.

XXI. The Cupbearer and the Baker

He [Ka'b] said: the day Yusuf entered jail, the king became angry with two of his servant boys and imprisoned them on the same day as Yusuf and in the same jail. And that is the saying of Allah, *be He exalted*, in His honored Qur'an, where it says: **"And two young men went to prison with him."**[58] Ka'b said: and the men in prison joined Yusuf and wept on account of his weeping. And whenever one of them had a dream, he recounted it to Yusuf, and he explained its meaning to them. And one day those two boys who were imprisoned on the same day as Yusuf came and said: "Let us go where Yusuf is and play a trick on him." And they went where Yusuf was. And one of them—it was the one who had served the king as his cupbearer—said unto Yusuf: "*Oh Yusuf*, I have seen in a dream that the king took me out of jail and returned me to his palace. And while I was in the palace, it was as if I saw a vineyard planted with many date palms, and as if they brought grapes and dates, and the grapes were mixed with the green dates. And I took three grapes and three green dates and squeezed them and gave the king of that wine to drink." Yusuf said: "Oh, what a good dream you have had!" And the other lad was the king's baker, and he said: "*Oh Yusuf*, I have seen in a dream that the king took me out of jail and held out to me a *basket.* In it was bread, and I was carrying it, and above my head were blackbirds who pecked my head and ate the bread. Oh truthful one,[59] tell us the meaning of my dream, for I see that you are of the good." Yusuf said: "Oh, what a bad dream you have had!" And it is as Allah, *glorified and exalted be He*, says in His honored Qur'an that he

---

[58] Qur'an 12:36.
[59] Joseph's chastity won him the epithet *ha-tzadik* ("the righteous") among the Jews, whence the Muslims gave him the title *al-ṣadak*; however, the cognate *ṣadak* in Arabic means "truthful."

said: "And two young men went to prison with him. One of them said: I dreamed that I was pressing wine. The other said: I dreamed that I was carrying upon my head bread whereof the birds were eating. Announce unto us the interpretation, for we see that you are of the good. Yusuf said: The food which you are given (daily) shall not come unto you but I shall tell you the interpretation ere it comes unto you. This is of that which my Lord Allah, *be He exalted*, has taught me. Lo! I have forsaken the *religion* of folk who believe not in Allah and are disbelievers in the *Torah of the world*.[60] And I have followed the *religion* of my fathers, Ibrahim, Isma'il, Ishaq, and Ya'qub. It never was for us to attribute aught as partner to Allah. This is of the bounty of Allah unto us and unto mankind; but most men give not thanks."[61] Then Yusuf turned to them and said: "Oh jailmates, as for the first of you, he will give the king his wine to drink. As for the other one, he will be hanged, and the birds will eat from his head." They said: "We have not dreamed any of what we told you. Rather, we were just playing a trick on you." Yusuf said: "Begone from me, for the matter is judged as it has been interpreted." Then Yusuf turned to the one who was destined to escape and said unto him: "Mention me to your lord." He said: "It pleases me, *oh* Yusuf." When dawn came, the king ordered the two boys who were imprisoned with Yusuf taken out of jail. As for the one who served the king his wine, the king pardoned him and restored him to his post. As for the other one, he ordered him to be stripped and hanged above the city gate. And Allah, *be He exalted*, sent blackbirds who ate off his head down to the brain. And it was as Yusuf said.

Ka'b al-Ahbar said: there was in Misra one of the king's enemies, a man they had captured from the towns of the *Arabs*. And he was very bad to the people and did many wrongs to the [other] prisoners in the jail, so that they complained to the king of his wickedness. And the king ordered him taken to a jail that he had in the lands of Falastin. And they handcuffed him and led him away. And they came to pass with him through the vale of Kin'an, where Ya'qub, *peace be upon him*, was. When Ya'qub heard them, he said unto them: "Oh people, whence are you coming, and whither are you going?" They said unto him: "We are coming from the lands of Misra, and we are going to the the lands of Falastin, for we are transporting a prisoner in chains, whom the king is sending to the jail in Falastin." And Ya'qub began to feel the prisoner and search him with his hand, and then he said: "Oh prisoner, I have a boy in jail in Misra. A light like the brightness of the moon shines from between his eyes and from his cheeks, [he

---

[60] The Arabic text of the Qur'an actually reads *al-akhira* ("the Hereafter"). Ursula Klenk speculates that the Spanish text may originally have read "la otra *ad-dunya*" (the other world), and that the copyist misread "la otra" as "la taura."

[61] Qur'an 12:36-38.

has] a green birthmark on his cheek, and he is of very gracious speech and of honored grandparents and parents." The prisoner said: "That description fits a boy who was with me in jail, but he died." He [Ka'b] said: and Ya'qub grew even sadder than before, and he begged Allah, *be He exalted,* to send him the *Angel of Death* to inform him about that. And the *Angel of Death* came to him and said: *"Peace be upon you, oh Ya'qub, and Allah's mercy and His blessing!"* Ya'qub said: *"And Allah's peace and mercy and blessing be upon you, oh Angel of Death!* I was very anxious to see you. Have you received the *soul* of my beloved Yusuf?" He said: "No, *oh* Ya'qub, for your beloved Yusuf is alive, and is given a great *honor."* He [Ka'b] said: and Ya'qub's anxiety was calmed when he heard that.

The narrator said: and Yusuf remained in jail for the time that Allah, *be He exalted,* willed. And it is said that he was in jail for twelve years. Then Zalikha longed to see Yusuf, and she sent word saying: "Bring Yusuf where I can see him, for I want to see him." And she ordered *brocade* and silk rolled out from the door of her palace to the door of the jail. And Zalikha and her maidens and servants went up to the door of the jail. And Yusuf came out unto her. When she looked at him and saw the woolen tunic that had scratched his back, and the chains that had eaten into his legs, she couldn't bear it and fell into a faint. And when she was taken back to her palace, she just kept on weeping until she wasted away.

XXII. The King's Dream

Yusuf was in jail twelve years, more or less. The compiler said: when Allah, *be He exalted,* willed to remove Yusuf from jail, Allah, *be He exalted,* made the king have that dream that Allah, *glory be to Him,* mentioned in His *book.* And he awoke terrified, frightened of what he had seen in that dream. And they said unto him: *"Oh* king, what is it that is worrying you and making you sad?" The king said: "I have seen in my dream, *oh* my people, very great wonders." Then he sent for the men of *knowledge* and of learning, and admonished them, saying: *"Oh* my sages, on *Friday* night I have seen the river al-Nil's water dry up until not a drop was left in it. And I wondered at that. And as I gazed at the al-Nil, marveling at its dryness, I saw seven fat cows come out, glistening as if they had been rubbed with oil, and each of them had a very large udder full of milk, and they kept coming until they stood in front of me. And as I gazed at them, behind them there came from the river seven very lean cows, dried up, lean; and it was as if sparks shot out from between their eyes, like sparks of fire. And each of them had a horn on the front of its head like a long lance. When I saw them, my fear deepened. And those seven cows kept coming until they stood in front of me, right next to the fat ones. And I wondered at that, and at how they remained apart from me. And lo, I beheld a very beautiful green meadow, and in it I saw seven dry ears of wheat. And I took one of them and rubbed it in my palm, and took out what was inside it, and I found not a single grain. Then I turned toward my right and I saw seven very beautiful green ears of wheat, and I rubbed them with my palm and my palm was filled with wheat. And that is the saying of Allah, *glorified and exalted be He*, where it says: **"And the king said: I saw seven fat kine which seven lean were eating, and seven green ears of wheat and other (seven) dry. Oh courtiers! Expound for me my dream, if you can interpret dreams. They answered: They are just dream fantasies! And we are not knowing in the interpretation of dreams."**[62] The [surviving] one of those two prisoners who had been taken out of jail said—for after a while he remembered [Yusuf]: "I will give you its interpretation, but let me think about it." And he went to the jail where Yusuf was. And this was the one to whom Yusuf had said: "Mention me to your lord." As soon as he had heard the king's dream, he went to Yusuf where he was in jail and said unto him: *"Peace be upon you, oh truthful one, and Allah's mercy and His blessing!"* And he sat down at his side and said unto him: "Oh Yusuf, I have dreamed that seven fat cows ate seven lean cows, and seven green ears of wheat and another seven dry ones [were] together. Interpret this dream for me, and peradventure I will declare it unto the people, and they will know it." Yusuf said: "You are lying, for you did not have this dream on *Friday* night. Tell me truthfully who dreamed this, *oh lad*, and if you tell me who dreamed this dream, I will tell you its interpretation, *Allah willing*." He said: "I will undeceive you and tell you the truth. Know, *oh truthful one*, that the king had this dream on *Friday* night." Yusuf said: "I knew that it was the king who had this dream. Go then, *oh lad*, and say unto them: sow for the next seven years, and whatever you harvest, set it aside with its ears of wheat except for the little that you eat. After that will come seven hard years when you will eat what you have stored except for a very little that you will save. After that will come years when the peoples will beg for relief, and they will be full of anguish and hard pressed." *He said:* and the lad left the jail very happy, joyful, and went straight to the king and told him the interpretation of his dream. The king said: "And who interpreted this dream for you?" He said: "I interpret it for you, *oh king*." The king said: "You are lying, *oh boy*, for that interpretation could only be from a very wise, very knowledgeable man, descended from sages. I promise you, *oh lad*, if you don't tell me the truth and let me know who the interpreter is, I will have your throat cut." Then the boy said: "Know, *oh king*, that Yusuf, the one who is in jail, interpreted it for me." The king said: "Yusuf is in jail?" The boy said: "Yes, *oh king*." When the king heard that, he wept. Then he turned [to

---

[62] Qur'an 12:43–44.

the boy] and said: "So much the worse for you! Go to the jail, and bring him out only if he is willing, for he is the one who chose jail for himself."

And the boy went to the jail and went up to Yusuf and said unto him: "Oh Yusuf, the king gives you the choice of whether to go out or to remain in jail. Decide whether you want to go out." Yusuf said unto him: "Go back to the king, and ask him why those women stained their hands, for my lord is very familiar with their wiles. And if they will exonerate me and hold me guiltless of what I was accused of in the presence of the king, I will go out of the jail, and if not, I would rather stay in jail than go out." And he informed him of what Yusuf said. The king said: "This lad Yusuf wants to be exonerated of what he was accused of?" And the king sent for the nine women, and when they had come, he had them sit down in their seats. Then he sent for Zalikha, and when she had come, he had her sit down among the women. Then he sent for the queen's sister, the mother of the baby that testified for Yusuf, and the child came with her. When they were all together, the king said unto them: "What were you thinking when you tried to seduce Yusuf?" They said: "We take refuge with Allah, we know no wickedness of him." The king's wife said: "Now the truth is out. I tried to seduce him, and he told the truth." Then the boy went to Yusuf: "Zalikha has exonerated you of what you were accused of and has admitted that it was she who tried to seduce you." And Yusuf rejoiced with a great joy when he heard it. Then he said: "That is so that [the king] may know that I didn't betray him when he was absent, and that Allah does not guide the wiles of slanderers."

XXIII. Yusuf Is Released from Prison

Then Jibril, *peace be upon him*, came down and said unto him: "Oh Yusuf, now you are free. Cleanse yourself, for you would have sunk in the sea of sinners had not Allah, *be He exalted*, preserved you and allowed you to understand the interpretation." Yusuf said: "And how can I cleanse myself? For my soul lusts after wickedness unless my Lord take pity, for my Lord is merciful to pardon." Then the king said: "I want to honor this lad with a very great honor." Zalikha rejoiced with a great joy and sent for the women of her city, and there was no one in Misra from her region that didn't show up for the day when Yusuf was released from jail. The king likewise summoned the men of his kingdom and they came on horseback from land and sea, so that there was no one in Misra and its region who didn't come for Yusuf's release from jail. The people of Misra dressed in very rich garments, both men and women, and adorned themselves, and adorned their marketplaces. And the king said: "I will honor him with an honor unlike any that has been given before or after, for he is a very wise young man." Then he ordered the palaces decorated, and they were decorated with the best cloths and ornaments. And he ordered the best horses adorned for him with ornaments of gold and silver and the precious colors of jewels, with clothing and rich cloths as well as jewels of gold and silver. And he said: "I shall adorn him with the king's own ornaments, and I shall gird on him the king's sword, and put the king's rings on his fingers, and I will have him ride the king's horse, and I will have the king's ensign unfurled above his head, and I will choose him for myself, because he is powerful, very faithful, and loyal."

He said: and Jibril, *peace be upon him*, came down to Yusuf and said unto him: "Oh Yusuf, I congratulate you on the honor Allah, *be He exalted*, has bestowed on you, for He has remedied your anguish, and has directed you to the right path and concord and joy." And Yusuf rejoiced, and magnified praise and blessings unto Allah, *glorified and exalted be He*, and *bowed down* and prolonged his *prostration* with *praises* and sanctifications unto his Lord Allah, *blessed and exalted be He. Said* Ka'b: wave after wave of *angels* unceasingly came to congratulate him and said: "May the honor Allah, *be He exalted*, has bestowed upon you do you good." And they said unto him: "Know that Allah, *be He exalted*, desires to honor and favor you above the sons of Ya'qub, and to give you all the land of Misra to rule, and to subject its kings and lords unto you." Yusuf said: "Oh my Lord, inspire me to praise You and thank You as is meet and right for Your honored Face and Your nobility, and the greatness of Your Lordship."

Then the king ordered a platform decorated. And its length was two miles, and one mile in width, and it was made of marble, and upon it were embroidered *hangings*. And its turrets were of gold, and upon the turrets green banners and red ensigns. And it had a very large door for the king, and there were seven doormen to guard the large door. And above the[63] door were seventy golden bells. And the width of the door was fifty cubits. Hanging over the door were brocade *hangings*. All of its areas were the loveliest things that Allah, *be He exalted, created*. And on a dais was a bird that waved its wings. And that dais and that building were the ones that 'Ad, son of 'Ad, son of Iram Dati Il'imadi, had built—the same ones the *Pharaohs* inherited until they ended up in the hands of King al-'Aziz. And he only opened it up when he wanted to have very great pleasure. And he ordered it opened, and ordered it spread with *silk* and *brocade*. Then he sent for the *hangings*, and they were hung upon it, along with the banners and ensigns. And the throne was put in its place, and it was of gold. Above it was a scarlet *dome*. Then he summoned the servants and maids, and they surrounded the throne. Then the *ministers* and the patriarchs came, with maces and golden swords in their hands, and they stood before the throne.

---

[63] The ms. has "cada puerta" ("each door"), but only one door is mentioned.

Then he ordered five hundred knights and five hundred infantrymen to surround the jail. And he ordered them to roll out *brocade* right up to the jail door.
And he ordered incense burners placed on the right and left sides of the road.
Then he sent for five hundred maidens, and he gave each one a pot of pure
musk. And he sent for saffron and all sweet smelling [herbs] and had them
strewn across the path. And he had the maidens stationed on the right and left
sides of the road. And scarlet cloths were spread on the ground the whole
length of the road, and they were covered with jasmine and roses and myrtle.

Then he summoned his *vizier* and ensign-bearer and gave him his chain and
his ring and his sword, and had his horse, which was called Alkifah, saddled.
No one rode that horse but the king. Then he said unto him: "Take all of this
and go to the jail, and dress him in these jewels, and put this crown of mine
and my rings on him, and gird my sword on him, and let him ride on this horse
of mine. And carry this staff before him and unfurl this ensign above his head,
for I want to single him out for myself."

He said: and the *vizier* went to the jail and found Yusuf in it weeping. And
the reason for his weeping was that the jailer had told him: "Oh Yusuf, the king
is making very great preparations to take you out of jail, and I think he is taking you out to kill you." And the *vizier* found him weeping and said unto him:
"Do not weep, *oh* Yusuf, for your fortune has changed. You are now more fortunate than anyone before or after you. Take off those garments of sadness."
And he took off the woolen tunic and put on the garments of honor and the
king's crown. And the *vizier* took him out of the jail and put him in the king's
own stirrups. Then he unfurled the king's ensign above his head, and the *vizier*
walked before Yusuf, and the king's armies received him. And Jibril, *peace be
upon him*, and seventy thousand *angels* met him, and greeted him, and said unto
him: "Congratulations, *oh* Yusuf, for this is [the fulfillment of] the promise your
Lord made unto you when you were in the cistern."

XXIV. Yusuf Becomes King

Said Ka'b: and the king's armies surrounded Yusuf, and the people crowded together to see him. And his face shone with joy and gladness. And he began to
make his way over the silk and the *brocade*, and the maidens received him with
the perfumes of *ambergris* and camphor and musk. And the towns gleamed in
his reflected light. When Yusuf reached the gate of the platform, the king's *ministers* and patriarchs hastened to him to carry the two-sided axes and staves before him, *may Allah grant him peace and save him*, and they said unto him: "Oh
honored king, enter; for you are now favored with good fortune, for you will
never again be unfortunate." And the standards and ensigns were raised above

his head. When Yusuf reached the *dais*, the king arose and made him sit in his own chair. And the king sat down facing him, *may Allah grant him peace and save him*, and the king said unto him: "Oh Yusuf, today you are given power, loyal one." Yusuf said: "Put me in charge of the *treasure houses* of the land, for I am a very good steward and very wise." And that is the saying of Allah, *be He exalted*.[64] The king said: "Oh Yusuf, but I am doing all of this because you are better suited to reign than I, and you are worthy of it." Allah, *glorified and exalted be He*, says: **"Thus gave We power to Yusuf in the land . . . where We pleased. We reach with Our mercy whom We will. We lose not the reward of the good."**[65]

He said: when Yusuf sat on the king's chair, the keys of the *treasure houses* of the kingdom were given to him. And the king stood up and said unto Yusuf: "Oh Yusuf, remain in charge of all the kingdom from this day forward, for you are wiser and more deserving of it than I." Then the king went away and settled down in a house that he had chosen for himself, and he left the kingdom to Yusuf, *peace be upon him*.

He said: only a few days passed before King al-'Aziz died, and the kingdom was left to Yusuf. And the king was forgotten because of Yusuf. *Said Ka'b:* then Yusuf ordered the people to sow all the land, the rugged as well as the flat land, during the good years for the years of drought, those that Allah mentioned in His honored Qur'an. And the people sowed, leaving neither flat nor rugged lands unsown up to the very tops of the hills and the bottoms of the valleys. And they prepared granaries to store the harvest of the seven years. When the good years were past, the water stopped for seven years, for not a drop came down from *heaven* nor did Allah cause a green leaf to sprout, until the River al-Nil dried up. And hunger fell upon the people. And they joined together and went to Yusuf and said unto him: "Oh king, sell us grain for doubloons and *dirhams*." And he sold it to them for doubloons and *dirhams* and gold and silver. Everything ended up in Yusuf's hands. In the third year they came to Yusuf: "Sell us provisions in exchange for our male and female slaves." And he sold it to them until all [the slaves] were his. When the fourth year came, they came to him and said unto him: "Sell us provisions in exchange for our camels and horses." And he sold it to them until everything was his. When the fifth year came, they said unto him: "Oh king, sell us provisions in exchange for the livestock and cows we have left." And he sold it to them until everything was his. When the sixth year came, they said unto him: "Oh king, sell us provisions in exchange for our houses and farms." And he sold it to them for their houses

---

[64] That is, a paraphrase of Qur'an 12:55: "He said: Set me over the storehouses of the land. Lo! I am a skilled custodian."

[65] Qur'an 12:56.

and farms. When the seventh year came, they said unto him: "Sell us provisions in exchange for our *seed pearls* and pearls and our own persons." And he sold it to them until everything was his, all the money and people in Misra.

XXV. The Aged Zalikha Becomes a Slave

And Zalikha experienced the same lack of provisions and hunger that befell the other people, and this was after the death of King al-'Aziz. And Zalikha sold all her jewels and farms and horses and estates, and everything she owned on the face of the earth, until she had nothing left with which to buy provisions. Then she sold herself to Yusuf and became one of Yusuf's slaves and captives. He [Ka'b] said: and Yusuf was going from his palace to the city and outside the city. And Zalikha had built herself a house to live in at the crossroads. After Yusuf had grown rich with governing the kingdom, he forgot Zalikha with the length of days, and Yusuf did not mention her. And Zalikha grew old, and her back was bent, and her eyes went blind, and she was in dire straits. And Zalikha built herself a house out of canes outside the city.

And Yusuf went out every day for a drive through the city and its outskirts so that those of his kingdom might see him, and to hear complaints and do justice to those who had been wronged. And he kept an eye on all that Allah had entrusted to his dominion and commanded good behavior and forbade wrongdoing. And when Yusuf wanted to go out riding, he rode on King al-'Aziz's horse. And when the stable boy saddled the horse, the horse neighed so that those of Misra heard its neighing and knew that the king was going out. And when he rode out, the people rode out to accompany him, and five hundred thousand rode on horseback on his right side, and five hundred thousand on horseback on his left side, and before him went a thousand squires with swords in their hands and a thousand with halberds, and a thousand young men with golden maces; and likewise behind him. And he never passed by anyone without their remarking: "This servant has been given a great kingdom." And that is the saying of Allah, *glorified and exalted be He*, that said: **"And the people did not care about that which Allah, *be He exalted,* of His bounty hath bestowed upon them. For We bestowed upon the house of Ibrahim the *book* and Wisdom, and We bestowed on them a mighty kingdom."**[66] Whatever Allah, *be He exalted*, makes great, that is a great thing.

And Zalikha was wearing a woolen tunic and was girdled with a rope around her waist, and she sat at the crossroads to await Yusuf's passing. And when he

---

[66] Qur'an 4:54.

passed by, she would cry out to him, but Yusuf didn't hear her cries. And Zalikha did that for many days, but it did her no good at all. When she saw that Yusuf did not hear her shouts, she turned to her idol that she worshipped instead of Allah, *be He exalted,* and broke it, and said: "Woe unto you, *oh* idol, for he who adores anything but Allah, the Lord of *creation,* is lost! Because I adored you, my kingdom has been taken from me and given to my slave. From this day forward I shall not believe in you."

He said. Ka'b said: when Zalikha broke her idol and withdrew from serving the idol and believed in Allah, *glorified and exalted be He,* Yusuf rode out one day, as was his wont, with his armies and his adornments; and she stood at the crossroads waiting for Yusuf. When he was near, she cried out in her loudest voice: "*Oh* king, blessed be He who makes obedient slaves into kings, and disobedient kings into slaves! And these are words that have been found and spoken with a broken heart." And Yusuf hearkened unto her and summoned one of his servants and said unto him: "*Oh* lad, go with that *old lady* to the money house, and see what she wants, and find out what she needs, and give her what she asks for." *He said:* and the boy took Zalikha by the hand and went with her to Yusuf's palace and said unto her: "*Oh old lady,* what do you need, for the king has ordered me to give you whatever you ask for?" She said: "It is *forbidden* for anyone but the king to remedy my need." And she sat down [to wait] until the king should return to the palace.

When Yusuf was back at the palace, he took off his rich raiment and put on a woolen garment and spread ashes beneath him. And he sat down on them *praising* Allah, *be He exalted,* and sanctifying Him. And while he was doing this, the boy came in, and Yusuf said unto him: "Did you find out what the old lady needed?" He said: "*Oh* king, she says that no one may know her need but you." And Yusuf ordered her sent for, and she came—now falling, now getting back up—until she stood before Yusuf. When Yusuf saw her, he wept, wept mightily, for he was very compassionate, *may Allah grant him peace and save him.* And he said unto her: "*Oh old lady,* I heard you say words that cut me to the heart." She said: "*Oh* king, I said: blessed be He who makes obedient slaves into kings, and disobedient kings into slaves!" Yusuf said: "*Indeed,* you speak the truth, *oh old lady,* for Allah, *be He exalted,* gives the kingdom to whom He wills, and honor to whom He wills; and He humbles whom He wills. In His hand is good, in His hand is evil, and He has power over everything." He said: "Oh, how good is what you have said, *oh old lady!* But who are you?" for Yusuf did not recognize her because of the change in her after her beauty and loveliness [had vanished]. She said: "*Oh* Yusuf, how quickly you have forgotten me! I am the one who prepared the king's own bed and honor for you, and prepared the king's chair for you. I am the one who offered you my body with my words. I am Zalikha, the one who bought you for much money! Oh, what a great grief, *oh* Yusuf!"

When Yusuf heard her, he wept, wept mightily, and said: "*There is no strength or power but in Allah, the High, the Great.* Oh, how sorry I am for you, oh Zalikha!" He [Ka'b] said: the two of them did not cease weeping until they dropped what they had in their hands." Then Yusuf turned to her and said: "Oh Zalikha, what has become of your beauty and loveliness and your kingdom?" She said: "Oh Yusuf, it has gone from me. He Who gave it to you took it from me." Yusuf said: "I shall give you three wishes. Ask whatever you want for your honor and to keep my promise." She said: "I will not ask you for anything until you swear with the oath you swore when I sought to seduce you, and you swore that you would never approach what is *forbidden.*" He said: "By the authority of the grey hair of Ibrahim, my grandfather, I swear to grant you three wishes, whatever you want. Ask for what you will." Zalikha said: "My first wish is for you to pray to Allah, *be He exalted,* that He restore my sight and my youth." And Yusuf prayed to his Lord, and Allah, *glory be to Him,* restored her sight and her youth. When she saw Yusuf and his beauty and comeliness, she said: "My second wish is for you to pray to Allah that He give me back my beauty and loveliness." And Allah gave her back her beauty and loveliness, and returned her to the age of an eighteen-year-old *maiden.* And Allah increased her beauty and loveliness to seven times what she had before. And that day she was a hundred and twenty years old. When Yusuf saw her, and saw her loveliness and beauty, he turned his face elsewhere so as not to look upon her, for he was afraid that what happened the first time would be repeated. She said: "Oh Yusuf, I still have my third wish." He said: "Ask, oh Zalikha." "I ask you—but my request is not to you but to Him Who judges and judgment is not passed upon Him, Who passes sentence but is not sentenced Himself." Yusuf said: "And what is your wish, oh Zalikha, for by the grey hair of my grandfather Ibrahim, I shall grant it, be it what it may?" Then she said: "My wish is for you to marry me, for long have you tormented me, and my body has wasted away with desire for you. But now that Allah, *be He exalted,* has given me dominion over you, I am content, *Allah willing.*"

XXVI. Yusuf Marries Zalikha

He said: and that was very grievous unto Yusuf, and he wept. And Allah, *be He exalted,* sent *a revelation* to Yusuf and said unto Yusuf: "It is necessary to grant her her wish." He said: "Oh Yusuf, by My Honor and My Nobility, it was already known unto Me that she must be your wife in this *world* and in the next." And she married Yusuf, *peace be upon him.* And Allah, *be He exalted,* sent him seventy thousand *angels* who said unto him: "May marriage do you good, oh Yusuf, for this is what Allah promised you when you were in the cistern." Yusuf said: "*Praise be to Allah, Lord of the universe!*" Then he lifted up his hands to *heaven* and said: "Lord, complete Your graciousness unto me, and remedy old Ya'qub, and let him as *a blessing* look upon me and be joined with me. *You are powerful over all things.*"

Said Ka'b al-Aḥbar: then Yusuf built for Zalikha a *pavilion* on twelve huge nuggets of reddish gold. And he put upon the *pavilion* a covering of silver, and before the *pavilion* pillars of yellow gold. And he inlaid *sandalwood* in the door, and had scarlet *hangings* hung over it. And under each of the nuggets of the *pavilion* he placed a golden vulture with its wings extended. And they were filled with musk and *ambergris*. Then he unfurled the *hangings* of the *pavilion*, and there were lamps of *seed pearls* hanging in it, their chains [being] of silver and of gold. Then he placed in the midst of the *pavilion* a very rich bed, garnished and covered with brocade, and he adorned it with all beautiful adornments. And he said unto Zalikha: "Oh Zalikha, this is the *pavilion* of obedience and not that of disobedience." And Yusuf, *peace be upon him*, was alone with her. *The author of the story said:* Allah gave Yusuf as *a blessing* by Zalikha twelve male children. He praised Allah, *be He exalted*, with them and the *angels* of the seven heavens.

XXVII. Yusuf's Brothers Go to Misra

Said Ka'b al-Aḥbar: and it was the saying and judgment of Allah, *be He exalted*, that there was a famine in al-Sham, so that the cattle and animals died, and the people perished of hunger. And Ya'qub turned to his sons and said unto them all together before him: "Oh sons, do you not see this time of straitness and very great famine that has befallen us?" They said: "Yes, *oh prophet* of Allah. What then would you like for us to do?" Ya'qub said: "I want you to go to Misra and buy us wheat from its king." They said: "*Oh prophet of Allah*, do you want to send us to the haughty of the earth and the *Pharaohs* of the earth; and do you not know their enmity toward us and our fathers before us?" Ya'qub said: "*Oh sons*, Allah, *blessed and exalted be He*, has commanded the king of Misra, and he died, and now there reigns in Misra a youth, the wisest and simplest and most sane of people. Go then unto him, and give him *greetings*, and inform him of our *misfortune* and necessity, for he will provide you with a remedy for our need." He [Ka'b] said: then they prepared for the journey. And there were ten of them, and he gave each one of them a belt of *dirhams* and a *she-camel* from his herd. And they bade Ya'qub farewell and set out.

And Yusuf had prayed to Allah, *be He exalted*, to let him see his brothers. And Yusuf had ordered guards placed along the road between al-Sham and Misra, and he ordered the man in charge of guarding the pass not to let anyone from al-Sham enter Misra without first requiring him to recount his lineage, and sending a written report of it to Yusuf. When the sons of Ya'qub, *peace be upon him*, came, and the guardian of the pass didn't recognize them, he said unto them: "Where are you from, and where are you going, and what are you seeking, for I consider you scouts and spies." They said: "By Allah, we are not scouts. Rather, we are from Kin'an, sons of Ya'qub." Ka'b *said* that the Lord of the Pass said unto them: "You are all sons of Ya'qub?" They said: "Yes." He said: "My king has ordered me not to let anyone pass without inquiring about what they are doing and their business. What is it that you want?" They said: "We want to enter Misra, for we want to ask the king to sell us bread." He said: "Stay [here] until I write the king, for he ordered me not to let anyone from al-Sham pass without first informing him." He [Ka'b] said: and he took them an awning of canes so that they would be in the shade, and he wrote to Yusuf saying: "*In the name of Allah, the Merciful, the Compassionate*. From the Lord of the Pass to the King: know that a caravan from al-Sham has reached me, and I have never seen a group of greater brightness nor of such beautiful faces. And they say that they are sons of Ya'qub. And they claim that a very great drought and famine has reached them, and they come that you may give them provisions in exchange for their money. Consider, *oh king*, what answer I shall give them, whether you will give them license to enter Misra or order them to return."

When the letter reached the king, he wept, wept mightily, and said: "May Allah comfort you concerning me, *oh prophet* of Allah!" And then he lifted up his hands and his head to the *heavens* and said: "Lord, do not punish me for what I am about to do!" Then he wrote to the Lord of the Pass: "*In the name of Allah, the Merciful, the Compassionate*. When you receive this letter, let that caravan go their way, for none more honorable than they have come from al-Sham nor will another equal to them pass by you."

When the king's letter reached him, he let them go their way. Then Yusuf gave orders for the city gates to be opened and the markets to be decorated and provided with provisions. And he ordered *hangings* of *brocade* hung over the doors of his markets, and he ordered doormen to be stationed at each door. And he ordered a *pavilion* erected, and it was done. And inside the *pavilion* he had his throne of *seed pearls* placed. And he arranged for a man who spoke Hebrew to stand on the right side of the throne, and for a man who spoke the *Coptic* language of Misra to stand on the left side. And he ordered that wheat and barley be brought before him.

When the sons of Ya'qub entered the city, they marveled at it, for they had never seen its like, and they were bewildered by its riches. And they traveled on until they reached the palace of King Yusuf, *peace be upon him*. When they tried to go in unto Yusuf, the king's doorman came out and said unto them:

"Where do you want to go?" They said: "We are sons of Ya'qub, the *prophet* of Allah, and we want to go in to the king to buy wheat and barley from him." And the doorman detained them for three days. And every day they were sent out a provision of dishes and good drinks from the king's table. And on the third day the doorman came out to them, just as [he had done] at first, and when he ordered them to enter, and they went inside the palace of Yusuf, *peace be upon him*, their sight was confused by what they saw of the king's riches and graces and puissance. They all marveled and signaled one to another, and said: "A great kingdom has been given to this youth."

XXVIII. Yusuf Receives His Brothers

When they arrived before the king, they bowed their heads and lowered their sight from the king's *face*. Then all together they gave the king their *greeting*, saying: "*Peace be upon you, your excellency, and Allah's mercy and blessing!*" And Yusuf, *peace be upon him*, looked at them and knew them, but they knew him not. And it is as Allah, *glorified and exalted be He*, said in his honored Qur'an. When Yusuf saw them, he could not help weeping very mightily. Then he said unto them: "Who are you?" as if he didn't recognize them. They said: "*Oh* king, we are the sons of Ya'qub." Yusuf said unto them: "May Allah, *be He exalted*, grant you life, *oh* sons of Ya'qub. Are you in need of anything?" They said: "Yes, *oh* king, for in our land a very great famine and drought has befallen, so that the people are dying from the force of the great famine, and the animals are all being lost to the great drought. And know that the *prophet* Ya'qub sends us to you that you may help us and sell us wheat in exchange for our money." Yusuf said: "It pleases me, by the honor of Ya'qub, and by your honor."

Then Yusuf ordered their money belts taken. Then he called one of his servant lads (and he had given him orders earlier and had said unto him: "When you see that I have measured the weight, take the belt of the man whose weight I have measured and put the money in his sack, mixed up with the wheat, and make sure that no one sees you"). He [Ka'b] said: then Yusuf sent for his measuring cup. And the wheat was brought and poured out before him. Then Yusuf took the cup and began to measure it out for them, and he let no one else but himself do the measuring, that the measure be not shortened during his turn. And every time Yusuf measured the grain, the lad put the belt in the sack, until they were all finished, and all the belts were in the sacks. And Yusuf did that so that they would find themselves with their money and return again to buy wheat and bring their brother Yamin.

When he had finished the measuring, and they had their loads, all came to-gether to thank the king, and they stood before him and said unto him: "May Allah, *glorified and exalted be He*, reward you for our sake and for the sake of the *prophet* of Allah, Ya'qub, *oh* king, with a good reward, for if you could see him, *oh* king, you would pity his great sorrow." And Yusuf said: "And what is the matter with him that I should feel sorry for him?" They said: "*Oh* king, he had a son whose name was Yusuf. And he went out one day with us—for we are his brothers—to keep watch over the cattle, and the wolf ate him. And a very great sadness has overcome him, and he has wept until he lost his eyesight, and his back is bent. And if you could see him, *oh* king, you would take pity and feel very sorry for him." Yusuf said: "Slow down, *oh* sons of Ya'qub, tarry a while, for I want to bid you *farewell*." And he went inside the palace until his grief abated. Then he went out to them and bade them farewell, and wished them *peace*. And they wished him *peace* and a good reward for the good [he had done done them] and Allah's gratitude.

Yusuf said unto them: "*Oh* sons of Ya'qub!" They said: "What is your plea-sure, *oh* king?" He said: "What do you think of my way of doing business?" They said: "*Oh* king, may Allah reward you with good, no one more God-fearing nor of better practice than you has been seen. Command what you wish us to do, and we will do it, *Allah willing*." Yusuf said unto them: "And do you not see how I give full measure, and how I am the best of those who show hospitality to-ward guests?" They said: "Indeed, *oh* king, and we will make known unto Ya'qub, our father, the hospitality and high honor with which you have re-ceived us." Yusuf said unto them: "I need something from you, *oh* sons of Ya'qub." "And what is it that you need, *oh* king?" He said: "For you to tell me how many children were born unto Ya'qub." They said: "*Oh* king, twelve male children and a maiden called Dunya." Yusuf said: "Then why do I see only ten of you? What has become of the other two?" They said unto him: "*Oh* king, as for one of them, the wolf ate the one named Yusuf. And he was the comeliest of us in his face and the best spoken and the most beloved of our father Ya'qub. One day he went out with us to graze the cattle, and the wolf ate him. And Ya'qub has wept for him until he lost his eyesight, and his bones have bent, and his eyes have turned white with sadness and grief." Yusuf said: "And did the wolf eat him before your very eyes?" They said: "Yes, *oh* king." He said: "What then has become of your other brother?" They said: "He is with the cat-tle, for he is keeping watch over it while we have come here, and he has been assigned to serve Ya'qub." Yusuf said as Allah, *be He exalted*, recounts in his honored Qur'an that Yusuf said when he saw them, and had honored them and filled their needs: **"Bring unto me a brother of yours from your father. See ye not that I fill up the measure and I am the best of hosts? And if ye bring him not unto me, then there shall be no measure for you with me, nor shall**

ye draw near."[67] They said: "We will ask his father for him, and we will do it."
Then they wished Yusuf *peace*, and bade him farewell.

XXIX. The Brothers Return to Ya'qub

And they returned to Ya'qub with the wheat, and they rejoiced and made
merry. When they got to Ya'qub, they went in unto him and all together *greeted*
him and said unto him: "*Oh* Ya'qub, the king of Misra sends you *greetings* and
wishes that Allah, *be He exalted*, may comfort you in the *misfortune* that has
befallen you concerning your son Yusuf, when the wolf ate him. *Oh prophet of
Allah*, know that he has shown us great honor and good company and a great
welcome and has given us full measure. We have never seen a king of better
customs or business practices nor more just nor more fearful of Allah. When
we left to come to you and bade him farewell and wished him *peace*, he asked
us how many children had been born unto the *prophet* Ya'qub, and we told him.
He said unto us: 'I would like for you to come back to me with your brother
Yamin, for I would like much to see him.' And if we don't take him, he said,
there would be no measure of bread for us. And we bade him farewell, and we
promised to bring him. And if we don't take him, there will be no measure of
bread for us, nor shall we be allowed to draw near him." Then they said as Allah
says in His Qur'an: **"Send with us our brother; surely we will guard him well.
Ya'qub said: Can I entrust him to you save as I entrusted his brother to you
aforetime? Allah is better at guarding, and He is the Most Merciful of those
who show mercy."**[68]

When they opened their sacks and found that their coins had been returned
to them, they said: "*Oh* father, this is our money that has been returned to us."
They said: "Father, give us our brother, and the measure will be increased unto
us, and we will guard him well." Ya'qub said: "I will not send him with you unless you swear by Allah to return him to me, unless he be 'surrounded' (which
means, 'unless he die')." When they gave their oaths, Ya'qub said: "May Allah
be the Guarantor of what I have said."

Ka'b al-Ahbar said: when Ya'qub said: "I will not send him with you unless
you swear by Allah . . . ," he meant for them to swear not to separate from him
nor to leave him alone. And they swore by the *prophet* Muhammad, *may Allah
grant him peace and save him*. After they swore, Ya'qub said: "Allah, *be He exalted*, is my Witness and my Guarantor."

---

[67] Qur'an 12:59–60.
[68] Qur'an 12:63–64.

He said. He [Ka'b] said: and Ya'qub was afraid that they would give them the evil eye when they entered Misra.[69] And he said unto his sons: "Oh sons, how many gates are there in Misra to go in unto the king?" They said: "There are many gates to go in unto the king." Ya'qub said as Allah, *be He exalted,* says in His Qur'an that Ya'qub said: **"Go not in by one gate; go in by different gates."**[70] After Ya'qub decided to send his son Yamin with them, when the day of their departure came, Ya'qub came to his son at the hour of *dawn* and dressed him and girded him with a belt, and that belt had been the belt of Ibrahim, *peace be upon him.* And he bade him farewell, and hugged him to his breast, and set him upon his *she-camel.* Then he wept and said: "Oh son, thus did I with your brother Yusuf, and I haven't seen him again up to this hour." Then he said: "I commend you to Allah, the Lord of *blessedness.*"

XXX. The Brothers Go Back to Misra with Yamin

He said: and the caravan set out for Misra. And Yusuf had built twelve doors in his palace, with the names of his brothers above them. And none of the doors was more beautiful than Yusuf's own door, but it was equaled by the door of his brother Yamin, his brother by both father and mother. When Ya'qub's sons reached the Lord of the Pass, he said unto them: "When I saw you the first time, it was not the same, for now there are eleven of you. Who is this that comes with you and whom you surround as if he were a fugitive?" They said: "Hush, for the king has ordered us to bring this lad to him." He said: "Stay here until I write the king and let him know about you." Then he wrote: "*In the name of Allah, the Merciful, the Compassionate.* From the Lord of the Pass to the King of Misra: When you receive this letter, you will know that eleven men have arrived [here], and they claim that they are all sons of Ya'qub. And they are not coming in the same manner as the first time, but with them comes a beardless youth with a beautiful face and eloquent of speech. Of all these people he is the one who most resembles you, *oh* king, and they claim and say that you have ordered them to bring him to you."

When the king saw the letter and read it, he rejoiced with very great joy over their coming. And he wrote the Lord of the Pass to keep them with him seven days. However, Yusuf did that in order to prepare the reception for his brothers and his brother Yamin. *He said.* Ka'b said: then Yusuf ordered silk spread

---

[69] Because for so many sons of a single man to appear in public together might provoke envy and thereby attract the "evil eye."

[70] Qur'an 12:67.

around, and he sent for brocade *hangings*, and they were hung, and he ordered the gates of the city to be opened, and he sent for banners and *hangings*, and they were unfurled along the wall. And he stationed a thousand patriarchs at each gate, with a naked sword in each one's hand. Then he sent for the candelabras, and had them lit; and he sent for the thrones, and had them put in their places. Then he sent for the cups, and they were set out full of precious drinks and placed before him. Then he ordered six golden tables lined up with the chairs, and the tables were adorned with precious drinks and foods. And he ordered silken tablecloths placed on the tables. Then he sent for his maidservants, and they surrounded the tables. Then he ordered his doormen stationed at the doors. And he ordered the markets of the city well provisioned, he ordered banners and ensigns hung on the city wall, and he ordered the citizens to go out to receive the sons of Ya'qub until they should come in unto him within the city.

Said Ka'b: each of the sons of Ya'qub entered through a [different] gate. And Shama'un and Yamin entered through the same gate. And it was not because they feared anything from Allah,[71] but because of Ya'qub's need for them to do this, which he had made manifest to them. And he was [a man] of *knowledge*, as we have shown, but most people don't understand.[72]

Said Ka'b: when Ya'qub's sons entered the city of Yusuf and beheld the markets and their wealth and the abundance of their goods, they marvelled at that, and said one unto another: "A great kingdom has been given unto this lad." And people [kept] staring at Yamin and his loveliness and beauty, and his resemblance to Yusuf. And they reached the king's palace, where they were denied entrance and detained three days. When it was the fourth day, they were given license to enter. When they reached the second door, the doorman said unto them: "Who are you?" They said unto him: "We are sons of Ya'qub, the *prophet* of Allah, and we want to go in unto the king." *He said:* and they were detained three days. And thus, every time they reached a door, they were detained three days, until they came to the seventh door. And they looked and beheld a very wondrous door. It was four hundred cubits high, fifty cubits wide, plated with reddish gold and white silver, and surmounted with turrets, and on each turret were shining pearls, and on the door were enameled figures of everything that Allah, *be He exalted, created* of birds and animals. In the middle of the door was a pearl date palm with golden branches. And the sons of Ya'qub lifted up their heads and saw that the king's young men and servants had spread out silk and *brocade* for them to walk upon.

---

[71] That is, they were not superstitious.
[72] Paraphrase of Qur'an 12:68.

XXXI. Yusuf Reunited with Yamin

When Yusuf saw Yamin, he wept, wept mightily. And they said one unto another: "What Allah gave this youth was never seen among the peoples, for he has been given a very great kingdom." And Yamin walked with his brothers, and he looked at Yusuf and saw his beauty and comeliness and radiance, but he didn't recognize him. And he turned to his brothers and said: "Oh brothers, how has this king been given a complete resemblance to my brother Yusuf?" And Yamin still didn't recognize him, nor did he take his eyes off him; but his brothers had their heads lowered, full of fear because of what they saw of the frightening demeanor of the *ministers* and doormen and patriarchs.

And when the sons of Ya'qub reached the king, they *greeted* him, and he returned their *greeting* and said: "May Allah grant you life, *oh* sons of Ya'qub!" And they said unto him: "*Oh* king, the *prophet* of Allah, Ya'qub, sends you *greetings* and prays that Allah give you the best of rewards, since you are such a good king. May Allah brighten your face and exalt your kingdom and heighten your esteem."

Then Yusuf had the tables brought, and they were put in their places, and on them were placed an indescribable variety of drinks and foods. Then Yusuf said: "*Oh* sons of Ya'qub, behold six tables here. Each one of you, take the hand of his brother by father and mother, and sit with him at a table. *He said:* Shama'un took the hand of his brother and sat down with him, and Niskakhur took the hand of his brother and sat down with him, and Raubil took the hand of his brother and sat down, and Shama'un[73] took the hand of his brother and sat down. And the ten sat down, and they sat at five tables and began to eat; but Yamin remained standing. And the king said unto him: "What is the matter with you? Why don't you sit down to eat with your brothers?" He said: "*Oh* king, you have ordered each one to sit down with his brother by father and mother. And thus have they done, *oh* king. I have remained alone, because, know, *oh* king, that I had a brother by father and mother named Yusuf, and one day he went out with these brothers of mine to keep watch over the cattle, and the wolf ate him." The king said: "*Oh* lad, would you like me to be your companion today to eat at this table?" *He said:* "Yes, *oh* king." And Yusuf took him by the hand and sat down with him, and they both ate at the same table. And Yusuf handed him morsels little by little and gazed upon his face. When Yamin saw that, he was overcome with grief, and he wept, wept very mightily, and Yusuf wept on account of his weeping.

---

[73] The copyist apparently forgot that he had already listed Shama'un.

When they had done eating, Yusuf said: "Oh Yamin, what made you weep?" Yamin said: "Do not chastise me, *oh* king, for my weeping, for know, *oh* king, that I see in your face resemblance and likeness to my brother Yusuf." *Said* Yusuf: "And what is your name?" He said: "Yamin." *He said:* "And what is your mother's name?" He said: "Rahil." *He said:* "And did she have another son besides you?" He said: "Yes, *oh* king." *He said:* "What then became of him?" *He said:* "These brothers of mine claimed that the wolf ate him." He said: "Are you married?" He said: "Yes [and Allah prepared the king],[74] 22 and two sons have been born unto me." He said: "And what did you name the first one?" *He said.* He said: "I have named him with my brother's name." He said: "And what was your brother's name?" *He said:* "Yusuf." He said: "And what did you name the second one?" He said: "I named him Wolf." He said: "And why did you do that?" He said: "So that the name of my brother, the joy of my eyes, should not be lost." And Yamin wept. And the king said: "And what makes you weep, *oh* lad?" *He said:* "The resemblance I see in you to my brother Yusuf; and I am overcome by the grief of longing for my brother." Then Yusuf could not bear the grief, and he got up and went to another part of his palace and wept until his grief passed. Then he went back and said unto him: "Rejoice, *oh* lad, for things will yet turn out well for you, if Allah wills."

He said: when the sons of Ya'qub had done eating, Yusuf sent for honey, and it was diluted with water, and he gave them that to drink. Then they washed their hands and got up from the tables. And Yusuf sat down in his chair and ordered the wheat and barley brought, and asked them for their payment, and it was taken from them. Then they said unto him: "Oh king, we will give you a very honest statement, that you may know it: when we opened our sacks, we found our money in the sacks. And our father sends you *greetings* and says unto you: "Know that we are from a House to whom it is not *permitted* to eat something without paying for it. And if you, *oh* king, offered this *gift* and present to the *prophet* Ya'qub, *prophet* of Allah, then he says unto you: may Allah, *be He exalted*, give you a reward for it, a copious reward." *He said:* and Yusuf wept. He said: "Yes, it is a present and a *gift* for the *prophet* Ya'qub, and a donation for his honor before Allah, *glorified and exalted be He*."

He said: then Yusuf took the measure and knelt on the floor and meted out the grain he wanted to measure for the ten brothers. When he was ready to measure the weight of his brother Yamin, he turned unto him and said: "Is this your sack, *oh* lad?" He said: "Yes, *oh* king." And Yusuf had [previously] ordered one of his servants: "When you see me weigh this lad's sack, take the silver measuring cup and put it very subtly in the sack. Be careful that no one see you." When it was weighed, he did as the king commanded, and no one saw

---

[74] The meaning of this clause ["y adobó Allah al rey"] is unclear.

him. When they had loaded up their sacks, they came to the king and wished him *peace* and bade him farewell. And they went on until they were outside the city.

XXXII. Yamin Accused of Theft

Then Yusuf said to his servant: "Go after that caravan, and cry out unto them, and say unto them: "You are thieves!" And he went after them. When the servant cried out, they stopped. And he [Ka'b] said, as Allah, *be He exalted*, recounts in His honored Qur'an, which says that the sons of Ya'qub said: **"What is it you are missing? They said: We are missing the king's silver measuring cup, and he who bringeth it shall have a camel-load, and I am answerable for it. They said: By Allah, well ye know we came not to do evil in the land, and are no thieves."**[75] Then they said: "*Oh* king, you know that we are of the house of *prophets* and are among the heirs of the *pious*, and we do not steal. He said unto them as Allah, *be He exalted*, says in His Qur'an that Yusuf said: **"And what shall be the penalty if it be found in the sack of one of you?"**[76] "That he be given the punishment due to him as a wicked man." And they began to search the brothers' loads before they looked at that of Yamin, his brother. Then they took the measure of the load of his brother Yamin. Thus We contrived for Yusuf that he might take his brother according to the king's law.[77] Allah raises whom He will by degrees, and He is Wise above all.

Said Ka'b: when the brothers saw that, they were confused and ashamed and frightened of Yusuf. Then they turned unto their brother Yamin and struck him in the face and said unto him: "Is this the payment you gave the king for the honor he did you, after he honored you by eating at the same table with you and out of the same plate? And you stole his measuring cup?" Yamin said: "Oh sons of Ya'qub, I did not take it, by the authority of the grey hair of Ibrahim our grandfather, nor do I know anything about it." Then they turned to Yusuf, and they said unto him, as Allah recounts in His Qur'an that the sons of Ya'qub said unto Yusuf: **"Oh king, if this one has stolen, a brother of his stole before."**[78] And Yusuf kept [his indignation] to himself and did not declare it unto them, but he said unto them: "You are a bad lot, and Allah knows what you are making up." Then they said unto him: "*Oh* king, this lad has a very old father. Take then one of us in his place, for we see that you are a good man."

---

[75] Qur'an 12:71–73.
[76] Qur'an 12:74.
[77] Paraphrase of Qur'an 12:76.
[78] Qur'an 12:77.

Yusuf said: "Allah forbid that I take anyone but the man in whose keeping we found our property, for we would then be among the wicked." Then the king said unto them: "Oh sons of Ya'qub, you already know that if a man steals from our property, we take him as a slave by the law we have in our land." They said: "You speak truth, oh king." He said: "In justice I can only take the one who took our property." Then he took Yamin by the hand and led him back to his palace. And when Yusuf was alone with Yamin, he said unto him: "Be not sad nor frightened, oh my brother, for I am your brother. Don't worry about what has happened." Ka'b al-Aḥbar said that Yusuf and Yamin embraced and could not be separated, each one weeping with joy over the other.

XXXIII. The Brothers Return to Ya'qub

When the sons of Ya'qub despaired of their brother Yamin, the eldest—he was Yahuda—said: "You know that your father required that you swear by Allah, and how you failed before this [in the case of] Yusuf, his brother. Therefore, I am ashamed to return to our father Ya'qub without taking our brother with us." They said unto him: "What then shall we do, oh Yahuda?" He said, as Allah, *be He exalted*, says: **"Return unto your father and tell him that his son Yamin has stolen, and that we testify only to that which we have seen; we are not guardians of [the unseen]. And if he asks you for the rest, tell him to ask the township where we were, and the caravan with which we traveled hither, for we speak the truth."**[79] And by "the township" is meant Misra, and "the caravan" refers to those who came with their loads from Misra. Then they went and returned unto Ya'qub, but Yahuda stayed where he was.

When Yusuf was alone with Yamin, he said unto him: "Oh brother, be not sad, for I am Yusuf, son of Ya'qub." They embraced and kissed each other between the eyes, and their sadness left them. And they magnified praise unto Allah, *glorified and exalted be He*, and gave Him many thanks.

And the others went on to al-Sham until they came to the vale of Kin'an. And they said: "Let us all go together and give Ya'qub our *greeting* with one voice, for when we *greet* him all together, he won't miss Yamin, and will not be anxious." Then they went in where Ya'qub was and gave him their *greetings*. However, Ya'qub had previously ordered Yusuf's sister, whose name was Dunya, to come to him with any news of her brothers. And when they arrived, and she didn't see her brother Yamin with them, she cried out a very great and loud cry, and she fell into a faint. And she said: "Oh my beloved Yamin! He is

---

[79] Qur'an 12:81–82.

lost just as Yusuf was lost!" And she came unto Ya'qub; but the brothers got there first and gave him their *greetings* all together. And they were nine.

And Ya'qub missed the voice of Yahuda and the voice of Yamin. And he lost control of himself, and fell on the ground, and did not come to for a period of three days. And his sons thought he had died, so deep was his faint. When he awoke, he turned to them and said unto them: "*Oh* sons, now I shall pray to Allah, *be He exalted,* against you, for I see you the lot of you as quarrelsome, discordant, and haughty. And what has become of your brother Yamin, he who was my consolation after Yusuf?" They said: "*Oh* father, Yamin has stolen, and we testify only to that which we have seen. Ask Allah and Misra—the township where we were—and the caravan with which we traveled hither, for we speak the truth. *Oh* father, your son Yamin has stolen the king of Misra's measuring cup, and the king has taken him in punishment of his theft. Be not afflicted, *oh* father, nor pray against us, for I attest by the authority of the *prophet, may Allah grant him peace and save him,* that it will be revealed in the fullness of time that we have not lost him nor been bad companions to him, but rather, the king has taken him in punishment of his theft. Ya'qub said: "What then has become of Yahuda?" They said: "*Oh prophet of Allah,* Yahuda stayed behind on the road, because he was ashamed for us to return to you without Yamin." And he [Ka'b] said: and Ya'qub wept, wept very mightily.

Then he said: "Allah forbid that Yamin should be a thief. He has been slandered with a lie to take him from you. Bring me ink and paper, and I shall write the king of Misra a letter. And they brought him ink and paper. He said unto Raubil: "Write me a letter that says as follows: '*In the name of Allah, the Merciful, the Compassionate.* From Ya'qub *Allah's Israelite,* son of Isḥaq, son of Ibrahim, friend of Allah, to the King of Misra: *Peace* upon you, etc. Praise be to Allah, He besides Whom there is no Lord. And I ask you, *oh* king, to greet that lay *prophet*[80] who will be sent at the end of time. Know, *oh* king, that we are of a House that has been tested with *troubles* and has suffered. My grandfather Ibrahim was thrown into the fire and suffered. And he relied upon Allah, *glorified and exalted be He,* and Allah made the fire cold and safe for him. Isma'il was to be sacrificed, but Allah saved him with a very great sacrifice.[81] As for myself, *oh* king, I have been tested with the loss of my son Yusuf. And his brother Yamin was my consolation after [the loss of] Yusuf, my beloved. *Oh* king, fear Allah in my son, for if you could see me, you would take pity on me. My body is ruined, and my back is bent, and my bones have wasted away, and my eyes have gone blind. Do me then the kindness to let me look upon him.

---

[80] That is, Muhammad.

[81] According to Muslim tradition, it was Ishmael (not Isaac, as in the Hebrew Bible) whom Abraham almost sacrificed.

It has been told me, *oh* king, that you claim that he has stolen. By Allah, *oh* king, I have not begotten a son who is a thief. Fear then Allah, *oh* king, and answer my petition. And Allah's *peace* be upon you and His blessing.' "

Said Ka'b al-Aḥbar: and Ya'qub prepared his sons for [the trip back to] Misra with butter and wool, and he gave the letter to Shama'un. And Ya'qub bade them farewell. And they went on to the place where Yahuda, their brother, was, and their brother Yahuda traveled on with them until they reached Yusuf. And they were not denied entry nor were they detained. And Yusuf had decorated his palace and hung up his *hangings*. And he summoned his governors and *ministers* and patriarchs, and they surrounded him and his throne. Then he ordered the sons of Ya'qub brought before him. And they were filled with fear and fright of what they had seen of the armies and of the great state. And Yusuf had gathered together in Misra those of his kingdom, and his tributaries, and he showed his brothers very great armies and power.

XXXIV. Yusuf Tests His Brothers

When they came before Yusuf, they *greeted* him, and he returned their *greetings* very summarily. And when they saw that, they grew sad, and fear came upon them, and they said: "Oh king, famine has touched us and our tribe, and we are come with butter and wool. Give us then full measure, and be *charitable* unto us." Then Yusuf lifted up his head toward them and said: "I think you are scouts and spies." And then he ordered many instruments of torture brought, and they were set before him. And they said: "By Allah, we are not scouts but the sons of Ya'qub, the *prophet* of Allah. Give us then full measure, and be *charitable*, for Allah rewards him who gives *charity* unto us." Yusuf said unto them: "*Oh* you lot of Hebrew servants, tell me your news, and speak the truth about yourselves, for your story is hidden and concealed from me, and I would like to know the facts. And I still think that you are spies, and that the king of your land has sent you in case he wants to make war against me. But Allah has given me dominion over you, and has made you submit to me. I think that you are ten brothers or more, and each one of you is a captain and governor over a thousand men, for you are ten thousand in all." They said: "Oh king, hear our saying from us, and know that we are all sons of Ya'qub, and we are not spies, nor are we warriors, but rather we are shepherds of flocks and farming people, and sons of Isḥaq, son of Ibrahim, friend of the Merciful."

He [Ka'b] said: and Yusuf turned to them and said: "Sit down, for I will keep talking with you until you explain your words and I understand your business. Inform me, *oh* sons of Ya'qub. How many sons did Ya'qub have?" They said: "Oh king, he had twelve sons." The king said: "Well, I don't see but ten here.

What became of the other two?" They said: "Oh king, the wolf ate one of them, and we left the other one in your custody." Yusuf said: "Is there among you one who reads Hebrew?" They said: "Oh king, we all read Hebrew." He [Ka'b] said: and the king put his hand under his chair and brought out a writing which they had written to Malik Ibnu Dugzi Al'uza'imu, lord of the caravan of Misra, when they sold him to him. And the sons of Ya'qub took it, and looked at the letter and what was in it, and they recognized it, and they gave the letter one unto another, and they all blushed, and a great sweat began to drip from them. And they said unto him: "Oh king, we don't know this handwriting." Yusuf said: "And how do you not know this handwriting, since it is yours?" They said: "No, oh king."

Then Yusuf asked for his measuring cup, and he tapped on it with his finger and raised his eyes to heaven and said: "Oh sons of Ya'qub, this measuring cup will test what you say against what the letter says." Then he tapped the cup a second time and said: "Know that the measuring cup tells me that you sold Yusuf for twenty *dirhams* and you divided them among yourselves, and that they were seventeen *dirhams* by weight." At this Yusuf stared at them, and they were dying of fear and fright. "And this is the letter that you wrote to the merchant who bought him from you." They said: "Allah forbid, oh king, we did no such thing." Then Yusuf tapped the measuring cup with his finger a third time, and listened a little. Then he raised his head and said: "Know, oh sons of Ya'qub, that the measuring cup informs me that you mistreated Yusuf, and took him from his father, and stripped him of his clothing, and tied his hands behind him with ropes, and threw him into the cistern. And then you beheaded a cow and wiped his clothing with the blood. And it further tells me that you went to his father Ya'qub and told him that the wolf had eaten him. All this you did with Yusuf."

He [Ka'b] said: when they heard his saying, they turned pale, and considered themselves lost, And they kept looked at one another. And Shama'un said unto them—and he was deaf—and he said: "Oh my brothers, what did the king say to you?" They said: "Oh brother, we are on the brink of ruin and our death, for the king says that we sold Yusuf, our brother, and we threw him in the cistern, and we claimed that the wolf ate him. And know that we are lost." Shama'un said unto them: "Oh brothers, give me license to cry out." And it so happened that whenever Shama'un cried out, any pregnant woman who heard him would abort the baby. And the brothers said: "Don't bother to cry out until you see what this king is going to do." Then they said: "Oh king, fear Allah and do not slander us concerning our brother, for this old Shama'un, when he gets angry, can't calm down until he cries out, and no pregnant woman hears him without aborting what she has in her belly." The king said: "Know then, oh sons of Ya'qub, that I have decided to cut off your heads and hang you on top of the city wall in punishment for what you did to your brother Yusuf and to

Ya'qub, *prophet* of Allah." Then he said as Allah, *be He exalted*, says that Yusuf said unto his brothers: **"Do you know what you did to Yusuf . . . , since you are a band of *ignorant men?*"**[82] They said: "We have done none of that, *oh* king." The king said unto them: "You seem confused to me." Shama'un said: "I don't see how we can be saved except by [my] shouting; and people will hear it, and all who hear me will be frightened, and will faint and fall to the ground."

XXXV. Yusuf Reveals Himself

[Ka'b] said that Yusuf turned to his eldest son and said unto him: "Oh Alfarashim, get up and [stand?][83] behind that old deaf man; for when he gets angry, his rage cannot be calmed until he cries out, and if he cries out, people will be frightened. [The only way to prevent this is for] someone of the family of Ya'qub, *prophet* of Allah, to touch him with his palm. If the palm touches him, his anger will be calmed." Then Alfarashim got up and stood behind his *uncle* Shama'un. And before Yusuf was a chunk of boulder which a hundred men would not be able to move if they got together. And Yusuf went toward his brothers and said unto them: "*Oh* sons of Ya'qub, I shall surely hang you in punishment for what you did to your brother; there is no doubt about it." Then they turned to Shama'un and said unto him: "Cry out now if it is to do us any good." The king said unto them: "If Shama'un cries out, I will take this boulder and hit you all with it." And Yusuf rolled up his sleeves and went to the boulder and picked it up and banged it on the ground. And it was smashed with a great smashing. And he didn't intend to hit them with the boulder, but he wanted to show them his marvels. [Ka'b] said that they were frightened and stunned by what they saw of Yusuf's strength and his might and his power with Allah, *be He exalted.* And Alfarashim went behind Shama'un's back and put his hand on his back, and he couldn't cry out. And Shama'un turned to his brothers and said unto them: "I have been touched by the palm of a relative of Ya'qub's." And they turned to the right and the left, and they saw the boy behind Shama'un. And they said unto him: "*Oh* boy, did you put your hand on this old man's back?" He said: "Yes." And they said unto him: "What is your name, *oh boy?*" He said: "My name is Alfarashim, son of Yusuf, son of Ibrahim, friend of Allah, *may Allah grant them peace and save them.*" They said unto him: "*Oh* lad, and where is your father?" He said: "My father is the King of Misra, Yusuf, son of Ya'qub, my grandfather." Then they said unto Yusuf as Allah, *be*

---

[82] Qur'an 12:89.
[83] A verb is missing after the word y in the manuscript.

He exalted, says that they said: **"Are you indeed Yusuf, oh king?"**[84] He said
unto them: "Yes, I am Yusuf, and this is my son.[85] And Allah has done graciously unto us; for he who is patient and fears Allah . . . Allah does not scorn
the patient nor the good."[86]

Ka'b al-Aḥbar said that the sons of Ya'qub threw themselves upon the feet
of Yusuf, their brother, and kissed his feet, and said unto him: "Allah has preferred you to us, and we sinned against you." Yusuf said: "There is no sin in you,
for I shall forgive you, and Allah will forgive me and you, for He is the Merciful Forgiver of the merciful." And Yusuf was very merciful and honorable. Then
Yusuf said unto his brothers: "Take this shirt of mine and hold it up to the face
of my father Ya'qub, and he will recover his eyesight. And then all of you, come
[back] to me with your wives and children." And Yusuf made provision for his
brother Yamin, and gave him a thousand *she-camels* and a thousand manservants with a thousand horses and a thousand pounds of camphor and *ambergris*
and a thousand loads of wheat, and he said unto him: "Go, *oh* brother, with
your brothers, and may all of this help you to return, and come back with all
your people."

XXXVI. The Brothers Go to Get Ya'qub

When they had left and bade Yusuf farewell, and Yamin with them carrying
Yusuf's shirt, they traveled on until they were ten miles from Ya'qub. And
Ya'qub sensed the smell of Yusuf from ten miles off, and he said unto his grandchildren, the sons of his sons: "I detect the smell of Yusuf." His grandsons said
unto him: "*Oh* grandfather, you are still under your old delusion."[87] Ka'b said
that his grief doubled because of that. He said: "I know from Allah what you
know not." And his sons arrived, and Yamin approached Ya'qub, and he
smelled the smell of Yusuf, and rays of light came to Ya'qub. When Yamin went
in unto Ya'qub, his father, and held Yusuf's shirt up to his eyes, then his eyesight returned to him. And he said as Allah, *be He exalted,* says in His Qur'an
that Ya'qub said unto them: **"Said I not unto you that I knew from Allah**

---

[84] Qur'an 12:90.

[85] The manuscript has "hermano" (brother), but the reference is clearly to Yusuf's
son Alfarashim.

[86] This is a paraphrase of the elliptical and somewhat obscure Qur'an 12:90, which
Pickthall translates: "Lo! he who wardeth off (evil) and endureth (findeth favour), for
verily Allah loses not the wages of the kindly."

[87] The meaning may be "you are senile." The sentence paraphrases Qur'an 12:95,
which Pickthall translates: "By Allah, lo! thou art in thine old aberration."

what you knew not?"[88] His sons said unto him: "*Oh* father, ask pardon for us for our sin, for we were wrongdoers." Ya'qub said: "I will yet beg pardon for you from my Lord, for He is a Merciful, Compassionate Pardoner."

XXXVII. Yusuf Receives Ya'qub in Misra

Then Ya'qub prepared for his departure and traveled with all his tribe toward Misra until they reached the city. And the king went out to receive them with six thousand banners, and six hundred thousand horsemen, and six hundred thousand infantrymen, and six hundred thousand maidens. And the king ordered proclamation made in all his kingdoms on sea and on land that they should come to Misra to welcome his father. And Yusuf dressed in his best clothes and raiment. And he ordered the patriarchs and the *ministers* to stand on the right and left sides of the road. And he ordered a thousand maidservants and manservants with pots of musk and camphor and *ambergris* to go among the people along the road. And he ordered silk spread out for three leagues long and wide. And Yusuf went out to receive his father with the greatest might, and he ordered the doors of his palaces opened; and he ordered his doormen and governors and patriarchs and prefects to keep order among the people, and to arrange them in groups and *rows* for a journey of three days. Then he had his throne decorated, and it was the *throne* that Allah mentioned in His honored Qur'an, where he says that **"When they came in before Yusuf, he approached his father and said: Come into Egypt safe and happy, if Allah wills. And he placed his father Ya'qub on the *throne*. And they both fell down *prostrate* to Allah, *be He exalted*."**[89] He [Ka'b] said that Yusuf ordered the *throne* decorated and spread over it *silk* and brocade. Then he went out to receive his father.

When Yusuf approached his father, they looked at each other and grieved for each other, and they fell down in gratitude to Allah. And Yusuf did not raise his head until his father raised his. And then Ya'qub embraced Yusuf, and hugged him to his breast, and they both embraced. And then they *bowed down*, giving thanks to Allah who had reunited them. Ka'b al-Aḥbar said: and Allah was praised by the two of them and by his *angels* of the seven heavens. And Ya'qub lifted up his hands toward *heaven* and said: "Oh my Lord, You have done graciously unto me, and I shall always magnify You. Receive my thanks and praises, *oh Merciful and Compassionate One, for You are powerful over all things*." Then Yusuf said unto him: "*Oh prophet* of Allah, get up and sit upon the chair." And Yusuf said unto him: "*Oh* father, this is the meaning of the

---

[88] Qur'an 12:96.
[89] Qur'an 12:99–100.

dreams that I told you before. **"And now the Lord has turned it to my good, for He has brought me out of jail to the great grace of seeing you, after *Satan* stirred up trouble between my brothers and me, for my Lord is very subtle in what He wants and very Wise. And, Lord, You have given unto me a great kingdom and taught me how to interpret dreams and stories. You are the Creator of the heavens and the earth, and you are my *friend* in this world and the next. Let me die a believer and a good *Muslim* and receive me among the good."**[90] This is what Allah said in His honored Qur'an. Ka'b al-Aḥbar said: and Yusuf never sat down at any hour of the night or day but he looked at the face of his father Ya'qub, may Allah greet him and all the *prophets* and messengers. *Amen.*

[Ka'b] said that Ibn al-'Abbas asked which one was more severely tried and patient, Yusuf or Ya'qub. Ibn al-'Abbas, *may Allah be pleased with him*, said that Yusuf wept over Ya'qub until a green birthmark he had on his cheek was worn away; and Ya'qub wept until his eyes turned white and he went blind out of longing and grief over Yusuf. And the reason why Ya'qub was tested with the loss of his son was, he said, because Ya'qub sold a slave woman who had a child, and Ya'qub ordered the child separated from its mother. Allah said: "By My Honor and My Nobility, I shall make a separation between you and the most beloved of your sons." And he separated him from Yusuf, for Allah had already said that he who separates a mother from her child before it has shed its baby teeth, Allah will separate that man from those he loves on the Judgment Day. Ibn al-'Abbas said that Allah, *be He exalted*, separated Ya'qub from his son for eighty two years. Then Ya'qub was reunited with him, and he lifted his hands to *heaven* and said: "Lord, You have separated me from my son for eighty two years. Praises and thanks be unto You, as is right. All graces and great praise are due unto Him forever." Ka'b al-Aḥbar said that Yusuf never coveted anything more than being reunited with his father and seeing his face. And after he obtained his wish, he desired the same with his fathers and grandfathers Ibrahim and Isma'il and Isḥaq and Ya'qub.

He [Ka'b] said that Ya'qub and Yusuf and his brothers remained in Misra for the time that Allah, *be He exalted*, willed. The number of them, between men and women, small and large, [was] three hundred persons. And thus Yusuf remained in his kingdom with his father and his tribe as long as Allah, *be He exalted*, willed. And this is what has come down to us of the story of Ya'qub and of his son Yusuf.

The grace of Allah be upon every *Muslim* man and *woman, amen. And praise be to Allah, Lord of the universe.*

---

[90] Qur'an 12:100–101.

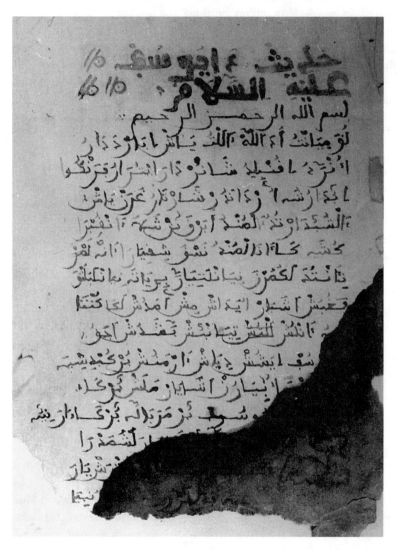

The first page of Manuscript A of the Ḥadīth of Yūsuf. Courtesy of Real Academia de la Historia, Madrid.

⇒ Ḥadith of Yusuf (c. 1250–1400)

Anonymous

This poem, usually referred to in Spanish as the *Poema de José*, is generally considered the outstanding example of Morisco *aljamiado* literature. Like the *Story of Yusuf, Son of Yaʿqub*, it is based on Surah XII of the Qurʾan and on the Muslim collections of legends of the prophets.

The poem has come down to us in two different manuscripts, both of which are incomplete. The longer manuscript, known as Manuscript B, belongs to Madrid's Biblioteca Nacional.[1] According to Ramón Menéndez Pidal, it dates from the second half of the sixteenth century.[2] It was first published, in a somewhat modernized version, in 1849 as an appendix to George Ticknor's *History of Spanish Literature*. It is missing at least two folios at the beginning and an unknown number at the end; it begins at the tenth stanza of the poem.

After the publication of Manuscript B, a second manuscript, known as A, was discovered hidden in a cave in Morés, Aragon. This manuscript, which is now in the library of the Real Academia de la Historia, Madrid, is thought to date from the late fourteenth or early fifteenth century.[3] Unlike Manuscript B, the text is written as if it were prose, and it is in at least two different handwritings. The lower part of the manuscript is considerably deteriorated, completely obliterating some stanzas. It does, however, contain the title and the stanzas missing from the beginning of Manuscript B. The copyist seems to have overlooked stanza 33, and one entire folio (from the middle of stanza 82 to the third line of stanza 92) is missing. The text ends with stanza 95. By combining the opening stanzas from Manuscript A with the material from Manuscript B, we attain a version consisting of 312 stanzas. It was at first widely believed that the Ḥadith was the work of a Castilian Morisco because the language of Manuscript B was heavily Castilianized, but the discovery of Manuscript A, the Aragonese characteristics of which are much more pronounced, proved beyond a doubt the Aragonese origin of the poem.

In 1864 Florencio Janer published an edition combining the text of the two manuscripts in Volume LVII of the *Biblioteca de Autores Españoles*, but the

---

[1] It is catalogued as Ms. Reserva 247 (G. g. 101).
[2] *Poema de Yuçuf: Materiales para su estudio* (Granada: Univ. of Granada, 1952), p. 64.
[3] D. Eduardo Saavedra, *Discursos leídos ante la Real Academia Española* (Madrid, 1878), p. 162.

transcription used in that edition is extremely defective and Janer does not list the many variant readings in the two manuscripts. The only reliable edition combining both manuscripts is that of William Weisiger Johnson, *The "Poema de José": A Transcription and Comparison of the Extant Manuscripts* (University, Miss.: Romance Monographs, 1974); I have used that edition as the basis for the present translation. Johnson points out in his introduction that

> both [manuscripts] are riddled with errors. Some of these errors are common to both, indicating the probability of an earlier manuscript—itself perhaps defective, and now lost—from which these two known versions were copied. There is even evidence that at some time the poem was transmitted orally: rhyming words at times appear in the middle of lines instead of at the end, and there are occasional attempts to correct this, usually at the expense of meter or sense, by changing the words which follow—but seldom by restoring the original wording. These would seem to be errors made during recitation and copied by the copyist, along with the attempts at correction, while the recitation was still in progress.[4]

George Ticknor described the Ḥadith as

> a curious and interesting production. It has the directness and simplicity of the age to which it is attributed, mingled sometimes with a tenderness rarely found in ages so violent. Its pastoral air, too, and its preservation of Oriental manners, harmonize well with the Arabian feelings that prevail throughout the work; while in its spirit, and occasionally in its moral tone, it shows the confusion of the two religions that then prevailed in Spain, and that mixture of the Eastern and Western forms of civilization which afterwards gives somewhat of its coloring to Spanish poetry.[5]

This hybrid nature of the text is immediately evident in its form. The Ḥadith is written in a meter known as *cuaderna vía*, consisting of "stanzas of four fourteen-syllable lines (alexandrines), each with a caesura in the middle, with full rhyme not assonance, and rhyming AAAA, BBBB, etc."[6] The *cuaderna vía*, an adaptation of an earlier French or Latin verse form, first made its appearance in narrative poems written by monks in Old Castile in the thirteenth century. The best-known examples of the genre are the *Poema de Fernán González*, an epic

---

[4] *"Poema de José,"* p. 11.
[5] *History of Spanish Literature*, 6th ed. (New York: Gordian Press, 1965 [orig. 1891]), I, 106.
[6] A. D. Deyermond, *A Literary History of Spain: The Middle Ages* (London: Ernest Benn Ltd., 1971), p. 58.

written in the monastery of San Pedro de Arlanza and dealing with the career of the first count of autonomous Castile, emphasizing his close relationship with the monastery; the *Libro de Alexandre*, a moralistic recounting of the rise and fall of Alexander the Great;[7] the *Libro de Apolonio*, a romance dealing with the adventures of the legendary king Apollonius of Tyre and illustrating the mysterious workings of divine providence; and several works by Gonzalo de Berceo,[8] a monk of the Benedictine monastery of San Millán de la Cogolla: lives of St. Emilian, the patron saint of Berceo's monastery, St. Dominic of Silos, and St. Oria, and an incomplete poem on the martyrdom of St. Lawrence; poems dedicated to the Virgin Mary—the *Miracles of Our Lady*, *Praises of Our Lady*, and *Lament of the Virgin on the Day of the Passion of Her Son Jesus Christ*—and two doctrinal poems, *The Sacrifice of the Mass* and *The Signs that Will Appear Before the Last Judgment*. All these poems can best be characterized as religious propaganda—sermons in verse—addressed to a popular audience and intended to stimulate religious devotion and, pointedly, pilgrimages and donations to the monasteries where they were written. Formerly, monks had usually composed their works in Latin (in fact, most of the poems I have mentioned are directly based on Latin sources), but these new compositions in Spanish were a response to the almost total disappearance of knowledge of Latin among laymen. Intended to entertain as well as to inspire, they were a direct attempt to compete with secular poetry, mainly epic poems and ballads. The monks who wrote them took pride in the care with which they were written, in their attention to meter and rhyme and the elegance of their language. Paradoxically, however, these poems "notwithstanding their greater formal perfection and frequent show of erudition, . . . recount their stories in a less elevated tone than that of the epic, since the latter, by the very heroic character of its subject matter, habitually tends to raise the narrative tone of its account."[9] Although all the poems I have mentioned are believed to have been written within a few decades of each other, in the mid-thirteenth century, the *cuaderna vía* continued to be cultivated until well into the following century.

It seems likely that the author of the *Ḥadith*—probably the imam[10] of a rural Aragonese Muslim community of the late thirteenth or early fourteenth century—saw this popular new literary form, with its appealing stories of the

---

[7] Interestingly, there is also an important Morisco legend on this subject, published by Francisco Guillén Robles in the same volume with his version of the *Story of Yusuf, Son of Ya'qub*.

[8] Berceo is the first Christian Spanish poet whom we can identify by name.

[9] Juan Luis Alborg, *Historia de la literatura española* (Madrid: Gredos, 1970), I, 114.

[10] Islam, of course, does not have ordained clergy in the Christian sense. An imam, like a rabbi, may serve his community as a legal expert, arbitrator, teacher, preacher, and prayer leader.

miracles of the Virgin and the deeds of Christian saints and heroes, as a threat to the faith of his flock. Just as the majority of Christians no longer had access to the Latin sources of their faith, most Spanish Muslims could no longer read Arabic. He therefore decided to use this popular and influential literary genre created by Christian monks and adapt it to his own Muslim purposes. If the Christians could draw on Latin writings to produce lives of their saints, he could equally well draw on Arabic sources to write a Spanish version of that "most beautiful of stories,"[11] the tale of Yusuf, which was likewise rich in miraculous demonstrations of divine providence.

The author of the *Ḥadith* proved himself a worthy rival of Berceo. The following assessment of Berceo's achievement could serve admirably as a description of the author of the *Ḥadith*:

> The lack of originality in subject matter does not . . . diminish Berceo's personality as a poet. The author modifies, amplifies, and enriches his models, clothing them in aspects of the everyday customs of his region. With tact and skill he selects the precise nuances, popular motifs, and picturesque expressions that will be most easily understood by his uneducated listeners. This technique enables him to humanize the cold aridity of the Latin text, giving it shape and color. Berceo's attempt to convey the flavor of something familiar and experienced to his narration—precisely because of the simple people whom he addresses—is manifest in all his work; and therein lies the root of his essential popularism. He strives to be graphic and familiar, and for that purpose he employs comparisons taken from farming practices, country ways of speaking, names of household utensils, and proverbs. This is why the subjects he addresses, which are universal—and nonetheless conventional as well—in the literature of his time, in his hands acquire the taste of immediate reality, of everyday landscape, of familiar localization. The world his eyes captured while gazing out from the tranquil cloister of his monastery is transmuted into poetry on his pages. And in this capacity for assimilation, which is an authentic creative force, resides all of Berceo's poetic grace and the miracle of his personality.[12]

When we compare the *Ḥadith* with the later *Story of Yusuf*, we are immediately struck by the poem's economy and directness. Eliminating all unnecessary details, the poet gets right to the point of the story, which he recounts with the simplicity and charm of a born storyteller. The motivations of the major characters are convincingly portrayed in a few deft strokes. Descriptions,

---

[11] Qur'an 12:3.
[12] Alborg, *Historia de la literatura española*, p. 119.

though brief, are unforgettably vivid and based on the author's own experience of rural life in medieval Spain. Thus, for example, the brothers describe the boy Yusuf "sleeping in the sheepfold / snuggled next to the sheep to keep out of the cold." Zaliqa's haste to see the beautiful slave boy the merchant is offering for sale is vividly captured in the lines: "Zaliqa left the table, her dinner untouched; / she jumped on her mule, and off she did rush." The seven dry ears of grain in the king's dream are described as "dried up and pale as a man long past his prime," [13] and after they have consumed the full ears, all are "as shriveled and white as mist at break of day." After Yusuf's appointment as viceroy, the people of Egypt are described as his "vassals." When Yusuf's brothers first arrive in Egypt they are directed to his house by a "squire." Yusuf assigns two thousand "knights" to serve his brothers. Later Yusuf will address his brother Benjamin as "squire," and Benjamin will address him as "knight." Yusuf is described as living in a "castle." Canaan is referred to in stanza 39 as the "Holy Land." [14] Like a wise and experienced farmer, Yusuf predicts the coming plenty or famine by the aspect of the moon. Yusuf has his brothers served not just any food but "the best fish." After Ya'qub and his family have eaten all the food his sons brought back from Egypt, not only is there no bread left, there is "no dough to knead." When the brothers return to Egypt with Benjamin and their arrival is celebrated by the burning of incense, the boy is portrayed as trying to catch the fragrant smoke in his hands, and this childish behavior angers his older brothers.

It is of course unfair to compare the Hadith to Berceo's poems, for the latter were lovingly preserved and copied in monastery scriptoria while the Hadith has come down to us only in a fragmentary and mutilated form. There are numerous instances in the poem where stanzas have obviously been transposed. Stanzas 63–66 in my translation appear as 65–67 in the manuscripts—thus absurdly placing the auctioneer's invitation for bids on Yusuf after he has already been sold to the king. Some material seems to have been deleted after stanza 88. When the king accuses Yusuf of plotting to rape his wife, Yusuf simply replies "I am not that sort of man," but the poem fails to state the king's reaction to this. As we have mentioned earlier, the poem's conclusion is missing. The longer manuscript ends abruptly with Ya'qub's command that his sons return to Egypt for a third time and search for Yusuf. Comparison with the version in *The Story of Yusuf, Son of Ya'qub* suggests that perhaps twenty five stanzas, or about eight percent of the poem, are lost.

In terms of its tone and treatment of the plot, the Hadith occupies a middle ground between *The Book of Heroes* and *The Story of Yusuf*. The first half of the

[13] The original Spanish literally says "as a hair gone grey."
[14] I have changed this to "Israel" in the translation for the sake of rhyme.

COAT OF MANY CULTURES

love story of Zaliqa and Yusuf is told in some detail, but the conclusion (Zaliqa's abandonment of idolatry and marriage to Yusuf) is omitted; of course, it might have been included in the missing final portion of the poem. The Ḥadith places greater emphasis on the heroic nature of Yusuf's brothers than The Story of Yusuf, and, as in The Book of Heroes, his confrontation with them is the poem's climactic scene. In the Ḥadith that confrontation is presented in two parts. After establishing his superiority, Yusuf at first seems to pardon his brothers (stanza 295), but then again threatens them, after pretending to hear from his magic measuring cup how they had mistreated their brother Yusuf. This final threat results in their abject surrender and admission of guilt, which makes possible their reconciliation with Yusuf. There is some evidence that the author of the Ḥadith may have had independent access to Jewish sources. In stanza 146 he refers to Yusuf's knowledge of the seventy languages (plus Hebrew), a particularly Jewish legend that does not occur in al-Kisai's Tales of the Prophets or in The Story of Yusuf. It is tempting to conjecture that the author may have discussed the story with the rabbi of his village or have heard or read a Jewish version of the story, just as he was familiar with the narrative poems of Christian monks.

The few modern critics who have studied the Ḥadith have tended to view it as having little, if any, literary merit. Some of their comments can surely be explained in terms of racial and religious prejudice; the very same qualities that in Berceo's work are praised as charming naïveté are criticized in the Ḥadith as crudeness and ignorance. Ramón Menéndez Pidal has voiced more serious and balanced reservations, which are surely shared by many modern readers. "The Morisco's narration," he writes,

> is half-hearted, with little delight in what he recounts; utterly absorbed in the details of his story, he is unable to express them vividly or even with complete clarity. To some extent, the same thing happened to the author of the Poem of Fernán González; perhaps both poets felt inhibited by the narrowness of the cuaderna vía and would have been able to give freer rein to their imagination in the looser verse form of an epic. It is only by comparison with other versions of the story of Joseph that we are able to understand some passages of the aljamiado Poem.[15]

As I have already pointed out, I disagree with Menéndez Pidal about the Ḥadith's vividness. The poem's elliptical nature—the omission of information needed to understand the story—is surely due to the fact that the poet was retelling a familiar and well-loved tale. For example, the first time he mentions

---

[15] Poema de Yuçuf, p. 100.

Zaliqa, in stanza 62, he doesn't even bother to tell us who she was. Some of Menéndez Pidal's other strictures may be simply due to the poor and incomplete state in which the Ḥadith has come down to us. However, my experience in teaching the Ḥadith has been that my students quickly grow impatient with its episodic nature. For them its chief defect is its lack of thematic unity and structure. They complain that the author seems content simply to recount one apparently disconnected episode after another without providing any sort of philosophical or exegetical framework to clarify the story's *global* meaning. This criticism is understandable. Nevertheless, it may to some extent merely reflect sophisticated modern readers' impatience with traditional folktales. As Jean Spiro observed in 1906, when the scholarly study of folklore was in its infancy, "Dealing with legends, taking an interest in stories—that is unworthy of a serious man, you will probably say; it is childish. I know that very well, and I reproach myself a lot for that reason; but, no matter how hard I try, I can't help preferring people's legends to their most accurate histories."[16] If we can approach the Ḥadith with something like a child's delight in hearing a good story, it can teach us a great deal about the inner life of the people who created it— their feelings, values, and aspirations—probably more than we could ever learn from the dry pages of history.

> ḤADITH[17] OF YUSUF
> *'Alayhi as-salamu*[18]
> *Bismi Illahi irrahmani rrahimi*[19]

1. All praise be to Allah, true God who reigns on high!
   His promises He keeps, on His justice we rely.
   Mighty and generous, He orders things aright.

2. Great is His power, the whole world overflowing!
   Nothing can happen without His surely knowing.
   He sees you on the land, and when a boat you're rowing;
   Allah will watch over you wherever you are going.

3. I'll tell you a story if you'll listen, my friends,
   of some strange things that happened away back when

---

[16] *L'histoire de Joseph selon la tradition musulmane* (Lausanne: Th. Sack, 1906), p. 5.
[17] Arabic: "tradition."
[18] Arabic: "Peace be upon him."
[19] Traditional Muslim invocation: "In the name of Allah, the Merciful, the Compassionate."

to Ya'qub and Yusuf and his brothers ten:
envy and greed would make them wicked men.

4. For Ya'qub loved Yusuf more than all the rest,
because he was spotless, of his children the best,[20]
and because his mother had been the loveliest
of his wives, the one whom he loved best.

5. They first began to envy him, it seems,
when late one night he had a troubling dream,
whose meaning his ten brothers quickly deemed
was that he'd be their master and their king.[21]

6. He dreamt that he had seen eleven stars
that with each other fought a bloody war,
until the sun and moon came from afar,
and all bowed down to Yusuf with great awe.

7. Since Yusuf was quite young, still but a child,
though Ya'qub warned him his dream he should hide,
he told his brothers all that he'd espied.
They sought to do him harm with stealth and guile.

8. They all agreed the best thing they could do
was beg their father, trusting old Ya'qub,
while feigning brotherly solicitude,
to let them have Yusuf in their keeping true.

9. When Ya'qub heard their words, he was aggrieved.
"No, no," he cried, "for how could I believe
you'd care for him? You think you can deceive,
but go away. With Yusuf you'll not leave."

10. His sons replied: "Think not such evil thoughts.
We are all brothers; to Yusuf we'd do nought.

---

[20] Only the words "Porque era ninno" are legible in this line. Florencio Janer added the words "puro e sin mansella" to complete the verse.

[21] The end of the first line and the beginning of the second line of this stanza are also illegible. This reconstruction is also based upon Janer's suggestions.

But if you will not trust us as we've sought,
then do as you think best; it matters not.[22]

11. But Allah our Maker knows our one desire
    is to teach Yusuf, that he may thus acquire
    the shepherd's art; then his brothers he'll admire.
    But do as you think best; for you are our sire."

12. So many loving words they spoke that day,
    so many fair promises they dared say,
    he gave them Yusuf, and he bowed to pray
    that no one his dear Yusuf would betray.

13. He gave him to them; would that he had not!
    Believing their false words, he did as they sought.
    He cried: "Hear me, my sons, and do as you ought;
    watch over my dear Yusuf, and forsake him not!

14. For the love of Allah, bring him back unto me soon!
    It will make him happy, and I'll consider it a boon.
    If you love me, have him here tomorrow at noon.
    I trust in mighty Allah to guard him from misfortune."

15. While Ya'qub watched, they carried him piggyback,
    but once out of sight, they began their attack.
    They dropped him to the ground with a loud whack.
    Longing for his father, he cried: "Alas, alack!"

16. Walking swiftly ahead, they left him in the lurch.
    He was but a child; he stumbled and was hurt.
    He cried: "I'm tired, brothers. Don't leave me in the dirt!
    Don't leave me here helpless! That crime you should avert.

17. Don't leave me here without father or mother!
    Don't let me die here of thirst and of hunger!
    Please give me water from some source or other!
    Think of our father's grey hair, my dear brothers!"

---

[22] The manuscript in the Biblioteca Nacional (Ms. B) begins with this stanza.

18. When one of his brothers heard these words resound,
    he seized Yusuf's water and poured it on the ground.
    Then he kicked him and with his fists he did pound
    the poor child as he lay with the water around.

19. His brothers then cursed him and said: "Little wretch,
    just see how much water your dreams now can fetch!
    You'll pay for those dreams, you'll be sorry yet,
    and your bragging and posturing you will regret!"

20. Then one of his brothers spoke up loud and clear;
    to murdering Yusuf he knew they were near.
    His name was Yahuda, and him they did fear.
    They did not then kill Yusuf. His prayer Allah did hear.

21. They took his advice, they thought it was fine
    to throw Yusuf in a well full of icy cold brine
    up high on a mountain. At its bottom recline
    monstrous beasts who'll eat Yusuf. Out of sight, out of mind.

22. But what would they say to their father so old?
    That Yusuf was sleeping in the sheepfold
    snuggled next to the sheep to keep out of the cold,
    when a wolf came and ate him; or so they were told.

23. Poor old Ya'qub was worried, knew not what to believe.
    It was long past noon, for Yusuf he did grieve.
    He said: "Oh Lord, in You I trust and believe;
    save Yusuf from beasts, and from cold him retrieve."

24. He went out to the road as far as he could go
    so the reason for his sons' delay he might know.
    Down the mountain they came, all nodding with woe:
    "Oh brother, dear Yusuf, whom we have loved so!"

25. When he saw them coming and heard what they said,
    Ya'qub fainted away as if he were dead.
    Thinking him lifeless, his sons were dismayed.
    "Grant him a full pardon!" to Allah they prayed.

26. Then Yahuda stood up and whispered in their ears:
    "Let's go back for Yusuf, and bring him back here,
    and we'll be forgiven by our father so dear.
    From my lips I promise your crime he'll not hear."

27. But his brothers replied: "We'll do no such thing.
    We'll go cut him in pieces. His corpse we will bring
    to our father; and then to one story we'll cling:
    that a wolf ate him up. We'll be convincing."

28. In just a few minutes their father woke up.
    He said to his sons: "Where's the one that I love?
    What have you done to him? Where have you put
    my dear Yusuf?" They answered: "A wolf ate him up."

29. "I don't trust you, my sons; I am sure that you lie.
    Go and catch me that wolf. Bring him here so that I,
    with Allah's assistance, can make him belie
    that story you're telling. The truth he will cry!"

30. So the wolf they pursued with that lie on their tongues,
    that the poor wolf had murdered Ya'qub's favorite son.
    They brought Ya'qub his shirt all covered with blood,
    so at last he'd believe that outrageous falsehood.

31. Ya'qub prayed to his Maker, and the wolf then did say:
    "Allah forbid that a *nabi*[23] I'd slay!
    They hunted me down in a land far away.
    Of this crime I am innocent. They'll not make me pay."

32. "My sons, you have wronged me!" These words Ya'qub spoke.
    "You gave me your promise, and your promise you broke.
    But Allah has taught me that where there is smoke,
    there is fire. For this you will pay, and that is no joke!"

33. With this curse on his breath, Ya'qub turned away weeping.
    Stunned and angry, all ten of the brothers went creeping

---

[23] Arabic: "prophet."

to where they'd left Yusuf; and there he was sleeping.
To the well they then dragged him, in spite of his shrieking.

34. He held on to the rope for dear life, Yusuf small,
    but they cut it in half, and allowed him to fall,
    and he fell 'twixt a rock and a boulder so tall,
    but Allah protected him. He was not hurt at all.

35. And Yusuf fell down in that water so cold,
    where often passed by many merchants who sold
    all sorts of things. It was hot, so they told
    their boys to fetch water. The lads quickly took hold

36. of the bucket, but when it had sunk out of sight,
    they tugged and they tugged with all of their might,
    but it wouldn't come up. Yusuf held to it tight.
    One last mighty tug, and they saw his face white!

37. They never had seen so astounding a creature!
    They were stunned and amazed by each gorgeous feature.
    To their master they took him. He took Yusuf's measure,
    and said he'd reward them for that living treasure.

38. Yusuf's brothers came running. The reason they gave
    was that they were hunting a runaway slave;
    and when they saw Yusuf, they said: "There's the knave!"
    The idea was Yahuda's, their interest to save.

39. The merchant then said: "Friends, if you'd like to sell
    this handsome young lad, I will pay you quite well—
    twenty pieces of silver!" They said: "Yes, we'll sell;
    but keep him in chains till you leave Israel."

40. Without further ado a bill of sale they decreed,
    and each hastened to sign his own name with a reed.
    As soon as the merchant that paper received,
    he took Yusuf in chains, as he had agreed.

41. The caravan started its way down the trail,
    but heartbroken Yusuf did nothing but wail:
    "Please, sir, let me bid my dear brothers farewell!"
    The merchant was moved, and replied: "Very well."

42. The merchant said: "I can't believe the words you speak.
    They've sold you as if you were but a sheep,
    and accused you of being a rascal and thief.
    For men such as these, I'd give not a fig!"

43. Loaded down with his chains, Yusuf slowly went creeping
    to his brothers. Yahuda that night watch was keeping.
    He cried out to his brothers, his voice choked with weeping:
    "Here's the one whom you've wronged, you wretches! Stop sleeping!"

44. Yusuf said unto them: "May our Maker refrain
    from punishing you, though your guilt is quite plain.
    Though you've split us asunder, one in love let's remain."
    He embraced every one, and then left with great pain.

45. How great was that caravan! It went on and on;
    but poor Yusuf in the midst of that crowd was alone.
    A lone grave in the wilderness they soon came upon;
    there next to a hill was his mother's tombstone.

46. All in a flash from his camel he leapt,
    without even disturbing his guard as he slept;
    and dragging his chain, to the grave soft he crept,
    where he called to his mother; and he wept, and he wept.

47. He said: "Mother dear, may our Maker forgive you!
    If you could see me, your heart would break in two!
    I'm a slave, I am chained so I hardly can move.
    My own brothers sold me. How can this be true?

48. They have done this to me, though I gave them no reason,
    with falsehood and cunning they have done me this treason.

My dear father is taken from me out of season.
For a few worthless coins they have taken my freedom."

49. At this the black slave on the camel stopped sleeping.
Gone was Yusuf, whom the merchants had left in his keeping.
Back the way they had come he went swiftly leaping.
As he passed by the grave, he heard Yusuf weeping.

50. "You rascal!" he cried then. "Have you no fear?"
And Yusuf he beat until death he was near.
"You're a runaway slave," he said. "It is quite clear
your masters weren't lying when they sold you here."

51. "That's a lie," Yusuf said. "I am not as you say.
I was honoring my mother in her grave where she lay.
But don't listen to me; for to Allah I pray,
as I am innocent, that He make you pay."

52. They continued their journey throughout the long night;
indeed, it seemed endless, for dawn brought no light.
It was darker at midday. They trembled with fright
as the wind howled, and they knew not where to take flight.

53. That merchant had never seen night last so long.
He knew Allah was punishing some terrible wrong.
"If anyone guilty of sin be among
us, come forward, this terror do not prolong!

54. Such darkness and woe could only have issued
from some terrible sin one of you has committed.
Come forward, confess, you can still be forgiven!
Our lives will be spared and our sins be remitted."

55. Then the black man admitted his cruel mistake,
though insisting he'd done it for his master's sake,
to bring Yusuf back when he'd tried to escape.
But the merchant told Yusuf his vengeance to take.

56. Yusuf said: "No indeed, not as long as I live.
    I come from a people who prefer to forgive.
    I will not take revenge. I may be your captive,
    but nevertheless to love mercy I'll strive."

57. When these words of kindness had scarcely been spoken,
    The sun brightly shone, of forgiveness a token.
    The merchant said: "Friend, I'd release you to your folk in
    Israel, but then my promise would be broken."

58. A few days after that, to their own land they came.
    They unchained Yusuf's hands, in the river he bathed.
    With fine purple and silks his body they draped,
    with rubies and pearls his face and hands arrayed.

59. When they got to the city, it was almost dark as night,
    shrouded in black clouds, it was a gloomy sight!
    But when Yusuf arrived, everything turned white;
    the people were amazed to see his shining light.

60. They asked the merchant why Yusuf shone that way.
    Was he a mortal man or some sort of saint?
    The merchant replied, "He is just my loyal slave.
    You can buy him if you wish; I'm offering him for sale."

61. The time of the sale he announced by the clock.
    All over the kingdom that news caused a shock.
    From far and from near that day people did flock
    to see Yusuf as he stood there on the auction block.

62. All kinds of people—men and women, old and young—
    were dying to see him, to him they did run.
    Zaliqa left the table, her dinner untouched;
    she jumped on her mule, and off she did rush.

63. The auctioneer his wares began to cry:
    "Who will buy my slave, so young and so bright;

as loyal as they come, and a handsome sight;
a true friend of Allah, who will always do right?"

64. Yusuf said: "Don't you mean: who'll buy this young mule,
who knows nothing of work and has scarce been to school?"
Quoth the auctioneer then: "Young man, don't be cruel!
It's my business to sell you, and I am no fool."

65. "In that case," said Yusuf, "why not just tell the truth?:
'A prophet of Allah I am offering you,
and one of the loftiest, a son of Ya'qub;
there's no better bargain than this godly youth.'" [24]

66. "I bid his weight in silver," one man quickly told
the auctioneer, but at once another offered gold.
Still another would pay his weight in precious stones;
but for his weight in pearls to the king he was sold.

67. But when the merchant saw what a treasure he had,
he implored the purchaser to sell him back the lad.
"I'll pay double the price—it wouldn't be too bad."
But the king said: "No, thanks," and the merchant was sad.

68. He kissed the king's hands, the king's feet he embraced,
but the king's words were written and could not be erased.
Then the merchant accepted his fate with good grace
and declined to take more than what he had paid.

69. But still he asked Yusuf one last parting boon:
"Pray Allah in heaven to give me a son!
I have twelve loving wives, but male children I've none.
And pray that I prosper, and that I live long!"

---

[24] The three previous quatrains are copied out of order in both of the extant manuscripts of the Ḥadith, where they appear as 65, 66, and 67. Obviously the auctioneer's cry must come before the sale of Yusuf to the king. Likewise, it seems to me that quatrain 64 in the original—the one where the king gives Yusuf to his wife—should come after the conversation between Yusuf and the auctioneer.

70. Then Yusuf bowed down and begged Allah on high
to give that man sons and to lengthen his life.
His prayer was soon heard, for all twelve of his wives
within the next month were heavy with child—

71. or should I say children?, for came the day when
they all were in labor, all gave birth to twins!
They were beautiful babies and grew to good men,
for that merchant was blessed by the Omnipotent.

72. The king with rejoicing took Yusuf away,
and gave him to Zaliqa that very same day;
for she was his wife, and long had she prayed
for a son. Little Yusuf she fondly embraced.[25]

73. Zaliqa raised Yusuf with motherly care.
Before long, the boy's beauty was beyond all compare.
Then her love turned to lust, and her passion she'd bare.
She longed for his body; to sin he'd not dare.

74. She said to her handmaid: "I know you have seen
how I've cared for Yusuf, what a mother I've been.
Day and night I have watched him with vigilance keen,
but he doesn't care. He is really quite mean!

75. He scarce knows I am here. It is just a disgrace!
I can't even get him to look me in the face.
If he could truly see me, he'd long for my embrace,
and he'd do all I ask; to my bed he would race!"

76. The handmaid spoke up then, to Zaliqa she said:
"I know just what to do, for I have a good head
for these things. A fine painter we must get.
Your worries are over! You'll soon have the lad in bed."

---

[25] This quatrain is number 64 in the original manuscripts.

77. Everything she asked for, she was given right away.
   In no time at all she had built a hideaway
   with white ceiling and walls. The very next day
   she hired a great painter that building to array.

78. In the painting before Yusuf Zaliqa did kneel.
   Both were utterly naked. One almost could feel
   the warmth of her lips as she strained to steal
   a kiss; for that painting was amazingly real!

79. When that building was done, it was a rare treasure.
   Zaliqa's delight was far beyond measure.
   She sent and asked Yusuf to come at his leisure,
   for she'd something to show him that would surely give pleasure.

80. When he saw Zaliqa on her mattress so thick,
   he tried to turn back; he suspected a trick.
   She'd not stand for that! Lust made her too quick
   for poor Yusuf. He began to feel sick.

81. Before he could flee, she took hold of his skirt.
   She pulled him against her, and continued to flirt.
   She promised him riches. He his faith did assert:
   "If I keep myself pure, I cannot be hurt."

82. But wherever he looked, he saw only temptation;
   scenes of lust and perversion were the sole decoration.
   "You're my slave," said Zaliqa. "This humiliation
   is too much to bear. I am growing impatient!" [26]

83. At that moment Yusuf in his loins felt a stirring.
   His veins with lust pounded, his eyesight was blurring,
   but he thought of his father while that was occurring.
   His veins filled with ice water, his desire overturning.

---

[26] One folio (the ninth), from the middle of this stanza to the third line of stanza 92, is missing from the manuscript in the Real Academia de la Historia (Ms. A).

84. Then Yusuf turned his back and tried to run from there,
    When she saw him escaping, Zaliqa despaired.
    Tearing his skirt, his buttocks she bared.
    "You can't do this to me!" she loudly declared.

85. The king heard her shouts as he came through the gate.
    Then he heard Yusuf sobbing and cursing his fate;
    his skirt was torn off, he was in a bad state.
    The king was afraid he had come home too late.

86. He rushed in to Zaliqa. She showed signs of distress:
    her eyes were bloodshot, and her hair was a mess.
    "Need I say what has happened? I am sure you can guess,"
    said Zaliqa. "Now your wisdom address

87. to this problem. Young Yusuf, your most trusted slave
    has just tried to rape me—the villainous knave!—
    in spite of the motherly love that I gave
    him, and all of my efforts to make him behave."

88. The king then asked Yusuf: "Was this always your plan?
    Have you sought to betray me since the day I began
    to love you and trust you? To deceive me you ran?"
    But Yusuf replied: "I am not that sort of man."

89. The ladies in the neighborhood gossiped a bunch:
    that Zaliqa wanted Yusuf they had a strong hunch.
    But Zaliqa always knew what to do in a crunch;
    she invited those ladies to the palace for lunch.

90. She gave them rich food and excellent wine.
    Before they knew it, they were all feeling fine.
    She served each one grapefruit, to each one assigned
    an elegant, jewel-studded, sharp little knife.

91. She had kept Yusuf hidden in the next room.
    She'd hired experts in beauty the young man to groom.

They draped him in silk from Egypt's best loom,
bejeweled his hands, doused his hair with perfume.

92. When those ladies saw him, they went totally insane.
They would have done anything his favor to gain!
They went berserk! Before their wits they could regain,
they'd sliced up their hands, but they felt no pain.

93. With their blood the grapefruits were stained bright red.
Zaliqa was thrilled. She laughed, and she said:
"What are you doing? Are you out of your heads?
Can't you see the blood dripping down on your breasts?"

94. When they saw the blood, they knew they were crazy.
Zaliqa said: "You all went mad just from seeing the way he
moves his body in an instant. So now I think maybe
you'll understand, and not say I'm no lady."

95. The women said: "You're right. We never should have done
what we did. We concede. This game you have won!
Therefore it's only right to finish what we've begun.
We'll help you get Yusuf. We'll join in the fun!" [27]

96. Zaliqa said: "That's wonderful!" She took them to the boy.
She thought they would persuade him, but that was just a ploy.
Each one hoped to have him for her own private toy.
When Zaliqa found out, she was really annoyed!

97. When Yusuf saw this, he called upon the Lord,
saying, "Father, have mercy, for You I have adored!
Now not one, but many women after me have whored;
but I'd rather rot in jail than do something untoward."

98. Zaliqa was gloomy. A great sadness befell
her. Without Yusuf's love life was nothing but hell;

[27] The text of the poem in the manuscript in the Real Academia de la Historia ends with this quatrain.

so she went to her husband, and him she did tell:
"Yusuf's slandering me. I have treated him well.

99. Please put him in jail. He'll soon see his mistake."
(She thought sure that Yusuf to go free would forsake
his virginity.) She had no idea the king would take
her in earnest. He intended to break

100. Yusuf's spirit, so he sentenced him to life
with no chance of parole. Poor Zaliqa cried
her eyes out. "Now I'll never be his wife!"
she said to herself. "I'm to blame for this strife."

101. "If I had suspected that this could befall,
I'd never have spoken to my husband at all.
Now I'll never be cured. I will choke on this gall.
My longing for Yusuf will be my downfall!"

102. When Yusuf in prison for ten years had lain,
the king gave an order to his chamberlain
to imprison two men, to cause them great pain:
his baker and cupbearer, for their guilt was quite plain;

103. at least the baker's guilt was proven beyond doubt.
He had poisoned the king's bread, and he had been found out.
But the cupbearer, his accomplice, was such a clever lout,
they couldn't be quite sure; still, rumors went about.

104. In prison Yusuf's beauty won him a special place;
he guarded all the others who'd fallen in disgrace.
When they were ill, he nursed them; to succour them he'd haste.
He had won the trust of all by the beauty of his face.

105. The cupbearer dreamt a mysterious dream;
he asked Yusuf what it could possibly mean:
Yusuf said: "Very soon you'll be restored, I deem,
to your former post by your master, the king.

106. Your master will forgive you, though I know you lied;
    but from this day forward let Allah be your guide.
    Do what you know is right. From Allah you can't hide.
    Return to your post with the greatest of pride!"

107. The baker laughed and said: "Do you believe that stuff?
    I'll show you, my friend, it's all a lot of guff.
    I'll make up a dream to tell this lad Yusuf;
    to know if I'm lying he's not smart enough!"

108. The baker to Yusuf a false dream then did say,
    but Yusuf its true meaning to him did convey,
    He said: "You were the king's baker for many a day,
    but you were brought here because him you'd betray."

109. "Three days from now you'll be taken out," he said,
    "and you will be hanged, askew will lie your head,
    and the birds of the gate on your marrow will be fed.
    There you will hang until you are dead."

110. The baker said: "I didn't really dream what I told you.
    I just said so to see how that dream you'd construe."
    Yusuf replied: "Nonetheless, it is true.
    What you said, Allah will now cause to ensue."

111. Yusuf said this to the cupbearer erelong:
    "Tell the king that in prison I do not belong;
    already this curse has lasted too long."
    He replied: "To defend you I will be strong."

112. Three days later a summons was sent.
    To the great king those men swiftly went.
    He sentenced the baker to be hanged with torment,
    but to give the cupbearer his old post was content.

113. The cupbearer his promise forgot to keep,
    for two long years didn't utter a peep,
    till one night the king dreamed while asleep.
    Twelve years had spent Yusuf in that dungeon-keep.

114. This was the dream the king had that night:
    that up from a river came cows to his sight,
    its name was al-Nil,[28] a river of might,
    and he saw seven cows emerge with delight.

115. They were lovely and fat and indeed great in size.
    Then seven scrawny cows from the river did arise.
    The lean ones ate the fat ones right before his eyes,
    leaving not a trace, not even their fat thighs.

116. He saw seven ears of corn—it was a sight sublime!—
    as green and beautiful as in the summertime,
    and seven ugly, dry ones, covered with grime,
    as dried up and pale as a man long past his prime.

117. The dry ones consumed the green without delay;
    no trace of their goodness did they now display.
    All turned very dry, until every one lay
    as shriveled and white as mist at break of day.

118. The king was amazed by the sight he had seen:
    how those seven dry ears consumed all the green.
    A sign very important he was sure this had been,
    but he couldn't imagine what it could mean.

119. He sent for his wise men and his dream did relate
    so they should explain it and elucidate.
    And they told him: "Sire, this task is very great,
    but we'll examine our books and your doubts will abate."

120. They came back and told him: "My lord, do not brood.
    Dreams do not come true, as we've understood.
    Worrying about them will do you no good.
    Turn your mind to your duties, as truly you should."

121. The king then dismissed them. In his wisdom he thought
    that all of their efforts had been but for naught.

---

[28] Arabic for Nile.

When the cupbearer heard that the king was distraught,
he came to the king, and this message he brought:

122. "A worthy sage, my lord, I have met,
who is wrongly imprisoned. I owe him a debt,
though for two years or more I did him forget.
Sorely I've wronged him, I admit with regret.

123. Once a dream he explained for me very well."
The king said: "Then perhaps my doubts he'll dispel.
Everything you have heard, to that man now please tell,
and we'll free him at once from that prison cell."

124. The cupbearer his way to Yusuf did wend.
and he said: "I'm sorry I forgot you, my friend.
I was afraid the king to offend,
but for my neglect I'll now doubly amend.

125. But first, oh brother, by the Creator you adore
my master's dream to explain I do you implore."
Yusuf said: "I'll be glad to do all you wish and more,
but I can't leave without permission from my jailer."

126. Then he told him all that dream did encompass,
so that Yusuf could see clearly as in a looking glass.
Yusuf's understanding his wishes did surpass.
Yusuf said: "The dream is true, and it will come to pass.

127. You should be aware that those cows so fat and nice
and the seven moist, green ears that were beyond all price,
of rain and plenteous water are seven years precise.
Wherever you sow, your seed will yield twice.

128. And the seven lean cows and the dry ears in a row
are seven long years of privation and woe.
They devour the good ones, no matter where they go.
No matter where you sow, there no grain will grow.

129. Hence you must sow heavily throughout the countryside
during those good years when you'll be well supplied.
First for yourselves and your cattle provide,
then bind what's left in sheaves and set it aside.

130. Keep the ears intact; don't thresh them at all;
and bind the straw up tightly, and into barns it haul,
so that no vermin into it can crawl,
and then in the dry times no harm will you befall.

131. Thus in those years you will have enough to eat,
and your animals and cows your water won't deplete.
If all of you work hard to accomplish this feat,
you'll make it through the lean years and the famine you'll cheat."

132. When the cupbearer heard Yusuf say that thing,
to his master a full account he did bring,
and he told that handsomely bearded king
that truly the dream had a beautiful meaning.

133. That message the king did greatly delight.
To jail a man like that seemed a terrible slight—
a wise man, and truthful, and indeed very bright,
so he then ordered Yusuf brought into his sight.

134. The cupbearer this news to Yusuf then passed,
and told him the king his presence had asked.
He must go there at once or be taken to task.
But Yusuf replied: "Hold on! Not so fast!

135. Please tell the king he should bear in mind
I am grateful indeed for his gesture so kind,
but for twelve lonely years have I been confined
in this jail. To that error I am not resigned!

136. Out of this prison cell I refuse to be led,
until comes to me," so Yusuf then said,

"one of those lovely ladies from whose lust I fled,
when, all unawares, their hands' blood they shed.

137. Let the king summon them, and them importune,
for they are the authors of my misfortune.
Perhaps now at last they will change their tune,
and the truth will come out. That would be a great boon!

138. If all those women and Zaliqa he will find,
and if to tell the truth for once they are inclined,
and he sees that the blame to them must be assigned,
right then I'll be glad to leave this place behind."

139. The king summoned them, and the truth did emerge,
for they said unto him: "Our guilt we must purge.
Only with loyalty did Yusuf's veins surge.
He never wanted sex; he never had the urge."

140. Then Zaliqa got up and swiftly did reply
to all those ladies: "We can no longer lie.
The time has come for us to eat humble pie.
I started all of this, that I cannot deny."

141. We all behaved quite badly, may God come to our aid!
May Allah forgive us! We'll call a spade a spade.
Yusuf is guiltless, no blame on him is laid."
Then the king with sad curses those women did upbraid.

142. And then the king to Yusuf a wondrous message sent,
saying he now knew Yusuf was innocent,
for those women to the truth had given their assent.
Then Yusuf out of that gloomy prison went.

143. On the door of that prison, he did these words inscribe:
"Prison is a sepulcher to men who are alive,
and a place of damnation; that abyss I've survived.
May Allah make our loved ones in freedom to thrive."

144. The king then sent him a richly bedecked steed
 and a grand escort to accompany him decreed.
 He rode like a prince who had never known need.
 To that wise king's palace did Yusuf proceed.

145 Then the king stood up—'twas an honor without peer!
 He walked up to Yusuf and told him to draw near,
 and sit at his side, and be of good cheer.
 Then the king said: "I will make you my vizier."

146. In the seventy languages known to mankind
 the king spoke to him. Yusuf answered in kind,
 then yet another tongue with those he combined.
 The king was amazed at Yusuf's brilliant mind.

147. Then the king turned to the following theme:
 "My cupbearer has already told you my dream.
 Now I'll hear your explanation with pleasure extreme,
 and then I will do whatever you deem."

148. "To your Maker I commend you," did Yusuf exclaim,
 "for by this dream you will receive great fame.
 Now to seek a valiant man must be your aim,
 to take charge of your affairs and guide them without blame.

149. As I have advised, be this your strategy:
 Let all the wheat be gathered from the earth prudently.
 Save the wheat from the good years for the hard times to be,
 when the whole world from hunger will suffer misery.

150. All people will come in desperate straits
 to buy the bread you did accumulate
 for money, and ivory, and gold and silver plate.
 Over high and low you'll be master in this state."

151. When the king heard that, he fell deep in thought.
 Yusuf, seeing that, this message to him brought:

"To save you from misfortune Allah will do naught,
until to give me power you have rightly sought."

152. The king said: "Dear friend, how happy you've made me.
I thank you, and Allah's gratitude you'll see.
You'll ensure that this land exalted will be.
This kingdom is yours from now on, I decree.

153. For it is your duty this kingdom to guide
and its people in winter and in summertide.
Young and old will obey you, over all you'll preside,
even me, for upon your wisdom I've relied.

154. As you well deserve, may Allah guide you, I pray.
My friendship I trust you will rightly repay,
and give me back my kingdom without delay
when the time is come. Don't your welcome outstay!

155. With this single condition, I give you free rein
like a king in his kingdom, to command and ordain,
and thus I now order throughout my domain,
for king I no longer wish to remain."

156. It was pleasing to Yusuf, his new task he embraced
and sat down right then in the king's very own place.
The king ordered the people to bow down to his face,
and they did him homage with very good grace.

157. And when Yusuf the slender new moon had beheld,
as into a house of good fortune it traveled,
he foresaw years of plenty unparalleled.
Then a great meeting of the people he held.

158. When his vassals had come into that council,
he informed all of them that it was his will
that both high and low that whole land should till,
and should sow everywhere, both valley and hill.

159. To sow they went out, so as Yusuf to obey.
They did as their natural lord did them say.
Twice the usual harvest their work did repay,
They were in awe as that sight they'd survey.

160. Yusuf ordered his stewards on whom he relied
strong granaries to build on every side
out of strong wood, and very long and wide,
where the bread of the good times they'd set aside.

161. Never had been seen buildings of that size!
Row upon row, like mountains did they rise.
That harvest with care did Yusuf supervise.
They bound the sheaves tightly as he did advise.

162. In the new granaries they stored all that wheat.
There the ears were stored up with precautions discreet,
so that no vermin their work could defeat.
Every year the same process did they repeat.

163. Stores of grain beyond count in that place were confined,
and when the moon entered a very bad sign,
that the drought was approaching did Yusuf divine.
No more work in the fields from that day he'd assign

164. until seven long years had come in and gone out,
for they would be years of famine and drought.
No water from earth or from heaven would spout.
Just as Yusuf had said, that's how it turned out.

165. To sell all that wheat the king then enrolled
good men and true, wise men and bold.
To give full measure those men he then told,
and to charge a high price for each bushel they sold.

166. He ordered those men to sell without stint
both to natives and foreigners who to them went,

but to inquire of each one his home and descent
if they were strangers, for that's what he meant.

167. In but a few days the land they did deplete.
No bread and merchandise remained on any street,
and in city or town there was nothing to eat.
Then they bought from Yusuf, who had all the wheat.

168. The first years with money and chattels they bought,
and silver and gold until they had naught.
Then to surrender their children they thought,
and when they were all gone, their own wives they brought.

169. In the seventh year their own bodies they sold,
and all became slaves—all of them, young and old.
At last everything by the king was controlled,
and in foreign lands too the famine took hold.

170. Thus everything into Yusuf's hands fell.
He owned more slaves than he could ever sell.
Then he went to the king and to him this did tell:
"Sire, what do you think? Have I done well?"

171. The king unto Yusuf this answer addressed:
"You're the man for the job; you are truly the best!
Since such skill at ruling you have possessed,
of that title right now myself I'll divest."

172. Then Yusuf said with great humility:
"Now all of my slaves I've decided to free,
and to restore the kingdom to your sovereignty."
But the king quickly replied: "I cannot agree."

173. The king continued: "That wouldn't be right.
So ungratefully my heart would not requite
your service, nor your great wisdom slight;
rather, from now on, you will be king outright."

174. And when Yusuf saw how the famine had spread,
throughout all the lands, his gentle heart bled,
for he feared that his father of hunger was dead.
"If word comes of him, please tell me," he said.

175. A few days later of bread fell quite short
the lands of Ya'qub. He could find no comfort,
for he had a large tribe and a beloved consort,
all of whom from his income he tried to support.

176. Ya'qub said: "My dear sons, I have heard tell,
that in Egypt a righteous king does now dwell;
in goodness and wisdom he does excel.
He has plenty of bread. He is willing to sell.

177. Now I'll give you some money, and at once you must leave,
and implore that good king you to receive.
Tell him of our pain, and I'm sure he'll believe.
With Allah's help, our suffering he will relieve."

178. His sons said: "We will gladly do as we should.
We'll seek out that king, since you say he is good.
We'll go straight through that kingdom to his neighborhood,
and with Allah's help, he will sell us some food."

179. When they reached that land with food replete,
they said they had come the king for to meet.
A squire said: "His palace is here in this street.
I'll get you some barley and also some wheat.

180. I'm the king's steward. I'm entitled to sell
to all those who outside this kingdom do dwell,
but first where you're from you must to me tell.
If you are from here, I will bid you farewell.

181. Tell me the land that you occupy,
and then for this bread you can surely apply,

and I'll give each of you what you want to buy.
Your money's worth I will gladly supply."

182. Then unto him their names they all told
and how they were brothers, and the land they did hold,
as dear sons of Ya'qub and Ishaq the old,
of their home in Jerusalem, that city extolled.

183. The squire right then to the mighty king went
and a full report to him did present
of those sons of a prophet, of noble descent:
"Sire," he said, "if you wish, to serve them I'm content."

184. "Bring them to me," said the king. "Be discreet,
and see that they're given the best fish to eat.
Follow their movements in every street.
Don't let them escape or your vigilance cheat."

185. When he saw them, the king was filled with delight,
and with beautiful garments those men did bedight.
A thousand knights on their left, and the same on their right,
he did post, and had all bow down at their sight.

186. The clothes they were brought were of very great price:
of gold and of silk, and embroidery precise,
and glittering jewels enormous in size;
all perfumed with civet, gaily colored and nice.

187. He ordered them to enter and to look upon his face,
while appropriate greetings they struggled to trace.
Politely then he seated each one in his place.
They were amazed by this kindness and grace.

188. While they were still standing, and the king was in his chair,
haughtily from that perch the king at them did stare;
but they were impervious to worry or care.
Lovingly the king his greetings did declare.

189. But even though the king had treated them that way,
Judah[29] said: "I may be mad, but I cannot but say
I fear this king, and near him I cannot bear to stay.
Perhaps he'll be so kind as to send us on our way."

190. But no matter what they said, he was deaf to their pleas.
For three days he kept them there and would not them release.
He showed them great honor and comfort and ease,
as if they were his children, attended to their needs.

191. His measuring cup was made of solid gold,
and a covering of jewels that cup did enfold.
Truly magic power that gorgeous cup did hold,
to let the king know when the truth to him was told.

192. The king asked them many questions, he coaxed and he pried,
while holding that cup on which he relied.
The king warned them to be careful what they replied,
for it would let him know if any of them lied.

193. Let them guard their tongues from lying, and all would be well.
Let no one say a word of falsehood or libel,
for if he did, that cup would ring like a bell,
and the cup spoke the truth, as I need hardly tell.

194. The king said to them: "Who's your father reverend?
Tell me, from what noble line do you descend?
I see you are strong, handsome, courteous men.
Answer my question, and I shall be your friend."

195. They said to him: "Sire, to tell the truth,
we are sons of a prophet, God's own people, forsooth.
We are sons of Ya'qub, true believers from our youth.
We came here to buy bread at your steward's booth."

---

[29] The manuscript alternates "Judas" (Spanish for "Judah") and the Arabic form Yahuda.

196. The king tapped his cup and hearkened thereunto.
     He held it to his ear, its message to construe.
     Then he said to them without further ado:
     "According to the cup, what you say is true."

197. The king then asked them: "How many are you, pray?"
     They told him: "We were twelve in our heyday,
     but the wolf ate one, we are sorry to say,
     and the other with our father at home had to stay."

198. The king said to them: "By my Maker I swear,
     if it were not for the honor due to your forebear,
     to throw you in prison right now I'd prepare,
     but for love of that old man, I'll let you go back there."

199. They replied: "Master, humbly do we pray,
     by the Lord of the world, who gave you such sway,
     please send us back to our father today,
     and our Maker your kindness will surely repay.

200. Regard not ourselves, but our honored old sire,
     for he is quite frail and soon will expire.
     If you knew him, to honor him you would desire,
     for he is a good man, of good deeds does not tire."

201. "Indeed, not for your sake, but for that old saint
     I will kindly give ear unto your complaint.
     May Allah one day with that man me acquaint.
     Like a son, I will love him without restraint.

202. Greet the old man for me. Say I hope he is fine.
     For that lost son of his does he still repine?
     By his youngest son have him drop me a line.
     If you forget this, you'll have no wheat of mine.

203. Yet I cannot but fear my trust you'd betray.
     I'll keep one of you here to be sure you obey

until your youngest brother that letter does convey.
Now all of you cast lots to decide who will stay."

204. Upon the one called Simeon[30] the unlucky lot fell,
the very one who had cut Yusuf's rope, truth to tell,
when the brothers were casting him into the well.
Now he had to stay in Egypt in a prison cell.

205. Then the king with diversions those men did distract;
while he had each one's money returned to his sack.
All awareness of this those brothers did lack.
He did it to give them more cause to come back.

206. They said their goodbyes, and went home to apprise
their father of that land, that great king to eulogize.
He was beyond compare, his land was of great size,
and he was rich in vassals, and in counsel was wise.

207. But strangest of all, that king did them remind
of their father Ya'qub, for he was wise and kind.
Anyone who came upon him for the first time would find
that he surely was a prophet, and the truth he divined.

208. Once at home, when their sacks of grain they had untied,
they found that all their money was still there inside.
"This king is very good," those men then testified.
"Our money he's restored, and honored us beside.

209. But he ordered us, dear father, to make you aware,
to send him your other son at once you must prepare,
and write him a letter with news of your welfare.
If you don't give it to us, we cannot go back there,

210. for he won't give us bread nor to us will attend.
But if you give it to us, to us he'll condescend,

---

[30] The text used this Latinized version of the Hebrew rather than the Arabic *Shama'un*.

and will trust us and believe us, and will kindly recommend,
and then we will get bread, and he will be our friend."

211. But their father said: "No indeed, that I will not do!
He is my life, and my only comfort too.
Furthermore, how could I ever trust you,
for you betrayed me before with a promise untrue?

212. "When you took Yusuf, and he never returned,
you broke your solemn vow, and my enmity you earned.
You lost me my son; your own brother you spurned.
To defend myself from your evil I have learned."

213. No matter what they said, he refused them to heed.
There was no way to persuade him to consent to that deed,
so they did not return, and they had to concede
till the bread was all eaten, and there was no dough to knead.

214. Then once again their father they implored
to entrust unto them that brother adored,
for to bring him back there they had promised that lord,
and the utmost protection to him they'd afford.

215. So much did they say, such pleas did prepare,
he had to give in, for the cupboards were bare.
They swore to protect him with vigilance rare,
to bring him back safely an oath did they swear.

216. Then to one of his sons did Ya'qub dictate:
"Oh mighty king of Egypt's great state,
Ya'qub sends you greetings, though sad is his fate,
for your kindness indeed he does appreciate.

217. "As for your question about how I have been,
I'm a worn-out old man, better times I have seen.
I am blind, and from sickness I have grown lean,
for my health was taken by my Maker serene

218. ever since Yusuf, a piece of my heart,
    and my strength at all times, from me did depart.
    He was my refuge, but now we're apart.
    I know not if he's dead or chained in some rampart.

219. Thus it seems I've been punished by the King on high.
    On your compassion and kindness I rely.
    As my earthly king, this request do not deny,
    and give me back my son, or for love of him I'll die.

220. If it weren't for this son, I'd already be dead.
    By him for dear Yusuf I have been comforted.
    I trust you'll command that back here he'll be led,
    and may Allah, the Powerful, His grace on you shed."

221. When that letter was finished, to his sons Ya'qub turned:
    "My sons, heed my words, for I am concerned.
    When back into Egypt you have returned,
    go through different gates, for thus I have learned."

222. Having said their farewells, they set out on their way.
    They all traveled together by night and by day,
    and they reached the city in the heat of the day.
    When the king heard the news, he became very gay.

223. The king then dressed up in his robes paramount,
    and had all his people their best horses mount,
    and take incense and perfume beyond any count.
    The smell was too wondrous for me to recount!

224. When all had been done just as the king spoke,
    he gave orders at once to bring him that folk,
    and as through the courtyard they came in a stroke,
    the youngest one tried to catch that fragrant smoke.

225. He smeared it on the garments in which he was clad
    and on his face, but his brothers thought that was bad:

"What are you doing?" they said. "Have you gone mad?
Do you think just for you is this welcome so glad?"

226. He replied: "Brothers, I beg you, do not complain.
Listen to my words and let me explain.
Control yourselves now, from anger refrain,
so the king will see you are of a good strain."

227. And then to his words they gave their assent,
for they saw his advice was indeed intelligent,
and they behaved well as to the king they went,
like worthy sons of that father excellent.

228. The king's magnificence those men did beguile,
though some thought him the same whom they had known erstwhile.
"What do you men want?" asked the king with a smile,
"and where did you acquire such a pleasing style?"

229. They told him that just now they had come back from their land,
and how they brought the letter by their youngest brother's hand,
just as they had promised, to obey his command.
The king was delighted that before him they did stand.

230. Then the youngest brother that letter to him gave,
in which their father told him of his condition grave.
When he read those things, to weep the king did crave,
and he turned away from them, his dignity to save.

231. Then the king ordered the men of his household
to prepare a fine table with vessels of gold
and still others of silver, and goblets manifold;
and those men to sit down and dine with him he told.

232. In pairs at the table the king did those men seat.
In the order of their birth they were served their meat.
Each with his closest brother that meal did then eat.
That's what the king decided, for such was his conceit.

233. As two by two those brothers dipped their hands into one plate,
the youngest one in silence and solitude ate.
As he thought of his own brother, he became disconsolate,
for the son of his mother should have been his messmate.

234. Sadly he stared at the food before him placed,
for each of his half brothers, his own brother faced.
Each morsel he brought to his lips with tears was laced,
and then he stopped eating; his food went to waste.

235. The handsome young lad then fell into a faint.
When the king saw that, he lost all restraint.
He held the boy's hand and joined in his complaint
until the poor lad his senses regained.

236. The king asked: "My friend, who has caused you to fret?"
He replied: "You, sir, are the cause of my regret,
for you're more like my brother than any I've met,
and that beautiful brother my heart can't forget."

237. "My friend, please forgive me," the king did entreat.
"We've only just met, but allow me to greet
you. Come and join me right here in my seat.
In place of your brother, with you I will eat."

238. The king attended the boy with gusto.
Dainty dishes before him were set in a row,
and with him he ate, his pity to show.
Such an honor the king on that lad did bestow.

239. The king gladly ate, the boy ceased to complain.
When his brothers saw that, they went truly insane.
Out of envy, they wished that their brother they'd slain,
saying: "Our little brother . . ."—this was their refrain—

240. ". . . right next to our father will take up his post.
As soon as we're home, he is certain to boast:

'That king felt quite honored to serve as my host,
for among all my brothers I am foremost.'"

241. The king then asked him if he'd taken a dame.
"I've a wife and three sons," the lad did exclaim.
"To remind me of Yusuf I gave each a name,
for thus in my heart his image I'd frame.

242. "One is called Wolf, and another is Blood,
the third one is Yusuf. His mother is good.
I have called them these names, for I've understood
that a wolf ate poor Yusuf when lost in the wood.

243. They brought us his blood stained shirt from that place,
but these names have helped me remember his face,
which the passing of time can never erase,
for he was my life and my only solace.

244. From the womb of one mother we both came to be,
but my unlucky father his loss lived to see.
I don't know if he's living, on land or on sea.
You reminded me of him and caused me misery."

245. Then the king his pain could no longer conceal,
and he longed to cry out, the truth to reveal.
He took him by the hand, to a corner did steal,
and then he spoke to him. His tone was virile.

246. The king then asked him: "Do you know me, squire?"
and the boy quickly answered: "Certainly not, sire."
He said: "I am your brother Yusuf, the one whom you desire,"
and they rejoiced to see such a wondrous thing transpire.

247. Then happiness the lad of his senses did deprive,
and Yusuf was afraid that he might not survive.
He took him by the hand, and the boy did then revive.
Yusuf said: "You have nothing to fear while I am alive."

248. The king then went on, and to the boy did confide:
    "From this day forward with me you will abide.
    but by neither man nor woman the truth will be espied,
    for very great precautions discreetly I'll provide.

249. To keep this secret I am sure you have the knack,
    but you must not be afraid or be taken aback.
    I mean to have my measuring cup placed in your sack.
    It is for love of you, for thus I'll have you brought back."

250. That secret of the king's by none of them was known.
    He had bidden them farewell, and on their way they'd gone.
    Together those brothers traveled on and on,
    and then all at once they heard a cry wanton.

251. They stopped to see the meaning of that cry so strong.
    It was the king pursuing them with a mighty throng,
    crying: "Stop, thieves, for you have done a great wrong!
    How dare you take something that to the king does belong?"

252. They stopped in their tracks to see those men draw nigh,
    for their angry shouts did the brothers terrify.
    At once they replied: "It's a sin to tell a lie.
    How dare you call us thieves? That charge we deny!

253. Of what you are seeking please give us some sign.
    Just tell us what's stolen, and cease to malign."
    They replied: "You have taken that measuring cup fine
    in which our king's accustomed secrets to divine.

254. Now let the wrongdoer admit his deceit,
    and we will reward him with a sack of good wheat."
    Then humbly the brothers those men did entreat:
    "We are all honest men, and your king we'd not cheat.

255. From a line of wrongdoers we do not descend.
    To such vile behavior we'd not condescend.

You have no evidence your charge to defend,
so you should stop shouting, and cease us to offend."

256. Then asked a nobleman who was nearby:
"What should we do if that is a lie?"
"Let the thief be enslaved," was the brothers' reply,
"With your good local custom we will gladly comply."

257. They searched through those brothers' sacks with rigor,
but the youngest one's sack did completely ignore.
When the brothers saw that, they were cut to the core.
How dare they commit such a blatant error?

258. Then to the king and his servant they whined:
"Our little brother's sack you should also unbind."
They replied: "It's no business of yours, never mind."
Then they searched it themselves, and the cup there did find.

259. When those brothers cast eyes on that cup justly famed,
they trembled with fear and their brother disclaimed.
They cried out: "Oh brother, aren't you ashamed?
Why have you done this? Now we'll surely be blamed."

260. He replied: "My dear brothers, do not me harrow!
First hear me out, and then you will know
that I have done nothing to deserve all this woe,
for nothing could drive me to an action so low.

261. Remember, my brothers, how your money you found
once before in your sacks. Did that not astound
all of you? As that money you stole, I expound,
likewise have I stolen this cup so renowned.

262. But if you are not guilty, you cannot ignore
I'm as innocent now as you were before."
His brothers, impressed by the poor boy's candor,
from that moment on held no more rancor.

263. Then to the king those men did report:
     "His brother the same way himself did comport.
     When a belt he stole, his aunt that theft did thwart.[31]
     They had the same mother, but we are a different sort."

264. In his heart the king smiled, though not without dread,
     to hear those words false and evil-minded.
     Then he told them: "Indeed it is just as I said,
     you all look like thieves. You are surely lowbred."

265. He ordered them to drag him away with abuse,
     but of course this was all just a clever ruse
     to convince his brothers, thus them to bemuse,
     that he was a prisoner and fought to get loose.

266. He was taken to the chamber where the king did reside,
     while his brothers to the dining room his servants did guide.
     When those men from his presence had been taken aside,
     the king made haste in his brother to confide.

267. Taking his brother gently by the hand,
     the king said: "I'm your brother Yusuf, you must understand,
     whose loss our old father had to withstand.
     He still mourns for me, and in grief for him I stand."[32]

268. The king in noble garments his brother did array,
     with all the elegance that kingdom could purvey.

---

[31] According to Muslim legend, after the death of Yusuf's mother, he was sent to live with his aunt. Later Ya'qub asked her to send Yusuf back to him. Reluctant to part with the beautiful child, she tied a belt that she had inherited from Isḥaq around his waist and then claimed that Yusuf had stolen it. According to the law, anyone caught in the act of theft became the slave of the owner of the stolen property. Hence Yusuf had to remain with her until she died. The Qur'an reports that the brothers told Yusuf: "If he has stolen (no wonder), his brother had stolen before" (12:77).

[32] It is obvious that the poem conflates two different traditions. Yusuf had already revealed his identity to his younger brother in stanza 246. In the Qur'an (12:69), as in the poem, Yusuf reveals his identity to his brother before hiding the cup in his sack. In the Bible (Gen. 45), it is only after his arrest that Benjamin learns Joseph's true identity.

Then the king told him: "Dear brother, today
please enjoy yourself and do as I say.

269. Now I'll go to our brothers, as truly I ought.
I'll ask them their plans and see what they've sought."
When the king went to them, he found them deep in thought,
they were sad and ashamed, and indeed quite distraught.

270. The king struck his cup, as he had done before.
He hearkened to the sound, its meaning to explore.
Then he asked his brothers: "Do you understand this lore?"
"No, indeed," they replied, "by the God Whom we adore."

271. "This sound says that you have all greatly sinned
seventy[33] years ago, and have yet to repent."
"Honored lord," they then sobbed in bitter torment,
"please forgive us for the sake of the Omnipotent.

272. Consider not us, for no merits have we,
but think of our venerable father's misery.
for if our old father you only could see,
you would send him our brother and set him free."

273. When the name of Ya'qub they mentioned again,
the king's heart from weeping could hardly refrain.
He said: "Friends, only that my wrath does restrain.
Were it not for Ya'qub, I would have you all slain."

---

[33] Thus the manuscript. In his edition Johnson comments that the word was probably meant to be "siete" (seven) rather than "setenta" (seventy). Neither number really
makes sense. We don't know how much time Yusuf spent in the king's house before his
arrest. However, the poem clearly states (stanza 135) that he spent twelve years in jail.
The seven good years, and probably at least the first year of famine, have now gone by,
so the brothers' sin (selling Yusuf) would have occurred at least twenty years before.
Muslim tradition tends to exaggerate the time Yusuf spent in Egypt before his reconciliation with his brothers. Zalikha grew old before Yusuf married her, and this is all presented as having occurred before Yusuf's brothers went to Egypt. Ibn al-'Abbas states
that Yusuf was separated from Ya'qub for eighty two years. Perhaps the figure seventy is
simply a round number meaning "a very long time."

274. Then the king said: "Leave this neighborhood.
Retaining you here will do me no good.
Your father wrote me, as I've understood,
I should send you back home as soon as I could."

275. They had promised their father they'd not leave that place
without taking their brother back to his embrace.
"Please give us our brother!" they begged the king's grace.
"Couldn't you take one of us in his place?"

276. But the king replied: "I'll not fall for that ploy!
Keep one of you and release that thieving boy?
Get out of here, and cease me to annoy.
If I hear another word, all of you I'll destroy!"

277. Then they took counsel as to what they should do,
or what sort of story for their father they'd construe;
or if it were possible the lad to rescue,
and thus make their word to their father come true.

278. Judah, as eldest, spoke first perforce:
"Tell our father the truth, we have no recourse.
That king's seized his son without any remorse.
Now he's the king's captive, and held with great force.

279. Know, my brothers, here my stay I'll prolong,
for we all promised our father to do him no wrong.
I'd not address my father with a lying tongue.
I'll make that king surrender, even though he's strong.

280. We must make that king understand that we're right.
Once again all our reasons to him we'll recite,
but if he persists in his obstinate spite,
we'll lay siege to his castle and his city we'll smite.

281. Nine different sectors in this city I've spied,
and the king's palace is off to one side.

I'll fight the king, and will soon crush his pride,
while each sector one of you has occupied."

282. Like a lion enraged, Judah went to the king.
He said: "Oh great king, please do me one thing.
Give me my brother, and your praises I'll sing,
or else of my vengeance you will soon feel the sting.

283. For if with the full strength of my voice I call,
all your people will die—young and old, great and small—
unborn babes from their mothers' wombs will fall.
Such a massacre the whole world will appall!"

284. The king then replied: "As you have said, do.
I dare you that vile threat to pursue.
You may be strong, but others are too.
You'll need all of your strength before you are through."

285. Then with anger did glower Judah's face.
A gigantic boulder he rushed to embrace.
Like an apple, he threw it with ease and with grace,
but the king just said: "Put it back in its place."

286. Quickly the king went up to that boulder,
with no effort he hoisted it up to his shoulder.
He aimed toward the wall, but that rock sailed right over,
for Judah was bold, but Yusuf was bolder.

287. Judah said nothing but inwardly cursed.
The king let him simmer, as his plan he rehearsed.
When he saw that Judah was ready to burst,
to go up and touch him, his son he coerced.

288. His son up to Judah that moment did dart.
As his father looked on, he touched that braggart.
Judah's anger right then to diminish did start,
and also his strength began to depart.

289. As he searched for his brothers, that boy he extolled:
"That handsome lad has touched my very soul;

he must be a descendant of Ya'qub the old."
Seeking his brothers, through that city he strolled.

290. When he found them, he asked: "Whose was that touch?"
They replied: "We swear unto you, it was none of us."
He said: "Are you sure? For its power was such,
only Ya'qub's descendant could affect me that much."

291. Then Yahuda spoke unto his kinsmen:
"This is the counsel of very bad men.
When I told you before: 'This is forbidden,'
you didn't believe me, and we fell into sin.

292. What I told you was good, but you weren't attentive;
now I'll grieve for my father as long as I live.
Let us beg our Creator His mercy to give,
and this noble king our deed to forgive."

293. Thus Judah the eldest to his brothers did preach:
"Let's go to the king with eloquent speech,
and in every way his pardon beseech.
Thus beyond the lion's realm we may reach."

294. They spoke these words unto the king erelong:
"Consider first of all your Creator so strong,
and then our father Ya'qub, who to Allah does belong."
But the king said: "You fought against me and did me wrong.

295. I wanted to show you the might of my hand,
so that at last you would understand
that our strength beyond yours does by nature expand."
Then the king pardoned them, and in peace they did stand.

296. When the king pardoned them, with joy did they swell,
but the king said: "My cup brings a message cruel.
It says that you threw your own brother in a well.
and I'm inclined to believe what to me it does tell.

297. When to put him on sale, you drew him out thence,
you lowered his price to a mere twenty pence."

"We beg you, kind sir, don't believe such nonsense!
We'd never do that!" This was their defense.

298. The king then proceeded a letter to unfold—
it was written in Hebrew and was very old—
recounting exactly how he had been sold.
That letter up to that day he did hold.

299. Judah took the letter and read it out loud.
Then he wept, and gloom did his brothers becloud.
They asked: "Who the king with this letter endowed?"
but the king asked: "Is this letter by you disavowed?"

300. Then they said: "Sir, if this letter you'll carefully read,
it deals with a slave whom we sold out of need."
Then Judah again that letter did read,
but the king said: "You are all wicked indeed."

301. He then struck that cup, as if casting a spell.
Its sound rang out there as clear as a bell,
and he told them: "This sound unto me does now tell
that your brother's alive and has done very well.

302. Don't imagine that in his grave he's been laid,
for soon he'll come here with a great cavalcade,
and will reveal to the world by whom he was betrayed,
and see that their treachery is duly repaid.

303. That you are all sinners is this cup's refrain,
and have wounded your father again and again,
for your sins have caused him unbearable pain.
Your duty as sons you did surely profane."

304. Then the king sent for his mightiest slaves
to cut off their hands, and they came there in waves.
When they saw them come there with knives and with staves,
they said: "We are lost, for truly we're knaves!"

305. They said to the king: "If we could see him now,
we'd all kiss his feet, and before him we'd bow.

Our former misdeeds we would all disavow,
and perhaps he'd have pity and forgive us somehow."

306. Then the king with kindness on those men did gaze,
for they had admitted the error of their ways.
They said they'd do good for the rest of their days
and they went to their father with joy and with praise.

307. But Judah and Simeon in Egypt remained.
Thus only eight brothers their homeland regained.
When their father cast eyes upon them, he complained:
"How dare you come here? Aren't you ashamed?"

308. Leaving three of your brothers, you come at your leisure?
I grieve for that little one, he is my treasure."
They said: "Father dear, he stole the king's measure.
But for you, the king would have killed him with pleasure.

309. Judah and Simeon with shame were undone.
They refused to come here for any reason."
Their father replied: "You have come here with treason.
If this should go on, you will leave me no son.

310. My sorrows increase, while of sons I have fewer.
How dare you yourselves insanely perjure,
saying that cup was stolen by my son so pure?"
They replied: "Father, we saw it, so we are quite sure."

311. He wrote them a letter to that king excellent,
and to search for their brother back to Egypt he sent.
Poor Yusuf they must seek, and never relent,
asking for him wherever they went.

312. "Have you lost your mind?" they asked him with a sigh.
"That Yusuf is dead you cannot deny."
He said: "Do as I say, for I've heard from on high,
what you cannot know, from the Lord of the sky . . ."[34]

---

[34] The manuscript in the Biblioteca Nacional ends with these words, the last on the fiftieth folio. An indeterminate number of pages—the poem's conclusion—are missing.

The first page of the Vatican manuscript of the Poem of Yosef.
Courtesy Biblioteca Apostolica Vaticana.

⇛ Poem of Yosef (c.1350)

Anonymous

This poem, usually known in Spanish as the *Coplas de José*,[1] is one of few surviving medieval Jewish *aljamiado* texts. The language of the poem is an archaic Castilian, with many forms paralleling fourteenth-century literary texts. It is based principally on Genesis 37–50, the *Sefer ha-Yashar*, the *Targum Jonathan*,[2] and King Alfonso X's *General History* (see following chapter).[3] Traditional Muslim accretions to the story, such as the talking wolf, the tear in Joseph's garment, and the banquet offered to the court ladies of Egypt, are notably absent from this version.

The poem has come down to us in three different manuscripts, all of which are both fragmentary and defective. It first came to public attention in 1910, when Moïse Schwab published a transcription of a fragment of sixteen stanzas[4] that had been discovered during the rebinding of some manuscripts in the Bibliothèque Nationale, Paris.[5] These pages had been used to stiffen the original bindings of one of those manuscripts. In 1935 Ignacio González Llubera published a considerably longer but still fragmentary manuscript[6] of the poem that he had found in the Cambridge University Library.[7] González Llubera either

---

[1] None of the manuscripts has a title. The title *Coplas de Yoçef* was first applied to the poem by Ignacio González Llubera, although he does not explain why he chose to use that term. In his recent edition, Moshe Lazar has adopted the title *Poema de Yosef* "to highlight [the poem's] being contemporaneous with the *Poema de Yuçuf*" (p. xv). Although I believe the Jewish poem is probably somewhat later than the Morisco one (and in any case I have rejected the traditional title *Poema de Yusuf* for the latter work, since Manuscript A is entitled *Ḥadith of Yusuf*) I have chosen to adopt Lazar's more general title for the Jewish poem. The vague Spanish term *coplas* misleadingly suggests parallels with satiric works such as the *Coplas de Mingo Revulgo* or with Jorge Manrique's *Coplas on the Death of His Father*.

[2] An Aramaic translation of the prophetic books of the Bible begun in Palestine in the first centuries of the Common Era and later revised in Babylonia, where it is thought to have attained its final form by the seventh century.

[3] See pp. 39–47 ("Parallels and Sources") of González Llubera's edition, and Saúl Sosnowski's article "Sobre las fuentes de las *Coplas de Yoçef*," *Sefarad* 29 (1969): 333–37.

[4] Corresponding to stanzas 5–19 of the present translation, plus stanza 22, which is inserted out of order after stanza 16.

[5] "Quatrains judéo-espagnols," *Revue Hispanique* 23 (1910): 9–32. Manuel Alvar López reprinted these stanzas on pages 349–51 of his anthology *Poesía española medieval* (Barcelona: Planeta, 1969).

[6] Catalogued as Ms. Add. 3355.

[7] *Coplas de Yoçef: A Medieval Spanish Poem in Hebrew Characters* (Cambridge: Cambridge Univ. Press, 1935).

was unaware of the fragment published by Schwab or failed to realize that it was part of the same poem—a somewhat excusable oversight since the text of the two fragments does not overlap. A water-mark on the Cambridge manuscript's paper establishes its date as between 1413 and 1473. The manuscript contains forty three stanzas. Fortunately, many of these are numbered, enabling González Llubera to determine that the first stanza in the manuscript was actually stanza 261 of the poem. González Llubera wrote of the Cambridge manuscript that

> the present text is a copy from an already defective MS. In two places (fols. 60 and 60v) the scribe has left a four-line blank, and in each case it is stated that a stanza is missing. Such omissions point to a dilapidated copy having existed from which the present one was made. That the copy was not only in a bad state of preservation, but defective as well, is apparent from the fact that after l. 28 no indication is forthcoming from the scribe with regard to those stanzas that both the sequence of the narrative and the numbering show to be missing at that spot. In conclusion, the present copy must be removed by at least two stages from the original version. Moreover, there is abundant proof of the corrupt state of the text: distorted lines (54–5), dittographies (e.g., l. 119), identical rime-words (146–7), and ll. 35, 46, 79, 108, 135, etc. show errors of transcription of one kind or another.[8]

In 1960 Moshe Lazar found still a third manuscript of the poem in the Vatican Library.[9] This manuscript, signed by a scribe named Gershon, was copied somewhere in the Ottoman Empire in 1533. By far the most nearly complete of the three manuscripts, it contains 309 stanzas and corresponds closely, with only minor variants, to the other two manuscripts. To judge by the numbering of the stanzas in the Cambridge manuscript, the Vatican manuscript is missing four stanzas from the early part of the poem (the stanza numbered 261 in the Cambridge manuscript corresponds to stanza 256 of the Vatican manuscript). It is also lacking one stanza (numbered 296 in the present translation) that appears in the Cambridge manuscript. Curiously, the Cambridge manuscript contains a notation after stanza 295 that "one stanza is missing," and then it adds a stanza that in fact is missing from the Vatican manuscript. Lazar first published an English translation by David Herman of the Vatican manuscript in

---

[8] *Coplas de Yoçef*, p. xiv.
[9] Catalogued as Ms. Neofiti 48.

1972 in the anthology *The Sephardic Tradition*.[10] He has published both the original *aljamiado* text and a Roman-alphabet transcription in 1990[11] and has promised to produce a future scholarly edition of the text, "with its complete listing of variant readings, notes and commentaries."[12] Unfortunately, Herman's translation contains numerous inaccuracies, does not scan as poetry— he is totally inconsistent in his use of rhymes, and seems merely to have inserted a rhyming word whenever he could think of one—and inexplicably omits six entire stanzas from the manuscript. The present translation is an entirely new one and takes into account the readings of all three manuscripts.

The meter of the poem has been described as a transitional form between the *cuaderna vía* and "a type of hexasyllable that would spring from it."[13] The poem's "alexandrines" are of six not seven syllables, rhyme may be either assonant or consonant, and the poet has introduced an internal rhyme in each line at the caesura. Further complicating matters, the fourth verse of each stanza must end with the word "Yosef." Hence the rhyme scheme is

_____ A	_____ B		
_____ A	_____ B		
_____ A	_____ B		
_____ A	_____ C		

As the *cuaderna vía* began to decline in popularity, some poets, such as Juan Ruiz (d. 1350?) and Rabbi Shem Tov (or Santob) of Carrión (d. after 1345), began to break away from the conventions of the genre in similar ways, and this too points to a date in the fourteenth century for our poem. Lazar has noted that the meter of the poem was probably influenced by medieval Hebrew *piyyutim*, liturgical poems composed for use as part of the synagogue service.[14] Indeed, one could point to examples such as the famous "Prayer for Dew" (*Ten tal lir'tzot*) for the first day of Passover composed by the seventh-century (?) poet Eleazar ben Kallir as a possible model. That poem consists of quatrains of verses ranging from six to ten syllables in length, with perfect rhyme, except that the final line of each stanza must always insert the word *tal* ("dew") after

---

[10] (New York: W. W. Norton, 1972), pp. 75–120.

[11] *Joseph and His Brothers: Three Ladino Versions* (Culver City, Calif.: Labyrinthos, 1990).

[12] Ibid., p. xv.

[13] González Llubera, *Coplas de Yoçef*, p. xxix.

[14] *Sephardic Tradition*, p. 77.

the common rhyme. As Ezra Fleischer has observed, the medieval *paytanim*, as the liturgical poets are called, especially "those of the Kallir school, attained great virtuosity in their methods of rhyming and playing with rhyme, and this lowered the level and content of the creations."[15] The *Poem of Yosef* is marred—at least as far as modern-day readers are concerned—by the poet's delight in metrical complication for its own sake. He constructed a veritable metrical straitjacket for himself that rendered the expression of ideas in anything approaching normal diction virtually impossible. I have naturally not attempted to duplicate the original metrical form in my translation, merely hinting at that form by including an internal rhyme in the last verse of each stanza (thus each stanza in the translation contains four monorhymes plus the word Yosef at the end). Perhaps the poet's intention was to outdo the Castilian monks, whose pride in the formal perfection of the *cuaderna vía* I have noted in the introduction to the Ḥadith of Yusuf.

Alec Moreno, a student in a seminar I have taught on the story of Joseph at Pomona College, has observed that the poet's use of the word Yosef at the end of each stanza actually serves to unify the poem by relating everything that happens to the perspective of its central character. By contrast, he argues, the Ḥadith seems purely episodic. Other students have pointed out that the Yosef of the *Poem* seems much more assertive and self-reliant than the somewhat passive Yusuf of the Ḥadith. This might be seen as reflecting a basic philosophical difference between the two religions—fatalism and the importance of submission to God's will in Islam, as opposed to Judaism's emphasis on personal responsibility. Furthermore, while the events narrated in the Ḥadith seem random, the *Poem* clearly applies the principle of causality: every action has necessary consequences. These considerations led another of my students, Lekha Shah, to comment that the *Poem* "seems almost an adult version of the Ḥadith." Elaborating on this, she writes: "The Ḥadith is gossipy and conversational in comparison to the relatively epic grandeur of the *Poem*. The reader can imagine an old, garrulous storyteller gleefully relating the Ḥadith to a mixed audience of common folk and bright-eyed children, whereas the *Poem* belongs before an assemblage in a great hall, to be recited for a solemn gathering of thoughtful onlookers." As an example of the differing level of sophistication of the two poems, she points out that in the Ḥadith Yusuf's goblet is presented as truly possessing magical properties, whereas in the *Poem* Yosef hoodwinks his brothers into thinking the goblet is magical in order to test them.

---

[15] "Piyyut," *Encyclopaedia Judaica* (Jerusalem: Keter Publishing House, c. 1972), XIII, 602.

González Llubera speculated that the *Poem* was originally composed as a vernacular narrative to be used during the celebration of the holiday of Purim, citing the parallel of Crescas ben Joseph ha-Levi Caslari's Provençal version of the story composed for that purpose. "In the Spanish lands as in Provence," he writes, "a certain demand for Purim narratives in the vernacular must have existed from the time when the decadence of Hebrew culture made itself felt and Jews began to write in the Peninsular Romance languages."[16] The Vatican manuscript confirms González Llubera's suspicion because the concluding note by the scribe Gershon states that he completed his transcription of the poem on the tenth of Adar, 1533—four days before Purim—suggesting that it was prepared for reading during the holiday celebration.

The Book of Esther—the scroll traditionally read in the synagogue on the Feast of Purim—shares with the story of Joseph its novelistic form and its essentially secular tone. Esther, like Joseph, attained a quasi-royal status, saved her fellow Jews from destruction and elevated them to a position of respect and honor. Even more than the story of Joseph, the Book of Esther is a highly ethnocentric narrative. Its vindictive conclusion, recounting how the Jews of Persia massacred 75,510 gentile foes in a single day—led the rabbis of Jamnia (c. 80 C.E.) to doubt whether it deserved to be included in the biblical canon and inspired Martin Luther to remark: "I am so hostile to this book that I wish it did not exist; for it Judaizes too much and has too much heathen naughtiness."[17] Nevertheless, the book's gleeful description of how the Jews survived a heinous plot to exterminate them has endeared it to Jews throughout the generations and has provided them with inspiration in other times of persecution. Jewish law regards Purim as a minor festival—that is, one is permitted to engage in servile work during it—but in the popular mind it became a major celebration in medieval Europe, probably because of its proximity to the Christian Carnival, with which it shares the customs of wearing masks and costumes, overindulgence in eating and drinking, and a general spirit of irreverent frivolity. Later, for many Spanish Jews who had converted to Catholicism but continued to maintain their Jewish identity in secret, the Fast of Esther which immediately precedes Purim replaced the Day of Atonement as the holiest day of the year. Cecil Roth has commented: "The reason is not far to seek. Was not the case of Esther 'telling not her race nor her birth,' yet still faithful to the religion of her fathers in an alien environment, almost identical with their

---

[16] Introduction to his edition, p. xxx.

[17] Cited in Madeleine S. Miller and J. Lane Miller, *Harper's Bible Dictionary* (New York: Harper & Brothers, 1952), p. 174.

own?"[18] Because they were unable to consult Jewish calendars to determine the exact date of Purim, they generally observed this fast on the full moon of February, precisely a month before their Passover celebration. In Sephardic communities outside the peninsula, the story of Joseph continued to serve as one of the most popular subjects of Purim songs, poems, and plays well into the twentieth century.[19]

Although for the most part the *Poem of Yosef* adheres closely to its sources, the poet does introduce some interesting innovations and vivid figures of speech. Nowhere else have I seen Joseph allege as an excuse for refusing to have intercourse with Potiphar's wife her ritual uncleanness for having failed to immerse herself in the ritual bath after her period (stanza 32). True to what we know of Joseph's psychology, Potiphar's wife almost persuades him by saying that he has nothing to fear, for she knows from astrology that "your lineage will be honored among your Jewish folk" (33). The similes used to describe Joseph's men fleeing from the mighty Simeon are unusually graphic: "He pounded them thoroughly, like a baker kneading dough; / like ashes from a fire, they were driven by his bellow" (106). The description of Menasheh as "light-footed as a zebra" (110) is also novel and adds a note of exoticism. Like the author of the Ḥadith, the poet specifies the food Joseph had prepared for his brothers, now described as "some tasty fat hens" (130). As Yosef anxiously prepares for his final confrontation with his brothers, he hears a lion roar and sees a deer run by (155). These omens, reminding him of his brothers' strength and swiftness, fill him with foreboding. When Joseph insists on retaining Benjamin as his slave, in a novel twist Judah informs him that they are aware of his unbridled sexual appetites and accuses him of lusting after the handsome Benjamin (180). The poet skillfully evokes the brothers' constantly changing emotions—fear, indignation, guilt—as they are tested by Joseph in the poem's long climactic scene, while Joseph (though inwardly also fearful) responds to them with heavy sarcasm. It is not death that Joseph fears but being buried in a foreign land (208). Having pushed his brothers to the very limits of endurance, he now changes his tactics and questions them kindly in an attempt to deter-

---

[18] *A History of the Marranos* (New York: Harper Torchbooks, 1966), p. 186.

[19] Moshe Lazar has reprinted a narrative poem with songs, *Coplas de Yosef ha-Tsaddik* by Abraham Toledo, first published in Constantinople in 1732, in his *Joseph and His Brethren*; Paloma Díaz-Mas lists a Purim play called *Historia de la vendida de Yosef de sus diez hermanos* (*History of the Sale of Joseph by His Ten Brothers*) performed in Constantinople in 1873 and 1874 and another called *Ya'qob y sus hijos* (*Jacob and His Sons*) performed in Shumen in 1915. See her *Sephardim: The Jews from Spain*, trans. George K. Zucker (Chicago: Univ. of Chicago Press, 1992), p. 140.

mine whether their feelings toward him have changed. Oddly, when he finally reveals himself to them their first impulse is to kill him, and they must be prevented from doing so by the intervention of an angel (224–25). In an interesting anachronism the *Poem* refers to Pharaoh's priests, who were exempted from confiscation of their lands, as "monks" (275) The *Poem* ends on an apocalyptic note, prophesying the coming of the Messiah Son of Joseph, who would be slain by Israel's foes but later restored to life by the Messiah Son of David. Such apocalyptic prophecies became common among the Jews of Spain after the terrible events of 1391, which many saw as the calamities that would usher in the Messianic era.

1. It is written in our scriptures, so I can promise you
    that the writer saw these things, and all the facts he knew,
    that once there was a man dignified and true,
    and beautiful to view, and his name was Yosef.

2. This Yosef always feared the mighty God of heaven,
    while shepherding the flocks with his brothers ten;
    but then he committed a terrible sin;
    against his closest kin, did incite his father Yosef.

3. His father loved him with a love so great
    that he bestowed on the lad a tunic ornate,
    but his brothers for Yosef felt only mortal hate.
    They envied the estate of their brother Yosef.

4. One day he called his brothers, and to them he revealed:
    "I dreamed we were binding our sheaves in the field,
    when your sheaves bowed down and to my sheaf did yield,
    the only one not to kneel was the sheaf of Yosef."

5. On the very next night once again he dreamed:
    that the sun and the moon came toward him, it seemed,
    and with eleven stars bowed down and esteemed
    Yosef's power. This dream to his father mentioned Yosef.[20]

---

[20] The Paris manuscript begins with this stanza.

6. His father understood its meaning was momentous,
   but his brothers were filled with a rage portentous.
   His father then dispatched him to the wilderness
   to his brothers ravenous, with food he sent young Yosef.

7. On the highway he encountered the angel Gabriel.
   Humbly he approached and asked him please to tell
   whether he had seen the sons of Yisra'el,
   and the holy angel made this reply to Yosef:

8. "As you hastened to this spot, you must hurry home today.
   Your brothers are enraged, they have sworn you to slay."
   He replied: "My father dear I cannot but obey."
   But with fear and dismay went on searching Yosef.

9. They'd tell him what they thought of those dreams with dispatch:
   "Do you really think that for us you are a match?
   You thought you'd be our master? As soon as we can catch
   you, for those dreams you hatch, you'll die, oh Yosef!"

10. In the wilderness he encountered all that wretched *dor*[21]
    They said: "Here comes that dreamer! Now let us therefore
    slay the little schemer. He'll vex us nevermore.
    In a deep well, furthermore, we'll toss that wicked Yosef."

11. Then Reuben said to them: "To murder him think not.
    Rather, let us leave him in that well to rot."
    Reuben's hasty words his soul did sorely blot,
    for to urge them he forgot: "Let's leave in peace Yosef."

12. In their strong arms his brothers hastened to ensnare
    Yosef. Of his tunic they stripped him quite bare.
    In that well full of snakes that would suffice to scare
    the bravest—it was there that they abandoned Yosef.

---

[21] Hebrew for "generation."

13. To do that wicked deed they did not hesitate.
    What's more, when they were done, they all sat down and ate.
    Just then some Moors passed by in a caravan great,
    and we must celebrate what Yehudah did for Yosef.

14. Yehudah with the strength of bears or bulls did swell.
    Remembering how his father loved Yosef so well,
    he said: "Let us not kill him, to the Moors let us him sell."
    And then from that deep well they hastened to draw Yosef.

15. They told the Moorish merchants that Yosef was for sale.
    They paid but a poor price, for he was wan and pale,
    for, lying in that pit, terrors did him assail.
    And now to Egypt's vale with those Moors went down Yosef.

16. Of his brothers nine were there, and so to make a minyan,[22]
    they required the Shekhinah's[23] divine intervention
    in their solemn oath to cast their malediction
    on any man who called attention to their sale of Yosef.[24]

17. When the brothers sold Yosef, Reuben was absent,
    but when he had eaten, back to the well he went.
    Not finding the lad there, he made a great lament
    and his garments he rent on account of Yosef.

18. Reuben wept for him; he cried out with great pain,
    and unto his nine brothers thus did he complain:
    "I searched for Yosef in that well where he had lain,
    but my search was all in vain, for there was no Yosef!"

19. Then they took a baby goat and cut off its head,
    smearing Yosef's tunic with the blood that they had shed.

---

[22] Hebrew: "quorum of ten men required for public prayer or to witness a solemn oath."

[23] Hebrew: "the divine Presence."

[24] See Arragel's commentary on Genesis 37:30. The Paris manuscript inserts stanza 22 here.

They besmirched it and stained it until it was quite red
and took it back with dread to the father of Yosef.[25]

20. When Ya'akob laid eyes on that dreadful sight,
    in horror and pain he cried out with all his might:
    "A lion must have eaten you, my son! Oh, woeful plight!
    Nonetheless, I'll remember to indite my love for Yosef."

21. Ya'akob then began his garments to rend.
    He forgot all Yosef's vices, all blame he did suspend.
    He refused to be comforted by family or friend
    for he knew there was no end to his mourning for Yosef.

22. Now they were leading Yosef on Ephratah's highway
    where in her sepulcher his honored mother lay,
    and thus he spoke to her, and unto her did say:
    "Oh, mother! Please pray to God for your son Yosef."

23. She replied, "Fear not my son, and cease to be in pain.
    Where they are taking you, great honor you'll obtain.
    Your dreams will come true, for so God did foreordain."
    Then its healthy color did regain the face of Yosef.

24. Down to the land of Egypt the Moors did Yosef lead,
    and there he was soon sold, as in the scriptures we read,
    to a kindly master, who loved him well indeed
    for the true facts did precede of the identity of Yosef.

25. God looked down with love on Yosef from His throne.
    His master soon relied on Yosef alone,
    for the lad had brought him luck, as was very well known.
    He put all that he did own in the hands of Yosef.

26. Like a rose among flowers was Yosef's comeliness.
    This awakened lust for him in the heart of his mistress.

---

[25] The Paris manuscript ends here.

Her constant talk of love caused Yosef deep distress.
With great licentiousness one day she summoned Yosef.

27. "Come to my waiting arms and comfort me today,
for if not, I am certain your beauty will me slay!
Fulfill your every longing, love me without delay,
for I will handsomely repay you if you do this, Yosef."

28. Prudently he answered her, her wishes did censor:
"My master has given me all I could wish for.
How then could I betray him with wickedness so sore?"
A solemn oath then swore not to do that, Yosef.

29. His mistress answered him like a woman without shame:
"How dare you despise me when my love you did inflame?
Lie with me now. This secret will not sully your name."
Then with horror did exclaim these words the righteous Yosef:

30. "Even if it were true that nobody would know,
God in heaven can see even what doesn't show.
He sees the evildoer and sentences him to woe.
To perform an act so low would surely condemn Yosef.

31. By that wedding band you are surely consecrated,
as a married woman, to your husband dedicated."
"But I care not at all for that nonsense you have prated.
I am liberated, and I will do as I wish, Yosef."

32. "Even if you were single, I could not do that thing
while you're having your period. It would be disgusting.
To the mikveh you must go till no blood to you does cling."[26]
This objection then did bring against his mistress Yosef.

---

[26] Jewish law forbids sexual relations with a menstruating woman from the time she expects her period until one week after her period is over. On the evening of the seventh day without sign of blood, the woman immerses herself in the mikveh (ritual bath), and only then may she resume sexual relations.

33. "Now do as I say, Yosef! No longer me provoke.
    Your lineage will be honored among your Jewish folk.
    I have seen it in your stars." To Yosef thus she spoke,
    and with that clever stroke lost his resistance Yosef.

34. Now Yosef said no more; with lust he was on fire.
    Intently he cast his eyes on the object of his desire.
    He saw her lying there, but when he looked up higher,
    as if him to inspire, there was the father of Yosef.

35. "Don't do that vile deed!" the figure to him said.
    "Twelve untainted stones in my mind's eye I see spread.
    If you commit this crime, yours will be stained with red,
    and I'd rather see you dead, my beloved son Yosef."

36. When Yosef saw that sight, terror did him compel.
    He ran straight out the door to escape his mistress' spell.
    He knew then that no arrow could inflict a wound so fell,
    It was the fear of hell that out of there drove Yosef.

37. His mistress was upset; her rage was plain to see.
    She chased after Yosef as he sought to flee,
    crying out: "Do not think you have seen the last of me!"
    Then in deep misery rent his garments Yosef.

38. And then she cried out in a feigned protest;
    when her husband arrived, these words to him addressed:
    "Your dear servant attempted your wife to molest,
    so now you must arrest your servant Yosef."

39. His master gave credence to that lie, it appears,
    for Yosef was arrested, thus fulfilling his fears.
    Of treason accused and subjected to jeers,
    for twelve tedious years lay in that prison Yosef.

40. The jailer in charge of the prisoners chained
    in that prison to see Yosef suffer was pained.

He comforted him, for Yosef his love had gained,
and his fathers' God remained always with Yosef.

41. One day the king was overcome with rage
against two of his servants. Their crimes he did allege,
and had his bodyguards, who were present at that stage,
throw them in the cage where then languished Yosef.

42. And since there was no one who could pay their bail,
those two men had to serve their time in jail.
There they had strange dreams, and began to weep and wail.
They didn't think to tell their tale to the wise Yosef.

43. When Yosef saw them so distressed that day,
he kindly asked them: "What causes your dismay?
Why are you so silent? Please, your trouble to me say."
Without further delay they confided then in Yosef.

44. The cupbearer told him, "In my dream I did obtain
some grapes from the vineyard, and then I would fain
squeeze them into the goblet of my sovereign."
This dream to explain brought great pleasure to Yosef.

45. He said: "Rejoice! To your health we'll drink a toast;
for the king will soon restore you to your former post.
Of the office of cupbearer once again you'll boast."
Among sages the most discerning was Yosef.

46. "When you are released from this fortress so strong,
Please tell the king that here I do not belong.
My cause please defend with your eloquent tongue,
for a terrible wrong has been done to Yosef."

47. "I dreamed that I had three baskets on my head;
in the topmost one there was delicious bread.
Then a flock of birds besieged me and filled me with dread."
This dream then sadly said the baker to Yosef.

48. "Though you may try to hide, your fate you can't forgo.
Hanged from the city gate, you will swing to and fro,
and your flesh will be devoured by vulture and by crow,
but this you cannot know as it is known to Yosef."

49. Three days after that, the king's decree went out:
the baker was hanged, as he deserved, no doubt,
but he restored his post to the cupbearer devout,
and thus it all turned out as was foretold by Yosef.

50. At that time the cupbearer out of jail was brought.
Yosef was certain his case would be well fought;
but in his joy the cupbearer for Yosef did naught,
not giving a moment's thought to his old friend Yosef.

51. King Pharaoh then had dreams that were destined to come true.
He declared them to his sorcerers and his wise men who knew
of dreams, and his astrologers, but none could them construe.
At last, all overdue, the cupbearer mentioned Yosef.

52. He came before the king and said on bended knee:
"When to prison you consigned your baker and me,
a flattering Jew in that place I did see,
and he was actually, as I recall, named Yosef.

53. The baker and I had dreams on the very same night,
and Yosef to us their true meaning did recite.
Everything he told us turned out exactly right.
I have never seen so bright an astrologer as Yosef."

54. As soon as the cupbearer that good news did impart,
Pharaoh had Yosef from prison depart.
Yosef then shaved and tried to look smart,
and with great joy in his heart to the king went Yosef.

55. The king was pleased with Yosef and to him his dream did tell.
Some of it confused him, but Yosef his doubts did dispel.

"In the river I saw seven cows in beauty excel.
Now listen to me well. They were all grazing, Yosef.

56. Then another seven cows all skinny and frail,
came after those first seven that were hearty and hale.
The lean ones ate the fat ones, but—strange is the tale!—
they were still thin and pale." The meaning saw Yosef.

57. "I fell back to sleep, and then I dreamed again.
On a single stalk I saw seven ears of grain
They were lovelier by far than any in my domain."
This was what the sovereign recounted to Yosef.

58. "Those first ears I saw in grain did abound,
but then came seven others that drooped to the ground.
Though they devoured the full ones, still empty they were found,
If this dream you can't expound, I'll be angry with you, Yosef."

59. "Those seven beauteous cows you did behold
and those seven ears of grain so manifold,
seven years of great abundance have foretold."
Very solemnly then told the king these words Yosef.

60. "The herd of cows that were like kindling dried,
and the ears of grain so sadly atrophied,
are seven years of famine throughout the countryside.
You will soon see verified all these words of Yosef.

61. Over the cities of your land this very day,
appoint a wise overseer and give him full sway—
a good man, who his Creator does obey.
Without any delay take this advice of Yosef.

62. Store up food in the seven good years to compensate
for the seven hungry years. This decree promulgate,
for if not, all your subjects will be disconsolate.
Famine will devastate, as was revealed to Yosef."

63. When Yosef finished speaking and was about to take his leave,
the king said to his courtiers: "I would not you deceive,
the requisite qualities in no man I perceive,
as I firmly believe, but in this righteous Yosef.

64. He is a man of wisdom, and furthermore, he's kind.
He can surely guide my cities with his brilliant mind.
If you agree with this, I will tell him he's assigned.
I'd be amazed if you could find so wise a man as Yosef."

65. With one voice those courtiers then did protest:
"Though Yosef may be of all sages the best,
all seventy languages he has not possessed."
To this arduous test they subjected Yosef.

66. Seventy letters the king had decreed
they slyly brought forth for Yosef to read.
Yosef dispatched them with ease and with speed.
They had to concede, and the king told Yosef:

67. "That test you have passed, all doubts you have suspended.
Now my kingdom to you I have fully commended.
You will be called 'lord,' by great merit attended,
and my people defended will be by Yosef."

68. Then a grievous famine that land did invade.
Before the king the people their grievance then laid:
"Save us from death, sire! With food come to our aid!"
The king was dismayed. He told them: "Go to Yosef!"

69. Fine garments of silk for Yosef he selected.
To ride the king's own horse Yosef was elected.
The people, by his beauty and virtue affected,
profoundly respected as their lord Yosef.

70. Then Yosef from that people a lovely wife chose,
such a wife as on her husband great honor bestows.

To give him two sons did God kindly dispose,
and Pharaoh did propose a new name for Yosef.

71. In the years of plenty that governor astute,
like the sands of the sea, took bread as tribute.
Indeed he stored up bread beyond all repute.
The sum no one could compute, not even wise Yosef.

72. And not a single vermin did that wheat infest
nor did any insect in that place make its nest.
Thus God showed His grace, may He be ever blessed,
saving only the best to be sold by Yosef.

73. Then ended those years of prosperity untold,
and the years of hardship began to unfold.
The people wept and wailed. They could not be consoled,
as had been foretold by discerning Yosef.

74. Yosef was overseer in that land, his word was law.
Much silver and gold in his coffers he saw.
Into the river he cast abundant straw;
a sign it did draw to the father of Yosef.

75. He summoned the guards who Egypt's gates controlled:
"Maintain a list for me in characters bold
of all the customers to whom wheat has been sold,"
and they did as they were told by the governor Yosef.

76. Back at home aged Ya'akob, blessed be his name,
went out for a stroll, to the river he came.
At much straw floating there his sight he did aim,
and that straw was the same that was put there by Yosef.

77. He said to his sons: "My boys, have no fear.
There is food in the cities, and though it be dear,
go and buy some, you ten; go now with good cheer,
but leave with me here the brother of Yosef.

78. Go on out there at once, don't stand here in vain,
    for I know there is food in Egypt's domain.
    Straw from the threshing does this river retain."
    It was once again that straw sent by Yosef.

79. "You know what to do so that you won't die.
    To enter that city together don't try.
    Use more than one gate, beware the evil eye!
    For as I can testify, that's what happened to Yosef."

80. To set out on the journey they all quickly ran,
    to buy food in Egypt, according to plan.
    As they entered, they followed their father's strict ban.
    and at once they began to seek their brother Yosef.

81. Of all of those who entered Egypt through any gate,
    each night they gave Yosef a list to evaluate.
    Yosef on those lists did carefully concentrate,
    and on them did locate his brothers' names Yosef.

82. A search throughout the city did Yosef execute,
    and finally in a house of ill repute
    they found them all hiding, thus ended their pursuit;
    and with harshness acute brought them to Lord Yosef.

83. They brought them to the palace, to Yosef's great hall,
    but they didn't know him, so handsome and tall.
    They bowed down to obey him, at his feet they did fall.
    At that moment did recall his youthful dreams Yosef.

84. When Yosef beheld them, he did of them demand:
    "Why have you come here in such a close-knit band?"
    They replied: "To buy food, as you'll surely understand,"
    and the name of their homeland they told unto Yosef.

85. Then Yosef said bad things to his brethren:
    "You look to me like very dangerous men,

in fact I am sure that of spies you are a den,"
and in like manner then continued to speak Yosef.

86. "My lord, please be assured such things we've never tried.
We're sons of one old father. To you we have not lied!
And back in our home town another brother does reside,
and still another died while but a lad—Yosef."

87. "As one band you have traveled to Egypt's great state,
which it's clear you intended to infiltrate,
because you did not all enter through a single gate."
These harsh words full of hate then spoke unto them Yosef.

88. "Our father's instructions in our ears still rang,
that we must not come into the city as a gang
to avoid the evil eye. Thus he did us harangue."
But an answer quickly sprang to the lips of Yosef.

89. "If it is true you came to Egypt only food to buy,
what made you think the prostitutes would have a good supply?
No, indeed your wicked actions you cannot justify."
And that's the reason why so furious was Yosef.

90. "My lord, a priceless treasure of ours had gone astray,
and we went unto that street to look for it today;
for all of us were certain we would find it right away."
But none of them dared say: "We went to look for Yosef."

91. "I know just what you lost. I look at you with dread.
In deeds of wickedness your whole lives you have led.
Of a whole town's stalwart men two of you the blood have shed."[27]
But to himself he said: "You were looking for Yosef!"

92. "If you are honest men, this is what you must now do:
Let the swiftest among you without further ado

---

[27] Reference to Simeon and Levi's massacre of the men of Shechem; cf. Gen. 34.

bring your other brother here within my purview."
Their chagrin did renew with this injunction Yosef.

93. "One of you to fetch the lad now must proceed,
the rest will be my prisoners; thus I have decreed.
Your innocence will be demonstrated by that deed.
And then you can indeed expect favors from Yosef."

94. Because they refused to obey his command,
right then and there to jail he did remand
his brothers, but after three days Yosef did demand
that once again they stand in the presence of Yosef.

95. Yosef then told them: "Go home. Do not object!
But first plenty of food from my granary collect,
for I fear almighty God, Whom you likewise respect."
They did not expect any favors from Yosef.

96. "One among you as a hostage I'll intern.
The rest of you with honor to the highway now turn,
and with your youngest brother to me soon return."
With countenance stern thus dismissed them Yosef.

97. "If to this city you do not bring that youth,
by Pharaoh's very life I swear to you, forsooth,
that in all you have told me there is not a word of truth,
and you are men uncouth, according to Yosef."

98. All of them then became worried and scared,
and in their holy language their anxiety they aired.
The men who were there uncomprehending stared,
but all they said was shared by their brother Yosef.

99. "We know that it is true," his brothers did exclaim,
"that when Yosef unto us in that wilderness came,
we said: 'here comes that dreamer!' To kill him was our aim,
but there was surely no blame in our brother Yosef.

100. We tore up that fine tunic in which he was clad,
     We put him in a pit of snakes and worms so bad.
     'My brothers, do not kill me!' implored the poor lad.
     We must have been quite mad to do that to Yosef.

101. A terrible sin against God was that act,
     when such a noble lad we cruelly attacked;
     which is why with suffering now we are racked,
     thus God vengeance does exact for our brother Yosef."

102. Then Reuben said to them: "You remember how that day
     I pleaded with you: 'Stop! Our brother do not slay!'
     God has truly judged us, as you see now with dismay;
     for we must surely pay for the blood of Yosef."

103. When Yosef heard that, he was deeply concerned,
     remembering how by his brothers he'd been spurned.
     He turned aside and wept, for his heart within him burned.
     But quickly returned to his brothers Yosef.

104. Though they were all strong men, and intelligent too,
     they were terrified of what would ensue,
     for who would be the hostage, not one of them knew,
     but it was Shim'on who was singled out by Yosef.

105. Shim'on to custody then he did remand.
     Said Yosef to his servants who before him did stand:
     "Shim'on is ferocious, so take him well in hand."
     They obeyed the command of their master Yosef.

106. Every one of Yosef's servants who up to him did go,
     he pounded thoroughly, like a baker kneading dough;
     like ashes from a fire, they were driven by his bellow.
     Against that fearsome foe reinforcements summoned Yosef.

107. Through the door came running strong men and bellicose,
     they were all as fierce as lions, and all as straight as arrows,

but to brave Shim'on they were like tiny sparrows.
Just see how he harrows those men for serving Yosef!

108. Shim'on considered all those men infirm and frail.
One by one they fell before him; over all he did prevail.
In defeat they gnashed their teeth and did their fate bewail.
Amid all that travail Menasheh spoke to Yosef.

109. "My lord, as matters stand, you cannot him defeat
but give me your leave, and I'll force him to retreat.
I will lead him to jail, I'll avenge his conceit."
What his son did entreat was then approved by Yosef.

110. Though he frightened all of them like a dreadful serpent,
light-footed as a zebra, Menasheh to him went.
He struck him on the head, and with bewilderment,
Shim'on to jail was sent on the orders of Yosef.

111. Shim'on ruefully remarked, as in jail he sat that night:
"I've never seen a man of such enormous might!
I cannot help suspecting he is an Israelite;
but thus God does requite the things I did to Yosef."

112. His brothers, leaving Shim'on in that sorry abode,
hastened to buy food, their money did unload,
and conducted their business in the proper mode;
and provisions for the road gave unto them Yosef.

113. With all their silver coins they conducted that affair,
so finding the money in their bags gave them a scare.
The man who had taken it had returned it there.
No one else was aware of this but he and Yosef.

114. They took enough food their families to feed.
Then Yosef from prison Shim'on freed.
He honored him and met his every need,
for very well indeed was Shim'on loved by Yosef.

115. To an inn that night went those brothers one and all.
There Levi took feed to his donkey in its stall,
but the sight of his coins in his bag did him appall.
His brothers he did call. They were frightened of Yosef.

116. "Would we had not been born!" they said. "Heaven forfend,
it appears we are doomed to a terrible end,
because God on high we did greatly offend
when so sorely we sinned against little Yosef."

117. They could not tell their father where Shim'on they did leave,
but each of them spoke of the abuse he did receive,
As they spoke, their father once again began to grieve,
for still he did cleave to the memory of Yosef.

118. "That we might survive the famine, to go there we did choose,
but the lord of the land to believe us did refuse.
It seems that with robbers he did us confuse."
They recounted the abuse heaped upon them by Yosef.

119. "We told him the truth. Unto him him we did say:
'In our land is our father; now he is old and gray,
and another brother there with him did stay.
Still another passed away, and his name was Yosef.'

120. For our sins, he disbelieves us, and against us he raves,
then he throws us into prison and treats us like knaves.
We thought we would drag those chains to our graves.
We were in fact like slaves, just like our brother Yosef.

121. Though in fact we had not done anything wrong,
imprisoned in that city we had to leave Shim'on
until we should return with our brother so young.
We were told to take along the full brother of Yosef."

122. They opened the sacks and the food displayed,
and there they found the money that each one had paid.

Those brothers and their father were sorely dismayed,
for nothing betrayed that it was the work of Yosef.

123. When that bread ran out, their father before them did stand:
"We must have more food the famine to withstand.
Where you left Shim'on, return now to that land.
Obey the command of the father of Yosef."

124. Ya'akob then told them: "It was foolish of you
to tell him of your brother; for even though it's true,
you should have realized it was a bad thing to do,
for now you would renew my suffering for Yosef."

125. "Yosef was eaten, as you know very well,
and you have left Shim'on in Egypt in a cell,
and now would take Binyamin, my precious jewel.
No words can retell my pain since I lost Yosef."

126. Yisra'el then told them: "I will do as you advise,
though I'm afraid that cruel man my son may victimize.
Take him wax and honey and things that he will prize,"
for he didn't realize they were talking about Yosef.

127. "Take all the best products of our patrimony,
to give unto that overseer as a testimony
of our affection and desire to live in harmony."
They didn't know that money had been put there by Yosef.

128. "Take double the money to buy food!" he exclaimed,
"and may the living God, for His mercy famed,
grant that the lord of that land my sons has not blamed,
since He has already reclaimed my beloved son Yosef."

129. They watched over Binyamin with great alacrity.
To Egypt they went, to that beautiful city.
They entered the palace with deep humility
and with formality they bowed down unto Yosef.

130. Yosef to his servant then did declare:
    "Some tasty fat hens for us please prepare,
    for I mean with these men my table to share."
    The man hurried from there with that order from Yosef.

131. While Yosef was occupied with his prefecture,
    that palace his brothers explored with great pleasure,
    and with his servants they conversed at their leisure,
    while a feast beyond measure the cook prepared for Yosef.

132. "As we returned home from our other trip here,
    we decided to stop at an inn that was near.
    One of us for food went into his gear,
    that from the overseer we had bought (that is, from Yosef).

133. When we got home, we had a shock quite rude,
    for there was all our money on top of the food.
    Both we and our father then began to brood.
    He was in a worse mood than when he lost Yosef.

134. Who could have dared such a vile trick to play?
    It could only be someone who desires us to slay.
    We are no thieves. Our debts gladly we pay."
    Thus heard them say their brother Yosef.

135. "We have brought back that money. We hope you're satisfied
    You will find it's all here; you will see we have not lied;
    and we will pay you again with food to be supplied."
    Then unto them replied that servant of Yosef:

136. "By this thing that has happened do not be dismayed.
    It must be the work of that God to Whom you've prayed,
    for the money you gave me in my coffers is laid."
    Then they were less afraid of that great man Yosef.

137. The servant spoke to them much more kindly than before.
    He sought to comfort them and showed them great favor.

When he brought Shim'on unto them, they hearts with joy did soar,
and then through the door came their brother Yosef.

138. When Yosef had dispatched the day's business,
his brothers had their gifts for him in readiness.
Yosef was delighted, and his pleasure did express.
Bursting with eagerness to question them was Yosef.

139. As soon as those gifts had been put on exhibition,
he asked: "Your old father, the one you did mention—
Is he well? Can you tell me his condition?"
for a grave premonition had been troubling Yosef.

140. "My lord, the truth to tell you we're content,
when we left him at home, his health was excellent;
by his authority we bring you this present,"
and to the ground they bent humbly before Yosef.

141. When he saw Binyamin, the mighty viceroy
asked them: "Your youngest brother is this boy?"
"Yes, indeed," they replied. "We would not you annoy,"
and with hearts full of joy they spoke those words to Yosef.

142. Then Yosef asked Binyamin in him to confide:
"Son, back at home have you taken a bride?"
"To me a loving wife God's goodness did provide,
and ten sons," he replied, "since the day that I lost Yosef.

143. Since the God of heaven took my brother to keep,
my poor old father has done nothing but weep.
He is cold as ice in summer, just as in winter deep.
On the floor does he sleep out of sorrow for Yosef.

144. When a man with his brother I see, thereupon
I am dying with longing for my companion.
Yosef was as lovely as the summer sun.
Beyond all comparison was my brother Yosef."

145. True words spoke Binyamin, his faithfulness did prove.
His heart to bestow this blessing him did move:
"May you always be guided by the great God above,"
for brotherly love attracted him to Yosef.

146. Then Yosef was filled with terrible distress.
He remembered all he'd suffered in that wilderness.
He went aside and wept with great bitterness,
but quickly did repress those memories Yosef.

147. When he had stopped weeping, Yosef did declare:
"Set the table with dainties delightful and rare!"
In the wink an eye, that meal they did prepare
for his brothers to share in happiness with Yosef.

148. Yosef urged them to drink an abundance of wine.
Quickly he seized his silver goblet fine,
and spoke to it as if that goblet could opine.
Thus pretended to divine with that goblet Yosef.

149. That the cup had told him, he said with sly deceit,
that Reuben was the oldest—they were startled by that feat!—
but Yehudah was their leader, for he was most discreet.
Thus in order then did seat all his brothers Yosef.

150. They were all arranged in the order they were bred.
"This one has lost a brother," of Binyamin he said.
"I too had a brother, but now he is dead,"
so Binyamin was led to the seat right next to Yosef.

151. Yosef treated them all with the utmost regard.
With jewels of great price each one he did reward.
but unto the youngest five times as great a hoard,
and then unto his guard privately spoke Yosef.

152. "Now do as I say and do not be remiss.
Give the food that they want to these men, with this twist:

put the money of each in the bag that is his,"
but no one knew of this but the servant and Yosef.

153. "Do just as I say, of my anger beware:
    put my divining cup so lovely and rare
    in the bag of that young man whom you see sitting there,
    but let no one be aware." Thus instructed him Yosef.

154. The servant did as his master him bade,
    Secretly he took the cup aforesaid,
    and put it into the bag of that handsome young lad,
    and in silence did pad back to his master Yosef.

155. At that time Yosef did gravely meditate.
    He heard a lion roar, saw a deer run by his gate.
    Yosef great danger then did anticipate,
    and of those Jews did relate the following Yosef:

156. "My brothers are just like them; that is a fact.
    They're as strong as a beast when they are attacked,
    as swift as the deer by a hunter tracked,
    and as quick to react as their brother Yosef."

157. Yosef thus pondered. His mood was abject.
    Next morning at dawn their donkeys they decked
    with food. To the highway they did them direct,
    and none did suspect any mischief of Yosef.

158. Yosef told his servant: "Now go and pursue
    those terrible men, and arrest that motley crew!"
    With anger that servant their crimes did review,
    and thus did he do as he was told by Yosef.

159. "Don't pretend to be meek. I know you are strong!
    Can you tell why you did this dreadful wrong?
    You stole that cup that to my master does belong."
    Against that mighty throng sent but one servant Yosef.

160. Those Jews strong as lions he pursued without ceasing,
as he chased after them, his insults increasing:
"You give evil for good, our property seizing!"
And indeed very pleasing were those words to Yosef.

161. Then they replied: "Enough of your abuse!
Though finding our silver in our bags did us confuse,
to bring it back here as honest men we did choose."
This was a good excuse of the brothers of Yosef.

162. He said: "You stole that cup, but for your crimes you'll pay.
You put it in in your bag and took it away.
Thus my lord's hospitality you chose to repay."
These dreadful things did say that servant of Yosef.

163. "If it is in our bags," to that servant they did rave,
"we will confess our crime, and all clemency we'll waive,
and every one of us will be your master's slave."
They thought that would save them from the wrath of Yosef.

164. He searched the bags with precision exquisite
and found the cup where he had hidden it,
in the bag of Binyamin. It seemed the culprit
was that youthful favorite so deeply loved by Yosef.

165. When the cup was found, they stopped in their tracks.
All those brave men turned the color of wax
They loaded their food back into their sacks.
Great fear then did tax the brothers of Yosef.

166. Then from no insult poor Binyamin was spared!
His mother was a thief, they solemnly declared.[28]
All of them with anger at the poor boy stared.
How badly they all fared! It was the fault of Yosef.

---

[28] Reference to Rachel's theft of her father Laban's household gods (see Gen. 31:32).

167. "Please do not kill me!" cried Binyamin with a grimace,
    "for I had no intention his precious cup to place
    in my bag. If I've done something so base,
    may I never see the face of my brother Yosef!"

168. Then they realized that he was innocent,
    for anyone could see his bewilderment.
    Then they left him alone, from cursing did relent.
    Back to Egypt they went, to the presence of Yosef.

169. That day Yosef his court did not hold,
    for he knew that his brothers he would soon behold.
    When they came back there, his feelings he controlled,
    but none was so bold as to speak before Yosef.

170. "That my cup you did take," he said, "I can surmise,
    though my power to divine you did thoroughly despise.
    You thought you would go home, but I thought otherwise.
    Is this then how you prize the benevolence of Yosef?"

171. Binyamin was still holding that cup in his hand.
    He asked it where his brother was, or in what land,
    and whether he was dead or still alive did stand.
    As he made this demand, Yehudah answered Yosef.

172. "My lord, of what has happened, truly we know naught,
    nor can we reply to you as we ought.
    We have nothing to say, though the truth we have sought,"
    and they were all distraught before mighty Yosef.

173. "Our sin chased us down, as heaven ordained,
    and today on that road, we were at last detained.
    Now in this land we will be surely be arraigned."
    He was sincerely pained by the wrong they had done Yosef.

174. "We men and our beasts till the day that we die,
    will do our best your every wish to satisfy.

The devil our people would thus mortify."
This humble reply they then gave unto Yosef.

175. But Yosef answered them in the following way:
"Binyamin is the culprit; he's the one who must pay.
You men take your food, and be on your way.
What more need I say?" was the answer of Yosef.

176. Yehudah to Yosef then addressed this complaint:
"Your honor, I beg you to act with restraint.
This lad's reputation, please do not taint."
His voice was quite faint as he spoke unto Yosef.

177. "Sir, for mercy I beg!" He bowed down to the ground.
"Instead of the boy, as your slave have me bound;
for if not, poor old Ya'akob in grief will abound.
His sobs will resound as before over Yosef."

178. Yosef then answered with pitiless ire,
"Binyamin did this act so loathsome and dire.
He must therefore serve me, for he is a liar.
That's what I require," was the judgment of Yosef.

179. Then mighty Yehudah spoke up with a sneer:
"You would have us believe you are quite austere,
but we've heard how for women you lust and you leer."
Thus without fear spoke Yehudah to Yosef.

180. "You are covetous, you are a *dayan*[29] unjust,
your filth you'd conceal with that office august.
Binyamin is good looking, for him do you lust!"
Not with fear but disgust spoke Yehudah to Yosef.

181. Then all Yosef's calm turned into alarm.
A fistful of wheat he proceeded to harm,

---

[29] Hebrew: "judge."

crushing it with the strength of his powerful arm.
This will surely disarm Yehudah, thought Yosef.

182. But like a beast Yehudah in blind rage did reel.
So furious was he, he could have crushed steel.
His brothers feared that in his righteous zeal,
a blow he might deal to his enemy Yosef.

183. "We came here fleeing from a terrible fate,
but you insulted us and treated us with hate,
you claimed we were thieves, and did us interrogate,
though we'd never perpetrate such crimes," said they to Yosef.

184. "You have done us wrong, but today our rage we'll vent.
We will slay the people here until our anger's spent.
Then you can truly say that on evil we were bent."
With malicious intent then said unto them Yosef:

185. "As everyone knows, and indeed we all have heard,
the people of one city you viciously murdered,
and on the paths of wickedness have constantly erred."
These dreadful words uttered to those strong men Yosef.

186. When Yosef finished speaking, thus did they inveigh:
"We may indeed have sinned, but never would we say
such slanderous words as you've spoken today."
With surprise and dismay then listened to them Yosef.

187. Yehudah then spoke up; he chose his words with care:
"To defend Binyamin to my father I did swear
against all enemies who sought him to ensnare."
A special grudge did bear against Yehudah Yosef.

188. "If it be true that such an oath you swore,
then it is only right that his fate you should deplore;
yet the suffering of Yosef you chose to ignore.
You sold him, furthermore. It was you who sold Yosef!"

189. But Yehudah wasn't frightened when those words he did hear.
Like a lion enraged he roared then loud and clear;
that sound would have terrified even the most severe.
Then overcome with fear was even intrepid Yosef.

190. On that deafening roar Yehudah relied
to summon his brother Naphtali to his side.
Now Naphtali as swiftly as a deer could stride.
In him he did confide, out of hearing of Yosef:

191. "My brother, pay attention. I expect you to be clever
Count all this city's streets, and examine wherever
its strong and mighty men are used to come together,
for today we will endeavor to find our brother Yosef."

192. Naphtali set out at once to do that deed.
He surveyed that city with incredible speed,
for to count its twelve streets little time did he need,
and then he did proceed to the palace of Yosef.

193. He told them secretly, "My brothers, now listen,
The streets of this city with armaments glisten,
There are twelve in all, and full of good men."
Right there and then they plotted against Yosef.

194. Strong Yehudah spoke up then, his brothers he bade:
"Give me three of those streets, I will fight like a cad.
The rest you'll attack like lions gone mad,
for we must protect the lad from the fate of Yosef."

195. They all told Yehudah that pleased them very well
They were sure those good men they could easily repel.
[. . . . .]30
for with strength did they swell beyond the ken of Yosef.

---

30 One line is missing from the manuscript here.

196. Thus Yehudah and his brothers did fume and did fret.
Then he went back to Yosef the young lad to get.
His demand for the boy with a firm 'no' was met.
And with this dire threat he then menaced Yosef:

197. "We will make war in Egypt. Young and old we will kill,
with gore and with blood all your streets we will fill.
We will teach you a lesson with our soldierly skill."
But uglier still was the answer of Yosef.

198. "Ah, yes," then said Yosef, "I'm sure that you could,
for truly at bloodshed you all are quite good.
You showed how that art you had understood
when you tainted with blood the tunic of Yosef.

199. The old man sought in vain his eyes to avert
from that tunic all covered with blood and with dirt.
Yea, a river of tears could not heal his hurt.
On seeing that shirt, he cried: 'My son, Yosef!' "

200. Yehudah then grieved to recall his handiwork.
He wailed just like a lion gone berserk,
His brothers in terror around him did lurk,
but he could not shirk those true words of Yosef.

201. "Heaven help me!" he cried with sorrow profound.
"To take the lad back to my father I'm bound.
For if not, in his tears this time he'll be drowned.
He will fall on the ground as he did for Yosef."

202. Yehudah then sought Yosef's kind heart to touch:
"At what straw of hope can my old father now clutch?
Binyamin was his light, his mirror, his nonesuch,
for he loved him just as much as his brother Yosef."

203. But this thought strong Yehudah's anger did renew:
"How could you such a wicked course pursue?

How could you make a promise so untrue?"
Thus fiercely did argue Yehudah with Yosef.

204. But Yosef replied: "Far worse was your action!
Like thieves you sold Yosef. What a vile transaction!
And how could you lie to your father in that fashion?
You showed no compassion to poor little Yosef."

205. When they heard those foul words that Yosef declared,
to start fighting right then they felt fully prepared.
Without lances or armor to fight him they dared:
no more were they scared of the mighty Yosef.

206. When Yosef saw that, things began to look bleak,
for he knew upon him their vengeance they'd wreak.
Then the help of his pagans he quickly did seek,
and in terror did sneak into hiding Yosef.

207. Then with a shock he proceeded to think:
"To conquer this town they are now on the brink;
the whole country from ruining they will not shrink,"
and with horror did sink the heart of Yosef.

208. "If they were to kill me, it would matter naught
for I've brought it on myself; but at the dreadful thought
of being buried here, I am totally distraught."
In this quandary was caught the unfortunate Yosef.

209. But at that very moment he made a stunning choice:
"I will give these Jews good reason to rejoice.
Indeed, before long they will make a joyful noise,
for the news I will voice that still living is Yosef."

210. At that moment Yosef from his hiding place did dart,
and unto all his servants this message did impart:
"All of you must now from my house depart!"
Then spoke from the heart unto his brothers Yosef.

211. Then very kindly those Jews he did implore:
     "Please tell me: when you came here before,
     what was it you were really looking for?"[31]
     Now they could not ignore that question of Yosef.

212. "We will tell you the truth, as certainly we should,
     The first time we came here and before you stood,
     we'd been searching for Yosef in a bad neighborhood,
     but it did us no good, for we didn't find Yosef."

213. "I thought you must be rascals, and not very astute
     to expect to find Yosef in a house of ill repute.
     What could have driven you there in your pursuit?
     In that street any brute would have known you'd not find Yosef."

214. "It had occurred to us, and indeed we did trust
     that those evil sluts after Yosef would lust.
     To their wiles he'd be forced to submit with disgust,
     for comely and robust was our brother Yosef."

215. "So in fact you failed to find that handsome lad.
     Did that failure of yours make you terribly sad?
     If you had found him, would you have been glad?"
     His brothers then bade assistance from Yosef.

216. Those Jews boldly spoke up to Yosef renowned:
     "Your questions our grief over Yosef compound.
     Do you know where he is? Is he safe and sound?
     Where can he be found? Surely woeful is Yosef."

217. Then he told them with a radiant face:
     "Rejoice for your brother! All sorrow efface,
     for he is safe and sound, and right here in this place.
     This day you'll embrace your brother Yosef."

---

[31] The first half of this line is illegible in the manuscript. The second half reads: "Dezidme: Que buscastes?"

218. Each tribe then to Yosef humbly did say:
    "If our brother is alive in this town today,
    please show him to us without further delay,
    for great love we'll display unto our dear Yosef."

219. "Since you desire Yosef with a love so sincere,
    and he is safe and sound, I'll bring him right here.
    No more of my vain words will you have to hear."
    At that moment drew near to his brothers Yosef.

220. "Oh, you whom the beauty of a rose does adorn!
    Yosef, come to these men, for they are forlorn.
    Now let old Ya'akob for his son cease to mourn.
    How could you scorn your own brothers, Yosef?"

221. When Yosef all those words did declare,
    he came up to his brothers and stood right there,
    but all those men into blank space did stare.
    They were all unaware that beside them stood Yosef.

223. Yosef no longer his impatience controlled:
    "I am your brother Yosef, the one whom you sold.
    Tell me: what is the condition of my father so old?"
    These words so bold then spoke unto them Yosef.

224. When Yosef's lovely face they did survey
    and heard the words he spoke to them that day,
    they were dumbfounded; they knew not what to say.
    Without a moment's delay they thought they would kill Yosef.

225. An angel, to prevent that homicide,
    all those angry men did swiftly divide,
    to the corners of that room did them sternly guide.
    With terror petrified at that moment was Yosef.

226. Then Yosef spoke in a tone of tenderness:
    "My brothers, don't cower in those corners' darkness.

Come here to me, hear the words I'll you address."
Then in shame and distress they went back to Yosef.

227. "Rejoice, my good brothers, so prudent and bold!
Don't be ashamed that your brother you sold.
As you see, all power in this nation I hold.
Thus God has extolled His servant Yosef.

228. For if you sold me, thus God did ordain
to govern the people of all this domain,
and with food all my family thus to sustain,
for always did remain our God with Yosef.

229. Now with great haste to our land you must go,
for a full account to my father you owe.
Tell him all that has happened, put an end to his woe.
Above all, let him know that still living is Yosef.

230. Tell him: When from my father I first departed
on my way to you, and left him broken-hearted,
a portion of Torah to study we'd just started."[32]
This sign then imparted to his brothers Yosef.

231. He knew that his father this sign would understand.
He said: "Come live and prosper here, as I have planned.
You need not fear the people of this land,
for with a mighty hand will provide for you Yosef."

232. "Go to my honored father and tell him I request
he should come here with his cattle and enjoy a well-earned rest.
Goshen is a good place with abundant pasture blessed.
Please do your best to hurry back to Yosef."

---

[32] The *Midrash Genesis Rabbah* attributes the following words to Joseph: "Say to him:
At the time when I left you, was I not studying the law of 'eglah 'arufah (the breaking
of the heifer's neck [Deut. 21:1])? Hence it is said: 'And he saw the wagons which
Joseph had sent.'" The Hebrew word for "wagons," 'agalot, is a homonym for the word
"heifers."

233. To these words they hearkened, as Yosef they faced.
Like ecstatic lions their voices they raised,
as Yosef their savior they honored and praised,
and all of them embraced their dear brother Yosef.

234. All of his servants by Yosef were dismissed,
so to show their true feelings those men did not resist.
To demonstrate his love Yosef did insist:
all were warmly hugged and kissed by a joyous Yosef.

235. Their joyful outcry by the king himself was heard.
To determine its meaning with his servants he conferred.
They told him: "Sire, unto us has come word
that this city have entered the brothers of Yosef."

236. As soon as the king of those brothers heard tell,
and learned that their veins with noble blood did swell,
he was overjoyed, though he was an infidel,
and wished to do them well on account of Yosef.

237. The king asked Yosef to come at his leisure,
saying: "Bring me your father, for him I will treasure.
I'll show him hospitality beyond measure,
and I'll give him pleasure for love of you, oh Yosef!

238. For your Jewish folk on my behalf pick
the choicest of food, and scour the district
for horses and wagons for them. My edict
is that they be quick. Don't delay them, Yosef!

239. Those wagons and horses I'd have you procure
a comfortable journey Ya'akob to ensure,
along with his women and infants so pure,
and you may be sure I'll provide for them, Yosef."

240. To return to his brothers Yosef was swift.
Of all that he told them this was the drift:

"This food for your households upon your beasts lift,
and tell them it's a gift from your brother Yosef.

241. Your belongings leave there, and don't think it misfortune.
Don't worry at all." Thus did Yosef importune:
"Here in Egypt I promise you'll have a rich portion,
for indeed a great fortune has God given Yosef."

242. He spoke now with pleasure, his mood had improved.
Gifts of robes rich and rare his benevolence proved.
But to give Binyamin five robes he was moved,
for Binyamin was beloved by his brother Yosef.

243. These noble garments to them he did assign,
and ten asses laden with fruit in a line.
To his father he sent a vintage old and fine,
the very same wine that was drunk by Yosef.

244. Yosef bade them farewell as they left his abode:
"Brothers, don't quarrel while you're on the road,
let no dissonance your hearts discommode.
This kindness you've owed to your brother Yosef.

245. As you leave my brother Binyamin with me here,
to set out on your journey, from the path do not veer
until you have brought me the father I revere,
and with greetings sincere give him the gifts of Yosef."

246. A granddaughter of Ya'akob stood in an embrasure,
and saw those wagons coming in the distance obscure.
"Look, grandfather dear," cried the maiden demure.
"It's a wagon, I'm sure. Still alive is Yosef!"

247. Then the grandfather unto the girl replied:
"If Yosef is alive, may you be sanctified!
God take you to His garden, may you with Him abide!"
Then to those men did stride that niece of Yosef.

248. Ya'akob struggled his emotion to subdue.
     Seeing his sons there his terror did renew,
     but they said: "Father, we are happy to tell you
     it's absolutely true that still alive is Yosef."

249. At those words poor Ya'akob almost fell into a faint.
     He was still tortured by doubt, and this was his constraint:
     he knew Yosef had been eaten, for his tunic blood did taint.
     He still uttered the complaint that he'd never see Yosef.

250. "Your beloved Yosef this sign to you betook,
     that when at your command his home he forsook,
     with you he had been reading in the Holy Book.
     Now, dear father, look! This message is from Yosef."

251. Just as his sons to Ya'akob with those words appealed,
     he saw those wooden wagons, and his happiness was sealed.
     Then he laughed out loud, and to gaiety did yield,
     and heaven to him revealed: "Still alive is Yosef."

252. No longer was he bitter, no grief did he then bear,
     but greatly rejoiced over what they did declare.
     At once the Holy Spirit to Ya'akob did repair,[33]
     and he started to prepare to go and see Yosef.

253. Ya'akob said: "I am nearing the end of my days,
     and yet before I die, on my dear son I will gaze,
     though in a wicked land my tent I must raise."
     He was still in a daze from the wondrous news of Yosef.

254. After traveling for a day, when it was twilight,
     to his Maker he performed a sacrificial rite,
     and God appeared to him in a vision that night.
     and good news did recite concerning his son Yosef.

---

[33] Cf. Arragel's commentary on Gen. 37:35.

255. Then these words from Ya'akob to God did ascend:
"I fear that foreign nation. How can I there descend?
For they despise us Jews and will surely us offend.
I cannot comprehend how has lived among them Yosef."

256. "No longer be afraid, for their hatred I'll defy.
Remembering your grandfather, the Jews I'll multiply;
I'll make of you a people like the stars in the sky.
Now joyously draw nigh unto your son Yosef."[34]

257. "I'll go down with you to Egypt, and there you will find
I'll defend you from that accursed nation unkind.
With My might I'll give you freedom when you are confined.
You should bear in mind what I have done for Yosef."[35]

258. With these words the true God Ya'akob inspired.
Then Ya'akob went on in that wagon he'd acquired.
Before him to Yosef Yehudah retired.
About Goshen inquired Yehudah of Yosef.

259. When to mighty Yosef that news they did relate,
to welcome his dear father he could no longer wait.
The old man's hand he kissed, his love to demonstrate,
and then did celebrate Ya'akob with Yosef.

260. Good old Ya'akob spoke these words as to Yosef he did cleave:
"Now I can die happy. Nevermore shall I grieve!
I never dared hope my Yosef I'd retrieve,
and no one could believe that I would yet see Yosef."

261. Then Yosef humbly said: "This is what I have thought:
I must go and tell the king, as certainly I ought,
that my father has come here just as the king had sought,
and with him he has brought the family of Yosef.

---

[34] The Cambridge manuscript begins with this stanza.
[35] At this point the Vatican manuscript repeats stanzas 256–57.

262. My brothers, pay attention, for this matter is deep.
Should the king question you, don't venture a peep,
but tell him that you are all shepherds of sheep.
You must faithfully keep this command of Yosef."

263. Five brothers to go with him he designated,
when to that great king their arrival he related.
Ya'akob with his herds to Goshen had migrated.
The king interrogated those brothers of Yosef.

264. To those honest men, he said: "Tell me, pray,
what was your work when at home you did stay?"
They replied: "We kept cattle by night and by day."
This they did say as instructed by Yosef.

265. Then Ya'akob's entry was announced by a page.
The king he did bless and bowed in homage.
Then the king asked him what was his age.
This answer most sage gave the father of Yosef:

266. "The years I have lived, since my age you would learn,
are one hundred and thirty, or so I discern,
and all marred by sadness and bitter concern.
Oh, how I did yearn for my dear son Yosef!"

267. Then Ya'akob pronounced this blessing so fair:
"May your god be zealous for your welfare,
and my God of pardon give me a full share."[36]
This was the prayer of the father of Yosef.

268. The king loved Ya'akob in all sincerity.
He gave him Goshen for his posterity.

---

[36] I have interpreted the word *shuvah* in the manuscript as a misspelling for *tshuvah*. Lazar's reading "Que suva encuentro" makes no sense. It appears that David Herman's reading was the same as mine, since he translates this line: "And may my God grant pardon to me."

Ya'akob and his sons lived there in dignity.
In great prosperity were they maintained by Yosef.

269. The famine grew severe, and the people then did cry:
"Oh, Yosef! Give us food, or else we will die.
Our money has run out. To your mercy we apply!"
At once this reply was given by Yosef:

270. "If indeed all your money you have spent,
I'll give you food and take your horses as payment."
"Gladly," said the people, for in their predicament
that seemed munificent of their master Yosef.

271. Some time later, they came to Yosef once again:
"Save us from death! Oh, Yosef, give us grain!
Of that food that you gave us nothing does remain.
Have mercy on our pain, lest we die, Yosef!

272. The money that we had, and our cattle as well,
for our sins, we have spent. What more is there to tell?
You can have our wretched bodies and the land where we dwell.
To you all this we'll sell in return for food, Yosef!"

273. Yosef answered: "Here is food and seed for you to sow.
Now return to your land, and when your crops you grow,
one-fifth of the harvest to the king will go.
For all time, you should know, is this ordinance of Yosef."

274. All those people went out and sowed their land.
They were all Yosef's slaves, they obeyed his command.
The fifth part they paid of all that came to hand,
for this was the demand imposed on them by Yosef.

275. There was a well-known land that the monks did occupy.
With rations of food Yosef did them well supply,
nor did they sell their lands those rations to buy,
for to them did not apply the ordinance of Yosef.

276. When Yosef heard all those people complain,
   he made a great prayer, and then God did deign
   in His kindness that famine at last to restrain,
   though still did retain some of that grain, Yosef.

277. Ya'akob in comfort that land did occupy
   seventeen years, as the Scriptures testify.
   In infinite numbers did his people multiply.
   When to death he drew nigh, he summoned Yosef.

278. Ya'akob then told him: "Please keep this in mind:
   to a grave here in Egypt I must not be consigned.
   Bury me in that land that God to us assigned.
   You will truly be kind if you do this, Yosef."

279. "Swear to me by our God Who everything knows
   to bury me where my grandparents repose.
   A space in that place for my coffin dispose."
   Like a good son then chose to swear that oath Yosef.

280. Then Ya'akob summoned his sons one and all.
   By the names of animals them did he call,
   and blessed them with blessings both great and small,
   but the best blessing of all he reserved for Yosef.

281. Words of wisdom to them did Ya'akob confide;
   with advice from his heart his sons he did guide.
   With a prayer on his lips the patriarch died.
   Then one last kiss applied to his father, Yosef.

282. At once Yosef hastened his father to obey.
   He was bathed and embalmed in the Egyptian way.
   Then a beautiful shroud did Yosef convey.
   In a rich coffin lay the father of Yosef.

283. When all had been done as Yosef had sworn,
   a great multitude for Ya'akob did mourn.

For seventy days was that nation forlorn,
for great love had they borne to the father of Yosef.[37]

284. Then Yosef unto the king did repair:
"I promised my father, and he made me swear,
to take him back home and bury him there."
The king did declare unto his servant Yosef:

285. "If indeed before God that oath you did indite
to take him back to that ancestral site,
go with good fortune, bury him out of sight,
and then, as is right, you'll return here, Yosef."

286. Yosef made his preparations on the journey's eve.
Many other people with him did leave,
in order that their loyalty he would believe,
and for Ya'akob did grieve all of them with Yosef.

287. By kings and emperors the sad cortege was met.
They did homage to Ya'akob with profound regret.
All of their crowns around his bier they set,
for indeed a great debt those kings owed to Yosef.

288. Yosef did everything as his father had rehearsed,
but was opposed by 'Esav, Ya'akob's brother accursed.
As those men approached the cave, their direction he reversed,
so that the very first to arrive there should be Yosef.

289. 'Esav then told him: "This is not Ya'akob's grave.
Don't you know I inherited this cave?
For I am the firstborn son, and that right I'll never waive."
This reply then gave unto his uncle, Yosef:

290. "This cave at first by Abraham was bought.
He bequeathed it to Yitzhak his son, as I was taught.

---

[37] At this point the Vatican manuscript repeats stanzas 258–59.

To my father Yitzḥak gave it, for he could deny him naught."
This answer then brought 'Esav unto Yosef:

291. "Why go on talking and this quarrel prolong?
Just show us the deed, and if the cave belong
to you, well and good. But I know you are wrong,
and before very long, you'll admit the truth, Yosef."

292. Then Yosef to his brother Naphtali did say:
"Hurry up! You must go to Egypt right away
and those papers notarized back to me convey."
Naphtali ran to obey the command of Yosef.

293. A deaf man who was digging Ya'akob's grave
said: "My master's body is here in the cave.
We should bury it now." With an angry wave
this answer then gave to that deaf man Yosef:

294. "Had not wicked 'Esav interfered with ill will,
my father's last wish I would surely fulfill."
Then that deaf man determined with courage virile,
the blood he would spill of that foe of Yosef.

295. Quickly his hand to his pickaxe did go.
On the forehead he struck mighty 'Esav a blow,
and when he was dead, his body did throw
in that grave far below the father of Yosef.

296. Those people then praised that deaf man's great deed,
and they buried Ya'akob. Their camp 'Esav besieged,
but victory to Yosef he was soon forced to cede.
To Egypt then did proceed those men with Yosef.[38]

297. As those Jews went back in Egypt to dwell,
they veered from the path to take counsel,

---

[38] This stanza is omitted from the Vatican manuscript.

for terror of Yosef upon them then fell,
because into that well they had cast young Yosef.

298. They said: "We tried to kill that favorite son,
and in that empty well did him abandon.
Now we'll surely be punished for what we have done.
We must beg his pardon or be killed by Yosef."

299. And when in Yosef's throne room they were found,
they threw themselves before him on the ground.
Their cries throughout that palace did resound,
and thus did they expound their repentance to Yosef.

300. They said: "Oh Yosef, can you our sins forgive?
We are guilty, but clemency is your prerogative.
We will be your slaves for as long as we shall live,
and obedience will give to your commands, oh Yosef!"

301. When Yosef heard that, he wept most bitterly.
He put them at ease with great civility:
"No harm will be done unto you in this city,"
for full of pity for his brothers was Yosef.

302. Then Yosef said these things to his brothers one and all.
He commended their good deeds and their virtues did recall.
Then profound peace upon their hearts did fall,
for greatly were they all beloved by Yosef.

303. Yosef supported them through thick and thin,
and he was well loved by both strangers and kin.
It is said that he lived to one hundred and ten,
and his last will did pen before he died, Yosef.

304. As he lay dying, Yosef said with agitation:
"I go to my death with great consternation,
for I know you will suffer bondage and privation
at the hands of this nation that was saved by Yosef."

305. He said: "Here in Egypt enslaved will you be,
    but at last you'll go out and again will be free.
    When that long-awaited day you shall see,
    please don't forget me! Take the bones of Yosef."[39]

306. To do Yosef's bidding his brothers were chary.
    (Later his mummy from Egypt they'd carry.)
    With a eulogy worthy of a great luminary
    in a grave temporary they buried Yosef.

307. Yisra'el in the land of Egypt did reside.
    There they were enslaved, and were sorely tried
    by that accursed people in their satanic pride,
    as had been prophesied in the words of Yosef.

308. But Yisra'el escaped from Egypt's stranglehold.
    They put Yosef's bones in an ark, as we've been told,
    and buried him in Shechem, their promise to uphold—
    the very place where was sold their father Yosef.

309. Out of Rome a false reformer yet will arise
    and the people of God with war will terrorize.
    Our honorable king with defeat he will chastise.
    Then death will surprise the *Mashiaḥ Ben Yosef*.[40]

310. Soon the *go'el*[41] will come to save us as of yore.
    With his awesome might he will triumph in the war,
    Then that traitor he will slay with rage and furor,
    and to life he will restore that mighty son of Yosef.

---

[39] The Cambridge manuscript ends with this stanza.

[40] Hebrew: "Messiah, Son of Yosef." Raphael Patai has summarized the tradition as follows: The Messiah ben Yosef "will achieve many signal victories, but his fate is to die at the hands of Armilus in a great battle in which Israel is defeated by Gog and Magog. His corpse is left unburied in the streets of Jerusalem for forty days, but neither beast nor bird of prey dares to touch it. Then, Messiah ben David comes, and his first act is to bring about the resurrection of his tragic forefunner." *The Messiah Texts* (New York: Avon Books, 1979), pp. 165–66.

[41] Hebrew: "redeemer."

This very noble story
another did declare
but without such care.
Now in its true glory
and in fine calligraphy,
by Gershon it is writ,
a scribe known for his wit,
a man of courtesy.
This is the thirteenth year
that has reigned o'er this state
Sultan Suleiman the great,[42]
whom God's people hold so dear,
five thousand two hundred ninety three
years since the world first came to be.
This task, as stated by the calendar,
was finished on the tenth day of Adar.[43]

ḤAZAK VE-NITḤAZEK.[44]

---

[42] The reign of the Ottoman Sultan Suleiman I the Magnificent began in September 1520. Thus the Vatican manuscript would date from 1533.

[43] The month of the Jewish calendar corresponding to February–March. The text was probably prepared to be read as part of the celebration of the holiday of Purim (14 Adar). González Llubera has argued that the original poem was also intended as a Purim narrative. See the Introduction to his edition of the *Coplas de Yoçef*, pp. xxix–xxx.

[44] "Be strong, and let us be strengthened!" Traditional exclamation recited by congregants in the synagogue upon completing the reading of a book of the Torah.

Alfonso X, the Learned, dictating to a scribe. From the Book of Chess, Dice, and Checkers. Illustrated parchment, c. 1293. El Escorial. Courtesy of Patrimonio Nacional, Madrid.

❯❯ General History (begun 1272)

Alfonso X the Learned, King of Castile (1221–1284)

Alfonso X of Castile inherited from his father Fernando III a vast kingdom stretching from the Atlantic to the Mediterranean, with a diverse Christian, Jewish, and Muslim population of over three million people. With the Reconquest virtually completed and Castile's future predominance in peninsular affairs assured, Alfonso took upon himself the enormous task of bringing "Castile itself into the mainstream of high civilization and [setting] afoot a process that would produce a united, educated, artistic, and religious people."[1] Perhaps his most important innovation was the adoption of the spoken Castilian language rather than Latin as the principal medium for the scholarly and literary works he wrote or sponsored, earning him the title "father of Castilian" and the accolade that "a greater service to the language was not rendered until Cervantes wrote his *Quijote*."[2] He is also remembered as one of history's greatest lawgivers. His *Siete partidas* achieved "the widest territorial force ever enjoyed by any law book" and is "one of the outstanding landmarks . . . of world law."[3] As if this were not achievement enough, Alfonso is also memorable as a poet (especially for his *Cantigas*, or *Canticles of Holy Mary*, which Burns characterizes as equal in importance to "Dante's *Divine Comedy* or . . . the best Gothic cathedral"[4]), historian, scientist, and sponsor and editor of translations (mainly from Arabic and Hebrew) of an encyclopedic variety of literary and scientific works.

Alfonso undertook two great historical projects. The first, known as the *Estoria de Espanna* or *Primera crónica general*, begins with the population of the world by the sons of Noah and traces the story of mankind down to the reign of Alfonso's father Fernando III, emphasizing the history of the Iberian peninsula. The *Estoria de Espanna* drew on the Bible, the works of classical and early medieval Latin historians (especially Paulus Orosius), and, heavily, on more recent ecclesiastical histories such as the *Chronicon mundi* (1236) of Lucas de Tuy and the *Historia Gothica* or *De rebus Hispaniae* of Rodrigo Jiménez de Rada (1170?–1247), as well as on Castilian epic poetry and on Arabic historical writings. As Nancy Joe Dyer has observed,

---

[1] Robert I. Burns, S.J., "*Stupor Mundi*: Alfonso X of Castile, the Learned," in Burns, ed., *Emperor of Culture: Alfonso X the Learned of Castile and His Thirteenth-Century Renaissance* (Philadelphia: Univ. of Pennsylvania Press, 1990), pp. 5–6.

[2] Richard E. Chandler and Kessel Schwartz, *A New History of Spanish Literature* (Baton Rouge: Louisiana State Univ. Press, 1961), p. 415.

[3] Charles Sumner Lobingier, cited in Burns, "*Stupor mundi*," p. 1.

[4] "*Stupor mundi*," p. 8.

> In the four decades between the composition of the Latin-ecclesiastical chronicles and the origins of the secularized Alfonsine project, the concept of writing about the recent past again evolved markedly toward greater narrativity and emplotment. Perhaps, as has been suggested, the shift was influenced by the more demographically representative Arabic historiographic models, and perhaps through inclusion of near-contemporary vernacular narratives which often included non-royal protagonists."[5]

Although this comment was inspired principally by the *Estoria de Espanna*'s treatment of the recent reign of Alfonso VIII, in fact both of Alfonso's histories as a whole can be said to constitute an important step forward in their treatment of history as a meaningful, coherent narrative and their inclusion of many humanizing details.

Alfonso began his second and more ambitious historical project, a history of the world known as the *General estoria* (*General History*), in 1272, before the *Estoria de Espanna* had been completed. The *General estoria* was the first attempt to write a history of the world in a modern language. It consists of six parts, only the first four of which were completed. In its final form, it covers the period from the creation of the world to the birth of the parents of the Virgin Mary. Amazingly, only the first two parts have ever been published. Antonio García Solalinde edited the *Primera parte*, published in Madrid by the Centro de Estudios Históricos in 1930; his edition of the *Segunda parte* was completed after his untimely death in 1937 by L. A. Kasten and V. R. B. Oelschläger and published in two volumes in 1957 and 1961. The present translation of the story of Joseph is based on Solalinde's edition of the *Primera parte*.

The principal sources of the *General estoria* are the Bible, Josephus's *Antiquities of the Jews*, Peter Comestor's twelfth-century *Historia Scholastica*, and the *Kitab al-Masalik wa-l Mamalik* (*Book of Roads and Kingdoms*) of Abu 'Ubaid al-Bakri (d. 1094), whom the distinguished Dutch orientalist Reinhardt Dozy described as "the most important geographer that Arab Spain produced."[6] Al-Bakri's version of the story of Joseph is based on the Qur'an and on various qur'anic commentaries, some of which are now lost. Interestingly, although it is generally assumed that the translations of Arabic materials were carried out by Jews, the influence of Jewish commentaries in the *General History* is very slight. The *General History* often follows Muslim tradition in direct contradiction to the Bible, as, for example, when Reuben states: "Let us not kill him,

---

[5] "Alfonsine Historiography: The Literary Narrative," in Burns, ed., *Emperor of Culture*, p. 146.

[6] Cited in Angel González Palencia, *Historia de la literatura arábigo-española* (Barcelona: Editorial Labor, 1945), p. 213.

for if his father and mother heard that he had died in that way, they would soon cry themselves to death in mourning for him." According to the Bible, Joseph's mother Rachel had died long before the incident in question; the Qur'an states that when Joseph was at last reconciled with his family in Egypt, "he gave his father and mother a place of honor . . . and seated his parents by his side on the throne" (12:97–99). An attempt to portray Joseph as fore-shadowing Christ can be seen in the text's statement that "they sold him to the merchants for thirty pieces of silver," as opposed to the Bible's "twenty pieces of silver" (Gen. 37:28). Likewise, in its treatment of Jacob's "blessings" or prophecies to his sons, the *General History* values Christian, messianic in-terpretations over Jewish ones. However, it is very interesting that in a case where the New Testament (Acts 7:14), following the Septuagint, contradicts the Hebrew text of Genesis 47:25–26, the *General History* insists on the ab-solute priority of the Hebrew text: ". . . it is our duty to say what Moses said literally in the biblical text, which is the source of all the others" (Book Nine, Chapter Two).

It is often difficult if not impossible to ascertain the extent of the monarch's personal involvement in his many great editorial projects. In the case of the *General History*, however, Alfonso explicitly stated that he "caused to be as-sembled" the various sources, "selected from them the most reliable and the best that I knew," and then "made this book" and "commanded" it to be writ-ten.[7] As Juan Luis Alborg has noted, "besides the factual events narrated, the work abounds in varied digressions and disquisitions which practically repre-sent an anthology of the most diverse fields of knowledge and reveal the ency-clopedic enthusiasm of the period, as well as the monarch's universalist con-cern."[8] For example, the section of the *General History* containing the story of Joseph includes digressions on crocodiles, dolphins, and other denizens of the Nile, on why the Libyans dislike shepherds, on the gentile kings who ruled var-ious parts of the world in the time of Joseph, on the introduction of wheat into Greece, on how men first began to breed mules, on the introduction of weights and measures in Greece, and on the story of Prometheus, who was believed to have been a contemporary of Joseph.

The *General History*'s account of the story of Joseph is noteworthy as one of the earliest attempts to treat that story as objective history, drawing on—and attempting to harmonize—all sources considered reliable, with remarkably lit-tle prejudice regarding the provenance of those materials. The attempts to har-monize material taken from such disparate sources are often awkward. For ex-

---

[7] John E. Keller, *Alfonso X, el Sabio* (New York: Twayne Publishers, 1967), p. 118; cited in Burns, *"Stupor mundi,"* p. 10.

[8] *Historia de la literatura española* (Madrid: Gredos, 1970), I, 167.

ample, the important scene when Joseph's mistress tries to force him to go to bed with her, and then Joseph encounters Phutiphar as he attempts to flee the palace and convinces Phutiphar of his innocence (Qur'an), is treated as a *separate* event from the scene where the "Lady Zulayme" feigns illness as an excuse to be left alone with Joseph on the day of the Nile festival, when she *again* attempts to seduce him, and he escapes, leaving his cloak in her hand (Bible). On this second occasion, Phutiphar "believes" her, as in the Bible, and imprisons Joseph, yet the reason given for the imprisonment follows Muslim tradition: he orders Joseph taken away "in order to save his wife's reputation and keep people from blaming her." The two incidents are separated by the qur'anic story of the banquet Zulayme gives for the court ladies, yet—like a joke without its punch-line—the narrative inexplicably omits the climactic moment of that scene, when the ladies, enraptured by Joseph's beauty, cut their hands with their knives. Also following Muslim tradition, the *General History* portrays Phutiphar as a eunuch and the Lady Zulayme as identical with Joseph's wife Asenath. One of the most charming interpolations in the *History* recounts how, after they are at last legally married, Joseph gently chides his wife, telling her that "what we have together now is better than what you wanted before," to which she indignantly replies: "By God, don't blame me, for my husband Phutiphar was no good as a husband, and you heard that before, and you were so handsome and so genteel that every woman who saw you lusted after you. And that's why I spoke to you of love. And you are an educated man, and wise, and a man of good fortune; therefore, I beg you not to bring this up again, nor embarrass me, for I don't consider it good nor courteous."

The *General History* also contains numerous contradictions, perhaps indicating that it was a composite of sections redacted by different scholars. Thus, for example, we are told in Book Eight, Chapter One, that Joseph was sold "thirteen years after the death of Isaac," but Chapter Twelve states that Isaac died when Joseph was twenty eight years old. Naturally, there are also numerous anachronisms, such as the reference to Zulayme's father as an "archbishop" or the various mentions of stained glass as figuring prominently in the luxurious palaces the *History* describes. Interestingly, the *General History* consistently presents ancient Egypt as a society composed of three different cultures or castes, like the Spain of Alfonso X. Thus many of the characters have three different names. Phutiphar, for example, was called "Tagui in the language of Egypt, and in Arabic al-'Aziz, and in Hebrew Phutiphar." There is evidence of confusion resulting from the fact that material translated from Arabic was later redacted by scholars who did not know that language, such as the absurd statement that Pharaoh called the town Joseph built for him Alf-yaum (Arabic, "a thousand days"), "which means work of seventy days."

On the whole, however, the *General History* is a remarkable example of Alfonso's syncretism, his conviction that all the sources available to him—pagan mythology, Muslim and Jewish folklore, as well as Christian writings—ultimately embodied the same universal truths, though expressed in different ways. It is admirable for its diligent efforts to recover those truths and convey them in a way that could be understood by all of Alfonso's subjects.

Here Begins the Eighth Book of the General History

This eighth book speaks of the matter of Joseph, of the dreams he had in his father's house, of his brothers' hatred and envy of him; and of how he was sold, and taken to Egypt, and there sold again; and of how he interpreted Pharaoh's dreams, and Pharaoh gave him power over all Egypt, and of what happened when his brothers went there to buy bread, and later went down into Egypt, and Joseph sent for his father Jacob.

Here ends the prologue, and the book begins.

I. Of the Wicked Deeds Joseph Saw His Brothers Commit, and of the Dreams He Dreamed in His Father's House, and of How He Was Sold and Taken to Egypt

Moses recounts in his history in the Bible that when Joseph was sixteen years old he watched over his father's cattle with his brothers, the sons of Bilhah and Zilpah, maids of Jacob's wives. And Master Godfrey[9] says that Joseph was in charge of his father's chamber. Hence Moses and Master Godfrey, who agrees with him and repeats his words, recount that Joseph observed that his brothers behaved badly in certain ways and committed some very great and very wicked sins. And Master Peter[10] says that he overheard how some of them despised their father, others committed bestiality, and Reuben had intercourse with his father's concubine Zilpah; and he told Jacob all of this.

And his father loved him more than all his other sons, first of all, because he begat him in his old age; and second, because he was more sensible, as

---

[9] The chronicler Godfrey of Viterbo (c. 1120–c. 1196).
[10] Peter Comestor (twelfth century), author of the *Historia scholastica*.

Josephus[11] says, and better behaved, and likewise of a noble heart, and more intelligent than all the others; and third, out of love for Rachel, his mother, whom he had loved very much. And he made him a noble garment with sleeves, and striped in many colors.

Around this time it came to pass that Joseph had two dreams. First, he dreamed that his father sent him and his brothers to harvest some grain, and as they each cut the grain and laid their sheaves down flat on the ground, his stood straight up where he had put it, and those of his brothers ran over to it and bowed down to it. And when he awoke, he told this dream to his brothers so that they could interpret it for him, according to Josephus. And they envied him greatly because of the partiality their father showed him. And Josephus says in this regard that they understood that dream to refer to the wealth and power he was going to have over them, and they were very upset about that. And if they had disliked him before, they really hated him from then on. And they pretended not to understand what the dream meant, and they refused to interpret it for him. Nevertheless, they answered him thus: "Will you indeed be our king, and will we be your vassals?" After saying that, they took counsel together about how they might prevent such a thing from happening. And Josephus recounts that from then on, they were much worse to him, and never spoke a kind or brotherly word to him, but rather always spoke to him rudely and angrily.

The second dream was that the sun and moon and eleven stars bowed down to Joseph. And Joseph told his father this dream. And when he heard it, he reprimanded him in front of his other sons, and said: "What does this mean? Shall I, and your mother, and your brothers indeed bow down you?" And Josephus further recounts that his brothers were saddened by these words when they heard them, and turned against Joseph in their hearts and also in their words. But his father kept silent and pondered these dreams.

After this, his brothers were wandering with their flocks in Shechem, which is a very good land with wonderful pasture, according to Josephus. And Joseph had stayed at home. And one day Israel ordered Joseph to go and see how his brothers and the cattle were doing, and come back and tell him; for it had been days since anyone had come from there who could bring him news of them or take them a message. And he was distressed about that and worried that peradventure some harm might have befallen them.

Joseph left Hebron, and went straight to Shechem to see how his brothers and their cattle were doing, as his father had commanded; but he didn't find them there. And as he was searching for them, he met a man who asked him

---

[11] Josephus Flavius (c. 38–after 100 C.E.), Jewish historian and one of the leading authors of Jewish Hellenistic literature.

where he was going and what he was looking for; and he replied that he was searching for his brothers. Then the man told him: "They left here, and I heard them say they were going to Dothan." Joseph went after them, and found them there. When they saw him coming in the distance, they said one to another: "Behold our dreamer. Come, let us kill him; and we'll say that a wild beast ate him, and then he'll see what good his dreams are." Then Reuben, who was the eldest brother, when he heard that, argued with the others as well as he knew how, to save him from being killed, and he said to them: "Let us not kill him, for if his father and mother heard that he had died in that way, they would soon cry themselves to death in mourning for him. Besides, God has found him worthy of those things he showed us in the dreams he told us, and wants to give them to him. And if we should oppose God's will or one whom He loves, we might incur His wrath and a great punishment on that account, and rightly so. Besides, he is our brother, and it would be treacherous for us to kill him for such a reason." But according to Josephus, neither these words nor many others that Reuben said could convince them nor dissuade them from killing him. And when Reuben saw the terrible crime they intended to commit, and was powerless to prevent it, he told them not to do so, but instead to throw him into a well he would show them that was there in the desert, and he would die there, and they would not stain their hands with their brother's blood. And he told them this so that he could get him out of there alive during the night—for there was no water in the well—and take him back to their father. At last he persuaded his brothers, and they accepted his idea.

As soon as Joseph arrived, they seized him, and took away the prized garment his father had given him, and Reuben tied him up in such a way as to do him no harm, and carefully put him into the dry well. And he went off to look for better pastures, to ensure Joseph's safety by luring the other brothers away from there. However, none of them left just then except Reuben; the others stayed there to eat after what they had done. And just then some merchants passed by who were coming from Gilead and transporting resin, and myrrh, and other spices to Egypt to sell. When Judah saw them, he suggested to his brothers—as soon as Reuben was gone—that they sell Joseph. He said it would be better than for him to die there, for after all, he was their brother and their own blood; and if he survived, he would be so far away that he could never become their master; and if he died, they wouldn't be responsible for his death. And, as Josephus recounts, they all liked what Judah said. And Master Godfrey says that these merchants were relatives of Joseph and his brothers, for they were descendants of Ishmael, Isaac's brother; however, neither the brothers nor the merchants were aware of this. And they sold him to the merchants for thirty pieces of silver, and those who bought him took him away with them to Egypt.

When Reuben came that night to take him out of the well, and didn't find him, he wept and rent his garments, and went to his brothers, and said: "The child is nowhere to be seen. What will become of me, and where will I go?" According to Josephus, they told him what they had done with Joseph, and then Reuben ceased his mourning. And so that their father might not suspect what they had done, they took the garment they had taken from the child, and tore it in pieces, and smeared it with the blood of a goat they killed, and sent it to their father by one of them. And they instructed him to tell him that they had found it like that, and ask him to examine it to see whether it wasn't his son's garment; and that is what they did. And as soon as their father recognized the garment, he said: "This is my son Joseph's coat; a wild beast has eaten him." And he rent his clothes, and put on mourning, and wept for a long time.

Afterwards, all his sons assembled to comfort him and take that pain from him, but he refused to be comforted, and he said: "Leave me alone, for I shall mourn for my son until I die and go down to Hades." Meanwhile, the merchants of Midian who had bought him sold him to Phutiphar, head of Pharaoh's cavalry.

And Joseph was sold in the 278th year since the birth of Abraham, and 107 years after Jacob's birth, and thirteen years after the death of Isaac. And he was then sixteen years old. And at that time were reigning King Baleus in Assyria, and Messapus in Sicionia, and Phoroneus in Argos, and Jupiter in Crete and in Europe, and the shepherd Pharaohs in Egypt.

Now we will set aside the Bible story, and we'd like to return to our account of the descendants of King Jupiter who were living at that time.

[Chapters II–IV purport to tell the true story of the human beings who inspired the myths of Saturn, Jupiter, Venus, Pluto, etc.]

V. Of Joseph's Coming to Egypt; and of His Master Phutiphar, Who Bought Him; and of Pharaoh Nicrao and His Conquests

Moses recounts in his history in the Bible that Joseph was sixteen years old when the merchants of Midian, which is in the land of Ishmael, bought him from his brothers; and that these merchants who bought him were going to Egypt with their merchandise, as we have said, and they took him with them, and they sold him to a potentate of King Pharaoh's house. And that potentate's name was Phutiphar, and he was a eunuch, and head of the king's cavalry. But Josephus states on this subject that Phutiphar was the king's steward and majordomo, and that he had all of Pharaoh's house under his keeping; and that Joseph was seventeen years old when he bought him. Master Godfrey says that the king of the Pharaohs who was reigning in Egypt when Joseph was sold there was known in Greek as Diapolita, but his proper name was Amosis. And Eusebius[12] and Sigebert[13] and Paulus Orosius[14] recount that this king was of a dynasty who were all known as the Diapolites, but he was called Amosis as his own proper name, as we have said. For you should be aware that, although some of the first Pharaohs of Egypt were called the Thebans, others, the shepherd kings, and still others, the Diapolites, this was because they ruled in dynasties; but each one of these Pharaohs had, besides these names that were common to the entire dynasty, his own proper name, and that was the case of this Pharaoh as well, and his name was Amosis, as has been stated.

But we have found that a wise king, who was lord of Niebla and Saltes, (which are towns in the kingdom of Seville, in the western part, near the great sea, next to a land called the Algarve—which means the westernmost part of the land of Spain) wrote a book in Arabic called *The History of Egypt*.[15] And a nephew of his gave it another name in Arabic: *Kitab al-Masalik wa-l Mamalik*, which means in our Castilian language *Book of Roads and Kingdoms*, because in it he speaks of all the lands and kingdoms, how many days' traveling time and how many leagues long and wide each one is. And the reason why the king's history recounts all of this was to determine where in the lands tolls should be collected. And this king of Niebla, when speaking in his book of the boundaries of Egypt, says that the Pharaoh of Joseph's time was called Rayon, son of al-Wadit, in Arabic, but that the people of Egypt called him Nicrao in Egyptian. And this Pharaoh was a great man, very handsome and intelligent, and a doer of good to men and to his peoples. And he canceled their taxes for three years, and ordered his treasury opened, and divided it among his rich men, and those of his household, and his peoples; and they all loved him because of that, and thanked him very much, and prayed to God for him.

And that Phutiphar, potentate in Pharaoh's house, likewise had these three names, as the histories recount: Tagui in the language of Egypt, and in Arabic al-'Aziz, and in Hebrew Phutiphar. And this Phutiphar was a man of very good judgment, and he loved justice and the law, and the king made him governor of all his dominions. Emboldened by the honor the king had done him, he had made in his house a silver bench on which he sat. For it was then the custom that kings sat on golden benches and judges on silver ones. And by the king's command this Phutiphar appointed constables and scribes in the towns, and

---

[12] The ecclesiastical historian Eusebius of Caesarea (c. 260–c. 340 C.E.).

[13] The chronicler Sigebert of Gembloux (c. 1030–1112).

[14] Historian and theologian (fl. 415) born in Spain.

[15] The author of the book, Abu 'Ubaid al-Bakri (see p. 332 above), was not actually a king but the son of King Abd al-'Aziz al-Bakri of Huelva and Saltes.

when he summoned them, or they came to him with lawsuits, he sat down and ordered them to sit down before him in an orderly manner, each one in his proper place. And he judged and settled all the lawsuits in the land, and in this way relieved the king; and he performed for him very well everything that was needed in the kingdom and among the peoples, so that the king had no cares or obligations but could live at his ease.

At this time the king ordered built for himself a house of glass and crystal of many colors, and he made water run around it, and he ordered large reservoirs built and filled with water, and he had fish of many different kinds put in them. And when the sun shone on the water, it caused a wonderful brightness in the house, and the king very much enjoyed seeing that brightness. And around those lagoons he ordered built as many terraces as there are days in the year; and each day he moved to a designated chamber with its particular view. And on each one of these terraces he had his palaces which did not resemble each other in their hangings, or their cloths, or in their vessels, nor in the other things that were there. And in each one of them the king lived for one day, and thus he went through them all in a year.

When his neighbor kings learned about this king's pleasures and enjoyments and his house, they were emboldened and began to make war against him. And a king of the land of Amalek, whose name was Abicauz, came against King Nicrao with great companies and a great army; and the king sent Phutiphar his governor against him. And the war lasted three years, and finally Phutiphar was defeated. And that king entered Egypt, and he did great damage in the land, and demolished castles and towers and many other fine constructions, and burned and destroyed whatever he found, and did whatever wickedness he could. Then the peoples of the kingdom complained grievously, so much so that their complaints and news of the terrible damage reached King Nicrao. Then he left those pleasures in which he was indulging, and went out and gathered his peoples together, and set matters aright, and went out with so great an army that there were six hundred thousand armed men in it, not counting the others he had had to begin with, who were numerous. And he fought his battle with that king of Amalek, and vanquished him, and pursued him to the borders of the lands of Shem, and killed him, and took many of that King Abicauz's companions captive, and entered the lands of Shem.

The kings of those lands were very frightened when they heard the deeds of King Nicrao, and they sent him their emissaries, and agreed to pay him tribute every year that he didn't make war against them. And Nicrao received the emissaries, and then returned to his kingdom and ordered his soldiers to prepare very well to go and make war on the kings of the West. And he took out against them an army of nine thousand armed men. When the neighboring kings and the others heard the news, some of them came to swear fealty to him, while others distanced themselves as much as they could, fleeing in order not to have to fight him. And he went out and marched across Africa, and reached Carthage the Greater, which is by the port of Tunis. And the people of that land made peace with him by a treaty whereby they promised to pay him tribute every year. Then he left there and marched through all the other lands until he reached the Green Sea, and came to a place where there was a copper idol, and he had his name engraved on it as a memorial of his arrival there. And they negotiated for all the people of that land to pay him tribute every year.

When the treaty was signed, he went on to Provence, and from there he came to Spain, which was then in the hands of King Roderic the Lesser. And King Nicrao fought him and killed many of his soldiers. And King Roderic and his people negotiated with him to pay every year a designated amount of gold per capita. When this was done and signed, Nicrao turned back toward the East, and crossed the sea, and entered the lands of the barbarians, and conquered all of them, and there was no place he passed through that he didn't bring under his control and make it pay him money, and there was no people he passed through where he didn't leave a monument to his arrival and a memorial to what he did there, as we've already mentioned. And the Latin writings call landmarks of warring and conquering kings such as these "gades," as when we say "gades Herculis," and it means the monuments of Hercules. And continuing in this way, and doing the same sorts of things, he reached Nubia, and the people of that land came to an agreement with him for a certain amount of property per year. And when this treaty was likewise completed and signed, he reached a place called Damacra, and they too negotiated to give him a certain amount per year. And he ordered a great tower built there, and had his name carved on a stone, and had it put in that tower. And when he had done this there and in the other places like a successful king, he returned to his own land.

We will have occasion to speak more about this King Nicrao later on, but for now we shall return to the story of Joseph.

VI. Of How Phutiphar Bought Joseph and Gave Him to His Wife Zulayme, and Phutiphar Built Pharaoh Some Very Noble Palaces

While Nicrao, this Pharaoh we were discussing, was traveling abroad, conquering and invading different lands, his governor Phutiphar, whom we have mentioned, began to travel through the cities and through all the kingdom of Egypt, appointing mayors and judges under himself, and maintaining the peoples in justice, and collecting what was due the king, and he did it very loyally and was very successful in everything. At this time he came to Manip,[16] which is a city in a very good area in Egypt, a very fertile place which the king greatly loved. And there he built some very rich palaces in which there were many chambers, each one with its terrace. And he made them with glass of very beautiful colors. And he put in each of those chambers and on each of those terraces many valuable hangings, and daises covered with gold-embroidered cloth and other wonderfully elegant things. And around the portals of these palaces he planted many very valuable trees that smelled very good, and much myrtle, which is a very noble and exotic tree, and which gives off a good odor.

And when he had finished these palaces, he went on traveling through the kingdom. And it happened that one day he returned to that city of Manip, and there he found those merchants from the land of Ishmael who were selling Joseph. And as they were putting him up for auction, he arrived; and as soon as he saw him, he looked good to him, and he was very pleased with him, and he strove to buy him for the king. The lad's price then went up to his weight in silver, but he bought him anyway, thinking that he would be good for the king's service because of his comely and genteel appearance; and he took him home with him.

And he had a wife whose name was Zulayme and who was also his cousin, the daughter of an uncle of his who was archbishop of a city which in Greek was called Heliopolis, which in our Castilian language means "City or Town of the Sun," and in Arabic it was called 'Ayin al-Shams, which means "Eye of the Sun," and in Egyptian it was called Damiata, which, according to those who explain the names of cities and places, means the same thing. And the city received its name from an idol of the sun that was there. And the reason for this name of the city was because in that idol and in that city were seen and appeared greater things than in any other place in the whole world, just as the eye of the sun is the greatest of all lights.

And Phutiphar showed that boy to Zulayme, his wife, and when she saw how beautiful and genteel he was she was delighted with him, and she begged her husband not to take him with him but to leave him there, for she would appreciate him very much. Phutiphar replied that it pleased him, and he did as she asked, and he left Joseph at home with his wife. And everything went very well for Phutiphar, and his wealth increased greatly, and he acquired great property, and the power he had held before likewise increased, and everything got better for him after he acquired that lad. And he understood well that God was with Joseph in all his actions, and that it was because of him that God gave him all those good things.

[16] Memphis?

And Joseph was very careful about everything he was given to do, and very intelligent. Hence a sage who wrote the histories of the things that happened in Egypt in those days, whose name was Pompey,[17] and another one named Justinus,[18] said about Joseph—for they learned all about him—that, although he was the youngest in days of his brothers, he surpassed them all in subtlety and understanding. And it was because they were afraid of him that they took him out into the wilderness and sold him to foreigners. Furthermore, they say that after those merchants brought him to Egypt he became an expert on the arts of magic, and because of that, he would be much loved by the king. For God gave him so much grace and so much knowledge that he was able to tell the things that were going to happen. And they even say that he was the first one who understood dreams and interpreted them in the land of Egypt; and his understanding set him apart from those who only pretended to know. And he knew and said so many things that it seemed that God rather than men revealed them to him. And because of his great intelligence, and because he was a good servant and everything he did turned out well, he was much loved by his master; and his master was so pleased with him that he didn't want to give him to the king, for whom he had bought him, but kept him for himself. And because he saw how prudent he was, he made him master of his house, and put him in charge of all his wealth, and didn't trouble himself about anything.

Then Phutiphar, governor of Egypt, received word that his master, King Nicrao, was coming home after conquering the lands we have mentioned. And he gathered together all the goodmen of the kingdom, and they went out to receive him with many minstrels and great rejoicing. And after that, in the palace they gave him many choice, noble, and rare presents, and many sweet-smelling spices, for thus it was the custom then in that land to receive princes. And the king was very pleased with Phutiphar, his governor, and with his reception. And after he got to Manip, he ordered all those who had gone out to receive him to stay with him, and he showed them great hospitality, and gave them everything they needed.

And then Phutiphar took him to those palaces that he had built there in a grand style, as we have said, in which there were many chambers with their windows made of colored glass. And each of those chambers was well decorated with many noble hangings and many couches embroidered with gold. And he had adorned them with leaves and branches of the many trees that we mentioned he had planted around these palaces, which smelled very good, and

---

[17] Gnaeus Pompeius Trogus, Roman historian of the age of Augustus, author of the *Historiae Philippicae*.

[18] Third-century C.E. Roman historian who wrote a digest of Trogus's *Historiae Philippicae*.

of the abundant myrtle, for they were now well established, and they gave off a good odor and made all the palaces and the whole area very beautiful and well disposed. And when he led the king to them, and the king saw them, he considered them very well built and a very fine residence for a king, and he stayed there and made that his home for a long time, so that he and his companions in battle could relax and recover from the pain and grief they had suffered for many years before that, while they were conquering the lands we have mentioned.

We will now leave this subject and return to the story of Joseph, in order to tell what happened to him with the wife of his master Phutiphar.

VII. Of How Joseph's Mistress Zulayme Fell in Love with Him, and of How She Behaved with Him before the Ladies of Pharaoh's House

At that time Joseph, who was held in such favor in his master's house, grew up and became very handsome and very genteel. And Lady Zulayme, his mistress, seeing him like that, fell in love with him. And the *History of Egypt* says that she hid her feelings as well as she could, so that men might not know how much she loved him, until at last she was overcome by her feelings and could no longer conceal them.

And one day she dressed up and adorned herself as well and as elegantly as she could. And she went to him and let him know, in the most beautiful and eloquent words she knew how, that she loved him, and was so deeply enamored that she could bear it no longer. And she confided to him that Phutiphar was no good as a husband, because he was a eunuch, and the king had had him castrated. And she pleaded with him, and told him that if he would do as she asked, she would give him great wealth, and make him a very rich man, and set him free, and place him in a great estate. And Joseph replied, as Moses says in the Bible story, that since his master had given him charge over his house and everything that was in it, he would not do such an imprudent thing to him, for it would be a great treachery. And the *History of Egypt* says that then she took hold of him and tried to make him kiss her, since she couldn't get anything more from him. And he refused and defended himself against her as well as he could until he finally had to run away from her, for she was grabbing him more and more tightly.

And thus it happened that, as Joseph was running away, at that very moment Phutiphar, his master, was coming in through the outer gate and looked toward the palace, and said to him: "What is this?" Joseph began to speak his choice and good words so as not to give his mistress away, but Lady Zulayme,

Phutiphar's wife, fearing betrayal, went out and said to him: "Phutiphar, I was lying asleep in my room, and this servant of yours came and tried to rape me." And Joseph excused himself as well as he could, still being careful to say nothing that would cast guilt or shame on his mistress. Phutiphar understood perfectly well, from the explanations he heard from both sides, that this was her doing, but he took her side, and said to Joseph: "Remove yourself from this matter, and don't ever do it again, and beg my pardon for the wrong you have done me." Joseph saw that he had done nothing wrong, and there was nothing for him to amend, nor any reason for him to beg pardon. And he kept silent, as Josephus recounts, but still he remained in his master's favor as before, for his master did not attach great importance to the matter.

News of what had occurred between Zulayme and Joseph soon reached the king's house; and the ladies who were there were determined to find out the truth of the matter, and discussed it among themselves. Even before this, however, King Nicrao had heard about Joseph and how Phutiphar had bought him for him. He asked [Phutiphar] about him, but Phutiphar denied the story. And he ordered Joseph not to leave the house, and to stay in a place where no one would see him. And while the king was taking his ease and enjoying himself in seclusion, Lady Zulayme, Phutiphar's wife, ordered many kinds of food prepared, and many wines brought, and invited a large group of the ladies from the king's palace. And when the ladies accepted her invitation, she took up residence in a palace which had another palace inside it, and both were painted and adorned with much gold. And she had them hung with silken cloths of bright yellow and many other colors, embroidered with gold with the technique known in Arabic as *dibeth*,[19] as the *History of Egypt* recounts. And all around she hung curtains[20] of that cloth.

And she summoned some women who shaved and beautified brides, and ordered them to shave and beautify Joseph as well as they knew how and were able, and to bring him beautified in that way to the palace where she had invited the ladies from the king's house. And this palace had its door facing East, so the morning sun came streaming in through it. And the women who beautified Joseph put a little net worked with seed pearls[21] and precious stones on his hair, and they dressed him in a bright yellow silk outfit embroidered with gold and silver, with bright red designs in the shape of wheels here and there, also decorated with gold. And inside the wheels were the figures of little green birds. And the outfit was lined with two layers of green gauze; and the openings of the sleeves were embroidered with precious stones of many colors. And

---

[19] Probably *dibaj* (that is, brocade or fine needlework).
[20] Old Spanish "acitaras," from Arabic "al-sitar."
[21] Spanish "aljofar," from Arabic "al-johar."

over that they put on him a transparent red shirt. And above all they put on his head a golden crown, all likewise studded with very noble precious stones. And they did this in such a way that his hair should show under the crown, and they arranged a lock of his hair in front so that it should hang over his chest, and they braided it like little nets. Then they darkened his eyes with kohl; and in his hand they placed a golden hyssop with green silk for him to use to sprinkle rose water on the ladies, as if he were a bishop or archbishop or a maiden of royal blood.

And when the ladies had eaten the other foods, they brought them citrons and other fruits of different kinds such as grow in the land of Manip; and they brought each one a knife with a handle studded with precious stones with which to peel the fruit. And then Lady Zulayme said to them: "Ladies, cut your fruit and eat." And then she had different kinds of wine brought to heighten their pleasure and rejoice them more, and she ordered many glasses put out so that each one could drink whichever wines she wished and as much as she wanted. And after they had eaten the fruit and drunk the wine, she said to them: "I have heard that the ladies in your palace have been talking about what occurred between me and my servant." They replied: "It is as you have said, but when we discussed this matter, we said that you are a great lady and would not do such a thing. For you are so honorable that we don't believe you would turn your head even for a prince, much less for your own servant." Then she replied: "It wasn't true that I wanted to do it, but even if it were as you heard, it wouldn't be so outrageous, because he is definitely the man to do it with."

Then she sent word for the women who had adorned him to bring him before her and the other ladies who were in that palace. And when he came to the place where his mistress was sitting with the ladies, the sun coming through the doorway shone on him as Lady Zulayme had arranged for him to be adorned, and the whole palace shone as well as Joseph's face and clothing. And Joseph kept walking along with his hyssop in his hand, as they had told him to do, until he reached his mistress and stood before her; and all the ladies stared at him. The Lady Zulayme started talking to them, but they were so preoccupied by Joseph's beauty that they paid no attention to what she was saying. She said: "Ladies, what is the matter with you? Why are you staring at my servant instead of paying attention to what I am saying?" And they replied: "God forbid he should be a servant! This is no servant. He looks more like a noble king."

As they stared at him, there was not one of them who was not moved in her heart and coveted a man with the great desire they had for him. And each one of them coveted him for herself, so much did he please them, and so handsome did he seem. When Lady Zulayme realized this, she was satisfied, and she said to them: "Ladies, this is the man you were accusing me of trifling with." They answered her: "Now we see, and we say that no one should criticize you for that. And we realize that whoever criticized you before was wrong. Go ahead and say whatever you like to Joseph." She said: "I've already spoken to him, but he refused to do any of the things I wanted him to; but you talk to him, and plead with him on my behalf, and peradventure he will do what I ask because of your request."

Then they all began to talk to him, each one in turn. But the one who was talking to him secretly sought him for herself, that he should give her the love that Lady Zulayme wanted. And every single one of them made this plea first, but none of them could get him to do what they wanted. Despairing of getting him for themselves, they at last advised and pleaded that he do what his mistress wanted and demanded, telling him that he would thereby win wealth and nobility. He answered that he had no need of it, for his master gave him enough, and they never succeeded in convincing him. When they saw this, they all agreed to take hold of him and rape him. And Lady Zulayme told them in Joseph's hearing: "Don't do that, it wouldn't be good for us! But since you know so much about our business, I may as well tell you what I plan to do if he won't give in to me. I shall put him in prison and give him a very hard life." Joseph heard that and answered: "Peradventure prison will be better for me than what you want me to do." Then she swore by her god that if he didn't do what she asked, she would have him arrested right away. And her god, according to the *History*, was an idol of green stone made in the name of the planet Mercury. But neither threats nor promises availed to persuade Joseph to do the things those women wanted.

VIII. Of How Lady Zulayme Seized Joseph and Had Phutiphar Throw Him in Jail; and of the Chronicle of the Kings of That Time

The *History* states that in Egypt every year they had a great holiday that all those who dwelled there honored very much. And according to their custom, all the women were supposed to be dressed up and adorned, each one as well as she knew how and was able. And they say that on the holiday of the year that Joseph was arrested, Lady Zulayme, his mistress, pretended to be ill and told her husband that since she was ailing, she wouldn't be able to attend the festival. And she did that to have a reason to stay home and be alone with Joseph and fondle him in every way, so persistently was she in love with him.

And she shut herself up that day in her room and sent the whole household out on different errands. And when most of the household were gone, she sent for Joseph, and he came at his mistress' command. And from the moment he entered the room, she began to speak to him of love, using the most eloquent and emphatic words she knew, and to implore him more than ever before, weeping mightily. But during all of this, he, always fearing God and remaining loyal to his master in his heart, steadfastly refused to do—or even to promise to do—what she asked. And he began leaving the room to go out.

When she saw this, she took hold of his cloak and held onto him tightly, insisting that he just go ahead and do it, even if he didn't want to and took no pleasure in it. But he absolutely refused to do it under any circumstances, and ran away, leaving his cloak in her hands. When she saw herself disdained like that, and [realized] that he had left his cloak behind, she was afraid that peradventure (notwithstanding that he had done such a good job of covering up for her on the previous occasion) he might betray her. Since the matter had come to such a pass, she called the men who were in the house and told them that Joseph had tried to rape her. And she ordered them to arrest him, just as she had sworn she would do. And the men of the house did as their mistress commanded—and even outdid themselves, given the circumstances—and they arrested him, and stripped him of the good clothes he was wearing, and took them away from him, and dressed him in rough woolen. And Lady Zulayme kept him locked up until her husband Phutiphar should come, so she could tell him what had happened and complain to him.

Phutiphar soon came home, and as soon as he came in, she complained to him and began acting as if she were on the verge of tears. And here the story says that she actually wept more out of her unrequited love and longing for Joseph than for the reasons she gave her husband, which were in any case false. And she said to Phutiphar very angrily: "You brought us a Hebrew man and servant here to mock us! I was lying in my room, weak and in pain, as I told you I was, and on that account I was unable to attend the festival. And the men of the house had gone out on their errands. And he came in, and when he saw me alone, he tried to rape me. Then I began to cry out, and he took flight, and I seized him by the cloak in order to keep him here until the men came so that they could see the treachery he had attempted; but he left the cloak in my hand, and here it is. Then the men of the house arrived, and I ordered them to arrest him and keep him like that until you should come, and they arrested him. And I complain unto you that they gave me a bad name because of him; and I beg you to take this to heart and order him thrown in jail."

When her husband heard these words and saw the cloak, he believed that his wife was telling the truth, and he was very angry about what had happened, and he did as his wife said, and ordered Joseph taken away in order to save his wife's reputation and keep people from blaming her. And they threw him in the king's jail where the other prisoners were, and he stayed there seven years. But he didn't suffer much in prison, for God still watched over him there, and was so gracious unto him that he won the favor of the jailer, who released him from his bonds and made him a guard over the other prisoners. And everything that was done there was done by the hand and command of Joseph. And he did it so intelligently and was so successful that he relieved the jailer of all his cares, so that he didn't have to worry about anything, for God guided Joseph in all his deeds.

When this happened, Joseph was twenty four years old, and it was seven years since he had first been sold, according to Eusebius and Jerome.[22] And these kings were then reigning: Baleus in Assyria, and Messapus in Sicionia, and Jupiter in Crete and in most of Greece and Spain. And that year Phoroneus, King of Argos died, and Appis, his son, reigned for thirty five years thereafter. And he was the third king of that place; and King Appis was the same one we have mentioned earlier who had been governor of the kingdom of Achaia, where he ruled. His brother's name was Egialeus, and he went to Egypt with many people and won a kingdom, and reigned there, as has been said. And the Pharaoh, whose name we have said was Nicrao, likewise reigned in Egypt then. And there were seven of those kings of Egypt who were called Pharaohs, and three of them had the following names: the first, Dauma; the second, al-Did; and the third, Nicrao. And this Nicrao was the one of Joseph's time, and they called him by that name in the language of Egypt, as we have said. Others, however, have called him by other names and said other things about this Pharaoh. They have affirmed that he was the Pharaoh of Moses, but it was not this one, as we shall explain further on at the appropriate time and place. We shall also discuss the other four Pharaohs further on in their proper places. Know, as the histories recount and say, that they called those kings of Egypt Pharaohs, because Dauma, who was the first one, did many arrogant things, and killed his father and most of his relatives, and ruled with arrogance and force. And for that reason from then on they called every king of Egypt Pharaoh, just as in Rome they gave the name of Caesar to those who came after Julius Caesar, who was the first of them, and first had this name; and likewise, after Octavian, emperors and Caesars alike.

IX. Of How Pharaoh's Cupbearer and Baker Had Dreams While They Were in Jail, and Joseph Interpreted Them, and They Came True

At the time when Joseph was in jail, it happened that two of the king's attendants did things that made them incur the king's wrath. And they were both eunuchs, for in ancient times it was customary in the houses of kings for kings and high-ranking princes to have all their servants and officials castrated, so

[22] St. Jerome (c. 340–420 C.E.), translator of the Bible into Latin.

that it might be safer to have them in their houses among their women, and that they might be better served. And even today the Moors have this custom, and those to whom this is done are called in Arabic *fitianes*.[23]

And one of those officials who incurred the king's wrath was the king's cup-bearer, and the other his baker. And the *History of Egypt* recounts that the king, Pharaoh Nicrao, had discovered those officials' guilt in the following way: it is said that one night as the king lay sleeping, someone in human form came to him in a dream and said to him: "Your cupbearer and your baker have plotted to kill you; beware of them." The king awoke when the dream was over, as usually happens to all men, and considered what had been said, and thought about the dream, and remembered it well. And early next morning he sent for the cupbearer and the baker, and told them what he had dreamed, and asked them to tell him if it was true. The cupbearer did not want to lie to his lord the king, and told him that it was as he had said. Then the king, in order to get more of the truth out of them and know more about the matter, said to them: "How did you think you could accomplish such a vile deed and act of treason as this, since I never spend much time alone with such as you, and I'm never by myself but always surrounded by courtiers? How then did you think you could kill me?" The cupbearer replied: "Sir, the idea was that I should give you poison in your wine, and the baker, in your bread—not that I agreed to do so, nor was I willing to do it. And just as I've told you the truth so far, I'm also telling you the truth about this." And all this while the baker kept silent and said nothing. And his name was Aracen, and the cupbearer's name was Matis. And the king, though he respected the cupbearer for not denying the truth, nevertheless finally ordered them both arrested in order to find out more about the matter, and they threw them into the king's jail, where Joseph was.

The jailer entrusted them to Joseph, as the Bible story tells; but the gloss[24] says that, although that was so, one must understand that the jailer entrusted them to Joseph after he had released him from his chains and given him license to wander freely about the jail and the house, as you will hear further along. For Josephus says that when they were brought to the jail, Joseph was still confined to the prison stocks; but the jailer would let him roam about the jail as he wished during the day. And it happened that they put the cupbearer next to him in prison. And, just as it happens in other places that the closest neighbors are more likely to see each other and to talk—and in those days they were still locking Joseph up at night—he and the cupbearer, since they dwelled closer together than any of the others, began to converse together and to comfort each other. And they opened their hearts to each other, and each one told

---

[23] The word *fitian* is the plural of *fatan*, which literally means "young man, lad."
[24] Probably a reference to the Targum Onkelos.

the other secretly the reason why he was thrown in jail; and since neither of them had really done anything to deserve it, they soon got well acquainted and became friends.

And a few days after this, the jailer learned that Joseph had been wrongfully imprisoned. And he liked him very much, and he did him a favor and removed him from confinement and put him in charge of the prison so that he could walk around in it freely. And then he entrusted all the prisoners who were there to him, and most especially Pharaoh's cupbearer and baker, telling him to guard them more than the others, but also to show them greater kindness.

And after these two had been there for a good while, it is said that one night each one had a dream. The next morning Joseph went in to them, and since he liked them and looked after them more than the other prisoners, he noticed that they were sad, and he took them aside and asked them why. They replied that they had had dreams, and that there was no one who could interpret them for them. Joseph said: "God grant that their meaning be good for you; tell me what you have dreamed." The cupbearer, since he was closer to Joseph than the other one, began first, and he said: "I saw a vine before me with three shoots bearing ripe and very good grapes; and I took some of them, and squeezed them into the king's cup, and made wine thereof, and gave it to the king to drink." Then Joseph said: "The three shoots are the next three days, and on the third day the king will remember you and will restore you to the favor you formerly enjoyed in his house. And I beg you, when you are prosperous and back in your former good estate, that you remember me, and tell the king, and ask him the favor of freeing me from this jail, for I was kidnapped from the land of the Hebrews, and they sold me here, and I am wrongfully imprisoned, as he can easily find out." And Joseph interpreted the dream in this way not because of his love for the cupbearer but because he understood that what he said was true. When the baker saw that Joseph had given such a favorable interpretation to the cup-bearer's dream, he told him his own dream. And he said that he had dreamed that he was carrying three little baskets of bread on his head, and in the top-most one were all the dishes prepared especially for the king; and birds came and ate them. Joseph answered him and said: "Would that you had dreamed things that I could interpret better than what you have said!" And he told him that in three days he would be executed, and the birds would eat his flesh.

And it so happened that three days after that, Pharaoh Nicrao gave a great feast in honor of his birthday, and the cupbearer and the baker begged their friends to remind the king of them, peradventure he might show them mercy in honor of the holiday. After considering when they should do this, the courtiers decided that the best time would be after the king had finished his lunch, for then he would be happy and in a good mood. They said to him: "Lord, be mindful of Matis, your cupbearer, and Arescem [sic], who was your baker, who have been in jail for some time now." The king, who was well versed in the whole affair, since they had spoken to him about it, restored the cupbearer to his office of pouring his wine, just as he had done before, because he had not lied to him and had told him the truth when he questioned him. Besides which, he had very little guilt in the matter. And he ordered the baker executed, because he found him guilty of high treason and of denying the truth. And Master Peter says in this place on this subject that thus was proven the truth of Joseph's skill as an interpreter of dreams. But he says that, although the cupbearer regained his post and his power, and got along very well with his master the king, he did not remember Joseph, who had interpreted his dream.

When all of this happened, Joseph was twenty five years old, and the kings whom we mentioned in the previous chapter were still reigning in their kingdoms.

X. Of How Joseph Interpreted Pharaoh Nicrao's Dreams in Jail, and Was Taken before Him

Meanwhile, Joseph remained in jail, and no one petitioned the king on his behalf. Two years later, Pharaoh dreamed one night that he was near the Nile, and he saw come out of it seven very beautiful and very fat cows and graze on the shore of the Nile; and then after them came seven lean and very ugly cows, and ate the seven fat ones. After Pharaoh had dreamed this dream, he awoke, and he thought about it and wondered what it could mean. And while he was thinking about it, he fell asleep again, and saw another dream. He dreamed that seven ears of corn grew from a single root, very full of grains and very beautiful; and after them came an equal number that were very thin and very empty, and they used up and consumed all the fatness and beauty of the first ones. The king awoke from this dream much more frightened than from the other dream, for it seemed to him that it was not a good sign, and he thought a lot about what it could mean.

The next morning he sent for the wise men of Egypt, and told them both of these dreams, and ordered them to interpret them and tell him what they meant. The wise men thought about them, but in the end not one of them dared interpret them nor say what they meant. And at that time Matis, the king's cupbearer, was there, and as they were pondering what to do, he remembered how Joseph had interpreted his dream in jail. And he went straight to the king, and knelt before him, and told him all that had happened to him with Joseph in prison, and how Joseph had interpreted his dream and that of Arescen, who had been the king's baker, and they had come true, just as he had told them. Then he likewise told him Joseph's story, how he had been kidnapped in the land of

Shem, where the Jews lived, and sold in Egypt. And, according to Josephus, he also told him how his master Phutiphar had thrown him in that jail without his having done anything to deserve it. And Moses says in the Bible story that after the king heard this, he ordered them to bring him before him right away. And they went and had him shaved and dressed well first, for thus the king had commanded, and then they brought him before him.

But the King of Niebla and the *History of Egypt* tell the story differently. They say that when the cupbearer told the king all about Joseph, Pharaoh ordered the cupbearer to go to him in jail, and to ask him what it was that he wanted to know, so that Joseph should first guess without asking or being told. And if Joseph replied that it was a dream he wanted to ask him about, then he would know that Joseph was wise and intelligent, and that he would tell him the truth; and only then should he tell him those dreams as the king had told him, and then ask for the interpretation of what they meant. Matis went and did as the king commanded. And Joseph said that he had come on account of the dreams, and interpreted them to him, and told him what they meant. As soon as Matis understood what Joseph said, he went back to the king and told it all to him, just as Joseph had shown him. It was then, according to the King of Niebla, that the king sent for Joseph to have him brought before him, and those who went to the jail told him that the king had summoned him. Joseph answered them and said: "I beg you to go back to my lord the king, and tell him that I kiss his feet, and ask him as a favor that before he takes me out of this jail, he find out the truth about why I was thrown in this prison." The messengers did as he asked, and went back to the king, and told him what Joseph had said.

The king thought that Joseph was right, and his request was appropriate and reasonable, and since he was so determined that the truth should be known, it seemed to the king that he must be innocent. And the king sought privately to learn the truth from Lady Zulayme, Joseph's mistress, for her husband Phutiphar was dead by then. And he had died while Joseph was in prison. And the king sent Lady Zulayme a trusted confidant of his to ask her on his behalf to tell him the truth of that matter. Lady Zulayme thought that it would be treason not to tell her lord the king the truth about what he was asking, and she didn't want to lie to him. And she sent him a message begging him to do her the favor of letting her see him personally about such a matter. The king, seeing that that was what she wanted, thought it was fine, and it pleased him, and he sent for her very honorably. And Lady Zulayme came and spoke privately with the king and revealed to him everything that had happened and the reason why Joseph was in that prison. When the king saw that Lady Zulayme was telling the truth, he considered her a very good woman, and he was likewise pleased to know that Joseph had behaved so well. And then he sent for him again and ordered him brought. And the king's men who went for him brought him out of the jail. And when they heard that the king was pleased with Joseph's behavior, they bathed him and shaved him and dressed him well.

Then they took him to the king. And as soon as the king saw him, he was well pleased with him, for God gave Joseph so much grace in his appearance that whoever saw him was well pleased with him. And likewise the king was immediately well pleased with him, and liked him very much in his heart. And, according to the Bible story, Pharaoh then told him what he had dreamed, and how he had found no wise man in Egypt who could interpret his dreams, and asked him to interpret them, and ordered him that neither out of fear of his anger nor for any other reason should he hide the truth of what he understood that those dreams showed. Then Joseph answered: "Sire, God will interpret them for you and will vouchsafe a good interpretation. This dream of yours is in two different manners, but the interpretation is the same. And God showed you this twice, in two different ways, so that you might be sure and believe that it will come true. And you should be very grateful to our Lord God that He chose to reveal you His secret plans. And I will tell you what I understand, and I will hide nothing. The seven fat cows and the seven ears full of grain that you saw in those visions of yours are seven years that are to come one after another, and they will be very abundant in bread and all the other fruits of the earth. The lean cows and the lean ears that came after them and ate them and consumed them, will be another seven very bad years and of very great famine without measure that will come after those first seven, and will consume all of their abundance. You, sire, should order that a search be made throughout your kingdom for a good man who should be wise and intelligent, and know how to weigh the things that are to come, and make him an overseer, and put him in charge of all the land of Egypt, and have him appoint others beneath him in all the land of Egypt to collect your taxes, so that they will answer to him, and he to you. For the Nile will flood in the seven good years, so that it will water all the land of Egypt in the usual and needful seasons, and the earth will produce so much bread and so many other fruits that there will be no counting or measuring them, and people will have no room to store them, and will give nothing for them, nor want them. And he whom you appoint to be your collector will take from all your kingdom the fifth part of the bread of the seven good years to come; for the people will give it to him very willingly, since they will have no place to put it, and there will be so much that they won't appreciate it. And have your steward store it up in your granaries and cellars for the seven bad years that are to come afterwards. And if you do this, you will ensure that your land will not suffer famine, nor will your people die of it, and you will preserve all Egypt and many other lands by doing great mercy to many; and furthermore, thereby you will save your soul."

XI. Of How King Pharaoh Nicrao Was Pleased with Joseph, and Tested Him in the City He Had Built at the Head of the Nile, and Placed Him in Charge of All His Kingdom, and Married Him to Lady Zulayme, Who Had Been His Mistress

When King Nicrao heard this, he considered how young Joseph was, and marvelled at his sayings, and even more at two things he saw in him: first, the great intelligence he had shown in interpreting the dreams; and second, the good and sensible advice he had given in that matter. And he was well pleased, as were all who were there, the overseers and guardians of the king's house. And the King of Niebla and his *History of Egypt* say that Pharaoh wanted to put Joseph in charge of his house and his kingdom. But it is said that, before placing him in power and giving him the honors we shall mention, as Moses tells in the Bible story, he decided, as a wise prince, to test Joseph's intelligence and knowledge in other ways.

And as a test of this, he then ordered him to build him a town with a very strong and very good castle for one of his daughters, where she could be securely kept. And he showed him the place where he should build it and explained how he wanted it built. And the place was a swamp with papyrus and hay fields and pastures flooded with the water of the Nile, which in that area still overflowed its banks, so that carrying out a construction such as the king wanted would be very difficult. But the water in that place was sweet, and hence the king thought the town would be better and more pleasant. Since the king had so ordered him, Joseph walked over the whole area, and went around it, and saw how the water was spread over all the land, forming lagoons and lakes and ponds in many places, and he examined and studied how he might get the water out of there and make that place dry.

And then he had many canals dug in the places where he saw that the water would most naturally flow. And in the midst of these he had built three large channels into which all the waters from those canals emptied. Once the construction of the canals and the channels was finished, all the waters gathered there and formed a riverbed and flowed together from there on. And the place was drained, as Joseph wanted and needed in order to do the construction.

And that is the place where the Nile first begins to enter a riverbed, and those three great channels into which all the water of the canals empties, each of which forms rivers on its own, are the ones we have heard called Astapus, Astusapes, and Astabores.

When Joseph saw that the place was well drained of water and dry, he gathered all the things he needed and began to do the construction, as the king had commanded, and all the construction was done and completed very quickly. In his *History of Egypt* the King of Niebla says it took Joseph four months to do it, but that seems like little time to build a town and castle, as the king commanded. In this regard the Latin histories say that it is not surprising, because all of Joseph's deeds came from God and were meant to teach us. And there are even some who say that Joseph finished all the work in seventy days, which is even less time.

When Pharaoh found out that the construction was finished, he marveled at how it could have been done so quickly, and he was very pleased that it was finished, and he summoned his ministers and his goodmen and went to see the construction. And when he saw that it had been done well and very quickly, he said to his ministers: "See what a wondrous and good job has been done here in such a difficult location and in so few days. There was work here for a thousand days!" And in Arabic seventy days is "sab'un," and hence the king called the town Alf-yaum, which means "work of seventy days."[25] And since he saw Joseph so sensible, and of such good understanding, and so successful in everything he undertook, he summoned his courtiers and the overseers and managers of his household, and said: "Can we find another man to whom God has given such a keen understanding as this one had of my dreams and the advice he gave me? Besides, I see that he succeeds very well at other things too." Then he said to Joseph: "God showed you everything you said in interpreting my dreams, and He guides you in your actions. It seems to me that I could not find in my kingdom a wiser man than you, nor even your equal. Hence I want you to take charge of my house, and for all the people of my lands to do your bidding and obey your command, and no one in the kingdom will be over you except the sovereign." Then he repeated: "I have made you lord over all the land of Egypt." Then he took the ring from his hand and gave it to him, and he dressed him in silk, which is a costly material, and it is the kind they call "shamet," and he put a golden chain around his neck, for that was the custom among the great men of the time, when one bestowed power on another, as Pharaoh Nicrao did to Joseph. And of the two chariots the king had, he made him ride one.

And the King of Niebla says that he ordered the knights of his guard to ride out with him, and protect him, and accompany him through the town. And they did so, and a crier went before them by the king's command, proclaiming

---

[25] There is obviously some corruption in the manuscript here. "Alf-yaum" (the manuscript has "Alfoym") means "a thousand days," and hence would refer to the king's exclamation, not to the time actually spent on construction.

that all should obey him, and kneel before him, and know that the king made this man governor and viceroy of all Egypt under himself. And after they had gone through the whole town, they returned to the king's palace, and the king said to Joseph before all the people: "I am the king who rules, but I order and command that no one but myself in the whole kingdom be exempt from obeying you, nor do anything but what you order." And then he changed his name, and called him Phaneth in Egyptian, which in our Castilian language means "savior of the world." And the King of Niebla says that he ordered him to sit on the bench Phutiphar had occupied in his lifetime, for the major ministers each had their designated and separate seat in Pharaoh's house. But in this passage that we take here from the King of Niebla, "minister" means "governor of the kingdom," and he appointed him governor in place of Phutiphar, who had been Joseph's master; and he married him to his wife Lady Zulayme. And in Arabic this is the name they give to that lady who was Phutiphar's wife, but we have found that in Egyptian they called her Asenath. And, as Moses recounts in the Bible, she was the daughter of a certain Phutipharis, who was bishop of Heliopolis, which is the city of the sun, where stood the idol whereby the sun gave answers to the gentile peoples, who considered them infallible.

And according to the King of Niebla, one day when Joseph and his wife Lady Zulayme were enjoying themselves, he said to her: "Lady, what we have together now is better than what you wanted before." She replied: "By God, don't blame me, for my husband Phutiphar was no good as a husband, and you heard that before, and you were so handsome and so genteel that every woman who saw you lusted after you. And that's why I spoke to you of love. And you are an educated man, and wise, and a man of good fortune; therefore, I beg you not to bring this up again, nor embarrass me, for I don't consider it good nor courteous." Joseph then replied: "Lady, I only said it because of the pleasure we take in each other now, but what you have said is right and fitting, and I will do as you say henceforth, for I consider myself very fortunate to be married to you."

XII. Of the Accounting of the Time when Joseph Was Placed in Charge of All Egypt, and of the Gentile Kings of That Year

When Joseph was twenty eight years old—and that was two years before he was put in charge of Egypt—Isaac was eighty five, according to Josephus, and a hundred and eighty, according to Moses and Jerome, and he died. And King Appis built that very strong and very good city in that part of Egypt where he reigned. And this Appis was the son of Phoroneus, King of Argos, who, as we mentioned, entrusted the kingdom of Achaia to his brother Egialeus, and great armies accompanied him to Egypt, where he won a land where he reigned. And this city that he populated is the one that we have said he named Mezraym;[26] and it is the same one we call Memphis in Latin. And Memphis is the name of both the city and the kingdom, just as in Spain we say León for both the kingdom and the city.

And Moses recounts—as do Josephus and others who agree with them—that Joseph was thirty years old when King Pharaoh raised him to honor and power, as we have said. And the year that Pharaoh put Joseph in charge of all his kingdom was 3,091 years since Adam; and 659 years since Noah's flood; and 558 years since the languages were divided; and 293 years since Ninus began to reign in Assyria; and 240 years since Abraham; and 185 years since Isaac's birth; and 120 since Jacob's. And Esau was the same age as Jacob. And Joseph was then thirty years old. And at that time Baleus ruled in Assyria, and Messapus in Sicionia, and Appis in Argos, and King Pharaoh Nicrao in Egypt. And know that from now on, we shall keep track of the stories and the other matters by the years of Joseph's rule, which altogether were eighty years from the day he was given power until the day he died, which was the first year of the first bondage of the children of Israel in Egypt, as you will hear later on in its place.

Now we shall leave these matters, and tell the story of Joseph.

XIII. Of How Joseph Converted Pharaoh Nicrao to His Customs, and How He Filled Pharaoh's Granaries with Much Bread, Because the People Didn't Care

Joseph always tried with good sense and good customs both to serve his master faithfully and to keep the law his fathers Abraham, Isaac, and Jacob had kept, as Moses and Josephus and all the others who tell of him stated. And in his *History of Egypt* the King of Niebla says that he always struggled with Pharaoh Nicrao, his master, from the time that he became his most trusted minister, to make him understand his religion and to attract him to it. And he was able to show and explain it to him so well that the king couldn't help thinking about it. And he saw that he said such good and righteous things about his religion and our Lord God that he had to believe what he said, and he considered himself well advised by him, both in this and in other things. And he ceased to believe in his god and the idols, for he saw and understood well from what Joseph told him, and the excellent explanations he gave, that it was all vanity. And

---

[26] This is the Hebrew *Mitzrayim* (Egypt).

he converted to belief in our Lord God, as Joseph believed and taught him, but he kept it secret so that the people wouldn't find out and rise up against him for that reason.

And as soon as Joseph was elevated to the high rank the king had given him, he began traveling through the whole kingdom, and overseeing all the lands and examining locations to decide which would be most appropriate and best for building granaries for the king there, to store up bread, as he had advised the king. Meanwhile, the seven good years came, as he had said, and the waters of the Nile overflowed and irrigated all the land at the seasons when it was needful; and all the fruits of the earth began to grow and abound, and the grain was so plentiful that when they came to harvest it, the piles of sheaves would not fit on the threshing floors where they used to bring the grain. And the abundance of wheat was so great that it was like the sands of the sea, so that there was no man who could measure it. And when the men saw such a great abundance of it, they thought that there would be no place large enough to store it; and even if they kept it and stored it to sell, they wouldn't find anyone to buy it, because there was no one in the whole land—not even the poor— who didn't have as much of it as he wanted. And they took as much of it as they thought they needed for themselves and their relatives and dependents and neighbors, and they left the rest lying on the threshing floors or in the fields, for no one wanted it.

Then Joseph began to travel through the kingdom, and he sent his overseers and collectors of the kingdom that he had appointed beneath him through every land, that they might require from all the peoples a fourth of the bread of that year as the king's share. And since they gathered so much that they had no place to store it, nor knew what to do with it, and they saw that it would be spoiled otherwise, they gave it to him willingly. Then Joseph had built in the cities and towns, in the places where the best bread was found, as he had planned, many warehouses and granaries for the king, and many cellars and other places such as silos outside the towns where they could put it. And these silos built in the wilderness or in the desert—for such places have need of silos and places to store bread—were known later in Egypt, and even now, as those who know that country and come from there say, as "Joseph's granaries." And Joseph ordered it all stored there, that of each land in its place. And when they sowed again and saw that they were going to have as good a year or better than the current one, they were annoyed by the bread they had saved, for they didn't appreciate it at all; and they gave it away, if they could find anyone who wanted it, and if not, they threw it out. And some said that Joseph's collectors, each one through the land where he went, picked up the bread wherever they found it, and stored it along with the fourth that Joseph had commanded them to ask as Pharaoh's portion.

And the Egyptians understood what sort of season they were going to have in the way we will explain here. The Egyptians have no other rains, for it doesn't rain in Egypt, nor is there a season of other precipitation except what comes from the River Nile, which naturally floods in its season every year, as we have already mentioned, and is so powerful that it irrigates the land; but some years more and others less, as it happens. And that's how the Egyptians get whatever fruits and whatever produce they pick from the earth. And when the Nile rises less, that year will be so much the worse; and when it floods more, so much the better; and depending on how much it rises each year, they know what to expect.

[Chapters XIV and XV are a digression dealing with crocodiles, dolphins, and other denizens of the Nile, and have no bearing on the story of Joseph]

XVI. Of What Joseph Did at This Time, and the Children He Had by Lady Zulayme, His Wife

As we have already said, Joseph then had built in the cities, the towns, and even the deserts many warehouses and granaries and other places for the king, and he ordered all the bread stored there, that of each land in its place; and, as Josephus points out, he didn't want to reveal to anyone why he was storing it all up like that.

Meanwhile, during those seven years that were good, Joseph begat two sons by his wife Lady Asenath or Lady Zulayme; and he called the first one Manasseh, which means "God made me forget the suffering I endured in my father's house"; the second one he called Ephraim, which is the same as to say "God gave me success in the land of my poverty."

XVII. Of How Pharaoh Nicrao Mercifully Ordered Bread Sold to All the People, and Changed Joseph's Name

When the good years were past, the bad ones started coming with great famine, as Joseph had told the king, in which, from the time they began, men all through the land suffered badly, as Josephus recounts. And because they hadn't bothered to store up bread—thinking that that plenty would last forever, not realizing that the times, and the things pertaining to them, always change and never remain in one state—lamenting the condition they were now in, they all hastened to the king's gates to implore his mercy, and beg him to command that they be given something to eat. The king said to them: "Go to Joseph, and do as he tells you, for he will satisfy you." And they did so, but Joseph didn't want to do anything without first informing the king. And when the king saw how his people and many foreigners who came from other lands were suffering very greatly and dying of hunger, he pitied them, for Joseph had made him compassionate, in keeping with the customs to which he had converted him. And he ordered Joseph to take measures to keep those people from perishing like that.

And from then on Joseph sold them all the wheat they needed, not only to those of the kingdom but to all the foreigners who came to buy, for they were all gentiles anyway. And Joseph did this gladly because his master had ordered him to, but also because, like the king, he felt great compassion for those whom he saw dying. And, according to Josephus, when the king saw that the seven good years had come, and were being followed by seven bad ones, and found that Joseph had given a true interpretation of his dreams, and saw him conduct himself so wisely and well and loyally in everything he did, and how exactly he understood and prophesied the things that were to come, he called him in his language Psomthaphanicos, which in our Castilian language means "revealer of hidden things that other men know not." And since they understood in their language what that meant, and they were all very pleased with Joseph, they called him that from then on.

When the years of famine began, the kings we mentioned in the earlier chapter were reigning in Assyria and in Sithionia and in Argos, and King Pharaoh Nicrao in Egypt.

XVIII. Of How Joseph's Brothers Came to Egypt for Bread, and They Didn't Recognize Him, But He Recognized Them and Had a Conversation with Them

These bad years came not only to Egypt nor its borders round about, but reached the land of Shem and many others. And the famine waxed great in Canaan, and the rumor began to spread through the land that there was plenty of bread in Egypt. And Jacob was then dwelling in the land of Canaan, and he called his sons, and said unto them: "I have heard that in Egypt they have much bread stored up from the good years that have gone by, and that they are selling it. Why don't you go there? Take provisions and what you need for the road and go down to Egypt, and if you find it for sale, buy us thence what we need, lest we perish of hunger. And let Benjamin, who is still small and could not endure the suffering of such a long journey, remain with me. For if he went, he would become exhausted or ill, or peradventure some other bad thing would befall him, which would cause you much trouble and be a hindrance to your journey, and you might have to leave him somewhere on the way. Go there, all the rest of you." The sons did as their father commanded, for they were in great distress because of the famine that was in the land. And they took what they needed for the road, and went with many others from that land who were likewise going there to buy bread, for everyone in Canaan lacked bread, and many were already dying of hunger.

And from the time they reached Egypt, they found that no bread whatsoever was being sold anywhere in all the land except by Joseph's command. So they had to go to him, and when they arrived, they bowed down as if in adoration. And Josephus says that they didn't realize that he was their brother Joseph, because when they sold him, he was little, and now he was grown, and also because a young man's face is often quite different from the face he had as a child. Furthermore, seeing that he was so powerful, they could hardly have believed that Joseph could have won such great power and honor as that, considering the way he he was brought to Egypt, the fact that he was in an alien land, and that so little time had gone by. Nor did they recognize him by his name, for the king had taken away his proper name of Joseph and given him those other names that we have mentioned: Psomthaphanicos when he interpreted his dreams, and Phanech when he advised him, and al-'Aziz when he appointed him governor. And these were the names by which he was called in Egypt. Hence, for all of these reasons, his brothers were unable to recognize Joseph. And then they bowed down unto him and adored him as if he were God, and began to beg him and petition that he grant them the favor of ordering bread sold to them.

And although they didn't recognize him, he knew them at once. For although he had been a child when they sold him, and hadn't seen them for many days, ever since Joseph was a little child, he had had a very good memory. And even though he knew them, he didn't want to reveal himself to them nor speak to them in the language of Canaan, because they would understand him, and peradventure recognize him, and be on their guard against him. So then he had a man who could understand them come, and he ordered him to translate his words to them, and theirs to him, and to ask them roughly, as if they were strangers, who they were, and where and from what land they came. They answered him: "We are from the land of Canaan, and we come thence, and our land is very short of food these days, and above all, bread; and it has been like this for a long time, and the famine is still increasing very much in these bad years we are in. And we have heard that there was much bread here in Egypt, and we have come here, as we see many others have done, to buy it."

Then Joseph recalled the dreams he dreamed in his father's house, and how Jacob had told them to his mother and his brothers. And he ordered the translator to tell them that they were spies of some powerful king or prince, and had come to examine the land and discover the weakest places in it whereby they might invade it. They answered Joseph: "Sir, we have come here to buy bread, just as we have told you, and we are men of peace, and your servants, and at your mercy, and we have not come here to do harm to anyone. And we are all brothers, and sons of one father, and he is a good man, and raises cattle, and works the land with us. And that is why we have come." When Joseph heard these words from them, he wanted to know still more, in their own words, what was their state of mind. And though he didn't answer them in their own tongue, he understood them very well, for he had been brought up in that language in his father's house with them, and he hadn't forgotten it, for he was a man of good memory. And he ordered the translator to reply in this way to the words they had said, as Josephus tells: "Nay, it is not as you say. You have not come to buy bread nor for anything of that sort, nor are you men of peace as you say, but you are spies of some king or powerful prince, as I said before; and you have come to scout out and discover the weaknesses of this land so that the one who sent you can invade and seize it. And you go about seeking damage and harm to our lord the king and his peoples. You say that you are all brothers, sons of one father, but I don't believe you. Rather, I think you have come from many places, and you say you are brothers to excuse yourselves and cover up what you are really doing. Nor can I believe that a farmer would bring up his sons in such a genteel manner as you appear to have been brought up." And furthermore he said to them: "Even kings, who are more honorable than other men, could hardly have such a genteel group of sons." And Joseph talked about their father, and said that a man such as they described, a shepherd and farmer, would not have such sons. And Joseph said this in order to find out whether his father was still alive and how he was. And another reason why he told them they were not brothers was in the hope that they would say how many of them there were altogether, and mention Benjamin, who was Joseph's brother by father and mother, whom he loved very much and longed to see. For he thought that because of their wickedness and jealousy, peradventure they had done some harm unto him, as they had done Joseph himself. But they were so frightened, and so worried that they were in danger of dying, that it didn't occur to them to mention Benjamin. And as they all stood around, they answered Joseph's questions. Then Reuben, who was the eldest of them all, began to speak, and the others fell silent, for among brothers and other relatives, the younger are very obedient to the elder and are ruled by them. And he answered everything Joseph said as follows.

XIX. Of the Words Reuben Spoke for Himself and His Brothers, and of Joseph's Words to Reuben and His Brothers

"You say that we are spies, and have come to scout out the land, and seek to harm the king and his peoples. We do not do so, for we would not want to harm your peoples nor interfere with your king in any way; nor are we your enemies. But we need salvation, and advice, and succor in the distress and the great scarcity that now exists throughout our land. And we heard of your courtesy, and of the kindness with which you have gone to the aid not only of those of your own land but even of strangers and pilgrims come from afar. You have made a wheat market so that all those in need might come to it, and you have saved them from dying of hunger.

You also said that we are not brothers, but we are, as is evident in our facial resemblance and the similarity in the shape of our bodies, which differ very little from each other, nor are we very unlike each other. You also said that we are not sons of one father, and that such a man would not have sons like us, but we are all sons of one father, and he is a Hebrew man, and his name is Jacob. And we were twelve brothers, and he begat us by four wives whose names were these: first was Rachel, whom he loved more than the others; next was Leah—and these two were sisters, daughters of Laban, our father Jacob's uncle—; after that came Bilhah, Rachel's maid; and fourth was Zilpah, Leah's maid. By Leah he had these six sons: Reuben, Simeon, Levi, Judah, Issachar, and Zebulun, and a daughter named Dinah. By Bilhah, Rachel's maid, he begat Gad and Asher.[27] By Rachel he had Joseph and Benjamin. And I am telling you about us now in this manner because we were all born one after another, in the order I have mentioned. And of these brothers, ten of us are here now. And Benjamin, who is the youngest of us all, because he was little and couldn't bear the travail of the journey, nor would it be suitable, our father didn't want him to go such a long way, lest he fall ill or have some misfortune that would hinder us in our travels, and he stayed at home. And the other brother, whose name was Joseph, is no longer living. When all twelve of us were alive, we were rich and wealthy, and things were going very well for us; but ever since our brother Joseph died, things have gone from bad to worse; for our father, since he lost that son, has never stopped grieving and weeping for him; and we too—both out of sorrow for the brother we lost and because of our father's grief

---

[27] The copyist seems to have deleted a line here. The children of Bilhah were actually Dan and Naphtali; Gad and Asher were Zilpah's sons.

and sadness—have fared badly, and our hearts have been broken. And sir, you can find out that all these things are true, as we have told you, by sending to our house to inquire."

And with all these words Reuben did his best to convince Joseph, and thereby to mollify him, and to quell his anger, and to stop him from thinking all those things he had said about them; for it seemed to him that Joseph had changed his attitude toward them. Joseph was very happy in his heart because of all he had seen of his brothers, which he would never have imagined. And when he heard that Jacob, his father, and Benjamin, his brother, whom he loved very much and longed to see, were alive, he was very happy in his heart, as we have said, but he didn't reveal it to his brothers. And he said to them: "This is what I say: you didn't say these things you're saying now to me at first. And I know very well that you are spies from the fact that you have changed your story, but I swear by Pharaoh's health that I shall test you in this, and you shall not leave my custody until you bring me that youngest brother you mentioned who stayed at home with your father. And send one of you for him, and bring him, and the others will stay here with me until we find out the truth."

And as soon as they heard these words, he ordered them thrown in jail, and they stayed there three days and three nights. On the third day he ordered them taken out and brought them before him, and said to them: "Do as I told you if you want to live." And Josephus says at this point that they, fearing that things would get even worse, were very sad before Joseph; and they thought that God sent them all the pain and misfortune they were suffering in revenge for their having sold their brother Joseph. And Reuben, who was the eldest, began to upbraid them—although his words could no longer be of any use to Joseph—and said to them: "Brothers, I told you, and advised you, and begged you not to kill your brother when you wanted to, and you didn't want to stop on my account, and I said that God would not let such treachery and such a wicked deed as that occur without avenging it. But you refused to believe me nor to stop on my account, nor because of all the good reasons I told you. And you thought that because you were doing that thing on a mountain, neither God nor man would see you, but I told you that God sees on the mountain and everywhere." Then they began to discuss the matter among themselves, confident that Joseph wouldn't understand them, because he was speaking to them through a translator. And the words of their brother Reuben made them all feel very guilty, and they hung their heads down toward the ground, since they were well aware of what they had done. And each of them began to sob, and they wept grievously, and said: "God is very just, and justly has He done this to us."

XX. Of How Joseph Took Pity on His Brothers, and Sent Them Home With the Grain and the Price of It; and They Asked Their Father for Benjamin, But He Said He Wouldn't Give Him to Them

When Joseph saw his brothers so distressed and weeping like that, he felt a great sorrow in his heart, and he couldn't help weeping, but he controlled himself as well as he could. But in the end he absolutely couldn't bear it, and his eyes filled with tears; and so that his brothers should not know, he went aside from them and wept. Then he cleansed his face of the tears, and returned to them, and said: "I am a God-fearing man, and I do this only to find out if you are telling me the truth, but I want to treat you better. If you are men of peace, as you said, let one of you stay as a hostage, and the rest of you go and take your father and his house the bread that you bought, and bring me your little brother to prove to me that you are telling the truth, and you shall not die." And with the anguish they then felt about their fate, they agreed to do as he told them. And he took Simeon and tied him up well before them. Then he ordered his men to fill their sacks with wheat, and he secretly admonished them to take the money and put that of each one in his load with the wheat, and to do it in such a way that they would not find out; and in addition to this, that they should give them provisions for the journey. And the men did as Joseph commanded them.

They loaded their bread on their beasts and went their way. And when they were on the road, one of them went aside and opened his sack to give food to his beast that he was riding. And when he looked inside, he saw in the mouth of the sack the money that he had given for the grain. And he returned to his brothers and said: "Do you not know? I found in my sack the money that I paid for the bread, and there it is." And they were frightened and said one another: "What is the meaning of this that God has done us?" And they continued their journey.

And as soon as they reached their father in Canaan, and he came out to receive them, he didn't see Simeon coming with them, and he said: "Where did you leave my son Simeon?" Then they began to recount what had happened to them in Egypt, and they said to him: "Father, the lord of the land spoke to us very angrily and said that we were spies of a king or of some great man, and we had come there to find out the weak places where one could go in and capture that land. And we told him that we were twelve brothers, all sons of one father, and that now we were eleven; and of these eleven, the youngest of all had stayed with you, and we ten were there, and the other one was dead. He thought we were lying to him, and refused to believe us, and detained us until we negotiated with him to leave one of us in his prison as a hostage, and the rest of us would come back and bring the bread, and then take Benjamin, who remained with you, to him; for he had a great desire to see him. And Simeon stayed with him, and after we did that, they sold us bread, and they also gave us everything we needed. For up to then, they wouldn't let us buy anything, nor did they want to sell it to us."

And when they had told their father all of this, they opened their sacks to empty out the wheat, and they found at the top of each one all the money they had paid for it. When Jacob saw that they were bringing back money they paid for the bread, and heard how they had negotiated over his son Benjamin, he was very distressed by that, and especially at their finding the price of the bread in their sacks, and he said to them: "You have left me without sons. Joseph is dead, Simeon is in jail; if you take Benjamin from me and something befalls him, all these ills come upon me." Reuben answered: "Father, give us Benjamin. Have no fear, for we will bring him back to you. I have two sons. If I don't bring him back, I will give them to you that you may kill them. Hand him over to me, and I will bring him back." Jacob said: "My son Benjamin will not go with you, for his brother Joseph is dead, and he alone is left of his mother, and if anything bad should befall him in the land of Egypt, you would bring my grey head down to hell in my old age with much grief."

XXI. Of How Jacob Gave In, and Gave Benjamin to His Brothers, and They Went to Joseph with Him, and He Received Them Very Well, and What He Did with Them after That

Jacob's sons begged him to give them Benjamin, as we have told you, so that they could keep their promise to Joseph, but they couldn't convince him. Then the famine increased fiercely, and there was great distress throughout the land. And once Jacob and his sons had eaten what they had brought before, their father at last said to them: "Sons, return to Egypt, and bring us something to eat." Then Judah replied and said to him: "Father, that powerful man of Egypt who gave us the bread this time told us thus: 'Bring me your brother, the youngest of you all. Otherwise, I swear to you that you shall not see my face, even if you come back here.' Now if you want us to go there, send Benjamin with us, and we will all go together and buy what we have need of; and God will grant that we all come back together. And, father, if you don't want to do this, we will not go there, for we would not dare appear before that potentate of Egypt, for he told us just as we have oft repeated to you—that even if we came back there, we should not see his face unless we brought him Benjamin, our youngest brother, whom he wants to see."

The father replied to Judah and the other sons: "You let that Egyptian governor and potentate know that you had another brother younger than you for no other reason than to bring me great misery." They answered him then: "Father, we told you truthfully that we would not have done it except that the man asked all about our affairs, and we answered him, and he asked us about our family, whether we had a father or any other brothers, and if so, whether they were still alive. And we answered what he asked straight away. We dared not do otherwise, for he had us under arrest. And we told him that we had a father and another brother younger than all the rest, and we told him the names, for we had no idea that he would have any reason to want us to bring him to him."

And Judah, who was a bold man in other things—as he would demonstrate later when he[28] entered the pathway through the Red Sea sooner than his brothers, as Josephus says and we shall discuss further on—dared then to confront Jacob and said to him: "Father, you should not fear for our brother, nor suspect us of wishing him any harm, for none of us would want to do anything to him. Besides, if it is fated that some harm must befall him, it would happen even if he were here with you. And if we wished to do him any harm, we would not tell you or anyone else so clearly. And for failing to take this lad with us to Egypt, we should not for no reason lose the chance to buy the food that they promised to sell us in abundance, since there is plenty of it in Pharaoh's land, if we take this boy with us. And likewise, father, you should be concerned about Simeon's survival, lest he perish because you failed to send Benjamin there. And above all of this, you should believe and trust that God will take care of this child, and give him to us, and we will go and bring food for us and for our little children, and they and we will not die for this reason. And if you will give him to me, I will take it upon myself, and you can hold me responsible, that if I bring him not back to you afterwards, I will be guilty of committing such a great crime against you that you should never forgive me. And if you hadn't delayed us with this scruple, we should already have gone and come back."

Then Jacob, partly because of Judah's good and forceful arguments and partly because of his distress over the great hunger in which he saw his people, said: "Sons, if it be so needful, take him, and do as you wish, and take the most noble things and the best spices that are in this land and are not in that land. And take them to him, and double the money that you found in your sacks, for it must have been by mistake that you brought it, and return it to the one who sold you the bread, so that he have nothing to say to us if that is how it hap-

---

[28] That is, the tribe of Judah, his descendants.

pened. And you will give the spices I order you to take to that potentate of the king of Egypt, and take your brother Benjamin, and go to him. And may our Lord, who is All Powerful, make him well pleased with you, and meek, and temperate, and may you find him in a good humor, and may he give you your brother whom he has in prison, and Benjamin whom you are taking, and let them come back with you, for I am as if bereft of sons until you return."

After Israel and his sons had spoken the words we have recounted, the sons took those gifts their father sent, and their money, and Benjamin their brother, and set out for Egypt. And when they had to part from their father, and were bidding him farewell, they all began to weep mightily, as Josephus tells, fearing that never again would they be together as then, and this fear endured until at last they did find themselves back together, as you will hear later. So they bade each other farewell, and the father was left alone, and the sons went away.

And when they reached Joseph, and he saw Benjamin with them, he was very happy and very delighted in his heart, and he called his steward and said to him: "Take these men in the house, and prepare us a great feast with many meats, for they will all be my guests, and will dine with me today." The steward did as his master ordered. And they were sore afraid, and said to themselves, one to another: "They have brought us here on account of the price of the food that we took away in our sacks last time, and the lord means to slander us, and say that we stole it, and use that as a ruse to to make us his servants." And Joseph's steward was standing by the door—and he was the one who had meted out the bread to them and put their money in their sacks—and they went up to him, and said to him: "Sir, we beg you to hear us. The other time when we came here to buy wheat and returned to our land and opened the sacks we were carrying full of wheat, we found in them the money we had paid for it. We are informing you of this. Take back the money. We have brought more money with which to buy what we need. And we insist that we don't know who put the money in our sacks, nor were we in any way guilty of that, but we will do whatever you think best and command." The steward replied: "Friends, be calm and have no fear. Your God and the God of your father gave you that money, and put it in your sacks, for I still have the money you gave me for the grain you bought." Then he went, by Joseph's orders, and took Simeon out of prison and brought him to them, and led them all once again inside his house, and brought them water to wash their feet, and gave food to their animals.

While all this was going on, Joseph was in the palace with the king. When they heard that they were going to eat there, and while he was at court, they took out the gifts they had brought to give him, and arranged them as well and attractively as they could, so that they would look good. And when

Joseph returned from the king's house, it was already midday. They took their presents in their hands and went up to him, and knelt before him, and prostrated themselves to the ground before him, and adored him, and presented him the things they had brought. Then he said very kindly: "God save you." And he asked them: "Is your father, the old man of whom you spoke to me, still alive?" They answered him: "He is alive, and is yours to command." And they bowed down again before him, and adored him as men adore God. Then Joseph raised his eyes and looked at Benjamin, who was his brother by father and mother, and said to them: "Is this the brother you told me about?" They answered him: "Yes, sir." Then he said to Benjamin: "Son, may God show you goodness and mercy." And his heart was moved because of his brother, and his eyes filled up with water, and he arose, and went into his chamber, and threw himself upon his bed and wept. Then he washed the tears from his face, so that he would not appear to have wept, and went back to them, and ordered the tables set.

His own table was set apart from theirs, as befitting a man of a different religion and an alien land; and there was a table for the Egyptians, who ate beside him as natives of the place; and a separate table for his brothers, as newcomers. For the Egyptians then considered it illegal and wrong to eat with Jews, who were not of their religion. And Joseph set each group a table of their own. And he said to his brothers: "You will be here before me on your side, for these Egyptians don't want to sit down at the same table with Hebrews, for they say it is against their law, and they consider it a great sin." And then he ordered them to sit down as they were accustomed to do in their father's house: the eldest first and in a higher seat than all the rest, and then the others, each one in the order in which they were born. And they gave them food, and he ordered a double portion of all the dishes and of everything that was served set before Benjamin, according to Josephus. But Moses says in the Bible that they gave him five times as much. And Master Peter comments on this, and says that peradventure Moses said this because there were five different courses, and they gave him an extra portion of each one; and thus the sayings of Moses and Josephus are not contradictory. And Joseph did this in order to honor him, because he loved him more than the others. And although he was very polite, and had exquisite table manners, and ordered each one given whatever he needed, they all marvelled at the preference and honor he showed Benjamin. And they all ate as much as they wanted and needed with Joseph until they were drunk, according to Moses. But Master Peter comments on Moses' words "until they were drunk," saying that when the Jews said "get drunk," they only meant to eat and drink in great abundance, as much as each one wanted.

XXII. Of How They Put Joseph's Cup in Benjamin's Sack, and Benjamin Was Arrested for That, and His Brothers Tried to Get Him Out of Prison

Josephus says that after these sons of Jacob had eaten and drunk, Joseph's servants took them to the chamber, and made up beds for them, and they lay down to sleep. And as they were sleeping, Moses says that Joseph summoned his steward and said to him: "Go and take these men's sacks, and fill them with as much wheat as will fit in them, and put as much money as the wheat is worth in each of their sacks, and take my silver cup in which I drink, and put it in the sack of the youngest." And the steward did everything as his master commanded him, and the young men knew nothing of this.

The next morning they got up, and loaded their animals, and left with great rejoicing, as Josephus recounts, because they were taking Simeon and Benjamin, whom they were to take back to their father, as we mentioned they had promised him. But Joseph arranged matters in the way you shall hear. As they were leaving the city, as soon as they had traveled a certain distance, Joseph summoned that steward of his who had given them their wheat and put the cup in Benjamin's sack, and ordered him to go with a company of armed men on horseback, and said to him: "Go after those men as quickly as you can, and arrest them." And he instructed him concerning everything he should say and do unto them. The steward went after them, as Joseph had commanded. And when they saw that company coming so swiftly after them, they wondered what it could mean, and they were very frightened. And as Joseph's men caught up with them, they began to insult them and mistreat them, and arrested them.

And the steward said to them: "What sort of men are you, who return evil for good? You stole my lord's cup in which he drank, and in which he saw the things that are to come. You did a bad deed." And the steward angrily spoke these and other words unto them. And they replied: "Sir, why do you accuse us of committing such a wicked deed? We gave you back the money that we found in our sacks in the land of Canaan, which nobody knew about. Why then should we steal gold or silver from your master's house, much less his cup?" According to Josephus, they thought the steward's words were insane, and so vehemently did they insist that they hadn't done what they were accused of, and so certain were they of their innocence—for they knew nothing of the trick that was being played on them—that they said forcefully: "Search us all, and if you find what you are looking for on any of us, let that man die, and the rest of us will become your master's servants." The steward said to them: "Let it be as you have judged. But I would deal more kindly with you; let him on whom I find it become a servant, and the rest of you may go merrily on your way." Then they unloaded their saddlebags, and each one opened his sack. The steward searched them, going from the eldest to the youngest, and he found the cup in the sack of Benjamin, who was the youngest.

When they saw that, they considered themselves dead men. And they began to weep grievously, and rend their garments, and make a great mourning—first of all, for Benjamin their brother, for they were very much afraid that they would execute him for the theft; and then because they would not be able to return him to their father, as they had promised, and he would be so grief-stricken that he would die. And they re-loaded, and went back to the city with their brother who had been arrested. And Judah had not yet left the town when they got back there. And he came out and met them on the road, and they went back weeping. And he went in with them unto Joseph, and they knelt and prostrated themselves on the ground before him.

Then Joseph noticed how concerned they were about Benjamin, and he saw them all crushed and grieved on his account, and he said to them: "It was wicked of you to pay no heed to my kindness and courtesy toward you, nor to remember that nothing is hidden from God. You dared do evil to the stranger who did you good; and you thought I didn't know; and you know not that in all the land there is no man who understands the things that are to be as well as I." They answered him: "Sir, what shall we say, or what excuse can we give, except to say that we are all your servants, since you have caught us in the theft? Give us any punishment you like, but do not harm Benjamin." Joseph, rejoicing in his heart over what he had heard them say, said: "God forbid that I should do such a thing! I want the one who was caught in the theft of the cup to stay here as my servant; for it is not right that the innocent should suffer for the guilty. The rest of you, go your way, and may good luck attend you, and return to your father. I will have you guided through Egypt so that you may have a safe journey." When they heard that Benjamin would remain there, they were all very dismayed, even though they had been found innocent. And from the great pain they felt, they grew silent and could not speak. And then they remembered Joseph, and they said to each other that he was more fortunate than they, if he was dead, for he had departed the misery and sadness of this life. Whenever they thought about that, Reuben always blamed them severely, and spoke ill of them, and reminded them that he had warned them that they were doing evil, but they had refused to believe him nor to stop what they were doing on his account.

While they were in such great anxiety, Judah, who had persuaded his father that Benjamin should come with them, was the only one of the brothers to stand up. And just as he was bold in other things, so he dared endanger himself to save Benjamin from death and prison. And he approached Joseph, and said to him forcefully but politely: "Sir, I would speak with you privately, if it please you. Hear me, and be so kind as not to get angry with me, for I am your servant, and you are my master from Pharaoh down." And then Joseph went aside with him, and Judah began to speak with him, and said, according to Josephus: "We have committed an imprudent act against you, which should not go unpunished. But it is your judgment that those of us who are not guilty should not suffer for it, but only the one who was caught in the theft. And they found your cup in the sack of Benjamin, our youngest brother. Hence we are very much afraid that you will order some harm done to him, and we would despair of his life if we did not trust in your great kindness, and this is a great comfort to us. Now, sir, regard not our ill advised deeds, but your kindness and reputation for good nature. Besides, sir, we insist that we did not commit this theft, nor was it done with our knowledge. We don't know whether it actually happened or not; but even if we did know, and wanted to say something about it, it wouldn't make any difference to you or your men. Above all, sir, you are very strong in goodness. Be not overcome by anger nor destroy us, for in you is our only salvation, now just as when you first sold us plenty of bread and food that we might not perish in these bad years of famine—we and our wives and our little children. Save us, whom you gave life, and in your kindness free from death the souls of those whom you did not suffer to die of hunger. And I firmly believe that God brought these bad years in our time so that we might have a reason to come to you in this place, and see how you protected us from death that we might not perish in bad years, and we might know your goodness. And now God has let us fall into this error against you so that you might pardon us, and thus He might show us how great was your mercy and goodness in everything, and make us know it. And in this regard, sir, if it be considered goodness in the powerful to forgive small wrongs, how much greater honor does he earn when he forgives great ones! And the greater the error of the wrongdoer, so much greater is the praise of the man who pardons him, for so much more is he like God, who pardons very great sins to those who repent, and even more so to those who peradventure are not guilty of a deed.

Furthermore, sir, the other time we came unto you, you asked us our business, and you asked whether we had a father or any other brother. And we answered that we have a father, and that we had left him alive, and a little brother with him; and that he had only that one child by the woman whose son he was, for another he had by her was no longer living; and that our father loved the one who stayed behind more than all the rest of us, because he is the youngest, and he begat him in his old age. And then you ordered us to bring that child so that you could see him. And we told you that his father would die of loneliness and longing for him if he left him, and that peradventure he would be unwilling to give him to us. And you were unhappy about that, as we understood, for you answered us then that if he didn't come back with us, we would not see your face. And we went away sadly when we heard you say those words. We returned to our father, and we told him all that you had said to us, and what had happened to us in this land, and he was deeply grieved about it. And there was no way to persuade him to hand over the child that he might come with us, except when we had eaten the bread we took, and he saw us in danger of dying because of the famine which waxed greater every day. And then he ordered us to come back for more, but we told him that we wouldn't dare come back here unless the child came with us. Then he answered us like this, to excuse himself for not giving him to us: 'You well know that I had but two sons by my wife Rachel, whom I loved very much. You were with the cattle in the wilderness grazing lands, and because I hadn't known nor heard anything from you for days, I sent one of those sons to you where you were wandering with the cattle—he was the older one—so that he might see you and find out your news, and come back and tell me how you were doing. And he went, and then he didn't come back or appear, and you came and brought me his torn and bloody garment, and you told me that a wild beast had eaten him. And if you take this one from me, I will soon die from worry and grief over him.' And, sir, you know that we have told you most of this before. And now, if I return to my father, your servant, and he doesn't see the child he loves as much as his own heart coming with me, he will die. And if this should happen to him on our account, I would never get over it, because I took this child as my responsibility, and I promised my father that I would return him to him, and if not, that I should always bear that guilt before him. And we are all ready and willing to suffer whatever punishment you wish to give us, provided that Benjamin be saved. And we all kiss the earth before your feet, and beg you mercifully to hear us and receive our petition."

When Judah had spoken these words, he bent his knees and prostrated himself on the ground before him, and said again: "Sir, I am your servant, and if you want to punish this deed, and take revenge for it, take me, and order all the punishments you like done unto me; but be so kind as to release Benjamin so that he may go with his brothers to his father, that his father not perish on his account. Unless he goes, I shall never return nor stand before my father to see him die of this pain. For all of us—both we and our father—are still grieving over the loss of the other one, and every day our grief over him weighs more heavily on our hearts, and our longing for him; and we are comfortless, and want to perish because of him. Sir, have pity on our father and on us. As I have just said, this is the great man's great honor: to forgive a great mistake and thereby be like God, Who does likewise, and thence to win grace and honor." When the other brothers who were waiting outside saw Judah lying before

Joseph's feet, they all went running and did the same thing, and said that they would be his servants or would gladly die for love of Benjamin, and to secure his release, that he might return safe and sound to his father.

XXIII. Of How Joseph Revealed Himself to His Brothers, and King Pharaoh Heard of It; and Then They Sent for Their Father Jacob

When Joseph saw his brothers' state of mind, he felt a great sorrow in his heart, and he couldn't go on any longer without revealing himself to them. And he ordered the others who were in that palace to leave them, because he wanted to speak privately with those foreign men. And when the others had gone outside, and he saw himself alone with his brothers, he began to weep mightily. And so great was the force of his weeping that it tightened its grip on his heart so that he could not speak to them in a low voice. And he raised his voice, so that those who had left the house and gone outside, and even those in Pharaoh's house, heard his cries, so loudly did he shout. And he said to them: "I am Joseph, your brother. My father Jacob is still alive!" When the brothers heard this, they were so frightened and terrified that they couldn't answer him. Then he said to them, now softly and piti-fully: "Come here to me." And when they came up to him, he repeated in an even softer voice, so as not to embarrass them if strangers heard: "I am your brother Joseph, he whom you sold to the Ishmaelite merchants who were going to Egypt. But fear not nor afflict yourselves because of that, nor because I am in this land. For I believe that that deed happened more because of God's will than your wickedness. And for that reason God will do you much good and much mercy now and later, and for your good God sent me to Egypt before you, and made me here like Pharaoh's father, and lord of his house and prince of all the land of Egypt. And I put you through all the reversals and travails you have experienced here only to see what you would do for Ben-jamin, your brother. But now I will behave differently toward you, for I see how well intentioned you are, and how you were ready to submit to slavery and even death for him, and even said that you grieved for me and missed me. And you lamented not having me, and not knowing what became of me, and I believe you. Likewise, because I've learned from you that my father is safe and sound.

Whatsoever you did unto me, and whatsoever bad feelings I harbored toward you because of that, henceforth I forgive you. Be not ashamed on my account, nor sad nor sorry, for it has come to what you now see. And now, go back, and do not tarry, and go to your father, so that no ill befall him, and peradventure he die not with worry and grief over your tarrying; but that instead, he come unto me; for otherwise, I should be so aggrieved that I would account all my good fortune as nothing. But go quickly, as I say, and tell him how I, his son Joseph, send him word that God did me much good and much mercy, and I am lord over all Egypt; and that he should come to me at once, before he dies, if only to fulfill the longing we have felt for one another, and receive much service from me, as a good father from his son. And he and you, his children and his grandchildren, will all live with me. And you will dwell in Goshen,[29] which is a very good land that I will obtain for you from the king. Your sheep, and your cows, and whatever else you own—bring it all with you, for I will advise you about everything and any need you may have. And know, and say unto my father, that of the seven bad years of famine that were to be, two are past and no more, and five more are yet to come. And make him come unto me with his tribe and all his household, and you come with him, with your tribes, with whatever you have, that you perish not in these bad years, for they are many. And you and Benjamin, my brother, can well see that everything I tell you about the power I hold is the truth."

After he had spoken these words, Joseph and Benjamin embraced, and both wept with joy at seeing each other. Then Joseph kissed all his other brothers, and likewise wept with them. And from then on they dared treat him as a brother. But Josephus says that they wept and their hearts were very sad, worrying about what had happened to him when they sold him, and they were very depressed on that account. And though it pleased them much, they were at the same time very embarrassed by their brother's kindness and good will toward them. Then they sat down to eat.

XXIV. Of How King Pharaoh Learned That Joseph's Brothers Had Come, and Rejoiced Greatly, and Sent for Them, and What He Said

Meanwhile, the news spread throughout the palace, and they told King Nicrao how Joseph's brothers had come. And the king was very happy about that, and so was all his retinue, but the king more than the others, because he loved Joseph more. And he ordered Joseph summoned, and he said to him: "I've heard that your brothers have come to you." Joseph replied: "Sire, they have come." The king said: "Their coming pleases me very much, and I would be very happy if your father came here, for I have heard that he is still alive.

[29] The manuscript has "Jersen."

Let them take everything they need, and go for him. And let them tell him to come here with all his household, and I will give them the best land they choose in all my kingdom to dwell in and populate, and they will have a great share in the goods of Egypt and the riches that are there." Joseph was very pleased with the promise his master had made regarding his father and his household. And he told it unto his brothers, and gave them plenty of gold and silver and everything they needed for their journey, and wagons from that land in which to bring their wives, and their little children, and the furniture of their houses, for thus the king had commanded him. In addition he ordered each one given two pairs of long, great garments, made in the Egyptian style. And he gave Benjamin three hundred silver dinars, and five of those very good garments, which were even better than those of his brothers, and he sent an equal amount with him to his father. And he ordered them to load twenty animals: ten of them with Egyptian products, and the best things to be found in all the land; and the other ten with wheat and barley. And when they were thus prepared, he let them go.

And as they began leaving, Joseph instructed them about what they should do, saying: "Go in peace and great harmony, and do not envy one another, observing peradventure that I have given more of my gifts to one of you than to any of the others; for you will come back, and, God willing, I will take care of all of you in such a way that you will be well pleased. And do not get angry at one another, so that you would fight during the journey." They heeded him, and considered their brother's advice very good. And they were happy with what he gave each one of them, and with what he sent their father, and they were very pleased that he gave Benjamin more than he gave them.

XXV. Of How These Sons of Jacob Left Egypt and Went to the Land of Canaan, and Told Their Father Everything Joseph Had Said to Them

They all left Egypt and went on their way, always in great harmony, and they came to the land of Canaan, where their father was, and they told him all these things. And they said to him: "Father, your son Joseph is alive, and he is lord over all Egypt." When Jacob heard this, he was filled with such great joy, and considered it such a wonder—if it was true—that he was like one who awakens from a nightmare, and can't believe it. When they saw that he doubted, they began to tell him all the things they had been through with him, and they showed him the wagons they were bringing, and the other things that Joseph sent, and they presented them to him as Joseph had commanded, and they all stood before him.

XXVI. Of How Jacob Came to His Senses, and Believed That His Son Joseph Was Truly Alive, and Acknowledged the Truth of Everything His Sons Told Him about This Matter

The father, when he saw all this, at last came to his senses, and his heart revived. And when he realized that his son Joseph, for whom he had lived in weeping for such a long time, was truly alive, and how well things had gone for him with King Pharaoh, and how because of his knowledge and his sense he governed all of Egypt, he thenceforth believed everything his sons told him. And he began to believe in the great deeds of God, and in His wonders and in His Providence. And he said: "From today forward, I care not what may come to me of bad nor of good, as long as my son Joseph is alive, for that suffices me. I want to go to him before I die, and see him, and bless him with you, my sons."

Here Begins the Ninth Book of the General History

This ninth book speaks of how Jacob went into Egypt with all his sons and his household and with all their belongings, to see Joseph, his son, and his grandsons, Joseph's sons, whom he had begotten there and who were with him. And likewise, of how Jacob went to see King Pharaoh Nicrao, and that Pharaoh received him well, and asked him his age, and gave him as an inheritance Goshen and Raamses, and Jacob dwelt there with his people; and of how Jacob's eyes grew dim, for he was old, and he blessed both of Joseph's sons with his hands crossed, and blessed them afterwards, mentioning each one by name; and about Jacob's prophecies to his sons; and of Jacob's death, and how his sons took him and buried him in Ephron; and of Joseph's death and his burial; and of Jacob's other sons, what became of them during Joseph's life and afterwards; and of the Pharaohs who reigned in Egypt at that time; and of the other gentile kings who reigned at that time in the other kingdoms of the earth; and of the other things that happened then in the lands of the gentiles, as you shall hear.

I. Of How Jacob Went to Egypt, and Inquired of God Concerning That Journey, and He Commanded Him to Go

Although Jacob was very frail and had grown old before his time because of his great grief over his son Joseph, whom he thought he had lost, as Josephus recounts, and also over Rachel, his wife and Joseph's mother, whom he loved so much, and she died on the road, as has already been recounted—because of all this he did not delay but made his preparations that much more rapidly to go to Egypt to see his son, once he had heard that good news. And he took all his sons, and the other sons of his household with everything he owned, and set out. And when he came to the Well of the Oath,[30] of which we have already spoken, he made his sacrifice to God there, and began to worry about that journey he was making. And he was afraid that peradventure his sons would see the land of Egypt rich and plentiful in food, and that for that reason they would be pleased with it, and fall in love with it, and that they would want to stay there and make it their home, and that afterwards they would not want to return to Canaan, and that this would aggrieve God, Who had promised it to them as an inheritance. And peradventure because of this failure to do what He wanted done, God would be angry; and God's anger was the one thing in this world that Jacob always tried hardest to avoid.

And Master Godfrey says that in his sacrifice and in his prayers that he said there, he asked God whether it was His command that he make this journey, and asked Him to show him what He wanted. And, according to Josephus, he fell asleep while worrying about this, and then night fell, and while he was asleep, God appeared to him in a vision, and called him, and said: "Jacob, it is only right that you should know God, Who was always with those from whom you come, and then with you; and guided them, and likewise you. For your father considered your brother Esau the eldest, but I chose you, and guided you when you went all alone to Mesopotamia and got married there, and I married you very well, and gave you many sons and great riches, and I watched over your son Joseph, whom you thought you had lost, and I led him to such great honor and power that today all of Egypt is his to command. And I am the very powerful and strong God of your father. Fear not to go to Egypt, for there I will make a great people come from you, and I will go with you, and I will guide you, and you will die there and end your life in this world. And your sons Joseph and his brothers will bury you with Abraham and Isaac, your fathers, and then I will bring your descendants back to the land of Canaan and give it to them for an inheritance, as I have promised. Go on down there."

II. Of How Jacob Went to Egypt, and an Accounting of Those Whom He Took with Him

When Jacob awoke from his dream, he was very happy with that vision he had seen, and he trusted in God that it would come true. And the next morning he

---

[30] That is, Beersheba.

ordered his companions to prepare for the road and move on. And his sons took their wives, and all the furniture of their houses that they had ready to take, and put it all in the wagons that Pharaoh had sent to Jacob to travel in. And they set out from that encampment they had made near the Well of the Oath, and began to travel. And they went on toward Egypt and then they entered it, Jacob and his eleven sons who were with him, and his grandsons, and his grand-daughters, and all his descendants who had come from him. And their names were those we shall say here: the father was called by these two names: Jacob and Israel. Jacob's first son was Reuben, but this has been mentioned earlier. And he had these four sons: Hanoch, and Pallu, and Hezron, and Carmi. The second son was Simeon, and he had these seven sons: Jemuel, and Jamin, and Ohad, and Jachin, and Zohar, and Shaul, who was the son of a Canaanite woman, and these he took with him. Levi, who was the third son, had these three sons there: Gershon, Kohath, and Merari. Also there were the sons of Judah, who was Jacob's fourth son, these three: Shelah, and Perez, and Zerah; and Judah also begat Er and Onan, but these two—Er and Onan—had already died in the land of Canaan, as was recounted. Perez, Judah's son, begat Hezron and Hamul. Issachar, who was the fifth, begat these four sons: Tola, and Phuvah, and Iob, and Shimron. Zebulun was the sixth of Jacob's sons, and he begat these three sons: Sered, and Elon, and Jahleel. And Jacob begat these six sons we have mentioned, and a daughter, whose name was Dinah, by Leah, in Mesopotamia, which is in the land of Syria. And their father Jacob, and their mother Leah, and these six children with their children, make thirty six persons.

By Zilpah, who was Leah's maid, Jacob begat these two: Gad and Asher. And Gad, who was the first of these two sons of Jacob and Zilpah, begat these seven sons: Ziphion, and Haggi, Shuni, and Ezbon, Eri, and Arodi, and Areli. Asher, Zilpah's second son, begat these four: Jimnah, and Ishuah, and Isui, and Beriah; and a daughter, whose name was Serah. Beriah, Asher's son, begat these two: Heber, and Malchiel. And these sons of Zilpah with their descendants were sixteen.

By his other wife, whose name was Rachel, whom he loved much, he begat these two: Joseph and Benjamin. And Joseph, Rachel's first son, begat these two in Egypt by Asenath his wife: Manasseh and Ephraim. Benjamin, Rachel's second son, begat these nine:[31] Belah, Becher, Ashbel, Gera, Naaman, Ehi, Rosh, Muppim, Huppim, and Ard. And these sons of Rachel with their sons are fourteen.

Bilhah, Rachel's maid, had these two by Jacob: Dan and Naphtali. Dan, Jacob and Bilhah's first son, begat Hushim. Naphtali, Bilhah's second son,

---

[31] Thus the text ("nueue"). In fact Benjamin had ten sons, as shown in the list immediately following.

begat Jahzeel, and Guni, and Jezer, and Shillem. And these descendants of Bilhah were seven.

And all the descendants of Jacob, whom we have counted here, those who went down with him into Egypt, were sixty six, not counting his sons' wives. But Manasseh and Ephraim, whom Joseph begat in Egypt and who were then there, do not enter into this count, nor Joseph, their father, nor even Jacob. And counting his sons' wives, they are seventy seven in all. About this reckoning of these persons Master Peter makes a commentary in his *History*, noting that the seventy translators[32] count that seventy five people entered Egypt with Joseph, and that the evangelist Luke agreed with them in the book of the Acts of the Apostles that he composed,[33] as well as Master Hugh,[34] whose book says the same thing; but we hold that this commentary is faulty,[35] and hence we say no more about it here, for it is our duty to say what Moses said literally in the Biblical text, which is the source of all the others. And when they began arriving in the land of Egypt, Jacob sent Judah ahead to let Joseph know that his father was coming with all his household, and that he should go out to the land of Goshen to meet them.

III. Of How Joseph Received His Father and His Brothers and Took Them to the King

When Joseph heard that his father was coming, he went out to receive him with great joy, to that land of Goshen, according to some; others say he went to the land of Raamses, and this appears to be a disagreement among those who spoke of this story. But Master Peter says, to resolve this doubt, that these two places—Goshen and Raamses—are in the same land. That land, which used to be known as Goshen, was later—and even before—called Thebes, whence came the Theban kings, who ruled in Egypt for a hundred and ninety years, as we have already mentioned. He goes on to say that these kings populated a town in their native land, and called it the City of Lords, after the first kings who came from there, who were the lords who held dominion over all the land of Egypt. And it was to this City of Lords[36] that Joseph went to receive his father, and it was there that they first saw each other, according to Josephus. And

---

[32] That is, the translators of the Greek version known as the Septuagint, prepared by a group of scholars at Alexandria, Egypt, in the third century B.C.E.

[33] Acts 7:14: "Joseph sent for his father Jacob and the whole family, seventy five persons in all. . . ."

[34] Hugh of St. Cher (c. 1200–1263), French cardinal and biblical commentator.

[35] The manuscript has "non tiene mengua," but the *non* seems to be a mistake.

[36] Apparently this was thought to be the meaning of Raamses.

Master Peter says that later on, when the Egyptians made the Jews slaves, they made them build a city in a place called Place of the Tents, and they named it Raamses, from the name of that land. And thus, all those names belong to the same land, and hence, although the sages and holy fathers appear to disagree about this, they really don't.

When Jacob got there and saw how great Joseph his son had become, he was so happy that he passed out and was in a swoon as if half dead for a long while, until Joseph revived him. However, the same thing happened to Joseph, but it didn't last as long. When both of them had regained consciousness, they embraced many times and wept together with the joy of seeing each other, and the father said: "Son, I shall die happy, since I have seen your face, and I know that I shall leave you alive to be my heir for many days afterwards." After Joseph had spoken with his father, he turned to his brothers, and greeted them, and spoke with them. Then he likewise greeted all the other members of their households, and took five of his brothers aside, and said to Jacob: "Father, rest here from your wandering, for this company can take care of you. And let the younger come with the older, and your cattle, so that none of your things remain on the road. And I will go before to tell the king that you are coming, with all your house and with all your belongings from the land of Canaan." And then he instructed his brothers, those who were going with him, and said to them: "When you get to the king, and he asks you about your life, tell him that you are shepherds and that you have always raised cattle, and that you have brought them here with you; for I will tell him the same thing. And therefore he will give you Goshen, which is good grazing land, where you can live apart from the Egyptians, which will be good for you, for the people of this land dislike shepherds who raise sheep."

IV. Of How Joseph's Brothers Spoke before the King, and He Ordered Joseph to Provide for Them and for His Father

When Joseph told his father and the other sons and members of the household who were remaining with him what to do, and also instructed, as you have heard, the other brothers who were going with him, he rode ahead of that other group of five, and went to Pharaoh, and went in, and said to him: "Sire, my father and my brothers are coming with their households and all their belongings from the land of Canaan, and they are bringing many sheep, and many cows and other cattle, and they are now in the land of Goshen, and they will remain there until they hear from you what you command them to do."

When Joseph had told the king this, he took those five brothers he had brought with him, and had them stand before him. As soon as the king found out who they were, he asked them how they earned their living, and they replied, as their brother had instructed them, and said: "Sire, we and our fathers are your servants. Since we began and up to this day, we have always raised cattle, and we own many. And now we have come to this your land seeking your kindness, as strangers seeking shelter with our cattle, for it has not rained in Canaan for many days, and we have no grass for our cattle, nor even bread for ourselves and our households; and both men and cattle were perishing of hunger. And we ask you as a favor to give us Goshen, where we may dwell and take shelter, for it is a good land and well suited for our needs, with pasture for our cattle." Then King Pharaoh said to Joseph: "Your father and your brothers have come to you, and you are overseer of the land of Egypt. Search out a good place for them to dwell, and if you know that among them are men who know about cattle, give them my cattle to watch, and in return I will do them much good and much kindness."

V. Of How King Pharaoh Received Jacob, and the Words of Both of Them

Joseph was very pleased that the king responded so well to the coming of his father and his brothers and received them so well. And since this was what he had arranged with him, he went back with those who were with him to his father and his other brothers, and he took Jacob and brought him with him to see the king. And when they reached him, Jacob bowed down and greeted him, and began to pray God to give him a good reign, and honor, and long life, and he blessed him. Then Pharaoh looked Jacob over, and found him to be a distinguished man, and well spoken, and handsome for an old man. And he liked him, and was pleased that he had come to see him. And he asked him how old he was. Jacob answered: "A hundred and thirty years—few and evil—and I have always been a stranger in strange lands." And the king marveled at the long life Jacob said he had lived. When Jacob saw the king's wonderment, he said to him: "I have not yet reached the number of days that my fathers lived." And Jacob told him about the lives and deeds of his fathers, and his own. When Pharaoh heard Jacob recount the lives of his fathers, which had been so long, he imagined that even he could live a few more years if he lived as they did. And then he deeded over and gave to him and his sons the City of the Sun, which we have said was called in Greek Heliopolis, and in Egyptian Damiata, where Phutiphar, the father of Joseph's wife, Lady Zulayme, had been lord.[37] And she was to inherit that city after her father's death. And he ordered that they should all live there, on account of the location, which was very good and pleasant and because of the great debt they owed the lord of that city because of Joseph and Lady Zulayme, who were now married.

VI. Of How Joseph Provided for His Father and His Brothers, by Pharaoh's Command

When Jacob learned the place where he was to dwell, he blessed the king and left. And Joseph entertained his father and his brothers there very lavishly, by the king's command. And then he conducted them very well and very honorably to that city where they were to dwell, and gave them there in the vicinity of that city the land of Goshen, because it was very rich in grazing land for their cattle. And Master Peter comments in this regard that something happens in Egypt which does not occur to the same extent elsewhere. That is, when wheat is plentiful in Egypt, there is little pasture; and when there is plenty of pasture, wheat is scarce. And they say that this occurs because of the abundance of water or the great drought. And he comments on this in this manner, saying that when the water abounds and stands a long time at the foot of the grain, the land becomes saturated, and the roots of the grain rot, and it dies and perishes. But grass flourishes with much water, and puts down deeper roots, and takes over the land, and grows and is plentiful. And in a dry year grain does better and grass worse, and in a year of moderate rainfall, the wheat does very well, and thrives, and gives bread abundantly if the rain falls in its seasons. And in a year of moderate rainfall the grass comes, but not as well as in a rainy year, because grass has a thin stem, and is weaker than grain, and needs water every day if the pasture is to grow and abound. And this happens in Egypt more than in other lands by reason of floodwaters of the Nile, which irrigate that land.

VII. Of the Reason Why the Libyans Dislike Those Who Raise Sheep

Master Peter says that the Egyptians acquired their dislike for those who raise sheep because in Libya, and in that part of Egypt which is near Libya, they

---

[37] Thus the manuscript. Earlier in the text Zulayme has been portrayed as Phutiphar's widow, not his daughter. The confusion of course stems from the fact that the Bible calls Joseph's master Potiphar and his father-in-law (the father of Asenath) Poti-phera.

adored as divine one of their kings whose name was Jupiter. And this was the same King Jupiter about whom we've said many things in the previous book, as we do in this one, and will do even further on; for this king endured so long, and was so wise and powerful, and did so many things that this is the only way to tell about him. And they made a great idol there to that Jupiter in the form of a sheep, for Jupiter was born under the sign of Aries. And they put it in a temple in Libya in the midst of the sand, and they called it Amon in the Egyptian language, which in our Castilian language means "Jupiter of the Sands," because this temple and its idol were in the land of the sands. And people from many lands came there to worship and sacrifice, and seek answers to the questions they asked that idol. And for that reason the people of that land did not eat sheep nor lamb nor anything of that sort, and they didn't like sheep around there. It was not that they disliked them altogether, but only that they hated those who raised them to eat, as Master Peter recounts.

Some mention here, in commenting on the boundaries of that place, that the land of Goshen marked the border of Egypt with Damiata.

VIII. Of How Joseph Settled His Father and His Brothers in Goshen and Raamses, and of the Year When That Happened

When Joseph had settled his father and his people in that land, which was very good for them, as it is said, and the king commanded him, he gave them all the bread and other things they needed for themselves and for their household, each one separately in his house, which they could not find in all the land. There was no one but the kings who possessed these things in Egypt, and even more so in Canaan. And besides the plague of famine which we mentioned, the drought was so great that the air was polluted by the water of the Nile, which did not rise nor irrigate the land as usual, nor was there any other form of precipitation, as Josephus recounts, and the people grew very sick. Both because of the pollution of the air, and because of the very great famine, most people died.

Jacob was a hundred and thirty two years old when he entered the land of Egypt with his sons and his household. And it was a hundred and eighty years since Isaac, his father, was born, and twelve years since he died; and two hundred and ninety two years since Abraham was born, and two hundred and fifteen since our Lord had ordered him to leave his land, and had given him and his descendants the land of Canaan as an inheritance; and sixteen since he had died. And Joseph was forty one years old, and it was eleven years since God had given him dominion over Egypt. And at that time were reigning King

Baleus in Assyria, and Messapus in Sicionia, and Appis in Argos, and King Pharaoh Nicrao in Egypt. And the third of the seven bad years that would come to pass was beginning. And here it is to be noted that the year when Joseph was placed in power was the very same year when the seven good years began. But the eighth year, which was the first of the seven that were to be bad, was not a year of famine. Not even the second year was altogether bad, for from the abundance of the seven good years at least those who had been prudent had enough of their own food to eat. And from then on began the very bad years and great famine throughout the land. Now we shall leave these other matters, and return to the story of Joseph, and recount how he dealt with the Egyptians in the bad years.

IX. Of How the Egyptians Sold Joseph All Their Cattle and Pasture Land for Pharaoh

Eleven years after Joseph had come to power in Egypt, the famine waxed greater every day throughout the land, and the men were in very great distress, and the Egyptians had already eaten everything they possessed themselves, and had sold all the furniture of their houses for food during the past three years. When the fourth year came, they had no money with which to buy bread, for Joseph had taken it all from them during those three years and put it in the king's treasury. And that year all the peoples of Egypt came to Joseph and said to him: "You have taken all our money and the furniture of our houses for the bread you have sold us in these three bad years that have gone by. Now we are in the fourth year, and the famine waxes greater every day, and we no longer have anything with which to buy bread. We beg you, since we have no more money, and that we perish not in so terrible a way before you, give us food to eat, for we are already all dying of hunger, small and great alike."

When Joseph saw the Egyptians complaining like that, he considered the matter of the bread and those sales and purchases that he had made with the peoples, and understood that the great dominion and power of King Pharaoh, his lord, over the kingdom would yet be established by means of the sales that would take place. And he decided the sales would be complete, as you shall hear. And his idea was that they completely sell all the cattle and pasture land of the kingdom, and he answered them in this way: "It is true that you sold me your furniture, but you still have your cattle. If you will sell them to me, I will give you food to eat this year." They were in such distress that they did so rather than die. And they wanted to bring him their oxen, and cows, and beasts, and all the other cattle they had. Joseph said to them: "I do not wish it so, but let the cattle remain in the pastures where they are, and you take what you need for now, and I will do this kindness you: I will give each one of you food in your own places, and I will send my men to investigate what cattle you have, and how much, and have them write it down as a precaution." They agreed, and it was done. And some even say that it was agreed that the pasture land would be deeded to the king along with the cattle. And in exchange for that, Joseph gave them enough food to live on through the year, on condition that from that time on, no one would raise cattle except by the king's consent, which he would give them in writing. Otherwise, all cattle would belong to the king from then on, and the pastures would also be his, by general purchase, as we have said that Joseph had calculated.

X. Of How the Egyptians Sold Joseph All Their Manservants and Maidservants for Pharaoh

When Joseph had been in power for twelve years, in the fifth year of the seven years of famine, the Egyptians again came to Joseph, and told him that they no longer had anything to sell except their lands and their bodies. And some say that Joseph replied and said to them: "I will show you that you have something else that you haven't thought of. And if you sell it to the king, I will buy it from you, and give you the bread you need for all this year in exchange." And they asked him what that could be. He said to them: "Your manservants and maid-servants." And when they heard that, they were relieved, and they gladly signed them over to him, for they were willing to sell themselves if he had wanted that, so how much more willingly would they sell their slaves! And right then they negotiated with him to sell the manservants and maidservants in exchange for food to eat that fifth year. And they say that the contract stated that from then on for this reason no man would have a slave in Egypt except the king alone, or the one to whom the king should give him or sell him. For the king bought them all, in accord with the general sale Joseph had calculated in this regard.

XI. Of How the Egyptians Sold Joseph All Their Lands and Even Their Own Bodies for Pharaoh

When Joseph had been in power for thirteen years, in the sixth year of famine, the Nile still did not rise as usual, which was a sign of another bad year, for they could foresee what kind of year they would have by how much the Nile rose. Nor did rain fall from heaven. And the councils of all the cities and towns and villages of all Egypt met together, and came to an agreement, and sent Joseph the following message: "We hide nothing from our lord, for we have given everything we had for bread. You know well that nothing is left to us but our bodies and our land. And you also know, and can see, that we are dying. But do otherwise with us; we and our lands are yours. Buy our lands and ourselves, and put us in servitude to our lord the king, and we will gladly be his slaves rather than die like this. Give us food to eat and seed to sow, that all we farmers die not, and the land become sterile for lack of anyone who would till it for grain and the other goods that come from it." Joseph in his wisdom responded that he would make a general purchase of them and their lands. And then they sold him all the land of Egypt with the great distress which oppressed them unto death. Most of them had already died, at least all the little children and the weak men and women, which caused the others great sadness and grief, for there were some such in every house. And Joseph bought their lands from them for Pharaoh, his lord, and also the bodies of all the people in the boundaries of Egypt, from one end to the other. And in this way King Pharaoh was made lord of all the men and of all the lands of Egypt, and of everything else that we have mentioned. And Master Godfrey and other histories recount that these sales and purchases were made privileges and laws and a decree in Egypt that it would always be thus.

In the seventh of the bad years, the Nile began to rise, and the men saw the signs of a good year, and they began to work the land, and they hastened to Joseph for the seeds he was to give them, and he gave them the seeds as he ought, and loaned them and their households enough to survive that year, for he still had grain. And in this way Joseph and the Egyptians spent those seven bad years of which you have heard, and the Bible story and the histories by many other sages recount it.

XII. Of How the Priests of Egypt and Their Possessions Were Exempt from This Sale and Servitude

When Joseph had been in power for thirteen years, the story says that the priests were exempted from being sold as slaves, and were allowed to retain their lands and property, for because they performed the sacrifices to their gods and said the hours[38] and the prayers, the king did not want them to enter into servitude like the other men. Furthermore, the story says that they gave a designated portion of Pharaoh's food to the priests for their stipends. And the king

---

[38] Anachronistic reference to the hours of the Christian Breviary (Matins, Lauds, Prime, etc.).

and Joseph, who had to oversee it by the king's command, did not want them to lack anything, but maintained them in their usual status, and this was another reason why they were under no pressure to sell themselves or alienate their lands or sell them, and they were exempt from all servitude. And Josephus recounts that many left Egypt for other lands at that time, and that the king thereby became even more powerful in holding the lands of his kingdom that he had bought, as it is said.

Joseph, because he had done all of this, proved himself sensible and altogether wise, and continued as the king's governor and overseer of his property even more firmly than before. And he governed very sensibly and cautiously, as was his wont, with all his heart, and even more than before. And thus he held power over all of Egypt, and continued all the years we have told and will yet tell.

Now we will tell you about the Pharaoh kings and matters concerning the other gentiles.

XIII. Of Pharaoh Nicrao and of King Pharaoh Amosis and Joseph's Power

When Joseph had been in power for fourteen years, Eusebius and Jerome say in this place in their chronicles that in the sixth year of those seven bad ones, Pharaoh Nicrao, about whom we have told you up to now, died. But some of the histories disagree, saying that he died in the seventh year, when, as we have said, all the dealings between Joseph and the Egyptians during the bad years were over. And it was then that the Pharaohs who were called the Shepherd Kings ceased to reign, for the reasons we have mentioned before. And then ended the hundred and three years that we have said these Shepherd Kings reigned. And likewise we have already mentioned that they belonged to a dynasty called the Diapolites, and then ended the power of the Diapolites and their manner of ruling, for they ruled arbitrarily as did the other kings of Egypt. And as we have already commented, they counted their times by the reckoning we have mentioned, which they called a dynasty, as the Romans say; and even now, we use the term Olympiad for a period of five years. And eighteen dynasties had passed since those Theban Pharaoh kings had come into power in Egypt. And it was two hundred and ninety four years since Abraham had been born, and a hundred and ninety years that the Thebans had reigned before, and a hundred and three the Shepherd Kings, so that these years numbered in all two hundred and ninety three since the beginning of the kingdom of Egypt. And there were eighteen dynasties of them according to their reckoning, as it is said, and in the eighteenth of them King Nicrao died, and afterwards his son King Amosis reigned. And our Latin chronicles don't mention any of the Thebans nor the Diapolite Shepherds by their proper names, nor do they say anything except that the Thebans reigned and then the Diapolite Shepherds, and they give the years of the reigns of each one of these. And they think this was why these Egyptians, since the kingdom was still new, didn't write when one died, nor when they removed one and installed another (and this is what happened for the most part). And they even say that one did not reign by himself, but instead the whole dynasty reigned jointly, and that dynasty had dominion over the other tribes or families and commanded them, which was the reason why they couldn't name the king individually. And from that time on, the kings of Egypt had greater power, and the sons ruled after the fathers, and from then on the chronicles and histories list them by their names, as you will hear from this point on in this history, in that we shall tell you about them and name them. And we will even tell you the names of the kings of the earlier time, if we find them.

And this Pharaoh in whose time Joseph was sold, and bought in Egypt, and whose dreams he interpreted when he saw the seven good years and after that the other bad ones, as he said, and gave the king dominion over all his land, as the *History of Egypt* says—that king's name was Nicrao in the Egyptian language and Rayen in Arabic. And that King Nicrao ruled twenty seven years, and he died.

XIV. Of King Pharaoh Amosis, and His Reign, and His Customs

When Joseph had been in power for fourteen years, during that seventh and last year of famine, after Joseph had bought all the land of Egypt for the king, and in that regard made his privileges and his decrees very strong and very great, Pharaoh Nicrao died, and after him ruled another Pharaoh named Amosis, son of of that Pharaoh Nicrao. And the *History of Egypt* recounts that in the Egyptian language they called this Pharaoh that we have said reigned after Nicrao, Amosis; and that in Arabic his name was Derith; and that he was the fourth Pharaoh, and he reigned for twenty five years. And Joseph remained his governor, and his counselor and potentate, just as he had been to his father. And that King Derith was guided by him, although he didn't have Joseph's belief, as his father Nicrao had secretly done. And Derith worshiped idols, which Nicrao had not done except in public and not willingly. And he knew by the art of the stars, as the *History of Egypt* recounts, how the sign of Cancer was his ascendant. And because, as those who are knowledgeable about the stars comment, this sign is especially the House of the Moon, King Amosis made an image of that planet and its likeness, and put it in the palace of the town Joseph had built by command of King Nicrao, at the source of the Nile. And that palace was built of marble, and King Amosis came there to worship that idol of the moon, and the others in the land did likewise, to honor the king and give him pleasure and win his favor, and also because it was those peoples' religion to worship idols.

When this occurred, it was two hundred and twenty years since our Lord had first promised the land of Canaan to Abraham for himself and his descendants. And Joseph was then forty three years old; and that year were reigning in Assyria and in Sicionia and in Argos the kings we named in the previous chapter.

XV. Of the Condition of the Egyptian Farmers, and How They Worked the Land, and Gave the King the Fifth Part

When Joseph had been in power for fifteen years, Josephus recounts that after the seven bad years were over and the eighth was beginning, that signs of good times to come began to appear definitively, and it seemed evident that that things were going to be as they had been before, when times were good. And he says that that year the Nile flooded as was its wont, and in other countries rain fell from heaven, and the famine waned, for the earth began to grow and show the fruits that men would be able to use for food in a little while. Then Joseph, as a sensible man and one guided by God and prudent with regard to things that might happen, guarded against the uprising of the people that could occur because of what he had done to the peoples for King Pharaoh, his lord, and his behavior up to the time that the king had firmly established his rule. Before anything else could happen, he quickly began to go through all the cities of Egypt, and in order to safeguard for the king his land and what he had won for him and his peoples, he called great meetings in the appropriate places. And Moses and Jerome recount in the Bible that he said thus: "You see well how Pharaoh has bought you and all your land for his property, and all of your goods, both fixed and portable. And everything is entirely his if he so desires. However, he wants to do you this favor: that you take of the seed and the lands, as has been agreed between me and you, and you work and sow, and of whatsoever you reap, each of you give the king the fifth part freely, without any cost or collection on his part. And you may keep for yourselves four fifths of what you have sowed, and maintain yourselves and your households. And you will have the lands as your possession with this condition: that you, and all those who come after you and possess them, will always give the king the fifth of whatsoever you reap, as I have said." When the people heard these words, as well as many other good things that Joseph said to them, they were relieved, and were very happy, and answered: "Sir, our survival and our well-being is in your hand. Have mercy on us, for we will gladly serve the king."

And in this regard they were all very glad to stay on the land, and they stayed. For although they had sold themselves to Joseph for Pharaoh, nevertheless they saw that even if Pharaoh wanted to seize them, he couldn't, because he couldn't make them stay there. And the *History* says in this regard that Joseph saw this even before he made that deal with them, although he didn't reveal it to anyone. And they wanted to leave, since they had no land either of their own or of anyone else's to work and to live on, but when they heard of this new arrangement, many of those who had left went back there. And they all praised Joseph, and spoke much good of him, and said that he had conducted this matter very sensibly and to the great benefit of his master and of all his peoples, and that he had discovered how to safeguard the king's property and ensure the success of his reign. And from that time on, the farmers in Egypt every year gave the king the fifth part of whatever they worked and reaped from the land. And, according to those who are familiar with those lands, today they consider it a statute and a law throughout Egypt, with the exception of the lands of the priests which were exempt and free from all exactions, as the kings had granted them, as you have heard.

Now we will leave these matters, and tell you about some of the gentile kings.

XVI. Of the Gentile Kings Who Were Reigning at That Time

When Joseph was fifty years old and had been in power for ten years, Messapus, King of Sithionia, died, and Eratus reigned for forty six years afterwards. And this Eratus was the tenth king of that land. And King Phoroneus of Argos had begotten a son whose name was Spartus, and in his lifetime he gave him a separate land in his kingdom. And when Joseph had been in power for twenty years, we find, as Eusebius and Jerome say, that this Spartus, son of King Phoroneus, populated the city of Sparta, which is now in that land that his father had given him. And there he made that good city, and called it Sparta from his own name, and afterwards they called the land Sparta, whence the gentile authors, such as Ovid and others, say Sparta for the city and Sparta for the land. And therefore the people of that land are today named the Spartans.

And when Joseph had been in power for twenty five years, Appis, King of Argos—the one who we earlier said had entrusted his kingdom of Achaia to his brother Egialeus, and had gone to Egypt with great hosts and had reigned in a land he had conquered there, and had been accepted as king by the inhabitants—died. And some say that King Appis's move to Egypt took place at this time, but others say it was before this, during the life of Jacob, when Jacob was a hundred and eleven years old. However, we believe that his move to Egypt probably took place that year, as we have already said, and that his death occurred in this year of Joseph. We have also found that at the time when he died, the people of the land where he reigned made an idol in his likeness to honor him, and they called it Serapis, which in Egyptian means "idol of Appis."[39] Others say that the Egyptians made that idol in honor of Joseph, who saved them from the famine in which they would have died but for him, and because of the fair arrangement he made with them about the lands, as we have said. And we will tell you more about this idol later, for we have found that it was the cause of the children of Israel's erring later on, as you will hear in this history. And Master Godfrey says that the Christians destroyed that idol afterwards, in the time of the Emperor Theodosius, as you will hear later. After this King Appis, his son Argo reigned in the land of Argos, and his reign lasted seventy years. And that land had been called Achaia up to then, and after Argo's reign, because he was such a good king, they gave it his name, and the people accepted their lord's command, and called the city and the kingdom Argos. And he was the fourth king of that land.

Now we will leave these matters and return to the Bible story, and we will tell you about how long Jacob lived in Egypt, and what he did, and how he died there.

XVII. Of How Jacob Fell Ill, and His Sons Came to See Him, and Their Conversation

When Joseph had been in power for twenty six years, Israel was dwelling in Egypt, in the land of Goshen, and he possessed it as an inheritance. And his descendants grew and increased greatly in that place, and great peoples came from them, as you will hear further on. And when Jacob was old, he was ill, and saw that the day of his death was approaching, and he sent for his son Joseph,

---

[39] A Greco-Egyptian god represented in the Serapeum of Alexandria, which depicted Hades or Pluto (the Egyptian bull-god Apis was assimilated to Osiris, god of the underworld, and therefore to Hades or Pluto) enthroned with a basket or corn measure on his head and Cerberus at his feet. The Serapeum was destroyed by Theodosius in 385 C.E.

and said to him: "Son, I beg you by the love and respect you have for me, and out of kindness, that you bury me not in Egypt, but take me out of this land and take me to Hebron, which is in the vale of Mamre, and bury me there, near the sepulchers of my fathers Abraham and Isaac. And if you love me well, that I may be sure you will do it, place your hand on my thigh, as is our custom, as a sign that you will carry out my request and petition and the oath that you have sworn, and thereby you will show me kindness." Joseph replied: "Father, I shall do what you command." Then Jacob said to him: "Swear then that you will keep your word in truth." Joseph swore unto him that he would do it in every particular. Then Israel turned toward the head of his bed, which was toward the east, according to Master Peter, and made his prayer to God, and praised His name for bringing him to the day when he should die in the hands of his son Joseph, and he greatly thanked that son for what he had promised and would surely do, by his oath that he would bury him with his fathers.

XVIII. Of How Jacob Recovered, But Soon Fell Ill Again, and Joseph Came to Him with His Sons, and the Words They Spoke Together

Joseph then bade his father farewell and went away. And Jacob recovered somewhat from that time. But a little afterwards—and this was the following year, when Joseph had been in power twenty seven years—Jacob fell ill again, and his sickness increased every day, for he was now very old and had always wandered in distress through alien lands. And they told Joseph that his father was near death, and as soon as he heard it he took both his sons, Manasseh and Ephraim, and came to him with them as soon as he could.

When they told Jacob that his son Joseph had come to see him, he was somewhat comforted, and he made an effort and sat up in his bed. And as soon as Joseph arrived, he went in to see him, and his sons Manasseh and Ephraim went in with him. And after they had greeted each other, they sat down, and Jacob then began to reveal to Joseph the visions he had seen, and to tell the ones we have already recounted in this history, but we must repeat them here, because Jacob repeated them to Joseph, as you will hear, and he had not told them unto him as he did that time, and he said: "Son, He Who is powerful over all things appeared to me at Luz, which is in the land of Canaan, and blessed me and promised me much good and much mercy, and that He would make great peoples come from me and my descendants, and that He would give us that land as ours, and that we would always be lords over it as long as we did as He commanded us, and relied not on ourselves. And now I want your sons, Ephraim and Manasseh, whom you begat in Egypt before I came to this place, to be mine like Reuben and Simeon, and for them to inherit from me like them and my other sons. And from both will come forth two lineages, and the other children you beget from now on will be yours."

And then he began to tell him what he had not completely told anyone up to then, not even him—for he was a child when his brothers sold him, and since then there had been no opportunity—and he told him of the death of his mother Rachel, how she had died on the road in the land of Canaan when they were coming from Mesopotamia, from the house of Laban, his father-in-law, and how it was winter then, and the weather was bad. And then they were entering Ephrath, which is the place they now call Bethlehem. And he also told him how he went in there on the road near that village of Bethlehem. And Jacob did this to bury her there, as Master Peter recounts, because Abraham and Isaac and the other holy fathers all understood through the spirit of God that he whom they expected to come to save the world would be born there, and in that land would receive death and suffering to save us, and there he would also be resurrected. And Jacob told his son these words, and made him understand why he should not be offended that he hadn't buried her where she had asked to be buried.

XIX. Of How Jacob Blessed His Grandsons, Ephraim and Manasseh, and Prophesied to Joseph Concerning Them

After this Jacob looked at Manasseh and Ephraim, and he couldn't distinguish them well, for he no longer saw well, since he was very old. And he asked Jacob who they were, and he said to him: "Father, these are my two sons that God gave me in this land." When Jacob realized that those were his grandsons, Joseph's sons, he was well pleased with them, and he ordered him to bring them near so that he could bless them. Joseph was very happy about that, and did his command, and took them to his father, and brought them to him, and put them in his lap, and he began to embrace and kiss them, and said to Joseph: "Son, I see well that I have not been deprived of seeing you, as I greatly feared a long time ago, for God shows me your descendants." Joseph then got up, and took them from his lap, and knelt and bowed down to the earth before him, humbling himself on account of what he was about to do. And, according to Master Peter, he begged him greatly, and asked him as a favor, to bless them. And he set Manasseh, who was the elder, on his right side, and Ephraim, who was the younger, on his left, and brought them near him.

And when Jacob blessed them, he crossed his hands, and put the left one on Manasseh, who was the elder, and the right one on Ephraim, who was the younger, and blessed them, and said: "May God, Whom my fathers Abraham and Isaac served, and Who has given me all that I needed from the day of my birth until today, and the angel that has always kept me from all evil, bless these children, and make their lineage increase greatly upon the earth." When Joseph saw that his father had put his right hand on Ephraim, who was the younger, and his left hand on Manasseh, who was born first, it grieved him, and he took his right hand to put it on Manasseh, and told him that he was the first-born son, and that he should bless him with his right hand. And his father then said to him: "I know it, son, and I know well what I am doing. The generation of Manasseh, who is older, will be great, but that of Ephraim, who is younger, will be very much greater, and many peoples will come from him."

XX. Of How Jacob Prophesied Concerning Manasseh,[40] and the Inheritance He Left Him

After this, Jacob said to Manasseh: "By you will be blessed the people of Israel, and hence men will say: May God make you like Ephraim and Manasseh." And he himself put Ephraim before Manasseh in saying these words. And according to Josephus, he then commanded his sons to accept them as brothers, and that they should have two shares in the division of Canaan like them. Then he said to Joseph: "Son, I am dying, but God will be with you, and will take you back to the land of your fathers. And I give you above your brothers the land of Shechem, which I bought for one hundred lambs, and always protected and defended with my arms."

XXI. Of Jacob's Words Concerning His Prophecies, and His Blessings to His Sons

When Joseph had been in power for twenty seven years, Jacob was sick unto death, and when he had told this to Joseph, he summoned his other sons to prophesy unto them, and tell each one of them the things that would come to pass unto their descendants in the fullness of time. And according to Master Peter, he spoke to them of the division of the land, and the status their descendants would later have. And he says that he told them words in which are

---

[40] The manuscript mistakenly says Benjamin.

comprehended very well both comings of our lord Jesus Christ—the first when he came in Saint Mary, and the second when he will come to judge the living and the dead, as you will hear later—and likewise the call of the peoples, who were later called to the faith of Christ and converted to it.

Now we will tell you how he spoke unto them, and the prophecies he told them, as they appear in the Bible story. And likewise, because otherwise they would be obscure to understand, we will give the commentaries we have found in the writings of the sages and holy fathers who spoke of this history.

And Jacob said unto his sons in this wise: "Gather together, my sons, and I will tell you the things that are to come to pass unto your descendants and in your last days. Gather together, and hear, sons of Jacob, hear Israel, your father." After saying this, he began to prophesy unto each one, in the order they were born, one after another. And first of all to Reuben, who was his eldest son, he said:

XXII. Of the Prophecy to Reuben

"Reuben, my firstborn son, you are my strength, for I begat you in my youth; and you are the beginning of my first sorrow that I had and the first complaint I had against my sons, because of the wrong you did me with my wife. You ought to be first in gifts and have a double portion and be greatest in domin-ion, in respect of your having been born before your brothers. But you were scattered abroad like unstable water in the vile deed of lust. May you not in-crease, because you went up to your father's bed, and soiled his couch. But be-cause of the sin you committed, may your increase only be equal to that of your brothers, for you didn't push ahead like water when it bubbles up, nor like the river when it raises up great waves. Nor shall you increase as you ought to have done, had it not been for the wickedness you committed."

After this, he spoke of Simeon, his second son, and of Levi, who was the third.

XXIII. Of Jacob's Prophecies to Simeon and to Levi

Concerning these two brothers, Jacob their father said: "Simeon and Levi, two brothers, vessels of wrongdoing and warriors, for with their madness they killed a man to my misfortune, and they dug under the city wall and demolished it in their self-will."

Many comment in different ways on these words which Jacob said to Simeon and Levi, his sons, about that man they killed. Some say he said it with refer-

ence to Shechem, son of King Hamor, whom they killed because he had taken
their sister Dinah, and raped her, and Shechem's men who died with him, as
you have already heard previously in this history. Others argue and say that this
was concerning what was to come, as if it had already happened, and they
reckon that it was said of Jesus Christ, for as Master Peter comments on this
place, and others who agree with him, the chancellors of the Jews came from
the lineage of Simeon, and these are those whom the holy scriptures of our
church of Christ call in Latin "scribes." For that is the meaning of *scriba* in
Castilian: "chancellor" or "notary." And the priests by whose counsel Jesus
Christ was taken and put on the cross and killed, according to the flesh, were
of the tribe of Levi. And they comment that thence Jacob said these words further on in his prophecy: "May my soul enter not into their counsel, nor my
glory in their company." And later on he even said unto them in this wise in
this prophecy: "Cursed be their anger, for they persisted, and their scorn, because it was harsh and wild. I will divide them in Jacob, and I will scatter them
in Israel." And this, as the holy fathers comment in their histories and glosses,
truly happened, for the descendants of Levi did not have a portion in the land
of promise with the other tribes, but only designated towns, and even these
were scattered through the portions of the other brothers in that they had no
separate boundaries, but only cities to dwell in for themselves and to maintain
their cattle, as you will hear further on in the division of the land, as you will
be informed in the history of the book of Joshua, who divided the land of
Canaan among these tribes by the command of God Who promised it to their
fathers for them and gave it to them. And likewise those of Simeon were so few
at that time that they didn't give them a designated separate portion, but they
were combined with those of Judah in theirs.

And because Simeon and Levi were united in the matter of Shechem, and
equal in the other wicked deeds you have heard of here, which their descendants committed, their father Jacob likewise united them in his prophecies
concerning both. After he had spoken to Simeon and Levi, he prophesied to
Judah, who was the fourth son, in his turn, and said unto him:

XXIV. Of Jacob's Prophecy to Judah, His Fourth Son, According to the Latin Biblical Text

"Judah, your brothers will praise you, your hands on the necks of your enemies.
The sons of your father will adore you and serve you. Judah, lion's whelp, my
son Judah, you went up to the prey. You stooped down and couched like a lion

and like a lioness. Who will awake you, and who will get you up? The lordship will not be taken from Judah, nor the chieftain from his thigh, until he who is to be sent comes; and that man will be the hope of the peoples. This son of mine will bind his foal to to the vineyard, and his ass to the grapevine. He will wash his stole or garment in wine, and his mantle in the blood of the grape. His eyes are more beautiful than wine, and his teeth are whiter than milk."

Now we shall tell you what these prophecies mean, and when these things Jacob prophesied will be fulfilled.

XXV. The Meaning of the Prophecies Concerning Judah

The first thing he told him—that his brothers would praise him—came to pass afterwards, and was fulfilled in the exodus from Egypt, when they reached the Red Sea, and all the other tribes hesitated to go in after Moses, but the tribe of Judah did not, saying: "Go on in, and let us follow our leader and our Lord God who commands us to do so." And then they went in after him. And Master Peter says in this regard that that is how the tribe of Judah came to merit the sovereignty they later held over the other tribes of Israel in the land of promise. And what the prophet said next—"your hands on the necks of your enemies, and the sons of your father will adore you"—likewise signifies the good and strong king they would have, who would spring from the tribe of Judah, who would break and oppress all their enemies, and would have dominion over all the tribes of Israel where they went; and it was King David who did all of this. And the words "Judah, lion's whelp" refer to the beginning of the reign of King David. In this prophecy Jacob called David "whelp," because, although he was the youngest of his brothers, he was chosen and taken to be king, as you will hear further on in the First Book of Kings. And beginning as a small thing, he increased and grew very mighty, and instructed all the people of Israel, and maintained them very well, and broke all their enemies, and made them pay him tribute, and oppressed them, just as the lion cub grows from very small into a great and very strong lion, and oppresses all the other wild beasts. And even those of his own tribe fear the one who turns out to be the strongest, and this is only natural, for among all animals the one who is smaller and weaker fears the one who is stronger than he and obeys him. And even among men the same thing often happens.

Regarding Jacob's words "my son, you went up to the prey, you stooped down and couched like a lion and like a lioness," the sages comment in their histo-

ries and glosses that when the strong lion is sleeping or resting, the other animals dare not approach him, nor even that place. And this is what happened
to David with the people of Israel and the other neighboring peoples round
about. And concerning what he said next—"who will get him up?"—some say
that it meant that he was a prophet and prophesied much, and who would
awake him and revive him but the Holy Spirit of our Lord God Who made him,
and through Whom he prophesied everything he said? Others argue that we
can apply it to King Solomon, his son, who was so wise, as you will hear later,
and left behind so many sensible and very wise sayings in writing.

As for that other saying—"the lordship will not be taken from Judah, nor the
chieftain from his thigh, until he who is to be sent comes," the holy fathers of
our religion comment that it seems very manifest that Jacob said this with reference to our Lord Jesus Christ, who would come in the flesh to save the gentiles as well as the Jews, those who would be converted to him, the former as
well as the latter. And all longed for his coming, both gentiles and Jews, as Master Peter and others who agree with him say. And Master Peter also comments
on this passage that up to the Babylonian captivity, there were twenty one kings
of Israel, as you will hear further on in the books of the Kings of Israel, and all
these were of the tribe of Judah. And from then on, up to Hyrcanus,[41] he says
they were dukes, and again they were kings there up to the time of Herod.[42] And
around the time of the coming of Jesus Christ, there ceased to be kings and
dukes of his tribe and of the people of Israel, and Herod, who was a foreigner,
reigned, as we will tell you when we come to the history of that time.

And with regard to the passage where the saying turned against Judah, and
he said unto him: "Son, this man whom I tell you will be sent, will bind his foal
to the vineyard, and his ass to the grapevine," Master Peter says that it referred
to the gentile peoples and the Jews, whom Jesus Christ would unite to himself,
for he is called "vine" and "vineyard."[43] And regarding what Jacob said next
about Judah, that "he would wash his garment in wine, and his mantle in the
blood of the grape," Master Peter and others with him, say that this signifies
the flesh of our Lord Jesus Christ, which would be stained with his own blood
in his passion.

---

[41] John Hyrcanus I, high priest of the Jews from 135 to 105 B.C.E.
[42] Herod the Great (c. 73–4 B.C.E.) king of Judaea (40–4 B.C.E.); or his son Herod
Antipas, tetrarch of Galilee and Peraea (4 B.C.E.–C.E. 39), to whom Jesus was sent by
Pilate to be tried.
[43] John 15:1–2: "I am the true vine, and my Father is the husbandman. Every branch
in me that beareth not fruit, he taketh away: and every branch that beareth fruit, he
purgeth it, that it may bring forth more fruit."

And concerning Jacob's final words in this prophecy, that "his eyes would be more beautiful than wine, and his teeth whiter than milk," the sages say that they refer to the apostles, whom the Holy Scripture calls the "eyes" of our Lord Jesus Christ in our religion and in our faith, because they were very strong, and said many good things, and in it did many good deeds, and founded it, and affirmed it, not hesitating on any account, even when it came to losing their own bodies, as they in fact lost them; except that such a loss is really more of a gain.[44] And they say that the teeth signify the other holy preachers and martyrs, whose holy souls were bleached by fire and other martyrdoms, like noble metals in the fire, and linen in water.

XXVI. Of Jacob's Prophecy to Zebulun, His Fifth Son

Jacob said of Zebulun: "He shall dwell on the seashore and in seaports, and will reach as far as Sidon." And Master Peter comments on this passage that it came true, for the descendants of Zebulun inherited the marshes of Canaan up to Sidon. And Jacob said nothing more about Zebulun, nor do the holy fathers expound his saying further.

XXVII. Of Jacob's Prophecy to Issachar, His Sixth Son

Jacob prophesied concerning Issachar, and said: "A strong ass that couches down between the borders of the land. He saw that rest was good, and the land was bountiful and pleasant. And he set himself to carry burdens and take them to the ports and serve taxes." Concerning this prophecy of Issachar Master Peter says at this point that Jacob said this about his descendants, because they were intelligent, muscular, and strong men, and very hardworking, and their portion among the tribes of Israel was the lands that lie between the mountains and the marshes, which are better and more fertile than others for raising fruit. And because of the great abundance of their possessions, he says that they set themselves to carrying to the ports many loads of very rich merchandise that they had in their lands. And they travailed to serve ships, and this means that they brought the kings' taxes and money over the seas, and they made their lands productive, and leveled them, and took from them. But the Hebrew explains this saying in another way, and says that

---

[44] Luke 9:24: "For whosoever will save his life shall lose it: but whosoever will lose his life for my sake, the same shall save it."

Issachar's descendants worked night and day at their studies, and that all the other tribes of Israel served them and brought them their gifts, because they were the teachers.

XXVIII. Of Jacob's Prophecy to Dan, His Seventh Son

Then Jacob said of Dan: "Dan shall judge his people, like one of the other tribes of Israel." And he continued: "May Dan become a serpent on the land, and a horned serpent on the path, that bites the horse's feet so that the rider falls backwards. But Lord, I shall await your savior." Those who speak of this passage comment in many different ways. And they say that what Jacob said about Dan's judging his people and the other things he said afterwards, had to do with the fact that Dan's tribe would be so small that men never thought that a person who would be a judge would come from it, but that a judge of Israel came from it just as from the other tribes, and that he was a very strong man, and guarded the highways of Israel so that their enemies should not enter there, nor cross their land, nor destroy it, nor tread upon it. And in his days they did not enter it as they had done before, and he broke the pride of the Philistines, and made them turn back, and contained them. And they say that this was Samson, and that this prophecy was fulfilled in him. And you will hear in his story that he did all this.

Others, however, argue that this refers to the Antichrist, who they say will come from the tribe of Dan. He will come armed with the horn of power, and the bite of mortal preaching against the saints. He will bite them and destroy them, for all the prophecies of the holy fathers say that many of those he will encounter who have known the faith of Christ—which is the highway of truth—and who are at the height of virtue, he will confuse and lead astray from the highway of truth and the good of Christ, the living God, and will make them fall backwards. And then will come in judgment our Lord, whom we await.

Still others explain that this prophecy refers to Judas Iscariot, and the horse signifies the flesh of our Lord Jesus Christ, and the rider of that horse, the soul of Jesus Christ; and that Judas wounded the flesh of our Lord Jesus Christ with the bite of perdition, casting him down to death, and made the Jews kill him. But our Lord Jesus Christ, whom the peoples awaited, rose on the third day, as was prophesied, and as he had told his disciples earlier. But some say that Judas Iscariot was of the tribe of Issachar.

XXIX. Of Jacob's Prophecy to Gad, His Eighth Son

The prophecy concerning Gad was: "Gad, armed and prepared, will fight before him, and afterwards will return armed to his land." Master Peter and others who agree with him comment on this prophecy that when Jacob said of Gad that he would fight before Israel, he meant that the tribe of Gad, and that of Reuben and the half-tribe of Manasseh would leave their wives and children beyond the Jordan in the desert when the other tribes passed over to the land of promise, and that there these two and a half tribes would receive their share of the land. Nevertheless, they went out in armor and fought before the others to help them win the land, as the other eleven and a half tribes had helped them win that land that they took before crossing the Jordan, and it was given to them on condition that they go armed before, awaiting the rest of the people of Israel, when they entered the land of promise. And thus they did later on, as you will hear in their history. At the end of fourteen years, once the others were settled in their land, those of this tribe returned to their households that they had left beyond the Jordan, and found the peoples thereabout warring against their people. And the men of Gad fought with their enemies, and wounded them fiercely, and broke them, and their enemies were conquered and in very bad shape. Hence Master Peter says that this was why Jacob said that Gad would return armed.

Now we will speak of Asher.

XXX. Of the Prophecy Concerning Asher, Jacob's Ninth Son

Concerning Asher, Jacob prophesied as follows: "Asher, fat his bread, and he will give delights to kings." And Master Peter comments that this was said with regard to the land of Asher's portion, which was very good land, and abounded greatly in all good things, and very pleasant. And Jacob his father said no more than this, nor did the holy fathers expound further on it.

XXXI. Of the Prophecy Concerning Naphtali, Jacob's Tenth Son

As regards Naphtali, his tenth son, Jacob said: "Naphtali, a swift deer sent, and thence words of beauty." Master Peter also comments on this, and others who agree with him, that it was said with reference to the land Naphtali would receive as his portion, which would be even better and more plentiful than that of Asher or the portions of his other brothers. And just as the deer is very swift among the other animals of the earth, in the portion that would be his, the fruits sprouted and showed earlier than in the other portions, and that land would grow them at the very beginning of the year more quickly and earlier than all the others. And in addition they said that Jacob's words to Naphtali— "and thence words of beauty"—signified that just as words are worth more when they are fine and lovely and well spoken, so the things and species that grow in Naphtali's portion are better than others, and of greater virtue, and greater value, and greater price. And that portion which fell to Naphtali is the one that lies in Israel on the lake called Gennesaret, and it is watered by the source of the river Jordan. Hence others say that this is why things grow so well there, as you have heard, because of the warm waters that are in that land, and that therefore the fruits sprout more swiftly there than in the other places in the land of promise, just as the deer is naturally swifter than other game.

Concerning Jacob's other saying about Naphtali, that he would give words of beauty, still others comment that this signifies Mount Tabor, which is in the portion of that land where afterwards dwelled the prophets who said the many and very good words that we find in their writings and in others, and you will hear them in their proper places in this history, or we will recount them to you, if God will. Others add that, either Jacob said that for the reason we have stated, or else with regard to the first fruits of that place, because they were the earliest of all those lands which the inhabitants always offered to God on the feast of Passover, and the people of Israel would make their sacrifices to God in the tabernacle of witness, where God would be praised with beautiful words of prayers that they said there. And later, still others commented that this could refer to Mount Tabor, because our Lord Jesus Christ and his apostles preached there, and there taught the beginning of the new law and of the faith of Christ to the people more than in any other place.

XXXII. Of the Prophecies Concerning Joseph, in Which Jacob Spoke Well of Him, and Praised Him

Concerning Joseph, his eleventh son, Jacob prophesied . . . ,[45] as the Bible story tells near the end of the book of Genesis, and said in this wise: "Increasing son, Joseph, increasing and beautiful to see. The daughters ran all over the wall.

---

[45] Here the manuscript reads: "quando delos otros en su firmamiento." I have not been able to decipher the meaning of this phrase. Perhaps "quando" is a mistake for "quanto," and the passage means that he prophesied as much about Joseph as about all his other sons put together.

And men sought to bring him grief and evil, and envied him, and shot at him, and they had darts. But his bow was firmly lodged in the strong one, and the cords binding his arms and his hands were untied by the hands of the Powerful One of Jacob; thence came forth a shepherd, the Rock of Israel. The God of your father will be your helper and He, who is powerful in all things, will bless you with the blessings of heaven from above, and with the blessings of the abyss which lies below, and with blessings of milk and of young cattle. The blessings of your father are reinforced by the blessings of his fathers, until the desire of the everlasting hills comes. Let them be on Joseph's head, and on the head of the Nazirite among his brothers."

This prophecy concerning Joseph is greater than any of those of his brothers, for there are many prophecies, and more good things in them, than in the others; for Joseph deserved it on account of all the goodnesses you have heard were in him, and all the services he performed for kings, and to the land, and to his father, and to his people. And in these prophecies there are words that are obscure to understand, and they appear in the Latin Bible story as we have told them here in the language of Castile. But we will comment on them here, as we did with those of the other brothers, so they can be understood.

XXXIII. Of the Meaning of the Prophecies Concerning Joseph

With regard to that statement the Scripture makes twice—"increasing son, Joseph, increasing son"—Master Peter and others who have expounded this story comment that it said it first, because he increased greatly in virtue of goodness, and continued to increase day by day, and did so as long as he lived; second, because of the distinguished position to which he rose, and the great power he held, and the fact that he managed to succeed in it very well and to maintain it. As for what it says next, that he was beautiful to see, and that the daughters ran around on the wall, St. Augustine, Master Peter, and others say that it referred to the fact that Joseph was so beautiful that he surpassed all the other men of that time in beauty; and you have already heard how we recounted this in the story of him and Lady Zulayme, his mistress and his wife, whom he later married; and how the ladies who were with him said that Joseph was so beautiful that no woman could see him without swooning. And from the time that he rose to great power, when he came to the towns where he traveled to collect the things and tribute due to his lord the king, the women went out and climbed up on the walls, and in the towers, and the high places, and stood at the windows to see a man so renowned for his beauty, and also for his great power.

Concerning what comes next in the prophecy, that men sought to bring him grief and evil, and envied him, and shot at him, and they had darts aimed at him, Master Peter recounts in his history that this referred to his brothers, because of their envy of him and what they did to him; but that was already past. For in these prophecies that you have heard Jacob prophesied concerning his sons, there are some sayings that referred to what had already happened, and that could be the case here, as the sages comment. Others say that this refers to the Egyptians, who envied the great favor in which the king held him, and the great wealth and power in which they saw him, and the evil they often would have done him if they could. But Joseph always kept himself with God, and God with him, and He helped him, and they could do him no harm. And this is how they explain Jacob's next saying, that his bow was firmly lodged in the strong one. And in this place, "the strong one," as the holy fathers comment, means God, for the strong one, by definition and without other modification, is the true God. And by Him the cords binding his arms and his hands were untied, on that occasion when you heard that his brothers seized him, and tied his hands, and threw him into the dry well, which the Latin calls "cisterna." And again when he was arrested and thrown in jail in Egypt by Lady Zulayme, the wife of his master Phutiphar, to whom his lord King Pharaoh later married him, as we have recounted earlier. And God, who was always the Powerful One of Jacob, Joseph's father, freed him.

And with regard to what the Bible says next, "thence came forth a shepherd, the Rock of Israel," Master Peter comments that Jacob said "shepherd" with reference to Joseph because he watched over all his family, like a shepherd to all the other sons, who gave them what they needed to eat and everything else, and supported them very well. And this saying was no longer a prophecy about Joseph, indicating that he would be a shepherd later, for Joseph had already been one, and was one then. Nor did Jacob say this so much as a prophecy about Joseph, as to recount and recall the good deeds of his good son; and because Joseph was a figure of Jesus Christ, who would yet come and be such a shepherd to his apostles, and his disciples would be shepherds to his peoples. "Rock of Israel" refers to Jeroboam, who would come from Joseph's lineage, and was a king, and ruled over the ten tribes, as we will recount in the history of the Third Book of Kings, and he maintained them like a man, and was in that way very strong like a rock. But the Hebrew text of this saying reads "rock of the shepherds," and concerning what the Hebrew calls "rock of the shepherds," the holy fathers comment that it means Joseph, who was the strength and defense of his brothers and their families, who came to Egypt as shepherds. And we judge that both those commentaries on the word "Rock" are good, and both have a place there, for thus it happened with Joseph, and also with Jeroboam, as we have told you, and you will hear concerning Jeroboam further on.

And you will find that the sages who have commented on the words Jacob said about Joseph up to this point, have explained that they were really praises of the good deeds Joseph performed—as we've already mentioned in this chapter—rather than prophecies, for prophecy speaks of the things that are to come, and some of these things had already happened, while others were happening at the time the words were spoken. Nevertheless, they were also prophetic, for the reason we have already mentioned, namely, that Joseph was a figure of Jesus Christ, who was to come.

XXXIV. Of Jacob's Blessings to His Son Joseph, Whom He Loved Much

After Jacob had praised Joseph for his deeds, as you have heard, he began to bless him, and he prayed that God might help him, and always give him His blessing, and an abundance of the goods that came from heaven and those of the earth, and an abundance of milk and of cattle, for those were then the greatest riches that men had, and those they sought the most. Many have commented in different ways on the words he said next: "The blessings of your father are reinforced by the blessings of his fathers, until the desire of the everlasting hills comes." Master Peter says that it is very difficult to explain the meaning of this biblical text, but he comments that it can be understood in the following way. You will hear farther on in the book of Numbers, which speaks of the census of the people of Israel and is the fourth of the five books of Moses, that in the desert there are some exceedingly great boulders, so high that their tops are hidden in the clouds of heaven, and they are called the boulders of Arnon, because of the mountain there named Arnon. And in them there are four peaks that are higher than all the rest, and hence the sages called them the *tetragon* hills, meaning "four," or "four blocks of stone," or four things like these hills and separated in like manner. And it means that they are either four peaks or four corners, wherefore Jacob speaks at this point of the four peaks of those boulders. And the sages who comment on this passage of this Bible story say that when the children of Israel were traveling through the desert with Moses, and they reached that mountain which has below it a great part of those boulders and those hills, they were brought low so that the people of Israel could pass through them more swiftly, and they seemed to rejoice greatly, as if rejoicing at the arrival of that people. Hence King David later said in his Psalter of this matter: "The mountains rejoiced like rams, and the little hills like lambs."[46] And interpreting this passage in this sense, it means that the

---

[46] Ps. 114:4.

hills of Arnon rejoiced at the coming of the people of Israel. Continuing their commentary, the sages say that Jacob blessed his son Joseph and prophesied at this point with these words: "The blessings of your father are reinforced by the blessings of his fathers, until the desire of the everlasting hills comes." And they say that Jacob was telling Joseph: "Son, you will be blessed until your descendants and the rest of the people of Israel come to the hills of Arnon, which will be pleased with them, and will humble themselves at their coming, and they will pass over to the land of promise which lies beyond." And some say that the half tribe of Manasseh took its portion of the land near those mountains. And in this wise others comment that this saying means: thus will Joseph be blessed, and he will yet possess that other property that comes later. Others say about this that Jacob prophesied concerning the Mount of Ephraim and the mountain of Samaria, where the people of Israel ruled, and they took and held part of those mountains from the Medes and the Persians. And some say in this regard that beyond those mountains are now exiled the descendants of Ephraim and Manasseh, and that the land rejoiced over their exile as if they were its enemies. For they comment that then ended the glory and the nobility and the fame of the power of the people of Israel, so great was their destruction then. The Hebrew comments in a different way on this passage and says: "until the everlasting hills be joined to heaven." And, as the histories comment, the meaning of this prophecy according to these Hebrew words is: "Blessed be Joseph's descendants until heaven and earth are joined together."

And concerning Jacob's final words—"Let them be on Joseph's head, and on the head of the Nazirite among his brothers"—the expounders comment that they mean that all these blessings you have heard should be fulfilled on the head and on the descendants of Joseph, who was holy among his brothers, for "Nazirite" means the same thing in their religion as "holy."

Now we will tell of the prophecy he spoke concerning Benjamin.

XXXV. Of Jacob's Prophecy Concerning Benjamin, His Last Son, in Which He Said as Follows:

"Benjamin, thieving wolf, in the morning he shall devour the prey, and in the evening he shall divide the spoil." Many expound this prophecy in different ways. Some say that this wolf whom Jacob called "thieving" here refers to the city of Jerusalem, which lies in the portion which Benjamin was to have in the land of promise. And the sages comment that that city must be the "thieving wolf" because in it was shed the blood of the prophets and that of our Lord Jesus Christ, as if it ate them like a devouring wolf. And they say that the prey that the prophecy says next that this thieving wolf would devour in the morning signifies the law that Moses took from our Lord Jesus Christ, and he took it away from him. The words "in the morning he shall devour" mean that the Jews understand that law literally and refuse to go on to its inner meaning. And even now it is as if the Jews were devouring it, but they don't swallow it nor chew it as long as they don't understand it nor want to do so. And as for the next saying—"in the evening he shall divide the spoil"—it means that at the end of the world the Jews will understand their former blindness, and arrive at the truth, and will take from the letter the understanding of what it means, which is the same as the spirit that gives life, for "the spirit gives life, and the letter kills,"[47] if a man does what it says, and not what it means. The Hebrew gives this other interpretation: it says that the "thieving wolf" refers to the altar in Jerusalem, which was like a wolf on account of its fire, which consumed the many sacrifices the priests placed on it to burn in honor of God and for the salvation of the people. And they say that the spoil that it would divide in the evening refers to the portions of the sacrifices to which the priests were entitled, which they would divide in the evening. Master Peter, and others who agree with him, give still another interpretation, saying that in reality these words refer to St. Paul, who was of the tribe of Benjamin, and at first he sought to do the Christians much evil, and persecuted them, and killed them; but he became a Christian later, and was a very great lord and prince of Christianity, and very faithful, and he commented on the words and scriptures of our Lord God and the graces of the Church. And he also says that this prophecy was said of Benjamin with reference to his tribe, who were always very warlike and fighting men, as you will hear in the book of the Judges of Israel, in the passage concerning the Levite's wife.[48]

These are the prophecies that Jacob prophesied to his sons when he was dying, and he told each of them exactly what would happen to their descendants.

XXXVI. Of How Jacob Commanded that He Be Buried, and Bade His Sons Farewell, and Died

And these tribes of Jacob were twelve in all, and in them were later fulfilled all these prophecies that you have heard their father spoke unto them. And when he was done prophesying, he blessed them, and said: "Sons, I am going to my

---

[47] 2 Cor. 3:6: "for the letter killeth, but the spirit giveth life."

[48] The reference is to the Levite whose concubine was raped and murdered by the Benjamites in Gibeah. The Benjamites chose to go to war against the other tribes rather than surrender the culprits (Judges 19–20).

people, and I beg you and command you to bury me with my own in the double cave that is in the field of Ephron the Hittite, over against Mamre, in the land of Canaan, the one that my grandfather Abraham bought from Ephron the Hittite, with its field, for his grave. And there lie buried he, and Sarah his wife, and his son Isaac, my father, and Rebecca, my mother, and Leah, my wife.

And after he had taught and instructed his sons in the manner we have said, and commanded what they should do, he gathered up his feet (which were outside) into the bed, and died. And he died as a good and holy man, as you have heard, and they buried him with his fathers in Hebron, where he had commanded them to do so. And we will tell you all about this burial here. Therefore we shall set aside the other words of the biblical text and tell you about this burial, but first of all, about the honor Pharaoh ordered done to Jacob upon his death, and which the Egyptians did then, and then he was honored by his sons and everyone else upon his burial.

XXXVII. Of the Mourning for Jacob, and of How Long the Ancients Mourned

When Joseph saw that his father was deceased, with the great grief and great sorrow that gave him, he ran and fell upon him, and began to kiss him, although he was already deceased, and he wept much and made a great mourning for him, as a very good son for a very good father. Then he ordered his sons, who were with him, to embalm him, and they bathed him very well, and then embalmed him. During this time, forty days passed while he remained unburied, and the Egyptians kept him those forty days, for it was the custom at that time to keep the dead that long.

In this regard Master Peter recounts that there were then in Egypt some gentiles called Enicos, and they differed from the other gentiles in their belief. And these people, according to their sect, had the custom of retaining and keeping their dead unburied for nine days. They didn't embalm them, and every day they washed them with warm water in order to see whether the soul had left the body yet, or if it was still there, as if asleep. And they kept the ones who were embalmed for forty days, for their flesh did not decompose nor stink. And the embalmed were bathed only once, but since they didn't decompose, they waited to see if they would revive, for many of them did return to life because of this waiting period and vigilance. And the Jews had the custom of keeping those they didn't embalm for sixteen days, and the embalmed for thirty days, which are ten less than the Enicos's custom.

And Joseph, in order to do greater honor to his father than had ever been done before to any man in that place, decided that both of those customs—

that of the gentiles and that of the Jews—should be observed in the case of his father Jacob's death. Therefore Jacob was kept unburied for seventy days, the thirty days of the Jews, and the forty days of the gentiles.

And it is for this reason that now Christians in some lands observe a thirty-day mourning period[49] for those who die, singing and offering Masses for them, according to that custom of the Jews, who waited thirty days to bury them. In Spain mourning is observed for men of honor—that is, *hidalgos*, and others who are so entitled because of their wealth—for forty days after they die. And this is according to the custom of the gentiles, from whom we Christians descend, who observe forty days, except that they don't keep them above the ground, but go to their graves and show their esteem by honoring them with prayers and offerings on the fortieth day. There are also some Christians who do this honor to the dead for seven days, and they say that they do this to show that in the seventh age all those who are to be in heaven will go there.

During all these seventy days we have mentioned, the gentiles of Egypt and the Jews who were there wept, and lamented, and mourned for Jacob.

XXXVIII. Of Jacob's Burial

When the mourning period was over, Joseph told those of Pharaoh's house how his father had adjured him to bury him with his fathers in the sepulcher he had made for himself in the land of Canaan. And then he implored them, if they loved him and wished him well and ever wanted to do him a favor, to beg the king to let him take him there, for he would come back right away. They went in with him, and told this to the king, and begged him to grant Joseph that favor that he requested. Then Pharaoh, with the great love he felt for Joseph, let him take him, and commanded him to do as his father had adjured him and he had promised him.

Then Joseph took him, and they set out with all the elders of the king's house, and all the other adult Egyptians, and Joseph's family, and his brothers with their families, except for those who were married and those who were unable to travel because of frailty, and the little children, and their mothers, and their maidservants, and their cattle, and those whom they left to guard the family members who stayed behind in the land of Goshen.

And also a large number of Egyptian horsemen accompanied them, and all together they made a great company, and they took wagons and much other baggage with everything they needed. And they came to a place called the

---

[49] Spanish: "treyntanario."

threshing floor of Atad, which is on this side of the Jordan as they were coming, and they stayed there seven days with the body, doing it much honor and
lamenting over it; and this was already in Canaan. And when the people who
dwelled there saw the Egyptians observing this great mourning, they named
that place "the Lament of Egypt," and thus it was called ever afterward. And
the route by which they came from Egypt to Canaan was not direct, but instead they went aside there with great fear of being attacked by the people of
those lands, according to Master Peter. Then they reached Hebron, and they
buried Jacob very honorably there where he had commanded.

Now we will tell you how long Jacob lived and when he died and was buried.

XXXIX. Of the Chronicle of Jacob's Years and His Burial

Jacob lived a hundred and forty seven years, as is told, and he spent his last seventeen years in Egypt, in the land of Goshen, where he was well treated by King
Pharaoh Nicrao and his son Joseph, and he died there, as we have said. And it
was then 4,198 years since Adam, according to the Hebrews, and 3,626 by the
reckoning of the seventy translators. It was 3,344 years since Noah, likewise by
the Hebrew accounting, and 2,392 according to the seventy translators. And
it was 942 years since the Deluge, according to the Hebrews, and 782 according to the seventy. And it was 841 since the division of languages, according
to the seventy. And it was 353 years since the reign of Ninus, King of Assyria.
And 310 since Abraham. And twenty seven years since the death of Isaac,
Jacob's father, for that was how many years Jacob lived after the death of his
father Isaac, and otherwise Isaac lived 180 years. And Joseph was then fifty
years old, and had been a potentate in Egypt for seventeen years. And the year
that Jacob died, these kings were reigning: Baleus in Assyria, Eratus in Sichio-
nia, Argo in Argos of Greece, and King Pharaoh Amosis in Egypt.

Now we will leave these matters and others in the Bible, and tell you about
other things that were happening among the gentiles at that time, and we will
relate them to you according to the years Joseph was in power, from here on
until he died.

[Chapter XL deals with the introduction of wheat into Greece, which is said to have
occurred around the time of Jacob's death; Chapter XLI is about how men began to
breed mules, twenty seven years after Jacob's death; and Chapter XLII deals with the
introduction of weights and measures in Greece.]

XLIII. Of How Joseph's Brothers Feared Him, and He Reassured Them, and Returned to Egypt with Them

After Joseph and his brothers had buried their father and performed there all the obsequies appropriate to his burial, Joseph prepared to return to Egypt with all the company that had come there to accompany and wait on him, and to honor his father. And he wanted to take his brothers with him, just as they had come with him. But his brothers were afraid that he would remember what they had done to him, and would want to take revenge on them now that he had them in his power (for his father was dead, and perhaps it was because of him that he had refrained from taking vengeance until then), and do them wrong, and oppress them. And they all discussed this among themselves. And they sent him a message that their father had told them in Goshen and had advised them to convey to Joseph if they should be afraid of him after his death. And the message said: "My son Joseph, I Jacob beg you to forget the sin and wickedness your brothers committed against you." And they sent envoys to him with this message, and also to beg him to forgive them for love of his father and out of his own goodness. When Joseph heard that his brothers were afraid of him, he was much aggrieved and wept on that account. And then they heard about this and went to him, and knelt before him, and all bowed down unto him, and told him that they were his servants, and that he should pardon them and show them kindness and mercy, and now they begged him themselves, face to face. Then Joseph replied that they should not be afraid, that what had happened was from God, and no one could oppose what God truly wanted to happen, and God had caused it all to turn out for the best, and He did it so that many should be saved by him, as they could see. Then he reassured them, and comforted them, and he told them again very meekly not to be afraid, for he would give them everything they needed for themselves and their families, just as he had done in the days of his father Jacob, and that they would see no change, except for the better. And then he pardoned them.

And Josephus says that then he gave them great gifts of many very rare things he had brought, and he gave much money to each of them, and also to the gentile Egyptians who had come with him and honored him. And they were very happy about this, and they believed him, and stayed with him, and were reassured, and all set out together for Egypt. And there they all lived with him. And Joseph did everything he had promised them and more.

Now we shall leave the Bible story and tell you how many Pharaohs there were in Egypt from the death of Jacob until that of Joseph, which was fifty three years, and also the kings of the other kingdoms we usually mention here, as they were at that time.

XLIV. Of the Pharaoh Kings and Other Gentile Kings at That Time

Twenty five years after Joseph had come to power in Egypt, Baleus had reigned fifty two years in Assyria, and he died. And after him Altadas reigned thirty two years, and Altadas was the twelfth king of that land. When Joseph had been in power for thirty eight years, that Pharaoh we told you was called Derith in Arabic and Amosis in Egyptian had reigned in Egypt for twenty five years, as we have already mentioned, and he died. And after him King Pharaoh his son—whose name was Chebron in Egyptian and Tsabedz in Arabic, according to the *History of Egypt,* and it is said that some called him Tsaden Chebron—reigned for thirteen years. And after him the sixth Pharaoh, whose name was Cashim in Arabic and Amenophes[50] in Egyptian, reigned for twenty one years.

Now we shall tell you some things about the other gentiles.

[Chapter XLV tells the story of Prometheus, who is supposed to have been a contemporary of Joseph's]

XLVI. Of the Power, and Descendants, and Death of Joseph, and His Admonition to His Brothers

During all these eighty years that we have recounted, Joseph was powerful, as we have said, and he continued to hold total power under all the Pharaohs of his time whom we have named, so that he never lost it, so much did he adhere to God and goodness and so successful did God make him because of that. And he saw the sons of his son Ephraim to the third generation, and those of Machir, his grandson, son of Manasseh. At the end of these years, Joseph realized that the time was coming when he must die, and he summoned his brothers and their families, and said unto them: "Brothers, I am now at the end of my life, and I die. But before doing so, I want to speak to you about your behavior, and thus do I instruct and counsel you: comfort one another and treat each other with perfect kindness, for when I am dead, I know that it will not go so well for you with your lords the Pharaohs nor with the Egyptians as it has been in my lifetime. And they will oppress you, and tax you sorely, and reduce you to oppressive and vile tasks, and make you their slaves. And so great will be their wickedness and cruelty to you—and even more so, that of the people,

---

[50] Amen Hotep?

for they are greedy and envious and have other bad habits that I well know—that they will greatly humiliate you. For kings, though they be naturally harsh, are better by themselves than when they are guided by evil counselors. And for this reason they will do you so much evil that it will grieve God, and He will look down and remember you. Therefore be strong, for after my death God will visit you and lead you to the land He swore to give to our fathers Abraham, Isaac, and Jacob."

After telling them this, he repeated that God would visit them, and begged them, and adjured them that, when God should take them out of that place to lead them to the Promised Land, they should not leave him there, but should take his bones with them and bury him with his father and his grandparents. And when he had finished saying these things, he asked them very insistently, by God and by the debts they owed him, to tell him whether all, or some, or any one of them had any complaints about him—for he would remedy them at once—and to forgive him. And they all replied that none of them had a big nor even a small complaint to make of him; but that they were all well aware that he had always shown them much generosity and kindness and mercy, and that our Lord God should pardon him and receive his soul. And that was their prayer, and they would repeat it as long as they lived. And then they all began to weep mightily, and he thanked them much, and divided his wealth among them, and gave it to them all, and then he prayed to God for them. And the *History of Egypt* says that he entrusted his family to Judah, his brother, and then he died. And when they told King Pharaoh Mephres[51] that Joseph was dead, he was very sorry about his death, for Joseph was a very wise man, and gave excellent advice in all matters, and particularly in the more intricate ones, and he had gotten along very well with him, as had the other Egyptians and the other Pharaohs whom Joseph had served before him. And he ordered much honor done to him upon his death, and had him embalmed. And the *History of Egypt* says that they wrapped him in his shroud with the kinds of cloth that were used for burying kings. And they put him in a marble urn made in the shape of an ark, and they enclosed it in lead, and they sealed it with that glue which is called *bitumen*[52] in Latin, in such a way that neither air, nor water, nor anything else could get into it. And some say that they cast it in the Nile, at the place where that river enters the Red Sea, but in such a way that they could remove it later. Others say that they buried it on the shore near the water, also in a place where they could remove it whenever they wished.

[51] The previous chapter mentions that this Pharaoh succeeded to the throne when Joseph was 104 years old.

[52] A kind of mineral pitch found in Palestine and Babylon.

And in this regard they say that every year the weather was good in the place where he lay, and whatever they sowed prospered, and the fruit likewise, but what was on the other side of the river suffered. And when men saw this, they understood, and they moved him up by the place where the Nile begins, and then the weather of that region improved, and everything prospered there, but the other place where he had lain earlier suffered. And when the people realized that this was the reason why they had good or bad weather in that land, they fell into a great quarrel over it. But it is said that to settle the quarrel and fight, and to keep it from getting any worse—for they saw that they stood to lose much by it—they figured out a way to ensure that the weather would be the same every year. And this is what they decided. At first, they thought they would have him taken completely out of the country, but they were afraid that that would make everything turn out worse. So they gave up that idea, and they decided the best thing would be to put him in the middle of the Nile. So they took him and put him in a coffin made in such a way that neither water nor rain could get into it, nor could the coffin sink too much beneath the water. And on it they put two very strong rings with a chain attached to each one. And they fastened one chain to one shore, and the other to the other equally, so that the coffin would stay in the middle of the Nile. And after they had done this, the weather improved, and the fruits of the earth prospered on both sides from then on.

Now we will tell you the years from the beginning of the world and from Adam, as we have found that Master Godfrey reckoned them in his *Pantheon*, and also by the accounts of other sages.

XLVII. Of the Number of Years from the Beginning of the World and from Adam to Joseph's Death

According to Master Peter in his *Book of the Generations of the Old Testament Patriarchs*, Joseph's death occurred 4,248 years after the beginning of the world and the creation of Adam, according to the reckoning of the Hebrews, and 3,676 according to the seventy translators. And it was 1,592 years since Noah, according to the Hebrews, and 1,432 according to the seventy translators. And it was 1,490 years since Noah's flood, according to the Hebrews, and 1,331 according to the translators. It was 1,389 years since the division of languages, according to the Hebrews, and according to the seventy translators 1,330. And it was 304 years since the reign of Ninus, King of Assyria, 360 years since Abraham's birth, 260 years since that of Isaac, 200 years since that of Jacob, and 110 years since Joseph's own birth.

And these gentile kings were then reigning in their kingdoms: Manitus in Assyria, Plenmeus in Sicionia, King Argo in Argos of Greece, and in Egypt the Pharaoh named Mephres.

At this point in our history and with these words concerning the gentiles, which we have inserted into the Old Testament in their proper places, the Book of Genesis, which is the first of the five books of Moses, comes to an end. From here on we will tell you about the time and the things that came after this until we get to the story of the Book of Exodus, which is the second of those five books of Moses.

Multiplices casus et longa pericula vitæ,
Fatidici Ioseph, gloria magna fuit.

Der Neid.

Ioseph durch Brüder Haß zur Schand,
verkauft wird in Egypten land.

*The story of Joseph as emblematic of envy. Engraving designed by Gottfried Eichler
the Younger for Johann Georg Hertel's edition of Cesare Ripa's* Iconologia *(Augsburg:
1758–1760); the first edition of the* Iconologia *was published without illustrations in Rome
in 1593. The allegorical character Envy appears in the foreground, with Joseph's sale to
the Ishmaelite merchants in the background. The Latin* fatto, *or statement of the event
illustrated, states:*

Many vicissitudes and long-lasting dangers occurred
To the prophet Joseph in his life, [but at last he won] great glory.

⇥ The Story of Joseph, Son of the Great Patriarch Jacob (before 1486)

Joan Roiç de Corella (1428?–1497)

Joan Roiç de Corella was born in Gandía, ancestral home of the Dukes of Borgia, forty two miles south of Valencia, around the year 1428, the eldest child and only son of Ausias Roiç de Corella and Aldonça de Corella. The family was a noble one which traced its ancestry back to the town of Corella in the Kingdom of Navarre, but they were only moderately wealthy. Roiç de Corella was a cousin of Ausias March (1397–1459), greatest Valencian poet of the fifteenth century. The family moved to Valencia around 1442, and Ausias Roiç de Corella died there in January 1450. Both the poet and his father are identified in many legal documents of the period as soldiers (*miles*), but neither is known to have had a military career and the word may be merely a reference to their knightly (*cavaller*) status.

Very little is known of the life of Roiç de Corella. The opulent Valencia of his time, closely linked to the royal court of Alfons V "the Magnanimous" of Aragon (1416–1458) in Naples, was famous for its literary academies and salons (*tertulias*), but Roiç de Corella's participation in the public intellectual life of the city seems to have been marginal. He did carry on an extensive correspondence with the distinguished humanist and patron of the arts Prince Carlos of Viana (1421–1461), nephew of Alfons V, but on the whole seems to have preferred a life of scholarly retirement.

Roiç de Corella earned his living as a professor of theology. He received the degree of Master of Sacred Theology in September 1469 and in November 1482 was appointed to the prestigious Chair of Theology in the Council Chamber of the city of Valencia. However, his writings reveal little interest in systematic theology. Instead, he applied the techniques he had acquired as a humanist well trained in the interpretation of the classics to scriptural exegesis. His first book, a *Life of St. Anne*, was published in Valencia in 1485. He also wrote a life of St. Mary Magdalen (*Historia de la gloriosa santa Magdalena*), adapted the Carthusian monk Ludolph of Saxony's life of Christ (*La Cartoxa*) from the Latin and published a translation of the book of Psalms in Venice in 1490.

He also produced elegant adaptations of Ovid's *Metamorphoses* and *Heroides*, Seneca's tragedies, and Boccaccio's *De claris mulieribus*. The great theme of Roiç de Corella's work is the nature of love. Both his prose and his poetry explore the whole range of the human experience of love, from mystical exaltation to sensual intoxication. In spite of his religious vocation, women figure prominently in his work and certainly did so in his life as well. He acknowledged having fathered two illegitimate children, Joan and Estefania, by a certain Isabel Martínez de Vera. One of his major works, the *Tragèdia de Caldesa,* in prose with intercalated passages of verse, recounts how the woman he calls Caldesa—apparently the great love of his life—betrayed him. Roiç de Corella spent the last years of his life in a Franciscan monastery.

Roiç de Corella is generally considered the last great writer of Valencian literature. That regional literature, which had begun as an outgrowth of the courtly love poetry of the Provençal troubadours in the late twelfth century and had been the first Iberian literature to introduce humanism and the innovations of Italian writers such as Dante, Boccaccio, and Petrarch to the peninsula, was already in its death throes in Roiç de Corella's time. Many of his contemporaries had already abandoned their native tongue in favor of Castilian. Indeed, the main reason Roiç de Corella has not received more recognition is the fact that he wrote all of his works in Valencian—and not only in Valencian, but in a highly stylized, rhetorical, Latinate style that limited their appeal to an élite readership. In the Prologue to his *Historia de Josep* he states that he chose to write that work in "vulgar de valençiana prosa," which I have translated, perhaps misleadingly, as "ordinary Valencian prose." Obviously, Roiç de Corella's prose is anything but ordinary. Scholars disagree about what he meant by that phrase. The adjective *vulgar* was commonly used in the Renaissance to distinguish the everyday spoken language from Latin. However, Jordi Rubió i Balaguer has argued that Roiç de Corella meant to distinguish his language from Catalan, with which Valencian is often confused.[1] Martín de Riquer, on the other hand, believes that the term *valençiana prosa* was intended to designate the "rhetorical and emphatic prose style" created by Roiç de Corella himself, not a characteristically Valencian style, which others have described as particularly "refined and delicate."[2] There has been a marked increase in scholarly interest in Spain's regional literatures since the death of the dictator Francisco Franco in 1975, and especially since the Constitution of 1978 provided for limited home rule by the seventeen "autonomous communities," one of which is Valencia. Josep Almiñana Vallés published the first critical edition of Roiç de Corella's *Obres* in Valencia in 1985. I have based my translation of the *Historia de Josep* on that edition (II, 638–667).

Modern critics have tended to appreciate Roiç de Corella's poetry more than his prose. Thus Marcelino Menéndez y Pelayo considered him a significant pre-

---

[1] "Literatura catalana," *Historia general de las literaturas hispánicas* (Barcelona: Barna, 1953), III, 881.
[2] *Historia de la literatura catalana* (Barcelona: Esplegues de Llobregat, 1964), III, 319.

decessor of Garcilaso de la Vega for having written Italianate iambic hen-
decasyllables with an accent on the sixth syllable (as opposed to the traditional
Provençal hendecasyllable, which accented the fourth syllable in the line).[3]
Commenting on the *Tragèdia de Caldesa*, Paul Russell-Gebbett has written that
"although in this work the customary emotional and formal exaggeration of the
prose set pieces seems to correspond to a real bitterness, and thus to confer
upon it an unwonted sincerity, it is in his verse that the writer appears most
sincere. It expresses more effectively because more economically his anger at
Caldesa's betrayal."[4] Russell-Gebbett's reference to the "unwonted sincerity"
of the *Tragèdia's* prose passages betrays the modern notion that rhetoric and
sincerity are at odds with one another. This view, as well as the idea that economy is necessarily more "effective" than expansiveness, would surely have puz-
zled Roiç de Corella. The highly artistic, poetic, and rhetorical prose style he
created was intended to elevate his native language and make of it a worthy
rival of Latin, capable of expressing humankind's deepest emotions and loftiest aspirations in the most exact, and therefore "sincere," way possible. He
would surely have viewed our modern, unvarnished prose—for all its vaunted
"sincerity"—as terribly inadequate, impoverished, and unlovely. He would
have wondered how modern writers could ever have voluntarily renounced the
use of the many expressive resources discovered by the ancients, and rediscov-
ered in his own time. The answer, of course, is that those devices were eventually so overused that they became worn out and hackneyed and therefore
ceased to produce the desired effects. In his time, however, they were a novel
and exciting reaction to the monotonous simplicity of so much medieval prose.

The *Historia de Josep, fill del gran Patriarcha Jacob* was first published in Valencia, probably in 1500, but it is known to have been written by 1486, since a
copy of it appears in the codex entitled *Jardinet d'Orats*, which was copied that
year. Only a single copy of the first edition has survived, in the library of the
University of Valencia. A Castilian translation appeared in Valladolid in 1507.

The most remarkable thing about the *Historia de Josep* is the utter absence
of any reference to Christianity, with the possible exception of a single sentence in chapter six ("Stripping him of that embroidered robe which his father
Jacob, out of singular love, had given him, they threw the meek lamb into the
old cistern"), which could be seen as an oblique reference to Jesus. The *Historia* is, for the most part, an artistic adaptation or paraphrase of the biblical text.
Just as he had done in his adaptations of Ovid, Roiç de Corella sees the whole

---

[3] *Antología de poetas líricos castellanos* in his *Obras completas* (Madrid: CSIC, 1945),
X, 169-170.
[4] "Medieval Catalan Literature" in P. E. Russell, ed., *Spain: A Companion to Spanish
Studies* (New York: Pitman, 1973), p. 259.

story as an allegory, in this case conveying the message that "God writes straight with crooked lines," that is, that, while respecting human free will, Divine Providence turns even the wicked actions of men to the benefit of the virtuous. This moral lesson is clearly stated in the Prologue and reiterated in Jacob's prayer in the penultimate chapter. Joseph is completely idealized as an "exemplar of virtues." The text gives no indication that he ever did anything to deserve his sufferings, and in this way, as in its straightforward moralizing, it is closer to the Muslim tradition than to the Jewish one. However, one might argue that the principal non-biblical influence on the work was the lives of the saints, and it is well to recall that Roiç de Corella himself had earlier composed lives of St. Anne and St. Mary Magdalene.

Nevertheless, it is clear that some of the non-biblical material in the work is adapted from Muslim and Jewish sources. Two passages in particular—Joseph's prayer in the cistern and his lament on the grave of his mother Rachel—are clearly of Muslim origin. Joseph's invocation in the cistern ("Oh, King of kings, immense Lord, God of Jacob, Isaac, and Abraham! Since nothing is hidden from Your majesty, and without Your power no creature is preserved, nor can any action be performed without Your will . . .") is remarkably similar to the prayer in chapter eight of the Muslim *Story of Yusuf, Son of Ya'qub* ("Oh Maker of all things made, Repairer of all things broken, oh Answerer of all prayers, oh Great above all the great, . . . oh Provider of sustenance to small creatures, . . . there is no power and strength but in Allah . . ."). Likewise, his lament on Rachel's grave recalls the similar lament in chapter ten of that version. We can only speculate about how Roiç de Corella became acquainted with that material. It seems most unlikely that he could have had access to Muslim texts. However, in fifteenth-century Valencia he would have had no difficulty in encountering knowledgeable Muslims who could have informed him of their traditions concerning the story of Joseph. As I. P. Harvey has observed, "the great number of Muslims who remained behind [in Valencia] at the conquest and the small number of Christian settlers at first willing to come live in such an alien land meant that for most of the period under examination [i.e., 1250–1500] the Muslims were still the majority community in many areas, and the outward and visible signs of Islamic civilization were much more numerous."[5] Furthermore, we know from a document dated November 1460 that Roiç de Corella's family, like so many other aristocratic Valencian families in his time, employed Muslim (*moros*) tenant farmers.[6] What is surprising is that he would have chosen to include material from a Muslim source at a time when

---

[5] *Islamic Spain, 1250–1500* (Chicago: Univ. of Chicago Press, 1990), p. 119.
[6] Cited in Almiñana, *Obres de Joan Roiç de Corella,* II, 119.

the Catholic monarchs were preparing their final onslaught on the kingdom of Granada and when the peninsula was in the grip of a fanatical anti-Muslim crusade mentality.

Equally surprising is his thorough knowledge and obvious respect for the commentary of Rabbi Solomon ben Isaac (1040–1105), commonly known by the acronym Rashi. It is obvious that he constantly consulted Rashi while writing his *Historia de Josep*. Roiç de Corella reports that the "humble youth" Joseph told his father: "It is a delightful burden for me to fulfill your commandments, obeying them without delay." Rashi had commented on the word *Hineni* ("Here I am") in Genesis 37:13: "*Hineni* denotes humility and quickness. He was quick to fulfill the commandments of his father . . ."[7] The unusual metaphor depicting Potiphar's wife as an "enraged she-bear" (*infuriada onssa*) seems to reflect Rashi's comment on Genesis 39:6 ("and Joseph was beautiful of form and fair to look upon"), according to which God, angered by Joseph's vanity, said: "Your father is in mourning, and you curl your hair! I shall incite the bear against you."[8] Also, Roiç de Corella rationalizes Joseph's charge that his brothers were spies by saying that they "had gone throughout the city, searching to see whether they might find Joseph." Rashi comments on Genesis 42:13 ("We thy servants are twelve brethren . . ."): "And because of that one son who is not here, we spread throughout the city to seek him."[9] When Roiç de Corella's Reuben offers his father his own two sons as security for Benjamin, Jacob replies: "I am amazed . . . that you say I should take what is already mine as a pledge; how can you fail to realize that your sons, too, are mine?" This reflects Rashi's citation of the *Midrash Genesis Rabbah* on Genesis 42: "He says that I should kill his two sons; are they his sons and not mine too?"[10] Roiç de Corella's statement that Joseph *struck* his divining cup, pretending that it revealed to him the order of his brothers' birth, and then said: "Let Reuben sit down first, for he is the first-born," and so forth, is based on Rashi's comment on Genesis 43:33 ("And they sat before him, the first-born according to his birthright, and the younger according to his youth"): "He struck his cup and exclaimed: 'Reuben, Simeon, Levi, Judah, Issachar and Zebulun, sons of one mother, be seated in this order, which is the order of your birth.'"[11] When Roiç de Corella has Judah tell Joseph that "in every way that Benjamin could serve you, doubtless I could serve your illustrious lordship better," he reflects Rashi's

---

[7] *The Pentateuch and Rashi's Commentary*, trans. Abraham Ben Isaiah and Benjamin Sharfman (Brooklyn: S. S. & R. Publishing Co., 1949), I, 374.

[8] Ibid., p. 393.

[9] Ibid., p. 422.

[10] Ibid., p. 429.

[11] Ibid., p. 440.

citation of the *Midrash Genesis Rabbah* on Genesis 44:33 ("And now, let thy servant, I pray thee, abide instead of the lad a bondman to my lord"): "In every respect I am superior to him: in strength, in war, and in service."[12]

Roiç de Corella could easily have had access to Rashi's commentaries as cited in the Franciscan Nicholas de Lyra's (c. 1270–1349) *Postilla literalis super totam Bibliam*. The *Postilla* was first printed in Rome in 1471, but hundreds of manuscripts had circulated long before that time. As we have seen, Rabbi Arragel had occasion to consult Lyra's *Postilla* when preparing his own commentary in the 1420s. The fact that both Arragel and Roiç de Corella had close connections with Franciscan monks is significant in this respect, for the Franciscan Order defended Lyra's literal, historical-grammatical interpretation of the Bible and his recourse to Jewish commentaries against the attacks of the Dominicans. By Roiç de Corella's time, however, the Dominicans had decisively triumphed in that battle, and their victory was nowhere more evident than in the Iberian peninsula. As a humanist with a strong interest in understanding the original, literal meaning of ancient texts, Roiç de Corella nevertheless sided with the Franciscans. It required considerable courage and dedication to the search for truth, regardless of its sources, to continue using Jewish texts in explicating the Scriptures in late fifteenth-century Valencia. The formerly sizeable Jewish community of Valencia had never recovered from the massacres and forced conversions of 1391. In Roiç de Corella's time many Jewish converts to Christianity flocked to the seaport of Valencia in an attempt to leave the peninsula. Between the establishment of the Spanish Inquisition in 1482 and the year 1488, "983 men and women in Valencia returned to the fold of the Church, while another 100 persons were burned at the stake."[13]

Roiç de Corella's *Historia de Josep,* written shortly before the fateful year 1492, is a final precious remnant of the tolerance for ethnic and religious differences that had so greatly enriched Spanish civilization during the Middle Ages and that would soon be tragically forgotten. It is also one of the most polished and elegant versions ever written of the story of Joseph.

I. Prologue

In order to demonstrate how our Lord God arranges things so as to exalt those who by their virtuous lives place their trust in His Majesty, I shall describe in ordinary Valencian prose that exemplar of virtues Joseph, son of the great

[12] Ibid., p. 449.
[13] Haim Beinart, "Valencia," *Encyclopaedia Judaica* (Jerusalem: Keter Publishing House, c. 1972), XVI, 57.

patriarch Jacob, in whose virtuous life one can clearly contemplate how Divine Providence, without force, directs human acts by means of our free will; and when He sends us tribulations, like a good lord and father, He intends them for our greater good.

II. Of the Hatred Which, out of Envy, Joseph's Brothers Felt toward Him

Wicked, sad, wretched envy, which with its jaundiced eyes always deplores prosperity, had wounded the souls and thoughts of the sons of the great patriarch Jacob with the poison of its mortal arrows so much that nothing was more offensive in their sight than the meek, benign presence of their brother Joseph, whom their father Jacob loved more than the others, because, born of a sterile mother when he was already very old, he was the son of that gracious and beautiful Rachel, for whom, in work at once exhausting and delightful, he had faithfully served his uncle Laban for fourteen years.

To Jacob's great sorrow, Rachel had paid the common debt to wicked death, leaving behind Joseph, her son, in virtue and beauty her very semblance and figure; whom Jacob retained as an esteemed token of his lost wife.

Joseph's brothers could not resist the power of so powerful an envy, fearing, with thoughts inflamed, the great love that Jacob felt for his son Joseph, more than for all the rest, to whom he had given a tunic of fine embroidery, a true indication and sign of how much more he loved him than the others.

III. Joseph Recites What He Had Dreamed

The wicked envy that was already burning within them grew still greater, enkindling great flames, because Joseph, in his benign simplicity, woke up and recited a dream, which, as a vision of profound mystery, troubled his humble and quiet thoughts: "Esteemed brothers, as I slept in the dark night, it seemed to me that I was with you binding sheaves in a fertile field, and that when my sheaf stood erect, yours bowed down to it. And after that, in another dream, it seemed to me that the sun, the moon, and eleven stars, bowing down, adored me."

A rage of terrible malice, piercing the hearts and thoughts of his brothers, split them asunder; their faces turned different colors, and with an altered voice they replied to Joseph: "Your errant thoughts betray your idle, fruitless life, Joseph; for after resting in a long sleep, without having done anything that could have tired you, stretching out your body and tossing and turning in your father's soft bed, you contemplate fictions of high poetry, in keeping with your ambition and pride, imagining yourself lord over our father Jacob and over the soul of your mother Rachel; and it is no wonder that if you lord it over them, you should subjugate us as well. Your dream, Joseph, may be interpreted as a sign of things to come, but for the present it is abundantly clear that the measureless love with which our father has loved you more than all of us, as your dream truly declares, would lead you now wickedly to subjugate both him and us."

Chiding him with many other insults, Joseph's brothers censured him; and even Jacob his father scolded that humble, meek lad with words of modest gravity, chiding him, while at the same time meditating on the profound mystery of so lofty a vision.

IV. Joseph Goes to the Wilderness to Approach His Brothers; and on the Attributes of Envy

In the flowery and green fields of the region of Shechem, Joseph's brothers were keeping watch over abundant animals and natural wealth when Jacob said these words to his beloved son Joseph: "Love and paternal solicitude arouse in my weary mind a great desire to know of your brothers and my sons, whether their life reposes in a prosperous state." The meek, humble youth answered his father without delay: "It is a delightful burden for me to fulfill your commandments, obeying them without delay, especially by going to see my brothers, on account of whose absence my soul was already not a little sad. I shall go, therefore, to carry out this delightful and happy task, approaching the fertile pastures of their flocks, until I reach the meadows where my brothers repose; and at the end of such a long journey, I shall bring them the present of some food, for it is necessary that they have such refreshment in the wilderness."

Thus the obedient son and loving brother set out, purposefully directing his steps and approaching with fraternal solicitude the green fields where his brothers gave abundant pasture to their flocks; and relieving the weariness of the journey by saying to himself: "By this task which I gladly undertake for my brothers, I shall please them and thereby mollify the malevolence they hold against me; and when they see how my mind is intent on serving them, they will forget what they suspected when I recited my dreams, and the love that my father showed me more than them, and even the anger they formerly felt toward me, when, out of brotherly zeal, I told my father about the discordant malevolence that was manifest among them."

Oh, pestilence of terrible strength! Oh, true iniquity, which first slays the one whom you inspire! Sad, wretched envy! Other hatreds and malices can be placated by service, gifts, or favors; but this one, increasing in power, only grows when the envious man thinks that the one whom he envies has carried out a virtuous act; though it be for his own benefit, it further enkindles the flames of malice when he thinks that, by acting virtuously, that man's honor and glory increase, whose total destruction the wretched envious man desires; and he does not accept the great joy of obtaining something useful, but rather feels only sadness and malice, which burn within him, thinking that that man has vanquished him; when the greatest good he desires is to see that man orphaned of every good thing.

V. Joseph's Brothers Plot His Death; Reuben Admonishes Them Not to Commit So Ugly a Crime

Meek, humble Joseph was approaching the fertile mountains where his brothers reposed, and from the farthest distance that human vision could attain, his brothers gazed upon that brother they detested with a hatred inflamed by envy. Yet even before that gaze had truly distinguished the figure of their brother, invincible malice already made them plot how they might slay him with a cruel, pitiless, wicked death; and speaking in an angry voice among themselves, they said: "Our king approaches us, he who in dreams of insane ambition foresaw our captivity; let us give his body as food to the wild animals, and may the birds exalt his flesh on high, since he desires to be above all; and let us send his wicked soul to hell, where he will experience the true meaning of what he dreamed, as he sees how that prophecy of his rulership is fulfilled."

The brothers had agreed to the wickedness of that unjust, cruel sentence, when Reuben, who was the first-born of them all, in the following words sought to dissuade the others from so abominable a crime: "What water, no matter how very clear it be, could be clean enough to wash our hands, if they be stained with innocent and fraternal blood; and if the adolescent age of our brother, the innocence of his actions, the confidence he feels as he comes to us, the happy expression he shows on having found us cannot dissuade us from committing a crime of so abominable a sort? Be moved to mercy by the memory of our aged father, whom you will slay at the same time if you spare not Joseph's life; and that knife, bloodied with our brother's blood, will traverse the very soul of our wretched father, and with lamentation, pain, and misery will send him to the dark prison of the bosom of our father Abraham before the days of his life have run their course. Restrain, then, brothers, the impetus of such insane malice; surely the world needed but a single Cain as an example of what envy could do. And if you are altogether unwilling to spare his life, alleviate the gravity of so ugly a crime; tear not his flesh asunder with a knife that your hands touch, but rather, allowing supreme Providence to dispose of his life, throw your innocent brother into an old cistern without water, which is only a short distance away from us. Thus, your hands will not be soiled by an abominable murder."

Reuben thought that if he saw Joseph live a little longer, he would be better able to mollify his brothers' rage and, saving Joseph's life, return him to his father's sight.

VI. Joseph's Brothers Throw Him into the Cistern, Where He Humbly Supplicates Our Lord God in Devout Prayer

The first-born Reuben had not altogether finished saying these words when the meek lamb Joseph, with humble countenance arriving on Jacob's mission, greeted his brothers in the following way: "Esteemed lords and brothers: our lord and father, out of paternal solicitude, desires to know of you, and, blessing you all with intense love, sends you his greetings. I bring you from your mothers well-prepared food to alleviate the travail of your continuous fatigue."

The last syllable of these words was followed by the cry of a wicked voice: "Let Joseph die! Since he has dreamed so clearly, it is a wonder that he hasn't dreamt of his own death!"

Stripping him of that embroidered robe which his father Jacob, out of singular love, had given him, they threw the meek lamb into the old cistern.

Not even the rage of his wicked brothers was able to rob Joseph of his innocent patience, as he supplicated the Divine Majesty in a humble and devout prayer: "Oh, King of kings, immense Lord, God of Jacob, Isaac, and Abraham! Since nothing is hidden from Your Majesty, and without Your power no creature is preserved, nor can any action be performed without Your will, do not permit, infinite, merciful Lord, my brothers to carry out such malice, for Your ineffable wisdom cannot fail to know that I never intended to offend them; and if, oh Lord of infinite justice, You have ordained that the term of my life extend no further than this, I accept this criminal death, for our greatest happiness is found in willing what You will. Hence, immense Lord, I beg You not for life, but rather that my brothers be not guilty of so great a crime; for though they may deserve to be abandoned by Your grace for having committed so ugly a crime, I wholeheartedly forgive them, Lord, begging that Your profound mercy not impute this sin to them, but lengthen the time of their lives, so that, repenting of their crime, they may calm Your just wrath."

VII. The Sale of Joseph to the Egyptian Merchants

Joseph's prayer, flying on wings of fervent devotion, entered the highest heaven and moved our Lord God, touching His sentiments of mercy and disposing Divine Providence to cause merchants to pass by at that time along the common highway, with camels bearing loads, transporting merchandise of great price to Egypt.

The wicked brothers were eating that food which Joseph with fraternal affection had given them, and as they beheld the merchants who were on their way to the kingdoms of Egypt, divine pity moved Judah's soul, ordaining that his tongue form the following words: "I have been thinking, brothers, that the acts of men, unlike those of the other animals that lack reason, are necessarily directed toward some purpose; therefore, I have been in suspense, wondering what purpose our brother's death could serve. We wrong ourselves, for no enemy of ours could do us greater harm; nor is my intellect convinced that we are any less guilty for causing his death without using the sword; rather, I am certain that if he should die of hunger in the dark cistern, his longer pain will only increase the guilt of our crime. Let us then save this lad's life, for he is our brother and our own flesh, for though another should slay him, we shall have left him alive; let us now absolve our hands of his life by drawing him out of the prison of the dark cistern, and in order that he may see the manifest falsehood of his dreams of power, let us sell his elegant person to the merchants who are going to Egypt, and thus the ambition of his haughty pride will be punished by a servitude of abject captivity."

Once Judah's argument had satisfied their malice, and the brothers' rage was quelled, they sold their brother as a slave to the merchants who were traveling to Egypt.

VIII. The Brothers Send Joseph's Bloodstained Robe to Jacob, His Father

The first-born Reuben was not present at that wicked sale, for in order to deliver his brother, he was wandering through the fertile fields in search of delightful pasture for the flocks; for in that way, by separating from his brothers, he might be able, returning Joseph his pristine freedom, to restore him to the sight of his father; and not finding Joseph in the dark cistern, Reuben wept with great grief. His brothers, having stained Joseph's robe with the blood of a kid, sent it to their miserable father.

Jacob, gazing with weeping eyes, recognized the bloody garment of the son whom he so loved, and in the laments, grief, and sadness with which everyone saw him complain, in grief lamented with true sorrow the false death of Joseph. The brothers all took counsel as to how they might alleviate Jacob's sadness, begging him, as an act of singular grace, that he should remit part of so extreme a mourning; but the grief-stricken old man, crying out for his son in a tearful voice, said: "Cursed be the wild beast that has devoured Joseph, whom I so rightly loved!" And, covered with a black garment, he persevered in his sorrowful complaint; and celebrating obsequies for that son who was still alive, weeping, he deplored the death of Joseph at his honored grave.

IX. Joseph Reaches the Tomb of His Mother Rachel

Toward the province of Egypt the merchants, rejoicing in their new purchase, made their way; as they observed the elegant form of the youthful slave, who had then attained the age of adolescence—for he appeared to be about sixteen or seventeen—gazing upon his face, his noble, elegant, figure, which was not that of a slave but of a free-man; but all these things, though they pleased the merchants' hearts, did not suffice to persuade them to untie Joseph's captive hands. They wondered greatly at the meekness of the benign lad.

As they traveled along, they approached the city of Bethlehem, and from afar Joseph glimpsed his mother's tall, sculptured tomb, which Jacob, as an honored sepulcher in her memory, had had carved with marvelous craftsmanship for the woman he so loved.

Rachel had died while giving birth to Benjamin, as Jacob came from serving Laban, his uncle. On the marble stone that covered the tomb, the following epitaph was written in Hebrew letters: "Having died in childbirth, under this marble stone lies Rachel, for whom Jacob lived."

No sort of human language, no words of the loftiest elegance could suffice to describe the grief and wretched complaint that the newly enslaved lad pronounced over his mother's grave; and weeping with tears that flowed abundantly from his eyes, he wet and cleansed the dusty marble of the high tomb. And, having read the inscription on the high sepulcher, with words, weeping, sobs, and barely audible sighs, he lamented his captivity as follows:

X. Joseph's Lament on His Mother's Grave

"Oh, death, you were kind to Rachel, for you have closed her eyes that she might not see the great misery of her son; but here now, by not closing my eyes, you allow me, living in slavery, to gaze upon her tomb with such sadness! So kind to the mother, so cruel to the son, promising me in Egypt, after a life of miserable slavery, a foreign burial! Now is the time to use your power on me, for since I am young, it will seem even greater; and if I die upon this tomb, my new masters will be content to give me burial in an urn with Rachel's corpse; if I found life bearable, I would not call upon you, oh cruel, wicked one; but as it is, breaking the marble of that high tomb with the force of my extreme sorrow, I would rest my weary person in an urn in there; and, mixing my flesh with her bones, either my soul would give life to her body, or her death would swiftly slay my life. I would not fear that narrow space nor the darkness of the closed tomb, since I grew accustomed to them during nine months in her womb."

The sorrowful slave was unable to state the full burden of his sad complaint before his master, haughtily commanding him with harsh mastery, took him away from the tomb where he wept with laments and tears that ran right down to the ground, bathing Joseph's own feet; he left there kissing the marble and looking back with weeping on the longed-for tomb; with his bound hands he wiped the abundant water from his weeping eyes so that, contemplating, he might gaze upon his mother's sorrowful sepulcher.

Exhausted from the long journey of many days, they at last reached Egypt, where they sold the meek slave Joseph to King Pharaoh's constable.

XI. Joseph's Mistress Falls in Love with Him

The adolescent slave showed an elegant, graceful, beautiful figure to all who looked upon him, multiplying that impression by virtuous acts.

The master whom he served placed him in charge of all his household, for his life was accompanied by such excellent virtues that the master who possessed him esteemed his new slave above everything else in the world; and Divine Providence kept watch over Joseph in such a singular way that both the natural and civil goods and riches of his master prospered with an admirable prosperity during the time that Joseph governed his house.

But the enemy of human nature, the devil, always lying in ambush, considered how he might defeat the virtuous adolescent, whose life was of such high perfection that he could in no way be faulted. And, recalling those first weapons with which, conquering, he had overthrown human nature, he thought that if he had managed to defeat and slay Adam, more perfect than other men, by means of a woman, likewise conquering, in a similar combat he could overthrow Joseph, that youth of beautiful and noble figure.

The diabolical enemy, hence, enkindled in the wounded mind of Joseph's mistress such ardent flames of love that her eyes, gazing, could contemplate nothing but the extreme beauty of the slave, whose graceful figure, chaste behavior, and humble, elegant words had transported that lady to such lofty thoughts of love that she did not presume to appear before Joseph without previously with her own hands having enhanced her natural beauty, changing every day upon her elegant person ornaments, jewels, rich garments, that in the chaste youth she might enkindle the slow flames of unchaste love, giving Joseph many an occasion to be alone with her, so that without being witnessed by any companion, by speaking she could make manifest and communicate to him secrets of great esteem, reciting stories, poems, past and present, of the sort of unchaste love that she desired to enkindle in Joseph's chaste mind.

XII. Joseph's Mistress Reveals Her Unchaste Love to Him

The chaste youth had sheltered his will and thoughts within the castle of chastity and purity, and he did not fear the strong artillery of unchaste love; and hence his virtuous soul was unaware of all baseness, for no suspicion that his lady might commit any crime had penetrated his chaste mind.

The inflamed Egyptian woman could no longer bear the flames of such a burning love; rather, her enamored madness only grew greater the more she beheld Joseph's chaste behavior. So much so that one day the squadrons of love, vanquishing those of fear or shame, forced her tremulous tongue to enunciate these words: "In my expression, words, and behavior, my slave and master, you could surely see that I would rejoice not a little if my ears could hear you speak the words which now my own tongue, ruled by extreme love, speaks; but wicked fortune, enemy of my chastity and shame, has blinded your chaste mind with a veil of such dark ignorance that you have been unaware of my desires, whose only goal is that I become your slave, as you are mine. You should not think that natural feminine shame has had no power over me, restraining my tongue from speaking words of such profound humility: your extreme beauty, accompanied by so many other good things, overthrowing the walls of my chastity, has opened the gates of my will to such an extent that, kneeling at your feet, I cannot help revealing my hope that you alone repair my life; if out of chaste cruelty you refuse to do that, by that greater cruelty you will only make matters worse; if you will not do this, take my husband's sharp sword and avenge him of the offense that I have committed against him on your account; tear my flesh, piercing my body and person, and you will make my extreme love worthy that my spirit may expire in your cruel arms; and may your harsh hands

give burial to my body, slain by you, writing on my tomb in the following words
how I lost my life:

Slain by love, in this dark sepulcher

lies the body of that Egyptian woman

who, for Joseph, departing this world

with great sorrow, abandoned her life."

XIII. Joseph Replies to His Mistress' Unchaste Words

What youthful slave would not be moved by the power of such loving words,
accompanied by humble, sad behavior, by sighs and other forces of unchaste
love, sufficient to overthrow the chastity of anyone else but Joseph?

The loyal, chaste man had cast anchor in the safe port of the fear of God,
and the ship of his upright will did not fear the high waves of the sea of Venus;
but with the chastity and shame which his unchaste mistress should have had,
with an expression of chaste intention he replied: "The fear of God, which is
the beginning of all good things; chastity, which I preserve for my legitimate
marriage; the loyalty I hold for your husband, my lord; and even more, the virtuous treatment I have experienced from you up to now, cause my thoughts to
be in suspense, making me think that your false words were just a test of my
loyalty to my master; for my intellect cannot understand how your soul could
be pierced by so cruel a wound as to subject your chastity to the ugliness of so
abominable a crime, offending God, who watches over our acts with judging
eyes, as well as your husband, my master, whom you so rightly love, by doing
him such great harm as to take pleasure with another in the chaste bed of his
chamber. But if indeed love has inflamed your soul with such infernal madness
that your will is on fire with such an ugly crime, you may be certain that before
such a notion could dwell for a moment in my chaste mind, the sun, dawning,
would bring darkness to the world, the night would be bright, the mountains,
running, would be moved, and the rivers in repose would cease their running.
As for me, I have already committed an offense, for which I am not without
grave guilt, for my ears have listened to words which so offend both God and
my master. Therefore, oh virtuous lady, change your mind, that fire may not
consume you, and live out the remainder of your chaste life as chastely as you
began, and improve your wounded thought, curing it, mindful of the offense
against God, of the loyalty of a chaste marriage, of the damage and shame and
loss of your reputation. And command Joseph, your slave, to do any subject
service within the limits of chaste loyalty."

XIV. His Mistress Tries to Take Joseph by Force; as He Flees, She Takes His Cloak

The force of such chaste words could not restrain a love enkindled with such burning flames; rather, many times the unchaste mistress sought to vanquish the youth's chastity. But, when she lost all hope of obtaining what she wanted, she thought by force to possess what she could not possess voluntarily.

Oh, terrible power of unchaste love, which, if it be not from the beginning overcome by virtue, thus subjects the wretched, enslaved mind to the ugliness of abominable acts! The maddened mistress waited for a day when Joseph entered her chamber alone, and, seizing the skirt of his cloak, said in a voice of extreme affection: "Since the sorrow and pain of my enamored and sad life has not succeeded in mollifying the ferocity and hardness of your implacable mind so that you should be content to be master of me, your mistress, I shall now find out whether by force, abandoning free will, I can take hold of your person, the beauty of which forces my chaste shame to the ugliness of so great a crime."

The wretched mistress had not yet finished pronouncing those unchaste words when the loyal, chaste slave, fleeing the vileness of abominable crime, leaving in unchaste hands his cloak, with anxious steps leaving her chamber, ran like the bird that, breaking the bond of its captivity, flapping its wings in the air, celebrates the great joy of its regained freedom.

Joseph's shameful mistress held in her unchaste hands without shame his cloak, a manifest sign of her unchastity; gazing upon which, without taking the time to consider what she did, her extreme love changed into a hatred of terrible wrath, following the natural female condition, which with fickleness hastens to do anything, good or bad. When that brave lioness cried out in a voice of enraged madness, all those who served her came running, thinking that some distress, tormenting her, afflicted her altered person; and holding the stolen cloak of the loyal, chaste slave, filled with implacable wrath, speaking in a loud voice, she cried out:

XV. Joseph's Mistress Accuses Him of Unchaste Boldness

"The fact that, on account of his benign condition, my lord and husband granted freedom and absolute command to the foreign slave, has emboldened him with such arrogance. And, since he was at complete liberty to dispose of everything else, his unchaste pride reached such a high degree that he decided to see whether he might possess me along with all those other things. For it is a common law that those whom fortune raises up from a vile condition exceed the limits of the status that benign chance has conferred upon them."

To the cries and moaning of so loud a voice, Joseph's master came with anxious steps; but before he could ask the reason for so much moaning, that enraged she-bear, with infuriated voice and gestures, cried out: "Those who place great trust in someone, without really knowing him, should not be surprised when they are brought to shame: you have so loved that foreign slave, whose condition you did not know, that you have enslaved your own house to a slave; you intended that my person, since it was yours, be exempt from such slavery; but that wicked, unchaste, abominable man has attempted—though you, his master, were its rightful owner—to take possession of what belonged to you alone, attempting with his two unchaste hands, destined for other bonds, to soil my person, that he might sully the conjugal bed of our chaste marriage! Behold his cloak—from which touch my chaste hands recoil— which he left behind in his flight, when he saw the hope of his wickedness altogether lost. And think not that the wicked slave is so very mighty; for the chastity and faith I have kept toward you in licit matrimony have given me renewed strength with which I have managed to defend my delicate person, as well as virtue, which always aids one who acts virtuously. My heart is trembling and still jumps with fear, and my tongue is weary of crying out, and my stomach is in knots, thinking upon my great misfortune: that a slave, filthy, abominable, without seeing a single sign of unchaste behavior in me, has dared attempt so abominable a wickedness."

XVI. Joseph's Master Orders Him Taken to Jail

Oh, common plague of those whom extreme love blindfolds! For it seems to them less than impossible that anything altogether false could proceed from the mouth of her whom they love; and, on the contrary, they consider it worse than false if they hear any truth that detracts from the chastity of the woman who, out of love, holds their will captive.

The master was blinded by the woman's wicked words with such profound wrath that he didn't wait to hear Joseph's just cause; but, without deliberating a well-advised decision, without seeing the slave's innocence, he ordered that they take Joseph to the common jail, where those guilty of grave crimes were kept; who, like a meek lamb, bore the irons and chains, as well as the words of abominable vituperation. And, in order to keep sublime faith, he didn't even reveal the unchaste guilt of his mistress, so that she might not suffer irreparable shame in the eyes of his master, hoping that Divine Providence, which never abandons those who hope in it, would at last set matters straight. Neither adverse nor prosperous fortune, freedom nor slavery, the darkness nor the bonds of the dark jail, could alter the perfect state of Joseph's virtuous life; and, just as prosperity, which he had worthily possessed in his master's house, never led his mind to long for the liberty of unchastity, so too adversity, which he unjustly suffered in that jail, could not sadden his soul to make him despair of divine clemency, nor make him cast the anchor of his hope in any other than in God.

The space of many days had not gone by when the jailor, knowing Joseph's virtuous life, put him in charge of all the prisoners, making him, in place of himself, master of the jail. The liberated prisoner ruled with benign meekness over those who were in the jail, and alleviated the sadness of their adversities with benign words.

XVII. King Pharaoh's Cupbearer and Baker Recite to Joseph What They Had Dreamt

Among the other prisoners whom, as was his wont, Joseph watched over, visiting them early every morning, one day, just as dawn promised the coming of Apollo, two of them were sighing with an expression of sadness; whom the captive jailer asked what was the cause of their showing such great sadness. One of them, sighing, was not slow to reply: "Your prudence is not unaware, oh virtuous youth, that King Pharaoh, our lord, angry at us, has ordered that, cast in this jail, we await the decree of his justice; and in the space of the darkness of last night, each one of us, in a vision of lofty meaning, has seen a dream that, suspending our minds, frightened them: it seemed to me that I was offering the great King Pharaoh his cup, and that a fertile grapevine put out three shoots whose green leaves, branches, and flowers, producing ripe clusters of grapes, were fruitful; which I grasped in my hand and squeezed a singular wine into a cup, and served it to the king, my lord, who was sitting at his royal table."

The cupbearer had just finished reciting his dream to Joseph when the other man, who served King Pharaoh as baker, sighing, began to say the following words: "It seemed to me, oh youth of profound intelligence, that I had three baskets of flour upon my head, and in the topmost of those three I bore all the delicacies that can be made of pastry, and that birds, without my being able to stop them, were seizing and eating them with great hunger."

XVIII. Joseph Interprets the Cupbearer's and Baker's Dreams

The king's gentlemen had finished reciting their dreams and were awaiting Joseph's reply, which they heard in the following words: "Only God, from Whose Majesty nothing is hidden, is capable of revealing the profound meaning indicated by such visions, as well as those to whom His Majesty, in its infinite freedom, reveals it. Your dreams indicate diverse and contrary sentences: the three shoots that you, oh cupbearer, have seen, are three days, after which, delivered from this jail, you will offer the cup with great honor to the king, your lord. Remember me, then, when you are restored to your pristine liberty and favor, for, though innocent of guilt, I have no one to speak to the king of my deliverance. To you, oh wretched baker, with great pity I shall tell the true meaning of your dream: the three baskets which you bore on your head in your vision are three days, after which King Pharaoh will command that your head be severed from your body, and your body will be hanged upon a cross and devoured by the birds of the air, who will use your flesh as pasture."

Now the third day had come, and the king celebrated his birthday with a solemn feast. At the banquet, remembering the two gentlemen he had arrested, he ordered that the cupbearer, restored to his former freedom and favor, again serve him his cup; but the baker was sentenced in accord with Joseph's true interpretation.

The cupbearer, once free and delivered, forgot the misery of the innocent slave in his own prosperous fortune.

XIX. The Cupbearer Tells the King of Joseph's Great Knowledge

Two years had passed since Joseph had interpreted those dreams in jail when King Pharaoh dreamed a dream of so profound a vision that his mind was overcome with fear; and summoning the most knowledgeable men of Egypt's kingdom, they could not interpret the truth hidden in the king's vision.

The cupbearer remembered Joseph, for thus Divine Providence had disposed; and with great joy he told King Pharaoh the cause of his ingratitude: "Excellent lord, I accuse myself, confessing my sin: for I have been ungrateful to an imprisoned slave who for two years, though innocent of guilt, has been detained in jail. For your excellency, unvanquished lord, is not unaware of how, for our faults, you ordered the baker and me imprisoned in that jail until such time as your excellent majesty should decide our just fate; and three days before, by your justice, the baker suffered death and, in your mercy, I was delivered, we dreamed dreams of a profound meaning, which the young slave of whom I have spoken promptly interpreted, revealing to us the sentence that your excellency within three days would decide to decree; so that if at present you lack a clear understanding, his intelligence is so great that nothing within the limits of human understanding can be hidden from his elevated mind."

XX. After Delivering Joseph from Jail, the King Tells Him His Dreams

The king rejoiced to hear the cupbearer speak of Joseph's great knowledge, and with extreme desire to hear and see Joseph, he ordered that, delivered from jail, richly dressed, he be brought as a free man before his majesty; addressing whom with an affable expression, he began to say the following words: "I cannot be excused, oh graceful youth, of negligent guilt, since, innocent of crime, you have been so long in jail. But now I wish, by repairing the damage done to you with favors and gifts of singular esteem, to diminish my fault. I have heard a reliable report that in the interpretation of visions and mysteries, nothing is hidden from your lofty intelligence."

With an expression and words of profound humility, the liberated slave replied: "Our Lord God in His infinite mercy reveals to you, oh clement and virtuous lord, mysteries of excellent prosperity; let your excellency, then, tell me the vision that has so suspended your mind."

"It seemed to me," said the concerned king, "that while sleeping in the darkness of the obscure night, I was on the bank of the great river, by whose abundant water my land of Egypt, being irrigated, bears fruit; that seven fat cows, beautiful and of lovely shape, emerging onto that shore, took fertile pasture in the green field; and seven others—lean, ill-formed, wretched—followed and caught up with the first ones, and, devouring them, showed no sign that having devoured them had filled them up, nor did they lose their former leanness. Once awake, concern about this dream and imagination of what it might signify occupied all my fantasy; and meanwhile, in another dream, it seemed to me that seven ears full of green grain sprouted up, after which came seven others—thin, sterile, withered—which devoured the first ones. This is the vision, Joseph, that has held my mind and thought in such suspense that my heart is filled with concern."

XXI. Joseph Interprets the Dreams of the King, Who Names Him Viceroy of Egypt

"Oh excellent king," replied Joseph, "the truth of your dream is one, though the representation be diverse: seven years of great fertility and abundance, most prudent lord, are to come in your land of Egypt, which will be followed by another seven, sterile and of great want, when the whole world will be in danger of perishing from famine; and the sterility and want will be so great that they will cause the former fertility to be forgotten. Let your majesty employ, therefore, most prudent lord, some prudent, just, and cautious man, who, with the general power of your excellency, will store up wheat during the seven years of great abundance, that all your kingdoms may not perish in the time of sterility."

Joseph's advice seemed very prudent to the king; and he replied, with a face of benign affability: "Since almighty God reveals the secrets of His ineffable prudence to you, oh virtuous youth, it would be impossible for me to find a man who could equal you in prudence, knowledge, and discretion. It is my will that my kingdoms and lands, obeying your commandments, consider you their lord in my place, after me; I would not be superior to you except in the dignity of the royal throne. I willingly entrust the care of my vassals to your discretion, commending them to you as to my own son, so that my life may be prolonged by the enjoyment of delightful leisure."

When the king finished saying these words, taking from his finger the seal with which he sealed his secret letters, he gave it to Joseph, ordering his servants to bring him rich, royal garments, along with other ornaments and jewels of inestimable price. It was his wish that, as he rode through the city in a triumphal chariot with public proclamation of his many and diverse titles, all the peoples should bend the knee before the viceroy Joseph; and because of the advice he had given concering the salvation of Egypt, he ordered that his name should be no longer "Joseph," but rather "Savior of the World," giving him a wife from his kingdoms, a noble, esteemed maiden.

XXII. Because of the General Famine, People Come to Joseph from All the Provinces to Buy Wheat

Joseph had completed thirty years of his virtuous life when, sitting in the viceroy's triumphal chariot, he ruled over the kingdoms of Egypt. The seven fertile years had come with such great abundance that the wheat was comparable to the sand of the sea, rendering an accurate count impossible because of its great multitude.

Two sons were born to Joseph of his noble, chaste wife during the time of great fertility, the first being Manasseh, the second, Ephraim. The seven years of abundance went by, and those of hunger, sterility, and misery came; and not only in the province of Egypt but throughout the world hunger, increasing, devoured the wretched people.

The people came crying out to King Pharaoh, who, crying out in a loud voice, said to them: "Go to the viceroy, obeying everything that he commands; his providence will restore your life."

As the famine increased, Joseph began to bring out the wheat from the barns and granaries, selling it first to those of Egypt, and then to those from other provinces who came unto him to buy it from all over the world, that they might mitigate the extreme misery of the great famine.

XXIII. Joseph's Brothers Come to Egypt to Buy Wheat

General want, occupying all the habitable land, devoured it, and especially the kingdoms of Egypt and of Canaan, where Jacob, Joseph's father, dwelled with his sons; he, hearing that wheat was sold in Egypt, spoke to his sons as follows: "What negligence occupies you, my sons, that you forget how, by going to Egypt, you could provide with little trouble that our lives not perish and that famine not altogether devour us, since the divine mercy shows us the remedy?"

The brothers decided to obey their father, leaving Benjamin, youngest of all, with Jacob, as a consolation and comfort in his old age. Having arrived in Egypt, they all bowed down prostrate on the ground, adoring Joseph—whom they did not recognize—as their master.

Joseph recalled that dream which was a manifest prophecy of his prosperity as he saw his brothers, whom he recognized, adore him as their master; nor was it any wonder that he was not recognized by them, because in the time that he had been absent from their sight, he had left off the figure of an elegant lad and taken on the beauteous form of a perfect man. And with a voice of harsh intonation and a not-at-all affable face, he asked his brothers with pretended suspicion: "What is the land where your journey began?"

"The land of Canaan," replied the brothers, "is where we, your servants, dwell, whence we set out to purchase our lives from the ministers of your lordship, that our death, insofar as it be pleasing to God, might be averted."

"Clear and manifest," replied the viceroy, "is the falsehood of what you have said, because, before you reached my palace, going around the city, you have observed the height and strength of the walls; whence the truth is shown that you are scouts or spies, considering at what place you might do damage to our city."

The brothers had gone throughout the city, searching to see whether they might find Joseph, remembering that they had wickedly sold him to merchants who were going to Egypt.

XXIV. The Brothers Reply to Joseph, Who Has Them Put in Jail

The brothers did not delay in responding to the irate words of the viceroy: "Let not your illustrious lordship believe, lord, that our occupation and livelihood consists of seeking harm to those who receive us in peace, giving us life; rather it suffices us, given the slightness of our strength, to offer what modest resistance we can to those who would procure our total destruction. We, your servants, were born twelve brothers, sons of a single father, Jacob, who is still alive, and will live on if our Lord God fulfills our desires. We have lost one brother, of whom for a long time no word has reached our ears; and the youngest of all stayed with his father, as consolation, comfort and support in his old age."

"By Pharaoh's health and prosperity, I swear to you," replied Joseph, "that you shall not leave this city until your brother, that young one of whom you have spoken, comes to Egypt, so that by manifest experience I may know the truth of your words. I shall release one of you to bring the brother you have spoken of; the others will await his arrival in jail until he comes; for my mind cannot accept what your tongues have spoken."

He concluded these words by commanding that, cast in jail, they promptly decide upon a course of action. Joseph wanted to know of his youngest brother—whom he loved very much, more than all the others, for he was his brother by father and mother, son of that lovely Rachel, for whom Jacob had suffered such great travail—to know in what condition he lived; for Joseph suspected that the malice his brothers had borne him, extending to his brother, might have brought him death or wicked slavery.

XXV. Simeon Stays in Jail for All the Brothers; the Others Return Home

The brothers spent three days in the dark jail, so that they might do some penance for that wicked sale; once they were brought out of jail, the viceroy, with a not-at-all affable countenance, said these words to them: "Though it is sufficently clear to me that you are scouts or spies, nevertheless the just administration of justice, as administered in Pharaoh's kingdoms, requires that you be not punished unless your guilt be proven. I have decided that one of you will remain in jail for all, and the rest will take food back to your houses; and if you would ransom that said brother of yours, as well as your reputation, returning without delay, let that little brother of whom you have spoken to me come with you. And thus will be manifestly shown the truth or falsehood of what you have said."

The brothers agreed to do as Joseph wished, for they could not oppose his will. And speaking among themselves, thinking that Joseph didn't understand them—for he spoke through an interpreter—they said to one another: "Oh, how deservedly we suffer this punishment and any other one, though it be greater still, for that grave, abominable sin of the attempted murder and enslavement of Joseph, our brother! That is why the viceroy understood the guilt of our wicked deeds, and he is administering justice for our brother; and indeed it is very merciful of him to spare our guilty lives, since we did not find it possible to spare the innocent life of our brother. Oh, if only we could find him now, so that, begging his pardon, we might alleviate our guilt! We would redeem his life at the cost of our own blood; we would return him to our father's sight, who rightly loved him more than all the others."

"I must remind all of you," said Reuben, the firstborn, "how greatly I struggled to prevent you from staining your hands with fraternal blood, and how you refused to let my sensible words quell your rage. I knew how much better it would be to refrain from such iniquity, for if so, almighty God, as just judge, would not now require Joseph's innocent blood of us."

The viceroy could hear no more, for tears were already beginning to well up in his eyes, and, withdrawing from his brothers, he wept from pity.

Then he ordered that in their presence Simeon, bound, be cast into jail, giving the others license to set out on their journey. He told his ministers to fill the sacks of the sons of Jacob with wheat beyond measure, and to put the money they had paid in the mouths of their bags.

XXVI. They Find the Money They Had Paid in Their Bags; and They Tell Jacob What Had Happened to Them in Egypt

The nine brothers set out with solicitude and anxiety for their brother Simeon, who remained captive in jail and, having reached the end of their first day's journey, opening their sacks to give food to their beasts, each one found in his sack that very price that he had taken to buy wheat. Frightened, they looked at each other, searching for the cause of so strange an occurrence.

Thus they reached Jacob, their father, who, counting the days of their travels with desire and paternal love, was awaiting them with worried and tearful thoughts, thinking they had delayed much more than they ought; and, kissing their venerable father's hands, as obedient sons, they showed him the foodstuffs that they had brought in great abundance from the kingdoms of Egypt, each one reciting what had happened to him on the road and how they could not return for more food nor get Simeon out of jail unless they took their brother Benjamin before the viceroy of Egypt.

Jacob, as abundant tears flowed down, bathing his aged face, answered them: "My stomach is tied in knots just from hearing what your words have said. Joseph, your brother, of whose bloodstained robe you made a miserable present to my weeping eyes, left this world long ago and is absent from our sight; and I am still suspended in doubt, wondering how some ferocious animal could have managed to tear apart the flesh of adolescent Joseph, while leaving his garment intact, or if perhaps some wicked man had first despoiled him of it, then how was it stained with his blood in such abundance; and now you tell me that Simeon is captive in the dark jail of Egypt and cannot be delivered thence unless you take Benjamin down to Egypt; and the end of your words is that I, miserable father, orphaned of my sons, shall send my soul with sorrow to the bosom of Abraham, my grandfather."

The other brothers said nothing, but Reuben, the first-born, replied: "Take two of my sons as security for Benjamin, and stab their flesh pitilessly with a knife if I do not return Benjamin to your sight."

"I am amazed at you, my son Reuben," replied Jacob, "that you say I should take what is already mine as a pledge; how can you fail to realize that your sons, too, are mine? Don't you think that if I were to lose Benjamin, I would lose much more if I then beheaded two other sons of mine? Let each of you, bewailing, weep for your own misfortunes, and I for those of all, for all are mine."

XXVII. Jacob Admonishes His Sons to Go Back for Wheat; They Reply That They Cannot Return Unless They Take Benjamin

Hunger and misery increased in the land of Canaan, and Jacob and his sons had consumed the wheat from Egypt. Their father told them: "My sons: I am not much concerned that my own old age should perish of hunger; but I am concerned for you and your children. Go back down, therefore, to Egypt, and save our lives, for divine Providence shows us how they can be saved."

Judah replied to these words: "We have told you again and again, oh lord and father, that the viceroy of Egypt, swearing with oaths that must be believed, has promised that we shall not see his face except covered with just wrath, nor shall we deliver Simeon, our brother, from jail unless Benjamin appears in his presence. If you want us to go back down to Egypt without Benjamin, send someone with us to bring back the wheat, for it is more than certain that if all of us enter Egypt without our brother, it will not be to buy grain but to ensure that we be sentenced to death, as the viceroy has already decreed; and we would consider it a lesser evil, indeed beyond compare, to abandon our lives to the hands of divine mercy rather than to the cruel sentence of a just judge in Egypt, who would hang us on a cross, where the birds will give our flesh a movable burial. You esteem Benjamin so much that you would rather see Simeon—no less your son than Benjamin, and whose father you have been for a longer time—perish in the sad jail of Egypt, and to see us, your sons, abandoned to miserable hunger, than for Benjamin to go from here to Egypt."

"It was only to increase my misery," replied Jacob, "that you, rejoicing over the affable reception the viceroy showed you, with a prolixity of vain words told him that you had another brother, so that it seemed that you had gone to Egypt not to buy wheat but to recite the chronicle of your family history. Is it possible that in Egypt they give wheat in exchange for fruitless words instead of money, since, bringing home your money, you have left behind words, the truth of which I shall now have to demonstrate at the cost of my life? What necessity, forcing, obliged you to reveal our circumstances so specifically to the viceroy?"

The other sons replied in a loud voice: "We were forced to reply to the viceroy; unless we spoke falsehood, we could have told him nothing other than what we said, because the viceroy questioned us about our status and life, as if he had lived among us for a long time. How could we have known that when we told the truth, saying that we had a younger brother, he would reply that we must bring him to his presence? And thus we hope that by the virtue, power, and strength of the truth, no harm will come to Benjamin, for the viceroy demanded him because we spoke the truth."

XXVIII. Jacob Consents for Benjamin to Go Down to Egypt with His Brothers

They had all just finished speaking these words when Judah replied with great effort: "Do not be afraid, oh lord and father, to place Benjamin in my charge: I alone, for all, wish that the burden of this charge weigh upon me; I pledge my life, which I esteem above all things in this world, here and now to you, father and lord, if I do not bring Benjamin back to your sight from Egypt; and if any harm should befall him, because of adverse fortune, hold me alone guilty, and with a cruel death remove my life from this world, and cursing my guilty soul, assure that I not attain the repose of our grandfather Abraham. Surely the love you hold for Benjamin is not sufficient for you to procure the death of our sons and ourselves, who are no less your sons than Benjamin. For if your great love can bear his absence for a little while, we shall again return from Egypt, having delivered Simeon, your son, from jail; who cannot be delivered without Benjamin."

With tears that washed his venerable face, and a great sigh proceeding from the depths of his heart, Jacob replied: "If you, my sons, consider it reasonable that Benjamin go down to Egypt, I cannot stand in your way by offering a contrary argument, because the virtue of prudence, in accordance with your wishes, has exhausted them. And since you are all in agreement about this, do not go empty-handed before the viceroy of Egypt; since we ask for nothing that is contrary to justice, make his illustrious lordship a gift of some of the singular things that are found in this land more than in Egypt: almonds, honey, balm, styrax, benzoin, and other aromatic gums and spices suitable for his majesty. And do not forget to return to his lordship the money that you have found within your bags, because, if that was ignorance of those who administer, your innocence will be clearly manifest. And I devoutly supplicate the Divine Majesty to calm and placate the viceroy so that he will return Simeon to you, as well as this lad Benjamin," whom, while saying these words, he kissed, weeping; "and in the meantime I shall be a father bereft of his sons."

XXIX. The Brothers Return to Egypt with Benjamin

In concord and the peace of brotherly love the ten brothers then set out, and all watched over Benjamin with solicitous care, remembering the solicitude with which their father Jacob had entrusted him to them.

And when they came before the presence of the viceroy in Egypt, Joseph rejoiced with ineffable joy on seeing Benjamin, whom he had so desired to see. He ordered his majordomo to prepare a great array of foods—for he intended those foreigners from the land of Canaan to eat with him in his great hall— and to give what they needed to their beasts in abundance, ordering that they be taken to his stables.

The viceroy Joseph, when he arranged these things, was in the great house of the city, where he celebrated general audience for all the people. The majordomo approached the ten brothers, telling them how the lord viceroy wanted them to come to the great palace where he dwelled; and they, with happy expressions, replied that they would be greatly delighted to obey the commands of his lordship.

And, following the majordomo, approaching the great house, fear began to worry their minds, as they said among themselves: "For the money that we found in our bags he will order us arrested, and, accusing us of theft, will sentence us all to slavery, both us and our beasts."

And with this hidden suspicion they reached the door of the lofty dwelling; and before they had even gone inside, they began to express their fear in the following words: "Very noble lord: may your nobility deign to lend your ears to our words for a little while. It is manifest to your prudence that we, to buy wheat, came before to the kingdoms of Egypt, the price of which, without fraud, we paid, in the presence your magnificence, to your ministers; and, once our sacks were filled and tied up, as we were on our way home, we found the money that we had paid, each one of us in his own bag. Therefore, very noble lord, we now bring that same price, so that, if it was an inadvertence of those who administered, your lordship's worship be not defrauded; and we have brought more than enough money to buy more wheat; and furthermore, with the good will of affectionate and devoted servants, we have brought to the respectable lord viceroy some things that are found in our land more than in Egypt."

With a gesture and expression of affable assurance, the majordomo replied: "Brothers, fear not that any harm may come to you by order of the viceroy; the money that you have found in your bags, our Lord God has put it in your sacks, because I still have those coins that, in payment for the wheat, without any damage you paid me. Do not fear anything that may happen to you, for I am taking you to the home of the lord viceroy not as prisoners but as guests to a solemn banquet."

As he finished saying these words, Simeon, freed from jail, appeared before his brothers.

XXX. The Brothers Appear before Joseph

The brothers felt such a great joy that it was easier to experience than to express when, while listening to the majordomo, they saw Simeon delivered, and with this joy, greater than could be written, they entered the great hall. The majordomo ordered their legs washed, to alleviate the travail of the long journey, and that they be given food in great abundance. And, awaiting the arrival of the viceroy, spreading out what they had brought, they discussed how they might best offer it to the viceroy, and each one taking part of the present, as Joseph entered the great hall, on bended knee they offered him the present with these words: "Our father Jacob, now grown very old, humbly kissing your hands, commends himself to your lordship, oh illustrious lord; and because some things are found in the land of our habitation that are not available in Egypt, with intense affection, he offers this poor present, begging your worship to accept it, in accord with the affection of the one who sends it. And, so that the truth of what your lordship doubted may be clearly shown, this is Benjamin, our youngest brother, whom your worship wished to see, to prove that we did not enter the land of Egypt with wicked intentions. As an inestimable favor, our father humbly supplicates your lordship that, without delay, you grant us license to return; for in his old age it is impossible for him to go on living without Benjamin, for he is his staff, comfort and support in his old age."

With benign meekness the viceroy replied: "I am very happy and content that no guilt is found in you; for it is not my desire to offend foreigners who come to Egypt with unjust, wicked suspicion, but only to protect the royal person of my lord, as well as the state of his kingdoms, from the attacks of wicked people. I am happy to know that your father is alive, and I desire him much health and long life; and I would be pleased if you would give me a fuller account of his condition."

"Our father, your servant," the brothers replied, "is in good health and as strong as one could expect, given his old age, always the obedient servant of your illustrious lordship."

And thus speaking, all bowed down to the ground. Joseph turned his eyes to Benjamin, saying: "This is your youngest brother, of whom you spoke?" They replied: "Yes, lord, that is your servant, as well as all of us." Joseph said to him: "My son, may our Lord God preserve you in His kindness and mercy."

Brotherly love could no longer withhold the tears from his eyes; but, going inside his private chamber, he shed them in great abundance, bathing his feet and even the very ground.

XXXI. Joseph Entertains His Eleven Brothers at a Solemn Banquet

Joseph asked for water to wash away the abundant tears from his tear-stained face; having covered his elegant person with rich garments, with a display of true joy, he entered the hall of the solemn banquet.

He ordered that they prepare a table on one side, at which his eleven brothers would sit; and on another side, for the barons and noblemen of the kingdoms of Egypt; for the Egyptians considered it sacrilegious to take food with the descendants of Abraham. And, holding in his hand a cup worked and carved with singular artifice, he struck it, pretending that, exercising an art of profound science, he divined. As the first sound rang out, he crying out in a loud voice, said—so that all his brothers should hear—: "Let Reuben sit down first, for he is the firstborn." And, as the cup sounded a second time, he said: "Let Simeon sit down next." And thus he commanded his brothers to sit down in the order of their birth; they were greatly astonished that he knew both their Hebrew names and the order of their birth. And, giving a command, he ordered that Benjamin's portion, greater than that of any of the others, be multiplied five times, to see whether that honor and love which he showed Benjamin more than all the others would cause them once again to be overcome by the poison of envy.

Thus they spent all that day in rest and delight of ineffable joy; and when the sun, traveling toward the west, hid its rays from human sight, he ordered the sacks of his eleven brothers filled beyond measure, and that their money be returned there at the same time, and that they put in the sack of the youngest one that cup with which he had pretended to divine their names and the order of their birth.

Before going to sleep, the eleven brothers asked the viceroy's license to depart; for they intended to begin their longed-for journey at daybreak, so that without delay they might take Benjamin, delivered from danger, back to the sight of their father; Joseph gave them that permission, with an affable face and gesture, sending affectionate greetings to Jacob.

XXXII. The Viceroy's Majordomo Arrests the Brothers, Accusing Them of Theft

Red dawn promised the coming of the sun when Jacob's sons with ineffable joy began their longed-for journey, discussing the benign reception they had been given by the meek lord. As they traveled along, they had distanced themselves a mile from the city when the viceroy ordered his majordomo to pursue the brothers, to whom, after arresting them, he spoke the following words: "Since you have committed this wickedness and ingratitude surpassing all others, it is clearly obvious that, from the very first day that you entered the kingdoms of Egypt, the illustrious lord viceroy understood the evil intentions of your malice. Is this the service that you render his lordship in return for the favors that you have received from that generous and benign man, that with the boldness of wicked audacity you have stolen the cup in which his lordship is accustomed to drink at banquets, and with which, in his great knowledge, he divines whatever he wishes to know?"

With the strength of a clear conscience, in a harmonious and lofty intonation, all the brothers replied: "We are very much amazed that your magnificence, most noble lord, should artfully accuse us of a crime so abominable to us, your servants; for your prudence cannot be unaware that we, without fraud, have returned the money that we found in our sacks, whence can be clearly seen that our lives are not concerned with what is not ours. How then, after all the benefits, honors, and favors that we have received from the lord viceroy in his kindness, could you think we could have changed so much for the worse as to be induced to commit thefts of abominable iniquity and ingratitude? But, so that our innocence may be promptly revealed, we are content that without delay, by searching us and our retinue, this be proven; and if any man be found to have stolen, let him die a cruel death without redemption; and the rest of us will be the lord viceroy's slaves for the remainder of our lives."

The majordomo did not delay in replying as follows: "My lord the viceroy is not of so cruel a condition that, beyond the limits of merciful justice, he should carry out any punishment; but a fair sentence will be that he who is guilty of such a theft will be a slave in the service of the lord viceroy; the rest of you, set free, may continue the journey you have begun."

The effect of these words was that the whole assembly then unloaded their beasts, anxious to manifest the truth of their innocence; and, opening the sacks, beginning with Reuben's, they found the golden cup in Benjamin's sack.

XXXIII. The Brothers Go before the Viceroy, Begging for Mercy

No style within the power of a human tongue would suffice to explain or describe the grief, sadness, and miserable complaints that all the brothers, weeping, poured out, while rending, as a sign of their true and extreme sorrow, their garments. Without delay they loaded their caravan and, returning to the city, entering the viceroy's house, Judah first, all cried out for mercy, although they were in no way guilty of the theft; but they thought they were more likely to be delivered by begging for mercy than by pleading the just cause of their innocence, for they had no other witness than the purity of a clear conscience, and furthermore, they rightly thought that the golden cup could not have been placed in Benjamin's sack except by the decree of the lord and judge.

It made Joseph happy to see his brothers complain in such a way out of love for Benjamin, and he realized how they had changed, since they had no envy of Benjamin, whom he had shown the singular grace of greater honor at the banquet. But in order to try the depths of their hearts, as penance for the wickedness they had committed by selling him, with a face of terrible false rage, he chose to reprehend them for their imputed crime as follows: "The benign reception you received from me was unable to restrain your wicked condition from committing so outrageous a wickedness or from the boldness of so foolish an enterprise: for surely you are not unaware that there is no one like me in the whole world when it comes to knowing hidden things."

Judah did not delay, with eyes that distilled tears in abundance, to answer the viceroy's words as follows: "With what tongue or what voice, in the presence of your worthy lordship, can we your servants excuse or defend a crime so manifestly proven? Since it pleases our Lord God that we bear the punishment for our crimes in Egypt, we neither can nor will answer anything to you, just judge; take our belongings and our persons, for our wrongdoing deserves that we all be slaves of your lordship, as well as the one in whose sack the stolen cup was found."

"It would not please the Divine Majesty," replied the viceroy, "for me to commit such an injustice; let only the one who committed the theft remain in Egypt as my slave; the others, free and cleared of guilt, may return to the land of your habitation."

These words so moved and pierced the hearts of all of them that at that point each one was extremely weary of life and would have accepted death as a great good fortune. Judah drew nearer to the worthy viceroy, and with a strained voice and expression of extreme pain, in an intonation at once loud and sad, began to speak the following true words:

XXXIV. Judah Begs the Viceroy to Take Him as Slave instead of Benjamin

"Imploring, I ask of you, oh virtuous and just lord, above all else, only a single favor: that your worthy lordship not be annoyed nor impatient if I, a little more than the others, lengthen my speech; for surpassing sorrow so torments my soul that he would be a merciful lord who without delay would in peace take my miserable life from me. I believe, oh respectable lord, that you cannot have forgotten—unless a multitude of arduous affairs have blotted it out of your mind—how, when you asked us, your servants, when we first came to Egypt, whether we had a father or other brother, we replied that we did—a man of exceedingly old age and a younger brother, an adolescent, who had stayed behind with him; whom our father dearly loved. Your lordship promptly ordered us to bring him to Egypt to your presence without delay. We replied that it was not possible for the lad to leave his father, without whom he would die. But your worship, replying, threatened that we should not again see your face in peace unless we came with our little brother; and your lordship, prudent lord, even saw fit to have our brother Simeon detained in jail until we should bring this Benjamin to your lordship.

"Having returned to the land where we customarily live, we gave our father a full account of the orders you had given us; and, when the famine grew so great as to threaten our perdition, our father Jacob begged us to come back to your lordship for wheat; but with a single voice we all replied that it was not possible for us to come unless he allowed our brother Benjamin to accompany us. And with abundant tears, which, washing, bathed his aged face, he replied: 'You, my sons, know that Rachel, for whom I served my uncle Laban during the best years of my life, bore Joseph, whom I loved as well as my own life; and then Benjamin, who took his place when he paid the common debt to death. I sent Joseph to you to visit you in the pastures of the flocks, and in place of him, you sent me his bloodstained robe, saying that a wild beast had made an end of his life; and up to now, no news of his survival or of his dead body has reached our ears. If you now take Benjamin, my only remaining token of Rachel and Joseph, to Egypt, and by my adverse fortune some accident befall so that you do not return him to my sight, before my time, you shall send my weary soul to the bosom of our grandfather Abraham with incomparable pain, sorrow, and misery.' And, since all my brothers said nothing, worthy lord, I answered: 'Commend Benjamin, your son, to me alone; let the burden of his life rest upon me, and cut the bodies of my children into little pieces if I return to your sight without Benjamin.' How then, benign lord, can I return to my father's presence without Benjamin, except to find myself at his miserable grave? For it is more than certain that his life will not endure if Benjamin's be lost.

"Hence, virtuous lord, since it is impossible for me or my brothers, who have an obligation like unto my own, to return without Benjamin, do us the kindness—which we will consider a favor—of allowing us to end our lives in Egypt as slaves of your illustrious lordship; for Divine Providence thus ordains, and thus we shall not see our father's painful death. As for what your prudent lordship has said—that it would be an unjust sentence that we all be slaves for the crime that only one has committed—doubtless, just lord, it would be a still more cruel justice to slay the father by slaying the son, who is guilty, than to retain all as slaves in the company of the one who committed the crime; but if your lordship will that only one slave stay here for this crime, let it not be Benjamin, for the result of that, even though he eventually be freed, would be the miserable death of our father.

"Bear in mind, benign lord, since you too have children—may God preserve them in every way like their father!—the strength of paternal love; and out of mercy alone, as a grace and favor that will be not a little esteemed, may your lordship grant that I serve you in place of Benjamin, and I will gladly stay here as your slave; for in every way that Benjamin could serve you, doubtless I could serve your illustrious lordship better, and all the more so, since I will serve you with joy, considering my slavery far better than freedom."

XXXV. The Viceroy Reveals to His Brothers Who He Is

The viceroy could no longer prevent tears of pity from flowing from his weeping eyes. Wishing to reveal the truth to his brothers, he ordered that all the others leave the great hall, and in a voice so loud that all those of his household could hear the sound of his words, crying out in the Hebrew language, with a tearful voice he said: "I am Joseph, your brother! Is it true that our father Jacob is still alive?"

With extreme astonishment mixed with unbearable fear, hearing these words, the brothers stood like statues sculpted of stone, staring at Joseph, beside themselves, and did not move at all. Joseph, with a low, soft, benign voice, weeping, cried to them: "Come up to me, brothers. I am Joseph, your brother, whom you sold at the field of Shechem, for thus Divine Providence allowed, for your salvation and that of Egypt. Now banish all fear from your minds, for my manifest awareness of your true repentance has altogether erased the offense from my mollified mind. Return without delay to our father, and tell him, kissing his hands on my behalf, that two years have gone by and the famine increases, and yet another five years will pass before the earth, for sterile draught, will suffer herself to be cultivated. Come then with all your descendants and take as your habitation the region of Goshen, which is known in the kingdoms of Egypt as most fertile and best disposed as pasture for your flocks."

Having recognized Joseph, the brothers were unable to speak out of extreme astonishment; Joseph, embracing them all, and Benjamin even more, wept tears of great love.

King Pharaoh rejoiced when his ears heard that the viceroy knew his brothers, and even more when he learned of their noble ancestry; commanding with generosity of great munificence that they send their father Jacob wheat in great abundance, together with a caravan of carts and many servants, that they might be able to bring all that they possessed in the land of Canaan, and select the part of the kingdoms of Egypt most fertile and suitable for their dwelling.

XXXVI. The Brothers Report Joseph's Survival and Triumph to Their Father

The viceroy Joseph dressed all his brothers in rich new garments, especially Benjamin, whom above all he made presents of jewels of great value; arranging for them to set out without delay, because in truth he thought that in their absence, and especially that of Benjamin, his father Jacob must be fearful and overcome with solicitous care.

With such great joy and happiness that it cannot be written, the brothers set out; and their father Jacob was counting the days, for the love of Benjamin tormented his soul with grave fears. But when he saw his sons coming with signs of such great joy, gazing on Simeon, and even more on Benjamin, he thought that they must be celebrating the arrival of those two.

The sons approached their aged father and, before saying anything else, with loud voices of happy intonation, cried out, saying: "We have found Joseph, your son, our brother, and he is the viceroy who rules the kingdoms of Egypt, and he desires to see you above all else. Behold the carts and servants that he sends so that we, our wives and children and all that we possess, may go down to Egypt."

Jacob's mind was seized above all with wonder on hearing news of such wondrous truth. And like a man awakened from a deep sleep by a loud, disturbing noise, gazing upon his sons, he could not answer them; for his intellect could not comprehend such great extremes in so short a time: that Joseph, whom he thought had been torn apart and slain by a wild beast, at the present should be seen living such a prosperous life as lord of Egypt. And turning his eyes toward the carts and servants that his son Joseph sent him, he realized that that happy news was true; and touching his knees to the hard ground, with his hands joined, raising his eyes full of happy tears to the celestial sphere, he gave thanks to the Divine Majesty for such great benefits in the following words:

XXXVII. The Prayer That Jacob Addressed to Our Lord When He Heard That Joseph Was Living in Great Prosperity

"Lord God, infinite essence, present everywhere, immutable being, interminable life, eternity without end, omnipotent, inexhaustible power, efficient and first cause, virtue and strength of every creature, incomprehensible intelligence! In You and through You is the design, mirror and idea of everything that can be made, infallible truth, bottomless source of infinite mercy, absolute goodness from which all other things devolve. No created thought suffices to contemplate how through paths inscrutable to us, Your Providence, disposing, administers human acts; allowing freedom to our free will, Your immense goodness permits the wickedness that our malice does, out of which Your infinite wisdom draws singular effects; and then Your customary mercy avenges and grants pardon to those who repent of such wicked acts. And therefore he is more than foolish, disloyal and rebellious who, by complaining, opposes what Your Majesty always works out for the best.

"Lord, I give thanks and all the praise I can to Your Highness, that Your power has delivered Joseph, Your creature, from the wickedness of his brothers, and that the gushing font of Your infinite mercy has washed them of such a black crime, and that Your inscrutable wisdom has provided sufficient food for the land of Canaan and Egypt.

"Multiply, oh Lord, now and always, Your mercy, which I humbly supplicate, as a special singular favor, that You grant that my eyes may see the face of Joseph, so that my soul may then go down content to the bosom of Abraham, your servant."

XXXVIII. Jacob Arrives in Egypt

As Jacob finished saying these words, his sons came up to him, kissing his hands and mouth. All wept; and without delay, with renewed strength and the power which the desire to see Joseph brought him, the aged father began, with all his descendants, their journey to the kingdoms of Egypt, and with anxiety greater than his age could bear, but safe and sound, his venerable person reached the land of Goshen, which was considered among the most fertile in the province of Egypt.

Judah sent a messenger to the viceroy, announcing the prosperous arrival of Jacob; Joseph followed in his noble, triumphal chariot of great excellence, accompanied by a magnificent retinue, and came to welcome his father, and touching his knee to the ground, kissed his hands, like a humble son of great obedience.

Jacob embraced and kissed Joseph, his son, whom he loved above everything in the world. Abundant tears of great love, bathing, washed both their faces. With a tremulous voice and the pleasure of so great a joy that no greater could be found in this world, weeping, he said: "Now the time has come that, if our Lord God please, paying the common debt to death, my soul should depart content from the old prison of this corporal dwelling, since I have seen you, my son and Rachel's, on account of whose absence, since the day I lost you, my life has been sad."

➤ Speculum Historiale[1]

Vincent of Beauvais (c. 1190–c. 1264)

CXVIII. From the *Story of Asseneth.*
Of Asseneth's arrogance

In the first of the seven years of plenty Pharaoh sent Joseph out to gather the grain. Joseph came to the region of Heliopolis, whose prince was the priest Putifar, Pharaoh's chief minister and counselor. Putifar's daughter Asseneth was the loveliest maiden in the world and was in every similar to the daughters of the Hebrews. She was haughty and proud, despising all men, albeit she had never yet seen a man.

There was a great, high tower connected to Putifar's house, the top floor of which contained ten chambers. The first of these was large and handsome, paved with porphyry; the walls were covered with precious stones, and the ceilings were fretted with gold. Within this chamber were Egyptian gods of gold and silver which Asseneth worshiped and feared, and to which she offered daily sacrifices. The second chamber held Asseneth's finery of gold and silver and jewels and precious linens. In the third chamber were all kinds of good food, for it was Asseneth's pantry. The remaining seven chambers were occupied by seven exceedingly beautiful virgins, who waited upon her. No man had ever spoken to them, not even a male child.

There were three windows in Asseneth's chamber. The first one, which was very large, faced the east; the second faced south, and the third faced north. In the room was a golden bed spread with splendid purple cloths woven out of jacinth and purple and byssus and embroidered with gold. Asseneth slept in that bed by herself, and no man had ever sat upon it.

A large courtyard encircled the house. Its walls were very high and were built of square stones. In them there were four iron gates, each of which was guarded by eighteen very strong young armed men. On the right side of the courtyard was a fountain of living water from which water flowed down into cisterns that watered all the trees that were planted in that courtyard, which were beautiful

---

[1]This translation is based on a facsimile reprint of a 1624 edition (Graz, Austria: Akademische Druck-u. Verlagsanstalt, 1965), IV, 42–44.

and fruitful. Asseneth was as great as Sarah, as lovely as Rebecca, as beautiful as Rachel.

CXIX. Of how Joseph dissuaded her from worshiping idols

Joseph sent Putifar a message that he would like to stay in his house. Putifar was delighted, and he told his daughter that Joseph, the Strong Man of God, was coming, and that he wanted to give her to him in marriage. She indignantly replied that she wanted to marry the king's son, not some slave. As they were speaking, someone came and announced Joseph's arrival. Asseneth fled up to her penthouse, and Joseph arrived sitting in Pharaoh's own chariot, which was entirely of gold and was drawn by four horses white as snow wearing gilded bridles. Joseph was wearing a very splendid white tunic and a cloak woven of purple and gold. He had a golden crown on his head, and all around the crown were twelve choice stones adorned with twelve golden stars. He had a royal scepter in his hand and an olive branch heavy with fruit. Putifar and his wife went out to meet him, and bowed down to him, and brought him into the courtyard, and the doors of the courtyard were closed. Asseneth saw Joseph and was very upset about what she had said concerning him. She said: "Behold, the sun has come down to us from heaven in this chariot! I did not know that Joseph was the son of God; for what man could beget such beauty, or what woman's womb could bear such light?" Joseph went into Putifar's house, and they washed his feet. And Joseph asked: "Who is that woman who was at the upstairs window? Get her out of this house!" for he was afraid she would bother him as all the other women did, excitedly sending him messages with all sorts of gifts, which he threw away with indignation and insults. But Putifar said: "Lord, that is my daughter who is a virgin and despises all men, albeit she has never before seen a man but me and now you. If you please, let her come and greet you." Thinking that, if she despised all men, surely she wouldn't force herself upon him, Joseph said to her father: "If your daughter is a virgin, I love her like my own sister. Have her mother go up and bring her here." When she stood before Joseph, her father said to her: "Greet your brother, who despises all foreign women just as you despise all men." Asseneth said: "Hail, you are blessed by God on high!" Joseph replied: "May God, Who gives life to everything, bless you." Putifar told his daughter to kiss Joseph, but when she tried to do so, Joseph held out his hand and put it on her chest, saying: "It is not fitting for a man who worships the living God, and eats the bread of life, and drinks from the chalice of incorruption, to be kissed by an alien women whose mouth kisses deaf and dumb idols, and who eats from their table bread of strangulation, and drinks from their sponges a chalice of insidiousness, concealing the chalice, and anoints herself with inscrutable oil."

CXX. Of Asseneth's penance and angelic consolation

When Asseneth heard Joseph's words, she was greatly saddened and wept, and Joseph took pity on her and put his hand on her head and blessed her. Asseneth took to her bed and fell ill on account of the fear and joy she felt. She did penance and renounced the gods she had worshiped. Joseph ate and drank, and when he was ready to leave, Putifar asked him to stay for a day. Joseph couldn't, but he promised to return on the eighth day. Asseneth put on a black tunic, which had been her mourning robe when her younger brother had died, and closing the door upon herself, shed wept and threw all her idols out the window that faced north. She also cast all her royal food to the dogs, and put ashes on her head and on the floor, and wept bitterly for seven days. At dawn on the eighth day the cocks crowed, and the dogs barked. Asseneth looked out the window that faced east and saw the morning star, and right beside her the heavens were split asunder, and a great light appeared. Seeing that, Asseneth fell upon her face in the ashes. Lo, a man came down from heaven and stood by Asseneth's head and called her by name, but she was too frightened to reply. He called out a second time: "Asseneth, Asseneth!" This time she answered: "Here I am. Tell me, my lord, who are you?" He replied: "I am a Prince of the House of God, and the Captain of the Lord's host. Arise and stand upon your feet, and I shall speak unto you." And Asseneth raised up her head and beheld a man who was in every way like Joseph, wearing a stole and a crown and holding a royal scepter. His face was like lightning, and his eyes were like the sun's rays, and the hair upon his head was like a flame of fire. Seeing that, Asseneth was struck by fear and fell upon her face, but the angel comforted her and raised her up, saying; "Take off that black hairshirt that you have put on, remove that sackcloth from your loins, put away all your sadness and shake off the ashes from your head, and wash your face and hands with living water, and put on your best clothes and jewelry, and I shall speak unto you." When she had done as he said, she hurried back to the angel, who said unto her: "Take that veil off your head, for you are a virgin. Be comforted and rejoice, virgin Asseneth, for your name is written in the Book of the Living and will never be erased. Behold, from today on you are renewed and given life, and you will never be erased. Behold, from today on you are renewed and given life, and you will eat the bread of blessing and drink the cup of incorruption, for you shall be anointed with holy chrism. Behold, today I have given you Joseph as your spouse, and your name will no more be called Asseneth but Many Refuges, for your penitence, which is the daughter of the Most High and an eternally joyful, laughing, modest virgin, has interceded with the Most High on your behalf. But when Asseneth asked the angel his name, he replied: "My name is written by the finger of God in the Book of the Most High, and everything written in that book is ineffable, and it is not fitting that mortal men should hear or say it."

CXXI. Of the table and the honey-comb which she set before the Angel

Taking hold of the top of his cloak, Asseneth said: "If I have found grace in your eyes, sit now a little while upon his bed, on which no man has ever sat, and I will prepare a table for you," and the angel replied: "Bring it quickly." And she set bread and fragrant old wine and a new table before him. The angel said: "Bring me a honey-comb too." She was very sad, because she had no honey-comb, but the angel said unto her: "Go into your pantry and you will find a honey-comb on your table." And she found a honey-comb as white as snow and very pure, sweet-smelling honey. And Asseneth said: "Lord, I had no honey-comb, but your holy mouth spoke, and there it was, exuding this fragrance like the breath of your mouth." And the angel smiled at what Asseneth said, and extending his hand, he touched her head saying: "Blessed are you, for you have put away idols and believed in the one God, and blessed are those who come to the Lord in penitence, for they will eat of this honey-comb, which the bees of God's paradise made from the dew of the roses of paradise. All of God's angels eat this, and he who eats it will never die." And extending his hand, he broke off a little piece of the honey-comb and ate it himself, and put the rest in Asseneth's mouth, and he said: "Behold, you have eaten the bread of life and have been anointed with holy chrism, and from today on your flesh will be renewed, and your bones will be healed, and your strength will never wane, and youth will not see old age, and your beauty will never decay, and you will be like unto a City built for all those fleeing to the name of God the Almighty King of the ages." And he extended his hand and touched the honey-comb he had broken, and it was whole again as before. Extending his right hand, he touched the top of the honey-comb with his index finger pointing east, drew his finger back toward himself, and stuck it into the edge of the honey-comb that was facing west, and the path of his finger was traced in blood. Then he extended his hand again, and touched the honey-comb with his fingertip on the north side of it and drew his finger over to the south side, and the path of his finger was traced in blood while Asseneth looked on. Then he said: "Look at the honey-comb," and many bees white as snow came out of it, and their wings were as purple as hyacinths. They all flew around Asseneth and made a honey-comb in her hands and ate of it, and Asseneth said to the bees: "Go to your place," and they all flew east toward paradise. The angel said: "Thus will be all the words I have spoken to you today," and the angel held out his hand a third time and touched the honey-comb, and fire sprang up from the table and consumed the honey-comb, but did not touch the table, and the fragrance of the smoke from the honey-comb was exceedingly sweet.

XCCII. Of the blessing of the seven virgins and Asseneth's marriage

And Asseneth said to the angel: "I have seven virgins who have been brought up with me since infancy, and were born on the same night as I. I will summon them, and you will bless them as you have blessed me." She ordered them summoned, and he blessed them, saying: "May the Lord God Most High bless you, and may you be like seven columns of the City of Refuge." Then he ordered Asseneth to clear the table, and when she had done so, the angel disappeared from her eyes. She turned around and saw what appeared to be a chariot with four horses flying eastward through the sky. Asseneth then begged him to forgive her for having spoken to him so boldly. Hardly had she said this when a young man of Putifar's household announced: "Behold, Joseph, the Strong Man of God, is coming; his servant is already at your door." Asseneth hastened out to meet Joseph, and stood by the stable. When Joseph entered the courtyard, Asseneth greeted him and told him the words the angel had said unto her, and washed his feet. The very next day Joseph asked Pharaoh to give him Asseneth as his wife, and Pharaoh gave her to him, and put the best crowns he had on their heads, and made them kiss each other. And he gave them a wedding and a great banquet that lasted seven days, and he gave orders that no one do any work during the days of Joseph's nuptials, and he called Joseph the son of God, and Asseneth daughter of the Most High.